יהושע
JOSHUA

AND

שופטים
JUDGES

SONCINO BOOKS OF THE BIBLE

EDITOR: REV. DR. A. COHEN M.A. Ph.D., D.H.L.

Joshua · Judges

HEBREW TEXT & ENGLISH TRANSLATION
WITH INTRODUCTIONS AND
COMMENTARY

Edited by
THE REV. DR. A. COHEN, M.A., Ph.D. D.H.L.

Revised by
RABBI A.J. ROSENBERG

THE SONCINO PRESS

LONDON · JERUSALEM · NEW YORK

FIRST EDITION 1950 (Ten Impressions)
REVISED EDITION 1982
SECOND IMPRESSION 1987

© THE SONCINO PRESS LTD. 1982

ISBN 900689-20-X

PUBLISHERS' NOTE

*Thanks are due to the
Jewish Publication Society of America
for permission to use their beautiful
English text of the Scriptures*

PRINTED IN THE UNITED STATES OF AMERICA

PUBLISHERS' INTRODUCTION
TO THE REVISED EDITION

JUST over thirty-five years ago THE PSALMS, the first in a series of the SONCINO BOOKS OF THE BIBLE, saw the light of day, to be followed in the next six years by the remaining thirteen books. Whereas the earlier edition drew from various non-Jewish, as well as Jewish, sources, the publishers now feel there is a need to acquaint the reader with the pure Jewish view of these holy books, and this revised edition therefore limits its scope to the traditional classic Jewish commentaries and source material.

We are indebted to The Judaica Press for allowing us to use material from the Judaica Books of the Prophets.

FOREWORD BY THE GENERAL EDITOR TO THE FIRST EDITION

THIS volume presents the first two post-Pentateuchal Books, *Joshua* and *Judges*. They relate the fulfillment of the Divine promise made to the patriarchs that their descendants would have possessions of the land which was to be the scene of their national life. The struggle to retain a precarious foothold after the conquest in the face of the hostility of neighbours is graphically described. The Books tell of stirring incidents and colorful personalities, but also reveal the feeble hold which the Mosaic faith had upon the nation. Familiarity with them is essential for an understanding of the remarkable development which was to take place in later ages.

The series is distinctive in the following respects:

(*i*) Each volume contains the Hebrew text and English translation together with the commentary. (*ii*) The exposition is designed primarily for the ordinary reader of the Bible rather than for the student, and aims at providing this class of reader with requisite direction for the understanding and appreciation of the Biblical Book. (*iii*) The commentary is invariably based upon the received Hebrew text. When this presents difficulties, the most probable translation and interpretation are suggested, without resort to textual emendation. (*iv*) It offers a *Jewish* commentary. It takes into account the exegesis of the Talmudical Rabbis as well as of the leading Jewish commentators.

All Biblical references are cited according to chapter and verse as in the Hebrew Bible. It is unfortunate that, unlike the American-Jewish translation, the English Authorized and Revised Versions, although made direct from the Hebrew text, did not conform to its chapter divisions. An undesirable complication was thereby introduced into Bible study. In the Hebrew the longer headings of the Psalms are counted as a separate verse; consequently Ps. xxxiv. 12, e.g., corresponds to verse 11 in A.V. and R.V. It is also necessary to take into account a marginal note like that found against 1 Kings iv. 21, 'ch. v. 1 in Heb.', so that the Hebrew 1 Kings, v. 14 tallies with iv. 34 in the English.

It is hoped that this Commentary, though more particularly planned for the needs of Jews, will prove helpful to all who desire a fuller knowledge of the Bible, irrespective of their creed.

A. Cohen

CONTENTS

יהושע

JOSHUA

INTRODUCTION AND COMMENTARY

by

RABBI DR. H. FREEDMAN, B.A., Ph.D.

Revised by
RABBI A.J. ROSENBERG

JOSHUA : יהושע

INTRODUCTION

I. CONTENTS

THE Book of Joshua, named after the national leader who succeeded Moses, relates the conquest of Canaan and its division among the tribes of Israel, in accordance with the Divine promise. This promise, first given to Abraham, inaugurated the history of the Jewish people. It was renewed to the other two patriarchs, Isaac and Jacob, and frequently repeated throughout the wanderings of the Israelites in the wilderness. It has been a constant factor in their long journey across the stage of history, their assurance in the past and hope for the future. The forty years in the desert were not a period of aimless wandering, but of preparation—spiritual, physical and mental—for its fulfilment, which was largely (but not completely) achieved by Joshua.

The twenty-four chapters of the Book fall into five divisions:

i. Chapters i–v, PREPARATION. God's charge to Joshua. The mission of the spies. The crossing of the Jordan. Circumcision of the people.

ii. Chapters vi–xii, IMMEDIATE FULFILMENT. The conquest of Canaan. This includes the miraculous fall of Jericho's walls, the setback at Ai and its subsequent capture, the building of an altar on mount Ebal, the surrender of the Gibeonites, the alliances against Joshua and the list of the defeated kings.

iii. Chapters xiii–xiv, FUTURE FULFILMENT AND PAST ACHIEVEMENT. This section contains a list of the territories still to be conquered and a historical retrospect of the conquests effected by Moses.

iv. Chapters xv–xx, BOUNDARIES. The frontiers of the tribes are described, to which is added an appendix enumerating the cities of refuge and the Levitical cities.

v. Chapters xxii–xxiv, EPILOGUE. The return of the two and a half tribes to their land in Transjordan. Joshua's farewell address, his death and burial.

II. PLACE OF THE BOOK IN THE CANON AND ITS IMPORTANCE

The Book of Joshua is the first of the Biblical section designated by the Jews 'the Former Prophets,' which also includes the Books of Judges, Samuel and Kings. Strictly speaking these Books are historical rather than prophetic in content. Nevertheless they constitute the Former Prophets. First, because they are written under Divine inspiration. Second, they do more than relate events in the early history of Israel; they also, and perhaps primarily, underline the doctrine that God and Israel are linked by a covenant, upon the faithful observance of which the national existence depended. They are written less from the standpoint of the historian than of the prophet. Hence these Books are rightly considered prophetical.

In the Hebrew the Book bears the superscription *Yehoshua*; in the LXX *Iesous* (in some MSS. with the addition of *uios Naue*, 'son of Naue'); in the Peshitta it is called 'Ketaba di Yeshu bar Nun talmideh d'Mushe' (the Book of Joshua, son of Nun, the disciple of Moses). In all but the last it immediately follows the Pentateuch, which is the natural order. The Peshitta, however, places the Book of Job between the Pentateuch and *Joshua*, in accordance with the Rabbinic view (B.B. 15a) that *Job* was written by Moses.

A passage in the Talmud (Ned. 22b) reads: 'Adda son of R. Chanina said: Had not Israel sinned, only the Pentateuch and the Book of Joshua would have been given to them, the latter because it records the disposition of the Land of Israel among the tribes.' This dictum summarizes its importance. It is the natural sequel to, and conclusion of, the Pentateuch through which run two central themes: the revelation of the Torah to Israel and the promise of Canaan. The realization of that promise is envisaged and begun, but not consummated, in the Pentateuch; the Book of Joshua tells of its achievement. In spite of this, and although its style is often reminiscent of *Deuteronomy,* there is no proof that it was an integral part of the Pentateuch, with which it is combined by modern critics to form a Hexateuch. The Books of Moses were held in such exceptional veneration by the Jews, that it is inconceivable that a whole section would ever have been allowed to be detached from them, all the more so because

it completes the Pentateuch, if it had been united therewith.

Joshua is important for what succeeds it in the Bible. The histories contained in *Judges*, *Samuel* and *Kings* are inexplicable without it. Furthermore, it confirms Israel's title-deeds, as it were, to the Promised Land.

III. STYLE OF THE BOOK

Joshua is written in straightforward prose, as dictated by its historical contents. The language is severely practical, and is characterized by an absence of literary ornamentation. This simplicity is found even in the account of Joshua's mysterious visitor, *the captain of the Lord's host,* where a more poetic and elevated style might have been expected.

The simplicity, however, does not exclude a certain vigour, almost amounting to vehemence, when matters have to be emphasized. Repetitions, couplets, antitheses and synonyms are employed for this purpose; e.g. *Be strong and of good courage* (i. 6, 9). *Be not affrighted, neither be thou dismayed* (i. 9). *I will not fail thee, nor forsake thee* (i. 5). *For then thou shalt make thy ways prosperous, and then thou shalt have good success* (i. 8). *Only be strong and very courageous, to observe to do according to all the law . . . turn not from it to the right hand or to the left* (i. 7). The next verse repeats the idea but in reverse order, the negative preceding the positive: *This book of the law shall not depart out of thy mouth, but thou shalt meditate therein day and night* (i. 8).

Verbs are piled one on another to drive home an important truth: *Only take diligent heed to do the commandment and the law . . . to love the Lord your God, and to walk in all His ways, and to keep His commandments, and to cleave unto Him, and to serve Him with all your heart and with all your soul* (xxii. 5). *Therefore be ye very courageous . . . that ye turn not aside . . . that ye come not among these nations . . . neither make mention of the name of their gods, nor cause to swear by them, neither serve them, nor worship them* (xxiii. 6f.). The condemnation of Achan's trespass is hammered out on the anvil of God's wrath, blow succeeding blow: *Israel hath sinned; yea, they have even transgressed My covenant . . . they have even taken of the devoted thing . . . and have also stolen, and dissembled also, and they have even put it among their own stuff* (vii. 11). The effect is

heightened in the original by *even* and *also* both being expressed by the same word *gam.*

As already stated, this Book marks the fulfilment of God's promise. Since this promise is one of the main themes of the Pentateuch, we naturally expect language and style to be affected by it. Moreover *Numbers* and *Deuteronomy* record the beginning of the conquest by Moses. Both he and his successor stressed its religious purpose and conditions; it is consequently not surprising to find a striking affinity of language, many expressions being almost identical. Cf., for instance, i. 3f. with Deut. xi. 24, i. 5 with Deut. xxxi. 8, i. 15 with Deut. iii. 20. Such examples could be multiplied and are what we would expect.

But the style is not a mere slavish imitation and contains many original expressions, some of which are found in later Books of the Bible, but not in the Pentateuch; e.g. *This book of the law shall not depart out of thy mouth,* etc. (i. 8). *His blood shall be on our head* (ii. 19). *Art thou for us, or for our adversaries?* (v. 13), which has become almost proverbial. *Wineskins, worn and rent and patched up* (ix. 4).

The only poetic passage is the Song of Victory in chapter x, quoted from *the book of Yashar.* The poem is, like all Biblical poetry, based on parallelism, here in a very simple form:

Sun, stand thou still upon Gibeon;
And thou, Moon, in the valley of Aijalon.
And the sun stood still, and the moon stayed,
Until the nation had avenged themselves of their
enemies (x. 12f.).

IV. RELIGIOUS TEACHINGS

As remarked above, the Book seeks to relate not only the conquest of the Land of Israel, but also to stress the spiritual and religious basis thereof. This concept has to be examined in detail.

From the outset it is made clear that the land is given to the people by God (i. 2, 6), but the gift is conditional upon faithful observance of the Torah (i. 7f.). It is probable that the circumcision at Gilgal (v. 2ff.), immediately before the campaign, was intended to underline that the land was theirs only in virtue of their covenant with God, of which circumcision was the outward symbol (Gen. xvii. 7ff.). It is noteworthy that one of Joshua's last acts was solemnly to

renew the covenant, after first warning Israel that the Lord was a holy and jealous God Who was exacting in His demands upon His worshippers (xxiv. 19–25).

While the narrative makes it evident that the greater part of the country was won by long and arduous fighting (cf. xi. 18, xiii. I, xvii. 12f.), the nation's Divine title to the land was manifested in the miracles which accompanied the early stages, starting with the passage of the Jordan, and the role allotted to the ark of the covenant in showing them the way. The purpose of the miracles was not only that all peoples should recognize God's might, but what was equally important, that Israel should fear Him always (iv. 24). The miraculous fall of Jericho doubtless served the same purpose, just as did Joshua's total ban on the city, which underlined that the Israelites were engaged in a holy task, and not in an ordinary war of plunder. Hence the severe punishment meted out to Achan for violating the ban.

In keeping with this aim, Joshua built an altar of stones on mount Ebal after the defeat of Ai and *wrote there upon the stones a copy of the law of Moses* (viii. 30ff.).

As the people were exhorted to keep in mind their Divine commission and its conditions before and during the campaign, so were they not allowed to forget them after the conquest. This is the theme of Joshua's farewell addresses: *Only take diligent heed to do the commandment and the law, which Moses the servant of the Lord commanded you, to love the Lord your God, and to walk in all His ways, and to keep His commandments, and to cleave unto Him, to serve Him with all your heart and with all your soul* (xxii. 5).

In their hour of triumph he warned them that they would suffer the same fate as the original inhabitants whom they had expelled, if they did not keep their part of the covenant (xxiii. 15f.). Two important religious ideas are enunciated in this connection. First, that their acceptance of God must be voluntary; the choice lay with themselves: *And if it seem evil unto you to serve the Lord, choose you this day whom ye will serve* (xxiv. 15); and their allegiance, if acknowledged, must be wholehearted. Second, there is the doctrine of collective responsibility. This was already implied in the incident of Achan and the defeat of Ai. It was left for the people

themselves to formulate this doctrine in remonstrating with the departed two and a half tribes for having set up an altar: *Did not Achan the son of Zerah commit a trespass . . . and wrath fell upon all the congregation of Israel? and that man perished not alone in his iniquity* (xxii. 20). It is a thought which has become integrated in Jewish life for all time.

V. AUTHORSHIP AND COMPOSITION

The Talmud declares: 'Joshua wrote the Book which bears his name. . . . But is it not written, *And Joshua the son of Nun, the servant of the Lord, died?* (xxiv. 29). Eleazar completed it. But it is also written in it, *And Eleazar the son of Aaron died!* (xxiv. 33). Phinehas completed it' (B.B. 14b, 15a). In this manner Rabbinic tradition asserts the unity and eponymous authorship of the Book, though admitting that passages in it must have been written after Joshua's death. An analysis does in fact point to two characteristics: unity of purpose and the impression of authorship by a contemporary eye-witness of the events described.

Unity of purpose. From first to last there is unmistakably one aim: to recount the conquest of the Promised Land and the conditions attached to the Israelites' possession of it. This is explicitly stated in the first chapter; it forms the theme of the farewell exhortations in the last chapters, and it is obviously the *motif* of almost every chapter in between. Each stage in the campaign and every incident—be it the fall of Jericho and the ban imposed upon it, the unexpected set-back at Ai, the sin of Achan, the treaty with the Gibeonites, the division of the land, the erection of an altar by the two and a half tribes and the reaction of the rest of the people—all tend to one goal and bear the impress of one consistent narrative.

A contemporary account. Equally strong is the impression that we have the work of an eye-witness. This is shown by the minuteness and accuracy of detail (see e.g., on x. 32). The exact delineation of the respective territories of the tribes and the local and topographical allusions point to the same conclusion. Even without the explicit statement in xxiv. 26 that *Joshua wrote these words in the book of the law of God*, we might have expected him to make a record of the stirring events. Though *these*

words in the verse quoted cannot be proved to be the whole Book, since none would be more competent than he to write the full account and it was natural for him to do so, we may credit him with its substantial authorship.

In the Talmudic extract cited above it was noted that the last few sentences were added by others. Later commentators point out that this must also apply to other statements; e.g. Caleb's expulsion of the three sons of Anak from Hebron and the capture of Leshem by the Danites (xv. 14, xix 47) are obviously of later date, since these events took place after Joshua's death (but see on xix. 47). Nevertheless, these few exceptions do not affect the hypothesis of Joshua's authorship of the work as a whole.

Against this claim it has been urged that the phrase *unto this day,* which occurs seven times, implies that the reference is to a much later date. But on examination it is found that the words are used idiomatically to denote stability of fact rather than lapse of time. The most illuminating example is found in vi. 25 where it is related that *Rahab dwelt in the midst of Israel unto this day.* The verb *dwelt* is in the feminine singular and refers to Rahab personally; consequently *unto this day* cannot denote more than her lifetime and she was a contemporary of Joshua.

A more serious objection arises out of the narrative itself which is alleged to be both self-contradictory and in disagreement with other parts of the Bible, particularly the Book of Judges. Whereas the Book as a whole represents the conquest as having been effected by the united nation under Joshua and almost complete, the first chapter of *Judges* depicts it as the work of the tribes acting independently. Again, the national unity implied in *Joshua* is at variance with the independent capture of Hebron and Debir by Caleb and Othniel respectively (xiv. 6ff., xv. 14ff.). The completeness of the conquest does not agree with the retention of Jerusalem in the hands of the Jebusites (xv. 63), and the failure to occupy Gezer (xvi. 10) as well as the cities from Beth-shean across the plain of Jezreel westwards (xvii. 11ff.). Again, cities described as captured or destroyed (e.g. Jericho) are subsequently found to be still standing or in the hands of the Canaanites.

These contradictions are readily resolved by a straightforward reading of the Book,

which not only reconciles them, but reveals precisely what we should expect. The seven people occupying Canaan were strongly organized, though not united at the beginning of the campaign. It is inconceivable that a piece-meal attack by the tribes of Israel acting separately and independently could have succeeded. The invasion in the first place must have been in force by the whole nation. Such a national invasion does not preclude local action, and to this category belong the exploits of Caleb and Othniel. Apart from the initial victory over Jericho, the war was fought on normal lines, the usual military tactics such as ambushes and ruses being employed. It met with a series of spectacular successes, aided by lack of unity among the defenders. The narrative makes it clear that only gradually, as the danger grew more pressing, was unity achieved among the Canaanite peoples. One city after another fell, and 'kings' were conquered in rapid succession. It must, however, be remembered that the cities were small, and the 'kings' only local petty chieftains. Thereafter the process slowed down. Joshua waged war for a long period, according to tradition seven years. Canaan is a small country; why, then, was so lengthy a campaign necessary? The inference is that after the initial victories by the Israelites the defenders rallied, perhaps at first carrying on guerilla warfare and afterwards coming more boldly into the open. Some towns may have been recaptured by them, and from others they could not be dislodged, though they were subdued. Hence the long war of seven years, and even then the country was not fully subjugated (cf. xiii. I, xviii. 2f.).

The division of the land had therefore to be made while the conquest was incomplete. An understandable war-weariness diminished their martial ardour (xviii. 3ff.), and they had to make do with what had been achieved thus far, postponing the final subjugation to later. In the meantime several tribes settled in their allotments, and the other lands still unconquered were assigned. This was psychologically necessary, but it weakened national ties. We can well understand that the Canaanites, emboldened by these conditions, won back many territories which, after Joshua's death, had to be re-taken. And because the national unity was affected, the people no longer acted as one

body but tribally. This tendency already manifested itself in Joshua's days, when the complaint of the Joseph tribes that insufficient land had been allocated to them was met by the answer that *they* (not the nation) should clear the hill-country. At that time this may have been the exception rather than the rule, occasioned by the fact that they had demanded what amounted to preferential treatment. After Joshua's death it became the normal attitude.

In all these events there is nothing contradictory, but a process often repeated in the course of history. Consequently we may conclude with the Rabbis of the Talmud that, apart from a few later additions added for the sake of completeness, the Book as we have it is the composition of Joshua.

VI. BOUNDARIES AND GEOGRAPHY

Boundaries. Both in the Pentateuch and in *Joshua* the frontiers of the Land of Israel fall into two categories. First there are the ideal boundaries as ultimately envisaged. These are variously given as *from the river of Egypt unto the great river, the river Euphrates* (Gen. xv. 18). *From the wilderness, and Lebanon, from the river, the river Euphrates, even unto the hinder sea* (Deut. xi. 24; cf. Josh. I. 4). *From the Red Sea even unto the sea of the Philistines, and from the wilderness unto the river,* i.e. the Euphrates (Exod. xxiii. 31). These boundaries were never fully realized and remained an ideal for the future. The promise was partially fulfilled in the latter days of David and in Solomon's reign, when they *ruled* as far as the Euphrates (I Kings v. 4), but the nation lived within the more limited boundaries of the second category.

This consists of the actual boundaries encompassing the land which Joshua was bidden to conquer and divide. The territory thus acquired is described as *the hill-country, and all the South, and all the land of Goshen, and the Lowland, and the Arabah, and the hill-country of Israel, and the Lowland of the same; from the bare mountain, that goeth up to Seir, even unto Baal-gad in the valley of Lebanon under mount Hermon* (xi. 16f., cf. xii. 7). This was west of the Jordan, Transjordan having been conquered by Moses. It embraced *from the valley of Arnon unto mount Hermon . . . all the cities of the plain, and all Gilead, and all Bashan* (Deut. iii. 8ff.; cf. Josh. xii. I). Accordingly the

actual boundaries were: the river of Egypt (Wadi el-Arish), *the bare mountain* and the river Arnon in the south, Lebanon in the north, going in a southerly direction to the valley of Mizpeh (xi. 8), thence north to the source of the Jordan and mount Hermon on the east.

Geography. The Land of Israel is divisible into the following regions:

i. The seashore (*choph hayyam,* Deut. i. 7): the low-lying strip of coast running the whole length of the country and forming its western boundary. This, together with the low hills south of Aijalon, is called the *Shephelah* (the Lowland).

ii. The hill-country (*har*): the ridge of mountains running down the centre from north to south.

iii. The *Negeb,* i.e. the dry region in the south.

iv. The wilderness of Judah to the east of the territory allotted to Judah and Benjamin.

v. The *Arabah* (plain): the plain of the Jordan which divides the country into two.

Transjordan falls into the following divisions:

i. The eastern *Arabah,* also called the *Emek* (xiii. 27).

ii. Bashan in the north down to the river Jarmuk.

iii. Gilead, stretching from the Jarmuk to the Arnon.

VII. LIFE AND CHARACTER OF JOSHUA

Joshua (for the name see on i. I), an Ephraimite and chief of his tribe (Num. xiii. 3, 8), was Moses' servant and successor. He was already recognized as the military leader of the people soon after their departure from Egypt, he having been chosen to head the men who fought against the Amalekites (Exod. xvii. 9ff.). As Moses' attendant he accompanied him up the mountain for the reception of the Torah (Exod. xxiv. 13). This fact is highly significant, since it indicates that even then he was not simply a military leader, but a spiritual disciple of Moses. Whenever God spoke to Moses *face to face,* Joshua was left in the sacred Tent to guard it (Exod. xxxiii. II). When Eldad and Medad prophesied in the camp (Num. xi. 27ff.), he was the zealous defender of Moses' prerogatives.

He was one of the twelve spies whom Moses sent to survey Canaan. Together with Caleb he vainly sought to counteract the defeatist attitude of the other ten. Their courage and faith were duly rewarded: of all the adults who left Egypt they alone entered the Promised Land (Num. xiv. 6ff., 22 ff.)

He was thus naturally marked out as his master's successor. Moses' plea to God to *set a man over the congregation* was answered by the command: *Take thee Joshua the son of Nun, a man in whom is spirit . . . and give him a charge. . . . And he shall stand before Eleazar the priest, who shall inquire for him by the judgment of the Urim before the* LORD (Num. xxvii. 16ff.). Two points are noteworthy: that in spite of Joshua's long apprenticeship Moses did not of his own accord choose his successor; and as leader Joshua had to submit to Divine guidance.

Moses' trusted servant from the time of the exodus, Joshua remained faithful to him to the end, having been his spokesman in the delivery of the farewell address (cf. Deut. xxxii. 44). He was in comparison with his master as the moon is to the sun ('The face of Moses was as the face of the sun; the face of Joshua was as the face of the moon,' B.B. 75a), but a moon which had absorbed and reflected the maximum brightness from the sun.

So the stage was set for his succession, and the opening verses of the Book follow in expected sequence on the account of Moses' death. Joshua came to his task both militarily experienced and spiritually prepared. He proved himself a strategist of high order; but had he been only a great general, he would not occupy the place he does in Biblical history. His military prowess was superimposed upon a foundation of deep faith and religious piety. Only a man with these qualities could lead an expedition which, in the final analysis, depended for its success on the extent to which the people were faithful to God and His covenant.

Loyal allegiance to God was ever foremost in his thoughts to the end of his life. His parting exhortations to the people are not those of a military conqueror but of a religious leader. They are as remarkable for what he did not say as for what he did. He did not urge the people to make themselves strong materially and in the martial sense. Their strength consisted in Divine help which they could only obtain through faithful service. *Therefore be ye very courageous to keep and to do all that is written in the book of the law of Moses, that ye turn not aside therefrom to the right hand or to the left* (xxiii. 6).

The uncompromising fidelity which he demanded from others he displayed in full measure himself; nowhere more so than when he threw down the challenge to Israel to choose their allegiance in full consciousness of the difficulties and sacrifices involved in serving God, and in his assertion that even if the whole nation abandoned Him for the gods of the Amorites, *as for me and my house, we will serve the Lord* (xxiv. 15).

He was a man of his word, modest and simple in his wants. He kept the promise made by the spies to Rahab and her family. He kept faith with the Gibeonites, though they had obtained his promise under false pretences. He did not use his exalted position for personal aggrandizement; his own needs were satisfied with a humble estate in an obscure region. Nor did he seek advantages for his family or tribe. He had the opportunity to do this when the Josephites demanded more extensive territory because of their numbers. He might have acceded to their request with every show of fairness and then enlarged the portion of his own tribe. Instead, he told them to use their superior numbers to clear the forest and drive out the Canaanites from their fastnesses. There spoke the fair-minded and intrepid leader.

His was an inspiring example to the people. No wonder that *Israel served the Lord all the days of Joshua, and all the days of the elders that outlived Joshua* (xxiv. 31).

VIII. NOTE ON THE COMMENTARY

The Bible is the Book of God's unfolding revelation to man. It is a spiritual pageant in which the present Book takes its place as one of the tableaux. From that standpoint the commentary has been written. No fanciful flights have been indulged in, and notes have been confined to the plain elucidation of the text. At the same time its inner spiritual essence has been brought out wherever possible. The Bible is the flowering of the Jewish religious and spiritual genius, for which reason the interpretation of the Rabbis, whether scientific in the modern sense of the term or not, often gets nearer to the spirit of

the writer. Hence the Talmud and Midrashic literature have been freely quoted.

The Book of Joshua, recording as it does the Israelite campaign for the Holy Land, is of especial interest to-day when Palestine is being rebuilt as the Jewish homeland. There is need now for research to locate and identify the newly established settlements in their relation to the numerous places mentioned in the Bible and particularly in Joshua. In this connection acknowledgment is made of the constant reference to the Hebrew commentary by Hershcovitz and Zidman (Jerusalem, published by the Mosad ha-Rav Kook, 5702–1942). Much archaeological research has been carried on during recent years in Bible lands, and use has been made of its results in the pages that follow.

JOSHUA

1. Now it came to pass after the death of Moses the servant of the LORD, that the LORD spoke unto Joshua the son of Nun, Moses' minister, saying: 2. 'Moses My servant is dead; now therefore arise,

1 וַיְהִי אַחֲרֵי מוֹת מֹשֶׁה עֶבֶד
יְהֹוָה וַיֹּאמֶר יְהֹוָה אֶל־יְהוֹשֻׁעַ
בִּן־נוּן מְשָׁרֵת מֹשֶׁה לֵאמֹר׃
2 מֹשֶׁה עַבְדִּי מֵת וְעַתָּה קוּם

v. 1. הפטרת שמחת תורה

CHAPTER I

GOD'S CHARGE TO JOSHUA

1–9 JOSHUA APPOINTED MOSES' SUCCESSOR

1. *now it came to pass.* lit. 'and it was,' which does not necessarily imply a continuation of what goes before; e.g. the Books of Ezekiel, Jonah, Ruth, Esther and others likewise begin with 'and it was,' although they are entirely disconnected. But here the beginning is closely connected with the end of Deuteronomy where the death of Moses is related. Consequently this chapter is appointed the Haphtarah (additional Scriptural lesson) on the festival of Simchath Torah (Rejoicing of the Law) in the diaspora and of Shemini Atsereth (Eighth Day of Tabernacles) in Palestine, when the annual cycle of the synagogal reading of the Torah is concluded with the final chapters of Deuteronomy.

the death of Moses. According to tradition, he died on the seventh of Adar, the twelfth month of the Jewish year.

the servant of the LORD. This is the highest title man is able to achieve. He is so designated in several passages (cf. Exod. xiv. 31; Num. xii. 7, etc.). Kimchi observes: This title was conferred upon those who dedicated all their actions, even those of a worldly nature, to the service of God. Abraham, David and the prophets were also called His servants.

Joshua. His name was originally Hoshea. Moses changed it to Joshua when he was sent nearly forty years earlier on the ill-fated mission of the spies (Num. xiii. 16). The name means 'the LORD will save,' or 'may the LORD save.' According to the Talmud, Sotah 34b the change expressed a prayer: 'The Lord save thee from the counsel of the spies,' viz. that Canaan could never be conquered.

Moses' minister. Cf. Exod. xxiv. 13; Num. xi. 28. Immediately after the exodus we find him acting as Moses' lieutenant and apparently the military leader of the people (Exod. xvii. 9). He was Moses' obvious successor, and was so designated during his lifetime (Num. xxvii. 18; Deut. i. 38). It is interesting to observe that Moses was not succeeded by one of his sons: they did not deserve it, and leadership is not hereditary, although the priesthood was. The Rabbis remark that when Moses asked God to appoint a successor to him, he was thinking of his own sons. But God answered him, *Whoso keepeth the fig tree shall eat the fruit thereof* (Prov. xxvii. 18), i.e. Joshua had earned the distinction by a lifetime of service, whereas Moses' son had not (Num. Rabbah xii. 9).

2. *is dead.* He died in the land of Moab, over against Beth-peor, facing Jericho, on the east side of the Jordan (Deut. xxxiv. 1, 6). From there the crossing had to be made. Since he is dead, *now therefore arise, go over this Jordan.* It having been decreed that he was not to enter the land, the crossing had to be deferred until after his death (Ralbag).

go over this Jordan, thou, and all this people, unto the land which I do give to them, even to the children of Israel. 3. Every place that the sole of your foot shall tread upon, to you have I given it, as I spoke unto Moses. 4. From the wilderness, and this Lebanon, even unto the great river, the river Euphrates, all the land of the Hittites, and unto the Great Sea toward the going down of the sun,

עֲבֹר אֶת־הַיַּרְדֵּן הַזֶּה אַתָּה
וְכָל־הָעָם הַזֶּה אֶל־הָאָרֶץ
אֲשֶׁר אָנֹכִי נֹתֵן לָהֶם לִבְנֵי
יִשְׂרָאֵל: כָּל־מָקוֹם אֲשֶׁר 3
תִּדְרֹךְ כַּף־רַגְלְכֶם בּוֹ לָכֶם
נְתַתִּיו כַּאֲשֶׁר דִּבַּרְתִּי אֶל־
מֹשֶׁה: מֵהַמִּדְבָּר וְהַלְּבָנוֹן 4
הַזֶּה וְעַד־הַנָּהָר הַגָּדוֹל נְהַר־
פְּרָת כֹּל אֶרֶץ הַחִתִּים וְעַד־
הַיָּם הַגָּדוֹל מְבוֹא הַשֶּׁמֶשׁ יִהְיֶה

Jordan. 'The descender from Dan.' It is a swiftly-flowing river, and takes its name from its descent from its source in Dan, a city in northern Eretz Israel, known later as Paneas, or Banias. It flows through the Lake of Sibkay, Tiberias, and the Dead Sea (Bek. 55a).

all this people. The new generation which had been less than twenty years old at the time of the exodus (Num. xiv. 29).

which I do give to them. Israel's claim to the land was based on a Divine decree. It began with Abraham (Gen. xiii. 14ff.) and persists all through Jewish history.

3. *every place,* etc. A reaffirmation of the promise in Deut. xi. 24.

that the sole of your foot shall tread upon. A figure of speech meaning that He would give them the strength to conquer (Kimchi). In actual fact, the land had to be won by hard fighting.

4. *the wilderness.* Of Zin (Kadesh) at the south-east corner of Canaan (Rashi from Num. xxxiv, 3).

this Lebanon. This fixed the northern boundary. It is a mountain-range, noted for its cedar trees. The Rabbis, citing Jer. xxii. 6, see in it an allusion to the Temple which whitened, through atonement, the sins of Israel (Siphrë, Ekeb). From where the people

stood it was visible in the distance; hence *this Lebanon* (Kimchi).

the river Euphrates. The ideal and furthermost eastern boundary. It was reached in the days of Solomon (I Kings v. 1).

all the land of the Hittites. The Hittites are the only tribe mentioned, as the most powerful and therefore the representative of all the seven tribes. The territory which they occupied in Canaan was only a small portion of a great empire. The Hittite empire proper lay between the Euphrates and the Orontes in north and north-east Syria (Daath Mikra).

the Great Sea. The Mediterranean, the western boundary. 'The Great Sea—that is the *whole* eastern flank of the Great Sea from its south-eastern to its north-eastern corner—shall be the western boundary of the land. If any point on the coast, between these corners were meant, the text would surely have designated that point. As it did not, the whole eastern shore of the Mediterranean must be intended. The western border of the Holy Land, therefore, begins at the south-eastern corner of the Mediterranean where the "Brook of Egypt" (the Wadi el-Arish), flowing into the Mediterranean about twenty miles south of Gaza, falls into it; hence it runs northward passing mount Carmel, Tyre, Zidon, the Lebanons, unto the northwestern border of the Bay of Alexan-

shall be your border. 5. There shall not any man be able to stand before thee all the days of thy life; as I was with Moses, so I will be with thee; I will not fail thee, nor forsake thee. 6. Be strong and of good courage; for thou shalt cause this people to inherit the land which I swore unto their fathers to give them. 7. Only be strong and very courageous, to observe to do accord-

5 נְבוּלְכֶם: לֹא־יִתְיַצֵּב אִישׁ
לְפָנֶיךָ כֹּל יְמֵי חַיֶּיךָ כַּאֲשֶׁר
הָיִיתִי עִם־מֹשֶׁה אֶהְיֶה עִמָּךְ
לֹא אַרְפְּךָ וְלֹא־אֶעֶזְבֶךָּ:
6 חֲזַק וֶאֱמָץ כִּי אַתָּה תַּנְחִיל
אֶת־הָעָם הַזֶּה אֶת־הָאָרֶץ
אֲשֶׁר־נִשְׁבַּעְתִּי לַאֲבוֹתָם לָתֵת
7 לָהֶם: רַק חֲזַק וֶאֱמַץ מְאֹד
לִשְׁמֹר לַעֲשׂוֹת כְּכָל־הַתּוֹרָה

פתח באתנח v. 6.

dretta' (S. H. Isaacs, *The True Boundaries of the Holy Land*). For a more detailed account of these boundaries, cf. Num. xxiv. 3-12.

shall be your border. In the future. So vast a territory far exceeded their needs at the time. This verse is a repetition of the promises made to Abraham (Gen. xv. 18) and Moses (Exod. xxiii. 31; Deut. xi. 24).

5. *as I was with Moses, so I will be with thee.* Both were charged with a tremendous task for which Divine aid was imperative. Each received the assurance of this help at the outset of his labours (cf. Exod. iii. 12) and subsequently (cf. iii. 7). Moses had given the same assurance to Joshua personally and to the people collectively (Deut. xxxi. 6-8).

fail thee. The root *raphah* means 'to be weak,' and the verb may be rendered here: 'I will not weaken thee,' or 'allow thee to become weak.' Elijah of Wilna comments: *I will not fail thee* in the war, *nor forsake thee* after the war.

6. *be strong and of good courage.* Do not think that My promises mean that the land will fall into your hands like ripe fruit. A strenuous campaign will be necessary which will demand all your strength and fortitude. The

phrase is repeated at the beginning of the next verse, so Rashi interprets: first in the physical sense, to fight and conquer; then in the moral sense, in observance of the Torah.

unto their fathers. To Abraham (Gen. xiii. 14f., xv. 18ff., xvii. 7ff.), to Isaac (Gen. xxvi. 3ff.) and to Jacob (Gen. xxviii. 13, xxxv, 12). In the narrower sense *fathers* denotes the three patriarchs; in a wider sense it means their ancestors in general, and the promise was made to the nation as a whole (e.g. Exod. vi. 8).

7. *very courageous.* The exhortation here is stronger and more urgent than in the preceding verse. To remain faithful to God's moral law would require even greater strength of character and steadfastness of purpose than the military operations of conquest (Daath Mikra, Daath Sofrim).

to observe, etc. Israel's possession of the land will depend on his observance of God's laws. For it is no ordinary invasion and conquest that are about to happen, but the expulsion of a people because it is morally unfit to own the land. Consequently Israel is explicitly warned of a similar fate if he lapses into similar abominations. Hence the stern admonition (cf. Lev. xviii. 25-28).

3

ing to all the law, which Moses My servant commanded thee; turn not from it to the right hand or to the left, that thou mayest have good success whithersoever thou goest. 8. This book of the law shall not depart out of thy mouth, but thou shalt meditate therein day and night, that thou mayest observe to do according to all that is written therein; for then thou shalt make thy ways prosperous, and then thou shalt have good success. 9. Have not I commanded thee? Be strong and of good courage; be not affrighted, neither be thou dismayed; for the LORD thy God is with thee whithersoever thou goest.'

10. Then Joshua commanded the officers of the people, saying: 11. 'Pass through the midst of the camp, and command the people, saying:

אֲשֶׁר צִוְּךָ מֹשֶׁה עַבְדִּי אַל־
תָּסוּר מִמֶּנּוּ יָמִין וּשְׂמֹאול
לְמַעַן תַּשְׂכִּיל בְּכֹל אֲשֶׁר
תֵּלֵךְ: לֹא־יָמוּשׁ סֵפֶר 8
הַתּוֹרָה הַזֶּה מִפִּיךָ וְהָגִיתָ בּוֹ
יוֹמָם וָלַיְלָה לְמַעַן תִּשְׁמֹר
לַעֲשׂוֹת כְּכָל־הַכָּתוּב בּוֹ כִּי־
אָז תַּצְלִיחַ אֶת־דְּרָכֶךָ וְאָז
תַּשְׂכִּיל: הֲלוֹא צִוִּיתִיךָ חֲזַק 9
וֶאֱמָץ אַל־תַּעֲרֹץ וְאַל־תֵּחָת
כִּי עִמְּךָ יְהוָה אֱלֹהֶיךָ בְּכֹל
אֲשֶׁר תֵּלֵךְ:
וַיְצַו יְהוֹשֻׁעַ אֶת־שֹׁטְרֵי הָעָם 10
לֵאמֹר: עִבְרוּ | בְּקֶרֶב 11
הַמַּחֲנֶה וְצַוּוּ אֶת־הָעָם לֵאמֹר

v. 7. סבירין ממנה v. 7. מלא ר v. 9. קמץ בז״ק

---

the law. Hebrew *torah,* lit. 'direction, teaching.' The Pentateuch is meant, along with the Oral Law, the entire body of divinely revealed Jewish teaching, ethical and legal. It thus implies far more than 'law.'

that thou mayest have good success (taskil). Lit. 'understand.' Since a successful person is thought to be wise and understanding, the term is used in this sense (Metsudath Zion).

Elijah of Wilna explains literally that through conscientious observance of the commandments, you will be given understanding and wisdom, to know how to be victorious and successful in battle.

8. *shall not depart out of thy mouth.* This is construed by some authorities as a promise and a blessing, and by others as an admoni-

tion and a command even to those fully conversant in all the intricacies of the Torah. Maimonides bases it upon the Pentateuchal command (Deut. iv. 19) *And lest they* (the words of the Torah) *be turned from thy heart all the days of thy life.* And one must necessarily forget unless constant study is maintained.

thou shalt make thy ways prosperous. This indicates that success depended upon himself. He could ensure it by faithful adherence to the Torah (Kimchi).

9. *have not I commanded thee?* On an earlier occasion, recorded in Deut. xxxi. 23.

10-11 THE OFFICERS GIVEN ORDERS

11. *command the people . . . within three days.* Ralbag argues that the order was not given

Prepare you victuals; for within three days ye are to pass over this Jordan, to go in to possess the land, which the LORD your God giveth you to possess it.'

12. And to the Reubenites, and to the Gadites, and to the half-tribe of Manasseh, spoke Joshua, saying:

13. 'Remember the word which Moses the servant of the LORD commanded you, saying: The LORD your God giveth you rest, and will give you this land. 14. Your wives, your little ones, and your cattle, shall abide in the land which Moses gave you beyond the Jordan; but ye shall pass over before your

הָכִינוּ לָכֶם צֵדָה כִּי בְּעוֹד |
שְׁלֹשֶׁת יָמִים אַתֶּם עֹבְרִים
אֶת־הַיַּרְדֵּן הַזֶּה לָבוֹא לָרֶשֶׁת
אֶת־הָאָרֶץ אֲשֶׁר יְהֹוָה
אֱלֹהֵיכֶם נֹתֵן לָכֶם לְרִשְׁתָּהּ:

12 וְלָרֽאוּבֵנִי וְלַגָּדִי וְלַחֲצִי שֵׁבֶט
הַֽמְנַשֶּׁה אָמַר יְהוֹשֻׁעַ לֵאמֹר:

13 זָכוֹר אֶת־הַדָּבָר אֲשֶׁר צִוָּה
אֶתְכֶם מֹשֶׁה עֶֽבֶד־יְהֹוָה
לֵאמֹר יְהֹוָה אֱלֹהֵיכֶם מֵנִיחַ
לָכֶם וְנָתַן לָכֶם אֶת־הָאָרֶץ

14 הַזֹּאת: נְשֵׁיכֶם טַפְּכֶם
וּמִקְנֵיכֶם יֵשְׁבוּ בָּאָרֶץ אֲשֶׁר
נָתַן לָכֶם מֹשֶׁה בְּעֵבֶר הַיַּרְדֵּן
וְאַתֶּם תַּעַבְרוּ חֲמֻשִׁים לִפְנֵי

then but after the two spies had set out, since they spent their first night in Jericho and then hid three nights in the hill-country. When they returned, the people stayed one night where they were and the next night by the Jordan, and only on the following day did they cross over.

12–18 JOSHUA REMINDS THE TWO AND A HALF TRIBES OF THEIR PROMISE

12. *the Reubenites,* etc. They had elected to settle on the east side of the Jordan. Moses had granted them permission to do this on condition that they crossed the Jordan and assisted the other tribes in the conquest. This they had solemnly promised to do (Num. xxxii), and now they were reminded of it by Joshua.

13. *Moses the servant of the* LORD. He made

use of this title of Moses to impress on them the solemnity and gravity of their promise to him (Daath Mikra).

this land. Transjordan, where they were encamped at the time.

14. *your little ones.* i.e. all below the age of twenty (cf. Num. xiv. 29, 31, where the expression is used to contrast to the adults of twenty and over).

beyond the Jordan. [Actually it was the same side of the Jordan where they were, since they had not yet passed over. But it is written from the standpoint of western Palestine which was always in the consciousness of Biblical writers as the territory of their home (cf. Deut. i, 1). In v. 1 it is used of western Palestine, but there *westward* is added. An exception occurs in ix. 1.]

before your brethren. See on iv. 12.

brethren armed, all the mighty men of valour, and shall help them; 15. until the LORD have given your brethren rest, as unto you, and they also have possessed the land which the LORD your God giveth them; then ye shall return unto the land of your possession, and possess it, which Moses the servant of the LORD gave you beyond the Jordan toward the sunrising.'

16. And they answered Joshua, saying: 'All that thou hast commanded us we will do, and whithersoever thou sendest us we will go. 17. According as we hearkened unto Moses in all things, so will we hearken unto thee; only the LORD thy God be with thee, as He was with Moses. 18. Whosoever he be that shall rebel against thy commandment, and shall not hearken unto thy words in all that thou commandest him, he shall be put to death; only be strong and of good courage.'

אֲחֵיכֶם כֹּל גִּבּוֹרֵי הַחַיִל
15 וַעֲזַרְתֶּם אוֹתָם: עַד אֲשֶׁר־
יָנִיחַ יְהֹוָה ׀ לַאֲחֵיכֶם כָּכֶם
וְיָרְשׁוּ גַם־הֵמָּה אֶת־הָאָרֶץ
אֲשֶׁר־יְהֹוָה אֱלֹהֵיכֶם נֹתֵן
לָהֶם וְשַׁבְתֶּם לְאֶרֶץ יְרֻשַּׁתְכֶם
וִירִשְׁתֶּם אוֹתָהּ אֲשֶׁר ׀ נָתַן
לָכֶם מֹשֶׁה עֶבֶד יְהֹוָה בְּעֵבֶר
הַיַּרְדֵּן מִזְרַח הַשָּׁמֶשׁ:
16 וַיַּעֲנוּ אֶת־יְהוֹשֻׁעַ לֵאמֹר כֹּל
אֲשֶׁר־צִוִּיתָנוּ נַעֲשֶׂה וְאֶל־
כָּל־אֲשֶׁר תִּשְׁלָחֵנוּ נֵלֵךְ:
17 כְּכֹל אֲשֶׁר־שָׁמַעְנוּ אֶל־מֹשֶׁה
כֵּן נִשְׁמַע אֵלֶיךָ רַק יִהְיֶה יְהֹוָה
אֱלֹהֶיךָ עִמָּךְ כַּאֲשֶׁר הָיָה עִם־
18 מֹשֶׁה: כָּל־אִישׁ אֲשֶׁר־יַמְרֶה
אֶת־פִּיךָ וְלֹא־יִשְׁמַע אֶת־
דְּבָרֶיךָ לְכֹל אֲשֶׁר־תְּצַוֶּנּוּ
יוּמָת רַק חֲזַק וֶאֱמָץ: ׃

נ״א אל v. 18.   ע״כ v. 18.

---

all the mighty men of valour. I.e. the mightiest of those of military age. According to the census of Num. xxvi, the Reubenites numbered 43,730, the Gadites numbered 40,500, and the entire tribe of Manasseh numbered 52,700. The soldiers who went to wage war with the Canaanites numbered about 40,000 (infra iv. 13). Apparently, the others remained behind to guard the women and children (Daath Mikra).

17. according as we hearkened unto Moses in all things. In spite of the people's frequent murmurings against Moses and Aaron, on the whole their authority had been unquestioned. There were, nevertheless. exceptions, as in the revolt of Korah and his associates (Num. xvi).

18. he shall be put to death. The basis of the Talmudic maxim: He who rebels against the kingdom is liable to death (Berakoth 32b).

2   CHAPTER II   ב

1. And Joshua the son of Nun sent out of Shittim two spies secretly, saying: 'Go view the land, and Jericho.' And they went, and came into the house of a harlot whose name was Rahab, and lay there. 2. And it was told the king of Jericho, saying: 'Behold, there came men in hither to-night of the children of Israel to search out the

וַיִּשְׁלַ֣ח יְהוֹשֻׁעַ־בִּן־נ֠וּן מִן־
הַשִּׁטִּ֞ים שְׁנַֽיִם־אֲנָשִׁ֤ים מְרַגְּלִים֙
חֶ֣רֶשׁ לֵאמֹ֔ר לְכ֛וּ רְא֥וּ אֶת־
הָאָ֖רֶץ וְאֶת־יְרִיח֑וֹ וַיֵּ֨לְכ֜וּ
וַ֠יָּבֹאוּ בֵּֽית־אִשָּׁ֥ה זוֹנָ֛ה וּשְׁמָ֥הּ
רָחָ֖ב וַיִּשְׁכְּבוּ־שָֽׁמָּה׃ 2 וַיֵּ֣אָמַ֔ר
לְמֶ֣לֶךְ יְרִיחֹ֖ו לֵאמֹ֑ר הִנֵּ֣ה
אֲנָשִׁ֗ים בָּ֣אוּ הֵ֧נָּה הַלַּ֛יְלָה מִבְּנֵ֥י
יִשְׂרָאֵ֖ל לַחְפֹּ֥ר אֶת־הָאָֽרֶץ׃

v. 1. הפטרת שלח לך

CHAPTER II

THE MISSION OF THE TWO SPIES

1. *Shittim.* In the Jordan valley, opposite Jericho. The word means 'acacia trees,' from the presence of which the place probably received its name. It was also known as Abel-shittim (Num. xxxiii. 49), i.e. 'the meadow (or, moist place) of Shittim.' It is now generally identified with Kefrein (Daath Mikra).

Jericho. The purpose of this mission was to see the land, but primarily Jericho, a fortified city situated on the boundary and acting as guardian for the hinterland. The victory over Jericho thus served as a psychological weapon to weaken the will to resistance of the entire land. This was Joshua's intent, not a strategic mission to determine the physical structure of the city, but the psychological makeup of its defenders. Thus, their report in v. xxiv, reads, *Truly the Lord hath delivered into our hands all the land, and moreover all the inhabitants of the land do melt away before us* (Alshich and Malbim). Ancient Jericho was situated near the Well of Elisha, north-west of the present Jericho, west of the Jordan and north of the Dead Sea (Daath Mikra). It was known as the 'City of Palms' and famed for

its fertility (Josephus, *Jewish War*, IV, viii. 3). Hence the Rabbis explained that Jericho was specially mentioned because it was worth all the rest put together (Siphrë).

harlot. Hebrew *zonah,* which the Targum and Jewish commentators connect with *mazon,* 'food,' and render 'an innkeeper.' It may be that she was both. The spies chose her house because strangers would not normally be noticed where travellers were constantly coming and going; also, from the conversation of those who resorted there they might learn about the spirit and morale of the people.

Rahab. According to Rabbinical tradition, she became the enchantress of eight prophets and priests, including Jeremiah. Some even assert that Joshua married her after she became a proselyte (Meg. 14b). This is evidence that her spiritual beauty matched her physical beauty.

2. *it was told,* etc. Their discovery is not surprising in spite of their precautions, because the country would be on the alert in face of imminent attack (Daath Mikra).

the king of Jericho. The numerous 'kings' mentioned in this Book (cf. xii. 7ff. where thirty-one are enumerated) were merely local

7

land.' 3. And the king of Jericho sent unto Rahab, saying: 'Bring forth the men that are come to thee, that are entered into thy house; for they are come to search out all the land.' 4. And the woman took the two men, and hid them; and she said: 'Yea, the men came unto me, but I knew not whence they were; 5. and it came to pass about the time of the shutting of the gate, when it was dark, that the men went out; whither the men went I know not; pursue after them quickly; for ye shall overtake them.' 6. But she had brought them up to the roof, and hid them with the stalks of flax, which she had spread out upon the roof.

3 וַיִּשְׁלַח מֶלֶךְ יְרִיחוֹ אֶל־רָחָב
לֵאמֹר הוֹצִיאִי הָאֲנָשִׁים
הַבָּאִים אֵלַיִךְ אֲשֶׁר־בָּאוּ
לְבֵיתֵךְ כִּי לַחְפֹּר אֶת־כָּל־
4 הָאָרֶץ בָּאוּ: וַתִּקַּח הָאִשָּׁה
אֶת־שְׁנֵי הָאֲנָשִׁים וַתִּצְפְּנוֹ
וַתֹּאמֶר כֵּן בָּאוּ אֵלַי הָאֲנָשִׁים
5 וְלֹא יָדַעְתִּי מֵאַיִן הֵמָּה: וַיְהִי
הַשַּׁעַר לִסְגּוֹר בַּחֹשֶׁךְ
וְהָאֲנָשִׁים יָצָאוּ לֹא יָדַעְתִּי אָנָה
הָלְכוּ הָאֲנָשִׁים רִדְפוּ מַהֵר
6 אַחֲרֵיהֶם כִּי תַשִּׂיגוּם: וְהִיא
הֶעֱלָתַם הַגָּגָה וַתִּטְמְנֵם
בְּפִשְׁתֵּי הָעֵץ הָעֲרֻכוֹת לָהּ

v. 5. קמץ בז״ק

chieftains. This is confirmed by the Tel el-Amarna Letters. They were vassals of great kings of other countries, many acknowledging the overlordship of the Pharaohs. Cf. Barton, pp. 441ff. for an interesting collection of these letters, some of which are appeals to Pharaoh for assistance against invaders, who may have been the Israelites (cf. Yalkut Shimeoni, *Joshua,* section xviii on *a goodly Shinar mantle,* vii. 21, where the dependence of these local 'kings' upon a powerful ruler elsewhere is described).

3. *the men that are come to thee, that are entered into thy house.* I.e. whether they stated their intention as having "come to thee," i.e. for intimacy with you, or having "come to thy house" to lodge.

for they are come to search out all the land. This was the sole purpose of their coming (Abarbanel).

4. *and the woman took.* Better *had taken.* i.e. she had taken them prior to the entry of the king's couriers (Kimchi).

hid them. i.e. had hidden them before the king's men came. The literal rendering is 'hid him,' but it is not unusual for the singular to be used thus instead of the plural. Rabbinic tradition asserts that the spies were Phinehas, son of Eleazar the High Priest, and Caleb. Phinehas stood before them unhidden. Yet, they were unable to see him because he was like an angel; hence she hid 'him,' Caleb (Tanchuma). The plural occurs in v. 6.

I knew not, etc. [Therefore she did not report the matter to the authorities.]

5. *about the time of the shutting of the gate.* i.e. the gate of the city (Abarbanel and Metsudath David).

when it was dark. When others take shelter within the walls (Abarbanel).

6. *the roof.* The flat roofs of houses in the East were put to various purposes (cf. Judg. xvi. 27; I Sam. ix. 25).

and hid them. i.e. in a new and better hiding

7. And the men pursued after them the way to the Jordan unto the fords; and as soon as they that pursued after them were gone out, the gate was shut. 8. And before they were laid down, she came up unto them upon the roof; 9. and she said unto the men: 'I know that the LORD hath given you the land, and that your terror is fallen upon us, and that all the inhabitants of the land melt away before you. 10. For we have heard how the LORD dried up the water of the Red Sea before you, when ye came out of Egypt; and what ye did unto the two kings of the Amorites, that were beyond the Jordan, unto Sihon and to Og, whom ye utterly destroyed. 11. And as

7 עַל־הַגָּג׃ וְהָאֲנָשִׁים רָדְפוּ
אַחֲרֵיהֶם דֶּרֶךְ הַיַּרְדֵּן עַל
הַמַּעְבְּרוֹת וְהַשַּׁעַר סָגָרוּ
אַחֲרֵי כַּאֲשֶׁר יָצְאוּ הָרֹדְפִים
8 אַחֲרֵיהֶם׃ וְהֵמָּה טֶרֶם
יִשְׁכָּבוּן וְהִיא עָלְתָה עֲלֵיהֶם
9 עַל־הַגָּג׃ וַתֹּאמֶר אֶל־
הָאֲנָשִׁים יָדַעְתִּי כִּי־נָתַן יְהוָה
לָכֶם אֶת־הָאָרֶץ וְכִי־נָפְלָה
אֵימַתְכֶם עָלֵינוּ וְכִי נָמֹגוּ כָּל־
10 יֹשְׁבֵי הָאָרֶץ מִפְּנֵיכֶם׃ כִּי
שָׁמַעְנוּ אֵת אֲשֶׁר־הוֹבִישׁ יְהוָה
אֶת־מֵי יַם־סוּף מִפְּנֵיכֶם
בְּצֵאתְכֶם מִמִּצְרָיִם וַאֲשֶׁר
עֲשִׂיתֶם לִשְׁנֵי מַלְכֵי הָאֱמֹרִי
אֲשֶׁר בְּעֵבֶר הַיַּרְדֵּן לְסִיחֹן
וּלְעוֹג אֲשֶׁר הֶחֱרַמְתֶּם אוֹתָם׃

v. 7. קמץ בז״ק

place, instead of the temporary one she had previously shown them (Metsudath David). Alternatively, she had previously put them in a place where the king's messengers would be unlikely to look. Now, she concealed them by covering them (Malbim).

7. *the way to the Jordan.* Their most likely route to rejoin their camp (Daath Mikra).

the fords. Of which there were several, linking the two sides of the Jordan (Daath Mikra).

the gate was shut. To trap them if still in the city (Abarbanel, Metsudath David).

9. *I know that the Lord hath given you the land.* I have two reasons for believing this: (1) *and*

that your terror is fallen upon us. Because we have become awestricken by your greatness, and (2) *that all the inhabitants of the land melt away before you.* They are terrorstricken by the prospect of your conquest of the land, lest you destroy them (Malbim).

10. *for we have heard,* etc. R. Simeon b. Eleazar said: When Israel fulfils the will of the Omnipresent, His name is magnified in the world, as it is said, *For we have heard,* etc. But when Israel does not do His will, His name is profaned in the world, as it is said, *And when they came unto the nations, whither they came, they profaned My holy name; in that men said of them: These are the people of the Lord, and are gone forth out of His land* (Ezek. xxxvi. 20) (Mechilta).

9

soon as we had heard it, our hearts did melt, neither did there remain any more spirit in any man, because of you; for the LORD your God, He is God in heaven above, and on earth beneath. 12. Now therefore, I pray you, swear unto me by the LORD, since I have dealt kindly with you, that ye also will deal kindly with my father's house—and give me a true token—13. and save alive my father, and my mother, and my brethren, and my sisters, and all that they have, and deliver our lives from death.' 14. And the men said unto her: 'Our life for yours, if ye tell not this our business; and it shall be, when the LORD giveth us the land, that we will deal kindly and truly with thee.' 15. Then she let them down by a cord through the window; for her house was upon the side of the wall,

11 וַנִּשְׁמַע וַיִּמַּס לְבָבֵנוּ וְלֹא־
קָמָה עוֹד רוּחַ בְּאִישׁ מִפְּנֵיכֶם
כִּי יְהֹוָה אֱלֹהֵיכֶם הוּא אֱלֹהִים
בַּשָּׁמַיִם מִמַּעַל וְעַל־הָאָרֶץ
12 מִתָּחַת: וְעַתָּה הִשָּׁבְעוּ־נָא
לִי בַּיהֹוָה כִּי־עָשִׂיתִי עִמָּכֶם
חֶסֶד וַעֲשִׂיתֶם גַּם־אַתֶּם עִם־
בֵּית אָבִי חֶסֶד וּנְתַתֶּם לִי אוֹת
13 אֱמֶת: וְהַחֲיִתֶם אֶת־אָבִי
וְאֶת־אִמִּי וְאֶת־אַחַי וְאֶת־
אַחְיוֹתַי וְאֵת כָּל־אֲשֶׁר לָהֶם
וְהִצַּלְתֶּם אֶת־נַפְשֹׁתֵינוּ
14 מִמָּוֶת: וַיֹּאמְרוּ לָהּ הָאֲנָשִׁים
נַפְשֵׁנוּ תַחְתֵּיכֶם לָמוּת אִם לֹא
תַגִּידוּ אֶת־דְּבָרֵנוּ זֶה וְהָיָה
בְּתֵת יְהֹוָה לָנוּ אֶת־הָאָרֶץ
וְעָשִׂינוּ עִמָּךְ חֶסֶד וֶאֱמֶת:
15 וַתּוֹרִדֵם בַּחֶבֶל בְּעַד הַחַלּוֹן
כִּי בֵיתָהּ בְּקִיר הַחוֹמָה

v. 18. אחיותי ק

11. *He is God,* etc. Cf. Deut. iv. 39. Jethro, who had worshipped idols, said, *Now I know that the Lord is greater than all gods* (Exod. xviii. 11), thus ascribing reality to them. Naaman went further and declared, *Behold now, I know that there is no God in all the earth, but in Israel* (2 Kings v. 15). Rahab, however, went still further, asserting, *He is God in heaven above, and on earth beneath* (Mechilta). The unity and omnipotence of God were one of the fundamental tenets impressed upon the children of Israel in the wilderness (cf. Deut. iv. 39). Strange though it must have appeared in those days, it may well have per-

colated to other peoples and gained credence from some individuals among them.

14. *our life for yours.* i.e. should our fellow-Israelites break the undertaking we give you, then our own lives will be forfeit.

this our business. lit. 'this our word,' viz. the sign we agree upon that Rahab's house should be distinguished by a scarlet thread in the window, because it might be used by others (Kimchi).

15. *upon the side of the wall.* lit. 'in the wall.' This explains how they escaped in spite of the

and she dwelt upon the wall.
16. And she said unto them: 'Get
you to the mountain, lest the
pursuers light upon you; and hide
yourselves there three days, until
the pursuers be returned; and
afterward may ye go your way.'
17. And the men said unto her: 'We
will be guiltless of this thine oath
which thou hast made us to swear.
18. Behold, when we come into the
land, thou shalt bind this line of
scarlet thread in the window which
thou didst let us down by; and thou
shalt gather unto thee into the house
thy father, and thy mother, and thy
brethren, and all thy father's household. 19. And it shall be, that
whosoever shall go out of the doors
of thy house into the street, his
blood shall be upon his head, and
we will be guiltless; and whosoever
shall be with thee in the house, his
blood shall be on our head, if any
hand be upon him. 20. But if thou
utter this our business, then we will
be guiltless of thine oath which thou
hast made us to swear.' 21. And
she said: 'According unto your
words, so be it.' And she sent them
away, and they departed; and she
bound the scarlet line in the window.

16 וּבַחוֹמָה הִיא יוֹשָׁבֶת: וַתֹּאמֶר
לָהֶם הָהָרָה לֵּכוּ פֶּן־יִפְגְּעוּ
בָכֶם הָרֹדְפִים וְנַחְבֵּתֶם שָׁמָּה
שְׁלֹשֶׁת יָמִים עַד שׁוֹב הָרֹדְפִים
וְאַחַר תֵּלְכוּ לְדַרְכְּכֶם:
17 וַיֹּאמְרוּ אֵלֶיהָ הָאֲנָשִׁים נְקִיִּם
אֲנַחְנוּ מִשְּׁבֻעָתֵךְ הַזֶּה אֲשֶׁר
18 הִשְׁבַּעְתָּנוּ: הִנֵּה אֲנַחְנוּ בָאִים
בָּאָרֶץ אֶת־תִּקְוַת חוּט הַשָּׁנִי
הַזֶּה תִּקְשְׁרִי בַּחַלּוֹן אֲשֶׁר
הוֹרַדְתֵּנוּ בוֹ וְאֶת־אָבִיךְ
וְאֶת־אִמֵּךְ וְאֶת־אַחַיִךְ וְאֵת
כָּל־בֵּית אָבִיךְ תַּאַסְפִי אֵלַיִךְ
19 הַבָּיְתָה: וְהָיָה כֹּל אֲשֶׁר־יֵצֵא
מִדַּלְתֵי בֵיתֵךְ הַחוּצָה דָּמוֹ
בְרֹאשׁוֹ וַאֲנַחְנוּ נְקִיִּם וְכֹל
אֲשֶׁר יִהְיֶה אִתָּךְ בַּבַּיִת דָּמוֹ
בְרֹאשֵׁנוּ אִם־יָד תִּהְיֶה־בּוֹ:
20 וְאִם־תַּגִּידִי אֶת־דְּבָרֵנוּ זֶה
וְהָיִינוּ נְקִיִּם מִשְּׁבֻעָתֵךְ
21 אֲשֶׁר הִשְׁבַּעְתָּנוּ: וַתֹּאמֶר
כְּדִבְרֵיכֶם כֶּן־הוּא וַתְּשַׁלְּחֵם
וַיֵּלֵכוּ וַתִּקְשֹׁר אֶת־תִּקְוַת

v. 18. הת׳ בצרי

locking of the gates. The wall of her house
was a continuation of the city wall.

16. *to the mountain.* Or, 'to the hill-
country,' westward instead of eastward, and
so throw the pursuers off the track. Moreover, the caves in the hills afforded excellent
shelter.

17. *guiltless.* If Rahab violated the conditions laid down in the following verses
(Rashi).

21. *she bound.* Later, when Jericho was
attacked by the Israelites (Kimchi).

22. And they went, and came unto the mountain, and abode there three days, until the pursuers were returned; and the pursuers sought them throughout all the way, but found them not. 23. Then the two men returned, and descended from the mountain, and passed over, and came to Joshua the son of Nun; and they told him all that had befallen them. 24. And they said unto Joshua: 'Truly the LORD hath delivered into our hands all the land; and moreover all the inhabitants of the land do melt away before us.'

22 הַשָּׁנִי בַּחַלּוֹן: וַיֵּלְכוּ וַיָּבֹאוּ
הָהָרָה וַיֵּשְׁבוּ שָׁם שְׁלֹשֶׁת יָמִים
עַד־שָׁבוּ הָרֹדְפִים וַיְבַקְשׁוּ
הָרֹדְפִים בְּכָל־הַדֶּרֶךְ וְלֹא
23 מָצָאוּ: וַיָּשֻׁבוּ שְׁנֵי הָאֲנָשִׁים
וַיֵּרְדוּ מֵהָהָר וַיַּעֲבֹרוּ וַיָּבֹאוּ
אֶל־יְהוֹשֻׁעַ בִּן־נוּן וַיְסַפְּרוּ־
לוֹ אֵת כָּל־הַמֹּצְאוֹת אוֹתָם:
24 וַיֹּאמְרוּ אֶל־יְהוֹשֻׁעַ כִּי־נָתַן
יְהוָֹה בְּיָדֵנוּ אֶת־כָּל־הָאָרֶץ
וְגַם־נָמֹגוּ כָּל־יֹשְׁבֵי הָאָרֶץ
מִפָּנֵינוּ:

---

3   CHAPTER III   ג

1. And Joshua rose up early in the morning, and they removed from Shittim, and came to the Jordan, he and all the children of Israel; and they lodged there before they passed over. 2. And it came to pass after three days, that the officers went through the midst of the camp; 3. and they commanded the people, saying: 'When ye see the ark of the covenant of the LORD your God,

1 וַיַּשְׁכֵּם יְהוֹשֻׁעַ בַּבֹּקֶר וַיִּסְעוּ
מֵהַשִּׁטִּים וַיָּבֹאוּ עַד־הַיַּרְדֵּן
הוּא וְכָל־בְּנֵי יִשְׂרָאֵל וַיָּלִנוּ
2 שָׁם טֶרֶם יַעֲבֹרוּ: וַיְהִי מִקְצֵה
שְׁלֹשֶׁת יָמִים וַיַּעַבְרוּ הַשֹּׁטְרִים
3 בְּקֶרֶב הַמַּחֲנֶה: וַיְצַוּוּ אֶת־
הָעָם לֵאמֹר כִּרְאֹתְכֶם אֵת
אֲרוֹן בְּרִית־יְהוָֹה אֱלֹהֵיכֶם

CHAPTER III

THE PARTING OF THE JORDAN

1. *early in the morning.* The zealous obey God's precepts at the earliest possible moment (Talmud). Traditionally, it was on the ninth of Nisan, the day after the return of the spies.

2. *after three days.* From the time of the proclamation, not from when they reached the Jordan. These three days corresponded to the three days the spies were in hiding (supra i.11).

3. *the ark of the covenant.* Also called *the ark of the testimony* (iv. 16). The *testimony* was the two tables of stone inscribed with the decalogue

and the priests the Levites bearing it, then ye shall remove from your place, and go after it. 4. Yet there shall be a space between you and it, about two thousand cubits by measure; come not near unto it, that ye may know the way by which ye must go; for ye have not passed this way heretofore.'

5. And Joshua said unto the people: 'Sanctify yourselves; for to-morrow the LORD will do wonders among you.' 6. And Joshua spoke unto the priests, saying: 'Take up the ark of the covenant, and pass on before the people.' And they took up the ark of the covenant, and went before the people.

וְהַכֹּהֲנִים֙ הַלְוִיִּ֔ם נֹשְׂאִ֖ים אֹת֑וֹ
וְאַתֶּ֣ם תִּסְע֔וּ מִמְּקוֹמְכֶ֖ם
4 וַהֲלַכְתֶּ֖ם אַחֲרָ֑יו: אַ֣ךְ | רָח֣וֹק
יִהְיֶ֗ה בֵּינֵיכֶם֙ וּבֵינָ֔ו כְּאַלְפַּ֥יִם
אַמָּ֖ה בַּמִּדָּ֑ה אַל־תִּקְרְב֣וּ
אֵלָ֗יו לְמַ֙עַן֙ אֲשֶׁר־תֵּדְע֣וּ אֶת־
הַדֶּ֙רֶךְ֙ אֲשֶׁ֣ר תֵּֽלְכוּ־בָ֔הּ כִּ֣י
לֹ֧א עֲבַרְתֶּ֛ם בַּדֶּ֖רֶךְ מִתְּמ֥וֹל
שִׁלְשֽׁוֹם:
5 וַיֹּ֧אמֶר יְהוֹשֻׁ֛עַ אֶל־הָעָ֖ם
הִתְקַדָּ֑שׁוּ כִּ֣י מָחָ֗ר יַעֲשֶׂ֧ה יְהוָ֛ה
6 בְּקִרְבְּכֶ֖ם נִפְלָאֽוֹת: וַיֹּ֣אמֶר
יְהוֹשֻׁ֙עַ֙ אֶל־הַכֹּהֲנִ֣ים לֵאמֹ֔ר
שְׂא֞וּ אֶת־אֲר֤וֹן הַבְּרִית֙ וְעִבְר֖וּ
לִפְנֵ֣י הָעָ֑ם וַיִּשְׂאוּ֙ אֶת־אֲר֣וֹן
הַבְּרִ֔ית וַיֵּלְכ֖וּ לִפְנֵ֥י הָעָֽם:

v. 4 וּבֵינֹו ק׳

which testified to the covenant between God and Israel, viz. that they would acknowledge and obey Him as their God, while He would recognize them as His people. There is naturally no reference here to the Tabernacle and its sacred appurtenances. The Tabernacle was dismantled during the journey, and its appurtenances would play no part as guide in the crossing of the Jordan, as did the ark.

the priests the Levites. The priests, who were all of the tribe of Levi. While all priests were Levites, the converse was not true, because the priesthood was confined to the descendants of Aaron (Rashi).

4. *about two thousand cubits.* i.e. one thousand yards. This was the extent of the permitted Sabbath day's journey. Joshua said to

them, 'In the future you will stand there and observe the Sabbath. Do not go more than two thousand cubits from the ark on any side, so that you can go and pray before it on the Sabbath' (Tanchuma).

come not near unto it. Crowding around the ark would lead to confusion and would also lessen reverence for its sanctity (Rashi, Kimchi).

5. *sanctify yourselves.* Thus was the sacred character of their task impressed upon them. The sanctification usually consisted in ritual purification which included the washing of garments and marital abstinence (cf. Exod. xix. 10, 14f.) (Metsudath David).

6. *the ark of the covenant.* This was usually in the centre of the camp (cf. Num. ii. 17). Now it was to be in front.

7. And the LORD said unto Joshua: 'This day will I begin to magnify thee in the sight of all Israel, that they may know that, as I was with Moses, so I will be with thee. 8. And thou shalt command the priests that bear the ark of the covenant, saying: When ye are come to the brink of the waters of the Jordan, ye shall stand still in the Jordan.'

9. And Joshua said unto the children of Israel: 'Come hither, and hear the words of the LORD your God.' 10. And Joshua said: 'Hereby ye shall know that the living God is among you, and that He will without fail drive out from before you the Canaanite, and the Hittite, and the Hivite, and the Perizzite, and the Girgashite, and the Amorite, and the Jebusite. 11. Behold, the ark of the covenant of the Lord of all the earth passeth on before you

7 וַיֹּאמֶר יְהֹוָה אֶל־יְהוֹשֻׁעַ
הַיּוֹם הַזֶּה אָחֵל גַּדֶּלְךָ בְּעֵינֵי
כָל־יִשְׂרָאֵל אֲשֶׁר יֵדְעוּן
כִּי כַּאֲשֶׁר הָיִיתִי עִם־מֹשֶׁה
8 אֶהְיֶה עִמָּךְ: וְאַתָּה תְּצַוֶּה
אֶת־הַכֹּהֲנִים נֹשְׂאֵי אֲרוֹן־
הַבְּרִית לֵאמֹר כְּבֹאֲכֶם עַד־
קְצֵה מֵי הַיַּרְדֵּן בַּיַּרְדֵּן
תַּעֲמֹדוּ:
9 וַיֹּאמֶר יְהוֹשֻׁעַ אֶל־בְּנֵי
יִשְׂרָאֵל גֹּשׁוּ הֵנָּה וְשִׁמְעוּ אֶת־
10 דִּבְרֵי יְהֹוָה אֱלֹהֵיכֶם: וַיֹּאמֶר
יְהוֹשֻׁעַ בְּזֹאת תֵּדְעוּן כִּי אֵל
חַי בְּקִרְבְּכֶם וְהוֹרֵשׁ יוֹרִישׁ
מִפְּנֵיכֶם אֶת־הַכְּנַעֲנִי וְאֶת־
הַחִתִּי וְאֶת־הַחִוִּי וְאֶת־
הַפְּרִזִּי וְאֶת־הַגִּרְגָּשִׁי וְהָאֱמֹרִי
11 וְהַיְבוּסִי: הִנֵּה אֲרוֹן הַבְּרִית
אֲרוֹן כָּל־הָאָרֶץ עֹבֵר

---

7. *unto Joshua.* As the campaign is about to begin, God renews to Joshua the assurance He had previously given to him (i. 5).

10. *the living God.* In contrast to the dead idols worshipped by other peoples (cf. Hos. ii. 1; Ps. xlii. 3).

the Canaanite, etc. The seven tribes inhabiting the land. Of these the Canaanites and the Amorites were the most important, and they sometimes gave their name to the whole country (cf. Gen. xv. 16; Amos ii. 9). The former inhabited the low-lying districts in the east and west, the latter the hilly area in the centre (Num. xiii. 29). We find, too, that

Sihon and Og, the kings of the Amorite, occupied the east bank of the Jordan. For the Hittites, see on i. 4. The Hivites were connected with Gibeon and Shechem (ix. 7, xi. 19; Gen. xxxiv. 2), also "under Hermon in the land of Mizpah"; (xi. 3) the Jebusites are mentioned in connection with Jerusalem, but, according to Rashi (xiv. 63), those were not of the Jebusite nation, but the descendants of Abimelech the Philistine, called Jebusites because of the city of Jerusalem, then called Jebus. The Perizzites were mentioned in connection with the Rephaim (xvii. 15) and the Canaanites (Gen. xiii 7). The Girgashites were of unknown locality. Per-

over the Jordan. **12.** Now therefore take you twelve men out of the tribes of Israel, for every tribe a man. **13.** And it shall come to pass, when the soles of the feet of the priests that bear the ark of the LORD, the Lord of all the earth, shall rest in the waters of the Jordan, that the waters of the Jordan shall be cut off, even the waters that come down from above; and they shall stand in one heap.' **14.** And it came to pass, when the people removed from their tents, to pass over the Jordan, the priests that bore the ark of the covenant being before the people; **15.** and when they that bore the ark were come unto the Jordan, and the feet of the priests that bore the ark were dipped in the brink of the water—for the Jordan overfloweth all its banks all the time of harvest—

12 לִפְנֵיכֶם בַּיַּרְדֵּן: וְעַתָּה קְחוּ
לָכֶם שְׁנֵי־עָשָׂר אִישׁ מִשִּׁבְטֵי
יִשְׂרָאֵל אִישׁ־אֶחָד אִישׁ־
13 אֶחָד לַשָּׁבֶט: וְהָיָה כְּנוֹחַ
כַּפּוֹת רַגְלֵי הַכֹּהֲנִים נֹשְׂאֵי
אֲרוֹן יְהֹוָה אֲדוֹן כָּל־הָאָרֶץ
בְּמֵי הַיַּרְדֵּן מֵי הַיַּרְדֵּן יִכָּרֵתוּן
הַמַּיִם הַיֹּרְדִים מִלְמָעְלָה
14 וְיַעַמְדוּ נֵד אֶחָד: וַיְהִי בִּנְסֹעַ
הָעָם מֵאָהֳלֵיהֶם לַעֲבֹר אֶת־
הַיַּרְדֵּן וְהַכֹּהֲנִים נֹשְׂאֵי הָאָרוֹן
15 הַבְּרִית לִפְנֵי הָעָם: וּכְבוֹא
נֹשְׂאֵי הָאָרוֹן עַד־הַיַּרְדֵּן
וְרַגְלֵי הַכֹּהֲנִים נֹשְׂאֵי הָאָרוֹן
נִטְבְּלוּ בִּקְצֵה הַמָּיִם וְהַיַּרְדֵּן
מָלֵא עַל־כָּל־גְּדוֹתָיו כֹּל יְמֵי

haps, because they evacuated when they heard of Israel's intention of conquering the land (Jerusalem Talmud, Sheviith, 6:1).

11. *the LORD of all the earth.* 'This phrase always designates God as He Who expels and brings in. Here it denotes that He will drive out the Canaanites and bring in the Israelites in their stead' (Pesikta).

12. *take you,* etc. The purpose is stated in iv. 1-3. Here Joshua instructs them to take twelve men to be prepared for further instructions (Rashi, Redak). Alternatively, these twelve men were to witness from close range, how the Jordan would split as soon as the priests rested their feet in its waters (Metsudath David). Alternatively, these

twelve men were to select the positions for their respective tribes behind the ark (Abarbanel).

15. *and when they that bore the ark were come unto the Jordan.* They did not need to step off the bank, but, immediately, *and the feet of the priests that bore the ark were dipped in the brink of the water* which overflowed the banks (Alshich).

overfloweth all its banks all the time of harvest. For the days of Nisan are the harvest season (Rashi). Even though it was the harvest season when there is no rainfall, the Jordan was overflowing its banks to make the miracle greater. It is also possible that during the spring season with the melting snows

16. that the waters which came down from above stood, and rose up in one heap, a great way off from Adam, the city that is beside Zarethan; and those that went down toward the sea of the Arabah, even the Salt Sea, were wholly cut off; and the people passed over right against Jericho. 17. And the priests that bore the ark of the covenant of the LORD stood firm on dry ground in the midst of the Jordan, while all Israel passed over on dry ground, until all the nation were passed clean over the Jordan.

16 קָצִיר: וַיַּעַמְד֣וּ הַמַּ֗יִם
הַיֹּרְדִ֨ים מִלְמַ֜עְלָה קָ֣מוּ נֵד־
אֶחָ֗ד הַרְחֵ֤ק מְאֹד֙ בָּֽאָדָם֙
הָעִ֔יר אֲשֶׁר֙ מִצַּ֣ד צָֽרְתָ֔ן
וְהַיֹּרְדִ֗ים עַ֣ל יָ֤ם הָֽעֲרָבָה֙ יָם־
הַמֶּ֜לַח תַּ֣מּוּ נִכְרָ֑תוּ וְהָעָ֥ם
17 עָבְר֖וּ נֶ֥גֶד יְרִיחֽוֹ: וְהַכֹּהֲנִ֣ים
נֹשְׂאֵ֣י הָֽאָרוֹן֩ בְּרִית־
יְהֹוָ֜ה בֶּחָרָבָ֗ה בְּת֣וֹךְ הַיַּרְדֵּ֖ן
הָכֵ֑ן וְכָל־יִשְׂרָאֵל֙ עֹֽבְרִים֙
בֶּחָ֣רָבָ֔ה עַ֤ד אֲשֶׁר־תַּ֙מּוּ֙ כָּל־
הַגּ֔וֹי לַֽעֲב֖וֹר אֶת־הַיַּרְדֵּֽן:

4   CHAPTER IV   ד

1. And it came to pass, when all the nation were clean passed over the Jordan, that the LORD spoke unto

1 וַיְהִ֗י כַּֽאֲשֶׁר־תַּ֤מּוּ כָל־הַגּוֹי֙
לַֽעֲב֖וֹר אֶת־הַיַּרְדֵּ֑ן · וַיֹּ֧אמֶר

v. 1. פסקא באמצע פסוק   .16 v מאדם ק׳

from the north, Jordan is always at its greatest depth. We find a similar instance in 1 Chron. xii. 16 (Kimchi).

16. *Adam, the city that is beside Zarethan.* The city of Adam is on the east bank of the Jordan, at the confluence of the Jabbok with the Jordan. This city is identified with Tel ed-Damieh 25–30 kilometers north of Jericho. The hill still retains its ancient name. Near it is the bridge named Jisr ed-Damieh.

that is beside Zarethan. Some identify this with Zeradah, mentioned in 1 Kings, xi. 26, the birthplace of Jeroboam son of Nebat. This is substantiated by the interchange of the two names in 1 Kings vii. 57 and 2 Chron. iv. 17. Some identify it with Sartaba, whence the fire signals were relayed to inform the public of the consecration of the new month. According to Rabbi Johanan (Jerusalem Talmud,

Sotah 7:5), Zarethan is twelve *mil* from Adam, as, indeed, Sartaba is.

and those that went down. Those that had previously flowed downstream from there.

the sea of the Arabah. The sea surrounded by wasteland (Daath Mikra).

even the Salt Sea. I.e. which is also known as the Salt Sea (Daath Mikra).

17. *firm on dry ground.* The miracle lasted so long as the priests stood there (Metsudath David).

CHAPTER IV

THE JORDAN CROSSED

1. *The LORD spoke.* See on iii. 12. These are the aforementioned twelve men, who were to be prepared for further instructions (Rashi).

Joshua, saying: 2. 'Take you twelve men out of the people, out of every tribe a man, 3. and command ye them, saying: Take you hence out of the midst of the Jordan, out of the place where the priests' feet stood, twelve stones made ready, and carry them over with you, and lay them down in the lodging-place, where ye shall lodge this night.'

4. Then Joshua called the twelve men, whom he had prepared of the children of Israel, out of every tribe a man; 5. and Joshua said unto them: 'Pass on before the ark of the LORD your God into the midst of the Jordan, and take you up every man of you a stone upon his shoulder, according unto the number of the tribes of the children of Israel; 6. that this may be a sign among

יְהֹוָה אֶל־יְהוֹשֻׁעַ לֵאמֹר׃

2 קְחוּ לָכֶם מִן־הָעָם שְׁנֵים עָשָׂר
אֲנָשִׁים אִישׁ־אֶחָד אִישׁ־אֶחָד
3 מִשָּׁבֶט׃ וְצַוּוּ אוֹתָם לֵאמֹר
שְׂאוּ־לָכֶם מִזֶּה מִתּוֹךְ הַיַּרְדֵּן
מִמַּצַּב רַגְלֵי הַכֹּהֲנִים הָכִין
שְׁתֵּים־עֶשְׂרֵה אֲבָנִים
וְהַעֲבַרְתֶּם אוֹתָם עִמָּכֶם
וְהִנַּחְתֶּם אוֹתָם בַּמָּלוֹן אֲשֶׁר־
תָּלִינוּ בוֹ הַלָּיְלָה׃

4 וַיִּקְרָא יְהוֹשֻׁעַ אֶל־שְׁנֵים
הֶעָשָׂר אִישׁ אֲשֶׁר הֵכִין מִבְּנֵי
יִשְׂרָאֵל אִישׁ־אֶחָד אִישׁ־
5 אֶחָד מִשָּׁבֶט׃ וַיֹּאמֶר לָהֶם
יְהוֹשֻׁעַ עִבְרוּ לִפְנֵי אֲרוֹן יְהֹוָה
אֱלֹהֵיכֶם אֶל־תּוֹךְ הַיַּרְדֵּן
וְהָרִימוּ לָכֶם אִישׁ אֶבֶן אַחַת
עַל־שִׁכְמוֹ לְמִסְפַּר שִׁבְטֵי
6 בְנֵי־יִשְׂרָאֵל׃ לְמַעַן תִּהְיֶה

According to the other commentators, this is a command, completely distinct from the previous one.

Alternatively, the first half may be connected with verse 4: *And it came to pass, when all the nation were clean passed over the Jordan . . . then Joshua called the twelve men,* etc.; the intervening passage would then be in parenthesis (Kimchi).

3. *out of . . . stood.* The Hebrew is literally 'from the standing-place of the feet of the priests.' In view of the preceding note, the rendering may be: 'out of the place where the priests' feet shall stand.'

5. *pass on before the ark.* Enter now into the Jordan and pass until you are in front of the priests (Rashi). This follows the tradition that the priests carrying the ark stood on the eastern side of the Jordan. Kimchi, however, explains that Joshua crossed after the entire nation, in order to assure them that the waters would remain standing. After all the people had crossed, he called the twelve men to cross the Jordan and to take twelve stones from the place the priests were standing.

6. *that this may be a sign among you.* The sense of history is very vivid and alive in Israel as a source of inspiration and a means of

you, that when your children ask in time to come, saying: What mean ye by these stones? 7. then ye shall say unto them: Because the waters of the Jordan were cut off before the ark of the covenant of the LORD; when it passed over the Jordan, the waters of the Jordan were cut off; and these stones shall be for a memorial unto the children of Israel for ever.' 8. And the children of Israel did so as Joshua commanded, and took up twelve stones out of the midst of the Jordan, as the LORD spoke unto Joshua, according to the number of the tribes of the children of Israel; and they carried them over with them unto the place where they lodged, and laid them down there. 9. Joshua also set up twelve stones in the midst of the Jordan, in the place where the feet of the priests that bore the ark of the covenant stood; and they are

זֹאת אוֹת בְּקִרְבְּכֶם כִּי־
יִשְׁאָלוּן בְּנֵיכֶם מָחָר לֵאמֹר
מָה הָאֲבָנִים הָאֵלֶּה לָכֶם:
7 וַאֲמַרְתֶּם לָהֶם אֲשֶׁר נִכְרְתוּ
מֵימֵי הַיַּרְדֵּן מִפְּנֵי אֲרוֹן
בְּרִית־יְהֹוָה בְּעָבְרוֹ בַּיַּרְדֵּן
נִכְרְתוּ מֵי הַיַּרְדֵּן וְהָיוּ הָאֲבָנִים
הָאֵלֶּה לְזִכָּרוֹן לִבְנֵי יִשְׂרָאֵל
8 עַד־עוֹלָם: וַיַּעֲשׂוּ־כֵן בְּנֵי־
יִשְׂרָאֵל כַּאֲשֶׁר צִוָּה יְהוֹשֻׁעַ
וַיִּשְׂאוּ שְׁתֵּי־עֶשְׂרֵה אֲבָנִים
מִתּוֹךְ הַיַּרְדֵּן כַּאֲשֶׁר דִּבֶּר
יְהֹוָה אֶל־יְהוֹשֻׁעַ לְמִסְפַּר
שִׁבְטֵי בְנֵי־יִשְׂרָאֵל וַיַּעֲבִרוּם
עִמָּם אֶל־הַמָּלוֹן וַיַּנִּחוּם שָׁם:
9 וּשְׁתֵּים עֶשְׂרֵה אֲבָנִים הֵקִים
יְהוֹשֻׁעַ בְּתוֹךְ הַיַּרְדֵּן תַּחַת
מַצַּב רַגְלֵי הַכֹּהֲנִים נֹשְׂאֵי אֲרוֹן
הַבְּרִית וַיִּהְיוּ שָׁם עַד הַיּוֹם

strengthening the bond between God and His people. The dedication of the firstborn to God and the observance of the Passover ritual are similarly explained (Exod. xiii. 1ff.; Deut. vi. 20ff.).

when your children ask, etc. This historical sense is to be made a medium for the education of the young, upon which Judaism has always laid the greatest emphasis.

9. *Joshua also set up twelve stones.* i.e. twelve other stones, in addition to those he set up in Gilgal (Rashi). Kimchi assumes that, although the divine command was not mentioned, this act was performed in fulfilment of a divine command. Abarbanel opines that

Joshua was not commanded to set up these stones, but decided to set up a monument in the Jordan, similar to the one in Gilgal.

in the place where . . . stood. So that the priests' feet would not sink into the mud (Rashi as quoted by Abarbanel). After the original twelve stones had been removed, it became necessary to replace them to prevent the priests' feet from sinking. Others maintain that they were set up near the place where the priests had been standing (Kimchi and Abarbanel).

unto this day. When this Book was written. The Talmud (Sot. 34a) asserts that they were still there in the generation after the destruc-

there unto this day. 10. And the priests that bore the ark stood in the midst of the Jordan, until every thing was finished that the LORD commanded Joshua to speak unto the people, according to all that Moses commanded Joshua; and the people hastened and passed over. 11. And it came to pass, when all the people were clean passed over, that the ark of the LORD passed on, and the priests, before the people. 12. And the children of Reuben, and the children of Gad, and the half-tribe of Manasseh, passed on armed before the children of Israel, as Moses spoke unto them; 13. about forty thousand ready armed for war passed on in the presence of the LORD unto battle, to the plains of Jericho.

10 הַזֶּה: וְהַכֹּהֲנִים נֹשְׂאֵי הָאָרוֹן
עֹמְדִים בְּתוֹךְ הַיַּרְדֵּן עַד־
תֹּם כָּל־הַדָּבָר אֲשֶׁר־
צִוָּה יְהֹוָה אֶת־יְהוֹשֻׁעַ לְדַבֵּר
אֶל־הָעָם כְּכֹל אֲשֶׁר־צִוָּה
מֹשֶׁה אֶת־יְהוֹשֻׁעַ וַיְמַהֲרוּ
11 הָעָם וַיַּעֲבֹרוּ: וַיְהִי כַּאֲשֶׁר־
תַּם כָּל־הָעָם לַעֲבוֹר וַיַּעֲבֹר
אֲרוֹן־יְהֹוָה וְהַכֹּהֲנִים לִפְנֵי
12 הָעָם: וַיַּעַבְרוּ בְּנֵי־רְאוּבֵן
וּבְנֵי־גָד וַחֲצִי שֵׁבֶט הַמְנַשֶּׁה
חֲמֻשִׁים לִפְנֵי בְּנֵי יִשְׂרָאֵל
כַּאֲשֶׁר דִּבֶּר אֲלֵיהֶם מֹשֶׁה:
13 כְּאַרְבָּעִים אֶלֶף חֲלוּצֵי
הַצָּבָא עָבְרוּ לִפְנֵי יְהֹוָה
לַמִּלְחָמָה אֶל עַרְבוֹת יְרִיחוֹ:

tion of the Second Temple and three Rabbis stood on the stones.

10. *according to all that Moses commanded Joshua.* The mention of Moses is unexpected and seems out of place. Probably Moses had given Joshua certain instructions before he died in connection with the crossing of the Jordan: these were now carried out. According to a Rabbinical tradition, these stones were first set up, on the day of the crossing, on mount Ebal, but were immediately removed and conveyed to Gilgal. This verse would then refer to the temporary erection of the stones at mount Ebal in accordance with Deut. xxvii. 4 (Kimchi). Possibly, however, the verse does not refer to the erection of the monument but to the crossing, and particularly to the exhortation to proceed with the conquest of Canaan (Rashi).

11. *and the priests, before the people* i.e. the priests left the river-bed and were miraculously transported over the river by the ark, in the presence of the people (Rashi).

12. *before the children of Israel.* This was done in accordance with their promise, "(Num. xxxii. 17) but we ourselves will be ready armed to go before the children of Israel . . ." Because of their military prowess, they led the troops (See Rashi ad loc).

13. *about forty thousand.* i.e. men of the two and a half tribes. Even so, they were only about one-third of the males of military age as enumerated in Num. xxvi. 7, 18, 34. The rest must have stayed behind to guard the cities and villages which they had already built, and some of them may have been unfit for military service.

14. On that day the LORD magnified Joshua in the sight of all Israel; and they feared him, as they feared Moses, all the days of his life.

15. And the LORD spoke unto Joshua, saying: 16. 'Command the priests that bear the ark of the testimony, that they come up out of the Jordan.' 17. Joshua therefore commanded the priests, saying: 'Come ye up out of the Jordan.' 18. And it came to pass, as the priests that bore the ark of the covenant of the LORD came up out of the midst of the Jordan, as soon as the soles of the priests' feet were drawn up unto the dry ground, that the waters of the Jordan returned unto their place, and went over all its banks, as aforetime. 19. And the people came up out of the Jordan on the tenth day of the first month, and encamped in Gilgal, on the east border of Jericho.

14 בַּיּוֹם הַהוּא גִּדַּל יְהוָה אֶת־
יְהוֹשֻׁעַ בְּעֵינֵי כָל־יִשְׂרָאֵל
וַיִּרְאוּ אֹתוֹ כַּאֲשֶׁר יָרְאוּ אֶת־
מֹשֶׁה כָּל־יְמֵי חַיָּיו:
15 וַיֹּאמֶר יְהוָה אֶל־יְהוֹשֻׁעַ
16 לֵאמֹר: צַוֵּה אֶת־הַכֹּהֲנִים
נֹשְׂאֵי אֲרוֹן הָעֵדוּת וְיַעֲלוּ מִן־
17 הַיַּרְדֵּן: וַיְצַו יְהוֹשֻׁעַ אֶת־
הַכֹּהֲנִים לֵאמֹר עֲלוּ מִן־
18 הַיַּרְדֵּן: וַיְהִי בַּעֲלוֹת הַכֹּהֲנִים
נֹשְׂאֵי אֲרוֹן בְּרִית־יְהוָה מִתּוֹךְ
הַיַּרְדֵּן נִתְּקוּ כַּפּוֹת רַגְלֵי
הַכֹּהֲנִים אֶל הֶחָרָבָה וַיָּשֻׁבוּ
מֵי־הַיַּרְדֵּן לִמְקוֹמָם וַיֵּלְכוּ
כִתְמוֹל־שִׁלְשׁוֹם עַל־כָּל־
19 גְּדוֹתָיו: וְהָעָם עָלוּ מִן־
הַיַּרְדֵּן בֶּעָשׂוֹר לַחֹדֶשׁ
הָרִאשׁוֹן וַיַּחֲנוּ בַּגִּלְגָּל בִּקְצֵה

v. 18. כעלות ק׳

---

14. Cf. iii. 7.

15–17. These verses obviously precede verse 11 chronologically. Yet it is natural to repeat here the command to the priests to go up from the Jordan, because verse 18 tells how, when they did so, the Jordan resumed its flow (Rashi).

19. *on the tenth day of the first month.* Nisan, or, as it was then called, Abib (cf. Exod. xii. 2 with xiii. 4), corresponding to March–April. On that day forty years earlier, they had taken the lamb for the paschal sacrifice

before their departure from Egypt (Exod. xii 3). 'R. Levi said: Their taking the paschal lamb in Egypt stood them in good stead at the Jordan' (Pesikta); i.e. the miracle at the Jordan was a reward for their act of faith in openly setting aside the lamb for the Passover sacrifice in the full knowledge that it might provoke the Egyptians, who worshipped the lamb, to drastic actions. R. Levi based his comment on the coincidence of the dates.

Gilgal. Cf. v. 9. The place is named Gilgal here in anticipation. The word really means

20. And those twelve stones, which they took out of the Jordan, did Joshua set up in Gilgal. 21. And he spoke unto the children of Israel, saying: 'When your children shall ask their fathers in time to come, saying: What mean these stones? 22. then ye shall let your children know, saying: Israel came over this Jordan on dry land. 23. For the LORD your God dried up the waters of Jordan from before you, until ye were passed over, as the LORD your God did to the Red Sea, which He dried up from before us, until we were passed over, 24. that all the peoples of the earth may know the hand of the LORD, that it is mighty; that ye may fear the LORD your God for ever.'

20 מִזְרַח יְרִיחוֹ: וְאֵת שְׁתֵּים
עֶשְׂרֵה הָאֲבָנִים הָאֵלֶּה אֲשֶׁר
לָקְחוּ מִן־הַיַּרְדֵּן הֵקִים
21 יְהוֹשֻׁעַ בַּגִּלְגָּל: וַיֹּאמֶר אֶל־־
בְּנֵי יִשְׂרָאֵל לֵאמֹר אֲשֶׁר֩
יִשְׁאָלוּן בְּנֵיכֶם מָחָר אֶת־
אֲבוֹתָם לֵאמֹר מָה הָאֲבָנִים
22 הָאֵלֶּה: וְהוֹדַעְתֶּם אֶת־־
בְּנֵיכֶם לֵאמֹר בַּיַּבָּשָׁה עָבַר
יִשְׂרָאֵל אֶת־הַיַּרְדֵּן הַזֶּה:
23 אֲשֶׁר־הוֹבִישׁ יְהוָֹה אֱלֹהֵיכֶם
אֶת־מֵי הַיַּרְדֵּן מִפְּנֵיכֶם
עַד־עָבְרְכֶם כַּאֲשֶׁר עָשָׂה
יְהוָֹה אֱלֹהֵיכֶם לְיַם־סוּף
אֲשֶׁר־הוֹבִישׁ מִפָּנֵינוּ עַד־
24 עָבְרֵנוּ: לְמַעַן דַּעַת כָּל־עַמֵּי
הָאָרֶץ אֶת־יַד יְהוָֹה כִּי חֲזָקָה
הִיא לְמַעַן יְרָאתֶם אֶת־יְהוָֹה
אֱלֹהֵיכֶם כָּל־הַיָּמִים:

'a circle' (see the note on the next verse).] The site is supposed to be indicated by a heap of ruins called Tel Etelch, formerly known as Tel Jeljal, about two miles from Jericho (Daath Mikra).

20. *set up.* [Possibly in the form of a circle, which is the meaning of Gilgal.]

21. See on verse 6.

23. *before you . . . before us.* [Though all this would happen in days to come, future generations would identify themselves with the

present generation for whom the miracle had been wrought. A similar identification runs through the *Haggadah* (the narrative of the exodus read in the Jewish home on the Passover eve), where all generations are bidden to regard themselves as having been liberated from the bondage of Egypt.]

24. *that ye may fear.* [This means either 'and *that ye may fear*,' 'and' being understood; or, recognition by *all the peoples of the earth* of God's might would intensify the fear of God among the Israelites.]

5   CHAPTER V   ה

1. And it came to pass, when all the kings of the Amorites, that were beyond the Jordan westward, and all the kings of the Canaanites, that were by the sea, heard how that the LORD had dried up the waters of the Jordan from before the children of Israel, until they were passed over, that their heart melted, neither was there spirit in them any more, because of the children of Israel.

2. At that time the LORD said unto Joshua: 'Make thee knives of flint, and circumcise again the children of Israel the second time.' 3. And Joshua made him knives of flint,

וַיְהִי כִשְׁמֹעַ כָּל־מַלְכֵי ¹
הָאֱמֹרִי אֲשֶׁר בְּעֵבֶר הַיַּרְדֵּן
יָמָּה וְכָל־מַלְכֵי הַכְּנַעֲנִי אֲשֶׁר
עַל־הַיָּם אֵת אֲשֶׁר־הוֹבִישׁ
יְהוָֹה אֶת־מֵי הַיַּרְדֵּן מִפְּנֵי
בְנֵי־יִשְׂרָאֵל עַד־עָבְרָנוּ וַיִּמַּס
לְבָבָם וְלֹא־הָיָה בָם עוֹד
רוּחַ מִפְּנֵי בְּנֵי־יִשְׂרָאֵל׃

בָּעֵת הַהִיא אָמַר יְהוָֹה אֶל־ ²
יְהוֹשֻׁעַ עֲשֵׂה לְךָ חַרְבוֹת צֻרִים
וְשׁוּב מֹל אֶת־בְּנֵי־יִשְׂרָאֵל
שֵׁנִית׃ וַיַּעַשׂ־לוֹ יְהוֹשֻׁעַ ³

v. 1. עברם ק׳   v. 2. הפטרת יום ראשון של פסח

CHAPTER V

OBSERVANCE OF CIRCUMCISION AND THE PASSOVER

1. *kings.* See on ii. 2.

Amorites . . . Canaanites. See on iii. 10.

westward. lit. 'seaward,' viz. the Mediterranean which is the western frontier of the Holy Land.

until they were passed over. This is the translation of the *kerĕ*, the *kethib* means 'until we were passed over.' In the *kethib*, Joshua addresses his generation. In the *kerĕ*, he addresses future generations (Daath Mikra).

their heart melted. D.M. plausibly explains that the terror which overwhelmed the native kings enabled the rite of circumcision to be performed. Had there been the likelihood of an attack upon them, the Israelite men of military age would have exposed themselves

to danger during the period of convalescence (cf. what is narrated in Gen. xxxiv. 24f.).

2-9 CIRCUMSION OF THE ISRAELITES

2. *at that time.* Before the kings had recovered from the shock of the news and could make an onslaught upon the Israelites.

knives of flint. An indication that previous practice was to perform the circumcision with sharp stones, as witness also the account in Ex. iv. 25, of Zipporah circumcising her son with a sharp stone (Yalkut Shimoni from Gen. Rabbah).

the second time. According to tradition, they were collectively circumcised before their departure from Egypt (see on verse 9). The present occasion would be the second collective circumcision. It is therefore clear that the passage has no bearing upon the institution of the rite; on the contrary, it was then recognized as an ancient practice (Rashi).

and circumcised the children of Israel at Gibeath-ha-araloth. 4. And this is the cause why Joshua did circumcise: all the people that came forth out of Egypt, that were males, even all the men of war, died in the wilderness by the way, after they came forth out of Egypt. 5. For all the people that came out were circumcised; but all the people that were born in the wilderness by the way as they came forth out of Egypt, had not been circumcised. 6. For the children of Israel walked forty years in the wilderness, till all the nation, even the men of war that came forth out of Egypt, were consumed, because they hearkened not unto the voice of the LORD; unto whom the LORD swore that He would not let them see the land which the LORD swore unto their fathers that He would give us, a land flowing with milk and honey. 7. And He raised up their children in

חַרְבוֹת צֻרֵים וַיָּמָל אֶת־בְּנֵי
יִשְׂרָאֵל אֶל־גִּבְעַת הָעֲרָלוֹת:
4 וְזֶה הַדָּבָר אֲשֶׁר־מָל יְהוֹשֻׁעַ
כָּל־הָעָם הַיֹּצֵא מִמִּצְרַיִם
הַזְּכָרִים כֹּל ׀ אַנְשֵׁי הַמִּלְחָמָה
מֵתוּ בַמִּדְבָּר בַּדֶּרֶךְ בְּצֵאתָם
5 מִמִּצְרָיִם: כִּי־מֻלִים הָיוּ
כָּל־הָעָם הַיֹּצְאִים וְכָל־
הָעָם הַיִּלֹּדִים בַּמִּדְבָּר בַּדֶּרֶךְ
בְּצֵאתָם מִמִּצְרַיִם לֹא־מָלוּ:
6 כִּי ׀ אַרְבָּעִים שָׁנָה הָלְכוּ בְנֵי־
יִשְׂרָאֵל בַּמִּדְבָּר עַד־תֹּם
כָּל־הַגּוֹי אַנְשֵׁי הַמִּלְחָמָה
הַיֹּצְאִים מִמִּצְרַיִם אֲשֶׁר לֹא־
שָׁמְעוּ בְּקוֹל יְהוָה אֲשֶׁר נִשְׁבַּע
יְהוָה לָהֶם לְבִלְתִּי הַרְאוֹתָם
אֶת־הָאָרֶץ אֲשֶׁר נִשְׁבַּע יְהוָה
לַאֲבוֹתָם לָתֶת לָנוּ אֶרֶץ זָבַת
7 חָלָב וּדְבָשׁ: וְאֶת־בְּנֵיהֶם

3. Gibeath-ha-araloth. i.e. 'the hill of the foreskins,' explained by the Midrash Rabba (Num. xi. 3) as 'the place which they had made into a hill by means of the foreskins'; i.e. it is not to be understood as a place-name.

4. the cause (dabar). He circumcised them at the Divine command (dibbur). Only the circumcised, Joshua told them, could possess the land; for God said to Abraham: I will establish My covenant between Me and thee and thy seed after thee. . . . And I will give unto thee, and to thy seed after thee . . . all the land of Canaan

. . . This is My covenant . . . every male among you shall be circumcised (Gen. xvii. 7-10) (Rashi).

died in the wilderness. In accordance with God's decree (Num. xiv. 28ff.).

5. had not been circumcised. The reason for this is not given. The Rabbis suggest that the fatigue of travelling in the wilderness made it inadvisable. Alternatively, they were circumcised, but not properly. (Rashi)

6. flowing with milk and honey. This is the classic description of the Holy Land, first mentioned in Exodus iii. 8, 17. Rashi Ex. xii. 5

their stead; them did Joshua circumcise; for they were uncircumcised, because they had not been circumcised by the way. 8. And it came to pass, when all the nation were circumcised, every one of them, that they abode in their places in the camp, till they were whole.

9. And the LORD said unto Joshua: 'This day have I rolled away the reproach of Egypt from off you.' Wherefore the name of that place was called Gilgal, unto this day.

10. And the children of Israel encamped in Gilgal; and they kept the passover on the fourteenth day

הֵקִים תַּחְתָּם אֹתָם מָל יְהוֹשֻׁעַ
כִּי־עֲרֵלִים הָיוּ כִּי לֹא־מָלוּ
8 אוֹתָם בַּדָּרֶךְ: וַיְהִי כַּאֲשֶׁר־
תַּמּוּ כָל־הַגּוֹי לְהִמּוֹל וַיֵּשְׁבוּ
תַחְתָּם בַּמַּחֲנֶה עַד חֲיוֹתָם:
9 וַיֹּאמֶר יְהוָה אֶל־יְהוֹשֻׁעַ הַיּוֹם
גַּלּוֹתִי אֶת־חֶרְפַּת מִצְרַיִם
מֵעֲלֵיכֶם וַיִּקְרָא שֵׁם הַמָּקוֹם
הַהוּא גִּלְגָּל עַד הַיּוֹם הַזֶּה:
10 וַיַּחֲנוּ בְנֵי־יִשְׂרָאֵל בַּגִּלְגָּל
וַיַּעֲשׂוּ אֶת־הַפֶּסַח בְּאַרְבָּעָה

---

explains it to mean that 'milk flows from the goats, and honey flows from the dates and the figs.' In Megillah 6a, he elaborates: The goats eat figs and the honey flows from them, and milk flows from the goats, forming a stream. Elsewhere (Kethuboth 111a), the Talmud apparently objecting to the inclusion of 'milk' in the description of the Holy Land, since it is not a product of the earth, explains the expression as a metaphor, "a land whose fruits are as fat as milk and as sweet as honey."

8. *till they were whole.* The Canaanites did not use the opportunity to attack because they were too terrified (see on verse 1); or, perhaps, they did not know of it.

9. *the reproach of Egypt.* The Egyptians had seen a sign of blood in the stars when the Israelites left Egypt. They interpreted this as a sign that the entire nation would be slaughtered in the desert. When Joshua circumcised the people, they realized that this sign of blood meant the mass circumcision, rather than a mass slaughter. Alternatively, the Egyptians would reproach them for their uncircumcised state, in which they showed

no superiority over the Egyptians. To Israel, this was considered a stigma, as in Gen. xxxiv. 14. This may also be rendered, "the shame of Egypt," the shameful beliefs of the idolatrous Egyptians would now be eliminated from among Israel by the observance of the Paschal rites, which signify the slaughter of the Egyptian lamb-deity. Also, the carnal lusts of the Egyptians would be modified by the circumcision (Ralbag). Or simply, the shame of being uncircumcised like the Egyptians (Kimchi).

Abarbanel explains that the Egyptians reproached the Israelites by saying that the LORD had no power to bring them to the Promised Land, and would slaughter them in the desert. Their entry into the land removed this stigma from them.

10-11 THE PASSOVER IS KEPT

10. *they kept the passover.* Having first been circumcised, for otherwise they would have been disqualified to observe it (cf. Exod. xii. 44, 48).

on the fourteenth day. As prescribed by the Torah (Exod. xii. 6).

of the month at even in the plains of Jericho. 11. And they did eat of the produce of the land on the morrow after the passover, unleavened cakes and parched corn, in the selfsame day. 12. And the manna ceased on the morrow, after they had eaten of the produce of the land; neither had the children of Israel manna any more; but they did eat of the fruit of the land of Canaan that year.

13. And it came to pass, when Joshua was by Jericho, that he lifted up his eyes and looked, and, behold, there stood a man over against him

עָשָׂר יוֹם לַחֹדֶשׁ בָּעָרֶב

11 בְּעַרְבוֹת יְרִיחוֹ: וַיֹּאכְלוּ מֵעֲבוּר הָאָרֶץ מִמָּחֳרַת הַפֶּסַח מַצּוֹת וְקָלוּי בְּעֶצֶם

12 הַיּוֹם הַזֶּה: וַיִּשְׁבֹּת הַמָּן מִמָּחֳרָת בְּאָכְלָם מֵעֲבוּר הָאָרֶץ וְלֹא־הָיָה עוֹד לִבְנֵי יִשְׂרָאֵל מָן וַיֹּאכְלוּ מִתְּבוּאַת אֶרֶץ כְּנַעַן בַּשָּׁנָה הַהִיא:

13 וַיְהִי בִּהְיוֹת יְהוֹשֻׁעַ בִּירִיחוֹ וַיִּשָּׂא עֵינָיו וַיַּרְא וְהִנֵּה־אִישׁ

11. *the produce of the land.* Since the manna ceased to fall, as stated in the next verse. The Rabbis held that the new harvest is meant, the Israelites first having brought the wave-offering of the 'sheaf' (*omer*), in accordance with Lev. xxiii. 10-14, *the morrow after the passover* here being identical with *the morrow after the sabbath* there (Rashi).

unleavened cakes. Cf. Exod. xii. 18ff.

parched corn. Cf. Lev. xxiii. 14. [Ears of grain, roasted at the fire, are still eaten as a substitute for bread in the East.]

12. *the manna ceased on the morrow.* No longer would their food come down to them from heaven. In their own land they must toil for their daily bread.

13-15 APPEARANCE OF THE CAPTAIN
OF THE LORD'S HOST

13. *by Jericho.* The text is literally 'in Jericho.' The Rabbis remark that he was in the outer environs of the city (since he was obviously not yet inside Jericho) which count as

the city (Rashi from Nedarim 56b).

Seventy cubits from the city are counted as the environs and are judged as part of the city.

The Almighty had sent the angel to encourage Joshua upon his impending invasion of Jericho. The sword symbolized victory. Thus the angel was saying, "I have given Jericho into thy hand." Joshua was unaware of the etherial character of his visitor, taking him for a soldier of flesh and blood. He queried, "Art thou for us, or for our adversaries?" Thereupon, the angel replied, "No, I am not a mere human. I am the archangel Michael, captain of the LORD's host of heaven and earth. I have come now, this very instant that you saw me. This is proof that I am an angel."

Ralbag understands this passage as a dream in which Joshua visualizes himself as actually standing within the walls of Jericho. He shares Maimonides' belief that it is impossible to perceive an angel except in a prophetic vision. Abarbanel, however, maintains that an angel who assumes a human form can be perceived in a conscious state.

with his sword drawn in his hand;
and Joshua went unto him, and said
unto him: 'Art thou for us, or for
our adversaries?' 14. And he said:
'Nay, but I am captain of the host
of the LORD; I am now come.'
And Joshua fell on his face to the
earth, and bowed down, and said
unto him: 'What saith my lord unto
his servant?' 15. And the captain
of the LORD's host said unto Joshua:
Put off thy shoe from off thy foot;
for the place whereon thou standest
is holy.' And Joshua did so.

עֹמֵד לְנֶגְדּוֹ וְחַרְבּוֹ שְׁלוּפָה
בְּיָדוֹ וַיֵּלֶךְ יְהוֹשֻׁעַ אֵלָיו וַיֹּאמֶר
לוֹ הֲלָנוּ אַתָּה אִם־לְצָרֵינוּ:
14 וַיֹּאמֶר ׀ לֹא כִּי אֲנִי שַׂר־
צְבָא־יְהוָה עַתָּה בָאתִי וַיִּפֹּל
יְהוֹשֻׁעַ אֶל־פָּנָיו אַרְצָה
וַיִּשְׁתָּחוּ וַיֹּאמֶר לוֹ מָה אֲדֹנִי
15 מְדַבֵּר אֶל־עַבְדּוֹ: וַיֹּאמֶר
שַׂר־צְבָא יְהוָה אֶל־יְהוֹשֻׁעַ
שַׁל־נַעַלְךָ מֵעַל רַגְלֶךָ כִּי
הַמָּקוֹם אֲשֶׁר אַתָּה עֹמֵד עָלָיו
קֹדֶשׁ הוּא וַיַּעַשׂ יְהוֹשֻׁעַ כֵּן:

8   CHAPTER VI   ן

1. Now Jericho was straitly shut up
because of the children of Israel:
none went out, and none came in.—
2. And the LORD said unto Joshua:

1 וִירִיחוֹ סֹגֶרֶת וּמְסֻגֶּרֶת מִפְּנֵי
בְּנֵי יִשְׂרָאֵל אֵין יוֹצֵא וְאֵין
2 בָּא: וַיֹּאמֶר יְהוָה אֶל־יְהוֹשֻׁעַ

v. 14.   v. 15. קָמֵץ בְּזָ"ק   חָסֵר יו"ד

his sword drawn. So did the angel appear to
Balaam (Num. xxii. 23) and to David (1
Chron. xxi. 16).

14. *'Nay, but I am captain.* See above,
Kimchi's commentary. Abarbanel explains:
'not as you think that you are the commander and I have come to help you. On the
contrary, I am the commander of Israel's
host, and you are my subordinate.' Thereupon, Joshua prostrated himself in subordi-
nation and asked, 'What saith my lord unto
his servant?'

the host of the LORD. Israel, who is the LORD's
host. Now this was Michael, as in Daniel x.
21 (Rashi).

15. *put off thy shoe.* As a mark of reverence;

Moses was similarly commanded at the
Burning Bush (Exod. iii. 5).

for the place whereon thou standest is holy. As
with the Burning Bush, no sanctity attached
to Jericho; its holiness resulted from the
appearance there of God's messenger.

CHAPTER VI

THE CAPTURE OF JERICHO

1. *now Jericho,* etc. A parenthetical verse,
interrupting the narrative of the appearance
of *the captain of the host of the* LORD (Malbim).

because of the children of Israel. From fear of
them (Daath Sofrim).

'See, I have given into thy hand Jericho, and the king thereof, even the mighty men of valour. 3. And ye shall compass the city, all the men of war, going about the city once. Thus shalt thou do six days. 4. And seven priests shall bear seven rams' horns before the ark; and the seventh day ye shall compass the city seven times, and the priests shall blow with the horns. 5. And it shall be, that when they make a long blast with the ram's horn, and when ye hear the sound of the horn, all the people shall shout with a great shout; and the wall of the city shall fall down flat, and the people shall go up every man straight before him.' 6. And Joshua the son of Nun called the priests, and said unto them: 'Take up the ark of the covenant, and let seven priests bear seven rams' horns before the ark of the LORD.'

רְאֵה נָתַתִּי בְיָדְךָ אֶת־יְרִיחוֹ
וְאֶת־מַלְכָּהּ גִּבּוֹרֵי הֶחָיִל:
3 וְסַבֹּתֶם אֶת־הָעִיר כֹּל אַנְשֵׁי
הַמִּלְחָמָה הַקִּיף אֶת־הָעִיר
פַּעַם אֶחָת כֹּה תַעֲשֶׂה שֵׁשֶׁת
4 יָמִים: וְשִׁבְעָה כֹהֲנִים יִשְׂאוּ
שִׁבְעָה שׁוֹפְרוֹת הַיּוֹבְלִים
לִפְנֵי הָאָרוֹן וּבַיּוֹם הַשְּׁבִיעִי
תָּסֹבּוּ אֶת־הָעִיר שֶׁבַע
פְּעָמִים וְהַכֹּהֲנִים יִתְקְעוּ
5 בַּשּׁוֹפְרוֹת: וְהָיָה בִּמְשֹׁךְ |
בְּקֶרֶן הַיּוֹבֵל בְּשָׁמְעֲכֶם אֶת־
קוֹל הַשּׁוֹפָר יָרִיעוּ כָל־הָעָם
תְּרוּעָה גְדוֹלָה וְנָפְלָה חוֹמַת
הָעִיר תַּחְתֶּיהָ וְעָלוּ הָעָם אִישׁ
6 נֶגְדּוֹ: וַיִּקְרָא יְהוֹשֻׁעַ בִּן־נוּן
אֶל־הַכֹּהֲנִים וַיֹּאמֶר אֲלֵהֶם
שְׂאוּ אֶת־אֲרוֹן הַבְּרִית
וְשִׁבְעָה כֹהֲנִים יִשְׂאוּ שִׁבְעָה
שׁוֹפְרוֹת יוֹבְלִים לִפְנֵי אֲרוֹן

v. 5. כשמעכם ק

2. *the LORD said.* Through His angel, this verse continuing v. 15 (Kimchi).

have given. The prophetic perfect.

4. *seven times.* This number in Hebrew is often symbolic of completeness.

5. *shall fall down flat.* lit. 'shall fall in its place.' Modern excavations have shown that the walls of Jericho were not breached, but sank down in their place, as from the effect of an earthquake. The miraculous manner of Jericho's capture was intended to emphasize to Israel at the outset of their task two thoughts: first, that God was with them; and second, that not by their own strength would they conquer, even when they fought in the usual manner. Moses had warned them against the presumption of saying, *My power and the might of my hand hath gotten me this wealth,* lest *thy heart be lifted up, and thou forget the LORD thy God* (Deut. viii. 17, 14).

7. And he said unto the people: 'Pass on, and compass the city, and let the armed body pass on before the ark of the Lord.' 8. And it was so, that when Joshua had spoken unto the people, the seven priests bearing the seven rams' horns before the Lord passed on, and blew with the horns; and the ark of the covenant of the Lord followed them. 9. And the armed men went before the priests that blew the horns, and the rearward went after the ark, [the priests] blowing with the horns continually. 10. And Joshua commanded the people, saying: 'Ye shall not shout, nor let your voice be heard, neither shall any word proceed out of your mouth, until the day I bid you shout; then shall ye shout.' 11. So he caused the ark of the Lord to compass the city, going about it once; and they came into the camp, and lodged in the camp.

12. And Joshua rose early in the morning, and the priests took up the

7 יְהֹוָה: וַיֹּאמְרוּ אֶל־הָעָם
עִבְרוּ וְסֹבּוּ אֶת־הָעִיר
וְהֶחָלוּץ יַעֲבֹר לִפְנֵי אֲרוֹן
8 יְהֹוָה: וַיְהִי כֶּאֱמֹר יְהוֹשֻׁעַ
אֶל־הָעָם וְשִׁבְעָה הַכֹּהֲנִים
נֹשְׂאִים שִׁבְעָה שׁוֹפְרוֹת
הַיּוֹבְלִים לִפְנֵי יְהֹוָה עָבְרוּ
וְתָקְעוּ בַּשּׁוֹפָרוֹת וַאֲרוֹן בְּרִית
יְהֹוָה הֹלֵךְ אַחֲרֵיהֶם:
9 וְהֶחָלוּץ הֹלֵךְ לִפְנֵי הַכֹּהֲנִים
תֹּקְעֵי הַשּׁוֹפָרוֹת וְהַמְאַסֵּף
הֹלֵךְ אַחֲרֵי הָאָרוֹן הָלוֹךְ
10 וְתָקוֹעַ בַּשּׁוֹפָרוֹת: וְאֶת־הָעָם
צִוָּה יְהוֹשֻׁעַ לֵאמֹר לֹא תָרִיעוּ
וְלֹא־תַשְׁמִיעוּ אֶת־קוֹלְכֶם
וְלֹא־יֵצֵא מִפִּיכֶם דָּבָר עַד
יוֹם אָמְרִי אֲלֵיכֶם הָרִיעוּ
11 וַהֲרִיעֹתֶם: וַיַּסֵּב אֲרוֹן־יְהֹוָה
אֶת־הָעִיר הַקֵּף פַּעַם אֶחָת
וַיָּבֹאוּ הַמַּחֲנֶה וַיָּלִינוּ בַּמַּחֲנֶה:
12 וַיַּשְׁכֵּם יְהוֹשֻׁעַ בַּבֹּקֶר וַיִּשְׂאוּ

‎v. 7. ויאמר ק׳   v. 9. תקעי ק׳

7. *he said.* So the *keré*; the *kethib* has 'they said,' viz. Joshua and the priests (Kimchi).

the armed body. The army was to be there, but would take no part in the attack. Jericho was not to fall through their prowess. This would confirm their dependence upon God for victory subsequently when the soldiers did fight.

8. *before the* Lord. The Divine Presence was symbolized by the ark.

9. *the armed men.* The men of the two and a half tribes who led the army (see on iv. 12) (Rashi, Kimchi, Metsudath Zion).

10. The strangeness of the procession, an army making a daily circuit round the city in silence, would strike terror in the hearts of its inhabitants.

15. *on the seventh day.* Tradition relates that

ark of the Lord. 13. And the seven priests bearing the seven rams' horns before the ark of the Lord went on continually, and blew with the horns; and the armed men went before them; and the rearward came after the ark of the Lord, [the priests] blowing with the horns continually. 14. And the second day they compassed the city once, and returned into the camp; so they did six days. 15. And it came to pass on the seventh day, that they rose early at the dawning of the day, and compassed the city after the same manner seven times; only on that day they compassed the city seven times. 16. And it came to pass at the seventh time, when the priests blew with the horns, that Joshua said unto the people: 'Shout; for the Lord hath given you the city. 17. And the city shall be devoted, even it and all that is there-

הַכֹּהֲנִים אֶת־אֲרוֹן יְהוָה:

13 וְשִׁבְעָה הַכֹּהֲנִים נֹשְׂאִים שִׁבְעָה שׁוֹפְרוֹת הַיֹּבְלִים לִפְנֵי אֲרוֹן יְהוָה הֹלְכִים הָלוֹךְ וְתָקְעוּ בַּשּׁוֹפָרוֹת וְהֶחָלוּץ הֹלֵךְ לִפְנֵיהֶם וְהַמְאַסֵּף הֹלֵךְ אַחֲרֵי אֲרוֹן יְהוָֹה הָלוֹךְ וְתָקוֹעַ

14 בַּשּׁוֹפָרוֹת: וַיָּסֹבּוּ אֶת־הָעִיר בַּיּוֹם הַשֵּׁנִי פַּעַם אַחַת וַיָּשֻׁבוּ הַמַּחֲנֶה כֹּה עָשׂוּ שֵׁשֶׁת

15 יָמִים: וַיְהִי בַּיּוֹם הַשְּׁבִיעִי וַיַּשְׁכִּמוּ כַּעֲלוֹת הַשַּׁחַר וַיָּסֹבּוּ אֶת־הָעִיר כַּמִּשְׁפָּט הַזֶּה שֶׁבַע פְּעָמִים רַק בַּיּוֹם הַהוּא סָבְבוּ אֶת־הָעִיר שֶׁבַע

16 פְּעָמִים: וַיְהִי בַּפַּעַם הַשְּׁבִיעִית תָּקְעוּ הַכֹּהֲנִים בַּשּׁוֹפָרוֹת וַיֹּאמֶר יְהוֹשֻׁעַ אֶל־הָעָם הָרִיעוּ כִּי־נָתַן יְהוָה לָכֶם אֶת־הָעִיר:

17 וְהָיְתָה הָעִיר חֵרֶם הִיא

v. 13. הלוך ק׳   v. 15. כעלות ק׳

it was the Sabbath which, however, was not allowed to interfere with the prosecution of the war (Num. Rabbah xiv. 1). [Hence, when in later times the Maccabeans determined to defend themselves on the Sabbath, after their first disastrous refusal to desecrate it by self-defence which had resulted in heavy slaughter, they did not make an innovation in Jewish law.]

17. *devoted*. Absolutely and irrevocably

consecrated so that it cannot be redeemed (cf. *no devoted thing . . . shall be sold or redeemed; every devoted thing is most holy unto the Lord*. Lev. xxvii. 28). The term *cherem* also connotes that which is sentenced to utter destruction (cf. Deut. xiii. 16). Both these connotations are intended here! what could be completely destroyed should be so treated. Indestructible materials, such as metals, were to be consecrated to God and not used for secular purposes (v. 19).

in, to the LORD; only Rahab the
harlot shall live, she and all that are
with her in the house, because she
hid the messengers that we sent.
18. And ye, in any wise keep yourselves from the devoted thing, lest
ye make yourselves accursed by
taking of the devoted thing, so
should ye make the camp of Israel
accursed, and trouble it. 19. But
all the silver, and gold, and vessels of
brass and iron, are holy unto the
LORD; they shall come into the
treasury of the LORD.' 20. So the
people shouted, and [the priests]
blew with the horns. And it came
to pass, when the people heard the
sound of the horn, that the people
shouted with a great shout, and the
wall fell down flat, so that the people
went up into the city, every man
straight before him, and they took
the city. 21. And they utterly

וְכָל־אֲשֶׁר־בָּהּ לַיהוָה
רַק רָחָב הַזּוֹנָה תִּחְיֶה הִיא
וְכָל־אֲשֶׁר אִתָּהּ בַּבַּיִת כִּי
הֶחְבְּאָתָה אֶת־הַמַּלְאָכִים
18 אֲשֶׁר שָׁלָחְנוּ: וְרַק־אַתֶּם
שִׁמְרוּ מִן־הַחֵרֶם פֶּן־תַּחֲרִימוּ
וּלְקַחְתֶּם מִן־הַחֵרֶם וְשַׂמְתֶּם
אֶת־מַחֲנֵה יִשְׂרָאֵל לְחֵרֶם
19 וַעֲכַרְתֶּם אוֹתוֹ: וְכֹל | כֶּסֶף
וְזָהָב וּכְלֵי נְחֹשֶׁת וּבַרְזֶל קֹדֶשׁ
הוּא לַיהוָה אוֹצַר יְהוָה יָבוֹא:
20 וַיָּרַע הָעָם וַיִּתְקְעוּ בַּשּׁוֹפָרוֹת
וַיְהִי כִשְׁמֹעַ הָעָם אֶת־קוֹל
הַשּׁוֹפָר וַיָּרִיעוּ הָעָם תְּרוּעָה
גְדוֹלָה וַתִּפֹּל הַחוֹמָה תַּחְתֶּיהָ
וַיַּעַל הָעָם הָעִירָה אִישׁ נֶגְדּוֹ
21 וַיִּלְכְּדוּ אֶת־הָעִיר: וַיַּחֲרִימוּ

---

18. *keep yourselves.* There is nothing corresponding to *yourselves* in the Hebrew. Kimchi
renders: 'Keep (everybody, yourselves and
others) from the devoted thing.' For this
reason Achan's trespass was imputed to all
Israel.

the camp of Israel accursed. Cf. Deut. vii. 25f.

and trouble it. 'All Israel are surety for one
another,' is a Rabbinic maxim. Here, too, we
have the doctrine of collective responsibility.

19. *brass.* Rather, 'bronze.'

holy unto the Lord. Synonymous with *devoted
. . . to the Lord* in verse 17.
    Since the city was taken on the Sabbath, it
was fitting that no one should benefit from
the booty (Rashi). Alternatively, since the city

was taken miraculously, without any effort
on their part, it was fitting that it come into
the treasury of the LORD (Abarbanel and
Malbim).

20. *So the people shouted, and the priests blew
with the horns.* The people shouted when they
heard the sound of the horns. Then they
shouted a great shout as predicted by Joshua
in v. 5 (Metsudath David and Malbim).
According to others, the people cried out for
joy before they heard the extended blast of
the horns. After the blast, they shouted
again, whereupon the walls fell (Abarbanel).

the wall fell down flat. Kimchi suggests that
only the portion of the wall opposite the
Israelite army fell, so that *every man* (went)
straight before him. It was on another part of
the wall that Rahab's house was situated.

destroyed all that was in the city, both man and woman, both young and old, and ox, and sheep, and ass, with the edge of the sword. 22. And Joshua said unto the two men that had spied out the land: 'Go into the harlot's house, and bring out thence the woman, and all that she hath, as ye swore unto her.' 23. And the young men the spies went in, and brought out Rahab, and her father, and her mother, and her brethren, and all that she had, all her kindred also they brought out; and they set them without the camp of Israel. 24. And they burnt the city with fire, and all that was therein; only the silver, and the gold, and the vessels of brass and of iron, they put into the treasury of the house of the LORD. 25. But Rahab the harlot, and her father's household, and all that she had, did Joshua save alive; and she dwelt in the midst of Israel, unto this day; because she hid the

אֶת־כָּל־אֲשֶׁר בָּעִיר מֵאִישׁ וְעַד־אִשָּׁה מִנַּעַר וְעַד־זָקֵן וְעַד שׁוֹר וָשֶׂה וַחֲמוֹר לְפִי־ 22 חָרֶב: וְלִשְׁנַיִם הָאֲנָשִׁים הַמְרַגְּלִים אֶת־הָאָרֶץ אָמַר יְהוֹשֻׁעַ בֹּאוּ בֵּית־הָאִשָּׁה הַזּוֹנָה וְהוֹצִיאוּ מִשָּׁם אֶת־ הָאִשָּׁה וְאֶת־כָּל־אֲשֶׁר־לָהּ 23 כַּאֲשֶׁר נִשְׁבַּעְתֶּם לָהּ: וַיָּבֹאוּ הַנְּעָרִים הַמְרַגְּלִים וַיֹּצִיאוּ אֶת־רָחָב וְאֶת־אָבִיהָ וְאֶת־ אִמָּהּ וְאֶת־אַחֶיהָ וְאֶת־כָּל־ אֲשֶׁר־לָהּ וְאֵת כָּל־ מִשְׁפְּחוֹתֶיהָ הוֹצִיאוּ וַיַּנִּיחוּם מִחוּץ לְמַחֲנֵה יִשְׂרָאֵל: 24 וְהָעִיר שָׂרְפוּ בָאֵשׁ וְכָל־ אֲשֶׁר־בָּהּ רַק׀ הַכֶּסֶף וְהַזָּהָב וּכְלֵי הַנְּחֹשֶׁת וְהַבַּרְזֶל נָתְנוּ 25 אוֹצַר בֵּית־יְהוָה: וְאֶת־ רָחָב הַזּוֹנָה וְאֶת־בֵּית אָבִיהָ וְאֶת־כָּל־אֲשֶׁר־לָהּ הֶחֱיָה יְהוֹשֻׁעַ וַתֵּשֶׁב בְּקֶרֶב יִשְׂרָאֵל עַד הַיּוֹם הַזֶּה כִּי הֶחְבִּיאָה

---

23. *they set them without the camp of Israel.* The two spies saved them as they had sworn to do, but they would not risk that intermingling with the Canaanites against which the Israelites had been repeatedly warned. Rahab and her family were placed outside the camp until they could be converted to Judaism according to the prescribed ritual.

Subsequently, they would be permitted to reside among the Israelites, like Rahab, as in v. 25 (Kimchi).

25. *unto this day.* i.e. some of Rahab's descendants were dwelling in the midst of Israel when this Book was written (Daath Mikra).

messengers, whom Joshua sent to spy out Jericho.

26. And Joshua charged the people with an oath at that time, saying: 'Cursed be the man before the LORD, that riseth up and buildeth this city, even Jericho; with the loss of his first-born shall he lay the foundation thereof, and with the loss of his youngest son shall he set up the gates of it.'

27. So the LORD was with Joshua; and his fame was in all the land.

אֶת־הַמַּלְאָכִים אֲשֶׁר־שָׁלַח
יְהוֹשֻׁעַ לְרַגֵּל אֶת־יְרִיחוֹ:
26 וַיַּשְׁבַּע יְהוֹשֻׁעַ בָּעֵת הַהִיא
לֵאמֹר אָרוּר הָאִישׁ לִפְנֵי יְהֹוָה
אֲשֶׁר יָקוּם וּבָנָה אֶת־הָעִיר
הַזֹּאת אֶת־יְרִיחוֹ בִּבְכֹרוֹ
יְיַסְּדֶנָּה וּבִצְעִירוֹ יַצִּיב
דְּלָתֶיהָ:
27 וַיְהִי יְהֹוָה אֶת־יְהוֹשֻׁעַ וַיְהִי
שָׁמְעוֹ בְּכָל־הָאָרֶץ:

---

7   CHAPTER VII   ז

1. But the children of Israel committed a trespass concerning the devoted thing; for Achan, the son of Carmi, the son of Zabdi, the son of Zerah, of the tribe of Judah, took

1 וַיִּמְעֲלוּ בְנֵי־יִשְׂרָאֵל מַעַל
בַּחֵרֶם וַיִּקַּח עָכָן בֶּן־כַּרְמִי
בֶּן־זַבְדִּי בֶּן־זֶרַח לְמַטֵּה

---

26. *buildeth this city.* i.e. as a city, complete with walls. But he did not forbid its resettlement; in fact, it was inhabited even in his own lifetime (xviii. 21; cf. also Judg. iii. 13; 2 Sam. x. 5).

with the loss of his first-born, etc. The opening phrase *cursed be* makes it clear that Joshua was not thinking of the heathen practice of human sacrifice at the founding of a city. Therefore it would appear that the statement in 1 Kings xvi. 34, concerning Hiel who rebuilt Jericho in the reign of Ahab—*with Abiram his first-born he laid the foundation thereof, and with his youngest son Segub he set up the gates thereof; according to the word of the Lord, which He spoke by the hand of Joshua*—refers to the fulfilment of the curse, and not human sacrifice (Rashi, Kimchi, Metsudath David).

CHAPTER VII

ACHAN'S TRESPASS

1. *the children of Israel committed.* Though only one man sinned, the trespass is ascribed to the whole people, in accordance with the doctrine of collective responsibility (Metsudath David).

trespass. Hebrew *maal*, a technical term for the misappropriation of property which was in a sacred category (cf. Lev. v. 15).

Achan. By changing the last letter, the name is altered to *Achar* (the troubler) in I Chron. ii. 7: *Achar, the troubler of Israel, who committed a trespass concerning the devoted thing.* Evidently the incident lingered for a long time in the memory of the people.

of the devoted thing; and the anger of the LORD was kindled against the children of Israel.

2. And Joshua sent men from Jericho to Ai, which is beside Beth-aven, on the east side of Beth-el, and spoke unto them, saying: 'Go up and spy out the land.' And the men went up and spied out Ai. 3. And they returned to Joshua, and said unto him: 'Let not all the people go up; but let about two or three thousand men go up and smite Ai; make not all the people to toil thither; for they are but few.' 4. So there went up thither of the people about three thousand men; and they fled before the men of Ai. 5. And the men of Ai smote of them about thirty and six men; and they chased them from

יְהוּדָה מִן־הַחֵרֶם וַיִּחַר־אַף
יְהֹוָה בִּבְנֵי יִשְׂרָאֵל׃

2 וַיִּשְׁלַח יְהוֹשֻׁעַ אֲנָשִׁים מִירִיחוֹ
הָעַי אֲשֶׁר עִם־בֵּית אָוֶן מִקֶּדֶם
לְבֵית־אֵל וַיֹּאמֶר אֲלֵיהֶם
לֵאמֹר עֲלוּ וְרַגְּלוּ אֶת־הָאָרֶץ
וַיַּעֲלוּ הָאֲנָשִׁים וַיְרַגְּלוּ אֶת־

3 הָעָי׃ וַיָּשֻׁבוּ אֶל־יְהוֹשֻׁעַ
וַיֹּאמְרוּ אֵלָיו אַל־יַעַל כָּל־
הָעָם כְּאַלְפַּיִם אִישׁ אוֹ
כִּשְׁלֹשֶׁת אֲלָפִים אִישׁ יַעֲלוּ
וְיַכּוּ אֶת־הָעָי אַל־תְּיַגַּע שָׁמָּה
אֶת־כָּל־הָעָם כִּי מְעַט הֵמָּה׃

4 וַיַּעֲלוּ מִן־הָעָם שָׁמָּה כִּשְׁלֹשֶׁת
אֲלָפִים אִישׁ וַיָּנֻסוּ לִפְנֵי אַנְשֵׁי

5 הָעָי׃ וַיַּכּוּ מֵהֶם אַנְשֵׁי הָעַי
כִּשְׁלֹשִׁים וְשִׁשָּׁה אִישׁ וַיִּרְדְּפוּם

2. *Ai.* A city known from the days of the Patriarchs. Its inhabitants at the time of the conquest were Amorites (v. 7). It was also known as Ayah (I Chron. vii. 28), and in Isaiah's time, Ayath (Isaiah x. 28). Some identify Ai with A-Tel (the ruins), northwest of Deir Diwan, neighboring Beitin (identified as Bethel). Others believe that it is buried under one of the mounds near Beitin, yet to be discovered (Daath Mikra).

Beth-aven, on the east side of Beth-el. The place is also mentioned in xviii. 12; I Sam. xiii. 5. Near Beth-el in a south-easterly direction lies the village of Deir Diwan, in the vicinity of which are mounds of ancient ruins. One of the mounds is the site of Ai; another the site of Beth-aven (see preceding).

go up and spy out the land. Joshua had similarly sent spies before crossing the Jordan (ii. 1). This may have been his regular practice.

3. *let not all the people go up.* i.e. there is no necessity for all of them to go up (Metsudath David). Moreover, let the inhabitants not think that we fear them (Meam Loez).

5. *about thirty and six men.* A small number even by ancient standards of warfare. But the Israelites were so imbued with the conviction of God's assistance in a holy war—a conviction strengthened by the supernatural fall of Jericho—that they saw in this incident more than a temporary setback; they interpreted it as the withdrawal of Divine aid.

Shebarim. Not mentioned elsewhere and so

before the gate even unto Shebarim, and smote them at the descent; and the hearts of the people melted, and became as water. 6. And Joshua rent his clothes, and fell to the earth upon his face before the ark of the LORD until the evening, he and the elders of Israel; and they put dust upon their heads. 7. And Joshua said: 'Alas, O Lord GOD, wherefore hast Thou at all brought this people over the Jordan, to deliver us into the hand of the Amorites, to cause us to perish? would that we had been content and dwelt beyond the Jordan! 8. Oh, Lord, what shall I say, after that Israel hath turned their backs before their enemies! 9. For when the Canaanites and all the inhabitants of the land hear of it, they will compass us round, and cut off our name from the earth; and what wilt Thou do for Thy great name?'

לִפְנֵי הַשַּׁעַר עַד־הַשְּׁבָרִים
וַיַּכּוּם בַּמּוֹרָד וַיִּמַּס לְבַב־
הָעָם וַיְהִי לְמָיִם: וַיִּקְרַע ⁶
יְהוֹשֻׁעַ שִׂמְלֹתָיו וַיִּפֹּל עַל־
פָּנָיו אַרְצָה לִפְנֵי אֲרוֹן יְהוָה
עַד־הָעֶרֶב הוּא וְזִקְנֵי יִשְׂרָאֵל
וַיַּעֲלוּ עָפָר עַל־רֹאשָׁם:
וַיֹּאמֶר יְהוֹשֻׁעַ אֲהָהּ | אֲדֹנָי ⁷
יֱהֹוִה לָמָה הֵעֲבַרְתָּ הַעֲבִיר
אֶת־הָעָם הַזֶּה אֶת־הַיַּרְדֵּן
לָתֵת אֹתָנוּ בְּיַד הָאֱמֹרִי
לְהַאֲבִידֵנוּ וְלוּ הוֹאַלְנוּ וַנֵּשֶׁב
בְּעֵבֶר הַיַּרְדֵּן: בִּי אֲדֹנָי מָה ⁸
אֹמַר אַחֲרֵי אֲשֶׁר הָפַךְ יִשְׂרָאֵל
עֹרֶף לִפְנֵי אֹיְבָיו: וְיִשְׁמְעוּ ⁹
הַכְּנַעֲנִי וְכֹל יֹשְׁבֵי הָאָרֶץ
וְנָסַבּוּ עָלֵינוּ וְהִכְרִיתוּ אֶת־
שְׁמֵנוּ מִן־הָאָרֶץ וּמַה־תַּעֲשֵׂה
לְשִׁמְךָ הַגָּדוֹל:

v. 7. הש׳ בצרי   v. 9. כצ״ל

---

far unidentified. The word means 'breakings' which may refer to pits and quarries in the neighborhood (Daath Mikra). The LXX and Targum render: 'until they had crushed them.'

6. *rent his clothes.* An ancient mourning rite (cf. Gen. xxxvii. 34; 2 Sam. xiii. 31), still practised by Jews (see Code of Jewish Law, ch. 145).

fell to the earth. In grief and supplication before God.

the elders of Israel. The leaders of the people. Perhaps they, with Joshua at their head, led the people in prayer.

they put dust upon their heads. This, too, was a mourning rite (cf. 2 Sam. i. 2; Job ii. 12), practiced at time of dire calamity (see Taanith 2:1).

7. *the Amorites.* See on iii. 10.

would that we had been content, etc. The Rabbis criticized Joshua for saying this (Sanh. 44a). Not even his grief justified him. True, such words had been spoken before (cf. Exod. xiv. 11f.; Num. xiv. 2f.); but then it was by the people, whereas Joshua was the leader.

8. *their backs.* Strictly speaking, this refers to the back of the head, directly behind the face (Ḥullin 19b).

10. And the LORD said unto Joshua: 'Get thee up; wherefore, now, art thou fallen upon thy face? 11. Israel hath sinned; yea, they have even transgressed My covenant which I commanded them; yea, they have even taken of the devoted thing; and have also stolen, and dissembled also, and they have even put it among their own stuff. 12. Therefore the children of Israel cannot stand before their enemies, they turn their backs before their enemies, because they are become accursed; I will not be with you any more, except ye destroy the accursed from among you. 13. Up, sanctify the people, and say: Sanctify yourselves against to-morrow; for thus saith the LORD, the God of Israel: There is a curse in the midst of thee, O Israel; thou canst not stand before thine enemies, until ye take

10 וַיֹּאמֶר יְהֹוָה אֶל־יְהוֹשֻׁעַ קֻם
לָךְ לָמָּה זֶּה אַתָּה נֹפֵל עַל־
11 פָּנֶיךָ: חָטָא יִשְׂרָאֵל וְגַם עָבְרוּ
אֶת־בְּרִיתִי אֲשֶׁר צִוִּיתִי אוֹתָם
וְגַם לָקְחוּ מִן־הַחֵרֶם וְגַם גָּנְבוּ
וְגַם כִּחֲשׁוּ וְגַם שָׂמוּ בִכְלֵיהֶם:
12 וְלֹא יֻכְלוּ בְּנֵי יִשְׂרָאֵל לָקוּם
לִפְנֵי אֹיְבֵיהֶם עֹרֶף יִפְנוּ לִפְנֵי
אֹיְבֵיהֶם כִּי הָיוּ לְחֵרֶם לֹא
אוֹסִיף לִהְיוֹת עִמָּכֶם אִם־לֹא
תַשְׁמִידוּ הַחֵרֶם מִקִּרְבְּכֶם:
13 קֻם קַדֵּשׁ אֶת־הָעָם וְאָמַרְתָּ
הִתְקַדְּשׁוּ לְמָחָר כִּי כֹה אָמַר
יְהֹוָה אֱלֹהֵי יִשְׂרָאֵל חֵרֶם
בְּקִרְבְּךָ יִשְׂרָאֵל לֹא תוּכַל
לָקוּם לִפְנֵי אֹיְבֶיךָ עַד־

9. *Thy great name*. Thy glory, which is bound up with the survival of Israel (cf. Num. xiv. 13ff.). 'The Holy One, blessed be He, linked His name with Israel's (j. Taan. 65d). The defeat may lead to the profanation of God's name (cf. Deut. ix. 28).

10. *get thee up*. lit. 'arise, to thee.' A Rabbi rendered: 'Get up, (the fault) is thine,' interpreting the words as a Divine rebuke to Joshua. The blame attached to him, either because he had imposed too great a trial upon the Israelites by devoting everything to God (hence he did not repeat it; cf. viii. 27); or because he failed in his duty by not personally leading the attack; for God had said to Moses, *Charge Joshua . . . for he shall go over before this people . . . he shall cause them to inherit the land* (Deut. iii. 28)—only when he leads them in person will he cause them to inherit

the land (Siphrë *ad loc.*; Sanh. 44a).

11. *Israel*. See on verse 1.

hath sinned. The reason for the defeat is not to be sought in Me but among the people. Joshua asked, 'But who of Israel? God retorted, 'Am I an informer? Go and cast lots' (Sanh. 43b).

they have even transgressed My covenant. The Rabbis see in this phrase an allusion to more serious sins committed by Achan (Sanh. 44a).

12. *they are become accursed*. 'They are themselves under the ban of destruction by the presence of the *cherem*, working, so to speak, automatically in their midst' as above, 6, 18 (Daath Mikra).

13. *sanctify*, etc. See on iii. 5.

away the accursed thing from among you. 14. In the morning therefore ye shall draw near by your tribes; and it shall be, that the tribe which the LORD taketh shall come near by families; and the family which the LORD shall take shall come near by households; and the household which the LORD shall take shall come near man by man. 15. And it shall be that he that is taken with the devoted thing shall be burnt with fire, he and all that he hath; because he hath transgressed the covenant of the LORD, and because he hath wrought a wanton deed in Israel.'

16. So Joshua rose up early in the morning, and brought Israel near by their tribes; and the tribe of Judah was taken. 17. And he brought near the family of Judah; and he took the family of the Zerahites. And he brought near the family of the Zerahites man by man; and Zabdi was taken. 18. And he brought near his household man by man; and Achan, the son of Carmi, the

הֲסִירְכֶם הַחֵרֶם מִקִּרְבְּכֶם:

14 וְנִקְרַבְתֶּם בַּבֹּקֶר לְשִׁבְטֵיכֶם וְהָיָה הַשֵּׁבֶט אֲשֶׁר־יִלְכְּדֶנּוּ יְהֹוָה יִקְרַב לַמִּשְׁפָּחוֹת וְהַמִּשְׁפָּחָה אֲשֶׁר־יִלְכְּדֶנָּה יְהֹוָה תִּקְרַב לַבָּתִּים וְהַבַּיִת אֲשֶׁר יִלְכְּדֶנּוּ יְהֹוָה יִקְרַב 15 לַגְּבָרִים: וְהָיָה הַנִּלְכָּד בַּחֵרֶם יִשָּׂרֵף בָּאֵשׁ אֹתוֹ וְאֶת־ כָּל־אֲשֶׁר־לוֹ כִּי עָבַר אֶת־ בְּרִית יְהֹוָה וְכִי־עָשָׂה נְבָלָה בְּיִשְׂרָאֵל:

16 וַיַּשְׁכֵּם יְהוֹשֻׁעַ בַּבֹּקֶר וַיַּקְרֵב אֶת־יִשְׂרָאֵל לִשְׁבָטָיו וַיִּלָּכֵד 17 שֵׁבֶט יְהוּדָה: וַיַּקְרֵב אֶת־ מִשְׁפַּחַת יְהוּדָה וַיִּלְכֹּד אֵת מִשְׁפַּחַת הַזַּרְחִי וַיַּקְרֵב אֶת־מִשְׁפַּחַת הַזַּרְחִי לַגְּבָרִים 18 וַיִּלָּכֵד זַבְדִּי: וַיַּקְרֵב אֶת־ בֵּיתוֹ לַגְּבָרִים וַיִּלָּכֵד עָכָן

---

14. *taketh.* The manner of selection is not stated; it was probably by lot. A Midrash (Pirkë de R. Eliezer xxxviii) explains that the choice was made by use of the Urim and Thummim.

tribes . . . families . . . households . . . man by man. 'All Israel consists of a number of tribes, a tribe of several clans (*mishpachah*), a clan of several "houses," a house of a number of individuals' (Rashi).

15. *wrought a wanton deed.* Or, better, 'committed a scandal.' The noun *nebalah* usually denotes a scandalous act of immorality (cf. Gen. xxxiv. 7; Deut. xxii. 21).

17. *the family of Judah.* The singular is apparently used generically and means the tribe of Judah subdivided into families (Kimchi).

and Zabdi was taken. As he was the head of the household (Metsudath David).

son of Zabdi, the son of Zerah, of the tribe of Judah, was taken. 19. And Joshua said unto Achan: 'My son, give, I pray thee, glory to the LORD, the God of Israel, and make confession unto Him; and tell me now what thou hast done; hide nothing from me.' 20. And Achan answered Joshua, and said: 'Of a truth I have sinned against the LORD, the God of Israel, and thus and thus have I done. 21. When I saw among the spoil a goodly Shinar mantle, and two hundred shekels of silver, and a wedge of gold of fifty shekels weight, then I coveted them, and took them; and, behold, they are hid in the earth in the midst of my tent, and the silver under it.' 22. So Joshua sent messengers, and they ran unto the tent; and, behold, it was hid in his tent, and the silver under it. 23. And they took them from the

בֶּן־כַּרְמִי בֶן־זַבְדִּי בֶּן־זֶרַח

19 לְמַטֵּה יְהוּדָה: וַיֹּאמֶר יְהוֹשֻׁעַ אֶל־עָכָן בְּנִי שִׂים־נָא כָבוֹד לַיהוָה אֱלֹהֵי יִשְׂרָאֵל וְתֶן־לוֹ תוֹדָה וְהַגֶּד־נָא לִי מֶה עָשִׂיתָ

20 אַל־תְּכַחֵד מִמֶּנִּי: וַיַּעַן עָכָן אֶת־יְהוֹשֻׁעַ וַיֹּאמַר אָמְנָה אָנֹכִי חָטָאתִי לַיהוָה אֱלֹהֵי יִשְׂרָאֵל וְכָזֹאת וְכָזֹאת עָשִׂיתִי:

21 וָאֵרְאֶה בַשָּׁלָל אַדֶּרֶת שִׁנְעָר אַחַת טוֹבָה וּמָאתַיִם שְׁקָלִים כֶּסֶף וּלְשׁוֹן זָהָב אֶחָד חֲמִשִּׁים שְׁקָלִים מִשְׁקָלוֹ וָאֶחְמְדֵם וָאֶקָּחֵם וְהִנָּם טְמוּנִים בָּאָרֶץ בְּתוֹךְ הָאָהֳלִי וְהַכֶּסֶף

22 תַּחְתֶּיהָ: וַיִּשְׁלַח יְהוֹשֻׁעַ מַלְאָכִים וַיָּרֻצוּ הָאֹהֱלָה וְהִנֵּה טְמוּנָה בְּאָהֳלוֹ וְהַכֶּסֶף

23 תַּחְתֶּיהָ: וַיִּקָּחוּם מִתּוֹךְ

ואֶרָא ק v. 21.

19. *give, I pray thee, glory to the Lord.* By confession, so vindicating God's justice and righteousness. The Rabbis derive from this passage that a criminal, after he has been proved guilty, must be exhorted to make confession (Sanh. 43b).

21. *a goodly Shinar mantle.* Shinar is a Hebrew name for Babylon (Gen. xi. 2) (Kimchi, Rashi, from Targum). Any sovereign who had not acquired a palace in the Land of Israel, experienced no satisfaction from his reign. . . . The king of Babylon had a palace in Jericho, and when he would visit it, he would wear this mantle (Rashi from

Tanhuma Mishpatim, 17). Achan rationalized his act by relating the origin of the garment. It was not a Canaanite garment. I had no idea that it was included in the ban (Malbim).

a wedge of gold. This was common currency in the ancient world. Such a wedge, about sixty shekels in weight, was found in the excavations at Gezer.

shekels. The silver shekel would be 384 grains troy (Rambam). The gold shekel weighs twice as much, partly because gold is heavier than silver, and partly because the coins were

midst of the tent, and brought them unto Joshua, and unto all the children of Israel; and they laid them down before the LORD. 24. And Joshua, and all Israel with him, took Achan the son of Zerah, and the silver, and the mantle, and the wedge of gold, and his sons, and his daughters, and his oxen, and his asses, and his sheep, and his tent, and all that he had; and they brought them up unto the valley of Achor. 25. And Joshua said: 'Why hast thou troubled us? the LORD shall trouble thee this day.' And all Israel stoned him with stones; and they burned them with fire, and stoned them with stones. 26. And they raised over him a great heap of

הָאֹהֶל וַיְבִאוּם אֶל־יְהוֹשֻׁעַ
וְאֶל כָּל־בְּנֵי יִשְׂרָאֵל וַיַּצִּקֻם
לִפְנֵי יְהֹוָה: וַיִּקַּח יְהוֹשֻׁעַ אֶת־ 24
עָכָן בֶּן־זֶרַח וְאֶת־הַכֶּסֶף
וְאֶת־הָאַדֶּרֶת וְאֶת־לְשׁוֹן
הַזָּהָב וְאֶת־בָּנָיו וְאֶת־בְּנֹתָיו
וְאֶת־שׁוֹרוֹ וְאֶת־חֲמֹרוֹ וְאֶת־
צֹאנוֹ וְאֶת־אָהֳלוֹ וְאֶת־
כָּל־אֲשֶׁר־לוֹ וְכָל־יִשְׂרָאֵל
עִמּוֹ וַיַּעֲלוּ אֹתָם עֵמֶק עָכוֹר:
וַיֹּאמֶר יְהוֹשֻׁעַ מֶה עֲכַרְתָּנוּ 25
יַעְכָּרְךָ יְהֹוָה בַּיּוֹם הַזֶּה וַיִּרְגְּמוּ
אֹתוֹ כָל־יִשְׂרָאֵל אֶבֶן וַיִּשְׂרְפוּ
אֹתָם בָּאֵשׁ וַיִּסְקְלוּ אֹתָם
בָּאֲבָנִים: וַיָּקִימוּ עָלָיו גַּל־ 26

thicker (*Tosafoth*). See Eduth L'Yisrael, pp. 191–5.

24. *the son of Zerah.* In verse 18 Achan is described as the great-grandson of Zerah; but *ben* (son) in Hebrew often means 'descendant' (Kimchi).

and his sons, and his daughters. R. Huna maintained that they were taken there, together with the rest of Israel (he construes *and all Israel with him* as the object of *took*), only to witness the execution (Sanh. 44a). The Mosaic law explicitly forbade the execution of children for their father's sin (Deut. xxiv. 16). If, however, the verse means that the children were also executed, they must have been punished as accomplices. Achan could hardly have dug the hole under his tent without their knowledge (Pirkei de Rabbi Eliezer, ch. 38).

and they brought them up unto the valley of Achor. lit. 'the valley of trouble' (cf. verse 26). The road to the valley led through a hill, therefore, 'they brought them *up*' (Kimchi and Metsudath David). It is identified by some with the Wadi el-Kelt which leads down from the hill-country to the Jordan Valley. The execution was not carried out in Gilgal itself, because there were no stones in the vicinity.

25. *the LORD shall trouble thee this day.* The Mishnah comments: only *this day,* but not in the hereafter, for all who confess (as Achan had done) have a share in the world to come (Sanh. vi. 2). With but few exceptions, confession and death were regarded in Judaism as expiation of one's misdeeds, and even the condemned criminal thereby secured his share in the after-life.

26. *and they burned them.* i.e the tent and the movable property (Rashi).

and stoned them. The ox and the other animals (Rashi).

a great heap of stones. Both as a monument of disgrace and as a deterrent (cf. viii. 29; 2 Sam. xviii. 17). Such cairns over the graves of criminals are still common in the East.

stones, unto this day; and the Lord turned from the fierceness of His anger. Wherefore the name of that place was called The valley of Achor, unto this day.

אֲבָנִים גְּדֹלִים עַד הַיּוֹם הַזֶּה וַיָּשָׁב יְהוָה מֵחֲרוֹן אַפּוֹ עַל־ כֵּן קָרָא שֵׁם הַמָּקוֹם הַהוּא עֵמֶק עָכוֹר עַד הַיּוֹם הַזֶּה׃

8   CHAPTER VIII   ח

1. And the Lord said unto Joshua: 'Fear not, neither be thou dismayed; take all the people of war with thee, and arise, go up to Ai; see, I have given into thy hand the king of Ai, and his people, and his city, and his land. 2. And thou shalt do to Ai and her king as thou didst unto Jericho and her king; only the spoil thereof, and the cattle thereof, shall ye take for a prey unto yourselves; set thee an ambush for the city behind it.' 3. So Joshua arose, and all the people of war, to go up to Ai;

1 וַיֹּאמֶר יְהוָה אֶל־יְהוֹשֻׁעַ אַל־תִּירָא וְאַל־תֵּחָת קַח עִמְּךָ אֵת כָּל־עַם הַמִּלְחָמָה וְקוּם עֲלֵה הָעָי רְאֵה ׀ נָתַתִּי בְיָדְךָ אֶת־מֶלֶךְ הָעַי וְאֶת־ עַמּוֹ וְאֶת־עִירוֹ וְאֶת־אַרְצוֹ׃
2 וְעָשִׂיתָ לָעַי וּלְמַלְכָּהּ כַּאֲשֶׁר עָשִׂיתָ לִירִיחוֹ וּלְמַלְכָּהּ רַק־ שְׁלָלָהּ וּבְהֶמְתָּהּ תָּבֹזּוּ לָכֶם שִׂים־לְךָ אֹרֵב לָעִיר מֵאַחֲרֶיהָ׃
3 וַיָּקָם יְהוֹשֻׁעַ וְכָל־ עַם הַמִּלְחָמָה לַעֲלוֹת הָעָי

v. 1. קמץ בז"ק

CHAPTER VIII
CAPTURE OF AI

1. *Fear not.* I.e. fear not to return to the city of Ai, the place that caused such havoc to the Jewish people (Abarbanel and Metsudath David).

take . . . with thee. This time you must lead the army (Abarbanel).

all the people of war. The battle shall be attributed to the entire army, not only to two or three thousand (Abarbanel).

the king of Ai. See on ii. 2.

and his land. Presumably the surrounding country which was the possession of Ai (Abarbanel).

2. *only the spoil thereof,* etc. In this respect Ai would differ from Jericho (cf. vi. 21) (Rashi).

set thee an ambush. Although Ai was a small town, it could not be conquered with ease, for it was highly fortified. Joshua, therefore, dispatched 30,000 men for an ambush, plus another 5,000 men for a second ambush, while the entire army was deployed in front of the city (Abarbanel).

and Joshua chose out thirty thousand men, the mighty men of valour, and sent them forth by night. 4. And he commanded them, saying: 'Behold, ye shall lie in ambush against the city, behind the city; go not very far from the city, but be ye all ready. 5. And I, and all the people that are with me, will approach unto the city; and it shall come to pass, when they come out against us, as at the first, that we will flee before them. 6. And they will come out after us, till we have drawn them away from the city; for they will say: They flee before us, as at the first; so we will flee before them. 7. And ye shall rise up from the ambush, and take possession of the city; for the LORD your God will deliver it into your hand. 8. And it shall be, when ye have seized upon the city, that ye shall set the city on fire; according to the word of the LORD shall ye do; see, I have commanded you.' 9. And Joshua sent them forth; and they went to the ambushment, and abode between Beth-el and Ai, on the west

וַיִּבְחַר יְהוֹשֻׁעַ שְׁלֹשִׁים אֶלֶף
אִישׁ גִּבּוֹרֵי הַחַיִל וַיִּשְׁלָחֵם
4 לָיְלָה: וַיְצַו אֹתָם לֵאמֹר רְאוּ
אַתֶּם אֹרְבִים לָעִיר מֵאַחֲרֵי
הָעִיר אַל־תַּרְחִיקוּ מִן־
הָעִיר מְאֹד וִהְיִיתֶם כֻּלְּכֶם
5 נְכֹנִים: וַאֲנִי וְכָל־הָעָם אֲשֶׁר
אִתִּי נִקְרַב אֶל־הָעִיר וְהָיָה
כִּי־יֵצְאוּ לִקְרָאתֵנוּ כַּאֲשֶׁר
בָּרִאשֹׁנָה וְנַסְנוּ לִפְנֵיהֶם:
6 וְיָצְאוּ אַחֲרֵינוּ עַד הַתִּיקֵנוּ
אוֹתָם מִן־הָעִיר כִּי יֹאמְרוּ
נָסִים לְפָנֵינוּ כַּאֲשֶׁר בָּרִאשֹׁנָה
7 וְנַסְנוּ לִפְנֵיהֶם: וְאַתֶּם תָּקֻמוּ
מֵהָאוֹרֵב וְהוֹרַשְׁתֶּם אֶת־
הָעִיר וּנְתָנָהּ יְהֹוָה אֱלֹהֵיכֶם
8 בְּיֶדְכֶם: וְהָיָה כְתָפְשְׂכֶם
אֶת־הָעִיר תַּצִּיתוּ אֶת־הָעִיר
בָּאֵשׁ כִּדְבַר יְהוָה תַּעֲשׂוּ רְאוּ
9 צִוִּיתִי אֶתְכֶם: וַיִּשְׁלָחֵם
יְהוֹשֻׁעַ וַיֵּלְכוּ אֶל־הַמַּאְרָב
וַיֵּשְׁבוּ בֵּין בֵּית־אֵל וּבֵין הָעַי

---

3. *thirty thousand men.* It is clear from the narrative that the thirty thousand represented the total attacking force which Joshua disposed as narrated, using some for the frontal attack and others (five thousand, verse 12) for the ambush. But see on verse 12.

5. *as at the first.* As described in vii. 5 when

the Israelites fled in earnest; on the present occasion, the flight was to be arranged for strategical purposes.

9. *Joshua lodged that night among the people.* His presence would hearten them for the attack, since they still smarted under the previous defeat (Abarbanel).

side of Ai; but Joshua lodged that night among the people.

10. And Joshua rose up early in the morning, and numbered the people, and went up, he and the elders of Israel, before the people to Ai. 11. And all the people, even the men of war that were with him, went up, and drew nigh, and came before the city, and pitched on the north side of Ai—now there was a valley between him and Ai. 12. And he took about five thousand men, and set them in ambush between Beth-el and Ai, on the west side of Ai. 13. So the people set themselves in array, even all the host that was on the north of the city, their rear lying in wait on the west of the city; and Joshua went that night into the midst of the vale. 14. And it came to pass, when the king of Ai saw it, that the men of the city hastened and rose up early and went

מִים לָעַי וַיֵּלֶךְ יְהוֹשֻׁעַ בַּלַּיְלָה
הַהוּא בְּתוֹךְ הָעָם:

10 וַיַּשְׁכֵּם יְהוֹשֻׁעַ בַּבֹּקֶר וַיִּפְקֹד
אֶת־הָעָם וַיַּעַל הוּא וְזִקְנֵי
יִשְׂרָאֵל לִפְנֵי הָעָם הָעָי:

11 וְכָל־הָעָם הַמִּלְחָמָה אֲשֶׁר
אִתּוֹ עָלוּ וַיִּגְּשׁוּ וַיָּבֹאוּ נֶגֶד
הָעִיר וַיַּחֲנוּ מִצְּפוֹן לָעַי וְהַגַּי

12 בֵּינָו וּבֵין הָעָי: וַיִּקַּח כַּחֲמֵשֶׁת
אֲלָפִים אִישׁ וַיָּשֶׂם אוֹתָם אוֹרֵב
בֵּין בֵּית־אֵל וּבֵין הָעַי מִיָּם

13 לָעִיר: וַיָּשִׂימוּ הָעָם אֶת־
כָּל־הַמַּחֲנֶה אֲשֶׁר מִצְּפוֹן
לָעִיר וְאֶת־עֲקֵבוֹ מִיָּם לָעִיר
וַיֵּלֶךְ יְהוֹשֻׁעַ בַּלַּיְלָה הַהוּא

14 בְּתוֹךְ הָעֵמֶק: וַיְהִי כִּרְאוֹת
מֶלֶךְ־הָעַי וַיְמַהֲרוּ וַיַּשְׁכִּימוּ
וַיֵּצְאוּ אַנְשֵׁי־הָעִיר לִקְרַאת־

v. 11. ‏נ"א וילן‎   v. 12. ‏לעי ק'‎   v. 13. ‏ביניו ק'‎

10. *numbered the people.* The morning of the attack seems rather late for numbering the forces (Kimchi and Metsudoth) 'mustered the people,' is preferable.

11. *all the people,* etc. The Hebrew construction is unusual, viz. the absolute form of the noun where the construct is required. The text is literally 'all the people, the war.'

12. *he took about five thousand men,* etc. This is not a repetition, but an amplification, of the data contained in verses 3–9 (cf. verse 3). Rashi and Kimchi suggest that Joshua set a double ambush, one nearer to the city than

the other, one consisting of thirty thousand men and the other of five thousand.

13. *so the people set themselves in array.* (Kimchi) It is also possible to render: 'so they set the people,' etc. *they* referring to Joshua and the elders mentioned in verse 10.

their rear. lit. 'his heel.'

and Joshua went. The tense is probably to be understood as a pluperfect: Joshua having marched *(went)* that night through the valley. Some MSS. read 'lodged' for *went*, which is also the reading in the Talmud (Sanh. 44b) and the LXX (cf. Eruvin 63b, Tos.).

out against Israel to battle, he and
all his people, at the time appointed,
in front of the Arabah; but he knew
not that there was an ambush against
him behind the city. 15. And
Joshua and all Israel made as if they
were beaten before them, and fled
by the way of the wilderness.
16. And all the people that were in
Ai were called together to pursue
after them; and they pursued after
Joshua, and were drawn away from
the city. 17. And there was not a
man left in Ai or Beth-el, that went
not out after Israel; and they left the
city open, and pursued after Israel.

18. And the LORD said unto
Joshua: 'Stretch out the javelin that
is in thy hand toward Ai; for I will
give it into thy hand.' And Joshua
stretched out the javelin that was in
his hand toward the city. 19. And
the ambush arose quickly out of

יִשְׂרָאֵל לַמִּלְחָמָה הוּא וְכָל־
עַמּוֹ לַמּוֹעֵד לִפְנֵי הָעֲרָבָה
וְהוּא לֹא יָדַע כִּי־אֹרֵב לוֹ
מֵאַחֲרֵי הָעִיר: וַיִּנָּגְעוּ יְהוֹשֻׁעַ 15
וְכָל־יִשְׂרָאֵל לִפְנֵיהֶם וַיָּנֻסוּ
דֶּרֶךְ הַמִּדְבָּר: וַיִּזָּעֲקוּ כָּל־ 16
הָעָם אֲשֶׁר בָּעִיר לִרְדֹּף
אַחֲרֵיהֶם וַיִּרְדְּפוּ אַחֲרֵי
יְהוֹשֻׁעַ וַיִּנָּתְקוּ מִן־הָעִיר:
וְלֹא־נִשְׁאַר אִישׁ בָּעַי וּבֵית 17
אֵל אֲשֶׁר לֹא־יָצְאוּ אַחֲרֵי
יִשְׂרָאֵל וַיַּעַזְבוּ אֶת־הָעִיר
פְּתוּחָה וַיִּרְדְּפוּ אַחֲרֵי
יִשְׂרָאֵל:
וַיֹּאמֶר יְהוָה אֶל־יְהוֹשֻׁעַ נְטֵה 18
בַּכִּידוֹן אֲשֶׁר־בְּיָדְךָ אֶל־
הָעַי כִּי בְיָדְךָ אֶתְּנֶנָּה וַיֵּט
יְהוֹשֻׁעַ בַּכִּידוֹן אֲשֶׁר־בְּיָדוֹ
אֶל־הָעִיר: וְהָאֹרֵב קָם 19

14. *at the time appointed.* Determined by the
king and his generals to be auspicious for
victory (Rashi).

the Arabah. i.e. 'the plain,' the valley broadening out into a plain, at the beginning of
which, viz. the end nearest Ai, the battle took
place.

15. *by the way of the wilderness.* i.e. eastward,
drawing the army of Ai farther from the
Israelite ambuscade to the west of the city.

16. *all the people.* Perhaps inclusive of the
civilians.

17. *Beth-el.* Near to, and west of, Ai. The
two cities must have united their forces to
repel the invader.

they left the city open. Their earlier victory had
lulled them into a sense of careless confidence.

18. *stretch out the javelin.* As a signal for the
group lying in ambush to emerge when they
would see the javelin stretched out toward
the city (Rashi).

20. *power.* (Rashi from Targum) lit. 'hands.'
Kimchi, Abarbanel, and Metsudath Zion
explain that the meaning here is 'space.'

42

their place, and they ran as soon as
he had stretched out his hand, and
entered into the city, and took it;
and they hastened and set the city
on fire. 20. And when the men of
Ai looked behind them, they saw,
and, behold, the smoke of the city
ascended up to heaven, and they
had no power to flee this way or that
way; and the people that fled to the
wilderness turned back upon the
pursuers. 21. And when Joshua
and all Israel saw that the ambush
had taken the city, and that the
smoke of the city ascended, then they
turned back, and slew the men of Ai.
22. And the other came forth out of
the city against them; so they were
in the midst of Israel, some on this
side, and some on that side; and they
smote them, so that they let none of
them remain or escape. 23. And
the king of Ai they took alive, and
brought him to Joshua.

24. And it came to pass, when
Israel had made an end of slaying all
the inhabitants of Ai in the field,
even in the wilderness wherein they
pursued them, and they were all
fallen by the edge of the sword,
until they were consumed, that
all Israel returned unto Ai, and
smote it with the edge of the sword.

מְהֵרָה מִמְּקוֹמָו וַיָּרוּצוּ כִּנְטוֹת
יָדוֹ וַיָּבֹאוּ הָעִיר וַיִּלְכְּדוּהָ
וַיְמַהֲרוּ וַיַּצִּיתוּ אֶת־הָעִיר
20 בָּאֵשׁ: וַיִּפְנוּ אַנְשֵׁי הָעַי
אַחֲרֵיהֶם וַיִּרְאוּ וְהִנֵּה עָלָה
עֲשַׁן הָעִיר הַשָּׁמַיְמָה וְלֹא־
הָיָה בָהֶם יָדַיִם לָנוּס הֵנָּה
וָהֵנָּה וְהָעָם הַנָּס הַמִּדְבָּר
21 נֶהְפַּךְ אֶל־הָרוֹדֵף: וִיהוֹשֻׁעַ
וְכָל־יִשְׂרָאֵל רָאוּ כִּי־לָכַד
הָאֹרֵב אֶת־הָעִיר וְכִי עָלָה
עֲשַׁן הָעִיר וַיָּשֻׁבוּ וַיַּכּוּ אֶת־
22 אַנְשֵׁי הָעָי: וְאֵלֶּה יָצְאוּ מִן־
הָעִיר לִקְרָאתָם וַיִּהְיוּ
לְיִשְׂרָאֵל בַּתָּוֶךְ אֵלֶּה מִזֶּה
וְאֵלֶּה מִזֶּה וַיַּכּוּ אוֹתָם עַד־
בִּלְתִּי הִשְׁאִיר־לָהֶם שָׂרִיד
23 וּפָלִיט: וְאֶת־מֶלֶךְ הָעַי
תָּפְשׂוּ חָי וַיַּקְרִבוּ אֹתוֹ אֶל־
יְהוֹשֻׁעַ:
24 וַיְהִי כְּכַלּוֹת יִשְׂרָאֵל לַהֲרֹג
אֶת־כָּל־יֹשְׁבֵי הָעַי בַּשָּׂדֶה
בַּמִּדְבָּר אֲשֶׁר רְדָפוּם בּוֹ
וַיִּפְּלוּ כֻלָּם לְפִי־חֶרֶב עַד־
תֻּמָּם • וַיָּשֻׁבוּ כָל־יִשְׂרָאֵל
הָעַי וַיַּכּוּ אֹתָהּ לְפִי־חָרֶב:

v. 22. נ״א לוֹ   v. 24. פסקא באמצע פסוק

43

25. And all that fell that day, both of men and women, were twelve thousand, even all the men of Ai. 26. For Joshua drew not back his hand, wherewith he stretched out the javelin, until he had utterly destroyed all the inhabitants of Ai. 27. Only the cattle and the spoil of that city Israel took for a prey unto themselves, according unto the word of the LORD which He commanded Joshua. 28. So Joshua burnt Ai, and made it a heap for ever, even a desolation, unto this day. 29. And the king of Ai he hanged on a tree until the eventide; and at the going down of the sun Joshua commanded, and they took his carcass down from the tree, and cast it at the entrance of the gate of the city, and raised thereon a great heap of stones, unto this day.

25 וַיְהִי כָל־הַנֹּפְלִים בַּיּוֹם הַהוּא
מֵאִישׁ וְעַד־אִשָּׁה שְׁנֵים עָשָׂר
26 אֶלֶף כֹּל אַנְשֵׁי הָעָי : וִיהוֹשֻׁעַ
לֹא־הֵשִׁיב יָדוֹ אֲשֶׁר נָטָה
בַּכִּידוֹן עַד אֲשֶׁר הֶחֱרִים אֵת
27 כָּל־יֹשְׁבֵי הָעָי : רַק הַבְּהֵמָה
וּשְׁלַל הָעִיר הַהִיא בָּזְזוּ לָהֶם
יִשְׂרָאֵל כִּדְבַר יְהֹוָה אֲשֶׁר צִוָּה
28 אֶת־יְהוֹשֻׁעַ : וַיִּשְׂרֹף יְהוֹשֻׁעַ
אֶת־הָעָי וַיְשִׂימֶהָ תֵּל־עוֹלָם
29 שְׁמָמָה עַד הַיּוֹם הַזֶּה : וְאֶת־
מֶלֶךְ הָעַי תָּלָה עַל־הָעֵץ
עַד־עֵת הָעָרֶב וּכְבוֹא הַשֶּׁמֶשׁ
צִוָּה יְהוֹשֻׁעַ וַיֹּרִידוּ אֶת־
נִבְלָתוֹ מִן־הָעֵץ וַיַּשְׁלִיכוּ
אוֹתָהּ אֶל־פֶּתַח שַׁעַר הָעִיר
וַיָּקִימוּ עָלָיו גַּל־אֲבָנִים גָּדוֹל
עַד הַיּוֹם הַזֶּה :

27. Cf. verse 2.

28. *unto this day.* From the standpoint of the writer. But it was subsequently rebuilt, as appears from Ezra ii. 28. Some, however, maintain that it continued in its ruined state for all time, the Ai mentioned in Ezra having been built on a different site.

29. *hanged.* After he was put to death (cf. x. 26).

on a gallows. A pole inserted into the ground, not a growing tree (Targum. See also Sanhedrin 46a).

until the eventide. In accordance with the law of Deut. xxi. 23. Man being made in the image of God, his dignity must be respected

even in a condemned criminal. It is noteworthy that the law was carried out even with a non-Israelite (Kimchi).

at the entrance of the gate of the city. The most conspicuous place where people congregated and public business was transacted (cf. Gen. xxiii. 10; Deut. xxii. 24; 2 Sam. xv. 2).

a great heap of stones. See on vii. 26. Here it would serve as a memorial of the victory and as a deterrent to the other kings of Canaan (Abarbanel and Ralbag).

30-35. The building of an altar; the inscription of the law of Moses upon stones; the proclamation of the blessing and curse as ordained in Deut. xxvii. 12ff.

30. Then Joshua built an altar unto the LORD, the God of Israel, in mount Ebal, 31. as Moses the servant of the LORD commanded the children of Israel, as it is written in the book of the law of Moses, an altar of unhewn stones, upon which no man had lifted up any iron; and they offered thereon burnt-offerings unto the LORD, and sacrificed peace-offerings. 32. And he wrote there upon the stones a copy of the law of Moses, which he wrote before the children of Israel. 33. And all Israel, and their elders and officers,

30 אָ֠ז יִבְנֶ֨ה יְהוֹשֻׁ֤עַ מִזְבֵּ֙חַ֙ לַֽיהֹוָ֔ה אֱלֹהֵ֖י יִשְׂרָאֵ֑ל בְּהַ֖ר עֵיבָֽל׃

31 כַּאֲשֶׁ֣ר צִוָּה֩ מֹשֶׁ֨ה עֶֽבֶד־יְהֹוָ֜ה אֶת־בְּנֵ֣י יִשְׂרָאֵ֗ל כַּכָּתוּב֙ בְּסֵ֙פֶר֙ תּוֹרַ֣ת מֹשֶׁ֔ה מִזְבַּח֙ אֲבָנִ֣ים שְׁלֵמ֔וֹת אֲשֶׁ֥ר לֹֽא־הֵנִ֤יף עֲלֵיהֶן֙ בַּרְזֶ֔ל וַיַּעֲל֤וּ עָלָיו֙ עֹל֣וֹת לַֽיהֹוָ֔ה וַֽיִּזְבְּח֖וּ שְׁלָמִֽים׃

32 וַיִּכְתָּב־שָׁ֖ם עַל־הָאֲבָנִ֑ים אֵ֗ת מִשְׁנֵה֙ תּוֹרַ֣ת מֹשֶׁ֔ה אֲשֶׁ֣ר כָּתַ֔ב

33 לִפְנֵ֖י בְּנֵ֣י יִשְׂרָאֵֽל׃ וְכָל־

---

30. *mount Ebal*. North of Shechem.

31. *an altar of unhewn stones . . . any iron.* Cf. Exod. xx. 22; Deut. xxvii. 5. 'The purpose of the altar was to preserve life (through atonement), whereas iron destroys it (by the sword). It is not fitting, therefore, that the destroyer shall be lifted up (exalted) over the preserver. Moreover, the altar promotes peace between Israel and his Father in heaven. Now, if the Torah stated, *Thou shalt lift up no iron tool upon them* concerning stones which neither see nor hear nor speak, because they promote peace between Israel and his Father in heaven, how much more so shall he who promotes peace between man and his neighbour, between husband and wife, between family and family, be spared tribulation' (Mechilta to Exod. xx. 22).

burnt-offerings . . . peace-offerings. The former were entirely consumed on the altar; of the latter only the fat (*cheleb*) was burnt, the rest being eaten (cf. Lev. i. 9, vii. 11ff.). The Rabbis teach that the burnt-offering made atonement for sins of omission. The peace-offering, on the other hand, was to bring peace to the world.

32. *the stones.* According to the Talmud (Sotah 36a), the Torah was written on the stones of the altar. After this event (of building the altar), they peeled the lime off them

and brought them to Gilgal (Rashi).

a copy of the law of Moses. Various explanations are given for this passage. Rav Saadiah Gaon asserts that the gist of all 613 commandments was recorded. Abarbanel quotes others who claim that the Decalogue, the basis of all the commandments, was written. Still others maintain that it was the Book of Deuteronomy, known as Mishneh Torah (Metsudath David after commentators quoted by Abarbanel). Nachmanides (Deut. xxvii. 3) states that the entire Pentateuch was copied on the stones, with crowns on all the letters as they are written in the Torah scrolls. He conjectures that either the stones were huge, or that the script fitted on them miraculously.

Rabbi Judah says that they wrote the words directly on the stones and subsequently whitewashed them with lime over the script. The Lord gave the heathens the power of extrasensory perception, whereupon they sent their clerks who peeled off the lime and copied the inscription. Rabbi Simeon maintains that they first whitewashed the stones with lime, and then wrote the words thereupon. The words were inscribed in all seventy languages to enable all the surrounding peoples to understand them (Kimchi' from Sotah 35b).

33. *officers.* Cf. i. 10.

and their judges, stood on this side the ark and on that side before the priests the Levites, that bore the ark of the covenant of the LORD, as well the stranger as the home-born; half of them in front of mount Gerizim, and half of them in front of mount Ebal; as Moses the servant of the LORD had commanded at the first, that they should bless the people of Israel. 34. And afterward he read all the words of the law, the blessing and the curse, according to all that is written in the book of the law. 35. There was not a word of all that Moses commanded, which Joshua read not before all the assembly of Israel, and the women, and the little ones, and the strangers that walked among them.

יִשְׂרָאֵל וּזְקֵנָיו וְשֹׁטְרִים |
וְשֹׁפְטָיו עֹמְדִים מִזֶּה | וּמִזֶּה |
לָאָרוֹן נֶגֶד הַכֹּהֲנִים הַלְוִיִּם
נֹשְׂאֵי | אֲרוֹן בְּרִית־יְהֹוָה כַּגֵּר
כָּאֶזְרָח חֶצְיוֹ אֶל־מוּל הַר־
גְּרִזִים וְהַחֶצְיוֹ אֶל־מוּל הַר־
עֵיבָל כַּאֲשֶׁר צִוָּה מֹשֶׁה עֶבֶד־
יְהֹוָה לְבָרֵךְ אֶת־הָעָם
יִשְׂרָאֵל בָּרִאשֹׁנָה: וְאַחֲרֵי־ 34
כֵן קָרָא אֶת־כָּל־דִּבְרֵי
הַתּוֹרָה הַבְּרָכָה וְהַקְּלָלָה
כְּכָל־הַכָּתוּב בְּסֵפֶר
הַתּוֹרָה: לֹא־הָיָה דָבָר מִכֹּל 35
אֲשֶׁר־צִוָּה מֹשֶׁה אֲשֶׁר לֹא־
קָרָא יְהוֹשֻׁעַ נֶגֶד כָּל־קְהַל
יִשְׂרָאֵל וְהַנָּשִׁים וְהַטַּף וְהַגֵּר
הַהֹלֵךְ בְּקִרְבָּם:

the priests the Levites. See on iii. 3.

as well the stranger as the home-born. This lack of discrimination between the stranger and the home-born is a practical example of the Brotherhood of Man as a corollary to the Fatherhood of God. It agrees with the oft-repeated insistence in the Pentateuch that the rights and feelings of the stranger be fully respected. The Rabbis observe that in no fewer than thirty-six places does the Torah command not to vex or oppress the stranger.

mount Gerizim. Cf. Deut. xi. 29; it faced mount Ebal.

the people of Israel. There is the same peculiarity of grammatical construction here as noted in verse 11.

at the first. to pronounce the blessings before the curses: Blessed be the man who will not make a graven or molten image (Rashi). The Levites turned their faces toward Mt. Gerizim and commenced with the blessings: Blessed be. . . . All the curses enumerated in the chapter were first pronounced conversely as blessings, after which the people replied, "Amen." The Levites turned their faces toward Mt. Ebal and pronounced the curses alternately, as enumerated in Scripture (Deut. xxvii).

35. *and the women.* Judaism has never held that women should be kept in ignorance. For the whole verse, cf. Deut. xxxi. 12.

the little ones. Education in the knowledge of God must begin with the young (cf. Deut. vi. 7).

that walked among them. i.e. accompanied the Israelites.

9 CHAPTER IX ס

1. And it came to pass, when all the kings that were beyond the Jordan, in the hill-country, and in the Lowland, and on all the shore of the Great Sea in front of Lebanon, the Hittite, and the Amorite, the Canaanite, the Perizzite, the Hivite, and the Jebusite, heard thereof, 2. that they gathered themselves together, to fight with Joshua and with Israel, with one accord.

3. But when the inhabitants of Gibeon heard what Joshua had done unto Jericho and to Ai, 4. they also did work wilily, and went and made as if they had been ambassadors,

1 וַיְהִי כִשְׁמֹעַ כָּל־הַמְּלָכִים
אֲשֶׁר בְּעֵבֶר הַיַּרְדֵּן בָּהָר
וּבַשְּׁפֵלָה וּבְכֹל חוֹף הַיָּם
הַגָּדוֹל אֶל־מוּל הַלְּבָנוֹן
הַחִתִּי וְהָאֱמֹרִי הַכְּנַעֲנִי הַפְּרִזִּי
2 הַחִוִּי וְהַיְבוּסִי: וַיִּתְקַבְּצוּ
יַחְדָּו לְהִלָּחֵם עִם־יְהוֹשֻׁעַ
וְעִם־יִשְׂרָאֵל פֶּה אֶחָד:
3 וְיֹשְׁבֵי גִבְעוֹן שָׁמְעוּ אֵת אֲשֶׁר
עָשָׂה יְהוֹשֻׁעַ לִירִיחוֹ וְלָעָי:
4 וַיַּעֲשׂוּ גַם־הֵמָּה בְּעָרְמָה
וַיֵּלְכוּ וַיִּצְטַיָּרוּ וַיִּקְחוּ שַׂקִּים

CHAPTER IX

STRATAGEM OF THE GIBEONITES

1. *the hill-country,* etc. Three districts are mentioned, viz. the Lowland, or *Shephelah,* properly the region of low hills, south of Aijalon, between the plain of Philistia (here *the shore of the Great Sea* (i. 4), i.e. the Mediterranean coast) on the one hand, and the central range (*the hill-country*) on the other (Daath Mikra).

Lebanon. See on i. 4.

the Hittite, etc. See on iii. 10. Of the seven peoples enumerated in that verse, the Girgashite is not mentioned here. According to tradition, the Girgashites evacuated and went to Africa (Jerusalem Talmud, Sheviith 6:1; Mechilta, end of *Bo*; Deut. Rabbah 5:13).

2. *with one accord.* lit. 'one mouth.' The Rabbis interpret 'against the mouth of the One' (Tanchuma), i.e. they determined to fight the Divine decree on the allocation of the land to Israel.

3. *but when,* etc. In contrast to these peoples, the Gibeonites, independent of their king, sought peace by submission (Abarbanel).

Gibeon. It has been identified with el-Jib, about five or six miles north-west of Jerusalem. It was larger than Ai (x. 2), and apparently the chief or capital of the four cities enumerated in verse 17. Its inhabitants were Hivites (verse 7), from which it is not to be inferred that not all the Hivites (mentioned in verse 1), joined in the campaign.

4. *they also did work wilily.* As Joshua had employed a stratagem to defeat Ai, so did they to escape their doom. Or they, too, like the kings mentioned in verses 1f., took defensive action, but used different means (Kimchi and Ralbag).

made as if they had been ambassadors. This translation connects the verb with *tsir,* 'envoy.' Several Hebrew MSS., the LXX and Targum read 'and took them provisions,' as in verse 12. The two verbs differ only in one consonant.

and took old sacks upon their asses, and wine-skins, worn and rent and patched up; 5. and worn shoes and clouted upon their feet, and worn garments upon them; and all the bread of their provision was dry and was become crumbs. 6. And they went to Joshua unto the camp at Gilgal, and said unto him, and to the men of Israel: 'We are come from a far country; now therefore make ye a covenant with us.' 7. And the men of Israel said unto the Hivites: 'Peradventure ye dwell among us; and how shall we make a covenant with you?' 8. And they said unto Joshua: 'We are thy servants.' And Joshua said unto them: 'Who are ye? and from whence come ye?' 9. And they said unto him: 'From a very far country

בָּלִים לַחֲמוֹרֵיהֶם וְנֹאדוֹת יַיִן
בָּלִים וּמְבֻקָּעִים וּמְצֹרָרִים:
5 וּנְעָלוֹת בָּלוֹת וּמְטֻלָּאוֹת
בְּרַגְלֵיהֶם וּשְׂלָמוֹת בָּלוֹת
עֲלֵיהֶם וְכֹל לֶחֶם צֵידָם יָבֵשׁ
6 הָיָה נִקֻּדִים: וַיֵּלְכוּ אֶל־
יְהוֹשֻׁעַ אֶל־הַמַּחֲנֶה הַגִּלְגָּל
וַיֹּאמְרוּ אֵלָיו וְאֶל־אִישׁ
יִשְׂרָאֵל מֵאֶרֶץ רְחוֹקָה בָּאנוּ
וְעַתָּה כִּרְתוּ־לָנוּ בְרִית:
7 וַיֹּאמְרוּ אִישׁ־יִשְׂרָאֵל אֶל־
הַחִוִּי אוּלַי בְּקִרְבִּי אַתָּה יוֹשֵׁב
וְאֵיךְ אֶכְרָות־לְךָ בְרִית:
8 וַיֹּאמְרוּ אֶל־יְהוֹשֻׁעַ עֲבָדֶיךָ
אֲנָחְנוּ וַיֹּאמֶר אֲלֵהֶם יְהוֹשֻׁעַ
9 מִי אַתֶּם וּמֵאַיִן תָּבֹאוּ: וַיֹּאמְרוּ
אֵלָיו מֵאֶרֶץ רְחוֹקָה מְאֹד

v. 7. ויאמר ק׳   v. 7. יתיר ר

---

old. lit. 'worn out.'

6. *Gilgal.* Cf. iv. 19. It was Joshua's base (cf. x. 15, 43).

the men of Israel. According to Abarbanel, this refers to the populace (cf. verse 18).

a far country. Only with such tribes was a treaty of peace permissible (Deut. xx. 15).

7. *the men of Israel.* As mentioned in the commentary on the preceding verse, this refers to the populace, who hesitated to enter into a treaty with the Gibeonites. The princes, on the other hand, even swore to them that they would keep the treaty, and it was the populace who complained about this.

Hivites. See on verse 3.

how shall we make a covenant with you? Since it is forbidden to us (cf. Deut. vii. 2)

8. *unto Joshua.* Seeing that the men of Israel were suspicious of them, they went to Joshua himself (Abarbanel).

we are thy servants. We wish to have no dealings with your entire people; we are servants to you alone (*Abarbanel* and *Metsudath David*).

who are ye? Why do you wish to be my servants, unless you are Canaanites and are trying to save yourselves? (Alshich)

9. *a very far country.* whose name is unknown to you, as well as the name of our nationality (Metsudath David).

thy servants are come because of the
name of the LORD thy God; for we
have heard the fame of Him, and all
that He did in Egypt, 10. and all that
He did to the two kings of the
Amorites, that were beyond the
Jordan, to Sihon king of Heshbon,
and to Og king of Bashan, who was
at Ashtaroth. 11. And our elders
and all the inhabitants of our country
spoke to us, saying: Take provision
in your hand for the journey, and go
to meet them, and say unto them:
We are your servants; and now make
ye a covenant with us. 12. This our
bread we took hot for our provision
out of our houses on the day we came
forth to go unto you; but now, behold, it is dry, and is become
crumbs. 13. And these wine-skins,
which we filled, were new; and,
behold, they are rent. And these
our garments and our shoes are worn
by reason of the very long journey.'
14. And the men took of their

בָּאוּ עֲבָדֶיךָ לְשֵׁם יְהֹוָה
אֱלֹהֶיךָ כִּי־שָׁמַעְנוּ שָׁמְעוֹ וְאֵת
כָּל־אֲשֶׁר עָשָׂה בְּמִצְרָיִם:
10 וְאֵת | כָּל־אֲשֶׁר עָשָׂה לִשְׁנֵי
מַלְכֵי הָאֱמֹרִי אֲשֶׁר בְּעֵבֶר
הַיַּרְדֵּן לְסִיחוֹן מֶלֶךְ חֶשְׁבּוֹן
וּלְעוֹג מֶלֶךְ־הַבָּשָׁן אֲשֶׁר
11 בְּעַשְׁתָּרוֹת: וַיֹּאמְרוּ אֵלֵינוּ
זְקֵינֵינוּ וְכָל־־יֹשְׁבֵי אַרְצֵנוּ
לֵאמֹר קְחוּ בְיֶדְכֶם צֵידָה
לַדֶּרֶךְ וּלְכוּ לִקְרָאתָם
וַאֲמַרְתֶּם אֲלֵיהֶם עַבְדֵיכֶם
אֲנַחְנוּ וְעַתָּה כִּרְתוּ־לָנוּ
12 בְרִית: זֶה | לַחְמֵנוּ חָם
הִצְטַיַּדְנוּ אֹתוֹ מִבָּתֵּינוּ בְּיוֹם
צֵאתֵנוּ לָלֶכֶת אֲלֵיכֶם וְעַתָּה
13 הִנֵּה יָבֵשׁ וְהָיָה נִקֻּדִים: וְאֵלֶּה
נֹאדוֹת הַיַּיִן אֲשֶׁר מִלֵּאנוּ
חֲדָשִׁים וְהִנֵּה הִתְבַּקָּעוּ וְאֵלֶּה
שַׂלְמוֹתֵינוּ וּנְעָלֵינוּ בָּלוּ מֵרֹב
14 הַדֶּרֶךְ מְאֹד: וַיִּקְחוּ הָאֲנָשִׁים

---

for we have heard the fame of Him. Their story
was quite plausible; hence it was accepted by
Joshua without more searching investiga-
tion.

10. *to the two kings,* etc. They carefully
omitted mention of more recent events, such
as the crossing of the Jordan and the capture
of Jericho and Ai, to give the impression that
they lived so far away that they had not heard
of them (Abarbanel, Malbim).

Heshbon. His capital to the north-east of
mount Nebo, 20 kilom. south-west of
Amman. It is now known as Kefar Hisban
(Daath Mikra).

Ashtaroth. Now Tel Ashtareh, fifteen miles
north of Edrei, a border town of Bashan.

11. *Our elders.* From artifacts dating from
the era of the conquest, we learn that the
council type of government was prevalent in

provision, and asked not counsel at the mouth of the LORD. 15. And Joshua made peace with them, and made a covenant with them, to let them live; and the princes of the congregation swore unto them.

16. And it came to pass at the end of three days after they had made a covenant with them, that they heard that they were their neighbours, and that they dwelt among them. 17. And the children of Israel journeyed, and came unto their cities on the third day. Now their cities were Gibeon, and Chephirah, and Beeroth, and Kiriath-jearim. 18. And the children of Israel smote them not, because the princes of the congregation had sworn unto them by the LORD, the God of Israel.

מִצֵּידָם וְאֶת־פִּי יְהוָה לֹא
15 שָׁאָלוּ: וַיַּעַשׂ לָהֶם יְהוֹשֻׁעַ
שָׁלוֹם וַיִּכְרֹת לָהֶם בְּרִית
לְחַיּוֹתָם וַיִּשָּׁבְעוּ לָהֶם נְשִׂיאֵי
הָעֵדָה:
16 וַיְהִי מִקְצֵה שְׁלֹשֶׁת יָמִים אַחֲרֵי
אֲשֶׁר־כָּרְתוּ לָהֶם בְּרִית
וַיִּשְׁמְעוּ כִּי־קְרֹבִים הֵם אֵלָיו
17 וּבְקִרְבּוֹ הֵם יֹשְׁבִים: וַיִּסְעוּ
בְנֵי־יִשְׂרָאֵל וַיָּבֹאוּ אֶל־
עָרֵיהֶם בַּיּוֹם הַשְּׁלִישִׁי
וְעָרֵיהֶם גִּבְעוֹן וְהַכְּפִירָה
18 וּבְאֵרוֹת וְקִרְיַת יְעָרִים: וְלֹא
הִכּוּם בְּנֵי יִשְׂרָאֵל כִּי־נִשְׁבְּעוּ
לָהֶם נְשִׂיאֵי הָעֵדָה בַּיהוָה

northern Syria, and, especially, in Asia Minor. This type of government was rare in Canaan, whose cities were ruled by kings (Daath Mikra).

14. *the men took of their provision.* i.e. the Israelites took some of the provisions of the Gibeonites to examine whether it was stale (Kimchi).

at the mouth of the LORD. By the Urim and Thummim on the High Priest's breastplate (Ralbag).

15. *Joshua . . . the princes of the congregation,* etc. Joshua, as leader, made the covenant of peace, while the oath ratifying it was taken by the princes who consulted neither Joshua nor the community (Abarbanel).

17. *on the third day.* The distance from Gilgal to Gibeon as the crow flies is nineteen miles; by road it would be more. Even so, they must have travelled very leisurely.

Chephirah, and Beeroth, and Kiriath-jearim. The first and third lay to the south-west of Gibeon. Beeroth, lit. 'wells,' may be the modern el-Bire, north of Gibeon and near Beth-el. Hershcovitz identifies Chephirah with the ruins which lie to the north of Kiriath-anabim, a settlement in modern Palestine just outside Jerusalem on the road to Tel-Aviv. Kiriath-jearim is also called Kiriath-baal in xv. 60.

18. *had sworn.* The covenant made by Joshua, being executed under the mistaken impression of Gibeon being a distant nation, had no legality. However, the abrogation of an oath is of such extreme gravity that, even if such oath was entered into by mistake, it must be abided by. Otherwise, non-Jews would be led to believe that the Jewish people are careless with their word, even though it is incorporated into a solemn oath (Gittin 46a, Rashi ad loc).

And all the congregation murmured against the princes. 19. But all the princes said unto all the congregation: 'We have sworn unto them by the LORD, the God of Israel; now therefore we may not touch them. 20. This we will do to them, and let them live; lest wrath be upon us, because of the oath which we swore unto them.' 21. And the princes said concerning them: 'Let them live' so they became hewers of wood and drawers of water unto all the congregation, as the princes had spoken concerning them. 22. And Joshua called for them, and he spoke unto them, saying: 'Wherefore have ye beguiled us, saying: We are very far from you, when ye dwell among us? 23. Now therefore ye are cursed, and there shall never fail to be of you bondmen, both hewers of wood and drawers of water for the house of my God.' 24. And they answered Joshua, and said: 'Because it was certainly told thy servants, how that the LORD thy God commanded His servant Moses to give

אֱלֹהֵי יִשְׂרָאֵל וַיִּלֹּנוּ כָל־
הָעֵדָה עַל־־הַנְּשִׂיאִים׃
19 וַיֹּאמְרוּ כָל־הַנְּשִׂיאִים אֶל־
כָּל־הָעֵדָה אֲנַחְנוּ נִשְׁבַּעְנוּ
לָהֶם בַּיהוָה אֱלֹהֵי יִשְׂרָאֵל
וְעַתָּה לֹא נוּכַל לִנְגֹּעַ בָּהֶם׃
20 זֹאת נַעֲשֶׂה לָהֶם וְהַחֲיֵה אוֹתָם
וְלֹא־יִהְיֶה עָלֵינוּ קֶצֶף עַל־
הַשְּׁבוּעָה אֲשֶׁר־נִשְׁבַּעְנוּ
21 לָהֶם׃ וַיֹּאמְרוּ אֲלֵיהֶם
הַנְּשִׂיאִים יִחְיוּ וַיִּהְיוּ חֹטְבֵי
עֵצִים וְשֹׁאֲבֵי־מַיִם לְכָל־
הָעֵדָה כַּאֲשֶׁר דִּבְּרוּ לָהֶם
22 הַנְּשִׂיאִים׃ וַיִּקְרָא לָהֶם יְהוֹשֻׁעַ
וַיְדַבֵּר אֲלֵיהֶם לֵאמֹר לָמָּה
רִמִּיתֶם אֹתָנוּ לֵאמֹר רְחוֹקִים
אֲנַחְנוּ מִכֶּם מְאֹד וְאַתֶּם
23 בְּקִרְבֵּנוּ יֹשְׁבִים׃ וְעַתָּה
אֲרוּרִים אַתֶּם וְלֹא־יִכָּרֵת
מִכֶּם עֶבֶד וְחֹטְבֵי עֵצִים
וְשֹׁאֲבֵי־מַיִם לְבֵית אֱלֹהָי׃
24 וַיַּעֲנוּ אֶת־יְהוֹשֻׁעַ וַיֹּאמְרוּ כִּי
הֻגֵּד הֻגַּד לַעֲבָדֶיךָ אֵת אֲשֶׁר
צִוָּה יְהוָה אֱלֹהֶיךָ אֶת־־מֹשֶׁה
עַבְדּוֹ לָתֵת לָכֶם אֶת־כָּל־־

21. *hewers of wood and drawers of water.* Terms for the lowliest and most servile occupations (cf. Deut. xxix. 10).

23. *for the house of my God.* In connection with the Tabernacle (Targum).

27. *which He should choose.* At some time in

51

you all the land, and to destroy all the inhabitants of the land from before you; therefore we were sore afraid for our lives because of you, and have done this thing. 25. And now, behold, we are in thy hand: as it seemeth good and right unto thee to do unto us, do.' 26. And so did he unto them, and delivered them out of the hand of the children of Israel, that they slew them not. 27. And Joshua made them that day hewers of wood and drawers of water for the congregation, and for the altar of the LORD, unto this day, in the place which He should choose.

הָאָרֶץ וּלְהַשְׁמִיד אֶת־כָּל־
יֹשְׁבֵי הָאָרֶץ מִפְּנֵיכֶם וַנִּירָא
מְאֹד לְנַפְשֹׁתֵינוּ מִפְּנֵיכֶם
וַנַּעֲשֶׂה אֶת־הַדָּבָר הַזֶּה:
25 וְעַתָּה הִנְנוּ בְיָדֶךָ כַּטּוֹב וְכַיָּשָׁר
בְּעֵינֶיךָ לַעֲשׂוֹת לָנוּ עֲשֵׂה:
26 וַיַּעַשׂ לָהֶם כֵּן וַיַּצֵּל אוֹתָם
מִיַּד בְּנֵי־יִשְׂרָאֵל וְלֹא הֲרָגוּם:
27 וַיִּתְּנֵם יְהוֹשֻׁעַ בַּיּוֹם הַהוּא
חֹטְבֵי עֵצִים וְשֹׁאֲבֵי־מַיִם
לָעֵדָה וּלְמִזְבַּח יְהוָֹה עַד־
הַיּוֹם הַזֶּה אֶל־הַמָּקוֹם אֲשֶׁר
יִבְחָר:

10   CHAPTER X   י

1. Now it came to pass, when Adoni-zedek king of Jerusalem heard how Joshua had taken Ai, and had utterly destroyed it; as he had done to Jericho and her king, so he

1 וַיְהִי כִשְׁמֹעַ אֲדֹנִי־צֶדֶק מֶלֶךְ
יְרוּשָׁלַ͏ִם כִּי־לָכַד יְהוֹשֻׁעַ
אֶת־הָעַי וַיַּחֲרִימָהּ כַּאֲשֶׁר
עָשָׂה לִירִיחוֹ וּלְמַלְכָּהּ כֵּן־

the future, when their menial duties would be transferred to the Temple (Metsudath David).

CHAPTER X

CONQUEST OF THE SOUTH

1. *Adoni-zedek.* lit. 'my lord is Zedek,' this being the name of a Phoenician god. The Midrash (Gen. Rabbah xliii. 6) interprets as 'king of Zedek,' i.e. of Jerusalem, which is called *zedek* (righteousness), as it is written, *Righteousness lodged in her* (Isa. 1. 21). Kimchi expresses the view that all the early kings of Jerusalem were called Adoni-zedek or Melchizedek (cf. Gen. xiv. 18).

Jerusalem. The Hebrew name is *Yerushalayim* written without the letter *yad,* indicating that the original pronunciation was *Yerushalim,* i.e. 'the city of Shalem' (cf. Gen. xiv. 18). In the Tel el-Amarna Letters it is called Urusalim. The meaning is 'the city of peace.'

had done to Ai and her king; and how the inhabitants of Gibeon had made peace with Israel, and were among them; 2. that they feared greatly, because Gibeon was a great city, as one of the royal cities, and because it was greater than Ai, and all the men thereof were mighty. 3. Wherefore Adoni-zedek king of Jerusalem sent unto Hoham king of Hebron, and unto Piram king of Jarmuth, and unto Japhia king of Lachish, and unto Debir king of Eglon, saying: 4. 'Come up unto me, and help me, and let us smite Gibeon; for it hath made peace with Joshua and with the children of Israel.' 5. Therefore the five kings of the Amorites, the king of Jerusalem, the king of Hebron, the king

עָשָׂה לָעַי וּלְמַלְכָּהּ וְכִי
הִשְׁלִימוּ יֹשְׁבֵי גִבְעוֹן אֶת־
יִשְׂרָאֵל וַיִּהְיוּ בְּקִרְבָּם:
2 וַיִּירְאוּ מְאֹד כִּי עִיר גְּדוֹלָה
גִבְעוֹן כְּאַחַת עָרֵי הַמַּמְלָכָה
וְכִי הִיא גְדוֹלָה מִן־הָעַי
3 וְכָל־אֲנָשֶׁיהָ גִּבֹּרִים: וַיִּשְׁלַח
אֲדֹנִי־צֶדֶק מֶלֶךְ יְרוּשָׁלַם
אֶל־הוֹהָם מֶלֶךְ־חֶבְרוֹן
וְאֶל־פִּרְאָם מֶלֶךְ־יַרְמוּת
וְאֶל־יָפִיעַ מֶלֶךְ־לָכִישׁ וְאֶל־
דְּבִיר מֶלֶךְ־עֶגְלוֹן לֵאמֹר:
4 עֲלוּ־אֵלַי וְעִזְרֻנִי וְנַכֶּה אֶת־
גִּבְעוֹן כִּי־הִשְׁלִימָה אֶת־
יְהוֹשֻׁעַ וְאֶת־בְּנֵי יִשְׂרָאֵל:
5 וַיֵּאָסְפוּ וַיַּעֲלוּ חֲמֵשֶׁת ׀ מַלְכֵי
הָאֱמֹרִי מֶלֶךְ יְרוּשָׁלַם מֶלֶךְ־

---

2. *as one of the royal cities.* The implication is that it was not a royal city. This is confirmed by ix. 11 where the *elders* and *the inhabitants* are mentioned, but no king (D.M.).

greater than Ai. Apparently, then, Ai was a large city, and the report of the men who spied out the place (vii. 3) was too optimistic and underestimated its strength. Gibeon's surrender, accordingly, indicated a state of demoralization which, if allowed to go unchecked, would lead to the rapid collapse of the other Canaanite tribes (Metsudath David).

3. *Hebron.* Nineteen miles south of Jerusalem, on the road to Beersheba. It was an ancient and important city, which first

appears in Biblical history as the place where Abraham settled after he parted from Lot (Gen. xiii. 18). It was also the first city visited by the spies sent by Moses (Num. xiii. 22).

Jarmuth. The modern Khirbet el-Yarkuk, sixteen miles west of Jerusalem (D.M.).

Lachish. Now Tel el-Hesy on the road from Egypt to Gaza.

Eglon. Two miles north of Lachish and twenty-three west of Hebron.

4. *Gibeon.* He did not propose an attack on Joshua. His appeal for a confederation shows that the country had not united in face of the invader.

5. *the Amorites.* See on iii. 10.

of Jarmuth, the king of Lachish, the king of Eglon, gathered themselves together, and went up, they and all their hosts, and encamped against Gibeon, and made war against it. 6. And the men of Gibeon sent unto Joshua to the camp to Gilgal, saying: 'Slack not thy hands from thy servants; come up to us quickly, and save us, and help us; for all the kings of the Amorites that dwell in the hill-country are gathered together against us.' 7. So Joshua went up from Gilgal, he, and all the people of war with him, and all the mighty men of valour.

8. And the LORD said unto Joshua: 'Fear them not; for I have delivered them into thy hand; there shall not a man of them stand against thee.' 9. Joshua therefore came upon them suddenly; for he went up from Gilgal all the night. 10. And the LORD discomfited them before Israel, and slew them with a great slaughter

חֶבְרוֹן מֶלֶךְ־יַרְמוּת מֶלֶךְ־
לָכִישׁ מֶלֶךְ־עֶגְלוֹן הֵם וְכָל־
מַחֲנֵיהֶם וַיַּחֲנוּ עַל־גִּבְעוֹן
6 וַיִּלָּחֲמוּ עָלֶיהָ: וַיִּשְׁלְחוּ אַנְשֵׁי
גִבְעוֹן אֶל־יְהוֹשֻׁעַ אֶל־
הַמַּחֲנֶה הַגִּלְגָּלָה לֵאמֹר אַל־
תֶּרֶף יָדֶיךָ מֵעֲבָדֶיךָ עֲלֵה
אֵלֵינוּ מְהֵרָה וְהוֹשִׁיעָה לָּנוּ
וְעָזְרֵנוּ כִּי נִקְבְּצוּ אֵלֵינוּ כָּל־
מַלְכֵי הָאֱמֹרִי יֹשְׁבֵי הָהָר:
7 וַיַּעַל יְהוֹשֻׁעַ מִן־הַגִּלְגָּל הוּא
וְכָל־עַם הַמִּלְחָמָה עִמּוֹ וְכֹל
גִּבּוֹרֵי הֶחָיִל:
8 וַיֹּאמֶר יְהוָה אֶל־יְהוֹשֻׁעַ אַל־
תִּירָא מֵהֶם כִּי בְיָדְךָ נְתַתִּים
לֹא־יַעֲמֹד אִישׁ מֵהֶם בְּפָנֶיךָ:
9 וַיָּבֹא אֲלֵיהֶם יְהוֹשֻׁעַ פִּתְאֹם
כָּל־הַלַּיְלָה עָלָה מִן־
10 הַגִּלְגָּל: וַיְהֻמֵּם יְהוָה לִפְנֵי
יִשְׂרָאֵל וַיַּכֵּם מַכָּה־גְדוֹלָה

ע. 8. יתיר י׳

---

6. *come up to us quickly.* The appeal of the Gibeonites to Joshua and his ready response indicate that the treaty between them (ix. 15) was not simply one of submission or even a non-aggression pact but a defensive alliance; and although it had been obtained by fraud, Joshua honoured it.

7. *all the people of war . . . and all the mighty men of valour.* The two terms appear to be synonymous; but the conjunction *and* seems to suggest that different groups are meant. Perhaps *the mighty men of valour* were the officers.

8. *fear them not.* It was the most powerful coalition which Joshua had so far to face; hence God's special assurance.

9. *from Gilgal all the might.* By forced marches. It was more than twenty miles, the road ascending all the way (*he went up*).

at Gibeon; and they chased them by the way of the ascent of Beth-horon, and smote them to Azekah, and unto Makkedah. 11. And it came to pass, as they fled from before Israel, while they were at the descent of Beth-horon, that the LORD cast down great stones from heaven upon them unto Azekah, and they died; they were more who died with the hailstones than they whom the children of Israel slew with the sword.

12. Then spoke Joshua to the LORD in the day when the LORD delivered up the Amorites before

בְּגִבְעוֹן וַיִּרְדְּפֵם דֶּרֶךְ מַעֲלֵה
בֵית־חוֹרֹן וַיַּכֵּם עַד־עֲזֵקָה
11 וְעַד־מַקֵּדָה: וַיְהִי בְּנֻסָם |
מִפְּנֵי יִשְׂרָאֵל הֵם בְּמוֹרַד
בֵּית־חוֹרֹן וַיהוָֹה הִשְׁלִיךְ
עֲלֵיהֶם אֲבָנִים גְּדֹלוֹת מִן־
הַשָּׁמַיִם עַד־עֲזֵקָה וַיָּמֻתוּ
רַבִּים אֲשֶׁר־מֵתוּ בְּאַבְנֵי
הַבָּרָד מֵאֲשֶׁר הָרְגוּ בְּנֵי
יִשְׂרָאֵל בֶּחָרֶב:
12 אָז יְדַבֵּר יְהוֹשֻׁעַ לַיהוָֹה בְּיוֹם
תֵּת יְהוָֹה אֶת־הָאֱמֹרִי לִפְנֵי

---

10. *Beth-horon.* i.e. the upper or more eastern Beth-horon, five miles north-west of Gibeon, to which an *ascent* of nearly two miles leads from the lower Beth-horon lying to the north-west (Daath Mikra).

Azekah. Mentioned in xv. 35 as part of Judah's allotment. Its exact site has not been discovered, but it is in or near to the Vale of Elah in the *Shephelah* (the Lowland).

Makkedah. Mentioned again in xii. 16, xv. 41. Its location is uncertain. Some identify it with el-Mughar, south-west of Ekron and twenty-five miles from Gibeon.

11. *the descent of Beth-horon.* i.e. to the lower Beth-horon, which lay about 700 feet below the level of the upper city (Daath Mikra).

great stones. i.e. hailstones. A reference to the incident occurs in Ecclus. xlvi. 6, 'With hailstones of mighty power He caused war to break violently upon the nation.'

These stones had been suspended in the air since the days of Moses, who caused hailstones to fall upon Egypt. Upon the cessation of the plague of hail, the falling hailstones

were suspended in the air. Only now, since Joshua was a fitting successor to Moses, did they fall from heaven (Berakoth 54b).

12-14. The miracle of the sun standing still. The Rabbis list this passage, *then spoke Joshua to the* LORD, as one of the occasions when Israel uttered song to God (Mechilta, Beshallach). Some modern commentators attempt to eliminate the supernatural element from the incident by stressing the poetical form of the language, which they understand as implying no more than, 'May God grant us victory before the sun sets.' That the narrative was early understood as relating a miraculous prolongation of the day is evident from Ecclus. xlvi. 4, 'Did not the sun go back by his hand? And did not one day become as two?' Although the text of the praise is absent from the text, the Scripture informs us that Joshua, nevertheless, praised the Almighty after his prayer to Him. It is also possible that the words: "Sun, stand thou still upon Gibeon, etc." comprise the prayer, while the entire verse 13 comprises the song of praises recited by Joshua to the Almighty. This latter theory is

the children of Israel; and he said in the sight of Israel:

'Sun, stand thou still upon Gibeon;

And thou, Moon, in the valley of Aijalon.'

13. And the sun stood still, and the moon stayed,

Until the nation had avenged themselves of their enemies.

Is not this written in the book of Jashar? And the sun stayed in the midst of heaven, and hasted not to go down about a whole day. 14. And there was no day like that before it or after it, that the LORD hearkened unto the voice of a man; for the LORD fought for Israel.

בְּנֵי יִשְׂרָאֵל וַיֹּאמֶר ׀ לְעֵינֵי
יִשְׂרָאֵל
שֶׁמֶשׁ בְּגִבְעוֹן דּוֹם
וְיָרֵחַ בְּעֵמֶק אַיָּלוֹן׃
13 וַיִּדֹּם הַשֶּׁמֶשׁ וְיָרֵחַ עָמָד
עַד־יִקֹּם גּוֹי אֹיְבָיו
הֲלֹא־הִיא כְתוּבָה עַל־סֵפֶר
הַיָּשָׁר וַיַּעֲמֹד הַשֶּׁמֶשׁ בַּחֲצִי
הַשָּׁמַיִם וְלֹא־אָץ לָבוֹא כְּיוֹם
14 תָּמִים׃ וְלֹא הָיָה כַּיּוֹם הַהוּא
לְפָנָיו וְאַחֲרָיו לִשְׁמֹעַ יְהוָה
בְּקוֹל אִישׁ כִּי יְהוָה נִלְחָם
לְיִשְׂרָאֵל׃

קמץ ברביע‎ .v. 13

---

supported by the Mechilta, which lists this among the ten songs mentioned in the Scriptures (Kimchi).

12. *valley of Aijalon*. This is the valley that spreads out beside the straight road that leads from Shaar Hagai to Ramlah. It was named for the city of Aijalon, an ancient city found above it and mentioned in the Tel-El-Amarna letters (Daath Mikra). At that time, the moon was standing opposite the valley of Aijalon, far from Gibeon, for Gibeon is in Benjamin's territory (in the south), and Aijalon is in Dan's territory (in the north) (Rashi.) Joshua asked that the sun remain suspended over Gibeon and the moon over the valley of Aijalon. According to the Midrash, the battle took place on Friday, and Joshua asked that the day be lengthened so that there would be no need to desecrate the approaching Sabbath (Kimchi). The battle extended from Gibeon, where it was fought, to the valley of Aijalon, where the Israelites pursued the enemy (Abarbanel).

13. *the book of Jashar*. lit. 'the book of the upright.' 'Upright' may denote Israel (the

upright nation; cf. Jeshurun, Deut. xxxii. 15). But it is more probable that 'upright' refers either to individuals who are celebrated in this work, such as Joshua and Saul; or to the great deeds which are recounted therein. David's lament over Saul and Jonathan is quoted from it (2 Sam. i. 18). This might lead one to infer that it was a compilation later than David. It is, however, possible that the collection was added to in course of time and the present quotation belongs to an earlier form. A similar collection, *the book of the Wars of the Lord,* is cited in Num. xxi. 14 (see Ralbag).

about a whole day. Maimonides (*Guide*, ii. 35) explains *about a whole day* (verse 13. lit. 'like a complete day') as 'the longest possible day,' and the phrase 'indicates that that day appeared to the people at Gibeon as their longest day in the summer.'

14. *and there was no day*, etc. This statement gives an indication of the recognition that a great miracle had occurred (Abarbanel).

or after it. These words seem to imply a late

15. And Joshua returned, and all Israel with him, unto the camp to Gilgal.

16. And these five kings fled, and hid themselves in the cave at Makkedah. 17. And it was told Joshua, saying: 'The five kings are found, hidden in the cave at Makkedah.' 18. And Joshua said: 'Roll great stones unto the mouth of the cave, and set men by it to keep them; 19. but stay not ye; pursue after your enemies, and smite the hindmost of them; suffer them not to enter into their cities; for the LORD your God hath delivered them into your hand.' 20. And it came to pass, when Joshua and the children of Israel had made an end of slaying them with a very great slaughter, till they were consumed, and the remnant which remained of them had entered into the fortified cities, 21. that all the people returned to the camp to Joshua at Makkedah in peace; none whetted his

15 וַיָּ֧שָׁב יְהוֹשֻׁ֛עַ וְכָל־יִשְׂרָאֵ֥ל עִמּ֖וֹ אֶל־הַֽמַּחֲנֶ֥ה הַגִּלְגָּֽלָה׃

16 וַיָּנֻ֕סוּ חֲמֵ֖שֶׁת הַמְּלָכִ֣ים הָאֵ֑לֶּה וַיֵּחָבְא֥וּ בַמְּעָרָ֖ה בְּמַקֵּדָֽה׃

17 וַיֻּגַּ֖ד לִיהוֹשֻׁ֣עַ לֵאמֹ֑ר נִמְצְאוּ֙ חֲמֵ֣שֶׁת הַמְּלָכִ֔ים נֶחְבְּאִ֥ים

18 בַּמְּעָרָ֖ה בְּמַקֵּדָֽה׃ וַיֹּ֣אמֶר יְהוֹשֻׁ֗עַ גֹּ֣לּוּ אֲבָנִ֤ים גְּדֹלוֹת֙ אֶל־ פִּ֣י הַמְּעָרָ֔ה וְהַפְקִ֧ידוּ עָלֶ֛יהָ

19 אֲנָשִׁ֖ים לְשָׁמְרָֽם׃ וְאַתֶּם֙ אַֽל־ תַּעֲמֹ֔דוּ רִדְפוּ֙ אַחֲרֵ֣י אֹיְבֵיכֶ֔ם וְזִנַּבְתֶּ֖ם אוֹתָ֑ם אַל־תִּתְּנ֗וּם לָבוֹא֙ אֶל־עָ֣רֵיהֶ֔ם כִּ֧י נְתָנָ֛ם

20 יְהוָ֥ה אֱלֹהֵיכֶ֖ם בְּיֶדְכֶֽם׃ וַיְהִ֡י כְּכַלּוֹת֩ יְהוֹשֻׁ֨עַ וּבְנֵ֤י יִשְׂרָאֵל֙ לְהַכּוֹתָ֛ם מַכָּ֥ה גְדוֹלָֽה־מְאֹ֖ד עַד־תֻּמָּ֑ם וְהַשְּׂרִידִים֙ שָׂרְד֣וּ מֵהֶ֔ם וַיָּבֹ֖אוּ אֶל־עָרֵ֥י

21 הַמִּבְצָֽר׃ וַיָּשֻׁ֣בוּ כָל־הָעָ֣ם אֶל־הַֽמַּחֲנֶ֛ה אֶל־יְהוֹשֻׁ֖עַ מַקֵּדָ֑ה בְּשָׁל֕וֹם לֹֽא־חָרַ֞ץ

---

date for the composition of this Book. They may merely express the intense conviction that never again would God so signally manifest that He was the Ally of Israel.

15. This verse is not in chronological order and is repeated in verse 43 (Metsudath David).

20. *and the remnant which remained,* lit. and the remnant remained of them, and they

entered . . . This may be explained thus: And the remnant remained because of them; i.e., because of the Israelites, who were slothful in pursuing the battle, and therefore, they managed to enter the fortified cities. Alternatively, only those destined to remain alive, remained of them, and entered the fortified cities (K'li Y'kar).

21. *none whetted his tongue.* Cf. *But against any of the children of Israel shall not a dog whet his*

tongue against any of the children of
Israel. 22. Then said Joshua: 'Open
the mouth of the cave, and bring
forth those five kings unto me out of
the cave.' 23. And they did so, and
brought forth those five kings unto
him out of the cave, the king of Jerusalem, the king of Hebron, the king of
Jarmuth, the king of Lachish, the
king of Eglon. 24. And it came to
pass, when they brought forth those
kings unto Joshua, that Joshua
called for all the men of Israel, and
said unto the chiefs of the men of
war that went with him: 'Come near,
put your feet upon the necks of
these kings.' And they came near,
and put their feet upon the necks of
them. 25. And Joshua said unto
them: 'Fear not, nor be dismayed;
be strong and of good courage; for
thus shall the LORD do to all your
enemies against whom ye fight.'
26. And afterward Joshua smote

לִבְנֵי יִשְׂרָאֵל לְאִישׁ אֶת־
לְשֹׁנוֹ: 22 וַיֹּאמֶר יְהוֹשֻׁעַ פִּתְחוּ
אֶת־פִּי הַמְּעָרָה וְהוֹצִיאוּ אֵלַי
אֶת־חֲמֵשֶׁת הַמְּלָכִים הָאֵלֶּה
23 מִן־הַמְּעָרָה: וַיַּעֲשׂוּ כֵן
וַיֹּצִיאוּ אֵלָיו אֶת־חֲמֵשֶׁת
הַמְּלָכִים הָאֵלֶּה מִן־הַמְּעָרָה
אֵת ׀ מֶלֶךְ יְרוּשָׁלַ͏ִם אֶת־מֶלֶךְ
חֶבְרוֹן אֶת־מֶלֶךְ יַרְמוּת אֶת־
מֶלֶךְ לָכִישׁ אֶת־מֶלֶךְ עֶגְלוֹן:
24 וַיְהִי כְּהוֹצִיאָם אֶת־הַמְּלָכִים
הָאֵלֶּה אֶל־יְהוֹשֻׁעַ וַיִּקְרָא
יְהוֹשֻׁעַ אֶל־כָּל־אִישׁ יִשְׂרָאֵל
וַיֹּאמֶר אֶל־קְצִינֵי אַנְשֵׁי
הַמִּלְחָמָה הֶהָלְכוּא אִתּוֹ
קִרְבוּ שִׂימוּ אֶת־רַגְלֵיכֶם
עַל־צַוְּארֵי הַמְּלָכִים הָאֵלֶּה
וַיִּקְרְבוּ וַיָּשִׂימוּ אֶת־רַגְלֵיהֶם
25 עַל־צַוְּארֵיהֶם: וַיֹּאמֶר
אֲלֵיהֶם יְהוֹשֻׁעַ אַל־תִּירְאוּ
וְאַל־תֵּחָתּוּ חִזְקוּ וְאִמְצוּ כִּי
כָכָה יַעֲשֶׂה יְהֹוָה לְכָל־
אֹיְבֵיכֶם אֲשֶׁר אַתֶּם נִלְחָמִים
26 אוֹתָם: וַיַּכֵּם יְהוֹשֻׁעַ אַחֲרֵי־

v. 24. א׳ יתיר

tongue (Exod. xi. 7), a proverbial phrase to
express the idea that there were no signs of
hostility.

24. *put your feet upon the necks of these kings.*

To demonstrate the complete subjugation of
the enemy. The practice is illustrated on
Assyrian sculptures.

26f. *See on viii. 29 (Daath Mikra).*

them, and put them to death, and
hanged them on five trees; and they
were hanging upon the trees until
the evening. 27. And it came to
pass at the time of the going down
of the sun, that Joshua commanded,
and they took them down off the
trees, and cast them into the cave
wherein they had hidden themselves, and laid great stones on the
mouth of the cave, unto this very
day.

28. And Joshua took Makkedah on
that day, and smote it with the edge
of the sword, and the king thereof;
he utterly destroyed them and all
the souls that were therein, he left
none remaining; and he did to the
king of Makkedah as he had done
unto the king of Jericho.

29. And Joshua passed from
Makkedah, and all Israel with him,
unto Libnah, and fought against
Libnah. 30. And the LORD delivered it also, and the king thereof,
into the hand of Israel; and he smote
it with the edge of the sword, and
all the souls that were therein; he
left none remaining in it; and he did
unto the king thereof as he had done
unto the king of Jericho.

כז וַיְמִיתֵם וַיִּתְלֵם עַל חֲמִשָּׁה
עֵצִים וַיִּהְיוּ תְּלוּיִם עַל־
הָעֵצִים עַד־הָעָרֶב: וַיְהִי
לְעֵת ׀ בּוֹא הַשֶּׁמֶשׁ צִוָּה יְהוֹשֻׁעַ
וַיֹּרִידוּם מֵעַל הָעֵצִים
וַיַּשְׁלִכֻם אֶל־הַמְּעָרָה אֲשֶׁר
נֶחְבְּאוּ־שָׁם וַיָּשִׂמוּ אֲבָנִים
גְּדֹלוֹת עַל־פִּי הַמְּעָרָה עַד־
עֶצֶם הַיּוֹם הַזֶּה:

כח וְאֶת־מַקֵּדָה לָכַד יְהוֹשֻׁעַ
בַּיּוֹם הַהוּא וַיַּכֶּהָ לְפִי־חֶרֶב
וְאֶת־מַלְכָּהּ הֶחֱרִם אוֹתָם
וְאֶת־כָּל־הַנֶּפֶשׁ אֲשֶׁר־בָּהּ
לֹא הִשְׁאִיר שָׂרִיד וַיַּעַשׂ לְמֶלֶךְ
מַקֵּדָה כַּאֲשֶׁר עָשָׂה לְמֶלֶךְ
יְרִיחוֹ:

כט וַיַּעֲבֹר יְהוֹשֻׁעַ וְכָל־יִשְׂרָאֵל
עִמּוֹ מִמַּקֵּדָה לִבְנָה וַיִּלָּחֶם
עִם־לִבְנָה: וַיִּתֵּן יְהֹוָה גַּם־
אוֹתָהּ בְּיַד יִשְׂרָאֵל וְאֶת־
מַלְכָּהּ וַיַּכֶּהָ לְפִי־חֶרֶב וְאֶת־
כָּל־הַנֶּפֶשׁ אֲשֶׁר־בָּהּ לֹא־
הִשְׁאִיר בָּהּ שָׂרִיד וַיַּעַשׂ
לְמַלְכָּהּ כַּאֲשֶׁר עָשָׂה לְמֶלֶךְ
יְרִיחוֹ:

v. 28. נ״א על v. 29. נ״א אותה

28. *destroyed them.* Several Hebrew MSS. read 'it.'

29. *Libnah.* Between Makkedah and Lachish, but its exact site is unknown.

31. And Joshua passed from Libnah, and all Israel with him, unto Lachish, and encamped against it, and fought against it. 32. And the LORD delivered Lachish into the hand of Israel, and he took it on the second day, and smote it with the edge of the sword, and all the souls that were therein, according to all that he had done to Libnah.

33. Then Horam king of Gezer came up to help Lachish; and Joshua smote him and his people, until he had left him none remaining.

34. And Joshua passed from Lachish, and all Israel with him, unto Eglon; and they encamped against it, and fought against it. 35. And they took it on that day, and smote it with the edge of the sword, and all the souls that were

31 וַיַּעֲבֹר יְהוֹשֻׁעַ וְכָל־יִשְׂרָאֵל
עִמּוֹ מִלִּבְנָה לָכִישָׁה וַיִּחַן
32 עָלֶיהָ וַיִּלָּחֶם בָּהּ: וַיִּתֵּן יְהֹוָה
אֶת־לָכִישׁ בְּיַד יִשְׂרָאֵל
וַיִּלְכְּדָהּ בַּיּוֹם הַשֵּׁנִי וַיַּכֶּהָ
לְפִי־חֶרֶב וְאֶת־כָּל־הַנֶּפֶשׁ
אֲשֶׁר־בָּהּ כְּכֹל אֲשֶׁר־עָשָׂה
לְלִבְנָה:
33 אָז עָלָה הֹרָם מֶלֶךְ גֶּזֶר לַעְזֹר
אֶת־לָכִישׁ וַיַּכֵּהוּ יְהוֹשֻׁעַ
וְאֶת־עַמּוֹ עַד־בִּלְתִּי
הִשְׁאִיר־לוֹ שָׂרִיד:
34 וַיַּעֲבֹר יְהוֹשֻׁעַ וְכָל־יִשְׂרָאֵל
עִמּוֹ מִלָּכִישׁ עֶגְלֹנָה וַיַּחֲנוּ
עָלֶיהָ וַיִּלָּחֲמוּ עָלֶיהָ:
35 וַיִּלְכְּדוּהָ בַּיּוֹם הַהוּא וַיַּכּוּהָ
לְפִי־חֶרֶב וְאֵת כָּל־הַנֶּפֶשׁ

---

32. *on the second day.* All the other cities fell to Joshua at once at Lachish. Of this city alone it is said that he took it *on the second day;* an indication of its strategic strength. Later when Sennacherib invaded Judah, he attacked and took *the fenced cities,* but Lachish successfully withstood him and he was compelled to raise the siege (2 Kings xix. 8).

33. *Gezer.* Tel Jezer, six miles south of Lydda. Excavations here have revealed many interesting remains of the Canaanite epoch, the Jewish (from the days of the First and Second Temples) and of later periods. 'M. Clermont Ganneau discovered the ancient site, with the very name itself still lingering on the spot. Not only that, but he found the Levitical boundaries. In no other case have these been found. They were cut in the rock itself—not on movable stones—in two separate places, in Greek and square Hebrew characters' (*Quarterly Statement of the Palestine Exploration Fund,* 1874).

him and his people. The city of Gezer lay too far north for Joshua's campaign, and he did not attempt its capture for the present. If he did later, he failed, because it remained for hundreds of years a Canaanite fortress (cf. xvi. 10; Judg. i. 29).

therein he utterly destroyed that day, according to all that he had done to Lachish.

36. And Joshua went up from Eglon, and all Israel with him, unto Hebron; and they fought against it. 37. And they took it, and smote it with the edge of the sword, and the king thereof, and all the cities thereof, and all the souls that were therein; he left none remaining, according to all that he had done to Eglon; but he utterly destroyed it, and all the souls that were therein.

38. And Joshua turned back, and all Israel with him, to Debir; and fought against it. 39. And he took it, and the king thereof, and all the cities thereof; and they smote them with the edge of the sword, and utterly destroyed all the souls that were therein; he left none remaining; as he had done to Hebron, so he did to Debir, and to the king thereof; as he had done also to Libnah, and to the king thereof.

40. So Joshua smote all the land, the hill-country, and the South, and the Lowland, and the slopes, and all

אֲשֶׁר־בָּהּ בַּיּוֹם הַהוּא הֶחֱרִים
בְּכֹל אֲשֶׁר־עָשָׂה לְלָכִישׁ:

36 וַיַּעַל יְהוֹשֻׁעַ וְכָל־יִשְׂרָאֵל
עִמּוֹ מֵעֶגְלוֹנָה חֶבְרוֹנָה
37 וַיִּלָּחֲמוּ עָלֶיהָ: וַיִּלְכְּדוּהָ
וַיַּכּוּהָ־לְפִי־חֶרֶב וְאֶת־
מַלְכָּהּ וְאֶת־כָּל־עָרֶיהָ וְאֶת־
כָּל־הַנֶּפֶשׁ אֲשֶׁר־בָּהּ לֹא־
הִשְׁאִיר שָׂרִיד בְּכֹל אֲשֶׁר־
עָשָׂה לְעֶגְלוֹן וַיַּחֲרֵם אוֹתָהּ
וְאֶת־כָּל־הַנֶּפֶשׁ אֲשֶׁר־בָּהּ:
38 וַיָּשָׁב יְהוֹשֻׁעַ וְכָל־יִשְׂרָאֵל
עִמּוֹ דְּבִרָה וַיִּלָּחֶם עָלֶיהָ:
39 וַיִּלְכְּדָהּ וְאֶת־מַלְכָּהּ וְאֶת־
כָּל־עָרֶיהָ וַיַּכּוּם לְפִי־חֶרֶב
וַיַּחֲרִימוּ אֶת־כָּל־נֶפֶשׁ אֲשֶׁר־
בָּהּ לֹא הִשְׁאִיר שָׂרִיד כַּאֲשֶׁר
עָשָׂה לְחֶבְרוֹן כֵּן־עָשָׂה
לִדְבִרָה וּלְמַלְכָּהּ וְכַאֲשֶׁר
עָשָׂה לְלִבְנָה וּלְמַלְכָּהּ:
40 וַיַּכֶּה יְהוֹשֻׁעַ אֶת־כָּל־הָאָרֶץ
הָהָר וְהַנֶּגֶב וְהַשְּׁפֵלָה
וְהָאֲשֵׁדוֹת וְאֵת כָּל־מַלְכֵיהֶם

---

37. *king.* The new king appointed after Horam's execution (verses 23ff.) (Kimchi and Metsudath David).

and all the cities thereof. This implies that Hebron was the capital of the district. It was assigned to Caleb (xiv. 13f., xv. 13).

38. *Debir.* Formerly known as Kiriath-sepher. It has been identified with ed-Dahariyeh, eleven miles south-west of Hebron. It was recaptured by the Canaanites, and had to be reconquered by Othniel the son of Kenaz after Joshua's death (see on xv. 15) (Daath Mikra).

their kings; he left none remaining;
but he utterly destroyed all that
breathed, as the LORD, the God of
Israel, commanded. 41. And Joshua
smote them from Kadesh-barnea
even unto Gaza, and all the country
of Goshen, even unto Gibeon.
42. And all these kings and their
land did Joshua take at one time,
because the LORD, the God of Israel,
fought for Israel. 43. And Joshua
returned, and all Israel with him,
unto the camp to Gilgal.

לֹא הִשְׁאִיר שָׂרִיד וְאֵת כָּל־
הַנְּשָׁמָה הֶחֱרִים כַּאֲשֶׁר צִוָּה
41 יְהוָה אֱלֹהֵי יִשְׂרָאֵל: וַיַּכֵּם
יְהוֹשֻׁעַ מִקָּדֵשׁ בַּרְנֵעַ וְעַד־
עַזָּה וְאֵת כָּל־אֶרֶץ גֹּשֶׁן וְעַד־
42 גִּבְעוֹן: וְאֵת כָּל־הַמְּלָכִים
הָאֵלֶּה וְאֶת־אַרְצָם לָכַד
יְהוֹשֻׁעַ פַּעַם אֶחָת כִּי יְהוָה
אֱלֹהֵי יִשְׂרָאֵל נִלְחָם
43 לְיִשְׂרָאֵל: וַיָּשָׁב יְהוֹשֻׁעַ וְכָל־
יִשְׂרָאֵל עִמּוֹ אֶל־הַמַּחֲנֶה
הַגִּלְגָּלָה:

11   CHAPTER XI   יא

1. And it came to pass, when Jabin
king of Hazor heard thereof, that he

1 וַיְהִי כִּשְׁמֹעַ יָבִין מֶלֶךְ־חָצוֹר

---

40. *the slopes.* Connected with Pisgah (Deut.
iii. 17, iv. 49). Here it seems to denote the
regions east and west of *the hill-country.*

41. *Kadesh-barnea.* Mentioned in Deut. i. 2.
It is identified with Ain Kadis, fifty miles
south of Beersheba, between mount Paran
(Jebel Paran) and the River of Egypt (Wadi
el-Arish) (Daath Mikra)

Gaza. The most southern of the chief Philistine cities.

the country of Goshen. This is not the Goshen in
Egypt where the Israelites dwelt (Kimchi).
No *country* or district of that name is known
in the south of Canaan, but a Goshen is
mentioned in xv. 51 as a town in Judah's
portion, and *the country of Goshen* may be the
district around it.

42. *at one time.* The conquest was swift, one
town falling rapidly after another (Kimchi).

43. Repeated from verse 15, but here in its
chronological order (Metsudath David).

CHAPTER XI

CONQUEST OF THE NORTH

1. *Jabin king of Hazor.* He took the lead
because his kingdom was preeminent (verse
10). Another Jabin is mentioned in Judg. iv.
2, described as *king of Canaan, that reigned in
Hazor.* It has been suggested that Jabin
(meaning perhaps 'the intelligent') may have
been a generic title of the kings of Hazor, like
Pharaoh for the kings of Egypt.

Hazor. Its location was near Kedesh-naphtali
and lake Huleh in the extreme north.

sent to Jobab king of Madon, and to the king of Shimron, and to the king of Achshaph, 2. and to the kings that were on the north, in the hill-country and in the Arabah south of Chinneroth, and in the Lowland, and in the regions of Dor on the west, 3. to the Canaanite on the east and on the west, and the Amorite, and the Hittite, and the Perizzite, and the Jebusite in the hill-country, and the Hivite under Hermon in the land of Mizpah. 4. And they went out, they and all their hosts with them, much people, even as the sand that is upon the sea-shore in multitude, with horses

וַיִּשְׁלַח אֶל־יוֹבָב מֶלֶךְ מָדוֹן וְאֶל־מֶלֶךְ שִׁמְרוֹן וְאֶל־מֶלֶךְ
2 אַכְשָׁף: וְאֶל־הַמְּלָכִים אֲשֶׁר מִצָּפוֹן בָּהָר וּבָעֲרָבָה נֶגֶב כִּנֲרוֹת וּבַשְּׁפֵלָה וּבְנָפוֹת דּוֹר
3 מִיָּם: הַכְּנַעֲנִי מִמִּזְרָח וּמִיָּם וְהָאֱמֹרִי וְהַחִתִּי וְהַפְּרִזִּי וְהַיְבוּסִי בָּהָר וְהַחִוִּי תַּחַת חֶרְמוֹן בְּאֶרֶץ הַמִּצְפָּה:
4 וַיֵּצְאוּ הֵם וְכָל־מַחֲנֵיהֶם עִמָּם עַם־רָב כַּחוֹל אֲשֶׁר עַל־שְׂפַת־הַיָּם לָרֹב וְסוּס וָרֶכֶב

v. 4. קמץ בזקף גדול

Madon. A few miles west of the Sea of Kinnereth; it is mentioned again only in xii. 19.

Shimron. About twenty miles west of the southern end of the Sea of Kinnereth, assigned to Zebulun (xix. 15), known today as Tel Simunia (Daath Mikra).

Achshaph. A few miles north-west of Shimron, part of the territory of Asher (xix. 25).

2. *the hill-country.* The district of Galilee is intended.

the Arabah south of Chinneroth. The Jordan Valley, south of the Sea of Gennasereth (xii. 3, xiii. 27; Num. xxxiv. 11). The town of Kinnereth (xix. 35; Deut. iii. 17), whose site is unknown, supplied the earlier name for the lake which is later called the sea of Galilee.

the Lowland. i.e. the coastal region north of Carmel.

the regions of Dor. A Phoenician coastal settlement between Carmel and Caesarea. The Hebrew for *regions* (*naphoth*) is also rendered 'heights' (Daath Mikra).

3. For the people enumerated in the verse, see on iii. 10.

the Canaanites, etc. Jabin appealed to them as racial entities although they were divided nationally, not ethnically.

Hermon. The eastern portion of the anti-Lebanon range.

the land of Mizpah. Mt. Hermon and the neighboring hill in the northern part of Upper Gallilee command a view of the entire surrounding region, thus the name "Mizpah," meaning lookout. Kimchi maintains that, after this mightiest of all Joshua's wars, against the northern alliance, an altar and a house of prayer and assembly were built in commemoration of the successful waging of this war. See also Jud. xi. 11, 1, Sam. vii. 5, x. 17.

4. *even as the sand . . . in multitude.* Josephus gives their combined forces as amounting to 300,000 infantry, 10,000 cavalry, and 20,000 war-chariots (*Antiquities* V, i. 18). Even if these figures are exaggerated, the text evidences the enlarged scope of the alliance against Israel. Apparently the sense of unity grew among the threatened inhabitants.

with horses and chariots very many. This military equipment makes the victory of the Israel-

and chariots very many. 5. And all these kings met together; and they came and pitched together at the waters óf Merom, to fight with Israel.

6. And the Lord said unto Joshua: 'Be not afraid because of them; for to-morrow at this time will I deliver them up all slain before Israel; thou shalt hough their horses, and burn their chariots with fire.' 7. So Joshua came, and all the people of war with him, against them by the waters of Merom suddenly, and fell upon them. 8. And the Lord delivered them into the hand of Israel, and they smote them, and chased them unto great Zidon, and unto Misrephoth-maim, and unto

5 רַב־מְאֹד: וַיִּוָּעֲדוּ כֹּל
הַמְּלָכִים הָאֵלֶּה וַיָּבֹאוּ וַיַּחֲנוּ
יַחְדָּו אֶל־מֵי מֵרוֹם לְהִלָּחֵם
עִם־יִשְׂרָאֵל:

6 וַיֹּאמֶר יְהֹוָה אֶל־יְהוֹשֻׁעַ אַל־
תִּירָא מִפְּנֵיהֶם כִּי־מָחָר כָּעֵת
הַזֹּאת אָנֹכִי נֹתֵן אֶת־כֻּלָּם
חֲלָלִים לִפְנֵי יִשְׂרָאֵל אֶת־
סוּסֵיהֶם תְּעַקֵּר וְאֶת־
מַרְכְּבֹתֵיהֶם תִּשְׂרֹף בָּאֵשׁ:

7 וַיָּבֹא יְהוֹשֻׁעַ וְכָל־עַם
הַמִּלְחָמָה עִמּוֹ עֲלֵיהֶם עַל־
מֵי מֵרוֹם פִּתְאֹם וַיִּפְּלוּ בָּהֶם:

8 וַיִּתְּנֵם יְהֹוָה בְּיַד־יִשְׂרָאֵל
וַיַּכּוּם וַיִּרְדְּפוּם עַד־צִידוֹן
רַבָּה וְעַד מִשְׂרְפוֹת מַיִם וְעַד־

ites, who had only infantry, the more remarkable (Daath Mikra).

5. *the waters of Merom.* Usually identified with lake Huleh, the most northern of the three lakes in the Jordan Valley. It is called the lake of Semechonitis by Josephus (*Antiquities* V, v. 1), perhaps to be identified with Samki in the Talmud (Yeb. 121a).

6. *be not afraid because of them.* This coalition, larger even than that of the five kings in the preceding chapter, called forth God's reassurance (Me-am Loez).

hough their horses. i.e. cut the tendon of the joint in the hind leg. The practice does not seem to have been unusual, its purpose being to make them unfit as war-horses and employable only for domestic occupations (cf. Gen. xlix. 6; 2 Sam. viii. 4). Kimchi offers

the reason that the Israelites' might not use them in war and so rely upon their military strength rather than upon God. They were to remember that *a horse is a vain thing for safety* (Ps. xxxiii. 17) and *salvation belongeth to the Lord* (Ps. iii. 9).

8. *great Zidon.* Mentioned again in xix. 28, and distinguished from a smaller city of that name. It was situated on the coast north of Tyre (Daath Mikra).

Misrephoth-maim. A coastal town a few miles south of Tyre, named again in xiii. 6. The name signifies 'the burnings of (by) the waters' and may probably refer to smelting pits. Rashi explains it as 'salt pans' formed by letting the sea-water into basins. The water evaporated (was 'burnt') by the sun, leaving a deposit of salt.

the valley of Mizpeh eastward; and they smote them, until they left them none remaining. 9. And Joshua did unto them as the LORD bade him; he houghed their horses and burnt their chariots with fire.

10. And Joshua turned back at that time, and took Hazor, and smote the king thereof with the sword; for Hazor beforetime was the head of all those kingdoms. 11. And they smote all the souls that were therein with the edge of the sword, utterly destroying them; there was none left that breathed; and he burnt Hazor with fire. 12. And all the cities of those kings, and all the kings of them, did Joshua take, and he smote them with the edge of the sword, and utterly destroyed them; as Moses the servant of the LORD commanded. 13. But as for the cities that stood on their mounds,

בִּקְעַת מִצְפֶּה מִזְרָחָה וַיַּכֻּם
עַד־־בִּלְתִּי הִשְׁאִיר־לָהֶם
9 שָׂרִיד: וַיַּעַשׂ לָהֶם יְהוֹשֻׁעַ
כַּאֲשֶׁר אָמַר־לוֹ יְהוָה אֶת־
סוּסֵיהֶם עִקֵּר וְאֶת־
מַרְכְּבֹתֵיהֶם שָׂרַף בָּאֵשׁ:
10 וַיָּשָׁב יְהוֹשֻׁעַ בָּעֵת הַהִיא
וַיִּלְכֹּד אֶת־־חָצוֹר וְאֶת־
מַלְכָּהּ הִכָּה בֶחָרֶב כִּי־חָצוֹר
לְפָנִים הִיא רֹאשׁ כָּל־
11 הַמַּמְלָכוֹת הָאֵלֶּה: וַיַּכּוּ אֶת־
כָּל־הַנֶּפֶשׁ אֲשֶׁר־בָּהּ לְפִי־
חֶרֶב הַחֲרֵם לֹא נוֹתַר כָּל־
נְשָׁמָה וְאֶת־חָצוֹר שָׂרַף בָּאֵשׁ:
12 וְאֶת־כָּל־עָרֵי הַמְּלָכִים
הָאֵלֶּה וְאֶת־כָּל־מַלְכֵיהֶם
לָכַד יְהוֹשֻׁעַ וַיַּכֵּם לְפִי־חֶרֶב
הֶחֱרִים אוֹתָם כַּאֲשֶׁר צִוָּה
13 מֹשֶׁה עֶבֶד יְהוָה: רַק כָּל־
הֶעָרִים הָעֹמְדוֹת עַל־תִּלָּם

---

10. *and Joshua turned back.* I.e. Joshua hastened at that time to take Hazor before they became aware of the details of the battles, and be alerted (K'li Y'kar).

and took Hazor. The survivors fled to Harosheth-goiim, where they reestablished their kingdom (See Judges iv. 3).

the head of all those kingdoms. It is not clear whether the text is to be understood that Hazor exercised authority over other *kingdoms,* or simply that his realm was the most important.

12. *as Moses . . . commanded.* Cf. Deut. vii. 2ff., xx. 16ff.

13. *that stood on their mounds.* Jonathan renders: that stood in their strength; i.e. whose walls are not destroyed like those of Jericho and Ai (Rashi and Kimchi). Metsudoth renders: that stood at their height, explaining it in like manner.

save Hazor only. Joshua made this exception perhaps because the king of Hazor had instigated the coalition against him (Kimchi and Abarbanel). Alternatively, he burnt it

Israel burned none of them, save Hazor only—that did Joshua burn. 14. And all the spoil of these cities, and the cattle, the children of Israel took for a prey unto themselves; but every man they smote with the edge of the sword, until they had destroyed them, neither left they any that breathed. 15. As the LORD commanded Moses His servant, so did Moses command Joshua; and so did Joshua; he left nothing undone of all that the LORD commanded Moses.

16. So Joshua took all that land, the hill-country, and all the South, and all the land of Goshen, and the Lowland, and the Arabah, and the hill-country of Israel, and the Lowland of the same; 17. from the bare mountain, that goeth up to Seir, even unto Baal-gad in the valley of Lebanon under mount Hermon;

לֹא־שְׂרָפָם יִשְׂרָאֵל זוּלָתִי
אֶת־חָצוֹר לְבַדָּהּ שָׂרַף
יְהוֹשֻׁעַ: וְכֹל שְׁלַל הֶעָרִים 14
הָאֵלֶּה וְהַבְּהֵמָה בָּזְזוּ לָהֶם
בְּנֵי יִשְׂרָאֵל רַק אֶת־כָּל־
הָאָדָם הִכּוּ לְפִי־חֶרֶב עַד־
הִשְׁמִדָם אוֹתָם לֹא הִשְׁאִירוּ
כָּל־נְשָׁמָה: כַּאֲשֶׁר צִוָּה יְהֹוָה 15
אֶת־מֹשֶׁה עַבְדּוֹ כֵּן־צִוָּה
מֹשֶׁה אֶת־יְהוֹשֻׁעַ וְכֵן עָשָׂה
יְהוֹשֻׁעַ לֹא־הֵסִיר דָּבָר מִכֹּל
אֲשֶׁר־צִוָּה יְהֹוָה אֶת־מֹשֶׁה:
וַיִּקַּח יְהוֹשֻׁעַ אֶת־כָּל־הָאָרֶץ 16
הַזֹּאת הָהָר וְאֶת־כָּל־הַנֶּגֶב
וְאֵת כָּל־אֶרֶץ הַגֹּשֶׁן וְאֶת־
הַשְּׁפֵלָה וְאֶת־הָעֲרָבָה וְאֶת־
הַר יִשְׂרָאֵל וּשְׁפֵלָתֹה: מִן־ 17
הָהָר הֶחָלָק הָעֹלֶה שֵׂעִיר
וְעַד־בַּעַל גָּד בְּבִקְעַת
הַלְּבָנוֹן תַּחַת הַר־חֶרְמוֹן וְאֵת

because all the nations gathered there to wage war against Israel (Midrash Genesis Rabbah 81:4), because all the refugees from the allied cities were hidden there (Azulai), or simply because Moses had transmitted instructions to Joshua to burn it, giving no reason (Midrash ibid., Rashi).

16. *the land of Goshen.* See on x. 41.

the Arabah. The Jordan Valley from the Sea of Kinnereth to the Dead Sea (Daath Mikra).

the hill-country of Israel. The mountainous

region around Samaria (Daath Mikra).

17. *the bare mountain.* Near Kadesh-Barnea in the south-west. This is the opinion of most archeologists. Daath Mikra, however, believes that it is further south. It was given this name because of its lack of vegetation (Kimchi).

Seir. In the south-east (Daath Mikra).

Baal-gad. [So called because it was the site of a shrine to the cult of Gad, the god of Fortune; mentioned again in xii. 7, xiii. 5.]

and all their kings he took, and smote them, and put them to death. 18. Joshua made war a long time with all those kings. 19. There was not a city that made peace with the children of Israel, save the Hivites the inhabitants of Gibeon; they took all in battle. 20. For it was of the LORD to harden their hearts, to come against Israel in battle, that they might be utterly destroyed, that they might have no favour, but that they might be destroyed, as the LORD commanded Moses.

21. And Joshua came at that time, and cut off the Anakim from the hill-country, from Hebron, from Debir, from Anab, and from all the hill-country of Judah, and from all the

כָּל־מַלְכֵיהֶם֙ לָכַ֣ד וַיַּכֵּ֔ם
18 וַיְמִיתֵ֑ם: יָמִ֣ים רַבִּ֗ים עָשָׂ֧ה
יְהוֹשֻׁ֛עַ אֶת־כָּל־הַמְּלָכִ֖ים
19 הָאֵ֑לֶּה מִלְחָמָֽה: לֹא־הָיְתָ֣ה
עִ֗יר אֲשֶׁ֤ר הִשְׁלִ֨ימָה֙ אֶל־בְּנֵ֣י
יִשְׂרָאֵ֔ל בִּלְתִּ֥י הַֽחִוִּ֖י יֹשְׁבֵ֣י
גִבְע֑וֹן אֶת־הַכֹּ֖ל לָקְח֥וּ
20 בַמִּלְחָמָֽה: כִּ֣י מֵאֵ֣ת יְהֹוָ֣ה ׀
הָיְתָ֗ה לְחַזֵּ֤ק אֶת־לִבָּם֙
לִקְרַ֤את הַמִּלְחָמָה֙ אֶת־
יִשְׂרָאֵ֔ל לְמַ֖עַן הַחֲרִימָ֑ם
לְבִלְתִּ֤י הֱיוֹת־לָהֶם֙ תְּחִנָּ֔ה כִּ֚י
לְמַ֣עַן הַשְׁמִידָ֔ם כַּאֲשֶׁ֛ר צִוָּ֥ה
יְהֹוָ֖ה אֶת־מֹשֶֽׁה:
21 וַיָּבֹ֨א יְהוֹשֻׁ֜עַ בָּעֵ֣ת הַהִ֗יא
וַיַּכְרֵ֤ת אֶת־הָֽעֲנָקִים֙ מִן־
הָהָ֤ר מִן־חֶבְרוֹן֙ מִן־דְּבִ֔ר
מִן־עֲנָ֕ב וּמִכֹּ֖ל הַ֥ר יְהוּדָ֑ה

---

18. *a long time*. Seven years, according to the Rabbis. See below xiv. 10.

20. *to harden their hearts*. Their opposition is attributed to God as serving His purpose, explained in the next verse (Kimchi).

that they might have no favour. If they had submitted without a fight, the Israelites might have treated them with leniency and not destroyed them. In that event, they would have been a menace to the community seducing them to heathenism. Cf. Ex. xxiii. 33.

21. *the Anakim*. The giants, the sight of whom had struck terror in the hearts of the

spies sent by Moses (Num. xii. 33). Although Caleb led the drive against Hebron, and Othniel conquered Debir, these campaigns were under the overall leadership of Joshua (Kimchi). Ralbag (Jud. i. 13) maintains that Debir mentioned in Judges, is distinct from this one.

Debir. See on x. 38.

Anab. Between Hebron and Beer-sheba. 'The name is still found near to Debir, fourteen miles south-west of Hebron' (Daath Mikra).

the hill-country of Judah . . . the hill-country of Israel. I.e. the hill-countries that were later known by these names (Kimchi). When the

hill-country of Israel; Joshua utterly destroyed them with their cities. 22. There was none of the Anakim left in the land of the children of Israel; only in Gaza, in Gath, and in Ashdod, did some remain. 23. So Joshua took the whole land, according to all that the LORD spoke unto Moses; and Joshua gave it for an inheritance unto Israel according to their divisions by their tribes. And the land had rest from war.

וּמִכֹּל הַר יִשְׂרָאֵל עִם־
עָרֵיהֶם הֶחֱרִימָם יְהוֹשֻׁעַ:
22 לֹא־נוֹתַר עֲנָקִים בְּאֶרֶץ בְּנֵי
יִשְׂרָאֵל רַק בְּעַזָּה בְּגַת
23 וּבְאַשְׁדּוֹד נִשְׁאָרוּ: וַיִּקַּח
יְהוֹשֻׁעַ אֶת־כָּל־הָאָרֶץ כְּכֹל
אֲשֶׁר דִּבֶּר יְהֹוָה אֶל־מֹשֶׁה
וַיִּתְּנָהּ יְהוֹשֻׁעַ לְנַחֲלָה
לְיִשְׂרָאֵל כְּמַחְלְקֹתָם
לְשִׁבְטֵיהֶם וְהָאָרֶץ שָׁקְטָה
מִמִּלְחָמָה:

---

12   CHAPTER XII   יב

1. Now these are the kings of the land, whom the children of Israel smote, and possessed their land beyond the Jordan toward the sunrising, from the valley of Arnon unto mount Hermon, and all the

1 וְאֵלֶּה ׀ מַלְכֵי הָאָרֶץ אֲשֶׁר
הִכּוּ בְנֵי־יִשְׂרָאֵל וַיִּרְשׁוּ אֶת־
אַרְצָם בְּעֵבֶר הַיַּרְדֵּן מִזְרְחָה
הַשָּׁמֶשׁ מִנַּחַל אַרְנוֹן עַד־הַר
חֶרְמוֹן וְכָל־הָעֲרָבָה

Book was written, Judah's territory was known, as well as the territories of the other tribes. Cf. Deuteronomy xxxiv. 2.

22. *Gaza*, etc. Three of the five principal cities of the Philistines. Goliath belonged to Gath (I Sam. xvii. 4).

23. *the whole land.* i.e. the land as a whole, though many regions remained in Canaanite hands (cf. xiii. 1ff., 13).

according to their divisions. As determined by lot (Num. xxxiv. 2ff.).

the land had rest from war. Organized and united resistance was at an end, but local opposition continued for a long time. The phrase is repeated in xiv. 15 (Kimchi).

CHAPTER XII

SUMMARY OF CONQUESTS

1–6 IN TRANSJORDAN

1. *beyond the Jordan toward the sunrising.* This victory was gained by Moses before the history of *Joshua* began. It is included for the sake of completeness (Rashi).

the valley of Arnon. It ran from west to east in the south of Transjordan through the original territory of Moab, emptying its waters into the Dead Sea. Before its conquest by Moses, Sihon, king of the Amorites, had driven the Moabites south of the Arnon.

Arabah eastward: 2. Sihon king of
the Amorites, who dwelt in Heshbon, and ruled from Aroer, which is
on the edge of the valley of Arnon,
and the middle of the valley, and
half Gilead, even unto the river
Jabbok, the border of the children of
Ammon; 3. and the Arabah unto the
sea of Chinneroth, eastward, and
unto the sea of the Arabah, even the
Salt Sea, eastward, the way to Beth-
jeshimoth; and on the south, under
the slopes of Pisgah; 4. and the
border of Og king of Bashan, of the
remnant of the Rephaim, who dwelt

2 מִזְרָחָה: סִיחוֹן מֶלֶךְ הָאֱמֹרִי
הַיּוֹשֵׁב בְּחֶשְׁבּוֹן מֹשֵׁל מֵעֲרוֹעֵר
אֲשֶׁר עַל־שְׂפַת־נַחַל אַרְנוֹן
וְתוֹךְ הַנַּחַל וַחֲצִי הַגִּלְעָד וְעַד
יַבֹּק הַנַּחַל גְּבוּל בְּנֵי עַמּוֹן:
3 וְהָעֲרָבָה עַד־יָם כִּנְרוֹת
מִזְרָחָה וְעַד יָם הָעֲרָבָה יָם־
הַמֶּלַח מִזְרָחָה דֶּרֶךְ בֵּית
הַיְשִׁמוֹת וּמִתֵּימָן תַּחַת אַשְׁדּוֹת
4 הַפִּסְגָּה: וּגְבוּל עוֹג מֶלֶךְ
הַבָּשָׁן מִיֶּתֶר הָרְפָאִים הַיּוֹשֵׁב

mount Hermon. In the North. The Sidonians
called it *Sirion* (Deut. iii. 9; Ps. xxix. 6), which
means 'breastplate.' The Amorites named it
Senir (Deut. iii. 9; cf. Ezek. xxvii. 5; Cant. iv.
8). It was also known as *Sion* (perhaps 'elevated,' Deut. iv. 48), rising as it does to a height
of over 9,000 feet.

the Arabah. See on xi. 16.

2. *Heshbon.* See on ix. 10.

Aroer. Slightly north of the Arnon. Its location is here specified to distinguish it from
the town of that name in the territory of the
Ammonites (xiii. 25).

and the middle of the valley. This phrase is to be
understood as part of the object of *ruled*; the
central area of the valley was included in the
kingdom of Sihon.

Gilead. North and south of the river Jabbok
(Daath Mikra).

Jabbok. Running from west to east between
the mountains of Gilead some fifty to sixty
miles north of the Arnon; the modern Wadi
Zerka. Josephus describes Sihon's territory as
'resembling an island, the river Arnon being

its southern limit, the river Jabbok bounding
its northern side . . . while the Jordan itself
runs along by it on the west, (*Antiquities* IV, v.
2).

3. *the sea of Chinneroth.* The second lake into
which the Jordan flows in the north, after
which it continues its course until it finally
reaches the Dead Sea. It is also known as the
Sea of Gennasereth and the Sea of Tiberias,
and is about fourteen miles in length and six
in breadth. The district was one of great
beauty and fertility, its fruits being famous.

Beth-jeshimoth. Immediately to the northeast
of the Dead Sea, in the south of the Plains of
Moab (Daath Mikra).

Pisgah. A few miles due east of the northern
end of the Dead Sea. It was the name of a
spur of mount Nebo (Deut. xxxiv. 1), from
whence Moses viewed the Holy Land which
he was not permitted to enter (D.M.).

4. *the Rephaim.* They are named among the
peoples whom Chedorlaomer, Abraham's
contemporary, defeated (Gen. xiv. 5), and as
one of the races whom the Israelites would
dispossess (Gen. xv. 20). They are described

at Ashtaroth and at Edrei, 5. and
ruled in mount Hermon, and in
Salcah, and in all Bashan, unto the
border of the Geshurites and the
Maacathites, and half Gilead, even
unto the border of Sihon king of
Heshbon. 6. Moses the servant of
the LORD and the children of Israel
smote them; and Moses the servant
of the LORD gave it for a possession
unto the Reubenites, and the
Gadites, and the half-tribe of
Manasseh.

7. And these are the kings of the
land whom Joshua and the children
of Israel smote beyond the Jordan
westward, from Baal-gad in the
valley of Lebanon even unto the
bare mountain, that goeth up to
Seir; and Joshua gave it unto the
tribes of Israel for a possession
according to their divisions; 8. in
the hill-country, and in the Low-

5 בְּעַשְׁתָּרוֹת וּבְאֶדְרֶעִי: וּמֹשֵׁל
בְּהַר חֶרְמוֹן וּבְסַלְכָה וּבְכָל־
הַבָּשָׁן עַד־גְּבוּל הַגְּשׁוּרִי
וְהַמַּעֲכָתִי וַחֲצִי הַגִּלְעָד גְּבוּל
6 סִיחוֹן מֶלֶךְ חֶשְׁבּוֹן: מֹשֶׁה
עֶבֶד־יְהוָה וּבְנֵי יִשְׂרָאֵל
הִכּוּם וַיִּתְּנָהּ מֹשֶׁה עֶבֶד־יְהוָה
יְרֻשָּׁה לָרֻאוּבֵנִי וְלַגָּדִי וְלַחֲצִי
שֵׁבֶט הַמְנַשֶּׁה:
7 וְאֵלֶּה מַלְכֵי הָאָרֶץ אֲשֶׁר הִכָּה
יְהוֹשֻׁעַ וּבְנֵי יִשְׂרָאֵל בְּעֵבֶר
הַיַּרְדֵּן יָמָּה מִבַּעַל גָּד בְּבִקְעַת
הַלְּבָנוֹן וְעַד־הָהָר הֶחָלָק
הָעֹלֶה שֵׂעִירָה וַיִּתְּנָהּ יְהוֹשֻׁעַ
לְשִׁבְטֵי יִשְׂרָאֵל יְרֻשָּׁה
8 כְּמַחְלְקֹתָם: בָּהָר וּבַשְּׁפֵלָה

in Deut. ii. 21 *as a people great, and many, and
tall, as the Anakim.* The etymology of the name
is obscure. It may be connected with 'shades,
ghosts' and, taken in conjunction with the
name *Zamzummim* given them by the
Ammonites (Deut. ii. 20) which means
'whisperers, murmurers,' may indicate the
awe which they inspired by their gigantic
stature.

Ashtaroth. See on ix. 10.

Edrei. [East of the southern end of the Sea of
Kinnereth in a slightly southerly direction.]

5. *Salcah.* To the east of Edrei. Some identify it with Salchad on Jebel Hauran (the
mount of the Druses) (Kaftor Vaferach).

the Geshurites and the Maacathites. Geshur lay

to the east of the Sea of Kinnereth and
Maacah east of lake Huleh, both in the Hermon range (Daath Mikra).

6. *Moses . . . smote them.* Cf. Num. xxi. 21ff.;
Deut. iif.

and Moses the servant of the LORD. The phrase is
repeated, probably to emphasize that both
the conquest and the allocation were by
Divine authority (Malbim).

7–24 IN CISJORDAN

7. *westward.* lit. 'seaward,' i.e. in the direction of the Mediterranean, the western
boundary of the land.

from Baal-gad, etc. See on xi. 17.

land, and in the Arabah, and in the slopes, and in the wilderness, and in the South; the Hittite, the Amorite, and the Canaanite, the Perizzite, the Hivite, and the Jebusite:

9 the king of Jericho, one;

the king of Ai, which is beside Beth-el, one;

10 the king of Jerusalem, one;

the king of Hebron, one;

11 the king of Jarmuth, one;

the king of Lachish, one;

12 the king of Eglon, one;

the king of Gezer, one;

13 the king of Debir, one;

the king of Geder, one;

14 the king of Hormah, one;

the king of Arad, one;

15 the king of Libnah, one;

the king of Adullam, one;

וּבָעֲרָבָה וּבָאֲשֵׁדוֹת וּבַמִּדְבָּר
וּבַנֶּגֶב הַחִתִּי הָאֱמֹרִי וְהַכְּנַעֲנִי
הַפְּרִזִּי הַחִוִּי וְהַיְבוּסִי׃

9 מֶלֶךְ יְרִיחוֹ אֶחָד
מֶלֶךְ הָעַי אֲשֶׁר־מִצַּד
בֵּית־אֵל אֶחָד׃

10 מֶלֶךְ יְרוּשָׁלַ͏ִם אֶחָד
מֶלֶךְ חֶבְרוֹן אֶחָד׃

11 מֶלֶךְ יַרְמוּת אֶחָד
מֶלֶךְ לָכִישׁ אֶחָד׃

12 מֶלֶךְ עֶגְלוֹן אֶחָד
מֶלֶךְ גֶּזֶר אֶחָד׃

13 מֶלֶךְ דְּבִר אֶחָד
מֶלֶךְ גֶּדֶר אֶחָד׃

14 מֶלֶךְ חָרְמָה אֶחָד
מֶלֶךְ עֲרָד אֶחָד׃

15 מֶלֶךְ לִבְנָה אֶחָד
מֶלֶךְ עֲדֻלָּם אֶחָד׃

---

8. *the wilderness.* i.e. the uncultivated land, serving as pasture. This includes all such regions bordering the land on the east, e.g. the wilderness of Judah (xv. 61), the wilderness of Beth-aven (xviii. 12), etc. (Daath Mikra).

the South. Of Judah, including the territory of Simeon (see below xv, xix).

9ff. The thirty-one 'kings' (see on ii. 2). The city named in connection with each king was his capital, his realm comprising other towns and villages (Kimchi).

11. *Jarmuth . . . Lachish.* See on x. 3.

12. *Eglon.* See on x. 3.

Gezer. See on x. 33.

13. *Debir.* See on x. 38.

Geder. A city not mentioned before. According to the Septuagint, this is Gerar, the Philistine city. Elijah of Wilna locates it on the slopes. Since it was located on a slope, it was necessary to construct a fence, hence the name *'Geder,'* meaning a fence.

14. *Hormah.* Cf. Num. xxi. 3 for the meaning and origin of the name. For its conquest, cf. Judg. i. 17.

Arad. About sixteen miles south-east of Hebron; it still bears this name. See Daath Mikra.

15. *Libnah.* See on x. 29.

Adullam. South-west of Bethlehem. Later it came into prominence as David's hiding-place when he fled from Saul (1 Sam. xxii. 1).

16 the king of Makkedah, one;

the king of Beth-el, one;

17 the king of Tappuah, one;

the king of Hepher, one;

18 the king of Aphek, one;

the king of the Sharon, one;

19 the king of Madon, one;

the king of Hazor, one;

20 the king of Shimron-meron, one;

the king of Achshaph, one;

21 the king of Taanach, one;

the king of Megiddo, one;

22 the king of Kedesh, one;

the king of Jokneam in Carmel,

one;

23 the king of Dor in the region of

Dor, one;

מֶלֶךְ מַקֵּדָה אֶחָד 16

מֶלֶךְ בֵּית־אֵל אֶחָד׃

מֶלֶךְ תַּפּוּחַ אֶחָד 17

מֶלֶךְ חֵפֶר אֶחָד׃

מֶלֶךְ אֲפֵק אֶחָד 18

מֶלֶךְ לַשָּׁרוֹן אֶחָד׃

מֶלֶךְ מָדוֹן אֶחָד 19

מֶלֶךְ חָצוֹר אֶחָד׃

מֶלֶךְ שִׁמְרוֹן מְראוֹן אֶחָד 20

מֶלֶךְ אַכְשָׁף אֶחָד׃

מֶלֶךְ תַּעֲנַךְ אֶחָד 21

מֶלֶךְ מְגִדּוֹ אֶחָד׃

מֶלֶךְ קֶדֶשׁ אֶחָד 22

מֶלֶךְ־יָקְנְעָם לַכַּרְמֶל אֶחָד׃

מֶלֶךְ דּוֹר לְנָפַת דּוֹר אֶחָד 23

v. 20. לא קרי א׳

16. *Makkedah.* See on x. 10.

Beth-el. See on viii. 17.

17. *Tappuah.* In mouth Ephraim, possibly on the site of the modern Tel Sheikh (Daath Mikra).

Hepher. North-east of Shechem, near the coast (Daath Mikra).

18. *Aphek.* North-east of Jerusalem, south of the Jarkon, near the modern city of Petach Tikvah (Daath Mikra).

the Sharon. The plain which stretches from mount Carmel southward to Joppa (Jaffa). Some regard the *lamed* in the Hebrew as part of the name and render 'the king of Lassharon' (Targum).

19. *Madon . . . Hazor.* See on xi. 1.

20. *Shimron-meron.* See on xi. 1. Shimronmeron is probably identical with the Shim-

ron mentioned there. The Assyriologist, Sayce, remarks that 'Samsimuruna is given by an Assyrian inscription as the name of a town in this neighbourhood.'

Achshaph. See on xi. 1.

21. *Taanach . . . Megiddo.* In the Valley of Jezreel, north-east of Jenin and still called by these names. The latter is a few miles southeast of the former, midway between the Jordan and the coast (Daath Mikra). It was a famous fortress in antiquity (Daath Mikra).

22. *Kedesh.* Kedesh-naphtali, a few miles north-west of lake Huleh. Others hold that it was a town in the Valley of Jezreel, north of Taanach (Daath Mikra).

Jokneam in Carmel. i.e. at the foot of mount Carmel; now Tel Kaymun, near the modern Jewish settlement of Jokneam (Daath Mikra).

23. *Dor.* See on xi. 2.

the king of Goiim in the Gilgal,
one;

24 the king of Tirzah, one.

(All the kings thirty and one.)

מֶלֶךְ־גּוֹיִם לְגִלְגָּל אֶחָד׃
24 מֶלֶךְ תִּרְצָה אֶחָד
כָּל־מְלָכִים שְׁלֹשִׁים וְאֶחָד׃

13 CHAPTER XIII יג

1. Now Joshua was old and well stricken in years; and the Lord said unto him: 'Thou art old and well stricken in years, and there remaineth yet very much land to be possessed. 2. This is the land that yet remaineth: all the regions of the Philistines, and all the Geshurites;

1 וִיהוֹשֻׁעַ זָקֵן בָּא בַּיָּמִים וַיֹּאמֶר
יְהוָה אֵלָיו אַתָּה זָקַנְתָּה בָּאתָ
בַיָּמִים וְהָאָרֶץ נִשְׁאֲרָה
2 הַרְבֵּה־מְאֹד לְרִשְׁתָּהּ׃ זֹאת
הָאָרֶץ הַנִּשְׁאָרֶת כָּל־גְּלִילוֹת

the king of Goiim in the Gilgal. i.e. the king of a district in the north called Goiim whose capital was Gilguli. Today a village named Gilguli still stands there. An alternative translation is: 'king of the nations belonging to Gilgal.' On either interpretation this is not the Gilgal between the Jordan and Jericho, nor the Gilgal north of Beth-el (Daath Mikra).

24. *Tirzah.* North of Shechem and east of Samaria in mount Ephraim. Later it was the capital of the Northern Kingdom and the royal residence of the kings from Jeroboam I to Omri. Its beauty was proverbial (cf. Song of Songs vi. 4).

all the kings thirty and one. The preceding narrative did not give an account of all the battles in the campaign, those of minor importance being omitted. In the enumeration we are provided with a complete list of the conquered kings. The first half of the book, narrating the story of the conquest, ends here; and the next section describes the allocation of the land to the tribes.

CHAPTER XIII

1–7 UNCONQUERED PORTIONS OF
THE COUNTRY

1. *Joshua was old.* He had been one of the

spies sent by Moses forty-five years before (cf. Caleb's statement in xiv. 7, 10). He must have been of mature age at the time of the mission and was now over eighty years old. According to Yalkut, he was eighty-two years old.

there remaineth yet very much land to be possessed. In spite of the many victories already achieved.

2. Verses 2–5 are in parenthesis and define the unconquered territory. The continuation of God's words to Joshua, begun in verse 1, are verses 6f.

the regions of the Philistines. The Philistines occupied a narrow strip of the coastland from the Book of Egypt to Joppa, the principal cities being Gaza, Ashkelon, Gath, Ashdod and Ekron. Their original home may have been Egypt, whence they settled first in Crete and then in Canaan (cf. Amos ix. 7), attaining to such importance that they gave their name to the country (Philistia). Highly skilled in war, they were Israel's most powerful enemy, and were not finally subdued until the reign of David. Even after that they remained a thorn in their side until Judas Maccabeus inflicted a crushing defeat upon them, after which they disintegrated and finally disappeared.

the Geshurites. A people in the extreme southwest of Canaan reaching to the Egyptian

3. from the Shihor, which is before Egypt, even unto the border of Ekron northward—which is counted to the Canaanites; the five lords of the Philistines: the Gazite, and the Ashdodite, the Ashkelonite, the Gittite, and the Ekronite; also the Avvim 4. on the south; all the land of the Canaanites, and Mearah that belongeth to the Zidonians, unto Aphek, to the border of the Amorites; 5. and the land of the

הַפְּלִשְׁתִּים וְכָל־הַגְּשׁוּרִי׃

3 מִן־הַשִּׁיחוֹר אֲשֶׁר ׀ עַל־פְּנֵי מִצְרַיִם וְעַד גְּבוּל עֶקְרוֹן צָפוֹנָה לַכְּנַעֲנִי תֵּחָשֵׁב חֲמֵשֶׁת ׀ סַרְנֵי פְלִשְׁתִּים הָעַזָּתִי וְהָאַשְׁדּוֹדִי הָאֶשְׁקְלוֹנִי הַגִּתִּי

4 וְהָעֶקְרוֹנִי וְהָעַוִּים׃ מִתֵּימָן כָּל־אֶרֶץ הַכְּנַעֲנִי וּמְעָרָה אֲשֶׁר לַצִּידֹנִים עַד־אֲפֵקָה

5 עַד גְּבוּל הָאֱמֹרִי׃ וְהָאָרֶץ

border (I Sam. xxvii. 8). They are not identical with the Geshurites in xii. 5 (Daath Mikra).

3. *the Shihor.* Some define it as the eastern (Pelusiac) arm of Nile, others as the Brook of Egypt, the Wadi el-Arish, which flows into the Mediterranean between Gaza and Pelusium (Kaftor Vaferach).

before Egypt. On the eastern border of Egypt in the south-west of Canaan (Daath Mikra).

Ekron. On the north-east border of Philistia. Akar, an Arab village, is now found in the district.

is counted to the Canaanites. And therefore included in the land promised to Abraham (Rashi).

the five lords, etc. This explains that Philistia consisted of a confederation of the five city-states here enumerated, each of which was ruled by a *lord (seren).*

the Gazite. The lord of Gaza (see on x. 41).

the Ashdodite. The modern Esdud, west of Beer Tubiah (Daath Mikra).

the Ashkelonite. Ashkelon lay on the coast between Ashdod and Gaza. It is now a heap of ruins called by the Arabs Asklan (Daath Mikra).

the Gittite. Some identify Fath with Arak el-Menshieh, west of Beth Gubrin (Daath Mikra).

also the Avvim. They alone of all the Canaanite tribes remained there when these were expelled by the Philistines (cf. Deut. ii. 23).

4. *on the south.* The ancient versions connect this with *the Avvim,* reading: 'also the Avvim on the south' (so also Kimchi). [The division of the verse in M.T. may be retained as indicating this. Thus verses 2f. treat of the south-west of Canaan, while *on the south; all the land of the Canaanites* refers to the south as distinguished from the south-west.]

all the land of the Canaanites. [i.e. the region of Arad which is by the wilderness of Paran, Zin and Kadesh.]

and Mearah, etc. Some understand *Mearah* as a proper noun, the name of a place which has not been identified. Others render: 'and the cave that belongeth to the Zidonians'; perhaps a cave well known in those days as a place of retreat from the enemy (Daath Mikra).

Aphek. At the mouth of the river Adonis (Nahr Ibrahim) at the foot of Lebanon. Its modern name is Aphaca (Daath Mikra).

to the border of the Amorites. The border of the territory of Og in the north-east of Trans-

Gebalites, and all Lebanon, toward the sunrising, from Baal-gad under mount Hermon unto the entrance of Hamath; 6. all the inhabitants of the hill-country from Lebanon unto Misrephoth-maim, even all the Zidonians; them will I drive out from before the children of Israel; only allot thou it unto Israel for an inheritance, as I have commanded thee. 7. Now therefore divide this land for an inheritance unto the nine tribes, and the half-tribe of Manasseh.' 8. With him the

הַגִּבְלִי וְכָל־הַלְּבָנוֹן מִזְרַח הַשֶּׁמֶשׁ מִבַּעַל גָּד תַּחַת הַר־
6 חֶרְמוֹן עַד לְבוֹא חֲמָת: כָּל־יֹשְׁבֵי הָהָר מִן־הַלְּבָנוֹן עַד־מִשְׂרְפֹת מַיִם כָּל־צִידֹנִים אָנֹכִי אוֹרִישֵׁם מִפְּנֵי בְּנֵי יִשְׂרָאֵל רַק הַפִּלֶהָ לְיִשְׂרָאֵל בְּנַחֲלָה כַּאֲשֶׁר צִוִּיתִיךָ:
7 וְעַתָּה חַלֵּק אֶת־הָאָרֶץ הַזֹּאת בְּנַחֲלָה לְתִשְׁעַת הַשְּׁבָטִים
8 וַחֲצִי הַשֵּׁבֶט הַמְנַשֶּׁה: עִמּוֹ

jordan. Sihon and Og were both called *kings of the Amorites* (Deut. iii. 8).

5. *the land of the Gebalites.* The entire land was named for the city Gebal, now called Jebeil, a famous Phoenician seaport, approximately 70 kilometers north of Sidon. Its inhabitants were renowned as builders (1 Kings v. 32). The ancient Greeks called it Byblus (Daath Mikra, Kaftor vaferach).

Baal-gad. See on xi. 17.

unto the entrance of Hamath. Often mentioned as the ideal boundary of Israelite territory in the north (cf. Num. xxxiv. 8; Amos vi. 14). The Targumim Jonathan (Num. xiii. 21), Yerushalmi (Num. xxxiv. 8), Rav Joseph (1 Chron. xiii. 5, 2 Chron. vii. 8), identify this with Antioch, the ancient capital of Syria, now in southern Turkey. According to later scholars, such as *Tevuath Ha-aretz,* it is Hama in Syria, 180 kilometers north of Damascus (Ha-aretz Ligvulotheha).

6. *Misrephoth-maim.* See on xi. 8.

Them will I drive out. After your death (Rashi).

only allot thou it unto Israel. And subsequently, each tribe will conquer what fell into its lot (Rashi). Each tribe was now strong enough to conquer the enemy within its borders (Abarbanel). According to Maimonides, the division was necessary to give subsequent conquests communal status.

7. *divide this land.* [The psychological danger of fighting indefinitely without tangible fruits of the conquest was evident. The tribes had to be given a sense of ownership. Therefore the division without delay was imperative. On the other hand, the division would tend to loosen national ties; tribes would come more and more to think of their own territories and less nationally. So long as Joshua lived, this tendency was suppressed; but with his death it clearly manifested itself, as is evident from the Book of Judges.]

this land. The land of Canaan (Cis-Jordan), whether conquered or not. In respect to the unconquered land, the division would act as a stimulus to still greater efforts.

8–12 SUMMARY OF THE INHERITANCE IN TRANSJORDAN

8. *with him.* i.e. with the other half of the tribe of Manasseh. Although this is not stated explicitly, the context makes it clear that such is the meaning (Rashi, Kimchi, Metsudath David).

75

Reubenites and the Gadites received
their inheritance, which Moses gave
them, beyond the Jordan eastward,
even as Moses the servant of the
LORD gave them; 9. from Aroer, that
is on the edge of the valley of Arnon,
and the city that is in the middle of
the valley, and all the table-land
from Medeba unto Dibon; 10. and
all the cities of Sihon king of the
Amorites, who reigned in Heshbon,
unto the border of the children of
Ammon; 11. and Gilead, and the
border of the Geshurites and
Maacathites, and all mount Hermon,
and all Bashan unto Salcah; 12. all
the kingdom of Og in Bashan, who
reigned in Ashtaroth and in Edrei—
the same was left of the remnant of
the Rephaim—for these did Moses
smite, and drove them out. 13.
Nevertheless the children of Israel
drove not out the Geshurites, nor
the Maacathites; but Geshur and
Maacath dwelt in the midst of Israel
unto this day. 14. Only unto the
tribe of Levi he gave no inheritance;

הָרֽאוּבֵנִי֙ וְהַגָּדִ֔י לָקְח֖וּ נַחֲלָתָ֑ם
אֲשֶׁר֩ נָתַ֨ן לָהֶ֜ם מֹשֶׁ֗ה בְּעֵ֤בֶר
הַיַּרְדֵּן֙ מִזְרָ֔חָה כַּאֲשֶׁר֙ נָתַ֣ן
לָהֶ֔ם מֹשֶׁ֖ה עֶ֥בֶד יְהוָֽה׃
9 מֵעֲרוֹעֵ֡ר אֲשֶׁר֩ עַל־שְׂפַת־
נַ֨חַל אַרְנ֜וֹן וְהָעִ֨יר אֲשֶׁ֧ר
בְּתוֹךְ־הַנַּ֛חַל וְכָל־הַמִּישֹׁ֖ר
10 מֵידְבָ֖א עַד־דִּיבֽוֹן׃ וְכֹ֖ל עָרֵ֣י
סִיחוֹן֙ מֶ֣לֶךְ הָאֱמֹרִ֔י אֲשֶׁ֥ר מָלַ֖ךְ
בְּחֶשְׁבּ֑וֹן עַד־גְּב֖וּל בְּנֵי־
11 עַמּֽוֹן׃ וְהַגִּלְעָ֗ד וּגְבוּל֙ הַגְּשׁוּרִ֣י
וְהַמַּ֣עֲכָתִ֔י וְכֹ֛ל הַ֥ר חֶרְמ֖וֹן
וְכָל־הַבָּשָׁ֖ן עַד־סַלְכָֽה׃
12 כָּל־מַמְלְכ֥וּת עוֹג֙ בַּבָּשָׁ֔ן
אֲשֶׁר־מָלַ֥ךְ בְּעַשְׁתָּר֖וֹת
וּבְאֶדְרֶ֑עִי ה֤וּא נִשְׁאַר֙ מִיֶּ֣תֶר
הָרְפָאִ֔ים וַיַּכֵּ֥ם מֹשֶׁ֖ה וַיֹּרִשֵֽׁם׃
13 וְלֹ֣א הוֹרִ֗ישׁוּ בְּנֵ֣י יִשְׂרָאֵ֔ל אֶת־
הַגְּשׁוּרִ֖י וְאֶת־הַמַּעֲכָתִ֑י וַיֵּ֨שֶׁב
גְּשׁ֤וּר וּמַֽעֲכָת֙ בְּקֶ֣רֶב יִשְׂרָאֵ֔ל
14 עַ֖ד הַיּ֥וֹם הַזֶּֽה׃ רַ֚ק לְשֵׁ֣בֶט

---

9. *Aroer*, etc. See on xii. 2.

Medeba . . . Dibon. Two towns of Moab. The
former is slightly north of the Arnon and a
few miles north-west of Aroer; the latter lies
north of Dibon in an easterly direction. Both
towns were subsequently retaken by the
Moabites (Is. xv. 2).

11.   *the Geshurites*, etc. See on xii. 5.
Salcah. See on xii. 5.

12.   See on xii. 4.

13.   The Geshurites and Maacathites
remained unconquered by Israel.

14 NO INHERITANCE FOR THE LEVITES

he gave no inheritance. As commanded by God
(cf. Deut. x. 9, xviii, I).

the offerings of the LORD, the God of Israel, made by fire are his inheritance, as He spoke unto him.

15. And Moses gave unto the tribe of the children of Reuben according to their families. 16. And their border was from Aroer, that is on the edge of the valley of Arnon, and the city that is in the middle of the valley, and all the table-land by Medeba; 17. Heshbon, and all her cities that are in the table-land; Dibon, and Bamoth-baal, and Beth-baal-meon; 18. and Jahaz, and Kedemoth, and Mephaath;

הַלֵּוִי לֹא נָתַן נַחֲלָה אֵשֵּׁי יְהֹוָה
אֱלֹהֵי יִשְׂרָאֵל הוּא נַחֲלָתוֹ
כַּאֲשֶׁר דִּבֶּר־לוֹ:

15 וַיִּתֵּן מֹשֶׁה לְמַטֵּה בְנֵי־
16 רְאוּבֵן לְמִשְׁפְּחֹתָם: וַיְהִי
לָהֶם הַגְּבוּל מֵעֲרוֹעֵר אֲשֶׁר
עַל־שְׂפַת־נַחַל אַרְנוֹן וְהָעִיר
אֲשֶׁר בְּתוֹךְ־הַנַּחַל וְכָל־
17 הַמִּישֹׁר עַל־מֵידְבָא: חֶשְׁבּוֹן
וְכָל־עָרֶיהָ אֲשֶׁר בַּמִּישֹׁר
דִּיבוֹן וּבָמוֹת בַּעַל וּבֵית בַּעַל
18 מְעוֹן: וְיַהְצָה וּקְדֵמֹת

v. 16. סבירין עד

offerings . . . made by fire. i.e. the priestly service at the altar and the perquisites which were given to the Levitical families.

15–23 THE INHERITANCE OF REUBEN

15. *Reuben.* Hitherto it has been related in general terms that Transjordan had been allotted to the two and a half tribes. Now the exact boundaries of each of these tribes are defined. 'The country between the Arnon and the Jabbok was divided between Reuben and Gad. It was bounded on the south by Moab, and on the eastern border by Ammon. The southernmost district was given to Reuben, and it extended from the river Arnon to the junction of the Jordan with the Dead Sea. Gad's portion lay along the banks of the Jordan and to the east, reaching northward to the Sea of Chinneroth (lake Gennasereth), the northern portion from Mahanaim being very narrow. North of this lay the territory of half-Manasseh, which embraced the whole of Bashan' (Friedeberg).

according to their families. i.e. the territory was further sub-divided among the clans, or *families* of the tribes.

16. *Aroer.* See on xii. 2.

Medeba. See on verse 9.

17. *Heshbon.* See on ix. 10.

Dibon. See on verse 9.

Bamoth-baal. lit. 'the high places of Baal,' the town being named after the cult of Baal which was practised there. It lay north of the Arnon and east of the Dead Sea (see Num. xxii. 41).

Beth-baal-meon. lit. 'the house of the lord of Meon,' 'lord' probably referring to the deity worshipped in Meon, which lies a few miles east of the Dead Sea.

18. *Jahaz.* A few miles north-west of Bamoth-baal. Sihon joined battle there with Israel (Num. xxi. 23). Subsequently it became a Levitical city (1 Chron. vi. 63). Some identify it with Azefran, south-east of Medeba (Daath Mikra).

Kedemoth. Not identified; possibly in the vicinity of the upper reaches of the Arnon.

19. and Kiriathaim, and Sibmah, and Zereth-shahar in the mount of the valley; 20. and Beth-peor, and the slopes of Pisgah, and Beth-jeshimoth; 21. and all the cities of the table-land, and all the kingdom of Sihon king of the Amorites, who reigned in Heshbon, whom Moses smote with the chiefs of Midian, Evi, and Rekem, and Zur, and Hur, and Reba, the princes of Sihon, that dwelt in the land. 22. Balaam also the son of Beor, the soothsayer, did the children of Israel slay with the sword among the rest of their slain. 23. And as for the border of the children of Reuben, the Jordan was their border. This was the inheritance of the children of Reuben

19 וּמֵפָעַת: וְקִרְיָתַיִם וְשִׂבְמָה וְצֶרֶת הַשַּׁחַר בְּהַר הָעֵמֶק:
20 וּבֵית פְּעוֹר וְאַשְׁדּוֹת הַפִּסְגָּה
21 וּבֵית הַיְשִׁמוֹת: וְכֹל עָרֵי הַמִּישֹׁר וְכָל־מַמְלְכוּת סִיחוֹן מֶלֶךְ הָאֱמֹרִי אֲשֶׁר מָלַךְ בְּחֶשְׁבּוֹן אֲשֶׁר הִכָּה מֹשֶׁה אֹתוֹ | וְאֶת־נְשִׂיאֵי מִדְיָן אֶת־אֱוִי וְאֶת־רֶקֶם וְאֶת־צוּר וְאֶת־חוּר וְאֶת־רֶבַע נְסִיכֵי
22 סִיחוֹן יֹשְׁבֵי הָאָרֶץ: וְאֶת־בִּלְעָם בֶּן־בְּעוֹר הַקּוֹסֵם הָרְגוּ בְנֵי־יִשְׂרָאֵל בַּחֶרֶב
23 אֶל־חַלְלֵיהֶם: וַיְהִי גְּבוּל בְּנֵי רְאוּבֵן הַיַּרְדֵּן וּגְבוּל זֹאת נַחֲלַת בְּנֵי־רְאוּבֵן

Mephaath. A Moabite city (Jer. xlviii. 21) in the neighbourhood of Jahaz.

19. *Kiriathaim.* lit. 'two cities, or twin-cities,' north of the Arnon and east of the Dead Sea. It is mentioned on the Moabite Stone as Kiriathan, and king Mesha declares that he had built it.

Sibmah. Conjectured to be the modern Sumieh, north-west of Heshbon (Daath Mikra).

Zereth-shahar. North of Kiriathaim. Some identify it with es-Sara on the spur of mount Attarus, east of the Dead Sea (Daath Mikra).

the mount of the valley. [Perhaps mount Nebo.]

20. *Beth-peor.* On the crest of a hill near mount Pisgah (Daath Mikra).

slopes of Pisgah . . . Beth-jeshimoth. See on xii. 3.

21. *all the kingdom of Sihon.* This is not to be understood precisely, because only the southern part was assigned to Reuben (cf. verse 27).

the chiefs of Midian. Their overthrow is related separately in Num. xxxi. 8, where they are described as *kings of Midian.* Kimchi maintains that at that time they were vassals of Sihon; hence their mention is in place here.

22. *the soothsayer.* Or, 'diviner.' Originally divination by drawing lots may be meant (cf. Ezek. xxi. 26), a practice prohibited in Deut. xviii. 10. Here the term seems to be employed in the more general sense of a man who gives oracular messages. Balaam's death is recorded in Num. xxxi. 8.

23. *the villages thereof.* The villages adjacent to the cities.

according to their families, the cities and the villages thereof.

24. And Moses gave unto the tribe of Gad, unto the children of Gad, according to their families. 25. And their border was Jazer, and all the cities of Gilead, and half the land of the children of Ammon, unto Aroer that is before Rabbah; 26. and from Heshbon unto Ramath-mizpeh, and Betonim; and from Mahanaim unto the border of Lidbir; 27. and in the valley, Beth-haram, and Beth-nimrah, and Succoth, and Zaphon, the rest of the kingdom of Sihon king of Heshbon, the Jordan being the border thereof, unto the uttermost part of the sea of Chinnereth beyond the Jordan eastward. 28. This is the inheritance of the children of Gad according to their families, the cities and the villages thereof.

לְמִשְׁפְּחוֹתָ֖ם הֶעָרִ֑ים
וְחַצְרֵיהֶֽן׃

24 וַיִּתֵּ֤ן מֹשֶׁה֙ לְמַטֵּה־גָ֔ד לִבְנֵי־
25 גָ֖ד לְמִשְׁפְּחֹתָ֑ם וַיְהִ֤י לָהֶם֙
הַגְּב֔וּל יַעְזֵ֕ר וְכָל־עָרֵ֖י
הַגִּלְעָ֑ד וַחֲצִ֗י אֶ֚רֶץ בְּנֵ֣י עַמּ֔וֹן
עַד־עֲרוֹעֵ֕ר אֲשֶׁ֖ר עַל־פְּנֵ֥י
26 רַבָּֽה׃ יּוּמֵחֶשְׁבּ֤וֹן עַד־רָמַ֣ת
הַמִּצְפֶּה֙ וּבְטֹנִ֔ים וּמִמַּחֲנַ֖יִם
27 עַד־גְּב֥וּל לִדְבִ֑ר׃ וּבָעֵ֗מֶק
בֵּ֣ית הָרָ֞ם וּבֵ֤ית נִמְרָה֙ וְסֻכּ֔וֹת
וְצָפ֕וֹן יֶ֖תֶר מַמְלְכ֔וּת סִיחוֹן֙
מֶ֣לֶךְ חֶשְׁבּ֔וֹן הַיַּרְדֵּ֖ן וּגְבֻ֑ל
עַד־קְצֵה־יָ֥ם־כִּנֶּ֖רֶת עֵ֥בֶר
28 הַיַּרְדֵּ֖ן מִזְרָֽחָה׃ זֹ֣את נַחֲלַ֤ת
בְּנֵי־גָד֙ לְמִשְׁפְּחֹתָ֔ם הֶעָרִ֖ים
וְחַצְרֵיהֶֽם׃

v. 26. חצי הספר בפסוקים

24–28 THE INHERITANCE OF GAD

25. *Jazer.* North-east of Heshbon (see Daath Mikra).

Aroer that is before Rabbah. According to the use of this expression in other Biblical passages, there is indication that Israel surrounded Rabbah from the east. This is substantiated by the Rabbinical interpretation of Moses' blessing to Gad, (Deut. xxxiii. 20). *Blessed be He that enlargeth Gad,* to imply that Gad's territory extended eastward (Siphre) (Daath Mikra). This Aroer should not be confused with the Aroer in Reuben's territory.

26. *Ramath-mizpeh.* lit. 'the height of Mizpeh,' a few miles north of Heshbon. Its site may be the modern Tel el-Mizpeh (Daath Mikra).

Betonim. North-west of Ramath-mizpeh, the modern Batne (Daath Mikra).

the border of Lidbir. It may be identical with Lo-debar in 2 Sam. ix. 4, xvii. 27. It is conjectured to be the modern Um Edabar (Daath Mikra).

27. *the valley.* Of the Jordan (Daath Mikra).

Beth-haram. The modern Beit Harran, east of the Jordan opposite Jericho (Daath Mikra).

Beth-nimrah. The modern Tel Nimrin, north of Beth-haram (Daath Mikra).

Succoth. Identified by the Rabbis (j. Shebi. 38d) with Deralla, near the Jabbok. This is accepted by several modern geographers.

Zaphon. lit. 'north,' of the Jabbok (Daath Mikra).

29. And Moses gave inheritance unto the half-tribe of Manasseh; and it was for the half-tribe of the children of Manasseh according to their families. 30. And their border was from Mahanaim, all Bashan, all the kingdom of Og king of Bashan, and all the villages of Jair, which are in Bashan, threescore cities; 31. and half Gilead, and Ashtaroth, and Edrei, the cities of the kingdom of Og in Bashan, were for the children of Machir the son of Manasseh, even for the half of the children of Machir according to their families.

32. These are the inheritances which Moses distributed in the plains of Moab, beyond the Jordan at Jericho, eastward. 33. But unto the tribe of Levi Moses gave no inheritance; the LORD, the God of Israel, is their inheritance, as He spoke unto them.

29 וַיִּתֵּן מֹשֶׁה לַחֲצִי שֵׁבֶט מְנַשֶּׁה
וַיְהִי לַחֲצִי מַטֵּה בְנֵי־מְנַשֶּׁה
30 לְמִשְׁפְּחוֹתָם: וַיְהִי גְבוּלָם
מִמַּחֲנַיִם כָּל־הַבָּשָׁן כָּל־
מַמְלְכוּת | עוֹג מֶלֶךְ־הַבָּשָׁן
וְכָל־חַוֹּת יָאִיר אֲשֶׁר בַּבָּשָׁן
31 שִׁשִּׁים עִיר: וַחֲצִי הַגִּלְעָד
וְעַשְׁתָּרוֹת וְאֶדְרֶעִי עָרֵי
מַמְלְכוּת עוֹג בַּבָּשָׁן לִבְנֵי
מָכִיר בֶּן־מְנַשֶּׁה לַחֲצִי בְנֵי־
מָכִיר לְמִשְׁפְּחוֹתָם:
32 אֵלֶּה אֲשֶׁר־נִחַל מֹשֶׁה
בְּעַרְבוֹת מוֹאָב מֵעֵבֶר לְיַרְדֵּן
33 יְרִיחוֹ מִזְרָחָה: וּלְשֵׁבֶט הַלֵּוִי
לֹא־נָתַן מֹשֶׁה נַחֲלָה יְהוָה
אֱלֹהֵי יִשְׂרָאֵל הוּא נַחֲלָתָם
כַּאֲשֶׁר דִּבֶּר לָהֶם:

the rest, etc. i.e. that which had not been allocated to Reuben.

sea of Chinnereth. See on xi. 2.

29–31 THE INHERITANCE OF THE HALF-TRIBE OF MANASSEH

30. the villages of Jair. So named because Jair had conquered them (cf. Num. xxxii. 41). The term for villages, chawwoth, is connected with the Arabic for 'a collection of tents,' and denotes 'tent-settlements.' According to Hershcovitz, the term chawwah denoted a fortified encampment, which the sixty cities mentioned here originally were. They retained the designation even when they lost their military significance.

which are in Bashan. This is added to distinguish them from the villages of Jair in Gilead (1 Kings iv. 13).

31. and half Gilead. Along the Jordan the heritage of Gad stretched from the Jabbok northwards to the sea of Chinnereth; but in the east, the Jabbok, which divides the mountain range into two, formed the border between Gad and Manasseh, the southern half belonging to Gad while the northern half belonged to Manasseh (Gordon).

Ashtaroth. See on ix. 10.

Edrei. See on xii. 4.

Machir. The first-born son of Manasseh (Below xvii. 1). Sometimes, the phrase the children of Machir is synonymous with the tribe of Manasseh (Daath Mikra).

33. no inheritance. See on verse 14. No continuous area was allotted to them, but only scattered cities in various parts of the country (cf. xxi).

14   CHAPTER XIV   יד

1. And these are the inheritances which the children of Israel took in the land of Canaan, which Eleazar the priest, and Joshua the son of Nun, and the heads of the fathers' houses of the tribes of the children of Israel, distributed unto them, 2. by the lot of their inheritance, as the LORD commanded by the hand of Moses, for the nine tribes, and for the half-tribe.—3. For Moses had given the inheritance of the two tribes and the half-tribe beyond the Jordan; but unto the Levites he gave no inheritance among them. 4. For

א וְאֵלֶּה אֲשֶׁר־נָחֲלוּ בְנֵי־
יִשְׂרָאֵל בְּאֶרֶץ כְּנָעַן אֲשֶׁר
נָחֲלוּ אוֹתָם אֶלְעָזָר הַכֹּהֵן
וִיהוֹשֻׁעַ בִּן־נוּן וְרָאשֵׁי אֲבוֹת
ב הַמַּטּוֹת לִבְנֵי יִשְׂרָאֵל: בְּגוֹרַל
נַחֲלָתָם כַּאֲשֶׁר צִוָּה יְהוָֹה
בְּיַד־מֹשֶׁה לְתִשְׁעַת הַמַּטּוֹת
ג וַחֲצִי הַמַּטֶּה: כִּי־נָתַן מֹשֶׁה
נַחֲלַת שְׁנֵי הַמַּטּוֹת וַחֲצִי הַמַּטֶּה
מֵעֵבֶר לַיַּרְדֵּן וְלַלְוִיִּם לֹא־
ד נָתַן נַחֲלָה בְּתוֹכָם: כִּי־הָיוּ

v. 2. הרי בפתח

CHAPTER XIV

1-2 INTRODUCTION TO THE DIVISION OF WESTERN CANAAN

1. *Eleazar the priest.* The son of Aaron and his successor as High Priest. He is named here for the first time in connection with the division of the territory. He, together with Joshua and a representative from each tribe, had been designated to apportion the land by lot (Num. xxxiv. 17ff.) Here and in *Numbers* he is given precedence over Joshua, because the allotment was presided over by the High Priest as representative of God under Whose direction the task was carried out.

and the heads, etc. [The purpose was to prevent arbitrary allocation and ensure that even the weakest received a fair share. We may see here the operation of the democratic principle which is a conspicuous feature of the Bible.]

2. *by the lot.* The land was first divided into seven regions (cf. viii. 6ff.), and then lots were cast to determine the portion of each

tribe. The method is not described, but the following traditional account is given in the Talmud: 'Eleazar was wearing the Urim and Thummim, while Joshua and all Israel stood before him. An urn containing the names of the tribes, and an urn containing descriptions of the boundaries were placed before him. Animated by the Holy Spirit, he gave direction, exclaiming, "Zebulun" is coming up and the boundary lines of Acco are coming up with it. Thereupon he shook well the urn of the tribes and Zebulun came up in his hand. Likewise he shook well the urn of the boundaries and the boundary lines of Acco came up in his hand'; and so with the other tribes (B.B. 122a).

for the nine tribes, etc. But, it would appear, the division made by Moses for the two and a half tribes (*and Moses gave,* xiii. 15, 24, 29) was not by lot. Probably as only two and a half tribes were involved, it was easier to make the allotment by mutual agreement.

4. *two tribes.* And so the total number of tribes participating in the division was twelve, in spite of the exclusion of Levi (Metsudath David).

the children of Joseph were two tribes, Manasseh and Ephraim; and they gave no portion unto the Levites in the land, save cities to dwell in, with the open land about them for their cattle and for their substance.—5. As the LORD commanded Moses, so the children of Israel did, and they divided the land.

6. Then the children of Judah drew nigh unto Joshua in Gilgal; and Caleb the son of Jephunneh the Kenizzite said unto him: 'Thou knowest the thing that the LORD spoke unto Moses the man of God concerning me and concerning thee in Kadesh-barnea. 7. Forty years old was I when Moses the servant of the LORD sent me from Kadesh-barnea to spy out the land; and I brought him back word as it was in my heart. 8. Nevertheless my

בְּנֵי־יוֹסֵף שְׁנֵי מַטּוֹת מְנַשֶּׁה
וְאֶפְרָיִם וְלֹא־נָתְנוּ חֵלֶק
לַלְוִיִּם בָּאָרֶץ כִּי אִם־עָרִים
לָשֶׁבֶת וּמִגְרְשֵׁיהֶם לְמִקְנֵיהֶם
וּלְקִנְיָנָם: כַּאֲשֶׁר צִוָּה יְהוָֹה ⁵
אֶת־מֹשֶׁה כֵּן עָשׂוּ בְּנֵי יִשְׂרָאֵל
וַיַּחְלְקוּ אֶת־הָאָרֶץ:
וַיִּגְּשׁוּ בְנֵי־יְהוּדָה אֶל־יְהוֹשֻׁעַ ⁶
בַּגִּלְגָּל וַיֹּאמֶר אֵלָיו כָּלֵב בֶּן־
יְפֻנֶּה הַקְּנִזִּי אַתָּה יָדַעְתָּ אֶת־
הַדָּבָר אֲשֶׁר־דִּבֶּר יְהוָֹה אֶל־
מֹשֶׁה ׀ אִישׁ הָאֱלֹהִים עַל
אֹדוֹתַי וְעַל־אֹדוֹתֶיךָ בְּקָדֵשׁ
בַּרְנֵעַ: בֶּן־אַרְבָּעִים שָׁנָה ⁷
אָנֹכִי בִּשְׁלֹחַ מֹשֶׁה עֶבֶד־יְהוָֹה
אֹתִי מִקָּדֵשׁ בַּרְנֵעַ לְרַגֵּל אֶת־
הָאָרֶץ וָאָשֵׁב אוֹתוֹ דָּבָר
כַּאֲשֶׁר עִם־לְבָבִי: וְאַחַי ⁸

save cities to dwell in. Which were located among the other tribes. Jacob's dying words were accordingly fulfilled: *I will divide them* (Simeon and Levi) *in Jacob, and scatter them in Israel* (Gen. xlix. 7). The tribe of Simeon also received no separate territory but part of Judah's (xix. 1).

with the open land about them. In accordance with Num. xxxv. 2ff. This inclusion of land for pasture was essential for a population mainly pastoral.

6–15 CALEB'S CLAIM TO HEBRON

6. *the children of Judah . . . Caleb.* The former to support Caleb's claim (Abarbanel and Metsudath David).

the Kenizzite. i.e. the stepson of Kenaz. Othniel was Caleb's half brother. His father's real name was Hezron, as in 1 Chron. ii. 18. He was called ben Jephunneh to indicate that he had turned away (פָּנָה) from the counsel of the spies (Sotah 11b).

concerning me and concerning thee. i.e. that we live to enter the land of Canaan, as opposed to the rest of the generation who died in the desert (Abarbanel and Metsudath David).

Kadesh-barnea. See on x. 41.

7. *as it was in my heart.* In Hebrew *heart* corresponds to the English word 'mind.' Caleb's report corresponded with the impressions made upon him by his observations.

brethren that went up with me made the heart of the people melt; but I wholly followed the LORD my God. 9. And Moses swore on that day, saying: Surely the land whereon thy foot hath trodden shall be an inheritance to thee and to thy children for ever, because thou hast wholly followed the LORD my God. 10. And now, behold, the LORD hath kept me alive, as He spoke, these forty and five years, from the time that the LORD spoke this word unto Moses, while Israel walked in the wilderness; and now, lo, I am this day fourscore and five years old. 11. As yet I am as strong this day as I was in the day that Moses sent me; as my strength was then, even so is

אֲשֶׁר עָלוּ עִמִּי הִמְסִיו אֶת־
לֵב הָעָם וְאָנֹכִי מִלֵּאתִי אַחֲרֵי
9 יְהוָה אֱלֹהָי: וַיִּשָּׁבַע מֹשֶׁה
בַּיּוֹם הַהוּא לֵאמֹר אִם־לֹא
הָאָרֶץ אֲשֶׁר דָּרְכָה רַגְלְךָ
בָּהּ לְךָ תִהְיֶה לְנַחֲלָה וּלְבָנֶיךָ
עַד־עוֹלָם כִּי מִלֵּאתָ אַחֲרֵי
10 יְהוָה אֱלֹהָי: וְעַתָּה הִנֵּה הֶחֱיָה
יְהוָה אוֹתִי כַּאֲשֶׁר דִּבֵּר זֶה
אַרְבָּעִים וְחָמֵשׁ שָׁנָה מֵאָז דִּבֶּר
יְהוָה אֶת־הַדָּבָר הַזֶּה אֶל־
מֹשֶׁה אֲשֶׁר־הָלַךְ יִשְׂרָאֵל
בַּמִּדְבָּר וְעַתָּה הִנֵּה אָנֹכִי הַיּוֹם
11 בֶּן־חָמֵשׁ וּשְׁמֹנִים שָׁנָה: עוֹדֶנִּי
הַיּוֹם חָזָק כַּאֲשֶׁר בְּיוֹם שְׁלֹחַ
אוֹתִי מֹשֶׁה כְּכֹחִי אָז וּכְכֹחִי

v. 11. כ׳ רבתי

---

8. *made . . . melt*, etc. Cf. Num. xiv. 1ff.; Deut. i. 28.

9. *Moses swore.* The oath is not recorded in the Pentateuch (Kimchi).

the land whereon thy foot hath trodden. For the promise, cf. Deut. i. 36. Although in the forty days spent by the spies in Canaan a considerable portion of the country must have been reconnoitred, particular mention is made of Hebron in the narrative (Num. xiii. 22). The Rabbis explained that only Caleb went to Hebron to pray at the tombs of the patriarchs, the literal rendering of Num. xiii. 22 being, *they went up into the South, and he came unto Hebron.*

10. *these forty and five years.* The spies were

sent in the second year of the exodus, after which the people spent thirty-eight years in the wilderness (Deut. ii. 14). Hence the conquest must have occupied seven years (Rashi).

while Israel walked, etc. Kimchi renders: 'because Israel walked,' i.e. wandered in the wilderness, this being the reason for the lapse of forty-five years.

11. *as yet I am as strong this day,* etc. The inference Caleb wished to be drawn was that he was capable of conquering Hebron, despite his advanced age. It was a bold claim, yet not improbable in view of the longevity of that period. Moses lived to 120 (Deut. xxxiv. 7) and Joshua to 110 (xxiv. 29) (Abarbanel and Metsudath David).

my strength now, for war, and to go out and to come in. 12. Now therefore give me this mountain, whereof the LORD spoke in that day; for thou heardest in that day how the Anakim were there, and cities great and fortified; it may be that the LORD will be with me, and I shall drive them out, as the LORD spoke.'
13. And Joshua blessed him; and he gave Hebron unto Caleb the son of Jephunneh for an inheritance. 14. Therefore Hebron became the inheritance of Caleb the son of Jephunneh the Kenizzite, unto this day; because that he wholly followed the LORD, the God of Israel. 15. Now the name of Hebron beforetime was Kiriath-arba, which Arba was the greatest man among the Anakim. And the land had rest from war.

עַתָּה לַמִּלְחָמָה וְלָצֵאת

12 וְלָבוֹא: וְעַתָּה תְּנָה־לִּי אֶת־
הָהָר הַזֶּה אֲשֶׁר־דִּבֶּר יְהֹוָה
בַּיּוֹם הַהוּא כִּי־אַתָּה שָׁמַעְתָּ
בַיּוֹם הַהוּא כִּי־עֲנָקִים שָׁם
וְעָרִים גְּדֹלוֹת בְּצֻרוֹת אוּלַי
יְהֹוָה אוֹתִי וְהוֹרַשְׁתִּים כַּאֲשֶׁר

13 דִּבֶּר יְהֹוָה: וַיְבָרֲכֵהוּ יְהוֹשֻׁעַ
וַיִּתֵּן אֶת־חֶבְרוֹן לְכָלֵב בֶּן־

14 יְפֻנֶּה לְנַחֲלָה: עַל־כֵּן
הָיְתָה־חֶבְרוֹן לְכָלֵב בֶּן־
יְפֻנֶּה הַקְּנִזִּי לְנַחֲלָה עַד הַיּוֹם
הַזֶּה יַעַן אֲשֶׁר מִלֵּא אַחֲרֵי

15 יְהֹוָה אֱלֹהֵי יִשְׂרָאֵל: וְשֵׁם
חֶבְרוֹן לְפָנִים קִרְיַת אַרְבַּע
הָאָדָם הַגָּדוֹל בָּעֲנָקִים הוּא
וְהָאָרֶץ שָׁקְטָה מִמִּלְחָמָה:

---

to go out and come in. An idiomatic phrase signifying to fulfil all one's duties.

12. *now therefore give me this mountain.* viz. of Hebron. [It is a tribute to the fair division of the country that he was the only one to ask for and receive preferential treatment, and even he requested a piece of land which had still to be subjugated. Hebron is situated among the Judean hills.]

13. *he gave Hebron.* i.e. the fields and villages around Hebron (xxi. 12), the city itself being a priestly habitation and a city of refuge (xxi. 13) (B.B. 122b).

15. *Kiriath-arba.* i.e. 'the city of Arba.' To make it clear that *Arba* is a proper noun and does not mean 'four,' the text continues, *which Arba was the greatest man,* etc. Some Rabbinical commentators nevertheless explain the name of the city as the burial place of 'four' couples, viz. Adam and Eve, Abraham and Sarah, Isaac and Rebekah, and Jacob and Leah (Gen. Rabbah lviii. 4).

had rest from war. Israel being too weary then to continue and complete the conquest (Kimchi).

CHAPTER XV

15   **CHAPTER XV**   טו

1. And the lot for the tribe of the children of Judah according to their families was unto the border of Edom, even to the wilderness of Zin southward, at the uttermost part of the south. 2. And their south border was from the uttermost part of the Salt Sea, from the bay that looked southward. 3. And it went out southward of the ascent of Akrabbim, and passed along to Zin, and went up by the south of Kadesh-barnea, and passed along by Hezron, and went up to Addar, and turned about to Karka. 4. And it passed along to Azmon, and went out at the Brook of Egypt; and the goings out of the border were at the sea; this shall be your south border.

1 וַיְהִי הַגּוֹרָל לְמַטֵּה בְּנֵי יְהוּדָה לְמִשְׁפְּחֹתָם אֶל־גְּבוּל אֱדוֹם מִדְבַּר־צִן נֶגְבָּה מִקְצֵה 2 תֵימָן: וַיְהִי לָהֶם גְּבוּל נֶגֶב מִקְצֵה יָם הַמֶּלַח מִן־הַלָּשֹׁן 3 הַפֹּנֶה נֶגְבָּה: וְיָצָא אֶל־מִנֶּגֶב לְמַעֲלֵה עַקְרַבִּים וְעָבַר צִנָה וְעָלָה מִנֶּגֶב לְקָדֵשׁ בַּרְנֵעַ וְעָבַר חֶצְרוֹן וְעָלָה אַדָּרָה 4 וְנָסַב הַקַּרְקָעָה: וְעָבַר עַצְמוֹנָה וְיָצָא נַחַל מִצְרַיִם וְהָיָה תֹצְאוֹת הַגְּבוּל יָמָּה זֶה־ 5 יִהְיֶה לָכֶם גְּבוּל נֶגֶב: וּגְבוּל

 v. 4. והיו ק׳

CHAPTER XV

1–12 THE INHERITANCE OF JUDAH

'ROUGHLY, the inheritance of Judah extended from the north of the Dead Sea to the Mediterranean on the south along the shore of the Dead Sea and continuing towards Kadesh-barnea, and thence westward to the Wadi el-Arish' (Friedeberg).

1. This verse gives the boundaries in general terms, which the following verses describe in detail.

according to their families. See on xiii. 15.

the border of Edom. The region of mount Seir (Deut. i. 2) in the south-east.

the wilderness of Zin. In the south-west corner of Canaan; it is the northern portion of the wilderness of Paran (Num. xiii. 26).

2. *the bay.* lit. 'the tongue,' i.e. from the narrow tip of the Dead Sea in the south-east, whence it expands tongue-shaped.

3. *the ascent of Akrabbim.* i.e. 'scorpions' pass,' identified by some as Akabah (Ha-aretz lig'vuloteha). Others identify it as the city of Akraba, known during the Second Commonwealth as an Idumean city. For other theories, see Daath Mikra.

Zin. i.e. the wilderness of that name.

Kadesh-barnea. See on x. 41.

Hezron. In the extreme south of the territory of Judah.

Addar. Named Hazar-addar in Num. xxxiv. 4; on the southern boundary of Canaan.

Karka. Only mentioned here; unidentified but also in the extreme south.

4. *Azmon.* Ain Kusemeh, east of Kadesh (Ha-aretz ligvulotheha).

the Brook of Egypt. See on xiii. 3.

this shall be your south border. [An expression conveying the finality of the arrangement,

85

5. And the east border was the Salt Sea, even unto the end of the Jordan. And the border of the north side was from the bay of the sea at the end of the Jordan. 6. And the border went up to Beth-hoglah, and passed along by the north of Beth-arabah; and the border went up to the Stone of Bohan the son of Reuben. 7. And the border went up to Debir from the valley of Achor, and so northward, looking toward Gilgal, that is over against the ascent of Adummim, which is on the south side of the brook; and the border passed along to the waters of En-shemesh, and the goings out

קֵדְמָה יָם הַמֶּלַח עַד־קְצֵה
הַיַּרְדֵּן וּגְבוּל לִפְאַת צָפוֹנָה
מִלְּשׁוֹן הַיָּם מִקְצֵה הַיַּרְדֵּן:
6 וְעָלָה הַגְּבוּל בֵּית חָגְלָה וְעָבַר
מִצְּפוֹן לְבֵית הָעֲרָבָה וְעָלָה
הַגְּבוּל אֶבֶן בֹּהַן בֶּן־רְאוּבֵן:
7 וְעָלָה הַגְּבוּל ׀ דְּבִרָה מֵעֵמֶק
עָכוֹר וְצָפוֹנָה פֹּנֶה אֶל־
הַגִּלְגָּל אֲשֶׁר־נֹכַח לְמַעֲלֵה
אֲדֻמִּים אֲשֶׁר מִנֶּגֶב לַנָּחַל
וְעָבַר הַגְּבוּל אֶל־מֵי עֵין־
שֶׁמֶשׁ וְהָיוּ תֹצְאֹתָיו אֶל־עֵין

like *le roy le veult* which signifies the royal assent to a Bill and gives it the force of law. It is perhaps copied from Num. xxxiv where the phrase is frequent.]

5. *the bay.* See on verse 2.

6. *Beth-hoglah.* lit. 'house of a partridge'; the modern Ain Hajla (Daath Mikra).

Beth-arabah. lit. 'house of depression'; the site is unknown. Some believe it to be located near Ein-el-araba, next to Wadi-el-kilt in the plains of Jericho (Daath Mikra).

the Stone of Bohan the son of Reuben. The place was called "Eben," and it was owned by one Bohan the son of Reuben (not of the tribe of Reuben). Perhaps there was a stone of sufficient size and importance to serve as a landmark, hence the name "Eben," meaning a stone (Kimchi). Some conjecture that Scripture refers to Hajar-al-atzba (the finger rock), in the environs of Jericho (Daath Mikra).

The location, according to Hershcovitz, may have been the modern Nebi Musa, which is that of Moses' tomb in Arab tradition.

7. *Debir.* Not the same as the city of this name mentioned in x. 38.

the valley of Achor. See on vii. 24.

Gilgal. This is not Joshua's base near Jericho (x. 43). In xviii. 17 it is called Geliloth. Since there were several places named Gilgal, Scripture identifies its location (Daath Mikra).

the ascent of Adummim. This is identified with Tala'at ed-Dumm (ascent of blood). This Gilgal is located opposite the ascent up the mountain on the road between Jericho and Jerusalem. Next to the ascent are red stones which contain phosphates.

En-shemesh. lit. 'the spring of the sun,' [possibly a spring which was the scene of sun-worship by the Canaanites.]

Some theorize that this refers to the spring on the side of the highway between Jericho and Jerusalem, known today as Ain-al-haftz. Ein Shemesh was probably the city, and the waters of Ein Shemen were the springs in its environs (Daath Mikra).

En-rogel. A spring south-east of Jerusalem, perhaps with the original meaning of 'the fuller's spring' (so the Targum), now called 'the spring of Job.' It is mentioned again in viii. 16 as situated upon the boundary between Judah and Benjamin (Daath Mikra).

thereof were at En-rogel. 8. And the border went up by the Valley of the son of Hinnom unto the side of the Jebusite southward—the same is Jerusalem—and the border went up to the top of the mountain that lieth before the Valley of Hinnom westward, which is at the uttermost part of the vale of Rephaim northward. 9. And the border was drawn from the top of the mountain unto the fountain of the waters of Nephtoah, and went out to the cities of mount Ephron; and the border was drawn to Baalah—the same is Kiriath-jearim. 10. And the border turned about from Baalah westward unto mount Seir, and passed along unto the side of

8 רֹגֵל׃ וְעָלָה הַגְּבוּל גֵּי בֶן־
הִנֹּם אֶל־כֶּתֶף הַיְבוּסִי מִנֶּגֶב
הִיא יְרוּשָׁלִָם וְעָלָה הַגְּבוּל
אֶל־רֹאשׁ הָהָר אֲשֶׁר עַל־פְּנֵי
גֵי־הִנֹּם יָמָּה אֲשֶׁר בִּקְצֵה
9 עֵמֶק־רְפָאִים צָפוֹנָה׃ וְתָאַר
הַגְּבוּל מֵרֹאשׁ הָהָר אֶל־מַעְיַן
מֵי נֶפְתּוֹחַ וְיָצָא אֶל־עָרֵי הַר־
עֶפְרוֹן וְתָאַר הַגְּבוּל בַּעֲלָה
10 הִיא קִרְיַת יְעָרִים׃ וְנָסַב
הַגְּבוּל מִבַּעֲלָה יָמָּה אֶל־הַר
שֵׂעִיר וְעָבַר אֶל־כֶּתֶף הַר־

8. *the border went up.* From En-rogel towards Jerusalem which stands on hills (Daath Mikra).

the Valley of the son of Hinnom. This may be one of three possible valleys south of Jerusalem, viz. the Wadi er-Rababi, the Tyropoeon and the Kidron, but probably the first (Robinson). Later it was associated with human sacrifices, whence its name (Gehinnom, more familiarly Gehenna) came to denote the place of the torment of souls. It was traditionally regarded as the entrance to Gehinnom (Suk. 32b). To put an end to the abominations, Josiah defiled the area (2 Kings xxiii. 10).

the side of the Jebusite. [The western hill of Jerusalem, part of which lies today within the walls of the Old City. It includes the Jaffa Gate and the Tower of David. Joshua penetrated, but did not subjugate it, so that the Israelites and Jebusites dwelt in it (verse 63). It was not finally conquered until the time of David.]

the vale of Rephaim. To the south-west of Jerusalem. It now includes the district of Mekor Chayyim and the railway station on the north. The verse accordingly includes the hill

west of the Old City where now stand the King David Hotel and the districts of Rehaviah and Talbieh (Daath Mikra).

9. *was drawn.* Better, 'inclined,' *ta'ar* being regarded as a form of the root *tur,* 'turn about.'

the fountain of the waters of Nephtoach. According to Rashi, this was the fountain known as Ein-etam. This fount was twenty-three ells higher than the floor of the Temple court, and was the source of the High Priest's immersion water on Yom Kippur.

mount Ephron. On the northern boundary of Judah; not mentioned elsewhere.

Baalah. Now Kiriath el-Enab, near Jerusalem (Daath Mikra).

Kiriath-jearim. See on ix. 17; lit. 'city of forests.' Remains of these forests are still there.

10. *mount Seir.* It is obvious that this is not the Seir of Edom, but a mountain in Judah. Rabbi Elijah of Wilna remarked that as *Seir* is connected with *sa'ir* (hairy), it was a place thickly covered with reeds and shrubs, like a long-haired person.

mount Jearim on the north—the same is Chesalon—and went down to Beth-shemesh, and passed along by Timnah. 11. And the border went out unto the side of Ekron northward; and the border was drawn to Shikkeron, and passed along to mount Baalah, and went out at Jabneel; and the goings out of the border were at the sea. 12. And as for the west border, the Great Sea was the border thereof. This is the border of the children of Judah round about according to their families.

13. And unto Caleb the son of Jephunneh he gave a portion among the children of Judah, according to the commandment of the LORD to Joshua, even Kiriath-arba, which Arba was the father of Anak—the same is Hebron. 14. And Caleb drove out thence the three sons of Anak, Sheshai, and Ahiman, and Talmai, the children of Anak.

יְעָרִים מִצָּפוֹנָה הִיא כְסָלוֹן וְיָרַד בֵּית־שֶׁמֶשׁ וְעָבַר תִּמְנָה:

11 וְיָצָא הַגְּבוּל אֶל־כֶּתֶף עֶקְרוֹן צָפוֹנָה וְתָאַר הַגְּבוּל שִׁכְּרוֹנָה וְעָבַר הַר־הַבַּעֲלָה וְיָצָא יַבְנְאֵל וְהָיוּ תֹּצְאוֹת הַגְּבוּל

12 יָמָּה: וּגְבוּל יָם הַיָּמָּה הַגָּדוֹל וּגְבוּל זֶה גְּבוּל בְּנֵי־יְהוּדָה סָבִיב לְמִשְׁפְּחֹתָם:

13 וּלְכָלֵב בֶּן־יְפֻנֶּה נָתַן חֵלֶק בְּתוֹךְ בְּנֵי־יְהוּדָה אֶל־פִּי יְהוָה לִיהוֹשֻׁעַ אֶת־קִרְיַת אַרְבַּע אֲבִי הָעֲנָק הִיא

14 חֶבְרוֹן: וַיֹּרֶשׁ מִשָּׁם כָּלֵב אֶת־שְׁלוֹשָׁה בְּנֵי הָעֲנָק אֶת־שֵׁשַׁי וְאֶת־אֲחִימָן וְאֶת־תַּלְמָי

Beth-shemesh. lit. 'house of the sun,' also called Ir'Shemesh (xix. 41), 'city of the sun,' now the ruins of Ain Shems, some seven miles from Ekron. 'Here (at Ain Shems) are the vestiges of a former extensive city, consisting of many fountains, and the remains of ancient walls of hewn stone' (Daath Mikra).

Timnah. South-west of Beth-shemesh. It was the scene of an episode in the life of Samson (Judg. xiv. 1ff.).

11. *Ekron.* See on xiii. 3.

Shikkeron. On the north-west border of Judah; otherwise unknown.

Jabneel. Near Ekron, between Joppa and Ashdod, four miles inland. In 2 Chron. xxvi. 6 it is named Jabneh. After the destruction of the Second Temple in 70 C.E., R. Jochanan b. Zakkai founded there a Rabbinical academy which, under the name of Jabneh

or Jamnia, became famous as the religious and national centre of the Jewish people for a time. It is now a large Arab village called Jibneh (see Daath Mikra).

12. *the Great Sea.* The Mediterranean.

13–19 THE INHERITANCE OF CALEB

13. *unto Caleb.* See on xiv. 12. Joshua did not take it upon himself to grant Caleb's request, but consulted the oracle (*according to the commandment of the Lord* to Joshua).

Kiriath-arba. See on xiv. 15.

14. *And Caleb drove out.* i.e. after Joshua's death, for Hebron was not taken during Joshua's lifetime, as is stated in Judges i. 20 (Rashi).

Sheshai, etc. Cf. Num. xiii. 22.

15. And he went up thence against the inhabitants of Debir—now the name of Debir beforetime was Kiriath-sepher. 16. And Caleb said: 'He that smiteth Kiriath-sepher, and taketh it, to him will I give Achsah my daughter to wife.' 17. And Othniel the son of Kenaz, the brother of Caleb, took it; and he gave him Achsah his daughter to wife. 18. And it came to pass, when she came unto him, that she persuaded him to ask of her father a field; and she alighted from off her ass; and Caleb said unto her: 'What wouldest thou?' 19. And she said:

15 יְלִידֵי הָעֲנָק: וַיַּעַל מִשָּׁם אֶל־
יֹשְׁבֵי דְּבִר וְשֵׁם־דְּבִר לְפָנִים
16 קִרְיַת־סֵפֶר: וַיֹּאמֶר כָּלֵב
אֲשֶׁר־יַכֶּה אֶת־קִרְיַת־סֵפֶר
וּלְכָדָהּ וְנָתַתִּי לוֹ אֶת־עַכְסָה
17 בִתִּי לְאִשָּׁה: וַיִּלְכְּדָהּ
עָתְנִיאֵל בֶּן־קְנַז אֲחִי כָלֵב
וַיִּתֶּן־לוֹ אֶת־עַכְסָה בִתּוֹ
18 לְאִשָּׁה: וַיְהִי | בְּבוֹאָהּ
וַתְּסִיתֵהוּ לִשְׁאוֹל מֵאֵת־
אָבִיהָ שָׂדֶה וַתִּצְנַח מֵעַל
הַחֲמוֹר וַיֹּאמֶר־לָהּ כָּלֵב
19 מַה־לָּךְ: וַתֹּאמֶר תְּנָה־לִּי

15. *Kiriath-sepher.* It appears that Scripture distinguishes between the ancient city, housing the fortress, known as Kiriath-sepher, and the newer sections augmented to the city, known by the new name of Debir. For this reason, Caleb says in the following verse, "He that smiteth Kiriath-sepher . . ." The city is also known as Kiriath-sannah further in verse 49 (Daath Mikra).

The Rabbis state that book (סֵפֶר) is called Debir in Persian (Kimchi). The same is true in the Canaanite tongue (Daath Mikra).

16. Verses 16–19 are repeated in Judg. i. 12–15.

to him will I give, etc. Saul made a similar promise when fighting against the Philistines (1 Kenaz. i.e. from his mother (Rashi). Following the death of Caleb's father, Jephun-neh, his mother married Kenaz, from whom she bore Othniel. Since Caleb was raised in the household of Kenaz, he is also known as the Kenizzite. Kimchi and Abarbanel state that the family name was Kenizzite after its progenitor, Kenaz. Thus, Caleb and Othniel were full brothers.

18. *when she came unto him.* The words *unto him* are not in the Hebrew. A proposed interpretation is: when she came to her husband's house (Kimchi and Metsudath David).

a field. In Judg. i. 14 the noun has the definite article, i.e. the adjoining land which has a source of water.

what wouldst thou? [Apparently Othniel refused to ask for it; so she sprang down from the ass herself, which surprised Caleb into asking his question.]

'Give me a blessing; for that thou hast sent me in the Southland, give me therefore springs of water.' And he gave her the Upper Springs and the Nether Springs.

20. This is the inheritance of the tribe of the children of Judah according to their families.

21. And the cities at the uttermost part of the tribe of the children of Judah toward the border of Edom in the South were Kabzeel, and Eder, and Jagur; 22. and Kinah, and Dimonah, and Adadah; 23. and Kedesh, and Hazor, and Ithnan; 24. Ziph, and Telem, and Bealoth; 25. and Hazor, and Hadattah, and Kerioth, and Hezron—the same is

בְּרָכָה כִּי אֶרֶץ הַנֶּגֶב נְתַתָּנִי
וְנָתַתָּה לִי גֻּלֹּת מָיִם וַיִּתֶּן־לָהּ
אֵת גֻּלֹּת עִלִּיּוֹת וְאֵת גֻּלֹּת
תַּחְתִּיּוֹת:

20 זֹאת נַחֲלַת מַטֵּה בְנֵי־יְהוּדָה
לְמִשְׁפְּחֹתָם:

21 וַיִּהְיוּ הֶעָרִים מִקְצֵה לְמַטֵּה
בְנֵי־יְהוּדָה אֶל־גְּבוּל אֱדוֹם
בַּנֶּגְבָּה קַבְצְאֵל וְעֵדֶר וְיָגוּר:

22 וְקִינָה וְדִימוֹנָה וְעַדְעָדָה:

23 וְקֶדֶשׁ וְחָצוֹר וְיִתְנָן: זִיף וָטֶלֶם
24

25 וּבְעָלוֹת: וְחָצוֹר | חֲדַתָּה
וּקְרִיּוֹת חֶצְרוֹן הִיא חָצוֹר:

---

19. *a blessing.* i.e. a gift (cf. Gen. xxxiii. 11).

the Southland. Hebrew 'the land of the Negeb,' lit. 'a dry land.'

the Upper Springs . . . the Nether Springs. Welling up in the hill and plain respectively.

20–32 DETAILED LIST OF THE JUDEAN CITIES IN THE NEGEB

Judah's territory was divided into four main regions: the Negeb in the south, the Shephelah (Lowland) in the west, the Har (hillcountry) in the centre, and the Midbar (wilderness) in the east.

21. *Kabzeel.* The name occurs again in 2 Sam. xxiii. 20; Nehem. xi. 25 (Jekabzeel); 1 Chron. xi. 22. The site has not been discovered.

Eder. Perhaps the present ruins of Adar, about four miles south of Gaza.

Jagur. Otherwise unknown. When this applies to other place-names in the following lists, they are not mentioned in the commentary.

22. *Dimonah.* Perhaps the same as Dibbon in Nehem. xi. 25; identified by some with Tel ed-Dheib.

Addadah. [Perhaps Bir el-Uded, south of Kadesh-barnea.]

23. *Kedesh.* Some identify this with Kedesh mentioned in Num. xx. 1, located at the border of Edom. Others maintain that they are distinct of each other, and that the location of this one is unknown (Daath Mikra).

Hazor. Not the same town as that in xi. 10.

24. *Ziph.* Not the same as the Ziph of verse 55.

Bealoth. [It perhaps occurs again in 1 Kings iv. 16.]

25. *Hazor.* Different from the town named in verse 23.

Kerioth. Some identify it with the ruins of el-Kiriathin, south of Maon (D.M.).

Hazor; 26. Amam, and Shema, and
Moladah; 27. and Hazar-gaddah,
and Heshmon, and Beth-pelet; 28.
and Hazar-shual, and Beer-sheba,
and Biziothiah; 29. Baalah, and Iim,
and Ezem; 30. and Eltolad, and
Chesil, and Hormah; 31. and Ziklag,
and Madmannah, and Sansannah;
32. and Lebaoth, and Shilhim, and

26 אֲמָם וּשְׁמַע וּמוֹלָדָה: וַחֲצַר
27 גַּדָּה וְחֶשְׁמוֹן וּבֵית פָּלֶט:
28 וַחֲצַר שׁוּעָל וּבְאֵר שֶׁבַע
29 וּבִזְיוֹתְיָה: בַּעֲלָה וְעִיִּים
30 וָעָצֶם: וְאֶלְתּוֹלַד וּכְסִיל
31 וְחָרְמָה: וְצִקְלַג וּמַדְמַנָּה
32 וְסַנְסַנָּה: וּלְבָאוֹת וְשִׁלְחִים

27. *Beth-pelet.* Known also at the time of
the return to Zion as a city settled by the
returnees from Babylonia (Nehem. xi. 21).
Its location is not known definitely. Some
conjecture, however, that it is identified with
Tel-al-meshash, five kilometers east of
Beersheba (Daath Mikra).

28. *Hazar-shual.* Mentioned again in
Nehem. xi. 27; 1 Chron. iv. 28; included
among the cities of Simeon (xix. 3).

Beer-sheba. Either 'the well of seven' or 'the
well of the oath' (Gen. xxi. 28-32). It lay in
the extreme south, so that coupled with Dan
in the north, it described the complete length
of the land, *from Dan even to Beer-sheba* (2
Sam. xxiv. 2). It was a very ancient city, first
mentioned in connection with Abraham
(Gen. xxi). Later it was the judicial seat of
Samuel's son (1 Sam. viii. 2). Still later, in
the time of Amos, it was the site of an idolatrous cult (Amos v. 5, viii. 14). It still retains its name in the modern form of Bir
es-Seba.

29. *Baalah.* See on verse 9.

Ezem. A Simeonite town (xix. 3).

30. *Eltolad.* A Simeonite city (xix. 4), probably identical with *Tolad* (1 Chron. iv. 29).

Chesil. A comparison with the parallel passage in xix. 4 suggests that *Chesil* is identical
with *Bethul* mentioned there (see Kimchi). It
may have been the shrine (*Bethul* being a
form of *Beth-el*, 'house of God') of the con-
stellation *Chesil*, i.e. Orion (Job ix. 9) (Daath
Mikra).

Hormah. See on xii. 14.

31. *Ziklag.* This town came into prominence later when Achish, king of Gath, into
whose possession it had passed in the meantime, presented it to David (I Sam. xxvii. 6).
During David's absence with Achish, the
Amalekites raided and burnt it (1 Sam. xxxi.
1). Some authorities think that it stood on
the site of Zuheilikah, eleven miles south-
east of Gaza; others identify it with Tel el-
Kuwelfeh, between Zuheilikah and Beer-
sheba (Daath Mikra).

Madmannah. Umm Demneh, about twelve
miles north-east of Beer-sheba (D.M.).
[Some regard *Madmannah* ('dung') and *Sansannah* ('thorn') as epithets of opprobrium
applied to the heathen cults which were practised in these places.]

32. *Lebaoth.* Doubtless the Simeonite city
Beth-lebaoth (xix. 6).

Shilhim. See on *Sharuhen*, xix. 6.

Ain, and Rimmon; all the cities are twenty and nine, with their villages.

33. In the Lowland: Eshtaol, and Zorah, and Ashnah; 34. and Zanoah, and En-gannim, Tappuah, and Enam; 35. Jarmuth, and Adullam, Socoh, and Azekah; 36. and Shaaraim, and Adithaim, and Gederah, with Gederothaim; fourteen cities with their villages.

37. Zenan, and Hadashah, and Migdal-gad; 38. and Dilan, and Mizpeh, and Joktheel; 39. Lachish,

וְעַיִן וְרִמּוֹן כָּל־עָרִים עֶשְׂרִים
וָתֵשַׁע וְחַצְרֵיהֶן:
33 בַּשְּׁפֵלָה אֶשְׁתָּאוֹל וְצָרְעָה
34 וְאַשְׁנָה: וְזָנוֹחַ וְעֵין גַּנִּים תַּפּוּחַ
35 וְהָעֵינָם: יַרְמוּת וַעֲדֻלָּם
36 שׂוֹכֹה וַעֲזֵקָה: וְשַׁעֲרַיִם
וַעֲדִיתַיִם וְהַגְּדֵרָה וּגְדֵרֹתָיִם
עָרִים אַרְבַּע־עֶשְׂרֵה
וְחַצְרֵיהֶן:
37 צְנָן וַחֲדָשָׁה וּמִגְדַּל־גָּד:
38 וְדִלְעָן וְהַמִּצְפֶּה וְיָקְתְאֵל:

Ain, and Rimmon. In xix. 7 the reading is *Ain, Rimmon,* without the conjunction; but in xxi. 16 *Ain* occurs as the name of a Levitical city. They were probably situated close together, and so reckoned as one place. The modern identification is with Umm er-Ramamin, eighteen miles south-west of Hebron (Daath Mikra).

twenty and nine. In fact, thirty-eight are enumerated. The other nine are not counted because they were allotted to Simeon (Rashi). Others explain that they were mere villages and are therefore not reckoned as towns.

33–44 CITIES IN THE SHEPHELAH

33. *Eshtaol . . . Zorah.* Below they are listed among the cities of Dan (xix. 41); here *the spirit of the Lord* began to move Samson (Judg. xiii. 25) and his body was brought for burial (Judg. xvi. 31).

Ashnah. Another town of this name is mentioned in verse 43.

34. *Zanoah.* The modern Zanna, occurring again in Nehem. iii. 13, xi. 30; 1 Chron. iv. 18. Another place of this name is enumerated in verse 56 (Daath Mikra).

En-gannim. lit. 'spring of gardens'; Ummgina, a mile south-west of Beth-shemesh. A town of this name was included in territory of Issachar (xix. 21) (Daath Mikra).

Tappuah. Not the same as the town in xii. 17.

35. *Jarmuth.* See on x. 3.

Adullam. See on xii. 15.

Socoh. The modern es-Suweke, south-east of Beth-shemesh. Another place of the same name was in the hill-country (verse 48) (Daath Mikra).

Azekah. See on x. 10.

36. *fourteen cities.* Fifteen places are enumerated. Rashi maintains that *Enam* in verse 34 was not a separate town, but a suburb of *Tappuah,* the sense being 'Tappuah and its well,' while Kimchi considers *Gederah* and *Gederothaim* in this verse to be identical.

37. *Zenan.* Perhaps identical with *Zaanan* in Mic. i. 11 (Daath Mikra).

Migdal-gad. Perhaps the modern Mejdel, east of Ashkelon (Daath Mikra).

and Bozkath, and Eglon; 40. and Cabbon, and Lahmas, and Chithlish; 41. and Gederoth, Beth-dagon, and Naamah, and Makkedah; sixteen cities with their villages.

42. Libnah, and Ether, and Ashan; 43. and Iphtah, and Ashnah, and Nezib; 44. and Keilah, and Achzib, and Mareshah; nine cities with their villages.

45. Ekron, with its towns and its villages; 46. from Ekron even unto the sea, all that were by the side of Ashdod, with their villages.

39 לָכִישׁ וּבָצְקַת וְעֶגְלוֹן: וְכַבּוֹן 40
41 וְלַחְמָס וְכִתְלִישׁ: וּגְדֵרוֹת
בֵּית־דָּגוֹן וְנַעֲמָה וּמַקֵּדָה
עָרִים שֵׁשׁ־עֶשְׂרֵה
וְחַצְרֵיהֶן:
42 לִבְנָה וָעֶתֶר וְעָשָׁן: וְיִפְתָּח 43
44 וְאַשְׁנָה וּנְצִיב: וּקְעִילָה
וְאַכְזִיב וּמָרֵאשָׁה עָרִים תֵּשַׁע
וְחַצְרֵיהֶן:
45 עֶקְרוֹן וּבְנֹתֶיהָ וַחֲצֵרֶיהָ:
46 מֵעֶקְרוֹן וָיָמָּה כֹּל אֲשֶׁר־עַל־
יַד אַשְׁדּוֹד וְחַצְרֵיהֶן:

39. *Lachish.* See on x. 3.

Bozkath. The home of Josiah's mother (2 Kings xxii. 1).

Eglon. See on x. 3.

40. *Lahmas.* This reading (with the final *s*) is supported by the transcription in some ancient versions. Many Hebrew MSS. read 'Lahmam.' In any case, it may be the modern el-Lahm, about thirteen miles north-west of Hebron (Daath Mikra).

41. *Beth-dagon.* lit. 'house of Dagon,' the fish-god, worshipped by the Philistines. Many towns in western Palestine bore that name, e.g. a town assigned to Asher (xix. 27), and there is still a village called Beit Dejan near the Jewish city of Rishon Lezion. The *Beth-dagon* in this verse was more to the south, near Lachish, and its exact site is not known (Daath Mikra).

42. *Libnah.* See on x. 29.

Ether. Assigned to Simeon (xix. 7), perhaps the modern Air, two miles north-west of Beit Jibrin (Daath Mikra).

Ashan. Included in the cities of Simeon (xix. 7; 1 Chron. iv. 32).

43. *Nezib.* The modern Beit Nasib, eight miles north-west of Hebron (Daath Mikra).

44. *Keilah.* Now Tel Kilah, about eight miles north-west of Hebron. It appears in the history of David (cf. 1 Sam. xxiii. 6f.), and after the massacre of the priests of Nob it became the depositary of the sacred ephod.

Achzib. Possibly identical with *Chezib* in Gen. xxxviii. 5, which may be En el-Kezbeh near Socoh. Others maintain that its site was at Tel Bezeh, north-west of Keilah. It occurs again in Mic. i. 14 (D.M.).

Mareshah. Its remains have been found at Tel Sandahaneh, now Merash. It was fortified by Rehoboam (2 Chron. xi. 8). Josephus names it Marissa, a town captured by Judas Maccabeus (*Antiquities* XII. viii. 6).

45–47 CITIES ON THE PHILISTINE COAST

45. *Ekron.* See on xiii. 3.

46. *Ashdod.* See on xiii. 3.

47. Ashdod, its towns and its villages; Gaza, its towns and its villages; unto the Brook of Egypt, the Great Sea being the border thereof.

48. And in the hill-country: Shamir, and Jattir, and Socoh; 49. and Dannah, and Kiriath-sannah—the same is Debir; 50. and Anab, and Eshtemoh, and Anim; 51. and Goshen, and Holon, and Giloh; eleven cities with their villages.

52. Arab, and Rumah, and Eshan; 53. and Janum, and Beth-tappuah, and Aphekah; 54. and Humtah, and Kiriath-arba—the same is Hebron, and Zior; nine cities with their villages.

55. Maon, Carmel, and Ziph, and Juttah; 56. and Jezreel, and Jokdeam, and Zanoah; 57. Kain,

47 אַשְׁדּוֹד בְּנוֹתֶיהָ וַחֲצֵרֶיהָ עַזָּה
בְּנוֹתֶיהָ וַחֲצֵרֶיהָ עַד־נַחַל
מִצְרָיִם וְהַיָּם הַגָּבוֹל וּגְבוּל׃

48 וּבָהָר שָׁמִיר וְיַתִּיר וְשׂוֹכֹה׃

49 וְדַנָּה וְקִרְיַת־סַנָּה הִיא דְבִר׃

50 וַעֲנָב וְאֶשְׁתְּמֹה וְעָנִים׃ 51 וְגֹשֶׁן
וְחֹלֹן וְגִלֹה עָרִים אַחַת־
עֶשְׂרֵה וְחַצְרֵיהֶן׃

52 אֲרַב וְדוּמָה וְאֶשְׁעָן׃ 53 וְיָנִים
54 וּבֵית־תַּפּוּחַ וַאֲפֵקָה׃ וְחֻמְטָה
וְקִרְיַת אַרְבַּע הִיא חֶבְרוֹן
וְצִיעֹר עָרִים תֵּשַׁע וְחַצְרֵיהֶן׃

55 מָעוֹן ׀ כַּרְמֶל וָזִיף וְיוּטָּה׃
56 וְיִזְרְעֶאל וְיָקְדְעָם וְזָנוֹחַ׃ 57 הַקַּיִן

v. 47. הגדול ק׳   v. 48. ב״א בה״א   v. 52. ב״א ורומה   v. 53. וינום ק׳

---

47. *Gaza.* See on x. 41.

48–60 CITIES OF THE HILL-COUNTRY

48. *Shamir.* Now the ruins of Somerah, north-east of En Rimmon (Daath Mikra).

Jattir. A Levitical city (xxi. 14), probably the same as the place named in 1 Sam. xxx. 27.

Socoh. Cf. verse 35. Now the ruins of Suweikeh, north of Jattir (Daath Mikra).

49. *the same is Debir.* See on verse 15.

50. *Anab.* See on xi. 21.

Eshtemoh. Doubtless the same as the Levitical city *Eshtemoa* (xxi. 14; 1 Chron. vi. 42), mentioned again in 1 Sam. xxx. 28 (Daath Mikra).

Anim. Perhaps the modern Ghuwain seventeen miles south-west of Hebron (Daath Mikra).

51. *Goshen.* See on x. 41.

Holon. A Levitical city (xxi. 15), conjectured to be the ruins of Alin, north-west of Halhul (verse 58) (Daath Mikra).

Giloh. Again in 2 Sam. xv. 12.

52. *Rumah.* According to another reading 'Dumah,' the modern Daume, south-west of Hebron (Daath Mikra).

53. *Beth-tappuah, and Aphekah.* Not the same as *Tappuah* and *Aphek* in xii. 17f.

54. *Kiriath-arba.* See on xiv. 15.

Zior. Perhaps Za'ir, five miles north-east of Hebron (Daath Mikra).

55. *Maon.* The home town of Nabal (1 Sam. xxv. 2); the modern Ma'in, eight miles south of Hebron (Daath Mikra).

Ziph. Now Tel Zif, south-east of Hebron (Daath Mikra).

Juttah. One of the levitical cities (xxi. 16).

Gibeah, and Timnah; ten cities with their villages.

58. Halhul, Beth-zur, and Gedor;
59. and Maarath, and Beth-anoth, and Eltekon; six cities with their villages.

60. Kiriath-baal—the same is Kiriath-jearim, and Rabbah; two cities with their villages.

61. In the wilderness: Beth-arabah, Middin, and Secacah; 62. and Nibshan, and the City of Salt, and En-gedi; six cities with their villages.

63. And as for the Jebusites, the inhabitants of Jerusalem, the children of Judah could not drive them out; but the Jebusites dwelt with the

גִּבְעָה וְתִמְנָה עָרִים עֶשֶׂר וְחַצְרֵיהֶן׃

58 חַלְחוּל בֵּית־צוּר וּגְדוֹר׃

59 וּמַעֲרָת וּבֵית־עֲנוֹת וְאֶלְתְּקֹן עָרִים שֵׁשׁ וְחַצְרֵיהֶן׃

60 קִרְיַת־בַּעַל הִיא קִרְיַת יְעָרִים וְהָרַבָּה עָרִים שְׁתַּיִם וְחַצְרֵיהֶן׃

61 בַּמִּדְבָּר בֵּית הָעֲרָבָה מִדִּין

62 וּסְכָכָה׃ וְהַנִּבְשָׁן וְעִיר־הַמֶּלַח וְעֵין גֶּדִי עָרִים שֵׁשׁ וְחַצְרֵיהֶן׃

63 וְאֶת־הַיְבוּסִי יוֹשְׁבֵי יְרוּשָׁלַ͏ִם לֹא־יָכְלוּ בְנֵי־יְהוּדָה לְהוֹרִישָׁם וַיֵּשֶׁב הַיְבוּסִי אֶת־

v. 63. יתיר ר

---

56. *Jezreel.* The town of Ahinoam, wife of David (1 Sam. xxv. 43), otherwise unknown. *Zanoah.* Perhaps Zanuta, south-west of Hebron.

57. *Kain.* The Hebrew reads *hakkayin*, 'the Kain'; possibly Yukin south-east of Hebron (Daath Mikra).

Gibeah. Not the oft-mentioned city of that name in the portion of Benjamin; it may be the village of Gabaa near Hebron (Daath Mikra).

Timnah. Not the place named in verse 10, but that mentioned in Gen. xxxviii. 12ff., south of Hebron (Daath Mikra).

58. *Halhul.* It still bears that name; about three miles north of Hebron (Daath Mikra).

Beth-zur. Beit Sur, twelve miles south of Jerusalem; prominent in the Maccabean wars (1 Macc. iv. 29, vi. 49f.).

59. *Beth-anoth.* Now Beit Anun, south-west of Jerusalem (Daath Mikra).

60. *Kiriath-jearim.* See on ix. 17.

Rabbah. Of unknown location; not the same as the *Rabbah* of xiii. 25.

61–62 CITIES OF THE WILDERNESS OF JUDAH

61. *Beth-arabah.* See on verse 6.

62. *the City of Salt.* It probably received its name from the salt of the Dead Sea, and has been identified with Kumran to its north-west (Daath Mikra).

En-gedi. lit. 'the spring of the goat,' now Ain Jidi, on the western shore of the Dead Sea. It is a famous desert site in the Desert of Judea, also called Hazezon Tamar (Gen. xiv. 7; 2 Chron. xx. 2). The Emorites dwelt there in Abraham's time (Daath Mikra).

children of Judah at Jerusalem, unto this day.

בְּנֵי־יְהוּדָה בִּירוּשָׁלַם עַד הַיּוֹם הַזֶּה:

16   CHAPTER XVI   טז

1. And the lot for the children of Joseph went out from the Jordan at Jericho, at the waters of Jericho on the east, going up from Jericho through the hill-country to the wilderness, even to Beth-el. 2. And it went out from Beth-el-luz, and passed along unto the border of the Archites to Ataroth. 3. And it went down westward to the border of the Japhletites, unto the border of Beth-horon the nether, even unto Gezer; and the goings out thereof

וַיֵּצֵא הַגּוֹרָל לִבְנֵי יוֹסֵף מִיַּרְדֵּן יְרִיחוֹ לְמֵי יְרִיחוֹ מִזְרָחָה הַמִּדְבָּר עֹלֶה מִירִיחוֹ בָּהָר בֵּית־אֵל: וְיָצָא מִבֵּית־אֵל לוּזָה וְעָבַר אֶל־גְּבוּל הָאַרְכִּי עֲטָרוֹת: וְיָרַד־יָמָּה אֶל־גְּבוּל הַיַּפְלֵטִי עַד גְּבוּל בֵּית־ חוֹרֹן תַּחְתּוֹן וְעַד־גֶּזֶר וְהָיוּ

CHAPTER XVI

1–4 THE TERRITORY OF JOSEPH

1. *the children of Joseph.* viz. Ephraim and the other half of the tribe of Manasseh. The portion of Joseph marked the northernmost limit of Joshua's conquest and was not contiguous with that of Judah, the land between them being allotted to other tribes. Nevertheless the account of Joseph's allotment follows immediately upon Judah's because of the outstanding importance of the tribe of Ephraim in the history of the people.

from the Jordan at Jericho. There the boundary commenced, but Jericho was included in Benjamin's territory (xviii. 21).

the waters of Jericho. A brook, now called Nuemeh, flows in the vicinity (Daath Mikra).

through the hill-country, etc. The boundary as here defined runs from east to west.

2. *from Beth-el-Luz.* Targum and Kimchi render: 'from Beth-el to Luz,' construing the letter *heh* as denoting the locative case. But this raises a difficulty since the two names

were applied to the same city (cf. Gen. xxviii. 19, *he called the name of that place Beth-el, but the name of the city was Luz at the first;* cf. also Judg. i. 23). Kimchi suggests that this was a different Beth-el. Another explanation offered by Hershcovitz is that the inhabitants sometimes distinguished the two parts of the city, naming the residential part *Luz,* and the area in the south-east, where the shrine was situated (now Burj Beithin), *Beth-el* (see Daath Mikra).

the Archites. Apparently a well-known family or clan (cf. *Hushai the Archite,* 2 Sam. xvi. 16). The name may signify a native of the town now called Ain Arik to the west of Beth-el.

Ataroth. There is now a Jewish settlement of that name in the neighbourhood of which are ruins called by the Arabs Khirbet Attra. It is nearly four miles south of Beth-el (Daath Mikra).

3. *the Japhletites.* They are otherwise unknown.

Beth-horon the nether. See on x. 10.

Gezer. See on x. 33.

were at the sea. 4. And the children of Joseph, Manasseh and Ephraim, took their inheritance. 5. And the border of the children of Ephraim according to their families was thus; even the border of their inheritance eastward was Atroth-addar, unto Beth-horon the upper. 6. And the border went out westward, Michmethath being on the north; and the border turned about eastward unto Taanath-shiloh, and passed along it on the east of Janoah. 7. And it went down from Janoah to Ataroth, and to Naarah, and reached unto Jericho, and went out at the Jordan. 8. From Tappuah the border went

4 תְּצְאֹתָיו יָמָּה׃ וַיִּנְחֲלוּ בְנֵי־
5 יוֹסֵף מְנַשֶּׁה וְאֶפְרָיִם׃ וַיְהִי
גְּבוּל בְּנֵי־אֶפְרַיִם לְמִשְׁפְּחֹתָם
וַיְהִי גְּבוּל נַחֲלָתָם מִזְרָחָה
עַטְרוֹת אַדָּר עַד־בֵּית חֹרוֹן
6 עֶלְיוֹן׃ וְיָצָא הַגְּבוּל הַיָּמָּה
הַמִּכְמְתָת מִצָּפוֹן וְנָסַב הַגְּבוּל
מִזְרָחָה תַּאֲנַת שִׁלֹה וְעָבַר
7 אוֹתוֹ מִמִּזְרַח יָנוֹחָה׃ וְיָרַד
מִיָּנוֹחָה עֲטָרוֹת וְנַעֲרָתָה וּפָגַע
8 בִּירִיחוֹ וְיָצָא הַיַּרְדֵּן׃ מִתַּפּוּחַ

v. 8. תרצאתיו ק

at the sea. At Joppa.

4. the children of Joseph. The foregoing defined the boundaries of both Ephraim and half-Manasseh. Each allotment is now described in detail.

5–10 THE INHERITANCE OF EPHRAIM

5. This verse is supplementary to the preceding and adds some details concerning the boundary.

Ephraim. He is given precedence over Manasseh, although the younger, in accordance with Gen. xlviii. 19f. (Keli Yekar).

eastward. i.e. running from east to west (see on verse 1).

Atroth-addar. The same as Ataroth in verse 2 (Daath Mikra).

Beth-horon the upper. See on x. 10.

6. westward. lit. 'seaward'; this corresponds to and the goings out thereof were at the sea in verse 3. From here the northern boundary is defined.

Michmethath. It has been identified with the ruins of Juleijil, south-east of Shechem, or with Mahaneh el-Fuka to its south. In xvii. 7

it is described as before Shechem (Daath Mikra).

on the north. From Michmethath it turned in two directions, south-east and south-west, the latter course being described in verse 8.

Taanath-shiloh. Now Tana, seven miles south-east of Nablus (Daath Mikra).

Janoah. The modern Yanun, south of Taanath-shiloh and about ten miles south-east of Nablus (Daath Mikra).

7. went down. From the hill-country to the Jordan Valley (Daath Mikra).

Ataroth. Not the town mentioned in verses 2 and 5. Some identify it with Tel Sheikh Eziab, south of mount Sart'ba, others with the ruins of Awjah el-Fuka (Daath Mikra).

Naarah. Now Tel Jisr (see Daath Mikra).

Jericho. i.e. the waters of Jericho of verse I (Metsudath David).

8. The verse describes the western half of the northern border.

Tappuah. Not the place named in xii. 17, xv. 34. It was an Ephraimite city in the territory of Manasseh (cf. xvii. 8).

97

along westward to the brook of Kanah; and the goings out thereof were at the sea. This is the inheritance of the tribe of the children of Ephraim according to their families; 9. together with the cities which were separated for the children of Ephraim in the midst of the inheritance of the children of Manasseh, all the cities with their villages. 10. And they drove not out the Canaanites that dwelt in Gezer; but the Canaanites dwelt in the midst of Ephraim, unto this day, and became servants to do taskwork.

יֵלֵךְ הַגְּבוּל יָמָּה נַחַל קָנָה וְהָיוּ תֹצְאֹתָיו הַיָּמָּה זֹאת נַחֲלַת מַטֵּה בְנֵי־אֶפְרַיִם לְמִשְׁפְּחֹתָם: ‏9 וְהֶעָרִים הַמִּבְדָּלוֹת לִבְנֵי אֶפְרַיִם בְּתוֹךְ נַחֲלַת בְּנֵי־מְנַשֶּׁה כָּל־ הֶעָרִים וְחַצְרֵיהֶן: ‏10 וְלֹא הוֹרִישׁוּ אֶת־הַכְּנַעֲנִי הַיּוֹשֵׁב בְּגָזֶר וַיֵּשֶׁב הַכְּנַעֲנִי בְּקֶרֶב אֶפְרַיִם עַד־הַיּוֹם הַזֶּה וַיְהִי לְמַס־עֹבֵד: ‏

17   CHAPTER XVII   יז

1. And this was the lot for the tribe of Manasseh; for he was the first-born of Joseph. As for Machir the first-born of Manasseh, the father of Gilead, because he was a man of war, therefore he had Gilead and Bashan. 2. And the lot was for the

‏1 וַיְהִי הַגּוֹרָל לְמַטֵּה מְנַשֶּׁה כִּי־ הוּא בְּכוֹר יוֹסֵף לְמָכִיר בְּכוֹר מְנַשֶּׁה אֲבִי הַגִּלְעָד כִּי הוּא הָיָה אִישׁ מִלְחָמָה וַיְהִי־לוֹ הַגִּלְעָד וְהַבָּשָׁן: ‏2 וַיְהִי לִבְנֵי

---

the brook of Kanah. The Wadi Kanah, southwest of Nablus, flowing into the Awjah which empties into the Mediterranean north of Joppa (Daath Mikra).

9. *the cities . . . Manasseh.* Cf. xvii. 9.

10. *Gezer.* See on x. 33.

unto this day. When the Book of Joshua was composed. It was finally subjugated by the king of Egypt who gave it to king Solomon as part of his dowry (cf. 1 Kings ix. 16).

servants to do taskwork. Cf. xvii. 13.

CHAPTER XVII

1–6 THE FAMILIES OF MANASSEH

1. *Machir the first-born of Manasseh.* [A comparison with Num. xxvi. 29ff. reveals an apparent discrepancy between that passage and verses 1f. There Machir is the son of Manasseh (cf. also Gen. 1. 23), and Abiezer, etc. are described as *the sons of Gilead.* The explanation is that the phrase *children of Manasseh* signifies, as often in Hebrew, his 'offspring,' not necessarily of the first generation.]

the father of Gilead. lit. 'the father of *the*

rest of the children of Manasseh according to their families; for the children of Abiezer, and for the children of Helek, and for the children of Asriel, and for the children of Shechem, and for the children of Hepher, and for the children of Shemida; these were the male children of Manasseh the son of Joseph according to their families. 3. But Zelophehad, the son of Hepher, the son of Gilead, the son of Machir, the son of Manasseh, had no sons, but daughters; and these are the names of his daughters: Mahlah, and Noah, Hoglah, Milcah, and Tirzah. 4. And they came near before Eleazar the priest, and before Joshua the son of Nun, and before the princes, saying: 'The Lord commanded Moses to give us an inheritance among our brethren'; therefore according to the command-ment of the Lord he gave them an inheritance among the brethren of their father. 5. And there fell ten parts to Manasseh, beside the land

מְנַשֶּׁה הַנּוֹתָרִים֙ לְמִשְׁפְּחֹתָ֔ם
לִבְנֵ֣י אֲבִיעֶ֗זֶר וְלִבְנֵי־חֵ֙לֶק֙
וְלִבְנֵ֣י אַשְׂרִיאֵ֔ל וְלִבְנֵי־שֶׁ֔כֶם
וְלִבְנֵי־חֵ֖פֶר וְלִבְנֵ֥י שְׁמִידָ֑ע
אֵ֗לֶּה בְּנֵ֛י מְנַשֶּׁ֥ה בֶּן־יוֹסֵ֖ף
הַזְּכָרִ֖ים לְמִשְׁפְּחֹתָֽם:

3 וְלִצְלָפְחָד֩ בֶּן־חֵ֨פֶר בֶּן־
גִּלְעָ֜ד בֶּן־מָכִ֣יר בֶּן־מְנַשֶּׁ֗ה
לֹא־הָ֥יוּ ל֛וֹ בָּנִ֖ים כִּ֣י אִם־בָּנ֑וֹת
וְאֵ֙לֶּה֙ שְׁמ֣וֹת בְּנֹתָ֔יו מַחְלָ֣ה
וְנֹעָ֔ה חָגְלָ֥ה מִלְכָּ֖ה וְתִרְצָֽה:

4 וַתִּקְרַ֡בְנָה לִפְנֵי֩ אֶלְעָזָ֨ר הַכֹּהֵ֜ן
וְלִפְנֵ֣י ׀ יְהוֹשֻׁ֣עַ בִּן־נ֗וּן וְלִפְנֵ֣י
הַנְּשִׂיאִים֙ לֵאמֹ֔ר יְהוָ֚ה צִוָּ֣ה
אֶת־מֹשֶׁ֔ה לָֽתֶת־לָ֥נוּ נַחֲלָ֖ה
בְּת֣וֹךְ אַחֵ֑ינוּ וַיִּתֵּ֨ן לָהֶ֜ם אֶל־פִּ֣י
יְהוָ֗ה נַֽחֲלָ֔ה בְּת֖וֹךְ אֲחֵ֥י
5 אֲבִיהֶֽן: וַיִּפְּל֣וּ חַבְלֵֽי־מְנַשֶּׁ֗ה
עֲשָׂרָ֔ה לְבַ֕ד מֵאֶ֖רֶץ הַגִּלְעָ֑ד

Gilead,' but in verse 3, where the son as an individual is named, the definite article is omitted. It is therefore probable that 'the clan of Gilead' is intended, and the rest of the verse should be translated: 'because it was warlike, therefore it had Gilead and Bashan.' This interpretation is borne out by Deut. iii. 14f. where it is related that *Jair the son of Manasseh* captured Bashan, and Gilead was assigned to Machir, i.e. clans and not individuals are to be understood.]

2. *Abiezer.* In Num. xxvi. 30 the form of the name is Iezer.

3. Cf. Num. xxvi. 33, xxvii. 1ff.

4. *the Lord* commanded Moses. Cf. Num. xxvii. 6f.

our brethren. i.e. our father's brothers (Metsu-dath David).

the brethren of our father. i.e. they were to receive their father's share among his brothers (See Rashi, Num. xxvii. 7).

5. *ten parts.* i.e. six for six fathers' houses enumerated above, and four for the daughters of Zelphehad: (1) Their father's share with those who left Egypt; (2) his share with his brothers in the property of Hepher; (3) their father's extra share as a firstborn; (4)

of Gilead and Bashan, which is beyond the Jordan; 6. because the daughters of Manasseh had an inheritance among his sons; and the land of Gilead belonged unto the rest of the sons of Manasseh.

7. And the border of Manasseh was, beginning from Asher, Michmethath, which is before Shechem; and the border went along to the right hand, unto the inhabitants of En-tappuah.—8. The land of Tappuah belonged to Manasseh; but Tappuah on the border of Manasseh belonged to the children of Ephraim. —9. And the border went down unto the brook of Kanah, southward of the brook, by cities which belonged to Ephraim among the cities of Manasseh; but the border of Manasseh was on the north side of the brook; and the goings out thereof were at the sea: 10. southward it was Ephraim's, and northward it was Manasseh's, and the sea was his border; and they reached to Asher on the north, and to Issachar on the east.

וְהַבָּשָׁן אֲשֶׁר מֵעֵבֶר לַיַּרְדֵּן:

6 כִּי בְּנוֹת מְנַשֶּׁה נָחֲלוּ נַחֲלָה בְּתוֹךְ בָּנָיו וְאֶרֶץ הַגִּלְעָד הָיְתָה לִבְנֵי־מְנַשֶּׁה הַנּוֹתָרִים:

7 וַיְהִי גְבוּל־מְנַשֶּׁה מֵאָשֵׁר הַמִּכְמְתָת אֲשֶׁר עַל־פְּנֵי שְׁכֶם וְהָלַךְ הַגְּבוּל אֶל־הַיָּמִין אֶל־

8 יֹשְׁבֵי עֵין תַּפּוּחַ: לִמְנַשֶּׁה הָיְתָה אֶרֶץ תַּפּוּחַ וְתַפּוּחַ אֶל־ גְּבוּל מְנַשֶּׁה לִבְנֵי אֶפְרָיִם:

9 וְיָרַד הַגְּבוּל נַחַל קָנָה נֶגְבָּה לַנַּחַל עָרִים הָאֵלֶּה לְאֶפְרַיִם בְּתוֹךְ עָרֵי מְנַשֶּׁה וּגְבוּל מְנַשֶּׁה מִצְּפוֹן לַנַּחַל וַיְהִי תֹצְאֹתָיו

10 הַיָּמָּה: נֶגְבָּה לְאֶפְרַיִם וְצָפוֹנָה לִמְנַשֶּׁה וַיְהִי הַיָּם גְּבוּלוֹ וּבְאָשֵׁר יִפְגְּעוּן מִצָּפוֹן וּבְיִשָּׂשכָר מִמִּזְרָח:

the share of their father's brother, who died childless (Rashi).

6. *the rest of the sons of Manasseh.* Presumably Peresh and Sheresh, named in 1 Chron. vii. 16 as the sons of Maachah the wife of Machir (Daath Mikra).

7–13 THE BOUNDARIES OF MANASSEH'S TERRITORY

7. *the border.* The south-west frontier (Metsudath David).

from Asher. i.e. beginning at the end of Asher's boundary in the north-west. Some authorities, however, hold that Asher here is not the tribe (cf. verse 10), but a city east of Shechem belonging to Manasseh (D.M.).

Michmethath. In the south-east (see on xvi. 6).

The two extremities of the boundary are accordingly defined.

the right hand. i.e. southward (Metsudath David).

En-tappuah. The well of Yasuph, a village south of Shechem (Daath Mikra).

8. *the land of Tappuah.* The district adjacent to the village (Rashi).

9. *the brook of Kanah.* See on xvi. 8.

cities which belonged to Ephraim. Cf. xvi. 9.

10. *to Asher on the north,* etc. This was the northern boundary. Its exact course and the towns which marked it are not specified, being described in detail in the boundaries of Issachar and Asher (xix. 17ff.).

11. And Manasseh had in Issachar
and in Asher Beth-shean and its
towns, and Ibleam and its towns,
and the inhabitants of Dor and its
towns, and the inhabitants of En-dor
and its towns, and the inhabitants of
Taanach and its towns, and the
inhabitants of Megiddo and its
towns, even the three regions.
12. Yet the children of Manasseh
could not drive out the inhabitants
of those cities; but the Canaanites
were resolved to dwell in that land.
13. And it came to pass, when the
children of Israel were waxen strong,
that they put the Canaanites to
taskwork, but did not utterly drive
them out.
14. And the children of Joseph
spoke unto Joshua, saying: 'Why

11 וַיְהִי לִמְנַשֶּׁה בְּיִשָּׂשכָר וּבְאָשֵׁר
בֵּית־שְׁאָן וּבְנוֹתֶיהָ וְיִבְלְעָם
וּבְנוֹתֶיהָ וְאֶת־יֹשְׁבֵי דֹאר
וּבְנוֹתֶיהָ וְיֹשְׁבֵי עֵין־דֹּר
וּבְנוֹתֶיהָ וְיֹשְׁבֵי תַעְנַךְ וּבְנוֹתֶיהָ
וְיֹשְׁבֵי מְגִדּוֹ וּבְנוֹתֶיהָ שְׁלֹשֶׁת
12 הַנָּפֶת: וְלֹא יָכְלוּ בְּנֵי מְנַשֶּׁה
לְהוֹרִישׁ אֶת־הֶעָרִים הָאֵלֶּה
וַיּוֹאֶל הַכְּנַעֲנִי לָשֶׁבֶת בָּאָרֶץ
13 הַזֹּאת: וַיְהִי כִּי חָזְקוּ בְּנֵי
יִשְׂרָאֵל וַיִּתְּנוּ אֶת־הַכְּנַעֲנִי
לָמַס וְהוֹרֵשׁ לֹא הוֹרִישׁוֹ:
14 וַיְדַבְּרוּ בְּנֵי יוֹסֵף אֶת־יְהוֹשֻׁעַ

v. 13. פתח באתנח   v. 14. נ״א אל

11. *Beth-shean.* lit. 'house of rest'; the name
probably indicates that it was a halting place
for caravans. It was an important Canaanite
city close to the modern Beisan in the Jordan
Valley, about twelve miles south of the Sea of
Galilee and four miles west of the Jordan.
The Philistines fastened the dead body of
Saul to its walls (1 Sam. xxxi. 10). In later
times it was named Scythopolis by the suc-
cessors of Alexander the Great. It was famed
for the sweetness of its fruits. 'R. Simeon b.
Lakish said, If the Garden of Eden is in the
Land of Israel, Beth-shean is the entrance
thereto' (Erub. 19a).

its towns. lit. 'its daughters,' i.e. the satellite
towns (Targum).

Ibleam. Now called Bel'ame, north of Nablus.
Here Ahaziah was mortally wounded when
fleeing from Jehu (2 Kings ix. 27).

the inhabitants of Dor, etc. The *inhabitants* are
mentioned because they remained in possession, as the next verse states.

Dor. Identical with the Dor in xi. 2 in the territory of Asher, though the Hebrew spelling
differs. The two cities mentioned here were in
the territory of Issachar (Rashi).

En-dor. South of mount Tabor, now En-dur.
It was here that Saul inquired of the spirit of
Samuel raised by the witch (1 Sam. xxviii.
7ff.).

Taanach . . . Megiddo. See on xii. 21.

the three regions. Or, 'the triple region,' viz. of
En-dor, Taanach and Megiddo with their
environs which have common boundaries.
See also on xi. 2 (Daath Mikra).

12f. Repeated in Judg. i. 27f.

13. *to taskwork.* Cf. xvi. 10.

14–18 DEMAND OF THE CHILDREN OF JOSEPH

14. *the children of Joseph.* The representatives
of the tribe of Manasseh (Rashi, Kimchi).

hast thou given me but one lot and one part for an inheritance, seeing I am a great people, forasmuch as the Lᴏʀᴅ hath blessed me thus?' 15. And Joshua said unto them: 'If thou be a great people, get thee up to the forest, and cut down for thyself there in the land of the Perizzites and of the Rephaim; since the hill-country of Ephraim is too narrow for thee.' 16. And the children of Joseph said: 'The hill-country will not be enough for us; and all the Canaanites that dwell in the land of the valley have chariots of iron, both they who are in Beth-shean and its towns, and they who are in the valley of Jezreel.' 17. And Joshua spoke unto the house of Joseph, even to Ephraim and to Manasseh, saying: 'Thou art a great people, and hast great power; thou

לֵאמֹר מַדּוּעַ נָתַתָּה לִּי נַחֲלָה
גּוֹרָל אֶחָד וְחֶבֶל אֶחָד וַאֲנִי
עַם־רָב עַד אֲשֶׁר־עַד־כֹּה
15 בֵּרְכַנִי יְהוָה: וַיֹּאמֶר אֲלֵהֶם
יְהוֹשֻׁעַ אִם־עַם־רַב אַתָּה
עֲלֵה לְךָ הַיַּעְרָה וּבֵרֵאתָ לְךָ
שָׁם בְּאֶרֶץ הַפְּרִזִּי וְהָרְפָאִים
כִּי־אָץ לְךָ הַר־אֶפְרָיִם:
16 וַיֹּאמְרוּ בְּנֵי יוֹסֵף לֹא־יִמָּצֵא
לָנוּ הָהָר וְרֶכֶב בַּרְזֶל בְּכָל־
הַכְּנַעֲנִי הַיֹּשֵׁב בְּאֶרֶץ־
הָעֵמֶק לַאֲשֶׁר בְּבֵית־שְׁאָן
וּבְנוֹתֶיהָ וְלַאֲשֶׁר בְּעֵמֶק
17 יִזְרְעֶאל: וַיֹּאמֶר יְהוֹשֻׁעַ אֶל־
בֵּית יוֹסֵף לְאֶפְרַיִם וְלִמְנַשֶּׁה
לֵאמֹר עַם־רַב אַתָּה וְכֹחַ

v. 14. קמץ בז"ק

---

one lot. In xvi. 1 *the lot* is singular.

and one part. i.e. one lot which consists of only one part. Though divided into two for Ephraim and Manasseh, the portion was really only one and insufficient (Metsudath David).

a great people. At the second census of the Israelites in the plains of Moab, shortly before they crossed into Canaan, the numbers of Ephraim and Manasseh were 32,500 and 52,700 respectively (Num. xxvi. 37, 34).

forasmuch as the Lord hath blessed me thus? In the first census, Manasseh numbered 32,200, whereas in the second census they numbered 52,700 (Rashi). Only the tribe of Manasseh had grounds for such a complaint because of their sharp increase. The tribe of Ephraim, however, experienced a decrease from 40,500 to 32,500.

the forest. Which then covered a considerable portion of the north-west of the mountain of Ephraim (cf. 1 Sam. xiv. 25; 2 Sam. xviii. 6).

the Perizzites . . . the Rephaim. See on iii. 10, xii. 4.

the hill-country of Ephraim. The mountain district which stretches from the Valley of Jezreel to the hill-country of Judah. The name is given here in anticipation.

16. *the Canaanites.* A generic term, including the Perizzites and the Rephaim just mentioned.

chariots of iron. Cf. xi. 4; war-chariots plated with iron.

17. *thou art a great people.* Joshua admits the justice of their original plea and gives them

shalt not have one lot only; 18. but the hill-country shall be thine; for though it is a forest, thou shalt cut it down, and the goings out thereof shall be thine; for thou shalt drive out the Canaanites, though they have chariots of iron, and though they be strong.'

גָּדוֹל לָךְ לֹא־יִהְיֶה לְךָ גּוֹרָל
18 אֶחָד : כִּי הַר יִהְיֶה־לָּךְ כִּי־
יַעַר הוּא וּבֵרֵאתוֹ וְהָיָה לְךָ
תֹּצְאֹתָיו כִּי־תוֹרִישׁ אֶת־
הַכְּנַעֲנִי כִּי רֶכֶב בַּרְזֶל לוֹ כִּי
חָזָק הוּא :

18   CHAPTER XVIII   יח

1. And the whole congregation of the children of Israel assembled themselves together at Shiloh, and set up the tent of meeting there; and the land was subdued before them.

1 וַיִּקָּהֲלוּ כָּל־־עֲדַת בְּנֵי־
יִשְׂרָאֵל שִׁלֹה וַיַּשְׁכִּינוּ שָׁם אֶת־
אֹהֶל מוֹעֵד וְהָאָרֶץ נִכְבָּשָׁה

assurance of their ultimate triumph over the mighty inhabitants.

18. *the goings out thereof.* i.e. to its furthest extent (Metsudath David). Kimchi explains the dialogue between Joshua and the children of Joseph in the following manner. The mountain belonged to Ephraim, while the valley belonged to Manasseh. Joshua advised the tribe of Manasseh to occupy Mt. Ephraim by clearing the forests and driving out the Perizzites and the Rephaim therefrom. The Ephraimites would surely agree to this plan. Upon this, the tribe of Manasseh rejoined, "The hill-country will not be enough for us; and all the Canaanites that dwell in the valley have chariots of iron . . ." Therefore, the valley that we need is impregnable. Thereupon, Joshua requested the children of Ephraim to join the children of Manasseh in their battle against the Canaanites.

CHAPTER XVIII

1 ERECTION OF THE TABERNACLE AT SHILOH

1. *Shiloh.* Now Seilun, twelve mile south of

Shechem and north of Beth-el (cf. Judg. xxi 19) (Daath Mikra).

and set up the tent of the meeting there. i.e. the tent of meeting that they had constructed in the wilderness. There was no ceiling, but a stone structure below, and curtains above. Thus we learned in Tract. Zeb. (118a) (Rashi). Shiloh is referred to as "the house of the Lord," and also as "the tent," and "the tent of Joseph." Hence, the Rabbis deduce that it was a combination of a house and a tent (Kimchi). The erection of this structure had been prophesied by Moses, who referred to it as *menuchah,* rest (Deut. xii. 9), as opposed to Jerusalem, to which he referred as *nachalah,* inheritance. Shiloh's halachic status was similar to that of Jerusalem insofar as high places were taboo during the existence of both sanctuaries. The tent of meeting remained there for 369 years, until the Philistines captured the ark of the covenant during the High Priesthood of Eli (1 Sam. iv. 11), from which time dates the destruction of Shiloh (cf. Jer. vii. 12; Ps. lxxviii. 60).

the tent of meeting. Where the Israelites could meet and commune with God (cf. Exod. xxix. 43).

subdued. But not completely (Elijah of Wilna).

2. And there remained among the children of Israel seven tribes, which had not yet received their inheritance. 3. And Joshua said unto the children of Israel: 'How long are ye slack to go in to possess the land, which the LORD, the God of your fathers, hath given you? 4. Appoint for you three men for each tribe; and I will send them, and they shall arise, and walk through the land, and describe it according to their inheritance; and they shall come unto me. 5. And they shall divide it into seven portions: Judah shall abide in his border on the south, and the house of Joseph shall abide in

² לִפְנֵיהֶם: וַיִּוָּתְרוּ בִּבְנֵי
יִשְׂרָאֵל אֲשֶׁר לֹא־חָלְקוּ
אֶת־נַחֲלָתָם שִׁבְעָה
³ שְׁבָטִים: וַיֹּאמֶר יְהוֹשֻׁעַ אֶל־
בְּנֵי יִשְׂרָאֵל עַד־אָנָה אַתֶּם
מִתְרַפִּים לָבוֹא לָרֶשֶׁת אֶת־
הָאָרֶץ אֲשֶׁר נָתַן לָכֶם יְהוָה
⁴ אֱלֹהֵי אֲבוֹתֵיכֶם: הָבוּ לָכֶם
שְׁלֹשָׁה אֲנָשִׁים לַשָּׁבֶט
וְאֶשְׁלָחֵם וְיָקֻמוּ וְיִתְהַלְּכוּ
בָאָרֶץ וְיִכְתְּבוּ אוֹתָהּ לְפִי
⁵ נַחֲלָתָם וְיָבֹאוּ אֵלָי: וְהִתְחַלְּקוּ
אֹתָהּ לְשִׁבְעָה חֲלָקִים יְהוּדָה
יַעֲמֹד עַל־גְּבוּלוֹ מִנֶּגֶב וּבֵית

2–10 A COMMISSION APPOINTED TO DIVIDE THE REST OF THE LAND

2. The literal translation of the verse is: 'And there remained among the children of Israel, whose inheritance they had not divided, seven tribes.'

3. *slack to go in to possess the land.* He should have said, "Why are ye slack to divide the land?" The intention was, however, that the Israelites realized that, as soon as they received their territory, they would have to wage war to possess it. They neglected to do so in order that the entire nation would wage war for the entire land, rather than each tribe for its inheritance. Their hesitancy to divide the land was, therefore, in effect, hesitancy to possess it (Abarbanel).

which the LORD ... *hath given you.* In these words Joshua reminded them of the Divine purposes behind the conquest and also of their obligation to take possession of the land. To those who were weary and perhaps disheartened by the slowness and incompleteness of the campaign these were words of encouragement. To those who were satisfied, now that they had their own territory, and perhaps to some of the landless who thought they could settle in the land of their more fortunate brethren or infiltrate into the unconquered portions, these were words of admonition and reproof. See Daath Mikra.

4. *three men for each tribe.* Of the remaining seven tribes (Rashi). Their purpose was to make a survey of the land still to be conquered.

describe. lit. 'write'; the area concerned was to be recorded in detail, upon which the allotment was to be made.

5. *divide it.* viz. the land both conquered and unconquered (Rashi).

the house of Joseph. Ephraim and the half-tribe of Manasseh.

their border on the north. 6. And
ye shall describe the land into seven
portions, and bring the description
hither to me; and I will cast lots for
you here before the LORD our God.
7. For the Levites have no portion
among you, for the priesthood of the
LORD is their inheritance; and Gad
and Reuben and the half-tribe of
Manasseh have received their inheritance beyond the Jordan eastward, which Moses the servant of the
LORD gave them.'

8. And the men arose, and went;
and Joshua charged them that went
to describe the land, saying: 'Go and
walk through the land, and describe
it, and come back to me, and I will
cast lots for you here before the
LORD in Shiloh.' 9. And the men
went and passed through the land,
and described it by cities into seven
portions in a book, and they came to
Joshua unto the camp at Shiloh.
10. And Joshua cast lots for them in
Shiloh before the LORD; and there

יוֹסֵף יַעַמְדוּ עַל־גְּבוּלָם
6 מִצָּפֽוֹן: וְאַתֶּם תִּכְתְּבוּ אֶת־
הָאָרֶץ שִׁבְעָה חֲלָקִים
וַהֲבֵאתֶם אֵלַי הֵנָּה וְיָרִיתִי
לָכֶם גּוֹרָל פֹּה לִפְנֵי יְהֹוָה
7 אֱלֹהֵינוּ: כִּי אֵין־חֵלֶק לַלְוִיִּם
בְּקִרְבְּכֶם כִּי־כְהֻנַּת יְהֹוָה
נַחֲלָתוֹ וְגָד וּרְאוּבֵן וַחֲצִי שֵׁבֶט
הַמְנַשֶּׁה לָקְחוּ נַחֲלָתָם מֵעֵבֶר
לַיַּרְדֵּן מִזְרָחָה אֲשֶׁר נָתַן לָהֶם
מֹשֶׁה עֶבֶד יְהֹוָה:
8 וַיָּקֻמוּ הָאֲנָשִׁים וַיֵּלֵכוּ וַיְצַו
יְהוֹשֻׁעַ אֶת־הַהֹלְכִים לִכְתֹּב
אֶת־הָאָרֶץ לֵאמֹר לְכוּ
וְהִתְהַלְּכוּ בָאָרֶץ וְכִתְבוּ
אוֹתָהּ וְשׁוּבוּ אֵלַי וּפֹה אַשְׁלִיךְ
לָכֶם גּוֹרָל לִפְנֵי יְהֹוָה בְּשִׁלֹה:
9 וַיֵּלְכוּ הָאֲנָשִׁים וַיַּעַבְרוּ בָאָרֶץ
וַיִּכְתְּבוּהָ לֶעָרִים לְשִׁבְעָה
חֲלָקִים עַל־סֵפֶר וַיָּבֹאוּ אֶל־
יְהוֹשֻׁעַ אֶל־הַמַּחֲנֶה שִׁלֹה:
10 וַיַּשְׁלֵךְ לָהֶם יְהוֹשֻׁעַ גּוֹרָל
בְּשִׁלֹה לִפְנֵי יְהֹוָה וַיְחַלֶּק־

6. *before the* LORD *our God*. i.e. before the
tent of meeting.
7. *For the Levites have no portion*. Therefore,
there were only seven remaining tribes.
Otherwise, there would have been eight
(Metsudath David).

the priesthood . . . inheritance. This passage is
parallel to Deut. xviii. 1: They shall eat the
offerings of the Lord made by fire, and His
inheritance (Kimchi). Another parallel passage is found in Num. xviii. 20: I am thy
share and thy inheritance. Onkelos para-

Joshua divided the land unto the children of Israel according to their divisions.

11. And the lot of the tribe of the children of Benjamin came up according to their families; and the border of their lot went out between the children of Judah and the children of Joseph. 12. And their border on the north side was from the Jordan; and the border went up to the side of Jericho on the north, and went up through the hill-country westward; and the goings out thereof were at the wilderness of Beth-aven. 13. And the border passed along from thence to Luz, to the side of Luz—the same is Beth-el —southward; and the border went down to Atroth-addar, by the mountain that lieth on the south of Beth-ḥoron the nether. 14. And the border was drawn and turned about on the west side southward, from the mountain that lieth before Beth-horon southward; and the goings out thereof were at Kiriath-baal—the same is Kiriath-jearim—

שָׁם יְהוֹשֻׁעַ אֶת־הָאָרֶץ לִבְנֵי
יִשְׂרָאֵל כְּמַחְלְקֹתָם:

11 וַיַּעַל גּוֹרַל מַטֵּה בְנֵי־בִנְיָמִן
לְמִשְׁפְּחֹתָם וַיֵּצֵא גְּבוּל גּוֹרָלָם
בֵּין בְּנֵי יְהוּדָה וּבֵין בְּנֵי יוֹסֵף:

12 וַיְהִי לָהֶם הַגְּבוּל לִפְאַת
צָפוֹנָה מִן־הַיַּרְדֵּן וְעָלָה
הַגְּבוּל אֶל־כֶּתֶף יְרִיחוֹ
מִצָּפוֹן וְעָלָה בָהָר יָמָּה וְהָיָה
תֹצְאֹתָיו מִדְבַּרָה בֵּית אָוֶן:

13 וְעָבַר מִשָּׁם הַגְּבוּל לוּזָה אֶל־
כֶּתֶף לוּזָה נֶגְבָּה הִיא בֵּית
אֵל וְיָרַד הַגְּבוּל עַטְרוֹת אַדָּר
עַל־הָהָר אֲשֶׁר מִנֶּגֶב לְבֵית־

14 חֹרוֹן תַּחְתּוֹן: וְתָאַר הַגְּבוּל
וְנָסַב לִפְאַת־יָם נֶגְבָּה מִן־
הָהָר אֲשֶׁר עַל־פְּנֵי בֵית־
חֹרוֹן נֶגְבָּה וְהָיָה תֹצְאֹתָיו אֶל־
קִרְיַת־בַּעַל הִיא קִרְיַת

v. 12. והיו ק׳   v. 14. והיו ק׳   v. 14. למדבחאי על

phrases: The gifts that I have given thee thy share and thy inheritance. Jonathan paraphrases our verse with the identical words: The gifts that the Lord gave them are their inheritance.

11–20 THE INHERITANCE OF BENJAMIN

Of Benjamin's portion Josephus remarked, 'This lot was the narrowest of all, by reason of the goodness of the land, for it included Jericho and the city of Jerusalem' (*Antiquities* V. i. 22).

12. *to the side of Jericho.* Including the city (cf. verse 21).

Beth-aven. See on vii. 2.

13. *Luz.* See on xvi. 2.

went down. Bethel is three thousand feet above sea level.

Atroth-addar. See on xvi. 5.

by the mountain. i.e. from Ataroth-addar it continued to the mountain.

Beth-horon the nether. Beth-horon did not come within Benjamin's territory (cf. xvi. 5). It belonged to Ephraim.

a city of the children of Judah; this was the west side. 15. And the south side was from the uttermost part of Kiriath-jearim, and the border went out westward, and went out to the fountain of the waters of Nephtoah. 16. And the border went down to the uttermost part of the mountain that lieth before the Valley of the son of Hinnom, which is in the vale of Rephaim northward; and it went down to the Valley of Hinnom, to the side of the Jebusite southward, and went down to En-rogel. 17. And it was drawn on the north, and went out at En-shemesh, and went out to Geliloth, which is over against the ascent of Adummim; and it went down to the Stone of Bohan the son of Reuben. 18. And it passed along to the side over against the Arabah northward, and went down unto the Arabah. 19. And the border passed along to the side of Beth-hoglah northward; and the goings out of the border were at the north bay of the Salt Sea, at the south end of the Jordan; this was

יְעָרִים עִיר בְּנֵי יְהוּדָה זְאת
15 פְּאַת־יָם: וּפְאַת־נֶגְבָּה
מִקְצֵה קִרְיַת יְעָרִים וְיָצָא
הַגְּבוּל יָמָה וְיָצָא אֶל־מַעְיַן
16 מֵי נֶפְתּוֹחַ: וְיָרַד הַגְּבוּל אֶל־
קְצֵה הָהָר אֲשֶׁר עַל־פְּנֵי
גֵּי בֶן־הִנֹּם אֲשֶׁר בְּעֵמֶק
רְפָאִים צָפוֹנָה וְיָרַד גֵּי הִנֹּם
אֶל־כֶּתֶף הַיְבוּסִי נֶגְבָּה וְיָרַד
17 עֵין רֹגֵל: וְתָאַר מִצָּפוֹן וְיָצָא
עֵין שֶׁמֶשׁ וְיָצָא אֶל־גְּלִילוֹת
אֲשֶׁר־נֹכַח מַעֲלֵה אֲדֻמִּים
וְיָרַד אֶבֶן בֹּהַן בֶּן־רְאוּבֵן:
18 וְעָבַר אֶל־כֶּתֶף מוּל־
הָעֲרָבָה צָפוֹנָה וְיָרַד
19 הָעֲרָבָתָה: וְעָבַר הַגְּבוּל
אֶל־כֶּתֶף בֵּית־חָגְלָה צָפוֹנָה
וְהָיָה | תֹּצְאוֹתָיו הַגְּבוּל אֶל־
לְשׁוֹן יָם־הַמֶּלַח צָפוֹנָה אֶל־
קְצֵה הַיַּרְדֵּן נֶגְבָּה זֶה גְּבוּל

v. 19. וְהָיוּ ק׳ v. 19. תֹּצְאוֹת ק׳

14. *Kiriath-jearim.* See on ix. 17.

a city of the children of Judah. Though a boundary of Benjamin, the city belonged to Judah (xv. 60).

15. *the waters of Nephtoah.* See on xv. 9.

16. *the Valley of the son of Hinnom.* See on xv. 8.

the vale of Rephaim. See on xv. 8.

En-rogel. See on xv. 7.

17. *En-shemesh.* See on xv. 7, where are also

notes on *Geliloth (Gilgal)* and *ascent of Adummim.*

the Stone of Bohan. See on xv. 6.

18. *unto the Arabah.* To the city of Beth-arabah (cf. xv. 6, 61) in the territory of Judah.

19. *Beth-hoglah.* See on xv. 6.

bay. See on xv. 2.

the south end of the Jordan. Where it flows into the Dead Sea.

the south border. 20. And the
Jordan was to be the border of it
on the east side. This was the
inheritance of the children of Benjamin, by the borders thereof round
about, according to their families.

21. Now the cities of the tribe of
the children of Benjamin according
to their families were Jericho, and
Beth-hoglah, and Emek-keziz; 22.
and Beth-arabah, and Zemaraim,
and Beth-el; 23. and Avvim, and
Parah, and Ophrah; 24. and
Chephar-ammonah, and Ophni, and
Geba; twelve cities with their
villages: 25. Gibeon, and Ramah,
and Beeroth; 26. and Mizpeh, and
Chephirah, and Mozah; 27. and
Rekem, and Irpeel, and Taralah;

נֶגֶב: וְהַיַּרְדֵּן יִגְבּוֹל--אֹתוֹ 20
לִפְאַת--קֵדְמָה זֹאת נַחֲלַת בְּנֵי
בִנְיָמֵן לִגְבוּלֹתֶיהָ סָבִיב
לְמִשְׁפְּחֹתָם:
וְהָיוּ הֶעָרִים לְמַטֵּה בְנֵי בִנְיָמֵן 21
לְמִשְׁפְּחוֹתֵיהֶם יְרִיחוֹ וּבֵית--
חָגְלָה וְעֵמֶק קְצִיץ: וּבֵית 22
הָעֲרָבָה וּצְמָרַיִם וּבֵית--
אֵל: וְהָעַוִּים וְהַפָּרָה וְעָפְרָה: 23
וּכְפַר הָעַמֹּנָי וְהָעָפְנִי וָגָבַע 24
עָרִים שְׁתֵּים--עֶשְׂרֵה
וְחַצְרֵיהֶן: גִּבְעוֹן וְהָרָמָה 25
וּבְאֵרוֹת: וְהַמִּצְפֶּה וְהַכְּפִירָה 26
וְהַמֹּצָה: וְרֶקֶם וְיִרְפְּאֵל 27

v. 24. העמונה ק

---

20. *of it.* Of the tribe of Benjamin (Rashi).

21–28 THE CITIES OF BENJAMIN

Having delineated the boundaries of Benjamin, the writer now lists its cities. They fall
into two groups: twelve cities in the east and
fourteen in the west.

21. *Beth-hoglah.* See on xv. 6.

22. *Zemaraim.* Perhaps es-Samra, north of
Jericho; not the same as *mount Zemaraim,
which is in the hill-country of Ephraim* (2 Chron.
xiii. 4).

23. *Avvim.* [This may be another name for
Ai.]

Parah. Tel Farah, south-east of Jerusalem,
near En Farah (Daath Mikra).

Ophrah. Also called Ephrain (2 Chron. xiii.
19), identified with et-Tayyibeh, a village
four miles north-east of Beth-el (Daath Mikra).

24. *Chephar-ammonah.* [Possibly the modern
village of Kefr Ana, three miles north of
Beth-el.]

Geba. Now Jeba, north-east of Jerusalem, a
Levitical city (xxi. 17).

25. *Gibeon.* Cf. ix. 17.

Ramah. Now er-Ram, five miles north of
Jerusalem (Daath Mikra).

Beeroth. See on ix. 17.

26. *Mizpeh.* Its remains may be Tel En-
nazbah, north of Ramah and near Ataroth;
but others identify it with Nabi Samwil, five
miles north-west of Jerusalem (Daath
Mikra).

Chephirah. See on ix. 17.

Mozah. In the Mishnah (Suk. iv. 5) it is called
Moza, which has been identified with Kefr
Kulanyah, north of Jerusalem. The ancient
name has been revived in a Jewish settlement
near the old site (Daath Mikra).

27. *Irpeel.* Some identify it with Rafat,
north of ej-Jib (Daath Mikra).

28. and Zela, Eleph, and the Jebusite—the same is Jerusalem, Gibeath, and Kiriath; fourteen cities with their villages. This is the inheritance of the children of Benjamin according to their families.

28 וְתַרְאֲלָה וְצֵלַע הָאֶלֶף וְהַיְבוּסִי הִיא יְרוּשָׁלַםִ גִּבְעַת קִרְיַת עָרִים אַרְבַּע־עֶשְׂרֵה וְחַצְרֵיהֶן זֹאת נַחֲלַת בְּנֵי־ בִנְיָמִן לְמִשְׁפְּחֹתָם׃

19   CHAPTER XIX   יט

1. And the second lot came out for Simeon, even for the tribe of the children of Simeon according to their families; and their inheritance was in the midst of the inheritance of the children of Judah. 2. And

1 וַיֵּצֵא הַגּוֹרָל הַשֵּׁנִי לְשִׁמְעוֹן לְמַטֵּה בְנֵי־שִׁמְעוֹן לְמִשְׁפְּחוֹתָם וַיְהִי נַחֲלָתָם בְּתוֹךְ נַחֲלַת בְּנֵי־יְהוּדָה׃

28. *Zela.* It is mentioned in 2 Sam. xxi. 14 as the burial-place of Saul and Jonathan. It may be Beit Jala, south of the plain of Rephaim. The Rabbis located it in the outskirts of Jerusalem (Num. Rabbah viii. 4).

Eleph. Unknown. It has been suggested that Zela ha-Eleph (the Hebrew has the definite article) is one name, which is shortened in 2 Sam. xxi. 14 to Zela (Elijah of Wilna).

the Jebusite. i.e. Jerusalem (cf. xv. 8).

Gibeath. More fully *Gibeath-benjamin* (1 Sam. xiii. 2), and *Gibeath-shaul* (1 Sam. xi. 4), now Tel el-Ful, north of Jerusalem (Daath Mikra).

Kiriath. This is doubtless Kiriath-jearim which is spelt *Kiriath-arim* in Ezra ii. 25. The second half, *arim,* corresponds with the word for *cities* in this verse which immediately follows *Kiriath.* It is therefore probable that the word must be understood twice and *Kiriath* taken as an abbreviated form of Kiriath-arim. Hershcovitz, quoting Prof. S. Klein, makes the following comment: *Kiriath* has the construct form, 'the city of,' and may be a shortened form for 'the city of . . . (an unnamed place)' as *Gibeath* (also in the construct state) stands for Gibeath-benjamin. This interpretation provides the requisite

fourteen cities. It is possible, however, that only one city is intended, and the meaning of the whole phrase is 'the hill of Kiriath-arim.' The *hill* of the place is emphasized because the city itself belonged to Judah. If this view is adopted, *arim* in the text must be read with both halves of the verse: 'and the hill of Kiriath-arim, cities fourteen.' This interpretation yields only twelve cities, and it would then have to be assumed that two have been ommitted. See Daath Mikra.

CHAPTER XIX

1–9 THE INHERITANCE OF SIMEON

1. *the second lot.* Of the seven tribes.

in the midst of . . . Judah. The reason is given in verse 9 (see also on xiv. 4). Nevertheless, the portion assigned to Simeon within the land of Judah was exactly defined, as the following verses show. In the course of time, the tribe merged with Judah and lost its separate identity; consequently when the country split into two kingdoms, the southern was known as the kingdom of the two tribes, viz. Judah and Benjamin, not three.

they had for their inheritance Beer-sheba with Sheba, and Moladah; 3. and Hazar-shual, and Balah, and Ezem; 4. and Eltolad, and Bethul, and Hormah; 5. and Ziklag, and Beth-marcaboth, and Hazar-susah; 6. and Beth-lebaoth, and Sharuhen; thirteen cities with their villages: 7. Ain, Rimmon, and Ether, and Ashan; four cities with their villages; 8. and all the villages that were round about these cities to Baalath-beer, as far as Ramah of the South. This is the inheritance of the tribe of the children of Simeon according

2 וַיְהִי לָהֶם בְּנַחֲלָתָם בְּאֵר־
3 שֶׁבַע וְשֶׁבַע וּמוֹלָדָה: וַחֲצַר
4 שׁוּעָל וּבָלָה וָעָצֶם: וְאֶלְתּוֹלַד
5 וּבְתוּל וְחָרְמָה: וְצִקְלַג
וּבֵית־הַמַּרְכָּבֹת וַחֲצַר
6 סוּסָה: וּבֵית לְבָאוֹת וְשָׁרוּחֶן
עָרִים שְׁלֹשׁ־עֶשְׂרֵה
7 וְחַצְרֵיהֶן: עַיִן רִמּוֹן וָעֶתֶר
וְעָשָׁן עָרִים אַרְבַּע וְחַצְרֵיהֶן:
8 וְכָל־הַחֲצֵרִים אֲשֶׁר סְבִיבוֹת
הֶעָרִים הָאֵלֶּה עַד־בַּעֲלַת
בְּאֵר רָאמַת נֶגֶב זֹאת
נַחֲלַת מַטֵּה בְנֵי־שִׁמְעוֹן

v. 8. בא' נתה כצ"ל

2. *Beer-sheba.* See on xv. 28.

with Sheba. The Hebrew is literally 'and Sheba.' Kimchi comments that both are counted as one city. Otherwise, the total would be fourteen instead of thirteen (verse 6). Perhaps one city was within the limits of the other, or the text is to be understood as 'the well of Sheba and the city of Sheba' (Daath Mikra). Malbim counts them as two cities, considering Beth-lebaoth and Sharuhen as one.

Moladah. See on xv. 26.

3. *Hazar-shual.* See on xv. 28.

4. *Eltolad, and Bethul.* See on xv. 30.

Hormah. See on xii. 14.

5. *Ziklag.* See on xv. 31.

Beth-marcaboth. The name signifies 'the house of chariots,' and *Hazar-susah* (*Hazar-susim* in 1 Chron. iv. 31) 'the village of horses.' They may be identical with Madmannah and Sansannah in xv. 31. The names indicate that 'they were stations of passage, and like those which are now to be seen on the great line of Indian transit between Cairo and Suez . . . depots and stations for the "horses" and "chariots" such as those which in Solomon's time went to and fro between Palestine and Egypt' (Stanley).

6. *Beth-lebaoth.* Called *Lebaoth* in xv. 32.

Sharuhen. Doubtless the same as Shilhim in xv. 32. Sharuhen was apparently the Egyptian name of the town. Ancient Egyptian records indicate that this city served as an Egyptian military base in the Negeb during the Israelites' bondage in Egypt (Daath Mikra).

7. *Ain, Rimmon.* See on xv. 32.

Ether, and Ashan. See on xv. 42.

8. *Baalath-beer.* In the Negeb, called *Baal* in 1 Chron. iv. 33.

Ramah of the South. To distinguish it from the other towns of that name (Ramah) elsewhere, e.g. *Ramoth in Gilead* (xx. 8). It is probably identical with *Ramoth of the South* (1 Sam. xxx. 27).

to their families. 9. Out of the allotment of the children of Judah was the inheritance of the children of Simeon, for the portion of the children of Judah was too much for them; therefore the children of Simeon had inheritance in the midst of their inheritance.

10. And the third lot came up for the children of Zebulun according to their families; and the border of their inheritance was unto Sarid. 11. And their border went up westward, even to Maralah, and reached to Dabbesheth; and it reached to the brook that is before Jokneam. 12. And it turned from Sarid eastward toward the sunrising unto the border of Chisloth-tabor; and it went out to Dobrath, and went up

9 לְמִשְׁפְּחֹתָם: מֵחֶבֶל בְּנֵי
יְהוּדָה נַחֲלַת בְּנֵי שִׁמְעוֹן כִּי־
הָיָה חֵלֶק בְּנֵי־יְהוּדָה רַב
מֵהֶם וַיִּנְחֲלוּ בְנֵי־שִׁמְעוֹן
בְּתוֹךְ נַחֲלָתָם:
10 וַיַּעַל הַגּוֹרָל הַשְּׁלִישִׁי לִבְנֵי
זְבוּלֻן לְמִשְׁפְּחֹתָם וַיְהִי גְּבוּל
11 נַחֲלָתָם עַד־שָׂרִיד: וְעָלָה
גְבוּלָם ׀ לַיָּמָּה וּמַרְעֲלָה וּפָגַע
בְּדַבָּשֶׁת וּפָגַע אֶל־הַנַּחַל
12 אֲשֶׁר עַל־פְּנֵי יָקְנְעָם: וְשָׁב
מִשָּׂרִיד קֵדְמָה מִזְרַח הַשֶּׁמֶשׁ
עַל־גְּבוּל כִּסְלֹת תָּבֹר וְיָצָא
אֶל־הַדָּבְרַת וְעָלָה יָפִיעַ:

9. *out of the allotment*, etc. Just as their allotments were together, so they fought together (cf. Judg. i. 3).

10–16 THE INHERITANCE OF ZEBULUN

10. *unto Sarid.* But not including that town. It is now Tel Sadud in the north of the Valley of Jezreel, where the Jewish settlement of Kvutzath Sarid has revived the ancient name (Daath Mikra).

11. *their border went up.* Over the sides of mount Carmel (Daath Mikra).

westward. lit. 'seaward,' reaching the sea by the bay of Acre, so fulfilling Jacob's prophecy, *Zebulun shall dwell at the shore of the sea* (Gen. xlix. 13). The strip which extended to the sea formed an enclave in the territory of Issachar (Daath Mikra).

Dabbesheth. [Some identify it with the ruins of Dabshah in the south of Upper Galilee.] Others identify it with Kefar Yehoshua (Daath Mikra).

the brook. A small tributary of the Kishon,

called by the Arabs Wadi Milh (Daath Mikra).

Jokneam. See on xii. 22.

12. *it turned from Sarid eastward.* i.e. discontinuing this direction, but beginning again from Sarid, the boundary from this point extended eastward.

unto the border of Chisloth-tabor. But not including it, the town belonging to Issachar (verse 18 where it is called Chesulloth). It is two miles south-east of Nazareth (Daath Mikra).

Dobrath. Now Deburije, near mount Tabor, four miles east of Nazareth. This city also belonged to Issachar (xxi. 28) (Daath Mikra).

Japhia. Now Yafa, south-east of Nazareth. The phrase *went up* is explained by the following description: 'For three quarters of an hour we wind through picturesque glens, their beds green with corn, and their banks dark with the foliage of the dwarf oak, hawthorn and wild pear. Yafa now appears

to Japhia. 13. And from thence it passed along eastward to Gath-hepher, to Eth-kazin; and it went out at Rimmon-methoar unto Neah. 14. And the border turned about it on the north to Hannathon; and the goings out thereof were at the valley of Iphtahel; 15. and Kattath, and Nahalal, and Shimron, and Idalah, and Beth-lehem; twelve cities with their villages. 16. This is the inheritance of the children of Zebulun according to their families, these cities with their villages.

13 וּמִשָּׁם עָבַר קֵדְמָה מִזְרָחָה גִּתָּה חֵפֶר עִתָּה קָצִין וְיָצָא
14 רִמּוֹן הַמְּתֹאָר הַנֵּעָה וְנָסַב אֹתוֹ הַגְּבוּל מִצְּפוֹן חַנָּתֹן וְהָיוּ
15 תֹּצְאֹתָיו גֵּי יִפְתַּח־אֵל וְקַטָּת וְנַהֲלָל וְשִׁמְרוֹן וְיִדְאֲלָה וּבֵית לָחֶם עָרִים שְׁתֵּים־עֶשְׂרֵה
16 וְחַצְרֵיהֶן זֹאת נַחֲלַת בְּנֵי זְבוּלֻן לְמִשְׁפְּחוֹתָם הֶעָרִים הָאֵלֶּה וְחַצְרֵיהֶן

on the top of a Tel, down in a glen on the right' (Porter, *Handbook,* II. p. 385).

13. *Gath-hepher.* The Rabbis identified it with Gobebatha of Sepphoris (Gen. Rabbah xcviii. II). It may be the modern Meshed, three miles north-east of Nazareth. It was the birthplace of Jonah (2 Kings xiv. 25).

Rimmon-methoar unto Neah. [R.V. renders: 'Rimmon which stretcheth unto Neah.' It is now Rummaneh, six miles north-east of Nazareth. Neah is otherwise unknown. It is named here only as a further delineation of Rimmon and is not included in the enumeration of the twelve cities (verse 15).]

14. *the border turned about it.* [It apparently refers to Neah. The boundary skirted Neah and proceeded to *Hannathon,* which some identify with Kephar Hanania of the Talmud, the modern Kefr Anan, on the border of Upper and Lower Galilee.]

the valley. This valley is mentioned again in verse 27. No one knows exactly where it is. Some believe that it is Wadi-al-chalidiah, which flows into Wadi-al-malich (tributaries of the Kishon), which flows into the valley of Beth Netofah. Some believe that it is one of the upper tributaries of the Naaman, which flows into the valley of Beth Hakerem in Galilee (Daath Mikra).

Iphtahel. Apparently a wadi in the south of Upper Galilee. The western boundary is not given because it marched with the border of Asher, defined in verses 24–31.

15. *and Kattath.* i.e. the border included the towns Kattath, etc. Kattath (in Judg. i. 30 *Kitron*) is called Kitonith in j. Meg. 70a, south of Sepphoris.

Nahalal. Identified by the Rabbis (*loc. cit.*) with Mahalal, west of Japhia. This city was not conquered until later (Judg. i. 30). There is now a Jewish settlement of that name in the Valley of Jezreel.

Shimron. See on xi. 1.

Idalah. Identified by the Rabbis (*loc cit.*) with Hawrayah, now Huwareh, near Shimron.

Beth-lehem. Of Galilee, north-west of Naha-lol, and not to be confused with the better known Beth-lehem of Judah (Kimchi).

16. *the inheritance of the children of Zebulun.* Dwelling by the coast and its territory consisting largely of mountainous regions, this tribe turned to seafaring and commerce, and became the entrepreneur for the rest of the nation. The Jewish Maritime League for developing the sea resources of modern Palestine has assumed the name of 'Zebulun.'

17. The fourth lot came out for Issachar, even for the children of Issachar according to their families. 18. And their border was Jezreel, and Chesulloth, and Shunem; 19. and Hapharaim, and Shion, and Anaharath; 20. and Rabbith, and Kishion, and Ebez; 21. and Remeth, and En-gannim, and En-haddah, and Beth-pazzez; 22. and the border reached to Tabor, and Shahazim, and Beth-shemesh; and the goings out of their border were at the Jordan; sixteen cities with their villages. 23. This is the inheritance of the tribe of the children of Issachar according to their families, the cities with their villages.

24. And the fifth lot came out for

17 לְיִשָּׂשכָר יָצָא הַגּוֹרָל הָרְבִיעִי
לִבְנֵי יִשָּׂשכָר לְמִשְׁפְּחוֹתָם:
18 וַיְהִי גְּבוּלָם יִזְרְעֶאלָה
19 וְהַכְּסֻלּוֹת וְשׁוּנֵם: וַחֲפָרַיִם
20 וְשִׁיאוֹן וַאֲנָחֲרַת: וְהָרַבִּית
21 וְקִשְׁיוֹן וָאָבֶץ: וְרֶמֶת וְעֵין־
גַּנִּים וְעֵין חַדָּה וּבֵית פַּצֵּץ:
22 וּפָגַע הַגְּבוּל בְּתָבוֹר
וְשַׁחֲצוֹמָה וּבֵית שֶׁמֶשׁ וְהָיוּ
תֹּצְאוֹת גְּבוּלָם הַיַּרְדֵּן עָרִים
23 שֵׁשׁ־עֶשְׂרֵה וְחַצְרֵיהֶן: זֹאת
נַחֲלַת מַטֵּה בְנֵי־יִשָּׂשכָר
לְמִשְׁפְּחֹתָם הֶעָרִים
וְחַצְרֵיהֶן:
24 וַיֵּצֵא הַגּוֹרָל הַחֲמִישִׁי לְמַטֵּה

v. 22. וּשְׂחֲצִימָה ק

---

18. *Jezreel.* Now Zerin, in the plain of that name (Daath Mikra).

Chesulloth. [Called *Chisloth-tabor* in verse 12; now Iksal on the western side of mount Tabor.]

Shunem. Now Shulem, north of Jezreel. It occurs several times in the Bible, as the encampment of the Philistines before their victorious battle of Gilboa against Saul in which he lost his life (1 Sam. xxviii. 4); Abishag's native town (1 Kings i.3); the place where Elisha often lodged (2 Kings iv. 8ff.).

19. *Hapharaim.* [Perhaps now the ruins of Parieh, between Megiddo and Jokneam.]

Anaharath. Now en-Na'ura, east of Shunem (Daath Mikra).

20. *Rabbith.* [The modern Raba, thirteen

miles north-east of Nablus, a large Arab village.]

Kishion. A Levitical city (xxi. 28) of uncertain location.

21. *Remeth.* A Levitical city called Jarmuth in xxi. 29 (Daath Mikra).

En-gannim. lit. 'the spring of gardens,' now the Arab city of Jenin in the southern extremity of the Valley of Jezreel. A spring rises in the hills behind the town and passes through it. Another place with this name occurs in xv. 34 (Kaftor vaferach).

En-haddah. [Probably Hadideh, south-west of Jabneel (verse 33).]

22. *Tabor.* A city by mount Tabor (D.M.).

Beth-shemesh. Now the ruins of Shemsin, south-east of Jabneel. There were towns of that name in the territory of Judah (xv. 10) and Naphtali (verse 38) (Daath Mikra).

the tribe of the children of Asher according to their families. 25. And their border was Helkath, and Hali, and Beten, and Achshaph; 26. and Allammelech, and Amad, and Mishal; and it reached to Carmel westward, and to Shihor-libnath. 27. And it turned toward the sun-rising to Beth-dagon, and reached to Zebulun and to the valley of Iphtahel northward at Beth-emek and Neiel; and it went out to Cabul on the left hand, 28. and Ebron, and Rehob, and Hammon, and Kanah, even unto great Zidon. 29. And the border turned to Ramah, and to

בְּנֵי־אָשֵׁר לְמִשְׁפְּחוֹתָם: וַיְהִי 25
גְּבוּלָם חֶלְקַת וַחֲלִי וָבֶטֶן
וְאַכְשָׁף: וְאַלַּמֶּלֶךְ וְעַמְעָד 26
וּמִשְׁאָל וּפָגַע בְּכַרְמֶל הַיָּמָּה
וּבְשִׁיחוֹר לִבְנָת: וְשָׁב מִזְרַח 27
הַשֶּׁמֶשׁ בֵּית דָּגֹן וּפָגַע בִּזְבֻלוּן
וּבְגֵי יִפְתַּח־אֵל צָפוֹנָה בֵּית
הָעֵמֶק וּנְעִיאֵל וְיָצָא אֶל־
כָּבוּל מִשְּׂמֹאל: וְעֶבְרֹן וּרְחֹב 28
וְחַמּוֹן וְקָנָה עַד צִידוֹן רַבָּה:
וְשָׁב הַגְּבוּל הָרָמָה וְעַד־עִיר 29

24–31 THE INHERITANCE OF ASHER

25. *Helkath.* A Levitical city (xxi. 31).

Achshaph. See on xi. 1.

26. *Allammelech.* Thought to be a city near the Wadi Malek, a tributary of the Kishon (Daath Mikra).

Amad. Perhaps Umm el-Amed, west of Beth-lehem in Galilee (Daath Mikra).

Mishal. A Levitical city (xxi. 30), called *Mishal* in 1 Chron. vi. 59. [Some identify it with Misalli in the extreme north of the plain of Sharon.]

to Carmel westward. i.e to Carmel, which is situated in the west (Metsudath David). Elijah of Wilna and Malbim render: in the sea of Carmel. This view is shared by Jonathan. The sea adjoins the mountain range of Carmel, near the Valley of Zebulun (Daath Mikra).

Shihor-libnath. The river of Libnath (Elijah of Wilna). This is one of the rivers in the north-ern sector of the country, probably called Libnath because of the white sands that abound there (Daath Mikra). [This is pro-bably the Nahr ez-Zerka, or 'crocodile brook,' which rises in the Carmel and flows into the Mediterranean just north of Caesarea.] This verse defines the boundary between Asher and Manasseh.

27. *Beth-dagon.* Beit Djen, near Akko.

and reached to Zebulun. i.e. the territory of Zebulun.

Iphtahel. See on verse 14.

northward. i.e the northern border of Zebu-lun.

Beth-emek. Now Amka, seven miles north-east of Akko.

Cabul. It still bears the ancient name and is situated nine miles south-east of Akko. This verse defines the boundary between Asher and Zebulun on the north and the west.

28. *and Ebron,* etc. Instead of continuing with the description of the border, the text enumerates important cities within the terri-tory.

Ebron. Many Hebrew MSS. read *Abdon* as in xxi. 30 and 1 Chron. vi. 59: now called Abde.

Rehob. A Levitical city (xxi. 31; 1 Chron. vi. 60). It has been identified with Rahubu, north of the Kishon.

Kanah. South-east of Tyre.

even unto great Zidon. See on xi. 8. All the cities up to Zidon were included in Asher's portion.

29. *and the border turned.* The frontier between Asher and Naphtali is defined.

the fortified city of Tyre; and the
border turned to Hosah; and the
goings out thereof were at the sea
from Hebel to Achzib; 30. Ummah
also, and Aphek, and Rehob; twenty
and two cities with their villages.
31. This is the inheritance of the
tribe of the children of Asher
according to their families, these
cities with their villages.

32. The sixth lot came out for the
children of Naphtali, even for the

מִבְצָר־צֹר וְשָׁב הַגְּבוּל חֹסָה
וְהָיוּ תֹצְאֹתָיו הַיָּמָּה מֵחֶבֶל
אַכְזִיבָה: וְעֻמָּה וַאֲפֵק וּרְחֹב 30
עָרִים עֶשְׂרִים וּשְׁתָּיִם
וְחַצְרֵיהֶן: זֹאת נַחֲלַת מַטֵּה 31
בְנֵי־אָשֵׁר לְמִשְׁפְּחֹתָם
הֶעָרִים הָאֵלֶּה וְחַצְרֵיהֶן:
לִבְנֵי נַפְתָּלִי יָצָא הַגּוֹרָל הַשִּׁשִּׁי 32

והיו ק‎ v. 29.

Ramah. Now Ramieh, east of Hanita.

the fortified city of Tyre. [Not the well-known
Phoenician city on the coast. It may perhaps
be the 'Ladder of Tyre' (Ras en-Kankurah) a
coastal town.]

from Hebel to Achzib. This is perhaps a reference to the city in Lebanon by this name,
mentioned in *Kaftor vaferach.* Jonathan,
however, renders: *from the lot of Achzib.* I.e.
from there, the border ended at the Mediterranean Sea (Metsudath David). Rashi, too,
follows this interpretation. Achzib is believed
by some to be the town of ez-Zib, on the
south coast of Tyre (Daath Mikra).

30. *Ummah.* A comparison with Judg. i. 31
suggests that this town is identical with Akko,
the modern Akka, on the coast north of Carmel, as in LXX (Daath Mikra).

Aphek. Called *Aphik* in Judg. i. 31; its site is
doubtful.

Rehob. See on verse 28. If this is a different
place, there were two towns of the same
name in the land of Asher.

twenty and two cities. This number is confirmed if *Hebel* in verse 29 is not the name of
a town; otherwise Achzib is not included as a
town of Asher, but as a region (Daath Mikra).

31. *this is the inheritance . . . Asher.* Much of
this territory remained in Canaanite hands
for a long time (cf. Judg. i. I), and many
cities, e.g. Zidon, Achzib, Rehob and Aphek,
were never conquered (Judg. i. 31). The two

northern kingdoms of Tyre and Zidon
retained their identity for hundreds of years
after the conquest. The Rabbis commented
on the extraordinary fertility of Asher's portion (Siphrë to Deut. xxxiii. 24f.). 'The territory of Asher extended from *Nahr Zerka* on
the south, to Zidon on the north, and contained some of the richest soil of the country,
and the maritime portion of the fertile plain
of Esdraelon, and commanded all the
approaches to Palestine from the sea on the
north. Its soil well fulfilled the prophetic
descriptions of Jacob and Moses. Here Asher
could *dip his foot* in the *oil* of his luxuriant
olive-groves (Deut. xxxiii. 24) such as still
distinguish this region, and fatten on the
bread, the fruit of the rich plain of Phoenicia
and his fertile upland valleys (Gen. xlix. 20).
He could *yield royal dainties (loc. cit.),* oil and
wine from his olives and vineyards, and milk
and butter from his pastures; while "under
his shoes" was the *iron* ore of the southern
slopes of the Lebanon, and the *brass* or cop-
per of the neighbouring Phoenician territory
(Deut. xxxiii. 25).' Possibly through its
wealth, aided by its proximity to the unconquered Phoenicians, the tribe degenerat-
ed and lost all importance. Its ties with the
rest of the nation were weak, and Deborah
contemptuously alluded to its isolation:
Asher dwelt at the shore of the sea (instead of
joining in the fight against Sisera) *and abideth
by its bays* (Judg. v. 17). By the time of David it
was so insignificant, that it was omitted from
the list of *the captains of the tribes of Israel* (1
Chron. xxvii. 16–22).

children of Naphtali according to their families. 33. And their border was from Heleph, from Elon-bezaanannim, and Adami-nekeb, and Jabneel, unto Lakkum; and the goings out thereof were at the Jordan. 34. And the border turned westward to Aznoth-tabor, and went out from thence to Hukok; and it reached to Zebulun on_the south, and reached to Asher on the west, and to Judah at the Jordan toward the sunrising. 35. And the fortified cities were Ziddim-zer, and

לִבְנֵי נַפְתָּלִי לְמִשְׁפְּחֹתָם:

33 וַיְהִי גְבוּלָם מֵחֵלֶף מֵאֵלוֹן בְּצַעֲנַנִּים וַאֲדָמִי הַנֶּקֶב וְיַבְנְאֵל עַד־לַקּוּם וַיְהִי

34 תֹצְאֹתָיו הַיַּרְדֵּן: וְשָׁב הַגְּבוּל יָמָּה אַזְנוֹת תָּבוֹר וְיָצָא מִשָּׁם חֻקֹּקָה וּפָגַע בִּזְבֻלוּן מִנֶּגֶב וּבְאָשֵׁר פָּגַע מִיָּם וּבִיהוּדָה

35 הַיַּרְדֵּן מִזְרַח הַשָּׁמֶשׁ: וְעָרֵי מִבְצָר הַצִּדִּים צֵר וְחַמַּת רַקַּת

32–39 THE INHERITANCE OF NAPHTALI

33. *Heleph.* [Probably somewhere near lake Huleh.]

Elon-bezaanannim. In the vicinity of Kedesh-naphtali (cf. Judg. iv. 11).

Adami-nekeb. A.V. construes as two separate places, with which interpretation the Rabbis agree, though the accentuation of M.T. supports A.J. The Rabbis (j. Meg. 70a) identified Adami with Damin, now Damieh, west of the sea of Kinnereth, and Hannekeb (understanding *ha-* as part of the name, not as the definite article (with Zaydetha, now Zeyadeh, also west of the sea of Kinnereth.

Jabneel. Identified by the Rabbis (*loc. cit.*) with Kephar Yama, south-west of the sea of Kinnereth. The ancient name has been revived in a modern Jewish settlement on that site.

34. *Aznoth-tabor.* [Perhaps lit. 'the ears of Tabor,' denoting some peaks of that mountain.]

Hukok. Now Yakuk, four miles north-west of the sea of Kinnereth (Daath Mikra).

and to Judah at the Jordan. i.e. the region on the east side of the Jordan inhabited by the Jairites (xiii. 30) who on their paternal side belonged to Judah (1 Chron. ii. 21f.). Others,

following the accentuation of M.T., which disjoins from what follows, render: 'and reached to Asher on the west, and to Judah; the Jordan was toward the sun-rising,' i.e. the Jordan marked its eastern boundary. Others explain that, since Judah bordered on the southern end of the Jordan, and the entire Jordan belonged to Naphtali, Naphtali's border met Judah's at the Jordan. Actually, Naphtali's border met that of all the tribes that bordered on Jordan. Judah is singled out to tell us that Naphtali's border met even Judah's, which was at the extreme south, and certainly that of all the other tribes north of it (Metsudath David). Other theories are: (1) This refers to the city of Bezek, conquered by Judah and Simeon (Judges i. 4–7). This was located south of the Kinnereth, in the vicinity of the valley of Beth-shean. (2) This refers to the village of Seid Judah on the eastern arm of the Jordan (Daath Mikra).

35. *and the fortified cities,* etc. i.e. the fortified cities of Naphtali (Rashi and Metsudath David). We do not find fortified cities in any other tribe, except 'the fortified city of Tyre,' which belonged to Asher (Daath Mikra). These were probably needed to protect the northern boundary.

Ziddim-zer. Some translate as two separate cities, which is in agreement with the

Hammath, and Rakkath, and Chinnereth; 36. and Adamah, and Ramah, and Hazor; 37. and Kedesh, and Edrei, and En-hazor; 38. and Iron, and Migdal-el, and Horem, and Beth-anath, and Beth-shemesh; nineteen cities with their villages. 39. This is the inheritance of the tribe of the children of Naphtali according to their families, the cities with their villages.

40. The seventh lot came out for the tribe of the children of Dan according to their families. 41. And the border of their inheritance was Zorah, and Eshtaol, and Ir-shemesh;

36 וְכִנֶּֽרֶת: וַאֲדָמָ֖ה וְהָרָמָ֑ה
37 וְחָצֽוֹר: וְקֶ֥דֶשׁ וְאֶדְרֶ֖עִי וְעֵ֥ין
38 חָצֽוֹר: וְיִרְאוֹן֙ וּמִגְדַּל־אֵ֣ל
חֳרֵ֔ם וּבֵית־עֲנָ֖ת וּבֵ֣ית שָׁ֑מֶשׁ
עָרִ֛ים תְּשַֽׁע־עֶשְׂרֵ֖ה
39 וְחַצְרֵיהֶֽן: זֹ֗את נַחֲלַ֛ת מַטֵּ֥ה
בְנֵֽי־נַפְתָּלִ֖י לְמִשְׁפְּחֹתָ֑ם
הֶֽעָרִ֖ים וְחַצְרֵיהֶֽן:
40 לְמַטֵּ֥ה בְנֵי־דָ֖ן לְמִשְׁפְּחֹתָ֑ם
41 יָצָ֖א הַגּוֹרָ֣ל הַשְּׁבִיעִ֑י וַיְהִ֗י
גְּב֤וּל נַחֲלָתָ֙ם צָרְעָ֖ה
וְאֶשְׁתָּא֖וֹל וְעִ֥יר שָֽׁמֶשׁ:

---

interpretation of the Rabbis. They identified Ziddim with Kephar Hittin (j. Meg. 70a). The exact location of Zer is unknown, but it was in the neighbourhood of the former.

Hammath. Near the hot springs (*cham* means 'hot') of Tiberias, or of Gerar (Meg. 6a).

Rakkath. The Rabbis identified it with Tiberias (Meg. 5b).

Chinnereth. See on xi. 2.

36. *Adamah.* Possibly identical with *Adami* in verse 33; it was accordingly both a border city and a fortress (Daath Mikra).

Ramah. West of Safed.

Hazor. See on xi. 1.

37. *Kedesh.* See on xii. 22.

Edrei. Not to be confused with the well-known Edrei in Bashan; it is otherwise unknown.

38. *Iron.* Now Yarun, north-east of Gush-halab (Daath Mikra).

Migdal-el. Some identify it with Mejdel-Islim, near Kedesh-naphtali; others hold that it is the ruins of Migdol, south of Mejdel-Islim (Daath Mikra).

Beth-anath. It may be the modern Ain Ata, six miles west of Kedesh. Beth-anath and Beth-shemesh, the latter being unidentified, were not conquered (Judg. i. 33).

nineteen cities. Since twenty-four are enumerated, it must be assumed that some of the places did not belong to Naphtali, but were only defined though not included in that tribe's territory (Metsudath David).

40–48 THE BOUNDARIES OF DAN

41. *the border.* This is not delineated in the same way as that of the other tribes, but only by the cities which it included. The reason is that Dan was enclosed by Ephraim and Benjamin in the north and east, and by Judah in the south and south-east; so his boundaries coincided with theirs.

Zorah . . . Eshtaol. See on xv. 33. They belonged to Judah and bordered on Dan (Rashi). It is also possible that these were not the same cities mentioned above (Metsudath David). Zorah is the modern Sar'a, fifteen miles west of Jerusalem; and Eshtaol, east of the former, is now called Eshua (Daath Mikra).

Ir-shemesh. See on xv. 10.

42. and Shaal-abbin, and Aijalon, and Ithlah; 43. and Elon, and Timnah, and Ekron; 44. and Eltekeh, and Gibbethon, and Baalath; 45. and Jehud, and Bene-berak, and Gath-rimmon; 46. and Me-jarkon, and Rakkon, with the border over against Joppa. 47. And the border of the children of Dan was too strait for them; so the children of Dan went up and fought against

42 וְשַׁעֲלַבִּין וְאַיָּלוֹן וְיִתְלָה:
43 וְאֵילוֹן וְתִמְנָתָה וְעֶקְרוֹן:
44 וְאֶלְתְּקֵה וְגִבְּתוֹן וּבַעֲלָת:
45 וִיהֻד וּבְנֵי־בְרַק וְגַת־רִמּוֹן:
46 וּמֵי הַיַּרְקוֹן וְהָרַקּוֹן עִם־
47 הַגְּבוּל מוּל יָפוֹ: וַיֵּצֵא גְבוּל בְּנֵי־דָן מֵהֶם וַיַּעֲלוּ בְנֵי־דָן

42. *Shaal-abbin.* The meaning is perhaps 'the place of foxes'; called *Shaalbim* in Judg. i. 35, where it is stated that it and Aijalon remained for a time in the hands of the Amorites. Some think it to be Selbith, west of Aijalon (Daath Mikra).

Aijalon. A Levitical city (xxi. 24), now Jalo, east of Emmaus. The valley of Aijalon is mentioned in x, 12, and was doubtless named after it (Daath Mikra).

Ithlah. Possibly Beit Tul, between Kiriath anavim and Aijalon (Daath Mikra).

43. *Elon.* Conjectured to be the ruins of Di Olin near Beth-shemesh (Daath Mikra).

Timnah. See on xv. 10.

Ekron. See on xiii. 3.

44. *Eltekeh, and Gibbethon.* Included among the Levitical cities in xxi. 23. The latter fell into Philistine hands (1 Kings xv. 27, xvi. 15). Their sites are unknown.

Baalath. Josephus (*Antiquities* VIII. vi. 1) places it near Beth-horon. It was fortified by Solomon (1 Kings ix. 18) where it is named in connection with Beth-horon the nether. [It may be the modern Bel'ain.]

45. *Yehud.* Now Yehudieh, eight miles east of Jaffa; a Jewish settlement is in its vicinity (Daath Mikra).

Bene-berak. To the west of Yehud, now Ibn-ibrak. In Mishnaic times it was the scene of the famous Passover Seder at which five

Rabbis spent the whole night expatiating upon the exodus from Egypt. A Rabbi who visited Bene-berak saw goats grazing under the fig-trees, while honey was flowing from the trees and milk ran from the goats, and these mingled with each other. 'This is, indeed,' he remarked, 'a land flowing with milk and honey' (Keth. 111b). In modern Palestine, a new settlement bearing the original Biblical name has been founded in the neighbourhood.

Gath-rimmon. A Levitical city (xxi. 24); its site is not precisely known. There is now a Jewish settlement of the same name, probably close to its Biblical site.

46. *Me-jarkon.* Near Jaffa.

Rakkon. Possibly Tel Rakkith (Daath Mikra).

with the border over against Joppa. This famous seaport did not pass into Jewish hands until it was captured in the second century B.C.E. by Simon Maccabeus (cf. 1 Macc. xiii. 11). It appears several times in Biblical history. To it the cedar and pinewood needed for Solomon's Temple were conveyed by Hiram, king of Tyre (2 Chron. ii. 15). The same materials were brought there for the rebuilding of the Second Temple (Ezra iii. 7). Jonah boarded a ship to flee *from the presence of the* LORD at Joppa (Jonah i. 3).

47. *was too strait for them.* This is not the rendering of the Hebrew, which is literally 'and the border (i.e. the territory) of the children of Dan went out from them.' A.J. is probably

Leshem, and took it, and smote it with the edge of the sword, and possessed it, and dwelt therein, and called Leshem, Dan, after the name of Dan their father. 48. This is the inheritance of the tribe of the children of Dan according to their families, these cities with their villages.

49. When they had made an end of distributing the land for inheritance by the borders thereof, the children of Israel gave an inheritance to Joshua the son of Nun in the midst of them; 50. according to the commandment of the LORD they gave him the city which he asked, even Timnath-serah in the hill-country of Ephraim; and he built the city, and dwelt therein.

51. These are the inheritances,

וַיִּלְכְּדוּ אוֹתָהּ וַיַּכּוּהָ לְפִי־חֶרֶב וַיִּירָשׁוּ אוֹתָהּ וַיֵּשְׁבוּ בָהּ וַיִּקְרְאוּ לְלֶשֶׁם דָּן כְּשֵׁם דָּן אֲבִיהֶם:

48 זֹאת נַחֲלַת מַטֵּה בְנֵי־דָן לְמִשְׁפְּחֹתָם הֶעָרִים הָאֵלֶּה וְחַצְרֵיהֶן:

49 וַיְכַלּוּ לִנְחֹל אֶת־הָאָרֶץ לִגְבוּלֹתֶיהָ וַיִּתְּנוּ בְנֵי־יִשְׂרָאֵל נַחֲלָה לִיהוֹשֻׁעַ בִּן־נוּן

50 בְּתוֹכָם: עַל־פִּי יְהוָֹה נָתְנוּ לוֹ אֶת־הָעִיר אֲשֶׁר שָׁאָל אֶת־תִּמְנַת־סֶרַח בְּהַר אֶפְרָיִם וַיִּבְנֶה אֶת־הָעִיר וַיֵּשֶׁב בָּהּ:

51 אֵלֶּה הַנְּחָלֹת אֲשֶׁר־נִחֲלוּ

v. 50. קמץ בז"ק

49-51 THE INHERITANCE OF JOSHUA

based on Kimchi and Metsudath David, who explain: The border of the children of Dan came out [in a lot that was] inadequate for them. They, therefore, required additional land, which they acquired by waging war with Leshem. Rashi explains the verse literally, interpreting it thus: The children of Dan took part [of their inheritance] here, and they also received a lot elsewhere far from their border, with other tribes intervening between them. Others explain that Dan's territory was unconquerable by them, since the Amorites did not allow them to go into the valley. They were able to conquer only on the western border. Leshem, or Laish was on the east. See Judges i. 34f. (Malbim).

fought against Leshem. Cf. Judg. xviii. *Leshem* is a variant of *Laish.*

Dan. Now Tel el-Kadi, 'the mound of the judge' (*Dan* in Hebrew signifies 'judge').

50. *according to the commandment of the* LORD. This command was possibly conveyed to them through the Urim and Thummim; or it may be that a Divine promise was made to him as to Caleb (cf. xiv. 9) although not recorded (Metsudath David). Unlike the rest of Israel, his portion was not chosen by lot (Baba Bathra 122a).

Timnath-serah. Also called *Timnath-heres,* 'the picture of the sun,' because they set up a figure of the sun on his grave to perpetuate the miracle he performed by halting the sun. Others maintain that its original name was Timnath-heres. It was called Timnath-serah because its fruit would rot because of its extreme richness (Rashi from Baba Bathra 122b). It is now the ruins of Tibneh, seventeen miles north-west of Jerusalem. Joshua was buried there (xxiv. 30) (Daath Mikra).

which Eleazar the priest, and Joshua
the son of Nun, and the heads of the
fathers' houses of the tribes of the
children of Israel, distributed for
inheritance by lot in Shiloh before
the LORD, at the door of the tent of
meeting. So they made an end of
dividing the land.

אֶלְעָזָר הַכֹּהֵן ׀ וִיהוֹשֻׁעַ בִּן־נוּן
וְרָאשֵׁי הָאָבוֹת לְמַטּוֹת בְּנֵי־
יִשְׂרָאֵל ׀ בְּגוֹרָל ׀ בְּשִׁלֹה לִפְנֵי
יְהֹוָה פֶּתַח אֹהֶל מוֹעֵד וַיְכַלּוּ
מֵחַלֵּק אֶת־הָאָרֶץ׃

20   CHAPTER XX   ב

1. And the LORD spoke unto Joshua,
saying: 2. 'Speak to the children of
Israel, saying: Assign you the cities
of refuge, whereof I spoke unto you
by the hand of Moses; 3. that the
manslayer that killeth any person
through error and unawares may
flee thither; and they shall be unto

1 וַיְדַבֵּר יְהֹוָה אֶל־יְהוֹשֻׁעַ
2 לֵאמֹר׃ דַּבֵּר אֶל־בְּנֵי
יִשְׂרָאֵל לֵאמֹר תְּנוּ לָכֶם אֶת־
עָרֵי הַמִּקְלָט אֲשֶׁר־דִּבַּרְתִּי
3 אֲלֵיכֶם בְּיַד־מֹשֶׁה׃ לָנוּס
שָׁמָּה רוֹצֵחַ מַכֵּה־נֶפֶשׁ בִּשְׁגָגָה
בִּבְלִי־דָעַת וְהָיוּ לָכֶם

he built the city. This probably means that he
added to the existing buildings.

It is, indeed, noteworthy that Joshua, the
great leader, who brought Israel into the
Holy Land, should request but a small town,
whose land is not fit for cultivation, or whose
fruits are inferior.

51. *Eleazar the priest, and Joshua the son of
Nun.* See on xiv. 1. This verse ends the
account of the division of the country.

the tent of meeting. The tent of meeting had
been erected in Shiloh fourteen years after
the Israelites had entered the land. See on
xviii. 1.

CHAPTER XX

THE CITIES OF REFUGE

1. *and the Lord spoke,* etc. The Talmud
(Mak. 11a) observes that the verb *dibber*

(which also has the meaning 'drive forward')
expresses strong emphasis. It is here intended to stress the thought that Joshua was
being commanded to fulfill an ordinance of
the Torah, viz. the establishment of cities of
refuge. Rashi, in his commentary on the Talmudic passage, remarks that nowhere else is
the fulfilment of a Pentateuchal injunction
recorded in the later Books of the Bible.

2. *speak to the children of Israel, saying.* This is
the only instance, outside the Pentateuch
where it is very frequent, of the use of this
formula.

assign you the cities of refuge. Now that the division of the Promised land was complete, the
Israelites were commanded to set aside cities
of refuge, as Moses had proclaimed in the
Torah (Deut. xix. 1f): "When the Lord thy
God will cut off the nations . . . and thou
dost succeed them and dwell in their cities
and houses, three cities shalt thou separate"
(Kimchi).

whereof I spoke unto you. Cf. Num. xxxv. 10ff.

you for a refuge from the avenger of blood. 4. And he shall flee unto one of those cities, and shall stand at the entrance of the gate of the city, and declare his cause in the ears of the elders of that city; and they shall take him into the city unto them, and give him a place, that he may dwell among them. 5. And if the avenger of blood pursue after him, then they shall not deliver up the manslayer into his hand; because he smote his neighbour unawares, and hated him not beforetime. 6. And he shall dwell in that city, until he stand before the congregation for judgment, until the death of the high priest that shall be in those days; then may the manslayer return, and come unto his own city, and unto his own house, unto the city from whence he fled.'

4 לְמִקְלָט מִגֹּאֵל הַדָּם: וְנָס
אֶל־אַחַת ׀ מֵהֶעָרִים הָאֵלֶּה
וְעָמַד פֶּתַח שַׁעַר הָעִיר וְדִבֶּר
בְּאָזְנֵי זִקְנֵי הָעִיר־הַהִיא אֶת־
דְּבָרָיו וְאָסְפוּ אֹתוֹ הָעִירָה
אֲלֵיהֶם וְנָתְנוּ־לוֹ מָקוֹם וְיָשַׁב
5 עִמָּם: וְכִי יִרְדֹּף גֹּאֵל הַדָּם
אַחֲרָיו וְלֹא־יַסְגִּרוּ אֶת־
הָרֹצֵחַ בְּיָדוֹ כִּי בִבְלִי־דַעַת
הִכָּה אֶת־רֵעֵהוּ וְלֹא־שֹׂנֵא
הוּא לוֹ מִתְּמוֹל שִׁלְשׁוֹם:
6 וְיָשַׁב ׀ בָּעִיר הַהִיא עַד־
עָמְדוֹ לִפְנֵי הָעֵדָה לַמִּשְׁפָּט
עַד־מוֹת הַכֹּהֵן הַגָּדוֹל אֲשֶׁר
יִהְיֶה בַּיָּמִים הָהֵם אָז ׀ יָשׁוּב
הָרוֹצֵחַ וּבָא אֶל־עִירוֹ וְאֶל־
בֵּיתוֹ אֶל־הָעִיר אֲשֶׁר־נָס
מִשָּׁם:

3. *the avenger of blood.* The *goël,* a near kinsman who regarded it as his duty to avenge the homicide by killing even its unintentional perpetrator. The provision of cities of refuge was consequently a humanizing measure of great ethical and social importance. If the goël killed the murderer outside the limits of the refuge cities, however, he was exempt from capital punishment (Makkoth 10b).

4. *and declare his cause.* He avows that the killing was accidental and not premeditated.

they shall take him into the city. This was done provisionally, until he stood his trial (verse 6).

and give him a place. i.e. rent free. Just as the Levites were given the right to live there, so also, the unwitting slayer had the right to live in these cities, and was therefore entitled to

live there rent free (Kimchi from Makkoth 13a).

5. *and hated him not.* That we should believe that he killed him stealthily (Metsudath David). If the murderer was an enemy of the murdered, he is not afforded the benefit of refuge, unless it is certain that the act of murder could not have been intentional (Makkoth 9b).

6. *until he stand before the congregation for judgment.* If he be freed from exile, he is dismissed. If, however, he is sentenced to exile, he is remanded to his refuge city, where he must dwell until the death of the High Priest (Rashi from Sifre Num. xxxv. 25). Thus, the Scripture gives two instances of the termination of the murderer's stay in the

7. And they set apart Kedesh in Galilee in the hill-country of Naphtali, and Shechem in the hill-country of Ephraim, and Kiriatharba—the same is Hebron—in the hill-country of Judah. 8. And beyond the Jordan at Jericho eastward, they assigned Bezer in the wilderness in the table-land out of the tribe of Reuben, and Ramoth in Gilead out of the tribe of Gad, and Golan in Bashan out of the tribe of Manasseh. 9. These were the appointed cities for all the children of Israel, and for the stranger that sojourneth among them, that whosoever killeth any

7 וַיַּקְדִּשׁוּ אֶת־קֶדֶשׁ בַּגָּלִיל
בְּהַר נַפְתָּלִי וְאֶת־שְׁכֶם בְּהַר
אֶפְרָיִם וְאֶת־קִרְיַת אַרְבַּע
הִיא חֶבְרוֹן בְּהַר יְהוּדָה:
8 וּמֵעֵבֶר לְיַרְדֵּן יְרִיחוֹ מִזְרָחָה
נָתְנוּ אֶת־בֶּצֶר בַּמִּדְבָּר
בַּמִּישֹׁר מִמַּטֵּה רְאוּבֵן וְאֶת־
רָאמֹת בַּגִּלְעָד מִמַּטֵּה גָד
וְאֶת־גּוֹלָן בַּבָּשָׁן מִמַּטֵּה
9 מְנַשֶּׁה: אֵלֶּה הָיוּ עָרֵי
הַמּוּעָדָה לְכֹל | בְּנֵי יִשְׂרָאֵל
וְלַגֵּר הַגָּר בְּתוֹכָם לָנוּס שָׁמָּה

v. 8. גולן ק

refuge city: (1) In the case of his being exonerated, he must stay only "until he stand before the congregation for judgment"; and (2) in the case of his being found guilty of unwitting murder, which could have been avoided, "until the death of the High Priest" (Azulai).

7. *and they set apart.* They assigned. Rather, they had assigned. These cities had already been assigned during Moses' lifetime, as is related in Deut. iv. 41ff. (Rashi). The cities were chosen for their accessibility from every part of the country.

Kedesh. See on xii. 22.

in Galilee. To serve the northern region, extending from the Valley of Jezreel to the foot of Lebanon.

Shechem. The modern Nablus; to serve the central region.

Kiriath-arba. See on xiv. 15; to serve the southern region.

8. *the Jordan at Jericho.* This phrase, as a rule, is to be understood literally, viz. the section of the Jordan facing Jericho. Here the entire length of the Jordan is meant.

The six cities of refuge, viz. the three already set aside by Moses on the eastern side of the Jordan, and the three now set aside by Joshua on the western side, were arranged in a double row running north and south, similar to two rows of vines in a vineyard (Makkoth 9b). The three cities on the west of the Jordan run parallel to the three cities on the east.

Bezer in the wilderness. It was the most southerly of the cities of refuge in Transjordan, corresponding to Jericho in western Canaan.

Ramoth in Gilead. Also called *Ramath-mizpeh* in xiii. 26 and *Ramoth-gilead* in 1 Kings iv. 13.

Golan in Bashan. The most northerly city in Transjordan, corresponding to Kedesh in western Canaan. It is perhaps the modern Jaulan, north of the Jarmuk (D.M.).

9. *might flee thither.* In later times precautions were taken to keep these roads free from obstructions, with signposts at every cross-road marked 'Refuge.' Once there, the slayer was assigned a dwelling (Rambam viii. 5).

person through error might flee thither, and not die by the hand of the avenger of blood, until he stood before the congregation.

כָּל־מַכֵּה־נֶפֶשׁ בִּשְׁנָגָה וְלֹא יָמוּת בְּיַד גֹּאֵל הַדָּם עַד־עָמְדוֹ לִפְנֵי הָעֵדָה׃

21

CHAPTER XXI

כא

1. Then came near the heads of fathers' houses of the Levites unto Eleazar the priest, and unto Joshua the son of Nun, and unto the heads of fathers' houses of the tribes of the children of Israel; 2. and they spoke unto them at Shiloh in the land of Canaan, saying: 'The LORD commanded by the hand of Moses to give us cities to dwell in, with the open land thereabout for our cattle.' 3. And the children of Israel gave unto the Levites out of their inheritance, according to the commandment of the LORD, these cities with the open land about them.

4. And the lot came out for the

1 וַיִּגְּשׁוּ רָאשֵׁי אֲבוֹת הַלְוִיִּם אֶל־אֶלְעָזָר הַכֹּהֵן וְאֶל־יְהוֹשֻׁעַ בִּן־נוּן וְאֶל־רָאשֵׁי אֲבוֹת הַמַּטּוֹת לִבְנֵי יִשְׂרָאֵל׃ 2 וַיְדַבְּרוּ אֲלֵיהֶם בְּשִׁלֹה בְּאֶרֶץ כְּנַעַן לֵאמֹר יְהוָה צִוָּה בְיַד־מֹשֶׁה לָתֶת־לָנוּ עָרִים לָשָׁבֶת 3 וּמִגְרְשֵׁיהֶן לִבְהֶמְתֵּנוּ׃ וַיִּתְּנוּ בְנֵי־יִשְׂרָאֵל לַלְוִיִּם מִנַּחֲלָתָם אֶל־פִּי יְהוָה אֶת־הֶעָרִים הָאֵלֶּה וְאֶת־מִגְרְשֵׁיהֶן׃ 4 וַיֵּצֵא הַגּוֹרָל לְמִשְׁפְּחֹת

v. 3. סבירין על

As already mentioned, the cities in Transjordan had already been set apart by Moses for this purpose, but they were not put into use until the three in Eretz Israel proper were set apart (Makkoth 9b). The Levitical cities, too, were classified as cities of refuge (Makkoth 10a).

CHAPTER XXI

THE LEVITICAL CITIES

1. the heads of fathers' houses. The phrase is defined in xxii. 14.

unto Eleazar the priest, etc. They were responsible for the division of the country among the tribes (xix. 51).

2. at Shiloh. Where the tent of meeting was set up (xvii. 1). After the sanctuary had become established in a more or less permanent location, and they had become servants of the LORD in this permanent sanctuary (Azulai).

in the land of Canaan. After all the tribes had received their shares of the land. Only then, could the Levites demand their cities, a number of which were to be given by each tribe from its inheritance (Azulai).

the LORD commanded. Cf. Num. xxxv. 1ff.

families of the Kohathites; and the children of Aaron the priest, who were of the Levites, had by lot out of the tribe of Judah, and out of the tribe of the Simeonites, and out of the tribe of Benjamin, thirteen cities.

5. And the rest of the children of Kohath had by lot out of the families of the tribe of Ephraim, and out of the tribe of Dan, and out of the half-tribe of Manasseh, ten cities.

6. And the children of Gershon had by lot out of the families of the tribe of Issachar, and out of the tribe of Asher, and out of the tribe of Naphtali, and out of the half-tribe of Manasseh in Bashan, thirteen cities.

7. The children of Merari according to their families had out of the tribe of Reuben, and out of the tribe of Gad, and out of the tribe of Zebulun, twelve cities.

8. And the children of Israel gave by lot unto the Levites these cities

הַקְּהָתִי וַיְהִי לִבְנֵי אַהֲרֹן הַכֹּהֵן
מִן־הַלְוִיִּם מִמַּטֵּה יְהוּדָה
וּמִמַּטֵּה הַשִּׁמְעֹנִי וּמִמַּטֵּה
בִנְיָמִן בַּגּוֹרָל עָרִים שְׁלֹשׁ
עֶשְׂרֵה:

5 וְלִבְנֵי קְהָת הַנּוֹתָרִים
מִמִּשְׁפַּחַת מַטֵּה־אֶפְרַיִם
וּמִמַּטֵּה־דָן וּמֵחֲצִי מַטֵּה
מְנַשֶּׁה בַּגּוֹרָל עָרִים עָשֶׂר:

6 וְלִבְנֵי גֵרְשׁוֹן מִמִּשְׁפְּחֹת מַטֵּה־
יִשָּׂשכָר וּמִמַּטֵּה־אָשֵׁר
וּמִמַּטֵּה נַפְתָּלִי וּמֵחֲצִי מַטֵּה
מְנַשֶּׁה בַבָּשָׁן בַּגּוֹרָל עָרִים
שְׁלֹשׁ עֶשְׂרֵה:

7 לִבְנֵי מְרָרִי לְמִשְׁפְּחֹתָם
מִמַּטֵּה רְאוּבֵן וּמִמַּטֵּה־גָד
וּמִמַּטֵּה זְבוּלֻן עָרִים שְׁתֵּים
עֶשְׂרֵה:

8 וַיִּתְּנוּ בְנֵי־יִשְׂרָאֵל לַלְוִיִּם
אֶת־הֶעָרִים הָאֵלֶּה וְאֶת־

---

4. *the Kohathites.* The Levites were divided into three families, named after Levi's sons (cf. Gen. xlvi. 11), viz. Gershonites, Kohathites and Merarites. They were enumerated in Num. xxvi. 57).

Aaron the priest. He was a descendant of Kohath (*loc. cit.*).

5. *the rest of the children of Kohath.* Apart from Amram, Aaron's father, they were Izhar,

Hebron and Uzziel (Exod. vi. 18). The descendants of Moses were also included.

by lot. To determine which tribe was to assign cities to which Levitical family.

6. *the children of Gershon.* They were Libni and Shimei (Exod. vi. 17).

7. *the children of Merari.* They were Mahli and Mushi (Exod. vi. 19).

with the open land about them, as the LORD commanded by the hand of Moses.

9. And they gave out of the tribe of the children of Judah, and out of the tribe of the children of Simeon, these cities which are here mentioned by name. 10. And they were for the children of Aaron, of the families of the Kohathites, who were of the children of Levi; for theirs was the first lot. 11. And they gave them Kiriath-arba, which Arba was the father of Anak—the same is Hebron—in the hill-country of Judah, with the open land round about it. 12. But the fields of the city, and the villages thereof, gave they to Caleb the son of Jephunneh for his possession.

13. And unto the children of Aaron the priest they gave Hebron with the open land about it, the city of refuge for the manslayer, and Libnah with the open land about it; 14. and Jattir with the open land about it, and Eshtemoa with the open land about it; 15. and Holon

מִגְרְשֵׁיהֶן כַּאֲשֶׁר צִוָּה יְהֹוָה
בְּיַד־מֹשֶׁה בַּגּוֹרָל:

9 וַיִּתְּנוּ מִמַּטֵּה בְּנֵי יְהוּדָה
וּמִמַּטֵּה בְּנֵי שִׁמְעוֹן אֵת הֶעָרִים
הָאֵלֶּה אֲשֶׁר־יִקְרָא אֶתְהֶן
10 בְּשֵׁם: וַיְהִי לִבְנֵי אַהֲרֹן
מִמִּשְׁפְּחוֹת הַקְּהָתִי מִבְּנֵי לֵוִי
כִּי לָהֶם הָיָה הַגּוֹרָל רִאשֹׁנָה:

11 וַיִּתְּנוּ לָהֶם אֶת־קִרְיַת אַרְבַּע
אֲבִי הָעֲנוֹק הִיא חֶבְרוֹן בְּהַר
יְהוּדָה וְאֶת־מִגְרָשֶׁהָ

12 סְבִיבֹתֶיהָ: וְאֶת־שְׂדֵה הָעִיר
וְאֶת־חֲצֵרֶיהָ נָתְנוּ לְכָלֵב בֶּן־
יְפֻנֶּה בַּאֲחֻזָּתוֹ:

13 וְלִבְנֵי ׀ אַהֲרֹן הַכֹּהֵן נָתְנוּ אֶת־
עִיר מִקְלַט הָרֹצֵחַ אֶת־
חֶבְרוֹן וְאֶת־מִגְרָשֶׁהָ וְאֶת־
לִבְנָה וְאֶת־־מִגְרָשֶׁיהָ:

14 וְאֶת־יַתִּר וְאֶת־־מִגְרָשֶׁהָ
וְאֶת־אֶשְׁתְּמֹעַ וְאֶת־

15 מִגְרָשֶׁיהָ: וְאֶת־חֹלֹן וְאֶת־
<hr/>
v. 10. ראשנה ק׳

---

11. *Kiriath-arba.* See on xiv. 15. According to xv. 13, Hebron was given to Caleb! The reconciliation is effected by distinguishing between the wider territory (*fields, villages* and the immediately neighbouring *towns,* all belonging to Hebron) as given to Caleb, whereas the city proper with the open land around it was given to the children of Aaron as a Levitical city. See the following two verses (Makkoth 10a).

12. *gave they.* Better, 'they had given.'

13. *the city of refuge.* The six cities of refuge enumerated in the previous chapter were all Levitical cities (cf. Num. xxxv. 6).

Libnah. See on x. 29.

14. *Jattir . . . Eshtemoa.* The names have a slightly different form in xv. 48, 50.

15. *Holon.* See on xv. 51.

with the open land about it, and
Debir with the open land about it;
16. and Ain with the open land
about it, and Juttah with the open
land about it, and Beth-shemesh
with the open land about it; nine
cities out of those two tribes.
17. And out of the tribe of Benjamin,
Gibeon with the open land about it,
Geba with the open land about it;
18. Anathoth with the open land
about it, and Almon with the open
land about it; four cities. 19. All
the cities of the children of Aaron,
the priests, were thirteen cities with
the open land about them.

20. And the families of the
children of Kohath, the Levites,
even the rest of the children of
Kohath, they had the cities of their
lot out of the tribe of Ephraim.
21. And they gave them Shechem
with the open land about it in the
hill-country of Ephraim, the city of
refuge for the manslayer, and Gezer

מִגְרָשֶׁהָ וְאֶת־דְּבִר וְאֶת־
16 מִגְרָשֶׁהָ׃ וְאֶת־עַיִן וְאֶת־
מִגְרָשֶׁהָ וְאֶת־יֻטָּה וְאֶת־
מִגְרָשֶׁהָ אֶת־בֵּית שֶׁמֶשׁ
וְאֶת־מִגְרָשֶׁהָ עָרִים תֵּשַׁע
מֵאֵת שְׁנֵי הַשְּׁבָטִים הָאֵלֶּה׃
17 וּמִמַּטֵּה בִנְיָמִן אֶת־גִּבְעוֹן
וְאֶת־מִגְרָשֶׁהָ אֶת־גֶּבַע וְאֶת־
18 מִגְרָשֶׁהָ׃ אֶת־עֲנָתוֹת וְאֶת־
מִגְרָשֶׁהָ וְאֶת־עַלְמוֹן וְאֶת־
19 מִגְרָשֶׁהָ עָרִים אַרְבַּע׃ כָּל־
עָרֵי בְנֵי־אַהֲרֹן הַכֹּהֲנִים
שְׁלֹשׁ־עֶשְׂרֵה עָרִים
וּמִגְרָשֵׁיהֶן׃
20 וּלְמִשְׁפְּחוֹת בְּנֵי־קְהָת הַלְוִיִּם
הַנּוֹתָרִים מִבְּנֵי קְהָת וַיְהִי עָרֵי
21 גוֹרָלָם מִמַּטֵּה אֶפְרָיִם׃ וַיִּתְּנוּ
לָהֶם אֶת־עִיר מִקְלַט הָרֹצֵחַ
אֶת־שְׁכֶם וְאֶת־מִגְרָשֶׁהָ בְּהַר
אֶפְרָיִם וְאֶת־גֶּזֶר וְאֶת־

Debir. See on x. 38.

16. *Ain.* lit. 'well'; in 1 Chron. vi. 44 instead
of *Ain* the reading is *Ashan.* [The full name
may have been Ain-ashan, perhaps the *Bor-
ashan* of 1 Sam. xxx. 30.]

Beth-shemesh. See on xv. 10.

17. *Gibeon.* See on ix. 3.

Geba. See on xviii. 24.

18. *Anathoth.* Now Anatha, three miles

north-east of Jerusalem (see Daath Mikra). It
was the birthplace of Jeremiah (Jer. i. 1).

Almon. Called *Alemeth* in 1 Chron. vi. 45; now
Almit, near Anathoth on the north-east
(Daath Mikra).

20. *the Levites.* Who were not descendants
of Aaron.

21. *Shechem.* See on xx. 7.

Gezer. See on x. 33.

with the open land about it; 22. and
Kibzaim with the open land about it,
and Beth-horon with the open land
about it; four cities. 23. And out
of the tribe of Dan, Elteke with the
open land about it, Gibbethon with
the open land about it; 24. Aijalon
with the open land about it, Gath-
rimmon with the open land about it;
four cities. 25. And out of the half-
tribe of Manasseh, Taanach with the
open land about it, and Gath-rimmon
with the open land about it; two
cities. 26. All the cities of the
families of the rest of the children of
Kohath were ten with the open land
about them.

27. And unto the children of
Gershon, of the families of the
Levites, out of the half-tribe of
Manasseh they gave Golan in
Bashan with the open land about it,
the city of refuge for the manslayer;
and Beeshterah with the open land
about it; two cities. 28. And out of
the tribe of Issachar, Kishion with

²² מִגְרָשֶׁהָ: וְאֶת־־קִבְצַ֫יִם
וְאֶת־מִגְרָשֶׁהָ וְאֶת־בֵּית חֹרֹן
וְאֶת־מִגְרָשֶׁהָ עָרִים אַרְבַּע:
²³ וּמִמַּטֵּה־דָ֫ן אֶת־אֶלְתְּקֵא
וְאֶת־מִגְרָשֶׁהָ אֶת־גִּבְּתוֹן
²⁴ וְאֶת־מִגְרָשֶׁהָ: אֶת־אַיָּלוֹן
וְאֶת־מִגְרָשֶׁהָ אֶת־גַּת־רִמּוֹן
וְאֶת־מִגְרָשֶׁהָ עָרִים אַרְבַּע:
²⁵ וּמִמַּחֲצִית מַטֵּה מְנַשֶּׁה אֶת־
תַּעְנַךְ וְאֶת־מִגְרָשֶׁהָ וְאֶת־גַּת
רִמּוֹן וְאֶת־מִגְרָשֶׁהָ עָרִים
²⁶ שְׁתָּֽיִם: כָּל־עָרִים עֶשֶׂר
וּמִגְרְשֵׁיהֶן לְמִשְׁפְּחוֹת בְּנֵי־
קְהָת הַנּוֹתָרִים:
²⁷ וְלִבְנֵי גֵרְשׁוֹן מִמִּשְׁפְּחֹת הַלְוִיִּם
מֵחֲצִי מַטֵּה מְנַשֶּׁה אֶת־עִיר
מִקְלַט הָרֹצֵחַ אֶת־גּוֹלָן בַּבָּשָׁן
וְאֶת־מִגְרָשֶׁהָ וְאֶת־בְּעֶשְׁתְּרָה
וְאֶת־מִגְרָשֶׁהָ עָרִים שְׁתָּֽיִם:
²⁸ וּמִמַּטֵּה יִשָּׂשכָר אֶת־קִשְׁיוֹן

v. 27. גּוֹלָן ק׳

22. *Kibzaim.* 1 Chron. vi. 53 substitutes *Jokmeam.*

Beth-horon. See on x. 10.

23. *Elteke . . . Gibbethon.* Mentioned in xix. 44.

24. *Aijalon.* See on xix. 42.

Gath-rimmon. See on xix. 45.

25. *the half tribe of Manasseh.* vix. that settled in western Canaan.

Taanach. See on xii. 21.

Gath-rimmon. Not the same town as that in verse 24 (Kimchi). It is mentioned in the Tel el-Amarna Letters, but its site is unknown. 1 Chron. vi. 55 substitutes *Bileam* which may be identical with *Ibleam* in xvii. 11 (Elijah of Wilna).

27. *the half tribe of Manasseh.* viz. that settled in Transjordan.

Golan. See on xx. 8.

Beeshterah. Called *Ashtaroth* in 1 Chron. vi. 56. See on ix. 10.

the open land about it, Dobrath with the open land about it; 29. Jarmuth with the open land about it, En-gannim with the open land about it; four cities. 30. And out of the tribe of Asher, Mishal with the open land about it, Abdon with the open land about it; 31. Helkath with the open land about it, and Rehob with the open land about it; four cities. 32. And out of the tribe of Naphtali, Kedesh in Galilee with the open land about it, the city of refuge for the manslayer, and Hammoth-dor with the open land about it, and Kartan with the open land about it; three cities. 33. All the cities of the Gershonites according to their families were thirteen cities with the open land about them.

34. And unto the families of the children of Merari, the rest of the Levites, out of the tribe of Zebulun, Jokneam with the open land about it, and Kartah with the open land about

וְאֶת־מִגְרָשֶׁהָ אֶת־דָּבְרַת
29 וְאֶת־מִגְרָשֶׁהָ: אֶת־יַרְמוּת
וְאֶת־מִגְרָשֶׁהָ אֶת־עֵין גַּנִּים
וְאֶת־מִגְרָשֶׁהָ עָרִים אַרְבַּע:
30 וּמִמַּטֵּה אָשֵׁר אֶת־מִשְׁאָל
וְאֶת־מִגְרָשֶׁהָ אֶת־עַבְדּוֹן
31 וְאֶת־מִגְרָשֶׁהָ: אֶת־חֶלְקָת
וְאֶת־מִגְרָשֶׁהָ וְאֶת־רְחֹב
וְאֶת־מִגְרָשֶׁהָ עָרִים אַרְבַּע:
32 וּמִמַּטֵּה נַפְתָּלִי אֶת־עִיר ׀
מִקְלַט הָרֹצֵחַ אֶת־קֶדֶשׁ
בַּגָּלִיל וְאֶת־מִגְרָשֶׁהָ וְאֶת־
חַמֹּת דֹּאר וְאֶת־מִגְרָשֶׁהָ
וְאֶת־קַרְתָּן וְאֶת־מִגְרָשֶׁהָ
33 עָרִים שָׁלֹשׁ: כָּל־עָרֵי
הַגֵּרְשֻׁנִּי לְמִשְׁפְּחֹתָם שָׁלֹשׁ־
עֶשְׂרֵה עִיר וּמִגְרְשֵׁיהֶן:
34 וּלְמִשְׁפְּחוֹת בְּנֵי־מְרָרִי הַלְוִיִּם
הַנּוֹתָרִים מֵאֵת מַטֵּה זְבוּלֻן
אֶת־יָקְנְעָם וְאֶת־מִגְרָשֶׁהָ
אֶת־קַרְתָּה וְאֶת־מִגְרָשֶׁהָ:

28. *Kishion.* Cf. xix. 20.

Dobrath. See on xix. 12.

29. *Jarmuth.* Called Remeth in xix. 21.

En-gannim. See on xix. 21.

30. *Mishal.* See on xix. 26.

Abdon. See on xix. 28.

31. *Helkath.* Cf. xix. 25.

Rehob. See on xix. 28.

32. *Kedesh.* See on xii. 22.

Hammoth-dor. Called *Hammon* in 1 Chron. vi. 61. [The name implies that it was a city near hot springs (cf. *Hammath* in xix. 35), possibly in the Plain of Gennesareth, but its exact site is not known.]

Kartan. [Possibly identical with *Rakkath* (xix. 35).]

34. *Jokneam.* See on xii. 22.

it; 35. Dimnah with the open land about it, Nahalal with the open land about it; four cities. [And out of the tribe of Reuben, Bezer with the open land about it, and Jahaz with the open land about it; Kedemoth with the open land about it, and Mephaath with the open land about it; four cities.] 36. And out of the tribe of Gad, Ramoth in Gilead with the open land about it, the city of refuge for the manslayer, and Mahanaim with the open land about it; 37. Heshbon with the open land about it, Jazer with the open land about it; four cities in all. 38. All these were the cities of the children of Merari according to their families, even the rest of the families of the Levites; and their lot was twelve cities.

39. All the cities of the Levites—forty and eight cities with the open land about them—shall be in the midst of the possession of the children of Israel, 40. even these

35 אֶת־דִּמְנָה וְאֶת־מִגְרָשֶׁהָ אֶת־
נַהֲלָל וְאֶת־מִגְרָשֶׁהָ עָרִים
36 אַרְבַּע׃ ٭ וּמִמַּטֵּה־גָד אֶת־
עִיר מִקְלַט הָרֹצֵחַ אֶת־רָמֹת
בַּגִּלְעָד וְאֶת־מִגְרָשֶׁהָ וְאֶת־
37 מַחֲנַיִם וְאֶת־מִגְרָשֶׁהָ׃ אֶת־
חֶשְׁבּוֹן וְאֶת־מִגְרָשֶׁהָ אֶת־
יַעְזֵר וְאֶת־מִגְרָשֶׁהָ כָּל־
38 עָרִים אַרְבַּע׃ כָּל־הֶעָרִים
לִבְנֵי מְרָרִי לְמִשְׁפְּחֹתָם
הַנּוֹתָרִים מִמִּשְׁפְּחוֹת הַלְוִיִּם
וַיְהִי גּוֹרָלָם עָרִים שְׁתֵּים
עֶשְׂרֵה׃
39 כֹּל עָרֵי הַלְוִיִּם בְּתוֹךְ אֲחֻזַּת
בְּנֵי־יִשְׂרָאֵל עָרִים אַרְבָּעִים
40 וּשְׁמֹנֶה וּמִגְרְשֵׁיהֶן׃ תִּהְיֶינָה

٭ בְּקְצַת סְפָרִים נִמְצְאוּ כָּאן ב׳ פְּסוּקִים הָאֵלֶּה. לְקוּחִים מִדִּבְרֵי הַיָּמִים א׳ ר׳ פְּסוּק ס״ג וְס״ד. וּכְפִי הַמָּסוֹרֶת אֵינָם רְאוּיִים לִהְיוֹת. וּלְמַעַן לֹא יֶחְסְרוּ לַקּוֹרֵא הַצֵּגְנוּם פֹּה בַּגִּלָּיוֹן: ٭

٭וּמִמַּטֵּה רְאוּבֵן אֶת־בֶּצֶר וְאֶת־מִגְרָשֶׁהָ וְאֶת־יַהְצָה וְאֶת־מִגְרָשֶׁהָ׃
אֶת־קְדֵמוֹת וְאֶת־מִגְרָשֶׁהָ וְאֶת־מֵיפָעַת וְאֶת־מִגְרָשֶׁהָ עָרִים אַרְבַּע׃

35. *Dimnah.* Called *Rimmono* in 1 Chron. vi. 62; perhaps identical with *Rimmon* in xix. 13.

Nahalal. See on xix. 15.

[*Bezer.* See on xx. 8.

Jahaz. See on xiii. 18.

Kedemoth . . . Mephaath. See on xiii. 18.]

36. *Ramoth in Gilead.* See on xx. 8.

Mahanaim. Cf. xiii. 26.

37. *Heshbon.* See on ix. 10.

Jazer. See on xiii. 25.

38. *twelve cities.* For this number the four cities in the two bracketed verses inserted from 1 Chron. vi. 63f., must be included; otherwise there are only eight. A parallel list of Levitical cities is given in 1 Chron. vi. with a number of variants. In some instances they are nothing more than different forms of the same name; in others different cities are indicated. That is because some of the cities which fell by lot to the Levites were then still in enemy hands and others had to be substituted (Kimchi on 1 Chron. vi. 39).

cities, every one with the open land round about it; thus it shall be with all these cities.

41. So the LORD gave unto Israel all the land which He swore to give unto their fathers; and they possessed it, and dwelt therein. 42. And the LORD gave them rest round about, according to all that He swore unto their fathers; and there stood not a man of all their enemies against them; the LORD delivered all their enemies into their hand. 43. There failed not aught of any good thing which the LORD had spoken unto the house of Israel; all came to pass.

הֶעָרִים הָאֵלֶּה עִיר עִיר
וּמִגְרָשֶׁיהָ סְבִיבֹתֶיהָ כֵּן
לְכָל־הֶעָרִים הָאֵלֶּה:

41 וַיִּתֵּן יְהֹוָה לְיִשְׂרָאֵל אֶת־כָּל־
הָאָרֶץ אֲשֶׁר נִשְׁבַּע לָתֵת
לַאֲבוֹתָם וַיִּרָשׁוּהָ וַיֵּשְׁבוּ בָהּ:

42 וַיָּנַח יְהֹוָה לָהֶם מִסָּבִיב כְּכֹל
אֲשֶׁר־נִשְׁבַּע לַאֲבוֹתָם וְלֹא־
עָמַד אִישׁ בִּפְנֵיהֶם מִכָּל־
אֹיְבֵיהֶם אֵת כָּל־אֹיְבֵיהֶם נָתַן

43 יְהֹוָה בְּיָדָם: לֹא־נָפַל דָּבָר
מִכֹּל הַדָּבָר הַטּוֹב אֲשֶׁר־
דִּבֶּר יְהֹוָה אֶל־בֵּית יִשְׂרָאֵל
הַכֹּל בָּא:

---

22   CHAPTER XXII   כב

1. Then Joshua called the Reubenites, and the Gadites, and the half-tribe of Manasseh, 2. and said unto them: 'Ye have kept all that Moses the servant of the LORD commanded you, and have hearkened unto my voice in all that I commanded you; 3. ye have not left your brethren

1 אָז יִקְרָא יְהוֹשֻׁעַ לָרֹאוּבֵנִי
וְלַגָּדִי וְלַחֲצִי מַטֵּה מְנַשֶּׁה:

2 וַיֹּאמֶר אֲלֵיהֶם אַתֶּם שְׁמַרְתֶּם
אֵת כָּל־אֲשֶׁר צִוָּה אֶתְכֶם
מֹשֶׁה עֶבֶד יְהֹוָה וַתִּשְׁמְעוּ
בְקוֹלִי לְכֹל אֲשֶׁר־צִוִּיתִי

3 אֶתְכֶם: לֹא־עֲזַבְתֶּם אֶת־

---

41. *all the land.* See on xi. 23.

43. *There failed not aught.* Although certain parts of the country were still left to conquer, this was because of neglect on the part of Joshua and Israel, not to the Almighty's

failure to fulfill His word (Ralbag).

any good thing, etc. [This verse summarizes the reiterated assurances which God made to the nation.]

these many days unto this day, but have kept the charge of the commandment of the LORD your God. 4. And now the LORD your God hath given rest unto your brethren, as He spoke unto them; therefore now turn ye, and get you unto your tents, unto the land of your possession, which Moses the servant of the LORD gave you beyond the Jordan. 5. Only take diligent heed to do the commandment and the law, which Moses the servant of the LORD commanded you, to love the LORD your God, and to walk in all His ways, and to keep His commandments, and to cleave unto Him, and to serve Him with all your heart and with all your soul.' 6. So Joshua blessed them, and sent them away; and they went unto their tents.

אֲחֵיכֶם זֶה יָמִים רַבִּים עַד
הַיּוֹם הַזֶּה וּשְׁמַרְתֶּם אֶת־
מִשְׁמֶרֶת מִצְוַת יְהֹוָה
4 אֱלֹהֵיכֶם: וְעַתָּה הֵנִיחַ יְהֹוָה
אֱלֹהֵיכֶם לַאֲחֵיכֶם כַּאֲשֶׁר
דִּבֶּר לָהֶם וְעַתָּה פְּנוּ וּלְכוּ
לָכֶם לְאָהֳלֵיכֶם אֶל־אֶרֶץ
אֲחֻזַּתְכֶם אֲשֶׁר ׀ נָתַן לָכֶם
מֹשֶׁה עֶבֶד יְהֹוָה בְּעֵבֶר
5 הַיַּרְדֵּן: רַק ׀ שִׁמְרוּ מְאֹד
לַעֲשׂוֹת אֶת־הַמִּצְוָה וְאֶת־
הַתּוֹרָה אֲשֶׁר צִוָּה אֶתְכֶם מֹשֶׁה
עֶבֶד־יְהֹוָה לְאַהֲבָה אֶת־
יְהֹוָה אֱלֹהֵיכֶם וְלָלֶכֶת בְּכָל־
דְּרָכָיו וְלִשְׁמֹר מִצְוֹתָיו
וּלְדָבְקָה־בוֹ וּלְעָבְדוֹ בְּכָל־
לְבַבְכֶם וּבְכָל־נַפְשְׁכֶם:
6 וַיְבָרֲכֵם יְהוֹשֻׁעַ וַיְשַׁלְּחֵם
וַיֵּלְכוּ אֶל־אָהֳלֵיהֶם:

ב״א וסער v. 4.

CHAPTER XXII

DEPARTURE OF THE TWO AND A
HALF TRIBES

1. *Then Joshua called.* i.e. upon the completion of the seven year period of conquest and the seven year period of division.

4. *hath given rest.* Cf. xxi. 44.

your tents. i.e. 'your homes'; the word *tent* was employed in this sense even when the

nomadic stage of existence had passed.

5. *only take diligent heed,* etc. The exhortation in this verse to remain faithful to the Torah was necessary. Separated from the rest of their brethren, they would be under constant pressure and temptation to forget their spiritual kinship with them, and abandon their religious heritage for the pagan cults of their neighbours. Joshua's words were therefore timely. Moreover, their retention of their land was dependent upon their fidelity to the Torah (cf. Deut. xxx. 20).

7. Now to the one half-tribe of Manasseh Moses had given inheritance in Bashan; but unto the other half gave Joshua among their brethren beyond the Jordan westward. Moreover when Joshua sent them away unto their tents, he blessed them, 8. and spoke unto them, saying: 'Return with much wealth unto your tents, and with very much cattle, with silver, and with gold, and with brass, and with iron, and with very much raiment; divide the spoil of your enemies with your brethren.'

9. And the children of Reuben and the children of Gad and the half-tribe of Manasseh returned, and departed from the children of Israel out of Shiloh, which is in the land of Canaan, to go unto the land of Gilead, to the land of their possession, whereof they were possessed, according to the commandment of the Lord by the hand of Moses. 10. And when they came unto the region about the Jordan, that is in the land of Canaan, the children of Reuben and the children of Gad and the half-tribe of Manasseh built

7 וְלַחֲצִי | שֵׁבֶט הַמְנַשֶּׁה נָתַן מֹשֶׁה בַּבָּשָׁן וּלְחֶצְיוֹ נָתַן יְהוֹשֻׁעַ עִם־אֲחֵיהֶם מֵעֵבֶר הַיַּרְדֵּן יָמָּה וְגַם כִּי שִׁלְּחָם יְהוֹשֻׁעַ אֶל־אָהֳלֵיהֶם וַיְבָרֲכֵם:

8 וַיֹּאמֶר אֲלֵיהֶם לֵאמֹר בִּנְכָסִים רַבִּים שׁוּבוּ אֶל־ אָהֳלֵיכֶם וּבְמִקְנֶה רַב־מְאֹד בְּכֶסֶף וּבְזָהָב וּבִנְחֹשֶׁת וּבְבַרְזֶל וּבִשְׂלָמוֹת הַרְבֵּה מְאֹד חִלְקוּ שְׁלַל אֹיְבֵיכֶם עִם־אֲחֵיכֶם:

9 וַיָּשֻׁבוּ וַיֵּלְכוּ בְּנֵי־רְאוּבֵן וּבְנֵי־גָד וַחֲצִי | שֵׁבֶט הַמְנַשֶּׁה מֵאֵת בְּנֵי יִשְׂרָאֵל מִשִּׁלֹה אֲשֶׁר־בְּאֶרֶץ כְּנַעַן לָלֶכֶת אֶל־אֶרֶץ הַגִּלְעָד אֶל־אֶרֶץ אֲחֻזָּתָם אֲשֶׁר נֹאחֲזוּ־בָהּ עַל־פִּי יְהוָה בְּיַד־מֹשֶׁה:

10 וַיָּבֹאוּ אֶל־גְּלִילוֹת הַיַּרְדֵּן אֲשֶׁר בְּאֶרֶץ כְּנַעַן וַיִּבְנוּ בְנֵי־ רְאוּבֵן וּבְנֵי־גָד וַחֲצִי שֵׁבֶט

v. 7. בעבר ק

---

8. *divide the spoil . . . with your brethren.* Who had stayed behind to guard the women and children. This was in accordance with the command of Num. xxxi. 27 (cf. 1 Sam. xxx. 24).

9. *out of Shiloh.* Where the division of the land had been determined (cf. xviii. 1).

10. *the land of Canaan.* The inference is that the altar was erected on the *western* side of the Jordan, thereby establishing a link between the land of the two and a half tribes and the land of the rest of Israel (Metsudath David). This is more probable than the view of Josephus that they built the altar after they 'were passed over the river' (*Antiquities* V. i. 26).

there an altar by the Jordan, a great altar to look upon. 11. And the children of Israel heard say: 'Behold, the children of Reuben and the children of Gad and the half-tribe of Manasseh have built an altar in the forefront of the land of Canaan, in the region about the Jordan, on the side that pertaineth to the children of Israel.' 12. And when the children of Israel heard of it, the whole congregation of the children of Israel gathered themselves together at Shiloh, to go up against them to war.

13. And the children of Israel sent unto the children of Reuben, and to the children of Gad, and to the half-tribe of Manasseh, into the land of Gilead, Phinehas the son of Eleazar the priest; 14. and with him ten

הַמְנַשֶּׁה שָׁם מִזְבֵּחַ עַל־הַיַּרְדֵּן
11 מִזְבֵּחַ גָּדוֹל לְמַרְאֶה: וַיִּשְׁמְעוּ
בְנֵי־יִשְׂרָאֵל לֵאמֹר הִנֵּה־בָנוּ
בְנֵי־רְאוּבֵן וּבְנֵי־גָד וַחֲצִי
שֵׁבֶט הַמְנַשֶּׁה אֶת־הַמִּזְבֵּחַ
אֶל־מוּל אֶרֶץ כְּנַעַן אֶל־
גְּלִילוֹת הַיַּרְדֵּן אֶל־עֵבֶר בְּנֵי
12 יִשְׂרָאֵל: וַיִּשְׁמְעוּ בְּנֵי יִשְׂרָאֵל
וַיִּקָּהֲלוּ כָּל־עֲדַת בְּנֵי־
יִשְׂרָאֵל שִׁלֹה לַעֲלוֹת עֲלֵיהֶם
לַצָּבָא:
13 וַיִּשְׁלְחוּ בְּנֵי־יִשְׂרָאֵל אֶל־
בְּנֵי־רְאוּבֵן וְאֶל־בְּנֵי־גָד
וְאֶל־חֲצִי שֵׁבֶט־מְנַשֶּׁה אֶל־
אֶרֶץ הַגִּלְעָד אֶת־פִּינְחָס
14 בֶּן־אֶלְעָזָר הַכֹּהֵן: וַעֲשָׂרָה

a great altar to look upon. The last three words do not mean 'in appearance' but describe the purpose of the altar. It was to serve as a monument. Consequently, the explanation given later (verses 22f.) was true and not an afterthought (Metsudath David).

11. *in the forefront of.* lit. 'in front of, over against, opposite to.'

on the side . . . Israel. More lit. 'towards the other side of the children of Israel.' This seems to support the interpretation that the altar was located on the west side of the Jordan.

12. *to go up against them to war.* i.e. if they would not rectify their error, for they thought that it was made for sacrifices (Metsudath David). As mentioned above, "high places," or private altars, had been banned since the establishment of the taber-

nacle at Shiloh (Rashi). The sacrificial service was to be performed in one place only, in Shiloh, where the Tabernacle had been set up. This was to impress upon the people the oneness of God. When they violated this ban and built high places, they were gradually drawn into idolatry, until the prophet Jeremiah denounced them by saying (ii. 28), ". . . for the number of thy cities were thy gods, O Judah." Therefore, the reaction was swift to this seeming wrong, just as in the case of the concubine of Gibeah (Judg. xx), lest this transgression spread throughout all Israel (Ralbag). See Hosea x. 9, where the prophet complains of the indifference and complacency of the people of his day, in comparison to the reaction at Gibeah.

13f. [The delegation which was sent consisted of the leading men, to impress the two and a half tribes with the gravity of their action.]

princes, one prince of a fathers' house for each of the tribes of Israel; and they were every one of them head of their fathers' houses among the thousands of Israel. 15. And they came unto the children of Reuben, and to the children of Gad, and to the half-tribe of Manasseh, unto the land of Gilead, and they spoke with them, saying: 16. 'Thus saith the whole congregation of the LORD: What treachery is this that ye have committed against the God of Israel, to turn away this day from following the LORD, in that ye have builded you an altar, to rebel this day against the LORD? 17. Is the iniquity of Peor too little for us, from which we have not cleansed ourselves unto this day, although there came a plague upon the con-

נְשִׂאִים֩ עִמּ֨וֹ נָשִׂ֜יא אֶחָ֨ד נָשִׂ֜יא
אֶחָ֤ד לְבֵ֣ית אָב֙ לְכֹ֖ל מַטּ֣וֹת
יִשְׂרָאֵ֑ל וְאִ֛ישׁ רֹ֥אשׁ בֵּית־
אֲבוֹתָ֥ם הֵ֖מָּה לְאַלְפֵ֥י יִשְׂרָאֵֽל׃
15 וַיָּבֹ֜אוּ אֶל־בְּנֵֽי־רְאוּבֵ֣ן וְאֶל־
בְּנֵי־גָ֗ד וְאֶל־חֲצִ֛י שֵׁבֶט־
מְנַשֶּׁ֖ה אֶל־אֶ֣רֶץ הַגִּלְעָ֑ד
וַיְדַבְּר֥וּ אִתָּ֖ם לֵאמֹֽר׃ כֹּ֣ה
16 אָֽמְר֞וּ כֹּ֣ל ׀ עֲדַ֣ת יְהֹוָ֗ה
מָֽה־הַמַּ֤עַל הַזֶּה֙ אֲשֶׁ֣ר
מְעַלְתֶּ֔ם בֵּאלֹהֵ֖י יִשְׂרָאֵ֑ל
לָשׁ֣וּב הַיּ֔וֹם מֵאַחֲרֵ֖י יְהֹוָ֑ה
בִּבְנֽוֹתְכֶ֤ם לָכֶם֙ מִזְבֵּ֔חַ
לִמְרָדְכֶ֥ם הַיּ֖וֹם בַּֽיהֹוָֽה׃
17 הַמְעַט־לָ֙נוּ֙ אֶת־עֲוֺ֣ן פְּע֔וֹר
אֲשֶׁ֤ר לֹֽא־הִטַּהַ֙רְנוּ֙ מִמֶּ֔נּוּ עַ֖ד
הַיּ֣וֹם הַזֶּ֑ה וַיְהִ֥י הַנֶּ֖גֶף בַּֽעֲדַ֥ת

14. *ten princes.* One from each of the tribes of Simeon, Judah, Issachar, Zebulun, Benjamin, Dan, Naphtali, Asher, Ephraim and half-Manasseh. Phinehas represented the Almighty, against Whom the two and a half tribes were suspected of rebelling (Malbim).

thousands. Better, 'clans.'

16. *to rebel this day against the Lord.* From the reply (verses 22f.), and also from the words of the delegation (cf. verse 19), it is clear that the objection was not the fear that the altar would be used for pagan worship. Even if it were intended for sacrifice to God, it still constituted rebellion in that it undermined the unity of the people for which a centralized sacrificial service was essential. The idea of centralization thus dates back to the very beginnings of the nation in the homeland (cf. Deut. xii. 13f.) (Rashi, Kimchi).

17. *the iniquity of Peor.* Cf. Num. xxv. 1ff.

we have not cleansed ourselves. i.e. we have not completely atoned for that sin (Metsudath David).

unto this day. A measure of the depth in which the incident had rooted itself in the national consciousness. Perhaps there was a suspicion that some of them still yearned after the lascivious rites of the cult, and would use the altar to corrupt the pure worship of God (Abarbanel).

a plague. In which 24,000 died (Num. xxv. 9).

gregation of the LORD, 18. that ye must turn away this day from following the LORD? and it will be, seeing ye rebel to-day against the LORD, that to-morrow He will be wroth with the whole congregation of Israel. 19. Howbeit, if the land of your possession be unclean, then pass ye over unto the land of the possession of the LORD, wherein the LORD's tabernacle dwelleth, and take possession among us; but rebel not against the LORD, nor rebel against us, in building you an altar besides the altar of the LORD our God. 20. Did not Achan the son of Zerah commit a trespass concerning the devoted thing, and wrath fell upon all the congregation of Israel? and

18 יְהֹוָה: וְאַתֶּם תָּשֻׁבוּ הַיּוֹם
מֵאַחֲרֵי יְהֹוָה וְהָיָה אַתֶּם
תִּמְרְדוּ הַיּוֹם בַּיהֹוָה וּמָחָר
אֶל־כָּל־עֲדַת יִשְׂרָאֵל
19 יִקְצֹף: וְאַךְ אִם־טְמֵאָה אֶרֶץ
אֲחֻזַּתְכֶם עִבְרוּ לָכֶם אֶל־
אֶרֶץ אֲחֻזַּת יְהֹוָה אֲשֶׁר שָׁכַן־
שָׁם מִשְׁכַּן יְהֹוָה וְהֵאָחֲזוּ
בְתוֹכֵנוּ וּבַיהֹוָה אַל־תִּמְרֹדוּ
וְאֹתָנוּ אַל־תִּמְרֹדוּ בִּבְנֹתְכֶם
לָכֶם מִזְבֵּחַ מִבַּלְעֲדֵי מִזְבַּח
20 יְהֹוָה אֱלֹהֵינוּ: הֲלוֹא | עָכָן
בֶּן־זֶרַח מָעַל מַעַל בַּחֵרֶם
וְעַל־כָּל־עֲדַת יִשְׂרָאֵל הָיָה

18. *He will be wroth with the whole congregation of Israel.* Collective guilt will have been incurred, because the community as a whole was responsible for seeing that its sections did not sin. The corollary was the responsibility of the individual to the community. Hence, we explain that God would be wroth with the whole congregation of Israel, i.e. with all those capable of protesting. Moreover, the other tribes would possibly be influenced to emulate the two and a half tribes in their worship of idols (Ralbag, Abarbanel, and Metsudath David).

19. *Howbeit.* If you had no idolatrous intentions, but intend to build a private altar to God (Abarbanel).

if the land of your possession be unclean. i.e. unfit for building an altar, even a private altar, as distinct from the communal altar, for the Lord did not choose it to cause His presence to rest therein (Rashi), judging by the fact that the tabernacle was not built on the eastern side of the Jordan (Kimchi).

wherein the Lord's *tabernacle dwelleth.* 'The land of Canaan is more holy than Transjordan, because the former is fit for a Temple for the Divine Presence, whereas the latter is not' (Num. Rabbah vii. 8).

and take possession among us. This was a magnanimous offer, since its acceptance would have appreciably diminished the territories of the other tribes. It indicates how far they were ready to go to preserve the nation's spiritual unity unimpaired.

nor rebel against us. It was a sin not only against God, but also against the unity of the people, and would involve them all in punishment (Abarbanel).

20. *upon all the congregation of Israel.* See on vii. 1. 'It is written, *Ye are standing this day all of you before the* Lord *your God . . . even all the men of Israel* (Deut. xxix. 9)—thus you are all responsible for one another. Even if there be one righteous man among you, you all *stand* (secure) for his sake. . . . Conversely, if one of

that man perished not alone in his iniquity.'

21. Then the children of Reuben and the children of Gad and the half-tribe of Manasseh answered, and spoke unto the heads of the thousands of Israel: 22. 'God, God, the LORD, God, God, the LORD, He knoweth, and Israel he shall know; if it be in rebellion, or if in treachery against the LORD—save Thou us not this day—23. that we have built us an altar to turn away from following the LORD; or if to offer thereon burnt-offering or meal-offering, or if to offer sacrifices of peace-offerings thereon, let the LORD Himself require it; 24. and if we have not rather out of anxiety about a matter done this, saying: In time to come your children might speak unto our children, saying: What have ye to do with the LORD, the God of Israel? 25. for the LORD hath

קֶצֶף וְהוּא אִישׁ אֶחָד לֹא גָוַע
בַּעֲוֹנוֹ:

21 וַיַּעֲנוּ בְּנֵי־רְאוּבֵן וּבְנֵי־גָד
וַחֲצִי שֵׁבֶט הַמְנַשֶּׁה וַיְדַבְּרוּ
אֶת־רָאשֵׁי אַלְפֵי יִשְׂרָאֵל:

22 אֵל ׀ אֱלֹהִים ׀ יְהֹוָה אֵל ׀
אֱלֹהִים ׀ יְהֹוָה הוּא יֹדֵעַ
וְיִשְׂרָאֵל הוּא יֵדָע אִם־בְּמֶרֶד
וְאִם־בְּמַעַל בַּיהֹוָה אַל־

23 תּוֹשִׁיעֵנוּ הַיּוֹם הַזֶּה: לִבְנוֹת
לָנוּ מִזְבֵּחַ לָשׁוּב מֵאַחֲרֵי יְהֹוָה
וְאִם־לְהַעֲלוֹת עָלָיו עוֹלָה
וּמִנְחָה וְאִם־לַעֲשׂוֹת עָלָיו
זִבְחֵי שְׁלָמִים יְהֹוָה הוּא יְבַקֵּשׁ:

24 וְאִם־לֹא מִדְּאָגָה מִדָּבָר
עָשִׂינוּ אֶת־זֹאת לֵאמֹר מָחָר
יֹאמְרוּ בְנֵיכֶם לְבָנֵינוּ לֵאמֹר
מַה־לָּכֶם וְלַיהֹוָה אֱלֹהֵי

25 יִשְׂרָאֵל: וּגְבוּל נָתַן־יְהֹוָה

you sin, the whole generation is punished' (Tanchuma Nitsabim 2).

22. *God, God, the* Lord. They referred to the Deity with the identical names mentioned in reference to the Creation (Ps. l.1) and to the giving of the Torah (Ex. xx. 5). Thus, they affirmed their belief in the One God Who created the world and Who revealed His Law to Israel. With this affirmation, they sought to refute the suspicions against them, both that of idolatry, since they believed that the Almighty Himself created the world, and also that of building an altar outside the tabernacle, since they believed firmly in the

revelation of the Torah, which forbids this (Minchath Shai).

and Israel he shall know. The Talmud (j. Shek. 47c) found in this verse, as also in Num. xxxii. 22 and Prov. iii. 4, the thought that a man must justify himself both in the sight of God and his fellows.

23. *let the* Lord *Himself require it.* i.e. then may He punish us. For the idiom, cf. Deut. xviii. 19; 1 Sam. xx. 16.

24. *a matter.* viz. the possibility that we and our descendants may be denied participation in God's worship (K'li Y'kar).

made the Jordan a border between us and you, ye children of Reuben and children of Gad; ye have no portion in the LORD; so might your children make our children cease from fearing the LORD. 26. Therefore we said: Let us now prepare to build us an altar, not for burnt-offering, nor for sacrifice; 27. but it shall be a witness between us and you, and between our generations after us, that we may do the service of the LORD before Him with our burnt-offerings, and with our sacrifices, and with our peace-offerings; that your children may not say to our children in time to come: Ye have no portion in the LORD. 28. Therefore said we: It shall be, when they so say to us or to our generations in time to come, that we shall say: Behold the pattern of the altar of the LORD, which our fathers made, not for burnt-offering, nor for sacrifice; but it is a witness between us and you. 29. Far be it from us that we should rebel against the LORD, and turn away this day from following the LORD, to build an altar

בֵּינֵ֖ינוּ וּבֵֽינֵיכֶ֑ם בְּנֵֽי־רְאוּבֵ֣ן
וּבְנֵי־גָ֔ד אֶת־הַיַּרְדֵּ֖ן אֵ֥ין־
לָכֶ֨ם חֵ֤לֶק בַּֽיהוָה֙ וְהִשְׁבִּ֣יתוּ
בְנֵיכֶ֣ם אֶת־בָּנֵ֔ינוּ לְבִלְתִּ֖י יְרֹ֥א
26 אֶת־יְהוָֽה׃ וַנֹּ֕אמֶר נַעֲשֶׂה־נָּ֣א
לָ֔נוּ לִבְנ֖וֹת אֶת־הַמִּזְבֵּ֑חַ לֹ֥א
27 לְעוֹלָ֖ה וְלֹ֣א לְזָ֑בַח׃ כִּי֩ עֵ֨ד
ה֜וּא בֵּינֵ֗ינוּ וּבֵֽינֵיכֶם֮ וּבֵ֣ין
דֹּרוֹתֵ֣ינוּ אַחֲרֵ֑ינוּ לַעֲבֹ֞ד אֶת־
עֲבֹדַ֤ת יְהוָה֙ לְפָנָ֔יו בְּעֹלוֹתֵ֥ינוּ
וּבִזְבָחֵ֖ינוּ וּבִשְׁלָמֵ֑ינוּ וְלֹֽא־
יֹאמְר֨וּ בְנֵיכֶ֤ם מָחָר֙ לְבָנֵ֔ינוּ
אֵֽין־לָכֶ֥ם חֵ֖לֶק בַּֽיהוָֽה׃
28 וַנֹּ֕אמֶר וְהָיָ֗ה כִּֽי־יֹאמְר֥וּ
אֵלֵ֛ינוּ וְאֶל־דֹּרֹתֵ֖ינוּ מָחָ֑ר
וְאָמַ֡רְנוּ רְא֣וּ אֶת־תַּבְנִית֩
מִזְבַּ֨ח יְהוָ֜ה אֲשֶׁר־עָשׂ֣וּ
אֲבוֹתֵ֗ינוּ לֹ֤א לְעוֹלָה֙ וְלֹ֣א
לְזֶ֔בַח כִּי־עֵ֣ד ה֔וּא בֵּינֵ֖ינוּ
29 וּבֵֽינֵיכֶֽם׃ חָלִ֨ילָה לָּ֜נוּ מִמֶּ֗נּוּ
לִמְרֹד֙ בַּֽיהוָ֔ה וְלָשׁ֤וּב הַיּוֹם֙
מֵאַחֲרֵ֣י יְהוָ֔ה לִבְנ֥וֹת מִזְבֵּ֖חַ

---

25. *fearing.* i.e. worshipping.

26. *let us now prepare to build us an altar.* This rendering is against the Hebrew accentuation which disconnects *us* from *to build,* and does not reproduce the meaning of the original, which is: 'let us now act for ourselves (to prevent the possibility of our exclusion) by building an altar' (Malbim).

27. *before Him with our burnt-offerings,* etc. Not upon *that* altar but by joining with our brethren on the other side of the Jordan (Daath Mikra).

28. *they so say to us.* That we have no portion in the LORD (Metsudath David).

pattern. The meaning here is 'replica.'

for burnt-offering, for meal-offering, or for sacrifice, besides the altar of the LORD our God that is before His tabernacle.'

30. And when Phinehas the priest, and the princes of the congregation, even the heads of the thousands of Israel that were with him, heard the words that the children of Reuben and the children of Gad and the children of Manasseh spoke, it pleased them well. 31. And Phinehas the son of Eleazar the priest said unto the children of Reuben, and to the children of Gad, and to the children of Manasseh: 'This day we know that the LORD is in the midst of us, because ye have not committed this treachery against the LORD; now have ye delivered the children of Israel out of the hand of the LORD.' 32. And Phinehas the son of Eleazar the priest, and the princes, returned from the children of Reuben, and from the children of Gad, out of the land of Gilead, unto the land of Canaan, to the children of Israel, and brought them back word. 33. And the thing pleased the children of Israel; and the children of Israel blessed God, and spoke no more of going up against them to war, to destroy the land wherein the

לְעֹלָה לְמִנְחָה וּלְזֶבַח מִלְּבַד
מִזְבַּח֩ יְהֹוָ֨ה אֱלֹהֵ֜ינוּ אֲשֶׁ֥ר לִפְנֵ֖י
מִשְׁכָּנֽוֹ׃

30 וַיִּשְׁמַ֣ע פִּֽינְחָ֣ס הַכֹּהֵן֮ וּנְשִׂיאֵ֣י
הָעֵדָ֣ה וְרָאשֵׁ֣י אַלְפֵ֣י יִשְׂרָאֵ֗ל
אֲשֶׁ֣ר אִתּ֔וֹ אֶת־הַדְּבָרִ֔ים
אֲשֶׁ֣ר דִּבְּר֞וּ בְּנֵֽי־רְאוּבֵ֣ן וּבְנֵי־
גָד֙ וּבְנֵ֣י מְנַשֶּׁ֔ה וַיִּיטַ֖ב בְּעֵינֵיהֶֽם׃

31 וַיֹּ֣אמֶר פִּֽינְחָ֣ס בֶּן־אֶלְעָזָ֣ר
הַכֹּהֵ֡ן אֶל־בְּנֵֽי־רְאוּבֵ֣ן וְאֶל־
בְּנֵי־גָ֣ד וְאֶל־בְּנֵ֣י מְנַשֶּׁה֒
הַיּ֣וֹם ׀ יָדַ֗עְנוּ כִּֽי־בְתוֹכֵ֣נוּ
יְהֹוָ֔ה אֲשֶׁ֛ר לֹֽא־מְעַלְתֶּ֥ם
בַּֽיהֹוָ֖ה הַמַּ֣עַל הַזֶּ֑ה אָ֚ז הִצַּלְתֶּ֣ם
אֶת־בְּנֵ֣י יִשְׂרָאֵ֔ל מִיַּ֖ד יְהֹוָֽה׃

32 וַיָּ֣שָׁב פִּֽינְחָ֣ס בֶּן־אֶלְעָזָ֣ר
הַכֹּהֵ֣ן ׀ וְהַנְּשִׂיאִ֡ים מֵאֵ֣ת בְּנֵֽי־
רְאוּבֵ֣ן וּמֵאֵ֣ת בְּנֵי־גָ֗ד מֵאֶ֤רֶץ
הַגִּלְעָד֙ אֶל־אֶ֣רֶץ כְּנַ֔עַן אֶל־
בְּנֵ֣י יִשְׂרָאֵ֑ל וַיָּשִׁ֥בוּ אוֹתָ֖ם
דָּבָֽר׃

33 וַיִּיטַ֣ב הַדָּבָר֮ בְּעֵינֵ֣י
בְּנֵ֣י יִשְׂרָאֵל֒ וַיְבָרְכ֥וּ אֱלֹהִים֙
בְּנֵ֣י יִשְׂרָאֵ֔ל וְלֹ֣א אָ֣מְר֔וּ לַעֲל֤וֹת
עֲלֵיהֶם֙ לַצָּבָ֔א לְשַׁחֵ֖ת אֶת־

---

31. *that the* LORD *is in the midst of us.* That we are indeed a holy people (cf. Num. xvi. 3, *seeing all the congregation are holy . . . and the*

LORD *is among them*). Another explanation is: no sin has been committed and the wrath of God has not been incurred (Daath Mikra).

children of Reuben and the children of Gad dwelt. 34. And the children of Reuben and the children of Gad called the altar—: 'for it is a witness between us that the LORD is God.'

הָאָרֶץ אֲשֶׁר בְּנֵי־רְאוּבֵן
34 וּבְנֵי־גָד יֹשְׁבִים בָּהּ: וַיִּקְרְאוּ
בְּנֵי־רְאוּבֵן וּבְנֵי־גָד לַמִּזְבֵּחַ
כִּי עֵד הוּא בֵּינֹתֵינוּ כִּי יְהֹוָה
הָאֱלֹהִים:

23 CHAPTER XXIII כג

1. And it came to pass after many days, when the LORD had given rest unto Israel from all their enemies round about, and Joshua was old and well stricken in years; 2. that Joshua called for all Israel, for their elders and for their heads, and for their judges and for their officers, and said unto them: 'I am old and well stricken in years. 3. And ye have seen all that the LORD your God hath done unto all these nations because of you; for the LORD your God, He it is that hath fought for

1 וַיְהִי מִיָּמִים רַבִּים אַחֲרֵי
אֲשֶׁר־הֵנִיחַ יְהֹוָה לְיִשְׂרָאֵל
מִכָּל־אֹיְבֵיהֶם מִסָּבִיב
וִיהוֹשֻׁעַ זָקֵן בָּא בַּיָּמִים:
2 וַיִּקְרָא יְהוֹשֻׁעַ לְכָל־יִשְׂרָאֵל
לִזְקֵנָיו וּלְרָאשָׁיו וּלְשֹׁפְטָיו
וּלְשֹׁטְרָיו וַיֹּאמֶר אֲלֵהֶם אֲנִי
3 זָקַנְתִּי בָּאתִי בַּיָּמִים: וְאַתֶּם
רְאִיתֶם אֵת כָּל־אֲשֶׁר עָשָׂה
יְהֹוָה אֱלֹהֵיכֶם לְכָל־הַגּוֹיִם
הָאֵלֶּה מִפְּנֵיכֶם כִּי יְהֹוָה
אֱלֹהֵיכֶם הוּא הַנִּלְחָם לָכֶם:

34. *called the altar.* The name given to it, *Ed,* is inferred from the explanation which follows (Rashi, Kimchi). Some Hebrew MSS. insert the word to be read orally. See Minchath Shai.

CHAPTER XXIII

JOSHUA'S FIRST FAREWELL EXHORTATION

1. *well stricken in years.* If, as is probable, Joshua addressed his exhortation to the people shortly before his death, he was one hundred and ten years old (xxiv. 29).

2. *their elders . . . their heads.* They represented *all Israel.* The *elders* were the leaders; the *heads* were the chiefs of the tribes. The former constituted the governing body of the community as a whole; the latter were concerned with tribal matters. See Abarbanel, Malbim.

officers. The Hebrew, *shoterim,* is the term which occurs in Deut. xvi. 18. They were subordinate officials who attended upon the *judges.*

3. *because of you.* On your behalf.

the Lord *. . . fought for you.* For that reason He had a claim upon the loyalty of the

you. 4. Behold, I have allotted unto you for an inheritance, according to your tribes, these nations that remain, from the Jordan, with all the nations that I have cut off, even unto the Great Sea toward the going down of the sun. 5. And the LORD your God, He shall thrust them out from before you, and drive them from out of your sight; and ye shall possess their land, as the LORD your God spoke unto you. 6. Therefore be ye very courageous to keep and to do all that is written in the book of the law of Moses, that ye turn not aside therefrom to the right hand or to the left; 7. that ye come not among these nations, these that remain among you; neither make mention of the name of their gods, nor cause to swear by them, neither serve them, nor worship them; 8. but cleave unto the LORD your God, as ye have done

4 רְאוּ הִפַּ֫לְתִּי לָכֶם אֶת־הַגּוֹיִם
הַנִּשְׁאָרִים הָאֵ֫לֶּה בְּנַחֲלָה
לְשִׁבְטֵיכֶם מִן־הַיַּרְדֵּן וְכָל־
הַגּוֹיִם אֲשֶׁר הִכְרַ֫תִּי וְהַיָּם
5 הַגָּדוֹל מְבוֹא הַשָּׁ֫מֶשׁ: וַיהֹוָה
אֱלֹהֵיכֶם הוּא יֶהְדָּפֵם
מִפְּנֵיכֶם וְהוֹרִישׁ אֹתָם
מִלִּפְנֵיכֶם וִירִשְׁתֶּם אֶת־
אַרְצָם כַּאֲשֶׁר דִּבֶּר יְהֹוָה
6 אֱלֹהֵיכֶם לָכֶם: וַחֲזַקְתֶּם
מְאֹד לִשְׁמֹר וְלַעֲשׂוֹת אֶת־כָּל־
הַכָּתוּב בְּסֵ֫פֶר תּוֹרַת מֹשֶׁה
לְבִלְתִּי סוּר מִמֶּ֫נּוּ יָמִין
7 וּשְׂמֹאול: לְבִלְתִּי־בוֹא
בַּגּוֹיִם הָאֵ֫לֶּה הַנִּשְׁאָרִים
הָאֵ֫לֶּה אִתְּכֶם וּבְשֵׁם אֱלֹהֵיהֶם
לֹא־תַזְכִּ֫ירוּ וְלֹא תַשְׁבִּ֫יעוּ
וְלֹא תַעַבְדוּם וְלֹא תִשְׁתַּחֲווּ
8 לָהֶם: כִּי אִם־בַּיהֹוָה
אֱלֹהֵיכֶם תִּדְבָּ֫קוּ כַּאֲשֶׁר

v. 6. יתיר ו

people. Similarly the Decalogue is introduced with the reminder, *I am the* LORD *thy God*, etc. (Exod. xx. 2).

4. *these nations that remain*. Still unconquered; they are enumerated in xiii. 2–6.

6. *be ye very courageous*. lit. 'be ye very strong,' i.e. do your uttermost.

7. *that ye come not among these nations*. [Joshua understood that this was their gravest danger, and their subsequent history only too

forcibly justified his forebodings.]

make mention. Cf. Exod. xxiii. 13.

cause to swear by them. i.e when imposing an oath, let it not be done in the name of a heathen god (Kimchi).

8. *but cleave unto the* LORD. Cf. Deut. iv. 4. Abarbanel construes; 'But cleave unto the Lord your God—since ye have done so until this day, (9) therefore the Lord hath driven out ... unto this day—(10) then one man of you *will chase* (so the Hebrew) a thousand.'

unto this day; 9. wherefore the LORD hath driven out from before you great nations and mighty; but as for you, no man hath stood against you unto this day. 10. One man of you hath chased a thousand; for the LORD your God, He it is that fought for you, as He spoke unto you. 11. Take good heed therefore unto yourselves, that ye love the LORD your God. 12. Else if ye do in any wise go back, and cleave unto the remnant of these nations, even these that remain among you, and make marriages with them, and go in unto them, and they to you; 13. know for a certainty that the LORD your God will no more drive these nations from out of your sight; but they shall be a snare and a trap unto you, and a scourge in your sides, and pricks in your eyes, until ye perish from off

9 עֲשִׂיתֶם עַד הַיּוֹם הַזֶּה: וַיּוֹרֶשׁ
יְהֹוָה מִפְּנֵיכֶם גּוֹיִם גְּדֹלִים
וַעֲצוּמִים וְאַתֶּם לֹא־עָמַד
אִישׁ בִּפְנֵיכֶם עַד הַיּוֹם הַזֶּה:
10 אִישׁ־אֶחָד מִכֶּם יִרְדׇּף־
אֶלֶף כִּי | יְהֹוָה אֱלֹהֵיכֶם הוּא
הַנִּלְחָם לָכֶם כַּאֲשֶׁר דִּבֶּר
11 לָכֶם: וְנִשְׁמַרְתֶּם מְאֹד
לְנַפְשֹׁתֵיכֶם לְאַהֲבָה אֶת־
12 יְהֹוָה אֱלֹהֵיכֶם: כִּי | אִם־
שׁוֹב תָּשׁוּבוּ וּדְבַקְתֶּם בְּיֶתֶר
הַגּוֹיִם הָאֵלֶּה הַנִּשְׁאָרִים
הָאֵלֶּה אִתְּכֶם וְהִתְחַתַּנְתֶּם
בָּהֶם וּבָאתֶם בָּהֶם וְהֵם בָּכֶם:
13 יָדוֹעַ תֵּדְעוּ כִּי לֹא יוֹסִיף יְהֹוָה
אֱלֹהֵיכֶם לְהוֹרִישׁ אֶת־הַגּוֹיִם
הָאֵלֶּה מִלִּפְנֵיכֶם וְהָיוּ לָכֶם
לְפַח וּלְמוֹקֵשׁ וּלְשֹׁטֵט
בְּצִדֵּיכֶם וְלִצְנִנִים בְּעֵינֵיכֶם
עַד אֲבׇדְכֶם מֵעַל הָאֲדָמָה

10. *one man of you hath chased a thousand.* The Rabbis interpret this literally. King David, who slew only eight hundred (2 Sam. xxiii. 8), attributed the missing two hundred to his own imperfection, which caused divine aid to be diminished (Moed Katan 16).

12. *if ye do . . . go back.* i.e. act to the contrary, by not cleaving to God but to the remainder of the Canaanite inhabitants.

make marriages with them. Cf. Deut. vii. 1ff. Intermarriage would defeat the purpose of

the Divine command to drive out the population of Canaan.

13. *a snare.* An enticement to idolatry.

pricks in your eyes. [The Hebrew for *pricks* is the usual word for *thorns*. They first cause only pain, then festering and finally, if not removed in time, loss of sight. So will you suffer from the Canaanites until you will be dispossessed of your land.]

until ye perish, etc. Cf. Deut. xi. 17. The threat was tragically verified in Israel's history.

this good land which the LORD your God hath given you. 14. And, behold, this day I am going the way of all the earth; consider ye therefore in all your heart and in all your soul, that not one thing hath failed of all the good things which the LORD your God spoke concerning you; all are come to pass unto you, not one thing hath failed thereof. 15. And it shall come to pass, that as all the good things are come upon you of which the LORD your God spoke unto you, so shall the LORD bring upon you all the evil things, until He have destroyed you from off this good land which the LORD your God hath given you. 16. When ye transgress the covenant of the LORD your God, which He commanded you, and go

הַטּוֹבָה הַזֹּאת אֲשֶׁר נָתַן לָכֶם
14 יְהֹוָה אֱלֹהֵיכֶם: וְהִנֵּה אָנֹכִי
הוֹלֵךְ הַיּוֹם בְּדֶרֶךְ כָּל־
הָאָרֶץ וִידַעְתֶּם בְּכָל־
לְבַבְכֶם וּבְכָל־נַפְשְׁכֶם כִּי
לֹא־נָפַל דָּבָר אֶחָד מִכֹּל ׀
הַדְּבָרִים הַטּוֹבִים אֲשֶׁר דִּבֶּר
יְהֹוָה אֱלֹהֵיכֶם עֲלֵיכֶם הַכֹּל
בָּאוּ לָכֶם לֹא־נָפַל מִמֶּנּוּ דָּבָר
15 אֶחָד: וְהָיָה כַּאֲשֶׁר־בָּא
עֲלֵיכֶם כָּל־הַדָּבָר הַטּוֹב
אֲשֶׁר דִּבֶּר יְהֹוָה אֱלֹהֵיכֶם
אֲלֵיכֶם כֵּן יָבִיא יְהֹוָה עֲלֵיכֶם
אֵת כָּל־הַדָּבָר הָרָע עַד־
הַשְׁמִידוֹ אוֹתְכֶם מֵעַל
הָאֲדָמָה הַטּוֹבָה הַזֹּאת אֲשֶׁר
נָתַן לָכֶם יְהֹוָה אֱלֹהֵיכֶם:
16 בְּעָבְרְכֶם אֶת־בְּרִית יְהֹוָה
אֱלֹהֵיכֶם אֲשֶׁר צִוָּה אֶתְכֶם

---

14. *the way of all the earth.* i.e. I am about to die. The same phrase was used by David (1 Kings ii.2) (Metsudath David).

not one thing hath failed thereof. [Joshua said this although he had emphasized that the conquest had been incomplete and some of the original inhabitants were still to be subdued. For him no contradiction was implied. Notwithstanding the incompleteness of the conquest, God's promise had been fulfilled: the slaves of Egypt were now masters in their

own country. That was the outstanding fact, and by contrast the failures were trivial setbacks which could not and should not affect their sense of obligation to God.]

15. *this good land.* [The adjective is added to stress the magnitude of national loss which would be the sequel of unfaithfulness.]

16. *when ye transgress the covenant . . . ye shall perish quickly.* A reminder that the Israelites could claim no greater privileges than the

and serve other gods, and worship them; then shall the anger of the LORD be kindled against you, and ye shall perish quickly from off the good land which He hath given unto you.'

וַהֲלַכְתֶּם וַעֲבַדְתֶּם אֱלֹהִים
אֲחֵרִים וְהִשְׁתַּחֲוִיתֶם לָהֶם
וְחָרָה אַף־יְהֹוָה בָּכֶם
וַאֲבַדְתֶּם מְהֵרָה מֵעַל הָאָרֶץ
הַטּוֹבָה אֲשֶׁר נָתַן לָכֶם:

24   CHAPTER XXIV   כד

1. And Joshua gathered all the tribes of Israel to Shechem, and called for the elders of Israel, and for their heads, and for their judges, and for their officers; and they presented themselves before God. 2. And Joshua said unto all the people: 'Thus saith the LORD, the God of Israel: Your fathers dwelt of old time beyond the River, even Terah, the father of Abraham, and the

1 וַיֶּאֱסֹף יְהוֹשֻׁעַ אֶת־כָּל־
שִׁבְטֵי יִשְׂרָאֵל שְׁכֶמָה וַיִּקְרָא
לְזִקְנֵי יִשְׂרָאֵל וּלְרָאשָׁיו
וּלְשֹׁפְטָיו וּלְשֹׁטְרָיו וַיִּתְיַצְּבוּ
2 לִפְנֵי הָאֱלֹהִים: וַיֹּאמֶר
יְהוֹשֻׁעַ אֶל־כָּל־הָעָם כֹּה־
אָמַר יְהֹוָה אֱלֹהֵי יִשְׂרָאֵל
בְּעֵבֶר הַנָּהָר יָשְׁבוּ אֲבוֹתֵיכֶם
מֵעוֹלָם תֶּרַח אֲבִי אַבְרָהָם

---

nations whom they had dispossessed. The latter had lost their country through sin, and they would suffer a similar fate if they were disloyal to the covenant in virtue of which alone they had taken possession of the Promised Land (Lev. xviii. 27f.).

CHAPTER XXIV

JOSHUA'S FINAL ADDRESS AND DEATH

FOLLOWING the example of Moses, Joshua before his death solemnly addressed the people, reviewing their history and drawing the moral therefrom. They owed their preservation to God, and to Him also was due their possession of their newly acquired land. Their future would be decided by whether they would remain loyal to His service or follow the worship of the deities of the peoples

whom they had dispossessed. See Kimchi.

1. *to Shechem.* The place was well chosen for the purpose, hallowed as it was by historical and religious associations. There the promise concerning the land had been made for the first time to Abraham, the founder of the nation, and there he had built an altar—his first—to God (Gen. xii. 6f.). There, too, the people had heard the solemn pronouncement of the blessings and curses and had renewed their covenant with God (viii. 30ff.) (Daath Mikra).

before God. Shechem was apparently the site of a temporary sanctuary (cf. verse 26) (Daath Sofrim).

2. *beyond the River.* The Euphrates, in Ur of the Chaldees (Targum).

they served other gods. According to tradition,

father of Nahor; and they served
other gods. 3. And I took your
father Abraham from beyond the
River, and led him throughout all
the land of Canaan, and multiplied
his seed, and gave him Isaac.
4. And I gave unto Isaac Jacob and
Esau; and I gave unto Esau mount
Seir, to possess it; and Jacob and
his children went down into Egypt.
5. And I sent Moses and Aaron, and
I plagued Egypt, according to that
which I did in the midst thereof; and
afterward I brought you out. 6. And
I brought your fathers out of Egypt;
and ye came unto the sea; and the
Egyptians pursued after your fathers
with chariots and with horsemen
unto the Red Sea. 7. And when
they cried out unto the LORD, He
put darkness between you and the
Egyptians, and brought the sea

וְאָבִי נָחוֹר וַיַּעַבְדוּ אֱלֹהִים
³ אֲחֵרִים: וָאֶקַּח אֶת־אֲבִיכֶם
אֶת־אַבְרָהָם מֵעֵבֶר הַנָּהָר
וָאוֹלֵךְ אוֹתוֹ בְּכָל־אֶרֶץ כְּנָעַן
וָאַרְבֶּ אֶת־זַרְעוֹ וָאֶתֶּן־לוֹ
⁴ אֶת־־יִצְחָק: וָאֶתֵּן לְיִצְחָק
אֶת־יַעֲקֹב וְאֶת־עֵשָׂו וָאֶתֵּן
לְעֵשָׂו אֶת־־הַר שֵׂעִיר לָרֶשֶׁת
אוֹתוֹ וְיַעֲקֹב וּבָנָיו יָרְדוּ
⁵ מִצְרָיִם: וָאֶשְׁלַח אֶת־מֹשֶׁה
וְאֶת־אַהֲרֹן וָאֶגֹּף אֶת־
מִצְרַיִם כַּאֲשֶׁר עָשִׂיתִי בְּקִרְבּוֹ
וְאַחַר הוֹצֵאתִי אֶתְכֶם:
⁶ וָאוֹצִיא אֶת־אֲבוֹתֵיכֶם
מִמִּצְרַיִם וַתָּבֹאוּ הַיָּמָּה
וַיִּרְדְּפוּ מִצְרַיִם אַחֲרֵי
אֲבוֹתֵיכֶם בְּרֶכֶב וּבְפָרָשִׁים
⁷ יַם־־סוּף: וַיִּצְעֲקוּ אֶל־
יְהוָֹה וַיָּשֶׂם מַאֲפֵל בֵּינֵיכֶם ׀
וּבֵין הַמִּצְרִים וַיָּבֵא עָלָיו

v. 3. וארבה ק׳

Terah was a manufacturer of idols some of
which Abraham broke (Gen. Rabbah xxxviii
13).

3. *led him throughout all the land of Canaan.*
To be possessed by his descendants (cf. Gen.
xiii. 17). According to Rabbinical tradition,
by traveling through the land, Abraham took
possession of it for posterity. Also, it is possible that Abraham was accepted as a ruler
and a Godly prince throughout the land
(Rambam loc. cit.)

4. *mount Seir.* [Better, *the mountainland of*

Seir, as A.J. in Gen. xxxvi. 8. When Esau was
given mount Seir, he lost any claim to the
land of Canaan (Metsudath David).

went down into Egypt. As the first act in the
drama of which Israel's possession of the
Promised Land was to be the dénouement.

6. *ye came.* There were many, who, like
Joshua, had been present at the Exodus and
the crossing of the Red Sea. They were over
sixty or under twenty at the time, and so were
not destined to perish in the wilderness
(Kimchi).

upon them, and covered them; and
your eyes saw what I did in Egypt;
and ye dwelt in the wilderness many
days. 8. And I brought you into
the land of the Amorites, that dwelt
beyond the Jordan; and they fought
with you; and I gave them into your
hand, and ye possessed their land;
and I destroyed them from before
you. 9. Then Balak the son of
Zippor, king of Moab, arose and
fought against Israel; and he sent
and called Balaam the son of Beor
to curse you. 10. But I would not
hearken unto Balaam; therefore he
even blessed you; so I delivered you
out of his hand. 11. And ye went
over the Jordan, and came unto
Jericho; and the men of Jericho
fought against you, the Amorite,
and the Perizzite, and the Canaanite,

אֶת־הַיָּם וַיְכַסֵּהוּ וַתִּרְאֶ֫ינָה
עֵינֵיכֶם אֵת אֲשֶׁר־עָשִׂ֫יתִי
בְמִצְרָ֫יִם וַתֵּשְׁבוּ בַמִּדְבָּר
8 יָמִים רַבִּים: וָאָבִיאָה אֶתְכֶם
אֶל־אֶרֶץ הָאֱמֹרִי הַיּוֹשֵׁב
בְּעֵ֫בֶר הַיַּרְדֵּן וַיִּלָּחֲמוּ אִתְּכֶם
וָאֶתֵּן אוֹתָם בְּיֶדְכֶם וַתִּ֫ירְשׁוּ
אֶת־אַרְצָם וָאַשְׁמִידֵם
9 מִפְּנֵיכֶם: וַיָּ֫קָם בָּלָק בֶּן־
צִפּוֹר מֶלֶךְ מוֹאָב וַיִּלָּחֶם
בְּיִשְׂרָאֵל וַיִּשְׁלַח וַיִּקְרָא
לְבִלְעָם בֶּן־בְּעוֹר לְקַלֵּל
10 אֶתְכֶם: וְלֹא אָבִ֫יתִי לִשְׁמֹעַ
לְבִלְעָם וַיְבָ֫רֶךְ בָּרוֹךְ אֶתְכֶם
11 וָאַצִּל אֶתְכֶם מִיָּדוֹ: וַתַּעַבְרוּ
אֶת־הַיַּרְדֵּן וַתָּבֹ֫אוּ אֶל־
יְרִיחוֹ וַיִּלָּחֲמוּ בָכֶם בַּעֲלֵי־
יְרִיחוֹ הָאֱמֹרִי וְהַפְּרִזִּי

v. 8. ואביא ק

7. *your eyes saw.* Strictly this was true only of
those who had been born in Egypt and had
personally witnessed God's miraculous
intervention on behalf of Israel, and only the
children under twenty years at the time of the
exodus had survived the journey in the wilderness. It is interesting to note that in the
Kuzari (philosophical presentation of
Judaism), Jehudah Halevi makes the exodus
the starting-point of the Jewish Faith, and
not any theological tenet; because while the
latter was open to argument, the former was
an indisputable historical fact witnessed by a
large number of people.

many days. Forty years, until the adults who
left Egypt, with the exception of Joshua and
Caleb, had died.

8. *the land of the Amorites.* See on iii. 10. Here
the reference is to the land of Sihon and Og
(Num. xxi. 21 ff.).

9. *fought against Israel.* Cf. Num. xxii. 2 ff.
The meaning of *fought* is 'opposed,' since
there is no record of a military attack by
Balak, although such was his intention (cf.
Num. xxii. 6, 11). The weapon he decided to
use was Balaam's power to curse, as the verse
goes on to relate (Kimchi).

10. *I would not hearken,* etc. God speaks
through Joshua.

11. *the men of Jericho.* The inhabitants of
Jericho; (Targum) the lords of Jericho
(Metsudath Zion). All the Canaanitish kings

and the Hittite, and the Girgashite, the Hivite, and the Jebusite; and I delivered them into your hand. 12. And I sent the hornet before you, which drove them out from before you, even the two kings of the Amorites; not with thy sword, nor with thy bow. 13. And I gave you a land whereon thou hadst not laboured, and cities which ye built not, and ye dwell therein; of vineyards and oliveyards which ye planted not do ye eat. 14. Now therefore fear the Lord, and serve Him in sincerity and in truth; and put away the gods which your fathers served beyond the River, and in Egypt; and serve ye the Lord.

וְהַכְּנַעֲנִי וְהַחִתִּי וְהַגִּרְגָּשִׁי הַחִוִּי וְהַיְבוּסִי וָאֶתֵּן אוֹתָם בְּיֶדְכֶם: 12 וָאֶשְׁלַח לִפְנֵיכֶם אֶת־הַצִּרְעָה וַתְּגָרֶשׁ אוֹתָם מִפְּנֵיכֶם שְׁנֵי מַלְכֵי הָאֱמֹרִי לֹא בְחַרְבְּךָ וְלֹא בְקַשְׁתֶּךָ: 13 וָאֶתֵּן לָכֶם אֶרֶץ אֲשֶׁר לֹא־יָגַעְתָּ בָּהּ וְעָרִים אֲשֶׁר לֹא־בְנִיתֶם וַתֵּשְׁבוּ בָּהֶם כְּרָמִים וְזֵיתִים אֲשֶׁר לֹא־נְטַעְתֶּם אַתֶּם אֹכְלִים: 14 וְעַתָּה יְראוּ אֶת־יְהֹוָה וְעִבְדוּ אֹתוֹ בְּתָמִים וּבֶאֱמֶת וְהָסִירוּ אֶת־אֱלֹהִים אֲשֶׁר עָבְדוּ אֲבוֹתֵיכֶם בְּעֵבֶר הַנָּהָר וּבְמִצְרַיִם וְעִבְדוּ

א׳ נחה v. 14.

owned parts of Jericho (Metsudath David).

the Amorites . . . All seven nations are mentioned here, since Jericho is situated on the border, and is the fortification of Eretz Yisrael, and the heroic soldiers of all seven nations assembled therein (Rashi). This battle was not mentioned previously.

12. *the hornet.* A flying insect resembling the bee in the structure of its body and in its way of life. It does not produce honey, however, Its stings are very painful and are sometimes fatal. Scripture refers to swarms of hornets.
Said Rabbi Simeon ben Lakish: The hornets stood on the banks of the Jordan and sprayed venom, which blinded their eyes from above and castrated them from below. Rav Pappa maintains that there were two types of hornets: one at the time of Moses and one at the time of Joshua. The one at the time of Moses did not cross the Jordan, whereas the one at Joshua's time did cross the Jordan (Sotah 36a; Tanchuma Buber

Devarim 9) (Daath Mikra). Others interpret *tzirah,* as akin to *tzaraath,* leprosy (Ibn Ezra, Lev. xiii. 19). Abarbanel explains that the dread of the Israelites, who had miraculously vanquished Sihon and Og, is compared to a hornet or wasp.

the two kings. Joshua is referring back to verse 8 to stress his point that the victories of the Israelites had not been due to their military prowess. What had been true of Sihon and Og also applied to the peoples enumerated in verse 11. See Kimchi, Metsudath David.

13. The verse describes the fulfillment of the promise recalled by Moses in Deut. vi. 10f.

14. *now therefore,* etc. Since God has bestowed upon you all these favours.

and in Egypt. Cf. Lev. xvii. 7: *And they shall no more sacrifice their sacrifices unto the satyrs, after whom they go astray,* which implies that they were continuing to do so. Ezek. xx. 8

15. And if it seem evil unto you to serve the LORD, choose you this day whom ye will serve; whether the gods which your fathers served that were beyond the River, or the gods of the Amorites, in whose land ye dwell; but as for me and my house, we will serve the LORD.'

16. And the people answered and said: 'Far be it from us that we should forsake the LORD, to serve other gods; 17. for the LORD our God, He it is that brought us and our fathers up out of the land of Egypt, from the house of bondage, and that did those great signs in our sight, and preserved us in all the way wherein we went, and among all the

15 אֶת־יְהֹוָה: וְאִם רַע
בְּעֵינֵיכֶם לַעֲבֹד אֶת־יְהֹוָה
בַּחֲרוּ לָכֶם הַיּוֹם אֶת־מִי
תַעֲבֹדוּן אִם אֶת־אֱלֹהִים
אֲשֶׁר־עָבְדוּ אֲבוֹתֵיכֶם אֲשֶׁר
בְּעֵבֶר הַנָּהָר וְאִם אֶת־אֱלֹהֵי
הָאֱמֹרִי אֲשֶׁר אַתֶּם יֹשְׁבִים
בְּאַרְצָם וְאָנֹכִי וּבֵיתִי נַעֲבֹד
אֶת־יְהֹוָה:

16 וַיַּעַן הָעָם וַיֹּאמֶר חָלִילָה לָּנוּ
מֵעֲזֹב אֶת־יְהֹוָה לַעֲבֹד

17 אֱלֹהִים אֲחֵרִים: כִּי יְהֹוָה
אֱלֹהֵינוּ הוּא הַמַּעֲלֶה אֹתָנוּ
וְאֶת־אֲבוֹתֵינוּ מֵאֶרֶץ
מִצְרַיִם מִבֵּית עֲבָדִים וַאֲשֶׁר
עָשָׂה לְעֵינֵינוּ אֶת־הָאֹתוֹת
הַגְּדֹלוֹת הָאֵלֶּה וַיִּשְׁמְרֵנוּ
בְּכָל־הַדֶּרֶךְ אֲשֶׁר הָלַכְנוּ

v. 15. מעבר ק׳

records: *neither did they forsake the idols of Egypt.* According to Rabbinic tradition, the Israelites in Egypt were steeped in idolatry.

15. *choose you,* etc. There could be no compromise, *for I the* LORD *thy God am a jealous God* (Exod. xx. 5), as Joshua immediately reminds them (verse 19), Who demands undivided allegiance. Similarly Elijah issued the challenge: *How long halt ye between two opinions? if the* LORD *be God, follow Him; but if Baal, follow him* (1 Kings xviii. 21). They could not serve both. This simple truth took

the Israelites hundreds of years to learn.

but as for me and my house, etc. A spirited note of defiance rings through the words. Were all to prove unfaithful, he would not fear to be in a minority of one. In the same spirit Mattathias declared many centuries later: 'Though all the nations that are under the king's dominion obey him, and fall away every one from the religion of their fathers . . . yet will I and my sons and my brethren walk in the covenant of our fathers (1 Macc. ii. 19f.).

peoples through the midst of whom we passed; 18. and the LORD drove out from before us all the peoples, even the Amorites that dwelt in the land; therefore we also will serve the LORD; for He is our God.'

19. And Joshua said unto the people: 'Ye cannot serve the LORD; for He is a holy God; He is a jealous God; He will not forgive your transgression nor your sins. 20. If ye forsake the LORD, and serve strange gods, then He will turn and do you evil, and consume you, after that He hath done you good.'

21. And the people said unto Joshua: 'Nay; but we will serve the LORD.' 22. And Joshua said unto the people: 'Ye are witnesses against yourselves that ye have chosen you

בָּהּ וּבְכֹל הָעַמִּים אֲשֶׁר עָבַרְנוּ
18 בְּקִרְבָּם: וַיְגָרֶשׁ יְהֹוָה אֶת־
כָּל־הָעַמִּים וְאֶת־הָאֱמֹרִי
יֹשֵׁב הָאָרֶץ מִפָּנֵינוּ גַּם־אֲנַחְנוּ
נַעֲבֹד אֶת־יְהֹוָה כִּי־הוּא
אֱלֹהֵינוּ:
19 וַיֹּאמֶר יְהוֹשֻׁעַ אֶל־הָעָם לֹא
תוּכְלוּ לַעֲבֹד אֶת־יְהֹוָה כִּי־
אֱלֹהִים קְדֹשִׁים הוּא אֵל־
קַנּוֹא הוּא לֹא־יִשָּׂא לְפִשְׁעֲכֶם
20 וּלְחַטֹּאותֵיכֶם: כִּי תַעַזְבוּ
אֶת־יְהֹוָה וַעֲבַדְתֶּם אֱלֹהֵי
נֵכָר וְשָׁב וְהֵרַע לָכֶם וְכִלָּה
אֶתְכֶם אַחֲרֵי אֲשֶׁר־הֵיטִיב
לָכֶם:
21 וַיֹּאמֶר הָעָם אֶל־יְהוֹשֻׁעַ לֹא
22 כִּי אֶת־יְהֹוָה נַעֲבֹד: וַיֹּאמֶר
יְהוֹשֻׁעַ אֶל־הָעָם עֵדִים אַתֶּם
בָּכֶם כִּי־אַתֶּם בְּחַרְתֶּם לָכֶם
v. 19. מלא ר

19. [Perhaps Joshua recalled the fervent reply in the past, *All the words which the Lord hath spoken will we do* (Exod. xxiv. 3) and how quickly it was forgotten. So he warns the people that the service of God is very exacting, and a mere facile declaration was not enough. To serve Him meant single-minded devotion and dedication to His will.]

19. *ye cannot serve the* LORD. In a half-hearted way (Azulai, Akedah).

He is a holy God. Who abhors everything that is impure, demanding holiness of living from His worshippers (Malbim).

He is a jealous God. [Who brooks no compromise between good and evil.]

He will not forgive . . . your sins. [He is not a God Who can be bribed to forgive by means of rich sacrifices.]

20. *and consume you, after that He hath done you good.* [Each generation has its own responsibility; it cannot rely on the virtues of former generations if it is itself unworthy.]

22. *ye are witnesses against yourselves.* Therefore you admit that Divine punishment will be justified if you incur it. See Rashi.

the LORD, to serve Him.—And they said: 'We are witnesses.'—23. Now therefore put away the strange gods which are among you, and incline your heart unto the LORD, the God of Israel.' 24. And the people said unto Joshua: 'The LORD our God will we serve, and unto His voice will we hearken.'

25. So Joshua made a covenant with the people that day, and set them a statute and an ordinance in Shechem. 26. And Joshua wrote these words in the book of the law of God; and he took a great stone, and set it up there under the oak that was by the sanctuary of the

אֶת־יְהֹוָה לַעֲבֹד אוֹתוֹ

23 וַיֹּאמְרוּ עֵדִים: וְעַתָּה הָסִירוּ
אֶת־אֱלֹהֵי הַנֵּכָר אֲשֶׁר
בְּקִרְבְּכֶם וְהַטּוּ אֶת־לְבַבְכֶם
אֶל־יְהֹוָה אֱלֹהֵי יִשְׂרָאֵל:

24 וַיֹּאמְרוּ הָעָם אֶל־יְהוֹשֻׁעַ
אֶת־יְהֹוָה אֱלֹהֵינוּ נַעֲבֹד
וּבְקוֹלוֹ נִשְׁמָע:

25 וַיִּכְרֹת יְהוֹשֻׁעַ בְּרִית לָעָם
בַּיּוֹם הַהוּא וַיָּשֶׂם לוֹ חֹק
26 וּמִשְׁפָּט בִּשְׁכֶם: וַיִּכְתֹּב
יְהוֹשֻׁעַ אֶת־הַדְּבָרִים הָאֵלֶּה
בְּסֵפֶר תּוֹרַת אֱלֹהִים וַיִּקַּח
אֶבֶן גְּדוֹלָה וַיְקִימֶהָ שָּׁם תַּחַת
הָאַלָּה אֲשֶׁר בְּמִקְדַּשׁ יְהֹוָה:

that ye have chosen you the LORD. [Of your free will, as all religious practice must be.

23. *put away the strange gods.* Joshua's stern challenge and reiterated demand for whole-hearted allegiance to God were evidently not without cause; he knew that some harbored heretic beliefs to which he referred as strange gods (Ralbag, Abarbanel, Metsudath David).

25. Joshua *made a covenant with the people that day.* On the strength of their unequivocal declaration, he renewed the covenant which God had first made with Israel at Sinai.

26. *in the book of the law of God.* This cannot mean that Joshua added this as an appendix to the Pentateuch and included it therein; firstly, because the Books of Moses were too sacred to be tampered with, and secondly, because the words are not to be found there. It may indicate that he wrote them on a scroll which he deposited in the same place together with *the book of the Law of God,* viz. the Pentateuch (so some commentators). It is, however, hard to read this meaning into the text. The difficulty disappears if we render: '*with* the book of the law of God.' The intention would be then that he wrote his book, including all the events recorded therein, as well as the covenant, as the book following the book of the law of God, i.e. following the Pentateuch (Abarbanel). The Rabbis explain the phrase as applying to the last eight verses of the Pentateuch (from *so Moses the servant of the* LORD died there to the end), or the chapter on the cities of refuge (Mak. 11a).

he took a great stone. It was a common practice to set up a stone to commemorate an event of importance (cf. Gen. xxviii. 18; Exod. xxi 4). Joshua commemorated the crossing of the Jordan in this manner (iv. 3).

the oak that was by the sanctuary. The Hebrew is

LORD. 27. And Joshua said unto all the people: 'Behold, this stone shall be a witness against us; for it hath heard all the words of the LORD which He spoke unto us; it shall be therefore a witness against you, lest ye deny your God.' 28. So Joshua sent the people away, every man unto his inheritance.

29. And it came to pass after these things, that Joshua the son of Nun, the servant of the LORD, died, being a hundred and ten years old. 30. And they buried him in the border of his inheritance in Timnath-serah, which is in the hill-country of Ephraim, on the north of the mountain of Gaash. 31. And Israel served the LORD all the days of Joshua, and all the days of the elders that outlived Joshua,

27 וַיֹּ֤אמֶר יְהוֹשֻׁ֙עַ֙ אֶל־כָּל־הָעָ֔ם הִנֵּ֤ה הָאֶ֙בֶן֙ הַזֹּ֔את תִּֽהְיֶה־בָּ֖נוּ לְעֵדָ֑ה כִּֽי־הִ֣יא שָׁמְעָ֗ה אֵ֣ת כָּל־אִמְרֵ֤י יְהוָה֙ אֲשֶׁ֣ר דִּבֶּ֣ר עִמָּ֔נוּ וְהָיְתָ֤ה בָכֶם֙ לְעֵדָ֔ה פֶּֽן־תְּכַחֲשׁ֖וּן בֵּאלֹֽהֵיכֶֽם׃

28 וַיְשַׁלַּ֤ח יְהוֹשֻׁ֙עַ֙ אֶת־הָעָ֔ם אִ֖ישׁ לְנַחֲלָתֽוֹ׃

29 וַיְהִ֗י אַֽחֲרֵי֙ הַדְּבָרִ֣ים הָאֵ֔לֶּה וַיָּ֛מָת יְהוֹשֻׁ֥עַ בִּן־נ֖וּן עֶ֣בֶד יְהוָ֑ה בֶּן־מֵאָ֥ה וָעֶ֖שֶׂר שָׁנִֽים׃

30 וַיִּקְבְּר֤וּ אֹתוֹ֙ בִּגְב֣וּל נַחֲלָת֔וֹ בְּתִמְנַת־סֶ֖רַח אֲשֶׁ֣ר בְּהַר־אֶפְרָ֑יִם מִצְּפ֖וֹן לְהַר־גָּֽעַשׁ׃

31 וַיַּעֲבֹ֤ד יִשְׂרָאֵל֙ אֶת־יְהוָ֔ה כֹּ֖ל יְמֵ֣י יְהוֹשֻׁ֑עַ וְכֹ֣ל ׀ יְמֵ֣י הַזְּקֵנִ֗ים אֲשֶׁ֨ר הֶאֱרִ֤יכוּ יָמִים֙ אַחֲרֵ֣י

---

literally 'in the sanctuary.' This was not a permanent sanctuary, but it was called the sanctuary of the LORD, because they brought the Ark there, as it is stated above: (verse 1) *And they presented themselves before God* (Rashi, Kimchi and Metsudath David). As mentioned above in the name of Daath Soferim, this was a temporary sanctuary. It was one of the high places, heretofore used for sacrifices, and still used for prayer even after the erection of the Tabernacle in Shiloh. In either case, it was not necessarily a building but a hallowed site, and an oak tree could easily be found within its confines.

According to the Midrash, this was the oak tree under which Jacob hid the idols and their ornaments that were part of the booty

of Shechem (Gen. xxxv. 4) (Rashi, Kimchi).

Others render: *under the doorpost which is in the sanctuary of the* LORD. (Targum) i.e. under the doorpost of the temporary sanctuary in Shechem (Rashi, Kimchi). Others conjecture that is was placed under the doorpost in the sanctuary in Shiloh (Daath Mikra).

29. *the servant of the* LORD. [A faithful disciple of Moses, he was now crowned with the same title as his master (cf. i. 1). He had begun his task with the solemn reminder that he was continuing the work of *the servant of the Lord*. He ends it with the proud consciousness that he too had earned that praise.]

30. *Timnath-serah.* See on xix. 50.

and had known all the work of the LORD, that He had wrought for Israel. 32. And the bones of Joseph, which the children of Israel brought up out of Egypt, buried they in Shechem, in the parcel of ground which Jacob bought of the sons of Hamor the father of Shechem for a hundred pieces of money; and they became the inheritance of the children of Joseph. 33. And Eleazar the son of Aaron died; and they buried him in the Hill of Phinehas his son, which was given him in mount Ephraim.

יְהוֹשֻׁעַ וַאֲשֶׁר יָדְעוּ אֵת כָּל־
מַעֲשֵׂה יְהֹוָה אֲשֶׁר עָשָׂה
לְיִשְׂרָאֵל: וְאֶת־עַצְמוֹת יוֹסֵף 32
אֲשֶׁר־הֶעֱלוּ בְנֵי־יִשְׂרָאֵל
מִמִּצְרַיִם קָבְרוּ בִשְׁכֶם
בְּחֶלְקַת הַשָּׂדֶה אֲשֶׁר קָנָה
יַעֲקֹב מֵאֵת בְּנֵי־חֲמוֹר אֲבִי־
שְׁכֶם בְּמֵאָה קְשִׂיטָה וַיִּהְיוּ
לִבְנֵי־יוֹסֵף לְנַחֲלָה: וְאֶלְעָזָר 33
בֶּן־אַהֲרֹן מֵת וַיִּקְבְּרוּ אֹתוֹ
בְּגִבְעַת פִּינְחָס בְּנוֹ אֲשֶׁר נִתַּן־
לוֹ בְּהַר אֶפְרָיִם:

חזק

32. *the bones of Joseph.* In accordance with his dying request (Gen. 1. 24f.).

which the children of Israel brought up out of Egypt. In fact, it was Moses who did this (cf. Exod. xiii. 19). The Rabbis point out that when a person leaves his task unfinished (as did Moses who brought the bones out of Egypt but could not bury them in the Land of Israel), Scripture regards those who complete it as having performed it (Sot. 13b).

buried they. [Perhaps better, 'they had buried.' They had probably buried him soon after their arrival in Canaan, but the historian records the incident here in fitting connection with Joshua's death.]

in Shechem. The Talmud remarks: 'From Shechem he was abducted (cf. Gen. xxxvii. 13); to Shechem he was returned' (Sot. 13b).

which Jacob bought. Cf. Gen. xxxiii. 19.

they became. viz. the city of Shechem and *the parcel of ground.*

33. *the Hill of Phinehas.* In the city of Gibeah (a name which occurs frequently, signifying that it stood on or near a hill) which had been given to him, and called by his name. It is conjectured to be the modern Jibieh, north-west of Gufna, or Et-tel, south of Senjil (Daath Mikra). The death of Phinehas marked the close of an era. The people were settled in their land: thus the first stage in God's design—first revealed to Abraham in the words, *And I will make of thee a great nation* (Gen. xii. 2)—was fulfilled. But it was as yet far from completion. A long period of spiritual development was to follow.

שופטים

JUDGES

INTRODUCTION AND COMMENTARY

by

JUDAH J. SLOTKI, M.A., Ph.D.

Revised by
RABBI A.J. ROSENBERG

JUDGES : שופטים

INTRODUCTION

THE TITLE

The traditional name of the Book, *Shophetim*, appears as early as the Talmudical period (B.B. 14b), and has the support of the LXX, *Sophateim*. Its antiquity is evidenced by the fact that it was adopted by the Vulgate (Jerome).

The name was determined by the contents. The greater part of the Book deals with the exploits of a series of national leaders who, by their victories over oppressive enemies, brought Israel independence for a time from a foreign yoke. The term *shophet* has a wider connotation in Hebrew than has the English word 'judge' or the corresponding nouns in Greek and Latin. It denotes both *judicare* and *vindicare*, the latter in the double sense of 'defending, delivering' and 'avenging, punishing.' The *shophet* was judge and governor. Though in power he was not, within his more limited sphere of influence, inferior to the later kings, there was no hereditary right of succession.

II. PLACE IN THE CANON

In the Hebrew Bible, *Judges* stands second in the section known as 'The Earlier Prophets' (cf. the Introduction to *Joshua*), consisting of the historical Books which narrate the story of Israel from the entry into Canaan to the destruction of the First Temple in 586 B.C.E. In the Greek version, *Ruth* is attached to *Judges,* either under the one name *Kritei* or under its own name. In some Greek MSS. *Judges* and *Ruth* are combined with the Pentateuch and *Joshua* to form a separate codex—the Octateuch.

The Book continues the story of Israel's rise to nationhood and deals with the period from the death of Joshua to the birth of Samuel.

III. DATE AND AUTHORSHIP

The problems when the Book was written and by whom are linked together. The work is anonymous, more regard having been paid to its message than to its authorship. The traditional view ascribes it to Samuel

who, it is said, composed it in addition to his own Book and *Ruth* (B.B. 14b).

From the chronological reference, four times repeated, *in those days there was no king in Israel* (xvii. 6, xviii. 1, xix. 1, xxi. 25), the deduction has been drawn that the earliest date of composition could not be before the reign of Saul. It is not inconceivable that the Book was composed in sections at different periods of Samuel's life, though it is unnecessary to assume that a passage like xviii. 30f. was added after his death; because it should be remembered that the ark was taken from Shiloh during his lifetime (cf. 1 Sam. iv. 11; on *the day of the captivity,* see the commentary *ad loc.*).

It may also be assumed that Samuel embodied in his work documentary material contemporaneous with the incidents it relates. In this category are the Ode of Deborah and the parable of Jotham. The judges may possibly have left monuments with inscriptions which commemorated their military feats. The contract between Jephthah and the Gileadite elders (xi. 9f.) may very probably have been committed to writing.

This view dispenses with the mutually contradictory conclusions of modern scholars, among which the following may be mentioned: (*i*) The Book was edited in its present form in the sixth century B.C.E., before the captivity (*ii*) It is of early origin, but the section xvii-xxi is a later addition. (*iii*) It was written in the first seven years of David's reign, before the capture of Jerusalem (*iv*) It was composed some time in the reign of David or Solomon, preferably between 1042 and 1023 B.C.E.

IV. CHRONOLOGY

When we approach the project of harmonizing the chronological data of the book of Judges, we must reconcile the years given for each judge along with the years of foreign oppression with the three hundred years that elapsed from Israel's entry into the Holy Land until Jephthah's judgeship (xi. 26). We must also reconcile these figures with the figure given in 1 Kings vi. 1, that the Temple

was built 480 years after the Exodus, in the fourth year of Solomon's reign. Consequently, Solomon took office 436 years after Israel's entry.

From the Book the following data are obtained:

Israel under Cushan-rishathaim
(iii. 8) .... 8 years
Othniel (iii. 11) .... 40 years
Subjection to Eglon, king of Moab
(iii. 14) .... 18 years
Peace after Eglon's death and dur
ing Ehud's rule (iii. 30) .... 80 years
Subjection to Jabin, king of
Canaan (iv. 3) .... 20 years
Peace after Barak's victory (v. 31) . 40 years
Incursions of the Midianites, etc.
(vi. 1) .... 7 years
Judgeship of Gideon (viii. 28) .... 40 years
Rule of Abimelech (ix. 22) .... 3 years
Judgeship of Tola (x. 2) .... 23 years
Judgeship of Jair (x. 3) .... 22 years
Gilead under the Ammonites (x. 8) 18 years
Judgeship of Jephthah (xii. 7) .... 6 years
Judgeship of Ibzan (xii. 9) .... 7 years
Judgeship of Elon (xii. 11) .... 10 years
Judgeship of Abdon (xii. 14) ..... 8 years
Philistine domination (xiii. 1) .... 40 years
Samson's career (xv. 20, xvi. 31) .. 20 years

This yields a total of 410 years.

By adding the 28 years of Joshua's reign, as recorded in Seder Olam, we arrive at a total of 438 from Israel's entry into the Holy Land until Samson's death. This is already two years too many before counting the years of Eli's and Samuel's judgeships and the reigns of Saul, Ish-bosheth and David. Moreover, from the beginning of the conquest to Jephthah's judgeship, we have 347 years, whereas Scripture states that there were 300 years.

According to Seder Olam, quoted by Rashi (xi. 26), Scripture sometimes includes the years of foreign subjugation in the years of the judge who followed. This is true in the case of Othniel, Ehud, and Deborah. In the case of Gideon, however, the years of subjugation are not included. Also, between the 23 years of Tola and the 22 years of Jair, there was one year overlapping.

Accordingly, the chronology from Joshua to Jephthah is as follows:

Joshua .... 28 years
Israel under Cushan-rishathaim .. 8 years
Othniel .... 32 years
Subjection to Eglon .... 18 years

Peace after Eglon's death and dur
ing Ehud's rule .... 62 years
Subjection to Jabin .... 20 years
Peace after Barak's victory .... 20 years
Incursions of the Midianites ..... 7 years
Judgeship of Gideon .... 40 years
Rule of Abimelech .... 3 years
Judgeships of Tola and Jair ...... 44 years
Gilead under the Ammonites .... 18 years

This yields a total of exactly 300 years.

Kimchi counts the 7 years of the incursions of the Midianites and their allies in the forty years of Gideon. He counts also 25 years for Tola and Jair. This makes us six years short. He, therefore, counts the six years of Jephthah's judgeship in the 300 years.

Elijah of Wilna, in his chronological table, concurs with Rashi, adding that the subjuction of Gilead under the Ammonites ended with the second year of Jephthah. Hence, we figure from Jephthah as follows:

Judgeship of Jephthah (xii. 7) .... 4 years
Judgeship of Ibzan (xii. 9) .... 5 years
Judgeship of Elon .... 9 years
Judgeship of Abdon .... 7 years
Samson's career .... 19 years
Judgeship of Eli (1 Sam. iv. 18) ... 39 years
Samuel and Saul .... 13 years
David (1 Kings ii. 11) .... 40 years

Thus we have a total of 436 years from the beginning of the conquest to the beginning of King Solomon's reign.

As mentioned before, the Ammonites still oppressed Israel until the second year of Jephthah's judgeship, leaving 4 years. Ibzan's 7 years include one year overlapping with Jephthah and one year overlapping with Elon. The last year of Elon overlaps with Abdon, as does Abdon's with Samson's and Samson's with Eli's. According to this computation, the Tabernacle in Shiloh, which was destroyed on the day of Eli's death, stood until the three hundred and eighty-third year counting from the conquest. By subtracting the fourteen years that the Tabernacle stood in Gilgal, we arrive at 369, as in Seder Olam, ch. 11. The 40 years of Philistine domination coincide with Jephthah's Elon's, Abdon's, and Samson's judgeships.

V. RELIGIOUS AND HISTORICAL VALUE

The value of the Book as source-material for the study of the religious and historical

development of Israel has been universally conceded. To the genuineness of the sources we have the testimony of the style, the life-like freshness of the narrative, the minute accuracy of detail, and the fact that they form an integral part of the historical writings.

The period with which the Book deals was crucial for the early Israelites. The campaign for the possession of their national home was virtually ended. They were inuring themselves to the life of agricultural settlers. The transition was beset with hindrances on all sides. Apart from the inevitable difficulties of adaptation to a new mode of living, they had to contend with the repeated onslaughts of invaders and marauders as well as with the lure of the fascinating but debasing form of religion practised by the peoples who surrounded them.

This moral and religious danger made their failure completely to drive out the native population so serious a matter; because it threatened to undermine both the spiritual character of the nation which had been built up by Moses and the material achievements effected by Joshua. The Book traces the people's struggle to hold and consolidate these achievements in the face of overwhelming odds. In spite of numerous setbacks, they succeeded in holding their own, even extending their gains, thereby paving the way for Israel's kings and especially the prophets who were to make their permanent mark upon the advancement of the human race.

VI. POLITICAL AND MORAL CONDITIONS

When the Israelites entered Canaan, they brought with them a theocratic form of government which held them together as one people. Soon, however, they began to yield to the seductions of nature worship and fall away from the austere morality of the desert. In consequence, they lost their sense of unity and broke up into separate tribes, each fighting for its own existence. Individual tribes had set their own form of governmental organization, and cities appointed their own elders. Several tribes might, as the result of outside pressure, combine for joint action; but not until the end of the period do we find the whole nation joined together for united action.

The confusion and disorganization are well summed up in the Midrashic comment on Ruth i. 1: 'It was a generation that judged its judges.' Only when a leader arose strong enough to curb them is there evidence of discipline and cohesion. On his death, the confusion returns with increased intensity. From the sources it appears that the tribe of Ephraim claimed the hegemony because of its possession of the principal city, its central position, the situation within its territory of the Tabernacle at Shiloh, and the fact that Joshua had belonged to this tribe. The claim was not generally recognized, and on several occasions gave rise to friction between it and the other tribes.

The powerful tribe of Judah including its neighbour Simeon, on the other hand, seems to have held aloof, safe in its mountain fastnesses and in its numerical superiority, until it lost its independence to the Philistines.

In the war against the Canaanites under Sisera, although Ephraim and western Manasseh, Benjamin and Issachar rallied to the standard, Reuben, Gad, Dan, Asher, and eastern Manasseh remained inactive. Zebulun and Naphtali appear to have borne the brunt of the struggle. When Gideon raised the battle-cry against Midian, the response came from western Manasseh and part of Asher; Ephraim arrived on the scene later. On Gideon's death, the city of Shechem set up its own petty king and brought on civil war. Jephthah ruled only over a part of Transjordan, while subsequent judges held sway over the northern tribes alone. Samson's authority was hardly that of a judge.

In spite of the political and military chaos that prevailed, the people as a whole settled down to peaceful pursuits. This emerges clearly from the story of Ruth, where we meet with a beautiful pastoral idyll, depicting a life of simplicity, piety, integrity and kindliness carrying with it an assurance of the ultimate triumph of the teachings inculcated by Moses and kept alive by men of God in public exhortation and by private example.

JUDGES

1. AND it came to pass after the death of Joshua, that the children of Israel asked of the LORD, saying: 'Who shall go up for us first against the Canaanites, to fight against them?' 2. And the LORD said: 'Judah shall go up; behold, I have delivered the land into his hand.'

וַיְהִי אַחֲרֵי מוֹת יְהוֹשֻׁעַ וַיִּשְׁאֲלוּ בְּנֵי יִשְׂרָאֵל בַּיהוָה לֵאמֹר מִי־יַעֲלֶה־לָּנוּ אֶל־הַכְּנַעֲנִי בַּתְּחִלָּה לְהִלָּחֶם בּוֹ : וַיֹּאמֶר יְהוָה יְהוּדָה יַעֲלֶה הִנֵּה נָתַתִּי

CHAPTER I

CONTINUATION OF THE CONQUEST OF CANAAN

1–2 THE ORACLE

1. *and it came to pass.* The usual introductory phrase in the Bible connecting the previous narrative with what follows. The thread of the story is taken up where it was left at the end of the preceding Book (Daath Mikra).

the death of Joshua. This event marked the end of the general campaign in Canaan as the death of Moses marked the termination of Israel's wandering in the wilderness. The formula is similar to that which introduces the Book of Joshua (Adne Keseph).

asked of the LORD. In the critical moment when they were deprived of their divinely appointed leader, the people sought Divine guidance by consulting the Urim and Thummim through the High Priest who, at the time, was Phinehas, the grandson of Aaron (Abarbanel, Malbim). The method of ascertaining God's will was, according to Rabbinical tradition, as follows: The Names of God were placed in the High Priest's breastplate, in which were set twelve precious stones, each engraved with the name of a tribe (Exod. xxviii. 15ff.). By the power of the Divine Names the letters of the tribal names became illuminated and God's will was discerned by noting the letters which were lit up following an enquiry. In the present instance, the stone bearing Judah's name was illumined and then four letters on

other stones which made up the word *ya'aleh,* 'shall go up' (Ramban, Exod. xxviii. 30).

who shall go up. To take the still unconquered territory included in the allotments made by Joshua. In the land of several tribes Canaanites continued to dwell as before, threatening the security as well as the moral and spiritual life of the Israelites. These dangerous elements had to be removed and the enquiry was to decide which tribe should take the initiative. The importance of victory in the earliest stage justified a special enquiry of God, because it would have a powerful effect upon the morale of the attackers and the attacked (Daath Soferim, Malbim).

[The verb *go up* may have been chosen because of the hilly nature of the country, or it may signify nothing more than 'march against.']

for us. i.e. for the common benefit of all the tribes. If the first would be victorious, it would instill fear in the adversaries' hearts and make it easier for the remaining tribes (Metsudath David).

first. lit. 'at the beginning.' It is not employed here in the sense of priority. The issue was not which tribe should lead a joint expedition or have the hegemony, but which should conduct a campaign in its alloted region (Daath Soferim).

the Canaanites. See on Josh. iii. 10.

2. *Judah.* As befitting his stature, and because he received his portion first (Malbim).

have delivered. In the purpose of God even

3. And Judah said unto Simeon his brother: 'Come up with me into my lot, that we may fight against the Canaanites; and I likewise will go with thee into thy lot.' So Simeon went with him. 4. And Judah went up; and the LORD delivered the Canaanites and the Perizzites into their hand; and they smote of them in Bezek ten thousand men.

3 אֶת־הָאָרֶץ בְּיָדוֹ: וַיֹּאמֶר
יְהוּדָה לְשִׁמְעוֹן אָחִיו עֲלֵה
אִתִּי בְגוֹרָלִי וְנִלָּחֲמָה בַּכְּנַעֲנִי
וְהָלַכְתִּי גַם־אֲנִי אִתְּךָ
בְּגוֹרָלֶךָ וַיֵּלֶךְ אִתּוֹ שִׁמְעוֹן:
4 וַיַּעַל יְהוּדָה וַיִּתֵּן יְהֹוָה אֶת־
הַכְּנַעֲנִי וְהַפְּרִזִּי בְּיָדָם וַיַּכּוּם
בְּבֶזֶק עֲשֶׂרֶת אֲלָפִים אִישׁ:

the future is already an accomplished fact; hence the use of the perfect tense (Rashi, Gen. xvi. 18; Bereshith Rabbah, 44:22).

3–20 JUDAH'S CAMPAIGNS

3. *Simeon.* Chosen as an ally because of the close proximity of his land which lay to the south of Judah. His towns were within the territory of Judah (cf. Josh. xix. 1–9 with Josh. xv. 26–32, 42) (Abarbanel).

his brother. The tribe is personified. [Judah was Simeon's *brother* not only in the sense that all the sons of Jacob were brothers, but the two had the same mother, Leah (Gen. xxix. 33, 35).] Moreover, their frontiers adjoined. Simeon was, in fact, the only full brother whose aid he could solicit since their lands were adjacent and there was great friendship between them. Although only Judah was instructed to go up, perhaps Simeon thought that he too should go up since his territory was within Judah's (Abarbanel).

'Come up with me into my lot. Rashi paraphrases: Come up with me and help me conquer what fell as my portion. He cites other exegetes who interpret, 'Judah shall go up,' as referring to Othniel, also known as Jabez, whom the Rabbis in Tractate Temurah (16a), identify with Judah, the brother of Simeon.

that . . . and. [In the Hebrew this is expressed by the simple conjunction *waw,* and can be rendered as a conditional clause: 'if you go with me, then I will go with you.']

4. *Judah.* [He alone is mentioned, being, so to speak, the major partner in the undertaking.]

Perizzites. Perhaps descendants of Canaan, although not listed under that name in Gen. x. 15–18). Possibly, they were called by another name (Ibn Ezra, Gen. xiii. 7). The name 'Perizzi' is derived from the root, *prz,* used in connection with open cities. Hence, the Perizzites were between the nomads, who dwelt in tents, and those who lived in permanent cities. The Perizzites occupied the mountains (Josh. xv. 3) and the forest of Ephraim (ibid. xvii. 15) (Kesseth Hasofer, Gen. xiii. 7).

smote . . . ten thousand men. This probably indicates the complete destruction of the enemy (Daath Mikra).

Bezek. Either a town or a district mentioned again in I Sam. xi. 8, though the same place may not be meant. The Bezek of I Sam. has been identified by Kaftor Vaferah with the modern Khirbet Ibzek, fourteen miles south-west of Beth-Shean, north-east of Shechem. But this is too far north for the Bezek of this verse, which is in the territory of Judah. Some identify it with the region of Abu Dis, near Jerusalem, approximately two kilometers east of Kefar Hashiloach, not far from the road to Jericho, which passes about one half kilometer north of Abu Dis (Daath Mikra). Rashi (I Sam. xi. 8), however, identifies it with that of I Sam. Accordingly, the latter is the site mentioned in our verse, i.e. the more southerly location.

5. And they found Adoni-bezek in Bezek; and they fought against him, and they smote the Canaanites and the Perizzites. 6. But Adoni-bezek fled; and they pursued after him, and caught him, and cut off his thumbs and his great toes. 7. And Adoni-bezek said: 'Threescore and ten kings, having their thumbs and their great toes cut off, gathered food under my table; as I have done, so God hath requited me.' And they brought him to Jerusalem, and he died there.

5 וַיִּמְצְאוּ אֶת־אֲדֹנִי בֶזֶק בְּבֶזֶק
וַיִּלָּחֲמוּ בּוֹ וַיַּכּוּ אֶת־הַכְּנַעֲנִי
6 וְאֶת־הַפְּרִזִּי: וַיָּנׇס אֲדֹנִי בֶזֶק
וַיִּרְדְּפוּ אַחֲרָיו וַיֹּאחֲזוּ אֹתוֹ
וַיְקַצְּצוּ אֶת־בְּהֹנוֹת יָדָיו
7 וְרַגְלָיו: וַיֹּאמֶר אֲדֹנִי־בֶזֶק
שִׁבְעִים | מְלָכִים בְּהֹנוֹת
יְדֵיהֶם וְרַגְלֵיהֶם מְקֻצָּצִים הָיוּ
מְלַקְּטִים תַּחַת שֻׁלְחָנִי כַּאֲשֶׁר
עָשִׂיתִי כֵּן שִׁלַּם־לִי אֱלֹהִים
וַיְבִיאֻהוּ יְרוּשָׁלַ͏ִם וַיָּמׇת שָׁם:

---

5. *they.* [i.e. the allies, Judah and Simeon.]

Adoni-Bezek. [Introduced somewhat abruptly, but the context makes it clear that he was the head of the force which the two tribes had just defeated, and that he was a powerful king.] The name means 'the lord of Bezek' (Kimchi). After Israel's conquest, the Canaanites did not have the audacity to call their leaders kings but lords (Daath Soferim. Cf. verse 7).

6. *cut off,* etc. This was done as a punishment for his cowardice. His thumbs were cut off as a punishment for not defending the city, and his toes were cut off as a punishment for fleeing, behavior unbefitting a king (Abarbanel). [Mutilation does not otherwise seem to have been practised by the Israelites. The same cannot be said of the other nations of antiquity, whether Persian, Greek, Phoenician, Roman or Arab whose records reveal appalling examples of cruelty to prisoners of war.]

7. *threescore and ten kings.* Canaan appears to have been divided into a host of petty states, and although Adoni-bezek was not important enough to rank among the Canaanite kings, he was sufficiently powerful to have defeated and captured many rulers (Rashi).

kings. i.e. rulers over cities (Ramban, Num. xxxv. 14). Adoni-bezek had captured them in war. We learn from the Tel-el-Amarna letters that there was extreme hatred between the kings of Canaan, with constant warfare ensuing (Daath Mikra).

table. The noun *shulchan* is connected with the Aramaic and Syriac *shelach,* 'to strip off' the skin of an animal. Originally it was a round mat of leather with a drawing-string along the edge. It served as a table or as a receptacle for food (See Shorashim, Kimchi and Ibn Jenach). [Later the *table* was a low stand, around which the diners sat on the ground, or it was placed before them as they sat on chairs or couches. We have to imagine the captive kings gathering up from the ground, like dogs, the fragments which fell while their master ate.]

requited. He recognized Divine retribution for his evil deeds. In a heathen this displays an unusually advanced state of moral consciousness. Even in those early days, the principle of measure for measure, later stressed by the Rabbis as God's method of punishment, was known (Daath Soferim).

and they. viz. the Israelites, as they now marched to attack Jerusalem (Rashi).

8. And the children of Judah fought against Jerusalem, and took it, and smote it with the edge of the sword, and set the city on fire. 9. And afterward the children of Judah went down to fight against the Canaanites that dwelt in the hill-country, and in the South, and in the Lowland. 10. And Judah went against the Canaanites that dwelt in Hebron—now the name of Hebron

8 וַיִּלָּחֲמוּ בְנֵי־יְהוּדָה בִּירוּשָׁלַם וַיִּלְכְּדוּ אוֹתָהּ וַיַּכּוּהָ לְפִי־חָרֶב וְאֶת־הָעִיר שִׁלְּחוּ בָאֵשׁ׃ 9 וְאַחַר יָרְדוּ בְּנֵי יְהוּדָה לְהִלָּחֵם בַּכְּנַעֲנִי יוֹשֵׁב הָהָר וְהַנֶּגֶב וְהַשְּׁפֵלָה׃ 10 וַיֵּלֶךְ יְהוּדָה אֶל־הַכְּנַעֲנִי הַיּוֹשֵׁב בְּחֶבְרוֹן וְשֵׁם־חֶבְרוֹן לְפָנִים

brought him. [Carried him with them as captive.]

8. *fought against Jerusalem, and took it.* The apparent contradiction between this statement and what is implied in verse 21 may be reconciled by supposing that the Judahites captured and destroyed the lower city but were unable to conquer the citadel. Subsequently the lower city was rebuilt and inhabited by the men of Judah and Benjamin as well as by Jebusites who, holding the citadel, were masters of the city until the time of David (Malbim). Another explanation is: after taking the city and burning it, the Judahites did not occupy the site. The Jebusites soon rebuilt and fortified it so strongly that neither Benjamin, in whose territory it lay, nor Judah, whose border it threatened, was able to retake it. Members of these tribes settled in the city as aliens until the reign of David when the Jebusites were finally driven out (2 Sam. v. 6ff.) (Daath Mikra).

edge. lit. 'mouth,' i.e. the sharp edge of the sword. See below iii. 16 (Kimchi in Shorashim).

set . . . on fire. lit. 'sent away in fire.' Perhaps the phrase originated in the idea of 'getting rid of by fire' (Malbim).

9. *went down.* Apparently, having reached the highest part of the Judean highlands, the invading army poured down into the remaining hill-country and thence into the Negeb in the south and the Lowland along

the Mediterranean coast, so overrunning the whole of what became the land of Judah (Malbim).

the hill-country. [The mountainous backbone of southern Palestine whose highest elevation is near Hebron, where the land rises to a height of nearly 3,000 feet.]

the South. [Hebrew *negeb,* the steppe which forms the transition to the true desert. Being the southernmost natural division of the country, the name acquired the meaning 'south' as *yam,* 'sea,' came to denote 'west.' The root is extinct in Biblical Hebrew, but in Aramaic and Syriac it means 'dry.']

the Lowland. The coastal plain, including the foothills of Judea, stretching from Jaffa to Gaza. Its fertility made it a great contrast to the austere and forbidding dry land of the Negeb (Daath Mikra).

10–15 CALEB'S EXPLOITS

10. *and Judah went.* We are to understand by this that a detachment of Judean warriors, headed by Caleb, turned south to the conquest of Hebron and the surrounding territory (Metsudath David).

Hebron. This ancient and historic city is situated twenty-two Roman miles south of Jerusalem, in the highest part of the mountains of Judah, 2,000 feet above sea level. The town lies in a valley which runs from northwest to south-east. The modern city is built partly at the bottom and partly on the slope of the eastern hill. The fields and the sur-

beforetime was Kiriath-arba—and they smote Sheshai, and Ahiman, and Talmai. 11. And from thence he went against the inhabitants of Debir—now the name of Debir beforetime was Kiriath-sepher. 12. And Caleb said: 'He that smiteth Kiriath-sepher, and taketh it, to him will I give Achsah my daughter to wife.' 13. And Othniel the son of Kenaz, Caleb's younger brother, took it; and he gave him Achsah his daughter to wife. 14. And it came to pass, when she came unto him,

קִרְיַת אַרְבַּע וַיַּכּוּ אֶת־שֵׁשַׁי
וְאֶת־אֲחִימָן וְאֶת־תַּלְמָי׃
11 וַיֵּלֶךְ מִשָּׁם אֶל־יוֹשְׁבֵי דְּבִיר
וְשֵׁם־דְּבִיר לְפָנִים קִרְיַת־
12 סֵפֶר׃ וַיֹּאמֶר כָּלֵב אֲשֶׁר יַכֶּה
אֶת־קִרְיַת סֵפֶר וּלְכָדָהּ
וְנָתַתִּי לוֹ אֶת־עַכְסָה בִתִּי
13 לְאִשָּׁה׃ וַיִּלְכְּדָהּ עָתְנִיאֵל
בֶּן־קְנַז אֲחִי כָלֵב הַקָּטֹן
מִמֶּנּוּ וַיִּתֶּן־לוֹ אֶת־עַכְסָה
14 בִתּוֹ לְאִשָּׁה׃ וַיְהִי בְּבוֹאָהּ

v. 10. פתח באתנח

rounding villages belonged to Caleb by divine bestowal (See Num. xiv. 24; Josh. xv. 13, xxi. 12).

Kiriath-arba. Cf. Gen. xxiii. 2, xxxv. 27. As mentioned in Josh. xiv. 15 and xv. 13, Arba was the name of the father of the giants who lived in that city, viz. Ahiman, Sheshai, and Talmai. Hence, the city was apparently called Kiriath-arba on his name, i.e. the city of Arba. It is, therefore, indeed puzzling that the Rabbis interpret Kiriath-arba as the city of the four, i.e. the four giants who lived there, the four righteous men, Abraham, Aner, Eshkol, and Mamre, or the four couples buried there, Adam and Eve, Abraham and Sarah, Isaac and Rebekah, and Jacob and Leah (Gen. Rabbah lviii. 4). Expositors, therefore, conclude that the city was originally called Arba for the reasons given by the Rabbis. The giant, Arba, was named after the city. They arrived at that conclusion since they could find no reason for calling a person Arba (Mizrachi, Gen. xxiii. 2).

11. For the episode, cf. Josh. xv. 15–19.

from thence he went. The subject is Judah and refers to the detachment under Caleb which

had set itself the conquest of the south (Metsudath David).

Debir. A place of strategical importance in the Negeb (cf. verse 15) or on the verge of the hill-country (cf. Josh. xi. 21, xv. 49). It has been equated with the modern village of Dahariyeh, four or five hours south-west of Hebron, standing in a conspicuous position on a flat ridge at a point where the roads meet from Gaza, Beersheba and other places south and east (Daath Mikra).

Kiriath-sepher. See on Josh. xv. 15.

12. [For a similar incentive, cf. I Sam. xvii 25.]

my daughter. [From the sequel it appears that the victor also received the captured city as a possession.]

13. *Caleb's younger brother.* Grammatically this may refer either to Kenaz or Othniel. Rashi quotes the view that Caleb was Othniel's brother from the same mother. See also on Josh. xiv. 6, xv. 17.

14. *when she came.* [The ambiguity is removed either by assuming that she had been summoned from a place of safety, perhaps Hebron, where she had been left during the campaign against Debir;] or that the

that she moved him to ask of her father a field; and she alighted from off her ass; and Caleb said unto her: 'What wouldest thou?' 15. And she said unto him: 'Give me a blessing; for that thou hast set me in the Southland, give me therefore springs of water.' And Caleb gave her the Upper Springs and the Nether Springs.

וַתְּסִיתֵהוּ לִשְׁאוֹל מֵאֵת־אָבִיהָ
הַשָּׂדֶה וַתִּצְנַח מֵעַל הַחֲמוֹר
וַיֹּאמֶר־לָהּ כָּלֵב מַה־לָּךְ׃
15 וַתֹּאמֶר לוֹ הָבָה־לִּי בְרָכָה
כִּי אֶרֶץ הַנֶּגֶב נְתַתָּנִי וְנָתַתָּה
לִי גֻּלֹּת מָיִם וַיִּתֶּן־לָהּ כָּלֵב
אֵת גֻּלֹּת עִלִּית וְאֵת גֻּלֹּת
תַּחְתִּית׃

incident happened as she was going from her father's house, where the marriage had taken place, to her husband's new home escorted on the way by her father (Metsudath David). Another explanation is given in the note on Josh. xv. 18.

to ask. I.e. Achsah persuaded her husband to permit her to ask her father for the field (Metsudath David). Alternatively, she persuaded him to ask her father for the field. After he had given her the field, he personally asked him for the Upper Springs and the Nether Springs (Ralbag). Others explain that she coaxed her husband to ask her father. When he hesitated, she took the initiative and asked him herself (Abarbanel).

alighted. As a mark of respect (cf. Gen. xxiv. 64; I Sam. xxv. 23; 2 Kings v. 21) (Metsudath David). The root is elsewhere used of something 'sinking to the ground' (iv. 21). Perhaps the word should be rendered 'she sank down' to the ground in the posture of a suppliant (Metsudath Zion and Metsudath David). [The modern East provides examples of the practice referred to.]

what wouldest thou? The Hebrew expresses a sense of anxiety, such as would be conveyed in English by 'what ails you?' (Metsudath David).

15. *a blessing.* The Hebrew noun also denotes a 'present' (Metsudath Zion).

Southland. lit. 'the land of the Negeb.'

springs of water. The text is difficult. According to Rashi, the reference is to ground sufficiently watered by rain. Curious are the variants found in the parallel version in Josh. xv. 19 where the plural *illiyyoth* and *tachtioth* occurs. Kimchi explains that the plural refers to *gulloth* whereas the singular refers to the land in which the wells were situated. The *springs* have been tentatively identified with the Seil-ed-Dilbeh on the road from Hebron to Dahariyeh where lies one of the best-watered valleys in southern Eretz Israel (Daath Mikra).

When Caleb heard his daughter's reasonable request, he gave her a fertile field watered constantly by two springs, in order to enable Othniel to engage in his studies without the concern of earning a livelihood (Me-am Loez).

16. MOVEMENT OF THE KENITES

A branch of the Kenites whose ancestor, Jethro, the father-in-law of Moses, had adopted the religion of Israel, accompanied the tribe of Judah southwards from Jericho to the vicinity of Arad. See below for details. The Kenites, like their forefather Jethro, renounced all their worldly possessions and entered a desert in order to acquire Torah (Me-am Loez).

16. And the children of the Kenite, Moses' father-in-law, went up out of the city of palm-trees with the children of Judah into the wilderness of Judah, which is in the south of Arad; and they went and dwelt with the people. 17. And Judah went with Simeon his brother, and they smote the Canaanites that inhabited Zephath, and utterly destroyed it. And the name of the city was called Hormah. 18. Also

16 וּבְנֵי קֵינִי חֹתֵן מֹשֶׁה עָלוּ מֵעִיר
הַתְּמָרִים אֶת־בְּנֵי יְהוּדָה
מִדְבַּר יְהוּדָה אֲשֶׁר בְּנֶגֶב עֲרָד
17 וַיֵּלֶךְ וַיֵּשֶׁב אֶת־הָעָם: וַיֵּלֶךְ
יְהוּדָה אֶת־שִׁמְעוֹן אָחִיו וַיַּכּוּ
אֶת־הַכְּנַעֲנִי יוֹשֵׁב צְפַת
וַיַּחֲרִימוּ אוֹתָהּ וַיִּקְרָא אֶת־
18 שֵׁם־הָעִיר חָרְמָה: וַיִּלְכֹּד

the Kenite. The Hebrew omits the definite article, as if *keni* were a proper name. It is, in fact, one of the seven names by which, according to the Rabbis, Jethro was known (Metsudath David).

father-in-law. The term *chothen* is used of the woman's father (cf. xix. 4) as distinct from *cham* which denotes the man's father (cf. Gen. xxxviii. 25). In the Mishnah, however, we find the latter term used for both (Kimchi in Shorashim).

the city of palm-trees. So again in iii. 13; Deut. xxxiv. 3; 2 Chron. xxviii. 15. Geographers agree that the description aptly applies to the cultivated area below the spring eastward of the deserted mound.

According to Rabbinic tradition, the city was assigned to the descendants of Jethro until the time the Temple was erected, when it became the possession of the tribe in whose territory it would be built. The children of Jethro thus enjoyed its ownership for four hundred and forty years. The reference in the verse is said to be to the students among them who left their homes and went to study at the feet of Othniel (Rashi).

Arad. Generally identified with Tel Arad, a round, detached, not very prominent, but well-defined hill, about sixteen miles south of Hebron. It stands among extensive ruins. Archaeology reveals that Arad was desolate at the time of the conquest. (Ruins of a Canaanite city destroyed in the third millennium before the common era, were discovered, along with the ruins of an Israelite fortress built at the beginning of the Com-

monwealth. Hence, at the time of the conquest it was desolate.) Consequently, the Kenites pitched their tents wherever they wished. This site is not identical with the Arad mentioned in Num. xxi. 1, which was further south, within the desert. Shishak, king of Egypt, lists two places among his conquests, one named Arad Rabbat, and one named Arad Beth Yerocham. Our Arad is probably Arad Rabbat, and the one in Num. is probably Arad Beth Yerocham (Daath Mikra).

they went. lit. 'he went,' explained by Kimchi as the head of the clan with his followers. The subject may be singular with a collective meaning (Metsudath David).

with the people. i.e. with the Israelites of the tribe of Judah (Metsudath David).

17–21 FURTHER CAMPAIGNS

17. In fulfillment of the agreement made at the beginning of the campaign (i. 3), the allies then invaded the territory assigned to Simeon in the south of Judah (Malbim).

Zepath. Not the modern Safed in Galilee but a place in the Negeb, identified by some authorities with the modern Sebaita, by others with es-Sufah or el-Melh, and by still others with Tel Abu-Hureirah (see Daath Mikra).

utterly destroyed. The act of extermination was in accordance with the command given by Moses (cf. Deut. vii. 2, xx. 16ff.) and was practised by all warring peoples, both before and after this period. The neglect of

Judah took Gaza with the border thereof, and Ashkelon with the border thereof, and Ekron with the border thereof. 19. And the LORD was with Judah; and he drove out the inhabitants of the hill-country; for he could not drive out the inhabitants of the valley, because they had chariots of iron. 20. And they gave Hebron unto Caleb, as Moses had spoken; and he drove out thence the three sons of Anak. 21. And the children of Benjamin

יְהוּדָה אֶת־עַזָּה וְאֶת־גְּבוּלָהּ
וְאֶת־אַשְׁקְלוֹן וְאֶת־גְּבוּלָהּ
וְאֶת־עֶקְרוֹן וְאֶת־גְּבוּלָהּ:

19 וַיְהִי יְהֹוָה אֶת־יְהוּדָה וַיֹּרֶשׁ
אֶת־הָהָר כִּי לֹא לְהוֹרִישׁ
אֶת־יֹשְׁבֵי הָעֵמֶק כִּי־רֶכֶב

20 בַּרְזֶל לָהֶם: וַיִּתְּנוּ לְכָלֵב
אֶת־חֶבְרוֹן כַּאֲשֶׁר דִּבֶּר מֹשֶׁה
וַיֹּרֶשׁ מִשָּׁם אֶת־שְׁלֹשָׁה בְּנֵי

21 הָעֲנָק: וְאֶת־הַיְבוּסִי יֹשֵׁב

the command was subsequently considered to be the cause of Israel's sufferings in the struggle for independence (See ch. ii).

18f. These two verses do not, as some modern scholars suppose, contradict one another. Verse 18 tells that the great cities of the plain were *conquered*; while verse 19, besides implying that the hill-country was also taken, adds the information that it was cleared of its inhabitants, but not so the plain (Daath Soferim). An alternative explanation is that after defeat the people of the plain recaptured their land.

18. [The places named were the principal cities of Philistia, south of Jaffa.]

19. *he could not.* lit. 'it was not to,' i.e. it was not possible to (Metsudath David).

drive out. The verb *horish* cannot always be translated by the same English word and must be understood from the context. It can mean 'conquer, occupy, possess and dispossess' (See Kimchi, Shorashim).

the inhabitants of the valley. They were left in possession as a test for Israel (Kimchi). The region indicated is the coastal plain west of Judah in which the cities enumerated in verse 18 stood. *Emek* denotes 'deep depres-

sion' and describes not a ravine but a broad valley, such as the Plain of Jezreel which now called the 'Emek' *par excellence* (See Targum).

chariots of iron. This is not the reason that the inhabitants could not be driven out, because iron chariots would not constitute an insurmountable obstacle when *the* LORD *was with Judah.* The Targum explains that the Israelites, after their victories, had lapsed into sin and so forfeited the Divine favour. The chariots of iron were not made of that material, but the metal served as a strengthening element or as studs in what was otherwise a wooden construction (Daath Mikra).

20. Caleb expels the giants of Hebron (see on verse 10).

as Moses had spoken. The promise of Moses was in general terms (cf. Num. xiv. 24, Deut. i. 36), but understood to mean Hebron (see Rashi loc. cit.) Joshua, therefore acceded to Caleb's request for that city (Jos. xiv. 12ff., xv. 13ff.).

the three sons. [Cf. verse 10.]

Anak. The word means 'neck' in the Semitic languages. It often occurs as a proper noun

did not drive out the Jebusites that inhabited Jerusalem; but the Jebusites dwelt with the children of Benjamin in Jerusalem, unto this day.

22. And the house of Joseph, they also went up against Beth-el; and the LORD was with them.   23. And the house of Joseph sent to spy out Beth-el—now the name of the city beforetime was Luz.   24. And the watchers saw a man come forth out of the city, and they said unto him: 'Show us, we pray thee, the entrance into the city, and we will deal kindly

יְרוּשָׁלַ֫ם לֹא הוֹרִ֫ישׁוּ בְּנֵ֣י בִנְיָמִ֔ן
וַיֵּ֙שֶׁב הַיְבוּסִ֜י אֶת־בְּנֵ֤י בִנְיָמִן֙
בִּירוּשָׁלַ֔ם עַ֖ד הַיּ֥וֹם הַזֶּֽה׃

22 וַיַּעֲל֥וּ בֵית־יוֹסֵ֖ף גַּם־הֵ֑ם

23 בֵּֽית־אֵ֖ל וַיהֹוָ֥ה עִמָּֽם׃ וַיָּתִ֙ירוּ֙
בֵית־יוֹסֵ֖ף בְּבֵֽית־אֵ֑ל וְשֵׁם־

24 הָעִ֥יר לְפָנִ֖ים לֽוּז׃ וַיִּרְאוּ֙
הַשֹּׁ֣מְרִ֔ים אִ֖ישׁ יוֹצֵ֣א מִן־הָעִ֑יר
וַיֹּ֣אמְרוּ ל֗וֹ הַרְאֵ֤נוּ נָא֙ אֶת־
מְב֣וֹא הָעִ֔יר וְעָשִׂ֥ינוּ עִמְּךָ֖

but it has been rightly pointed out that the article is unusual with a personal name, and the suggestion is that the phrase 'sons of the Anak' means that the sun appears to be a necklace around their necks (Rashi, Num. xiii. 33).

21. *the children of Benjamin did not drive out.* In Josh. xv. 63 the statement is made that *the children of Judah could not drive them out.* Jerusalem was in the territories of both tribes (Kimchi).

Jerusalem. [According to the Amarna Letters, almost contemporary with this period, Jerusalem, under its king Abdi-Hipa, remained loyal to the Egyptian overlord Akhenaton (1375-1358 B.C.E.), although the rest of the country was falling away before the onslaught of the Habiru. This testimony explains why the city resisted conquest for a considerable time.]

unto this day. i.e. until the time of this writing by Samuel (Kimchi, Ralbag).

22-29 THE TRIBE OF JOSEPH'S CAMPAIGNS

22. *house of Joseph.* [The tribes of Ephraim and Manasseh.]

also went up. As Judah had done (verse 4) (Metsudath David).

Beth-el. The modern Beitin, at the head of the ravine which runs among the mountains from Jericho to Ai, barely two miles west of the latter. Excavations have revealed the remains of a stout defensive wall and a layer of destruction dating about this period [See Daath Mikra].

23. *sent to spy out.* This rendering construes *wayyathiru* as the Hiphil conjugation. The meaning given to the form by some commentator is: 'they caused an examination to be made' to find out the best way of surprising the town (Targum, Rashi, Kimchi). [The verb can either be a direct causative ('they caused men to spy out') or a form of the Kal on the analogy of *wayyalinu* for *wayyalunu*.]

Luz. See on Josh. xvi. 2.

24. *The watchers.* The Israelite scouts or pickets (Kimchi, Metsudath David).

show us. If they saw him coming out of the city, they would surely see whence he came! See the next note.

the entrance. Not the gate which would be obvious and heavily guarded, but a secret

with thee.' 25. And he showed them the entrance into the city, and they smote the city with the edge of the sword; but they let the man go and all his family. 26. And the man went into the land of the Hittites, and built a city, and called the name thereof Luz, which is the name thereof unto this day.

27. And Manasseh did not drive out the inhabitants of Beth-shean and its towns, nor of Taanach and its

25 חָסֶד: וַיַּרְאֵם אֶת־מְבוֹא
הָעִיר וַיַּכּוּ אֶת־הָעִיר לְפִי־
חָרֶב וְאֶת־הָאִישׁ וְאֶת־כָּל־
26 מִשְׁפַּחְתּוֹ שִׁלֵּחוּ: וַיֵּלֶךְ הָאִישׁ
אֶרֶץ הַחִתִּים וַיִּבֶן עִיר וַיִּקְרָא
שְׁמָהּ לוּז הוּא שְׁמָהּ עַד הַיּוֹם
הַזֶּה:
27 וְלֹא־הוֹרִישׁ מְנַשֶּׁה אֶת־
בֵּית־שְׁאָן וְאֶת־בְּנוֹתֶיהָ
וְאֶת־תַּעֲנַךְ וְאֶת־בְּנוֹתֶיהָ

---

entrance. The Hebrew might be rendered: 'the way to enter,' and they inquired about a path along which an unexpected assault could be made (Malbim).

25. *he showed them.* He indicated the direction by means of a gesture (Rashi, Kimchi from Sot. 46b).

with the edge. lit. 'to the mouth.' The sharp edge of the sword is referred to as the mouth. See below iii. 16 (Kimchi, Shorashim).

all his family. For the practice of benefiting the whole family, cf. Josh. ii. 12f., vi. 22f., 25. Family is employed in the wider sense of all his kindred.

26. *the man went.* [He migrated beyond the reach of his townsmen and settled for safety in a foreign land.] Perhaps he left Canaan because he did not wish to accept the seven Noachide commandments (Daath Soferim).

the land of the Hittites. If the reference is to the ten powerful kingdom of Hatti in Asia Minor the man travelled a considerable distance. The Hittites of this verse are, of course, not the people who were reckoned among the seven nations of Canaan. About this time (1400 B.C.E.) the Hittite empire was on the eve of a great expansion under Subbiluliu who overran Mesopotamia and

wrested from Egypt the suzerainty of Syria. He rivalled the greatness of the Assyrian kings (See Kimchi) (Daath Mikra).

built a city. [This explains how a city by the name of Luz should have existed in the days of the judges so far away from Canaan.] As a reward for supporting the Israelites, he eventually built a city (Daath Soferim).

Luz. There is no clue to the site beyond the statement that it was in the land of the Hittites. The Talmud (Sot. 46b) describes it as the place where the blue dye was made for the fringes (cf. Num. xv. 38), which Sennacherib did not disturb or Nebuchadnezzar destroy. Even the Angel of Death had no power over it, and old people, when tired of life, would go outside the city to die.

27–36 THE INACTIVITY OF THE OTHER TRIBES

27f. The statement corresponds to Josh. xvii. 11–13. The house of Joseph was separated from the other tribes, both on the north and south, by a line of Canaanite towns. It was thus cut off from the fertile plain, and from the tribes which struggled for a foothold in Galilee, by a chain of fortified cities guarding the passes. At the eastern end was Beth-shean on the main road to Damascus, at the western extremity

towns, nor the inhabitants of Dor
and its towns, nor the inhabitants
of Ibleam and its towns, nor the
inhabitants of Megiddo and its
towns; but the Canaanites were
resolved to dwell in that land.
28. And it came to pass, when Israel
was waxen strong, that they put the
Canaanites to taskwork, but did in
no wise drive them out.

29. And Ephraim drove not out
the Canaanites that dwelt in Gezer;
but the Canaanites dwelt in Gezer
among them.

30. Zebulun drove not out the
inhabitants of Kitron, nor the

וְאֶת־יֹשֵׁב֙ דּוֹר וְאֶת־בְּנוֹתֶ֔יהָ
וְאֶת־יֹשְׁבֵ֤י יִבְלְעָם֙ וְאֶת־
בְּנֹתֶ֔יהָ וְאֶת־יֹשְׁבֵ֥י מְגִדּ֖וֹ
וְאֶת־בְּנוֹתֶ֑יהָ וַיּ֨וֹאֶל֙ הַֽכְּנַעֲנִ֔י
לָשֶׁ֖בֶת בָּאָ֥רֶץ הַזֹּֽאת׃ וַֽיְהִי֙ 28
כִּֽי־חָזַ֣ק יִשְׂרָאֵ֔ל וַיָּ֥שֶׂם אֶת־
הַֽכְּנַעֲנִ֖י לָמַ֑ס וְהוֹרֵ֖ישׁ לֹ֥א
הוֹרִישֽׁוֹ׃
וְאֶפְרַ֗יִם לֹ֤א הוֹרִישׁ֙ אֶת־ 29
הַֽכְּנַעֲנִ֖י הַיּוֹשֵׁ֣ב בְּגָ֑זֶר וַיֵּ֧שֶׁב
הַֽכְּנַעֲנִ֛י בְּקִרְבּ֖וֹ בְּגָֽזֶר׃
זְבוּלֻ֗ן לֹ֤א הוֹרִישׁ֙ אֶת־ 30
יוֹשְׁבֵ֣י קִטְר֔וֹן וְאֶת־יֹשְׁבֵ֖י

was Megiddo on the road from the Mediterranean coast, commanding the commercial
and military route between Egypt and the
east. For the cities enumerated, see on Josh.
ad loc (see Daath Mikra).

28. *when Israel was waxen strong*. This was
after the defeat of Jabin and Sisera, below iv.
23f. (Daath Mikra).

taskwork. As below iv. 23, *So God subdued on
that day Jabin the king of Canaan before the children of Israel* (Daath Mikra). They impressed
the Canaanites in the working gangs which
were employed in the East on public work
(cf. 1 Kings iv. 11f.).

did in no wise drive them out. The population
remained largely Canaanite, and Beth-
Shean in later times was more foreign than
Israelite (See 1 Sam. xxxi. 10ff.). Although
Israel had waxen strong and was able to aid
Manasseh in driving out the Canaanites, the
tribe of Manasseh was content in putting
them to taskwork and was not interested in
driving them out (Abarbanel).

29. *dwelt in Gezer*. The Canaanites here
formed an enclave in the territory of Ephraim on the south-western border (cf. Josh.
xvi. 10). For Gezer, see on Josh. x. 33.

30–35 THE NORTHERN TRIBES

The achievements of the northern tribes
were less spectacular and of minor importance as compared with those of Judah and
Joseph. The Israelites there settled among
the older population which for many centuries remained predominantly heathen. A
noteworthy omission is mention of Issachar.
Perhaps the tribe of Issachar did indeed
comply with the commandment to drive out
the Canaanites in their territory (Daath
Soferim).

30. *Zebulun*. This tribe settled in the hilly
country of Lower Galilee, north of the
Great Plain towards the west (cf. Josh. xix.
10–16).

Kitron. Mentioned only here; traditionally
identified with Sepphoris (Meg. 6a).

165

inhabitants of Nahalol; but the Canaanites dwelt among them, and became tributary.

31. Asher drove not out the inhabitants of Acco, nor the inhabitants of Zidon, nor of Ahlab, nor of Achzib, nor of Helbah, nor of Aphik, nor of Rehob; 32. but the Asherites dwelt among the Canaanites, the inhabitants of the land; for they did not drive them out.

33. Naphtali drove not out the inhabitants of Beth-shemesh, nor the inhabitants of Beth-anath; but he dwelt among the Canaanites, the inhabitants of the land; nevertheless the inhabitants of Beth-shemesh and of Beth-anath became tributary unto them.

נַהֲלֹל וַיֵּשֶׁב הַכְּנַעֲנִי בְּקִרְבּוֹ
וַיִּהְיוּ לָמַס׃
31 אָשֵׁר לֹא הוֹרִישׁ אֶת־יֹשְׁבֵי
עַכּוֹ וְאֶת־יוֹשְׁבֵי צִידוֹן וְאֶת־
אַחְלָב וְאֶת־אַכְזִיב וְאֶת־
חֶלְבָּה וְאֶת־אֲפִיק וְאֶת־
32 רְחֹב׃ וַיֵּשֶׁב הָאָשֵׁרִי בְּקֶרֶב
הַכְּנַעֲנִי יֹשְׁבֵי הָאָרֶץ כִּי לֹא
הוֹרִישׁוֹ׃
33 נַפְתָּלִי לֹא־הוֹרִישׁ אֶת־יֹשְׁבֵי
בֵית־שֶׁמֶשׁ וְאֶת־יֹשְׁבֵי בֵית־
עֲנָת וַיֵּשֶׁב בְּקֶרֶב הַכְּנַעֲנִי יֹשְׁבֵי
הָאָרֶץ וְיֹשְׁבֵי בֵית־שֶׁמֶשׁ
וּבֵית עֲנָת הָיוּ לָהֶם לָמַס׃

Nahalol. See on Josh. xix. 15.

31. *Asher.* Located in the highlands behind the Phoenician coast. Its territory had Zebulun on the south and Naphtali on the east (See Josh. xixi. 24–31).

Acco. The modern Acre on the north coast of the Carmel headland. As Akka it appears in the Amarna Letters. In the Ptolemaic period it was renamed Ptolemais, and in the days of the Crusades St. Jean d'Acre. The ancient site is assumed to have lain a little further eastward (Daath Mikra).

Zidon. The famous Phoenician city which the Arabs called Saida, on the coast further to the north than Acco. In Homeric days it was celebrated as the home of the arts and the centre of Canaanite culture.

Ahlab. Identified by some with Gush Halab, the Gischala of Josephus, the modern el-Jish, north-west of Safed (Daath Mikra).

Achzib. See on Josh. xv. 44.

Aphik. Found (in the form *Aphek*) with

Rehob in the list of Asher's cities in Josh. xix. 30. [They were probably both more inland, in the plain of Acco.]

Rehob. To be distinguished from Beth-rehob (xviii. 28), near Dan. The Egyptian texts mention Rehob, which is probably the place referred to here. Kaftor Vaferach mentions that in his time it was called Rachab. Archaeologists identify it with Tel Berweh, an imposing and well-watered site seven miles inland from Acco (See Carta Atlas).

32. *among the Canaanites.* They lived among them as best they could without effecting a conquest; unlike their brothers in the south who asserted their military supremacy at the start and became the predominant element in the population (Kara, Malbim, Abarbanel, Metsudath David).

33. *Naphtali.* Their territory lay in the eastern part of Upper Galilee, north of Zebulun and Issachar and east of Asher (Josh. xix. 32–39).

Beth-shemesh ... Beth-anath. See on Josh.

34. And the Amorites forced the children of Dan into the hill-country; for they would not suffer them to come down to the valley. 35. But the Amorites were resolved to dwell in Har-heres, in Aijalon, and in Shaalbim; yet the hand of the house of Joseph prevailed, so that they became tributary.   36. And the border of the Amorites was from the ascent of Akrabbim, from Sela, and upward.

34 וַיִּלְחֲצוּ הָאֱמֹרִי אֶת־בְּנֵי־
דָן הָהָרָה כִּי־לֹא נְתָנוֹ
35 לָרֶדֶת לָעֵמֶק׃ וַיּוֹאֶל הָאֱמֹרִי
לָשֶׁבֶת בְּהַר־חֶרֶס בְּאַיָּלוֹן
וּבְשַׁעַלְבִים וַתִּכְבַּד יַד
בֵּית־יוֹסֵף וַיִּהְיוּ לָמַס׃
36 וּגְבוּל הָאֱמֹרִי מִמַּעֲלֵה
עַקְרַבִּים מֵהַסֶּלַע וָמָעְלָה׃

	2	**CHAPTER II**	**ב**

1. And the angel of the LORD came

1 וַיַּעַל מַלְאַךְ־יְהוָה מִן־

v. 35. פתח בס״פ

xix. 38. [The latter is supposed to have been the seat of the worship of the war-goddess Anath. Others identify it with Tel-el-Khurbeh, a mound in Upper Galilee. The name occurs in lists of conquests by the Egyptian kings Seti and Rameses II where the determinative shows that it is the name of a deity.] The late Prof. Samuel Klein identified it with Hineh, between the Hermon Mt. range and the Parpar River, approximately 30 kilometers south-west of Damascus.

34. *Amorites.* To the end of the chapter this name is used of the inhabitants instead of Canaanites. They were the tallest and strongest of the seven nations of Canaan, as is evident from Amos ii. 9 (Kesseth Hasofer). It may also be a general term for all the nations of Canaan.

Dan. This tribe attempted to gain a foothold south-west of Ephraim, but was checked by the native population who confined them to the district around Zorah and Eshtaol. The main body of the tribe was accordingly compelled to seek a new home and finally established itself in and around Laish (cf. xviii. 1ff.; Josh. xix 47f.).

35. *were resolved to dwell.* Initially, the Amorites caused Dan to retreat to the mountains, where they too advanced, thereby necessitating aid from their neighbors,

the house of Joseph. The latter, however, did not destroy them but were content to subjugate them (Metsudath David, Malbim).

Har-heres. The meaning is 'sun mountain.' It is doubtless the equivalent of Beth-shemesh (see on Josh. xv. 10) or Ir-shemesh (Josh. xix. 41), both of which are mentioned in the same context as Aijalon and Shaalbim. The site has been sought at modern Ain Shems, on the south side of the wadi Surar, opposite Surah (Zorah).

Aijalon . . . Shaalbim. See on Josh. xix. 42.

36. *ascent of Akrabbim.* At the south-eastern extremity, near Aqaba (Ha-aretz ligvulotheha).

Sela. lit. the cliff, or the rock. Location unknown.

CHAPTER II

1–5 ORIGIN OF THE NAME BOCHIM

The period of warlike activity was over, and the newcomers, now firmly established, settled down to a normal life; but the fears of Moses and Joshua with regard to the evil effects, which would ensue from Israel's contact with the native cults soon proved to be well founded.

1. *the angel of the* LORD. The Hebrew may

up from Gilgal to Bochim. And he said: '... I made you to go up out of Egypt, and have brought you unto the land which I swore unto your fathers; and I said: I will never break My covenant with you; 2. and ye shall make no covenant with the inhabitants of this land; ye shall break down their altars; but ye have not hearkened unto My voice; what is this ye have done? 3. Wherefore I also said: I will not drive them out from before you; but they shall be

הַגִּלְגָּל אֶל־הַבֹּכִים ׃ וַיֹּאמֶר
אַעֲלֶה אֶתְכֶם מִמִּצְרַיִם
וָאָבִיא אֶתְכֶם אֶל־הָאָרֶץ
אֲשֶׁר נִשְׁבַּעְתִּי לַאֲבֹתֵיכֶם
וָאֹמַר לֹא־אָפֵר בְּרִיתִי
² אִתְּכֶם לְעוֹלָם ׃ וְאַתֶּם לֹא־
תִכְרְתוּ בְרִית לְיֽוֹשְׁבֵי הָאָרֶץ
הַזֹּאת מִזְבְּחוֹתֵיהֶם תִּתֹּצוּן
וְלֹא־שְׁמַעְתֶּם בְּקֹלִי מַה־
³ זֹּאת עֲשִׂיתֶם ׃ וְגַם אָמַרְתִּי
לֹא־אֲגָרֵשׁ אוֹתָם מִפְּנֵיכֶם

v. 1. פסקא באמצע פסוק

be translated 'a messenger of the LORD.' In Rabbinic tradition, echoed in the Targum, he was Phinehas.

Gilgal. See on Josh. iv. 19. Here the messenger of God received the Divine communication and to this spot, later known as Bochim, he summoned the people for condemnation. It is also possible that the people were already assembled at Bochim for another purpose, and were condemned by Phinehas at that gathering (Kimchi).

Bochim. A mountainous site near Beth-el (Daath Mikra). Some, supported by the LXX, seek a connection with Allon-bacuth (Gen. xxxv. 8), below Beth-el. M.T. marks a lacuna, indicating a pause, perhaps alluding to the assembling of the people, prior to the prophet's rebuke. See preceding paragraph.

made. lit. 'will make'; the use of the future for the past is common in Biblical Hebrew (Targum, Kimchi). Rashi explains the tense as referring to the intention of God when He redeemed Israel from Egypt. Although the subject of *he said* is the messenger, the words that follow reproduce the form in which the Divine communication was made to him to be reported to the people.

covenant. Not the oath just mentioned, but

the covenant with conditions attached to its fulfillment, as described in Exod. xxxiv. 10f.

2. The verse refers to the prohibition against coming to terms with the native population.

break down. Cf. Exod. xxxiv. 13. The root means 'pull down, pull to pieces,' and is applicable to an altar constructed from a number of stones (See Ramban, Lev. xi. 35).

what is this ye have done? The question is rhetorical and carries a note of indignation. It is commonly used in the Bible, e.g. in Gen. xii. 18, infra viii. 1, xv. 11. Ehrlich understands it as: how could ye have done this!

3. *wherefore.* This is not the meaning of the Hebrew *wegam* and is obviously introduced in order to give the sequence of protasis and apodosis to the whole passage; viz. 'I said I will not break My covenant on condition that you keep your share of the contract, but you have not hearkened; therefore I have now also said,' etc. Another way of construing the text is to translate: 'and I also,' etc., and suppose that the reference is to a previous warning such as is found in Num. xxxiii. 55 or Josh. xxiii. 13 (Abarbanel).

unto you as snares, and their gods shall be a trap unto you.' 4. And it came to pass, when the angel of the LORD spoke these words unto all the children of Israel, that the people lifted up their voice, and wept. 5. And they called the name of that place Bochim; and they sacrificed there unto the LORD.

6. Now when Joshua had sent the people away, the children of Israel

וְהָיוּ לָכֶם לְצִדִּים וֵאלֹהֵיהֶם
4 יִהְיוּ לָכֶם לְמוֹקֵשׁ: וַיְהִי
כְּדַבֵּר מַלְאַךְ יְהֹוָה אֶת־
הַדְּבָרִים הָאֵלֶּה אֶל־כָּל־
בְּנֵי יִשְׂרָאֵל וַיִּשְׂאוּ הָעָם אֶת־
5 קוֹלָם וַיִּבְכּוּ: וַיִּקְרְאוּ שֵׁם־
הַמָּקוֹם הַהוּא בֹּכִים וַיִּזְבְּחוּ־
שָׁם לַיהֹוָה:
6 וַיְשַׁלַּח יְהוֹשֻׁעַ אֶת־הָעָם
וַיֵּלְכוּ בְנֵי־יִשְׂרָאֵל אִישׁ

---

snares. The noun *tsiddim* is lit. 'sides.' Kimchi regards the word as elliptical and explains it as 'thorns in the sides.' He suggests alternatively, that we may render it as 'snares,' making the noun a derivation of the root, *tsud,* 'to hunt' (cf. Assyrian *tsaddu,* 'trap spring'), the *daggesh* in the *dalleth* being a substitute for the missing long vowel (Rabbi Jonah ibn Janach in Sefer Hashorashim). The figures of *snares* and *trap* are reminiscent of such passages as Exod. xxiii. 33, xxxiv. 12; Deut. vii. 16.

4. *wept.* The national and religious conscience was dormant, but not dead. An appeal to it always drew an emotional response from the people (cf. xxi. 2; 1 Sam. xi. 4).

5. *they called.* [The subject is either those present at the assembly or men generally. If the latter, the Hebrew may be rendered: 'the place was called.']

Bochim. The name means 'weepers,' but no place so called is otherwise known. Similar sounding names are found in *Allon-bacuth* (Gen. xxxv. 8) and *the valley of Baca* (Ps. lxxxiv. 7).

6 – XVI. 31 HISTORY OF ISRAEL IN THE TIME OF THE JUDGES

6 – iii. 6. The writer, before resuming the narrative, makes a recapitulation by recall-

ing that after the assembly at Shechem (Josh. xxiv. 1ff.) Joshua had dismissed the people to their allotted territories, and Israel remained faithful to God during his lifetime and of the elders who had assisted him in the leadership. The new generation abandoned the old paths and succumbed to the heathen influences around them. God's anger was aroused and punishment fell heavily upon them in the form of enslavement and subjection to foreign powers. Consequent repentance led to deliverance by the hand of leaders appointed by God who judged and temporarily recalled them to His worship. But the death of a judge was the signal for a fresh and even graver lapse into local idolatry. God accordingly vowed that He would not drive out the inhabitants of the land but leave them as a test of Israel's steadfastness. Events demonstrated that the test had failed. It is correct to assume from the tone of the passage that, in the author's view, what really mattered was not the facts of Israel's history, but the moral and religious lessons which it taught (Rashi, Kimchi, Metsudath David).

6–10. Almost a verbatim repetition of Josh. xxiv. 28ff.

6. *when Joshua had sent the people away.* An introductory clause connecting what follows with the narrative as it ends in the Book of Joshua.

went every man unto his inheritance to possess the land. 7. And the people served the LORD all the days of Joshua, and all the days of the elders that outlived Joshua, who had seen all the great work of the LORD, that He had wrought for Israel. 8. And Joshua the son of Nun, the servant of the LORD, died, being a hundred and ten years old. 9. And they buried him in the border of his inheritance in Timnath-heres, in the hill-country of Ephraim, on the north of the mountain of Gaash. 10. And also all that generation were gathered unto their fathers; and

לְנַחֲלָתֽוֹ לָרֶשֶׁת אֶת־הָאָרֶץ׃

7 וַיַּעַבְד֤וּ הָעָם֙ אֶת־יְהֹוָ֔ה כֹּ֚ל יְמֵ֣י יְהוֹשֻׁ֔עַ וְכֹ֣ל ׀ יְמֵ֣י הַזְּקֵנִ֗ים אֲשֶׁ֨ר הֶאֱרִ֤יכוּ יָמִים֙ אַחֲרֵ֣י יְהוֹשֻׁ֔עַ אֲשֶׁ֣ר רָא֗וּ אֵ֣ת כׇּל־מַעֲשֵׂ֤ה יְהֹוָה֙ הַגָּד֔וֹל אֲשֶׁ֥ר עָשָׂ֖ה

8 לְיִשְׂרָאֵֽל׃ וַיָּ֛מׇת יְהוֹשֻׁ֥עַ בִּן־נ֖וּן עֶ֣בֶד יְהֹוָ֑ה בֶּן־מֵאָ֥ה וָעֶ֖שֶׂר

9 שָׁנִֽים׃ וַיִּקְבְּר֤וּ אוֹתוֹ֙ בִּגְב֣וּל נַחֲלָת֔וֹ בְּתִמְנַת־חֶ֖רֶס בְּהַ֣ר אֶפְרָ֑יִם מִצְּפ֖וֹן לְהַר־גָּֽעַשׁ׃

10 וְגַם֙ כׇּל־הַדּ֣וֹר הַה֔וּא נֶאֶסְפ֖וּ

ז. ‏v. 7. יתיר ר

---

his inheritance. [The portion allotted to each tribe by Joshua.]

to possess. In the manner described in chapter i of this Book.

7. *elders.* The leaders as defined in Num. xi. 16ff. They were the guardians of Israel's laws and religion. Cf. 'Moses received the Torah on Sinai, and handed it down to Joshua, and Joshua to the elders' (Aboth i. 1).

outlived. lit. 'prolonged days.' See Rashi.

who had seen. In verse 10 and Josh. xxiv. 31 the verb used is *had known.* The idea implied in both verbs is personal experience as distinct from hearsay or tradition (Malbim).

all the great work of the LORD. [The deliverance from Egypt, the miracles in the wilderness and the successful campaigns over the Jordan as well as in Canaan.]

8. *a hundred and ten years.* The same age as his ancestor Joseph (Gen. L. 26).

9. *border.* [i.e. territory.]

Timnath-heres. In *Joshua* it appears as Tim-

nath-serah (xix. 50, xxiv. 30; see the note of the first-mentioned verse). In Rabbinic tradition the origin of the name, 'picture of the sun,' is traced to an image of that luminary which was placed over Joshua's grave, as if to say, 'There lies the man who caused the sun to stand still' (Rashi from unknown Rabbinic source.)

the hill-country of Ephraim. The highlands stretching from the north of Jerusalem to the Valley of Jezreel.

Gaash. The root meaning is 'to quake,' indicating that at one time the mountain was volcanic. The Rabbis, indeed, tell us that the mountain quaked over them to kill them for neglecting to mourn Joshua fittingly (Rashi from Shab. 105b).

10. *all that generation.* [The contemporaries of Joshua who survived him.]

were gathered unto their fathers. i.e. their souls were gathered in with those of their forefathers. This is a common expression frequently used in the Bible to denote death (Metsudath David, Rashi Gen. xlvii. 30). Cf. 'gathered unto his people,' 'slept with his fathers.'

there arose another generation after
them, that knew not the LORD, nor
yet the work which He had wrought
for Israel.

11. And the children of Israel did
that which was evil in the sight of
the LORD, and served the Baalim.
12. And they forsook the LORD, the
God of their fathers, who brought
them out of the land of Egypt, and
followed other gods, of the gods of
the peoples that were round about
them, and worshipped them; and
they provoked the LORD. 13. And
they forsook the LORD, and served

אֶל־אֲבוֹתָיו וַיָּקָם דּוֹר אַחֵר
אַחֲרֵיהֶם אֲשֶׁר לֹא־יָדְעוּ
אֶת־יְהֹוָה וְגַם אֶת־הַמַּעֲשֶׂה
אֲשֶׁר עָשָׂה לְיִשְׂרָאֵל׃

11 וַיַּעֲשׂוּ בְנֵי־יִשְׂרָאֵל אֶת־הָרַע
בְּעֵינֵי יְהֹוָה וַיַּעַבְדוּ אֶת־
12 הַבְּעָלִים׃ וַיַּעַזְבוּ אֶת־יְהֹוָה
אֱלֹהֵי אֲבוֹתָם הַמּוֹצִיא אוֹתָם
מֵאֶרֶץ מִצְרַיִם וַיֵּלְכוּ אַחֲרֵי
אֱלֹהִים אֲחֵרִים מֵאֱלֹהֵי
הָעַמִּים אֲשֶׁר סְבִיבוֹתֵיהֶם
וַיִּשְׁתַּחֲווּ לָהֶם וַיַּכְעִסוּ אֶת־
13 יְהֹוָה׃ וַיַּעַזְבוּ אֶת־יְהֹוָה

that knew not the LORD, nor yet the work. Sixty-seven years had passed from the Exodus. Although there probably were other people living (who were in their eighties) who had also witnessed many of the miracles, since they possessed no Torah wisdom, this experience was not enough to protect the Jews from the ideologies of the natives, and they succumbed (Ralbag). Metsudath David explains that they knew not the LORD through logic, nor did they remember the work He had wrought.

11–13 ISRAEL'S APOSTASY

11. *children of Israel.* [There is a note of pathos in the phrase. How tragic that the children of the great and pious ancestor, who had 'striven with God and with men and prevailed,' should sink to idolatry!]

evil in the sight of the LORD. i.e. first they did what was evil by violating the commandments in general. Then they rebelled and worshipped idols; first in conjunction with their worship of God (verse 12), and then by abandoning His worship and denying His existence completely (v. 13) (Malbim).

Baalim. Plural of *baal,* 'lord, master'; so-called because they stood in this relationship with their devotees (Kimchi). The term doubtless applies not to the numerous images of the gods or the various local forms of one god, but to the different deities worshipped in the land. The Baalim were generally nature-gods and had their priests who carried on a cult often associated with immoral rites and human sacrifice (Daath Mikra).

12. *out of the land of Egypt.* The memory of Israel's bondage in that country lingered in the mind of posterity; and it should have aroused the gratitude of the people to keep them loyal to the God Who had redeemed them (Abarbanel).

followed other gods. i.e. they abandoned monotheistic worship and followed other gods in conjunction with their worship of God (Alshich).

provoked. [Almost in the sense of 'defied.']

13. *they forsook the LORD.* This is not a mere repetition, as supposed by modern com-

Baal and the Ashtaroth. 14. And the anger of the LORD was kindled against Israel, and He delivered them into the hands of spoilers that spoiled them, and He gave them over into the hands of their enemies round about, so that they could not any longer stand before their enemies. 15. Whithersoever they went out, the hand of the LORD was against them for evil, as the LORD had spoken, and as the LORD had sworn unto them; and they were

וַיַּעַבְדוּ לַבַּעַל וְלָעַשְׁתָּרוֹת׃

14 וַיִּחַר־אַף יְהֹוָה בְּיִשְׂרָאֵל וַיִּתְּנֵם בְּיַד־שֹׁסִים וַיָּשֹׁסּוּ אוֹתָם וַיִּמְכְּרֵם בְּיַד אוֹיְבֵיהֶם מִסָּבִיב וְלֹא־יָכְלוּ עוֹד

15 לַעֲמֹד לִפְנֵי אוֹיְבֵיהֶם׃ בְּכֹל | אֲשֶׁר יָצְאוּ יַד־יְהֹוָה הָיְתָה־ בָּם לְרָעָה כַּאֲשֶׁר דִּבֶּר יְהֹוָה וְכַאֲשֶׁר נִשְׁבַּע יְהֹוָה לָהֶם וַיֵּצֶר

mentators, but an indication of complete abandonment of their worship of God (Malbim, Alshich). It should not be understood that all the Israelites had completely forsaken the worship of God, but that many of them worshipped the idols to such an extent that it appeared as though they had completely abandoned the worship of the Almighty. Moreover, this was only for short periods of time. Since the faithful should have protested, it is counted as though the entire generation had worshipped idols exclusively (Daath Soferim).

Baal and the Ashtaroth. [Often mentioned together (cf. x. 6; 1 Sam. vii. 4, xii. 10). *Baal* is not a proper name and is frequently joined to a complement; e.g. Baal of Tyre, Baal of Peor, etc. There was consequently many a Baal in Canaan. Sometimes the plural is used and at other times the singular for the whole group of false gods. *Ashtaroth* is the plural of *Ashtoreth*, the Phoenician *Ashtart*. She was one of the most widely worshipped deities in the ancient Semitic Near East. The word is found as *Ishtar* in Babylonia and Assyria, *Ashtar* in Arabia and *Athar* in Syria. The Philistines erected a temple in her honour (cf. 1 Sam. xxxi. 10). Her name appears in the place *Ashteroth-karnaim* (Gen. xiv. 5; cf. Deut. i. 4) and on the Moabite Stone as *Ashtar-kemosh*. No satisfactory explanation has yet been given of the etymology of the word.] Kimchi con-

nected it with *the young* (ashteroth) *of the flock* (Deut. xxviii. 4) which he explains as 'the females of thy flock.'

14–15 GOD'S PUNISHMENT

14. *spoiled.* The punctuation indicates that the root of this verb is *shasas*, while that of *shosim* (spoilers) is *shasah*, both having the same meaning (Kimchi). In the Amarna Letters *sha-see* and *sha-sa* denote the nomadic robber tribes of the desert south of Canaan (Daath Mikra).

gave them over. lit. 'sold them,' i.e. made them subject to (Metsudath Zion).

their enemies round about. Israel is punished by those very nations with whom they had made treaties (Abarbanel).

could not any longer stand. As they had done in the days of Joshua. For the idea that sin was the cause of their discomfiture, cf. Josh. vii. 12, and also Lev. xxvi. 36f; Num. xiv. 42ff.

15. *went out.* The Hebrew verb is often used in the sense of 'marching out to war, make a foray' (cf. xi. 3), 'setting out on a campaign' (cf. Deut. xxviii. 7; 2 Sam. xi. 1). The Midrash sees here an allusion to the misfortunes of Elimelech, Mahlon and Chilion, described in Ruth i. 3ff (Kimchi).

the LORD *had sworn.* Cf. Lev. xxvi. 14ff. and Deut. xxviii. 15ff.

sore distressed. 16. And the LORD
raised up judges, who saved them
out of the hand of those that spoiled
them. 17. And yet they hearkened
not unto their judges, for they went
astray after other gods, and worshipped them; they turned aside
quickly out of the way wherein their
fathers walked, obeying the commandments of the LORD; they did
not so. 18. And when the LORD
raised them up judges, then the
LORD was with the judge, and saved
them out of the hand of their
enemies all the days of the judge;
for it repented the LORD because of
their groaning by reason of them
that oppressed them and crushed
them. 19. But it came to pass,
when the judge was dead, that they
turned back, and dealt more corruptly than their fathers, in following

16 לָהֶם מְאֹד: וַיָּקֶם יְהוָה
שֹׁפְטִים וַיּוֹשִׁיעוּם מִיַּד
17 שֹׁסֵיהֶם: וְגַם אֶל־שֹׁפְטֵיהֶם
לֹא שָׁמֵעוּ כִּי זָנוּ אַחֲרֵי אֱלֹהִים
אֲחֵרִים וַיִּשְׁתַּחֲווּ לָהֶם סָרוּ
מַהֵר מִן־הַדֶּרֶךְ אֲשֶׁר הָלְכוּ
אֲבוֹתָם לִשְׁמֹעַ מִצְוֺת־יְהוָה
18 לֹא־עָשׂוּ כֵן: וְכִי־הֵקִים
יְהוָה ׀ לָהֶם שֹׁפְטִים וְהָיָה
יְהוָה עִם־הַשֹּׁפֵט וְהוֹשִׁיעָם
מִיַּד אֹיְבֵיהֶם כֹּל יְמֵי הַשּׁוֹפֵט
כִּי־יִנָּחֵם יְהוָה מִנַּאֲקָתָם מִפְּנֵי
19 לֹחֲצֵיהֶם וְדֹחֲקֵיהֶם: וְהָיָה ׀
בְּמוֹת הַשּׁוֹפֵט יָשֻׁבוּ וְהִשְׁחִיתוּ
מֵאֲבוֹתָם לָלֶכֶת אַחֲרֵי

16–19 JUDGES SENT BY GOD

16. *judges.* Champions and leaders whom
the critical conditions of the time brought
to the fore (Daath Mikra).

17. *they hearkened not.* This cannot mean
that the relief obtained for them by their
deliverers had no effect upon them; that
would be contrary to the accounts in this
Book; but the repentance was only temporary. Disobedience recurred after the death
of the judge, as stated in verse 19 (Daath
Mikra).

went astray. The verb, lit. 'acted adulterous-
ly,' aptly describes Israel's lust for the Baalim, 'strange husbands.' [To Hosea, with his
personal bitter experience, the adulterous
wife became the figure of Israel's faithlessness to the covenant with God (Hos. i–iii)]
(Metsudath Zion).

quickly. [Only a few years after the death of
Joshua and the elders.]

18. *for it repented the* LORD. [Better, 'it
would repent the LORD.' This phrase does
not signify that He changed His mind,
because God is not man that He should
repent (cf. Num. xxiii. 19), but He was
moved to pity. The language has been
described as a condescension to the imperfection of human speech.]

19. *turned back.* They relapsed into their
former idolatry. The tense in the Hebrew is
the imperfect frequentative, expressing
habitual action (Rashi).

dealt more corruptly. They naturally went a
step further than their fathers, disregarding
the scruples which in some measure still re-
strained their forebears (Daath Soferim,
Daath Mikra).

their fathers. Not the righteous generation of
Joshua, but the generation which preceded
the evildoers (cf. verse 10) (Daath Soferim,
Daath Mikra).

other gods to serve them, and to worship them; they left nothing undone of their practices, nor of their stubborn way. 20. And the anger of the Lord was kindled against Israel; and He said: 'Because this nation have transgressed My covenant which I commanded their fathers, and have not hearkened unto My voice; 21. I also will not henceforth drive out any from before them of the nations that Joshua left when he died; 22. that by them I may prove Israel, whether they will keep the way of the Lord to walk therein, as their fathers did keep it, or not.' 23. So the Lord

אֱלֹהִים אֲחֵרִים לְעָבְדָם
וּלְהִשְׁתַּחֲוֹת לָהֶם לֹא הִפִּילוּ
מִמַּעַלְלֵיהֶם וּמִדַּרְכָּם
20 הַקָּשָׁה: וַיִּחַר־אַף יְהוָה
בְּיִשְׂרָאֵל וַיֹּאמֶר יַעַן אֲשֶׁר
עָבְרוּ הַגּוֹי הַזֶּה אֶת־בְּרִיתִי
אֲשֶׁר צִוִּיתִי אֶת־אֲבוֹתָם וְלֹא
21 שָׁמְעוּ לְקוֹלִי: גַּם־אֲנִי לֹא
אוֹסִיף לְהוֹרִישׁ אִישׁ מִפְּנֵיהֶם
מִן־הַגּוֹיִם אֲשֶׁר־עָזַב יְהוֹשֻׁעַ
22 וַיָּמֹת: לְמַעַן נַסּוֹת בָּם אֶת־
יִשְׂרָאֵל הֲשֹׁמְרִים הֵם אֶת־
דֶּרֶךְ יְהוָה לָלֶכֶת בָּם כַּאֲשֶׁר
23 שָׁמְרוּ אֲבוֹתָם אִם־לֹא: וַיַּנַּח

---

their. viz. of the predecessors (Daath Mikra).

practices. In a bad sense (ibid.).

20–23 WHY GOD LEFT SOME NATIONS IN CANAAN

20. *this nation.* The writer uses the noun *goi* which is seldom employed as a term for Israel. It has been suggested that a deliberate slight may have been the reason for the choice of the word here. Even the addition of *zeh* (this) is thought to carry a tone of alienation, like the Latin *iste* (cf. Isa. vi. 9, viii. 12) (Daath Soferim).

21. *I also.* The sequence of thought is: because Israel failed to keep his part of the compact, I also will not keep Mine (Metsudath David).

left. The use of *azab* is unusual (cf. 2 Sam. xv. 16). These nations are specified in the next chapter.

22. The verse states the reason that God considered it desirable that Joshua should leave some of the Canaanite nations unconquered.

prove. The text has the infinitive without a subject, a construction which creates ambiguity. The commentators interpret it as the writer's explanation of the Divine purpose (Ralbag, Metsudath David).

keep the way of the Lord. [i.e. observe the ordinances laid down by Him, carry out the practical precepts.]

23. This verse is an explanation of the preceding. Between them the two verses attempt to answer the questions raised by the statement in 21b, viz. why did God allow any nations to remain after Joshua's conquests? Why did He not enable him to exterminate them at once? The answer is: because He wished to prove Israel, etc., therefore He left them unconquered by Joshua (Metsudath David).

left those nations, without driving them out hastily; neither delivered He them into the hand of Joshua.

יְהֹוָה אֶת־הַגּוֹיִם הָאֵלֶּה לְבִלְתִּי הוֹרִישָׁם מַהֵר וְלֹא נְתָנָם בְּיַד־יְהוֹשֻׁעַ׃

8   CHAPTER III   **ג**

1. Now these are the nations which the LORD left, to prove Israel by them, even as many as had not known all the wars of Canaan; 2. only that the generations of the children of Israel might know, to teach them war, at the least such as beforetime knew nothing thereof; 3. namely, the five lords of the Philistines, and all the Canaanites,

1 וְאֵלֶּה הַגּוֹיִם אֲשֶׁר הִנִּיחַ יְהֹוָה לְנַסּוֹת בָּם אֶת־יִשְׂרָאֵל אֵת כָּל־אֲשֶׁר לֹא־יָדְעוּ אֵת כָּל־ 2 מִלְחֲמוֹת כְּנָעַן׃ רַק לְמַעַן דַּעַת דֹּרוֹת בְּנֵי־יִשְׂרָאֵל לְלַמְּדָם מִלְחָמָה רַק אֲשֶׁר־ 3 לְפָנִים לֹא יְדָעוּם׃ חֲמֵשֶׁת ׀ סַרְנֵי פְלִשְׁתִּים וְכָל־הַכְּנַעֲנִי

CHAPTER III

1–6 THE UNCONQUERED CANAANITE PEOPLES

1. The first half of the verse continues the last verse of the previous chapter.

had not known. This alludes to the new generation in Israel (cf. ii 10). The older generation, which had experienced the impact of Canaanite warfare and the ensuing victories, did not require 'proving,' because they had demonstrated their faithfulness to God (cf. 11 7) (Metsudath David).

all the wars of Canaan. The conquests achieved by Joshua and later by individual tribes.

2. The essential message of the verse is the need for future generations to know that in consequence of their sins they would be compelled to learn the art of war. If they walked in the ways of God this would be unnecessary (cf. verse 4) (Kimchi, Metsudath David).

thereof. i.e. of the wars of the Canaanites and

their tactics; hence the plural in the Hebrew (Rashi, Kimchi).

3. *five.* viz. Gaza, Ashkelon, Ashdod, Gath, Ekron and the surrounding territory (Josh. xiii. 3).

lords. See on Josh. xiii. 3. The Hebrew word *seren* is used only of the Philistines and is probably a native term (Daath Mikra).

Philistines. They formed a confederacy of the five cities. The difficulty of reconciling the statement that these territories were left unconquered with the statement in i. 18 that at least three of these cities had been taken by Joshua leads Kimchi to conjecture that the Philistines had meanwhile regained what they had lost. The Philistines, after whom the Holy Land was called Palestine, arrived in Eretz Yisrael in two waves from Crete, the first at the time of the Patriarchs, when they settled in the south-west. At the time of the judges, a new wave arrived, overrunning the land and threatening to crush the Israelites (Universal Jewish History, Biberfeld; Daath Mikra).

Canaanites. Here are probably intended the

and the Zidonians, and the Hivites that dwelt in mount Lebanon, from mount Baal - hermon unto the entrance of Hamath. 4. And they were there, to prove Israel by them, to know whether they would hearken unto the commandments of the LORD, which He commanded their fathers by the hand of Moses. 5. And the children of Israel dwelt among the Canaanites, the Hittites, and the Amorites, and the Perizzites, and the Hivites, and the Jebusites; 6. and they took their daughters to be their wives, and gave their own

וְהַצִּידֹנִי וְהַחִוִּי יֹשֵׁב הַר
הַלְּבָנוֹן מֵהַר בַּעַל חֶרְמוֹן עַד
לְבוֹא חֲמָת: וַיִּהְיוּ לְנַסּוֹת בָּם 4
אֶת־יִשְׂרָאֵל לָדַעַת הֲיִשְׁמְעוּ
אֶת־מִצְוֹת יְהוָה אֲשֶׁר־צִוָּה
אֶת־אֲבוֹתָם בְּיַד־מֹשֶׁה: וּבְנֵי 5
יִשְׂרָאֵל יָשְׁבוּ בְּקֶרֶב הַכְּנַעֲנִי
הַחִתִּי וְהָאֱמֹרִי וְהַפְּרִזִּי וְהַחִוִּי
וְהַיְבוּסִי: וַיִּקְחוּ אֶת־ 6
בְּנוֹתֵיהֶם לָהֶם לְנָשִׁים וְאֶת־

inhabitants of the Lowland from a point north of Philistia to a point just south of Zidon. There is no necessity to suppose that the name included all the population west of the Jordan (Daath Mikra).

Zidonians. Cf. Josh. xiii. 4; there it is a collective term for the Phoenicians, as in Homer (Odyssey IV, 84), named after the metropolis, Zidon. Later the Philistines rebelled and established Tyre as the metropolis until it fell into the hands of Alexander of Macedon (Kesseth Hasofer).

Hivites. The Hebrew pointing is 'Hivvites,' often mentioned in the Bible (cf. Gen. xxxiv. 2; Josh. ix. 7). At this time they were in the central region of Canaan. Attempts have been made by modern scholars, in the light of recent archaeological discoveries, to identify them with the Achaeans (Biberfeld).

Lebanon. This would complete the picture of encirclement provided by the list of unconquered places mentioned in this verse.

Baal-hermon. According to Josh. xiii. 5 the boundary ran, more precisely, *from Baal-gad under mount Hermon unto the entrance of Hamath.* Baal-gad (Josh. xi 17, xii 7) was the northern limit of Joshua's conquests and

was situated in the Lebanon valley; hence probably on the western side of mount Hermon, variantly identified as the modern Hasbeiya or as Baal-bech (See Daath Mikra).

the entrance of Hamath. See on Josh. xii. 5.

4. This verse explains the nature of the test mentioned in verse 1. It clears up any ambiguity that may have arisen out of the statement in verse 2 (See Daath Soferim).

to know. Not that God should know, but that it might be proved to the Israelites. The same theological problem arose in the 'proving' of Abraham (Gen. xxii. 1, Ibn Ezra and Ramban ad loc.).

5. Here the nations are mentioned in whose midst the Israelites dwelt; in verse 3 are listed the peoples on the frontiers (Daath Soferim).

Canaanites. Six nations are enumerated, as often elsewhere. The total of seven includes the Girgashites (cf. Josh. iii. 10, xxiv, 11).

Hittites. See on i. 26.

Amorites. See on i. 34.

6. The Israelites ignored the warning of Moses (Deut. vii. 3f) and intermarried with

daughters to their sons, and served their gods.

7. And the children of Israel did that which was evil in the sight of the Lord, and forgot the Lord their God, and served the Baalim and the Asheroth. 8. Therefore the anger of the Lord was kindled against Israel, and He gave them over into the hand of Cushan-rishathaim king of Aram-naharaim; and the children of Israel served Cushan-rishathaim eight years. 9. And when the children of Israel cried unto the

בְּנוֹתֵיהֶם נָתְנוּ לִבְנֵיהֶם
וַיַּעַבְדוּ אֶת־אֱלֹהֵיהֶם׃
7 וַיַּעֲשׂוּ בְנֵי־יִשְׂרָאֵל אֶת־
הָרַע בְּעֵינֵי יְהֹוָה וַיִּשְׁכְּחוּ
אֶת־יְהֹוָה אֱלֹהֵיהֶם וַיַּעַבְדוּ
אֶת־הַבְּעָלִים וְאֶת־
8 הָאֲשֵׁרוֹת׃ וַיִּחַר־אַף יְהֹוָה
בְּיִשְׂרָאֵל וַיִּמְכְּרֵם בְּיַד כּוּשַׁן
רִשְׁעָתַיִם מֶלֶךְ אֲרַם נַהֲרָיִם
וַיַּעַבְדוּ בְנֵי־יִשְׂרָאֵל אֶת־
כּוּשַׁן רִשְׁעָתַיִם שְׁמֹנֶה שָׁנִים׃
9 וַיִּזְעֲקוּ בְנֵי־יִשְׂרָאֵל אֶל־

the natives, the consequence being the adoption of their seductive cults (Metsudath David).

7-xvi. 31. This section recounts the thirteen judges who governed the people and demonstrates the truth of the thesis stated in ii. 11-22.

7-11 OTHNIEL

7. *forgot the* Lord. A very common phrase, found in many books of the Bible, to denote the faithlessness and ingratitude of the Israelites when they abandoned His worship for that of false gods (Targum, and forgot the worship of . . .).

Baalim. See on ii. 11.

Asheroth. Singular *Asherah,* a different word from *Ashtaroth* in ii. 13. These were trees planted at the entrance of the pagan temples, perhaps as a sort of sign directing the worshippers to the shrine. See below vi. 25 (Ramban, Deut. xvii. 21). Undoubtedly, these trees themselves became objects of worship, as is indicated in numerous places in the Bible and Talmud, including our verse.

8. gave them over. See on ii. 14.

Cushan-rishathaim. The name is curious and, if Semitic, would mean 'Cushan of double wickedness.' As the dual form is unknown with Hebrew abstract nouns, it is assumed that we have here a proper name (according to Kimchi *rishathaim* is a place-name), or a Hebraized version of a foreign name like Casha Rishati found in Mesopotamian inscriptions of that period (D.M.), or descriptive term, something like 'the double-dyed monster' (so the Talmud, Sanh. 105a).

Aram-naharaim. 'Aram of the two rivers,' denoting the land between the Tigris and the Euphrates, known as Mesopotamia. At that time, a large portion of Mesopotamia was in the hands of the Kashites, a nation originating from the Zagros mountains. Cushan was one of the Kashite kings, and emulating many of his Mesopotamian predecessors (cf. Gen. xiv), he set out on an expedition of conquest in Syria and Palestine (Daath Mikra).

served. By paying tribute (ibid.)

9. *cried unto the* Lord. In their distress; this recurring phrase suggests the remorse of the

LORD, the LORD raised up a saviour to the children of Israel, who saved them, even Othniel the son of Kenaz, Caleb's younger brother. 10. And the spirit of the LORD came upon him, and he judged Israel; and he went out to war, and the LORD delivered Cushan-rishathaim king of Aram into his hand; and his hand prevailed against Cushan-rishathaim. 11. And the land had rest forty years. And Othniel the son of Kenaz died.

12. And the children of Israel again did that which was evil in the

יְהֹוָה וַיָּקֶם יְהֹוָה מוֹשִׁיעַ לִבְנֵי
יִשְׂרָאֵל וַיּוֹשִׁיעֵם אֵת עָתְנִיאֵל
בֶּן־קְנַז אֲחִי כָלֵב הַקָּטֹן
מִמֶּֽנּוּ: וַתְּהִי עָלָיו רֽוּחַ־יְהֹוָה 10
וַיִּשְׁפֹּט אֶת־יִשְׂרָאֵל וַיֵּצֵא
לַמִּלְחָמָה וַיִּתֵּן יְהֹוָה בְּיָדוֹ
אֶת־כּוּשַׁן רִשְׁעָתַיִם מֶלֶךְ
אֲרָם וַתָּעָז יָדוֹ עַל כּוּשַׁן
רִשְׁעָתָיִם: וַתִּשְׁקֹט הָאָרֶץ 11
אַרְבָּעִים שָׁנָה וַיָּמָת עָתְנִיאֵל
בֶּן־קְנַז:
וַיֹּסִפוּ בְּנֵי יִשְׂרָאֵל לַעֲשׂוֹת 12

people, their sufferings having created a sense of guilt.

Othniel. Cf. i. 13. [Since Othniel was Caleb's brother, it is not likely that he was very much younger. It is, therefore, likely that he was born before the Exodus. In order to avoid dying in the wilderness because of the decree of the spies, he could not be older than 95. To assume that he was born after the Exodus would make him more than forty years younger than Caleb.]

10. *the spirit.* The Targum has 'the spirit of prophecy.' It signifies a sudden and powerful emanation from God which took possession of the individual and endowed him with gifts transcending the ordinary limits of human power. It manifests itself in the valour of the judge, the wisdom of the ruler, the genius of an artist (Exod. xxxi. 3, xxxvi. 1) the outpourings of a poet (2 Sam. xxiii. 2) and the ecstasy of a prophet (1 Sam. x 10). Kimchi indeed suggests that it refers to extra strength and valour with which he was endowed to wage war against the oppressors. Metsudath David adds that he was endowed with wisdom to judge justly. Rashi quotes

Midrash Tanchuma that it was a divinely endowed insight into understanding his mission to save Israel despite their shortcomings.

came. lit. 'was.'

judged. First he elevated them spiritually and then he was able to be victorious (Meam Loez).

delivered. Josephus (*Antiquities* V, iii. 3) relates that the victory was achieved by a band of resolute men under Othniel's command who surprised the king's bodyguard.

prevailed. i.e. he enjoyed many victories over the foe (Abarbanel). The same verb is used in vi. 2.

11. *had rest.* i.e. from war (Metsudath David).

forty years. According to the traditional chronology, this includes the eight years of oppression by Cushan (Rashi from Seder Olam, ch. 12). Thus we explain, And the land rested, making a total of forty years since Cushan commenced to oppress Israel (Elijah of Wilna on Seder Olam).

sight of the LORD; and the LORD strengthened Eglon the king of Moab against Israel, because they had done that which was evil in the sight of the LORD. 13. And he gathered unto him the children of Ammon and Amalek; and he went and smote Israel, and they possessed the city of palm-trees. 14. And the children of Israel served Eglon the king of Moab eighteen years. 15. But when the children of Israel cried

הָרַע בְּעֵינֵי יְהֹוָה וַיְחַזֵּק יְהֹוָה אֶת־עֶגְלוֹן מֶלֶךְ־מוֹאָב עַל־יִשְׂרָאֵל עַל כִּי־עָשׂוּ אֶת־ 13 הָרַע בְּעֵינֵי יְהֹוָה: וַיֶּאֱסֹף אֵלָיו אֶת־בְּנֵי־עַמּוֹן וַעֲמָלֵק וַיֵּלֶךְ וַיַּךְ אֶת־יִשְׂרָאֵל וַיִּירְשׁוּ 14 אֶת־עִיר הַתְּמָרִים: וַיַּעַבְדוּ בְנֵי־יִשְׂרָאֵל אֶת־עֶגְלוֹן מֶלֶךְ־מוֹאָב שְׁמוֹנֶה עֶשְׂרֵה 15 שָׁנָה: וַיִּזְעֲקוּ בְנֵי־יִשְׂרָאֵל

12–30 EHUD

12. *strengthened.* The meaning is: enabled him to prevail. It was not Eglon's prowess but Israel's sinfulness that led God to raise up this new foe as an instrument of punishment (Malbim).

Eglon. As the name of a man it occurs only in this chapter. As the name of a place it appears in Josh. x. 3, 5, 23, 37, xii. 12, xv. 39.

Moab. The territory east of the Dead Sea extending eastward to the desert, southwest to Edom, north-west to Ammon and north to Reuben and Gad. The river Arnon was the northern boundary. Only one literary record has come down to us from this ancient land, viz. the so-called Moabite Stone discovered in 1868.

13. *he gathered.* i.e. he formed an alliance.

children of Ammon. Neighbours and close kinsmen of the Moabites (cf. Gen. xix. 36ff.). They appear again as allies against king Jehoshaphat in 2 Chron. xx. 1.

Amalek. A Bedouin people roaming the Sinaitic peninsula whose name Israel always recalled with loathing as that of the first

enemy to attack him when he left Egypt (cf. Deut. xxv. 17ff.). Although practically exterminated by Saul (1 Sam. xv), they appear again in 1 Chron. iv. 43 in conflict with Israel, and in the days of Esther, Haman the Agagite, traditionally a descendant of the Amalekites, plotted to destroy the Jews in Persia.

and they possessed. They did not loot the city only to abandon it, but, on the contrary, they dwelt in it to show possession (Kimchi).

city of palm-trees. viz. Jericho (Targum, see on i. 16). The difficulty of reconciling the occupation of the city by Eglon with its destruction by Joshua can hardly be overcome by assuming that the Moabites built a fortress on the ruins, because the statement *they possessed* implies that it had been wrested from the people previously in occupation. That the Israelites had rebuilt it is impossible because Joshua had pronounced a curse on the one who would rebuild it or even rebuild another city with the same name. It is, therefore, likely that *the city of palm-trees* was a settlement which was built adjacent to Jericho and called by a different name to distinguish it from the old Jericho (Malbim).

unto the LORD, the LORD raised them up a saviour, Ehud the son of Gera, the Benjamite, a man left-handed; and the children of Israel sent a present by him unto Eglon the king of Moab. 16. And Ehud made him a sword which had two edges, of a cubit length; and he girded it under his raiment upon his right thigh. 17. And he offered the present unto Eglon king of Moab—now Eglon was a very fat man. 18. And when he had made an end of offering the present, he sent away the people that

אֶל־יְהוָֹה וַיָּקֶם יְהוָֹה לָהֶם
מוֹשִׁיעַ אֶת־אֵהוּד בֶּן־גֵּרָא
בֶּן־הַיְמִינִי אִישׁ אִטֵּר יַד־
יְמִינוֹ וַיִּשְׁלְחוּ בְנֵי־יִשְׂרָאֵל
בְּיָדוֹ מִנְחָה לְעֶגְלוֹן מֶלֶךְ
מוֹאָב: 16 וַיַּעַשׂ לוֹ אֵהוּד חֶרֶב
וְלָהּ שְׁנֵי פֵיוֹת גֹּמֶד אָרְכָּהּ
וַיַּחְגֹּר אוֹתָהּ מִתַּחַת לְמַדָּיו
17 עַל יֶרֶךְ יְמִינוֹ: וַיַּקְרֵב אֶת־
הַמִּנְחָה לְעֶגְלוֹן מֶלֶךְ מוֹאָב
18 וְעֶגְלוֹן אִישׁ בָּרִיא מְאֹד: וַיְהִי
כַּאֲשֶׁר כִּלָּה לְהַקְרִיב אֶת־
הַמִּנְחָה וַיְשַׁלַּח אֶת־הָעָם

v. 16. הכ׳ בצרי

15. *but when.* Or, 'then,' lit. 'and.'

Ehud. As the name of a clan it appears in 1 Chron. vii. 10.

Gera. The name of a son of Benjamin (Gen. xlvi. 21; cf. Shimei the son of Gera in 2 Sam. xvi. 5).

Benjamite. Israel's saviour on this occasion hailed from the tribe whose land had been invaded.

left-handed. The LXX and Vulgate translate 'ambidexterous.' Rashi explains the Hebrew *itter* as 'hand contracted by disease or mishap.' According to Kimchi, it signifies simply the loss of the natural use of the right arm (cf. xx. 16). The defect is mentioned because it figured in the sequel (Metsudath David).

a present. This was doubtless the periodic tribute imposed by the Moabites. The term *minchah* is used of the meal-offering to God. Generally it denotes a gift brought as a token of subservience or goodwill (cf. Gen. xxxii. 14, 2 Sam. viii. 2, 6).

16. *a sword.* [Not a dagger a span in length as the old translators thought, but a long dirk.]

a cubit. The distance from the elbow to the end of the thumb. The text has instead of the common word for *cubit* (*ammah*), which measures from the elbow to the end of the middle finger, the noun *gomed* which does not occur elsewhere in the Bible (Kara).

his raiment. It was a wide flowing garment in which the weapon could easily be concealed (See Daath Mikra).

his right thigh. To avoid rousing suspicion when about to draw the weapon with his left hand (Metsudath David).

17. *now Eglon was a very fat man.* The clause is introduced as a parenthesis in anticipation of what is narrated in verse 22 (Ralbag).

18. *he sent away.* It is evident from the next verse that Ehud accompanied them part of the way and then returned to Eglon's palace alone. He did not wish to be encumbered

bore the present.   19. But he himself turned back from the quarries
that were by Gilgal, and said:
'I have a secret errand unto thee,
O king.' And he said: 'Keep
silence.' And all that stood by him
went out from him.   20. And Ehud
came unto him; and he was sitting
by himself alone in his cool upper
chamber.   And Ehud said: 'I have

19 נְשֹׂאֵי הַמִּנְחָה: וְהוּא שָׁב מִן־
הַפְּסִילִים אֲשֶׁר אֶת־הַגִּלְגָּל
וַיֹּאמֶר דְּבַר־סֵתֶר לִי אֵלֶיךָ
הַמֶּלֶךְ וַיֹּאמֶר הָס וַיֵּצְאוּ
מֵעָלָיו כָּל־הָעֹמְדִים עָלָיו:
20 וְאֵהוּד ׀ בָּא אֵלָיו וְהוּא יֹשֵׁב
בַּעֲלִיַּת הַמְּקֵרָה אֲשֶׁר־לוֹ
לְבַדּוֹ וַיֹּאמֶר אֵהוּד דְּבַר־

v. 19. ‏קמץ בז״ק

by his followers in his subsequent flight, because it would be easier for one man to escape than for several (Kimchi, Metsudath David).

the people that bore the present. [A large retinue was required to carry the tribute which was payment in kind.]

19. *but he.* [The Hebrew construction makes use of the nominal sentence instead of the normal verb with *waw* consecutive, a literary device which serves to emphasize the contrast: he dismissed the retinue, but he returned.]

the quarries. The Hebrew noun is *pesilim* to which the LXX and Vulgate give the usual meaning 'graven images.' Perhaps they were rude stone images marking an ancient shrine or Moabite idols placed as boundary stones by Eglon (Daath Mikra). Daath Soferim conjectures that this was the quarry from which graven images were hewn.

Gilgal. This is Tel Eteleh, south-east of ancient Jericho. Accordingly, Ehud crossed the Jordan both going and returning. Others explain that Pesilim was the ford of the Jordan near Gilgal. He escorted his men as far as the Jordan but did not cross (Daath Mikra).

and said. [He spoke from a distance, as is shown from the following verse.]

a secret errand. He therefore could not con-

vey it to Eglon in the presence of the retinue who carried the present, but had to return alone. Some such excuse was essential to cover up his leaving and returning (Metsudath David).

keep silence. This is addressed by Eglon to his attendants, and indicates his desire not only for silence, but for complete privacy (Rashi, Pidanki).

20. *And Ehud came unto him.* i.e. Ehud drew closer, like one who is going to whisper a secret into someone's ear (Metsudath David, Daath Mikra).

he was sitting, etc. It is not clear whether the king retired to his room for the purpose of holding a private conversation. Probably he had been there all the time. The present tense supports this conjecture (Daath Mikra).

cool upper chamber. [More lit. 'upper chamber of cooling.' The *aliyyah* was a one-roomed apartment, built in a corner of the flat roof of a house. It was fitted on all sides with latticed windows which shut out the sun and gave both free ventilation and privacy. In the heat of summer it was the coolest part of the house. The *aliyyah* is often mentioned in the Bible as part of a private residence, serving as a guest-room (I Kings xvii. 19, 23; 2 Kings iv. 10f.), or of a palace (2 Kings i. 2). At times it was very spacious (cf. Jer. xxii. 13f.)].

a message from God unto thee.'
And he arose out of his seat.
21. And Ehud put forth his left
hand, and took the sword from his
right thigh, and thrust it into his
belly. 22. And the haft also went
in after the blade; and the fat closed
upon the blade, for he drew not the
sword out of his belly; and it came
out behind. 23. Then Ehud went
forth into the porch, and shut the
doors of the upper chamber upon
him, and locked them. 24. Now
when he was gone out, his servants
came; and they saw, and, behold,

אֱלֹהִים לִי אֵלֶיךָ וַיָּקָם מֵעַל
הַכִּסֵּא: וַיִּשְׁלַח אֵהוּד אֶת־יַד 21
שְׂמֹאלוֹ וַיִּקַּח אֶת־הַחֶרֶב
מֵעַל יֶרֶךְ יְמִינוֹ וַיִּתְקָעֶהָ
בְּבִטְנוֹ: וַיָּבֹא גַם־הַנִּצָּב אַחַר 22
הַלַּהַב וַיִּסְגֹּר הַחֵלֶב בְּעַד
הַלַּהַב כִּי לֹא שָׁלַף הַחֶרֶב
מִבִּטְנוֹ וַיֵּצֵא הַפַּרְשְׁדֹנָה:
וַיֵּצֵא אֵהוּד הַמִּסְדְּרוֹנָה וַיִּסְגֹּר 23
דַּלְתוֹת הָעֲלִיָּה בַּעֲדוֹ וְנָעָל:
וְהוּא יָצָא וַעֲבָדָיו בָּאוּ וַיִּרְאוּ 24

---

a message from God. The text has *Elohim*, a
term which could apply to any deity. The
view of the Rabbis is opposed to that of
some modern commentators who explain
that Eglon's mark of respect arose from his
belief that the message came from his own
god, Chemosh. On the contrary, they maintain that he knew from Whom the Hebrew
emissary brought his message and deliberately stood up as a mark of respect (Sanh.
60a). As a reward for this action God gave
him a daughter, Ruth, who became the
ancestress of a long line of Hebrew kings
(Midrash Rabbah on Ruth i. 9).

he arose. While the king was occupied with
what to an exceedingly fat man would be
the laborious act of rising, the movement of
Ehud's left hand would escape notice or not
arouse suspicion (Ralbag).

22. *went in.* The dirk was evidently not
provided with a cross-piece or guard (see
illustration in Daath Mikra).

he drew not. The subject is Ehud.

excrement. The Hebrew word *parshedonah* is
difficult and occurs nowhere else. Some
scholars connect it with *peresh,* 'dung' and

explain it of the excrement which issued
from the abdominal wound. It is so understood in the Midrash Rabbah on Gen. xlix.
27.

23. *porch.* The noun *misderon* is found
only here. The ancient versions all seemed
to favour a connection with *seder,* 'order,
row, rank' and understood it as the ante-
chamber where the common people waited
in 'orderly rows' when seeking to petition
the king (Kimchi).

the doors. [The plural doubtless refers to the
two leaves of the door, common in the East.
Archaeologists describe the doors of the
ancient Hebrews as consisting of slabs, four
and a half feet high, four feet wide and eight
inches thick which hung on pivots.]

upon him. i.e. Eglon and not, as the Hebrew
might imply, upon Ehud.

locked. [The tense in the Hebrew is unusual
and difficult to explain.] The locked doors
would deceive the waiting servants and give
Ehud time to make his escape (Kimchi).

24. *his servants came.* i.e. shortly after Ehud
left, Eglon's servants entered (Rashi).

the doors of the upper chamber were
locked; and they said: 'Surely he is
covering his feet in the cabinet of
the cool chamber.' 25. And they
tarried till they were ashamed; and,
behold, he opened not the doors of
the upper chamber; therefore they
took the key, and opened them; and,
behold, their lord was fallen down
dead on the earth. 26. And Ehud
escaped while they lingered, having
passed beyond the quarries, and
escaped unto Seirah. 27. And it
came to pass, when he was come,
that he blew a horn in the hill-
country of Ephraim, and the children
of Israel went down with him from
the hill-country, and he before them.
28. And he said unto them: 'Follow

וְהִנֵּה דַּלְתוֹת הָעֲלִיָּה נְעֻלוֹת
וַיֹּאמְרוּ אַךְ מֵסִיךְ הוּא אֶת־
רַגְלָיו בַּחֲדַר הַמְּקֵרָה: 25 וַיָּחִילוּ עַד־בּוֹשׁ וְהִנֵּה אֵינֶנּוּ
פֹּתֵחַ דַּלְתוֹת הָעֲלִיָּה וַיִּקְחוּ
אֶת־הַמַּפְתֵּחַ וַיִּפְתָּחוּ וְהִנֵּה
אֲדֹנֵיהֶם נֹפֵל אַרְצָה מֵת: 26 וְאֵהוּד נִמְלַט עַד הִתְמַהְמְהָם
וְהוּא עָבַר אֶת־הַפְּסִילִים
27 וַיִּמָּלֵט הַשְּׂעִירָתָה: וַיְהִי
בְּבוֹאוֹ וַיִּתְקַע בַּשּׁוֹפָר בְּהַר
אֶפְרַיִם וַיֵּרְדוּ עִמּוֹ בְנֵי־
יִשְׂרָאֵל מִן־הָהָר וְהוּא 28 לִפְנֵיהֶם: וַיֹּאמֶר אֲלֵהֶם

v. 25. קמץ בז"ק

---

surely. The Hebrew *ach* is restrictive in force,
as if to say: 'there is nothing wrong; he is
only . . . (Metsudath David.)'

covering his feet. Again 1 Sam. xxiv. 3, an
euphemistic circumlocution for answering
nature's call (Kimchi, Metsudath Zion).

25. *till they were ashamed.* Better *till it became
late.* i.e. until it became too late to be
accounted for by the suggested reason
(Malbim).

the key. They found it where Ehud had left it
(Kimchi), or perhaps they too had a key
(Metsudath David).

26. *beyond the quarries.* See on verse 19.
After passing the pagan shrine, frequented
constantly by the Moabites, he considered
himself safe, and fled to Seirah, which was
in Israelite territory (Ralbag).

Seirah. A place doubtless on the edge of the

Ephraimite highlands (Daath Mikra). Rashi
derives the name from *sa'ir,* 'woody district,'
and explains it as a thicket, a suitable place
to hide in. The scene of Ehud's adventure
was scarcely Jericho (verse 13), since this
would create geographical difficulties in the
description of his flight. Gilgal, to which he
fled, was not on the way from Jericho to
mount Ephraim, but in the opposite direction towards the fords of the Jordan and the
land of Moab. It is best to assume, with
Rashi, that Eglon was in his own land across
the Jordan and there Ehud went to assas-
sinate him.

27. *when he came back.* Back to the Land of
Israel (Rashi, Metsudath David).

blew a horn. As a summons to arms (cf. vi.
34; 1 Sam. xiii. 3) (Metsudath David).

went down. To the plain of Jericho (D.M.).

28. *follow.* lit. 'pursue.' Metsudath David

after me; for the Lord hath delivered
your enemies the Moabites into
your hand.' And they went down
after him, and took the fords of the
Jordan against the Moabites, and
suffered not a man to pass over.
29. And they smote of Moab at that
time about ten thousand men, every
lusty man, and every man of valour;
and there escaped not a man.
30. So Moab was subdued that day
under the hand of Israel. And the
land had rest fourscore years.

31. And after him was Shamgar
the son of Anath, who smote of the

רִדְפ֣וּ אַחֲרַ֗י כִּֽי־נָתַ֨ן יְהֹוָ֧ה
אֶת־אֹיְבֵיכֶ֛ם אֶת־מוֹאָ֖ב
בְּיֶדְכֶ֑ם וַיֵּרְד֣וּ אַחֲרָ֗יו וַיִּלְכְּד֞וּ
אֶת־מַעְבְּר֤וֹת הַיַּרְדֵּן֙ לְמוֹאָ֔ב
29 וְלֹֽא־נָתְנ֥וּ אִ֖ישׁ לַעֲבֹֽר׃ וַיַּכּ֨וּ
אֶת־מוֹאָ֜ב בָּעֵ֣ת הַהִ֗יא
כַּעֲשֶׂ֤רֶת אֲלָפִים֙ אִ֔ישׁ כָּל־
שָׁמֵ֖ן וְכָל־אִ֣ישׁ חָ֑יִל וְלֹ֥א נִמְלַ֖ט
30 אִֽישׁ׃ וַתִּכָּנַ֤ע מוֹאָב֙ בַּיּ֣וֹם
הַה֔וּא תַּ֖חַת יַ֣ד יִשְׂרָאֵ֑ל וַתִּשְׁקֹ֥ט
הָאָ֖רֶץ שְׁמוֹנִ֥ים שָׁנָֽה׃
31 וְאַחֲרָ֤יו הָיָה֙ שַׁמְגַּ֣ר בֶּן־עֲנָ֔ת
וַיַּ֤ךְ אֶת־פְּלִשְׁתִּים֙ שֵֽׁשׁ־

---

explains the meaning to be: 'follow me
quickly.'

took the fords of the Jordan. By doing this they
achieved a double purpose. They cut off the
retreat of those Moabites who were residing
on the Israelite side of the river (Ralbag),
and intercepted any aid that might attempt
to cross from Moab (Kimchi). The fords of
the river were near Gilgal (Josh. ii. 7; 2
Sam. xix. 16). There is still a ford near the
site of ancient Jericho.

against the Moabites. lit. 'to Moab,' which had
led some interpreters to explain: 'the fords
towards Moab' (so Metsudath David).

29. *about ten thousand.* [A round number, as
often.]

lusty. lit. 'fat.' The meaning of the clause is:
all of them were vigorous and valiant men
(Kimchi). The Moabites must have formed
an army of occupation on Israelite territory
(Ralbag).

30. *fourscore years.* i.e. two generations,
counting from the beginning of the oppression, thus leaving a period of actual peace
of sixty-two years' duration (Ralbag). The
spirit of the Moabites was effectively broken.
They dared no more to harass the Israelites,
but returned to their land on the other side
of the Arnon (D.M).

31 SHAMGAR

Shamgar. He was the first of the six minor
judges. His name is foreign and his father's
is that of a goddess of war. Neither the
period nor the duration of his judgeship is
given, and it is the Rabbinic view that he
died in the first year of his office (Abarbanel). As iv. 1 ignores him, it is suggested
that during his administration Israel was
sinful and that he was unable to protect
them from Canaanite oppression even in his
lifetime. In v. 6 the time of Shamgar is mentioned as Israel's darkest hour before the
dawn of deliverance under Deborah (Kimchi, Metsudath David).

Philistines six hundred men with an ox-goad; and he also saved Israel.

מֵאוֹת אִישׁ בְּמַלְמַד הַבָּקָר
וַיּשַׁע גַּם־הוּא אֶת־יִשְׂרָאֵל:

4 **CHAPTER IV** ד

1. And the children of Israel again did that which was evil in the sight of the LORD, when Ehud was dead. 2. And the LORD gave them over into the hand of Jabin king of Canaan, that reigned in Hazor; the captain of whose host was Sisera, who dwelt in Harosheth-goiim. 3. And the children of Israel cried

¹ וַיֹּסִפוּ בְּנֵי יִשְׂרָאֵל לַעֲשׂוֹת
הָרַע בְּעֵינֵי יְהֹוָה וְאֵהוּד מֵת:
² וַיִּמְכְּרֵם יְהֹוָה בְּיַד־יָבִין מֶלֶךְ־
כְּנַעַן אֲשֶׁר מָלַךְ בְּחָצוֹר וְשַׂר־
צְבָאוֹ סִיסְרָא וְהוּא יוֹשֵׁב
³ בַּחֲרֹשֶׁת הַגּוֹיִם: וַיִּצְעֲקוּ

an ox-goad. A formidable weapon, sometimes eight to ten feet long, with a spike at one end and a chisel-shaped blade at the other. It is called a *malmad* because it 'teaches' the ox to plough. The Hebrew letter *lamed* is so-called because in the ancient script it bore a resemblance to this instrument (Biberfeld).

CHAPTER IV

THE JUDGESHIP OF DEBORAH

1–3 ISRAEL'S OPPRESSION BY KING JABIN

1. *when Ehud was dead.* lit. 'and Ehud was dead (or, had died).' Grammatically the construction is explained as a postponed circumstantial clause introducing a fact essential to the understanding of the situation. The reason that Shamgar is ignored in this narrative is perhaps to be sought in the fact that he left no mark on Israel's history. He had effected only a partial and temporary deliverance and failed to prevent the people's backsliding (Kimchi, Metsudath David).

Rabbi Jacob Pidanki conjectures that Ehud was still alive at the time of Shamgar, but he was very old. Malbim maintains that some evil was done while yet in Ehud's lifetime but his merit protected them.

2. *gave them over.* See on ii. 14. Whereas they were previously given over to Aram and Moab, who did not belong to the seven nations of Canaan, now they were given over into the hands of the Canaanites, to fulfill the prophecy of ii. 3 (Malbim).

Jabin. Like Abimelech among the Philistines and Pharaoh among the Egyptians, Jabin (probably meaning 'intelligent') may have been a common name among the kings of Hazor (cf. Josh. xi. 1 where a different king is intended).

Canaan. Here used as a general term for Hazor. The reason is supplied in Josh. xi. 10: *Hazor beforetime was the head of all those kingdoms.* At this time, it was an honorary title, since the house of Jabin no longer ruled over all Canaan but over the remnant of the Canaanites (Daath Mikra).

reigned. i.e. had his capital (cf. Josh. xiii. 12, 21).

in Hazor. The difficulty arising from this statement, viz. that Hazor had been destroyed by Joshua (Josh. xi. 11) over one hundred and fifty years before, is removed by assuming with Kimchi that a remnant of the population had escaped to Harosheth-goiim where they set up a new city-State under a king who also called himself Jabin, king of Hazor.

Hazor. See on Josh. xi. 1.

Harosheth-hagoiim. The meaning of the name

unto the LORD; for he had nine hundred chariots of iron; and twenty years he mightily oppressed the children of Israel.

4. Now Deborah, a prophetess, the wife of Lappidoth, she judged Israel at that time. 5. And she sat under

בְּנֵי־יִשְׂרָאֵל אֶל־יְהוָה כִּי
תְּשַׁע מֵאוֹת רֶכֶב־בַּרְזֶל לוֹ
וְהוּא לָחַץ אֶת־בְּנֵי יִשְׂרָאֵל
בְּחָזְקָה עֶשְׂרִים שָׁנָה:
4 וּדְבוֹרָה אִשָּׁה נְבִיאָה אֵשֶׁת
לַפִּידוֹת הִיא שֹׁפְטָה אֶת־
5 יִשְׂרָאֵל בָּעֵת הַהִיא: וְהִיא

v. 4. הפטרת בשלח ויש מתחילין ותשר דבורה

is difficult. The Targum renders it as: the strongest of the cities of the nations. The meaning of the word *harosheth* is obscure. Kimchi relates it to *chorshah*, 'forest,' explaining that the Canaanites had fortresses in the forest. Ralbag and Abarbanel relate it to *harash*, a craftsman. Ralbag explains that the city was built by the craftsmanship of many nations, thus making it impregnable. Abarbanel explains that it was a large city in which the craftsmanship of all nations was available. Others identify *goiim* with the nation mentioned in Gen. xiv. 1, which settled in lower Galilee, known as *gelil hagoiim*, 'the district of the nations.' This city may have been founded by that nation and inherited by the Canaanites (Daath Mikra). Its location is believed to be at Tel-Amer (known today as Tel-geba-shemen), near el-Harithiyeh, on the north side of Kishon, not far from Megiddo (Daath Mikra).

3. *cried.* A similar root with a changed consonant was used in iii. 9.

nine hundred. This was a huge number, considering that the Egyptians had only six hundred (Exod. xiv. 7) (Pes. 118b).

chariots of iron. See on i. 19. [These gave Jabin mastery over the Plain of Jezreel.] According to inscriptions, the vehicles were two-wheeled, open behind and carrying a driver, who was simultaneously a warrior and a shield-bearer (Illustrations in Daath Mikra).

twenty years. Half a generation.

mightily. lit. 'with force'; again in 1 Sam. ii. 16.

4–16 VICTORY OF DEBORAH AND BARAK

4. *Deborah.* She was the moving spirit in the episode now narrated. The name means 'bee.'

a prophetess. lit. 'a woman, a prophetess.' The title, signifying that her activities were Divinely inspired, is applied also to Miriam and Huldah (Exod. xv. 20; 2 Kings xxii. 14). The description is not used of any other judge.

wife of Lappidoth. Deborah's identity as the wife of the unknown Lappidoth tells us nothing about her. The Rabbis, sought other meanings in these words: She was a 'woman of torches,' i.e. she made wicks for the sanctuary in Shiloh (Meg. 14a); she was the wife of Barak, also known as Lappidoth. He was called Barak because his face shone like lightning, which is the meaning of 'Barak,' and Lappidoth, because he brought wicks to the Sanctuary (Eliyahu Rabba, ch. 9). Ralbag interprets that her degree of Divine inspiration was so intense as to create sparks and flames during the moments of its reception. Alternatively, because of her zeal and quickness, she is compared to a torch (Metsudath David).

judged. Decided cases between litigants, or, perhaps, merely publicized the laws of the Torah (Tos. Git. 88b). She also directed the people in the right way of life (Ralbag).

at that time. This limiting phrase led to the inference that her prophetic utterances were restricted in application to her own generation (Kimchi).

the palm-tree of Deborah between Ramah and Beth-el in the hill-country of Ephraim; and the children of Israel came up to her for judgment. 6. And she sent and called Barak the son of Abinoam out of Kedesh-naphtali, and said unto him: 'Hath not the LORD, the God of Israel, commanded, saying: Go and draw toward mount Tabor, and take with thee ten thousand men of

יוֹשֶׁבֶת תַּחַת־תֹּמֶר דְּבוֹרָה
בֵּין הָרָמָה וּבֵין בֵּית־אֵל בְּהַר
אֶפְרָיִם וַיַּעֲלוּ אֵלֶיהָ בְּנֵי
יִשְׂרָאֵל לַמִּשְׁפָּט: וַתִּשְׁלַח 6
וַתִּקְרָא לְבָרָק בֶּן־אֲבִינֹעַם
מִקֶּדֶשׁ נַפְתָּלִי וַתֹּאמֶר אֵלָיו
הֲלֹא־צִוָּה ׀ יְהוָה אֱלֹהֵי־
יִשְׂרָאֵל לֵךְ וּמָשַׁכְתָּ בְּהַר
תָּבוֹר וְלָקַחְתָּ עִמְּךָ עֲשֶׂרֶת

5. [This verse is to be understood as a circumstantial addition, providing the information that, unlike Samuel (1 Sam. vii. 16f.), she did not go on a circuit but received inquiries at her place of residence. This was undoubtedly due to feminine modesty.]

sat. To settle disputes (Metsudath David). Others rendering 'dwelt,' explain that her house was under a palm-tree (Kimchi).

the palm-tree of Deborah. Modern scholars look for the location at Dobrath (Josh. xix. 12, xxi 28), the modern Deburije, at the western foot of Tabor; but this seems too far north to fit in with the other details in the verse.

Ramah. The region in which Samuel also judged Israel (1 Sam. vii. 16.), the modern er-Ram, about five miles north of Jerusalem on the road beyond Gibeah in the territory of Benjamin (Daath Mikra). It has been suggested that the memories surrounding the place since the time of Jacob (cf. Gen. xxxv. 8) led Deborah to choose it as her seat (Abarbanel from unknown Rabbinic sources).

Beth-el. See on i. 22.

6. *Barak.* The name has been found in Palmyrene and Sabean inscriptions as well as Carthaginian. If he was Deborah's husband, she must have separated from him on

account of her constant communication with God; therefore she now sent for him (Ralbag).

Kedesh-naphtali. See on Josh. xii. 22.

commanded. By Moses in the words *thou shalt utterly destroy them* (Deut. vii. 2) (Rashi). Others hold that Deborah was referring to a command delivered to her by God (Metsudath David). [The question is rhetorical compelling the hearer to make a reply in the affirmative.]

draw. By persuasion and encouragement, since the Israelites were afraid to take up arms against the Canaanites (Kimchi and Ralbag).

toward mount Tabor. lit. 'in mount Tabor,' i.e. persuade them and encourage them to come with you upon Tabor (Kimchi, Metsudath David). Daath Mikra suggests: draw them [from their places and assemble them] on mount Tabor.

Tabor. [The well-known mountain at the head of the northern arm of the Great Plain. The Arabs call it Jebel et-Tor, and it is easily recognizable as a symmetrical, rounded hill, presenting from the south the aspect of a segment of a sphere and from the north of a truncated cone. In the war with the Canaanites it proved a most advantageous strategic spot, from the point of view of position and natural strength.]

the children of Naphtali and of the children of Zebulun? 7. And I will draw unto thee to the brook Kishon Sisera, the captain of Jabin's army, with his chariots and his multitude; and I will deliver him into thy hand.' 8. And Barak said unto her: 'If thou wilt go with me, then I will go; but if thou wilt not go with me, I will not go.' 9. And she said: 'I will surely go with thee; notwithstanding the journey that thou takest shall not be for thy honour ; for the LORD will give Sisera over into the hand of a woman.' And Deborah arose, and went with Barak to Kedesh.

10. And Barak called Zebulun and

אֲלָפִים אִישׁ מִבְּנֵי נַפְתָּלִי
7 וּמִבְּנֵי זְבֻלוּן: וּמָשַׁכְתִּי אֵלֶיךָ
אֶל־נַחַל קִישׁוֹן אֶת־סִיסְרָא
שַׂר־צְבָא יָבִין וְאֶת־רִכְבּוֹ
וְאֶת־הֲמוֹנוֹ וּנְתַתִּיהוּ בְּיָדֶךָ:
8 וַיֹּאמֶר אֵלֶיהָ בָּרָק אִם־תֵּלְכִי
עִמִּי וְהָלָכְתִּי וְאִם־לֹא תֵלְכִי
9 עִמִּי לֹא אֵלֵךְ: וַתֹּאמֶר הָלֹךְ
אֵלֵךְ עִמָּךְ אֶפֶס כִּי לֹא תִהְיֶה
תִּפְאַרְתְּךָ עַל־הַדֶּרֶךְ אֲשֶׁר
אַתָּה הוֹלֵךְ כִּי בְיַד־אִשָּׁה
יִמְכֹּר יְהֹוָה אֶת־סִיסְרָא
וַתָּקָם דְּבוֹרָה וַתֵּלֶךְ עִם־
10 בָּרָק קֶדְשָׁה: וַיַּזְעֵק בָּרָק

Naphtali . . . Zebulun. [The omission of Issachar may be explained by the assumption that they were so closely associated with Zebulun as to be included in them. The tribe is mentioned in the poetic description of the rising in v. 15.]

7. *I will draw*. God, speaking through the prophetess, promises to lure the enemy to destruction (Metsudath David).

Kishon. After the Jordan, it is the most considerable river in Palestine. Having its rise near mount Tabor, it flows in a north-westerly direction through the Plain of Jezreel and empties itself into the Mediterranean at the foot of mount Carmel in the Haifa harbour. The bed is often dry in summer.

captain. Or 'general'; i.e. the leader of the national militia.

chariots. Manned by trained warriors of rank.

multitude. The common force of soldiers comprising the infantry.

8. *if thou wilt go, etc.* It was not cowardice which prompted the condition, but a sense of the powerful influence exercised by the prophetess over the people. Her presence would be a source of inspiration and an assurance of Divine aid (Ralbag).

9. *a woman*. The context makes it clear that the reference is to Deborah and not to Jael. Her compliance with his condition will deprive Barak of the glory of the victory. If it were Jael whom she meant, the remark would be pointless, because Jael's part in the enemy's defeat was not dependent on whether the prophetess accompanied Barak or not (Kimchi). According to Ralbag, Deborah was prophesying Sisera's fall by the hand of a woman in a double sense, her own and Jael's.

to Kedesh. Where he mustered his troops.

Naphtali together to Kedesh; and there went up ten thousand men at his feet; and Deborah went up with him.

11. Now Heber the Kenite had severed himself from the Kenites, even from the children of Hobab the father-in-law of Moses, and had pitched his tent as far as Elon-bezaanannim, which is by Kedesh.

12. And they told Sisera that Barak the son of Abinoam was gone up to mount Tabor. 13. And Sisera gathered together all his chariots, even nine hundred chariots of iron, and all the people that were with him, from Harosheth-goiim, unto

אֶת־זְבוּלֻן וְאֶת־נַפְתָּלִי
קֶדְשָׁה וַיַּעַל בְּרַגְלָיו עֲשֶׂרֶת
אַלְפֵי אִישׁ וַתַּעַל עִמּוֹ
דְּבוֹרָה:

11 וְחֶבֶר הַקֵּינִי נִפְרָד מִקַּיִן מִבְּנֵי
חֹבָב חֹתֵן מֹשֶׁה וַיֵּט אָהֳלוֹ
עַד־אֵלוֹן בְּצַעֲנַנִּים אֲשֶׁר אֶת־
קֶדֶשׁ:

12 וַיַּגִּדוּ לְסִיסְרָא כִּי עָלָה בָּרָק
בֶּן־אֲבִינֹעַם הַר־תָּבוֹר:

13 וַיַּזְעֵק סִיסְרָא אֶת־כָּל־
רִכְבּוֹ תְּשַׁע מֵאוֹת רֶכֶב בַּרְזֶל
וְאֶת־כָּל־הָעָם אֲשֶׁר אִתּוֹ
מֵחֲרֹשֶׁת הַגּוֹיִם אֶל־נַחַל

v. 11. הר׳ בקמץ   v. 11. בצעננים ק׳

10. *there went up*. The form of the verb can be construed either as Kal (*went up*) or Hiphil ('he led up'). If the former, the subject, notwithstanding the singular verb, is *ten thousand men* (Targum); if the latter, it is Barak (Kimchi and Metsudath David).

at his feet. i.e. 'behind him, with him'; so most commentators (Rashi, Metsudath David). Some understand it as 'on foot,' contrasting Barak's poorly equipped force with that of Sisera (Malbim).

11. The information provided by this verse is essential for the understanding of the part played by the Kenites in the battle about to begin. The narrator chose this point to give the relevant details in order to avoid the need for interrupting the story of the battle (Daath Mikra).

Heber. Although the name of a Kenite, it is Hebraic and was borne by a grandson of Asher (Gen. xlvi. 17; Num. xxvi. 45) and by a Judahite (1 Chron. iv. 18).

severed himself. But still adhered to the reli-

gion of Israel, adopted by their ancestor Jethro. This explains Jael's patriotism and Sisera's trust in her (Ralbag).

the Kenites. i.e. the main body of this tribe, which roamed the desert south of Judah (Metsudath David).

Hobab. One of the seven names by which Jethro was known (Mechilta, Jethro 1). For father-in-law, see on 1. 16.

Elon-bezaanannim. lit. 'plain of the marshes,' mentioned in J.T. Meg. 1:1 as the marshes of Kedesh (Daath Mikra). It was the northernmost limit of Heber's wanderings, on the boundary of Naphtali (Josh. xix. 33). He was staying there at the time of the battle with Sisera.

12. *they told*. Indefinite subject, corresponding to 'he was told.'

13. *gathered together*. The verb *za'ak* in the Hiphil signifies 'call out, assemble' by means of the war-cry or trumpet blast (Metsudath Zion).

the brook Kishon. 14. And Deborah said unto Barak: 'Up; for this is the day in which the LORD hath delivered Sisera into thy hand; is not the LORD gone out before thee?' So Barak went down from mount Tabor, and ten thousand men after him. 15. And the LORD discomfited Sisera, and all his chariots, and all his host, with the edge of the sword before Barak; and Sisera alighted from his chariot, and fled away on his feet. 16. But Barak pursued after the chariots, and after the host, unto Harosheth-goiim; and all the host of Sisera fell by the edge of the sword; there was not a man left.

17. Howbeit Sisera fled away on

14 קִישׁוֹן: וַתֹּאמֶר דְּבֹרָה אֶל־
בָּרָק קוּם כִּי זֶה הַיּוֹם אֲשֶׁר
נָתַן יְהֹוָה אֶת־סִיסְרָא בְּיָדֶךָ
הֲלֹא יְהֹוָה יָצָא לְפָנֶיךָ וַיֵּרֶד
בָּרָק מֵהַר תָּבוֹר וַעֲשֶׂרֶת
15 אֲלָפִים אִישׁ אַחֲרָיו: וַיָּהָם
יְהֹוָה אֶת־סִיסְרָא וְאֶת־כָּל־
הָרֶכֶב וְאֶת־כָּל־הַמַּחֲנֶה
לְפִי־חֶרֶב לִפְנֵי בָרָק וַיֵּרֶד
סִיסְרָא מֵעַל הַמֶּרְכָּבָה וַיָּנָס
16 בְּרַגְלָיו: וּבָרָק רָדַף אַחֲרֵי
הָרֶכֶב וְאַחֲרֵי הַמַּחֲנֶה עַד
חֲרֹשֶׁת הַגּוֹיִם וַיִּפֹּל כָּל־מַחֲנֵה
סִיסְרָא לְפִי־חֶרֶב לֹא נִשְׁאַר
עַד־אֶחָד:
17 וְסִיסְרָא נָס בְּרַגְלָיו אֶל־אֹהֶל

---

nine hundred chariots of iron. See on verse 3.

14. up! lit. 'arise,' a call to action (Metsudoth, Ralbag).

is not the LORD, etc. [As in verse 6, the question is rhetorical, serving as a forceful asseveration.]

gone before. i.e. to battle. The phrase is used of a leader at the head of his army (cf. ix. 39) (Ralbag).

went down. To attack Sisera's army. The text does not convey the suddenness of the onslaught and the surprise of the enemy.

15. discomfited. Struck them with panic, resulting in confusion and mad flight. According to Josephus (Antiquities V, v. 4), a hail-storm occurred, 'and the wind blew the rain in the faces of the Canaanites, and so darkened their eyes that their arrows and slings were of no advantage to them; nor

would the coldness of the air permit their soldiers to use their swords, while the storm did not so much incommode the Israelites, because it came on their backs.'

all his host. The infantry (cf. verse 7).

before Barak. i.e. before Barak's arrival. The entire army had become confused and demoralized until their commander abandoned his floundering chariot in the morasses of the Kishon and fled for his life from the field on foot (Abarbanel).

16. not a man. lit. 'not unto one'; no fugitive reached the safety of the city (Metsudath David).

17–22 DEATH OF SISERA

17. Sisera escaped to the tent of Jael, fleeing in the opposite direction to that of his defeated army so as to elude pursuit (Kimchi).

his feet to the tent of Jael the wife
of Heber the Kenite; for there was
peace between Jabin the king of
Hazor and the house of Heber the
Kenite. 18. And Jael went out to
meet Sisera, and said unto him:
'Turn in, my lord, turn in to me;
fear not.' And he turned in unto
her into the tent, and she covered
him with a rug. 19. And he said
unto her: 'Give me, I pray thee, a
little water to drink; for I am
thirsty.' And she opened a bottle
of milk, and gave him drink, and
covered him. 20. And he said unto
her: 'Stand in the door of the tent,
and it shall be, when any man doth
come and inquire of thee, and say:
Is there any man here? that thou
shalt say: No.' 21. Then Jael

יָעֵל אֵשֶׁת חֶבֶר הַקֵּינִי כִּי
שָׁלוֹם בֵּין יָבִין מֶלֶךְ־חָצוֹר
18 וּבֵין בֵּית חֶבֶר הַקֵּינִי׃ וַתֵּצֵא
יָעֵל לִקְרַאת סִיסְרָא וַתֹּאמֶר
אֵלָיו סוּרָה אֲדֹנִי סוּרָה אֵלַי
אַל־תִּירָא וַיָּסַר אֵלֶיהָ
הָאֹהֱלָה וַתְּכַסֵּהוּ בַּשְּׂמִיכָה׃
19 וַיֹּאמֶר אֵלֶיהָ הַשְׁקִינִי־נָא
מְעַט־מַיִם כִּי צָמֵאתִי וַתִּפְתַּח
אֶת־נֹאוד הֶחָלָב וַתַּשְׁקֵהוּ
20 וַתְּכַסֵּהוּ׃ וַיֹּאמֶר אֵלֶיהָ עֲמֹד
פֶּתַח הָאֹהֶל וְהָיָה אִם־אִישׁ
יָבֹא וּשְׁאֵלֵךְ וְאָמַר הֲיֵשׁ־פֹּה
21 אִישׁ וְאָמַרְתְּ אָיִן׃ וַתִּקַּח יָעֵל

v. 18. מלרע   v. 19. חסר א׳   v. 19. מלא וא״ו

---

the tent. Being in southern Galilee, it was
probably not far from the field of battle
(Daath Mikra).

Jael. As a noun it means 'wild goat.'

the wife of Heber the Kenite. Apparently, Jael
and Heber occupied separate tents. Since
Heber was obligated to aid Sisera, the latter
hoped that his wife, too, would honour that
treaty (Abarbanel, see below).

for there was peace. Jael, however, was not
obliged to aid Sisera, since the treaty had
been enacted only with Jabin himself, not
with his dignitaries. Alternatively, women
were not bound by their husbands' political
alliances, since they did not participate in
politics (Abarbanel). Moreover, the treaty
was probably a general treaty enacted by the
Kenites, not by Heber himself. Therefore,
since Heber had broken away from the
main body of the Kenites, his household
was not bound by the treaty. Furthermore,
since the Kenites were converts to Judaism,

they could not be expected to side with the
Canaanites against their own people and
God (Malbim). Others theorize that Heber
entered into the treaty under duress, out of
fear of the Canaanites (Daath Mikra).

18. *rug* Though common in this sense in
modern Hebrew, the exact meaning of the
noun *semichah* in the Bible is uncertain. The
LXX understood it as 'tent curtain.' Kimchi
connects it with a Semitic root with the
meaning 'be thick,' and in Jewish Aramaic
the word denotes 'thick material.'

19. *bottle.* Made of goat's or lamb's skin
(Rashi, A.Z. 29b).

gave him drink. By providing milk instead of
water, she succeeded in making him drowsy,
since milk slackens the body and brings on
sleep (Rashi).

20. *stand.* The Hebrew has the masculine
singular of the imperative. Kimchi construes
as the infinitive without the preposition *lamed*

Heber's wife took a tent-pin, and took a hammer in her hand, and went softly unto him, and smote the pin into his temples, and it pierced through into the ground; for he was in a deep sleep; so he swooned and died. 22. And, behold, as Barak pursued Sisera, Jael came out to meet him, and said unto him: 'Come, and I will show thee the man whom thou seekest.' And he came unto her; and, behold, Sisera lay dead, and the tent-pin was in his temples. 23. So God subdued on that day Jabin the king of Canaan before the children of Israel. 24. And the hand of the children of Israel prevailed more and more against Jabin the king of Canaan, until they had destroyed Jabin king of Canaan.

אֵשֶׁת־חֶבֶר אֶת־יְתַד הָאֹהֶל
וַתָּשֶׂם אֶת־הַמַּקֶּבֶת בְּיָדָהּ
וַתָּבוֹא אֵלָיו בַּלָּאט וַתִּתְקַע
אֶת־הַיָּתֵד בְּרַקָּתוֹ וַתִּצְנַח
בָּאָרֶץ וְהוּא־נִרְדָּם וַיָּעַף
22 וַיָּמֹת׃ וְהִנֵּה בָרָק רֹדֵף אֶת־
סִיסְרָא וַתֵּצֵא יָעֵל לִקְרָאתוֹ
וַתֹּאמֶר לוֹ לֵךְ וְאַרְאֶךָּ אֶת־
הָאִישׁ אֲשֶׁר־אַתָּה מְבַקֵּשׁ
וַיָּבֹא אֵלֶיהָ וְהִנֵּה סִיסְרָא נֹפֵל
23 מֵת וְהַיָּתֵד בְּרַקָּתוֹ׃ וַיַּכְנַע
אֱלֹהִים בַּיּוֹם הַהוּא אֵת יָבִין
מֶלֶךְ־כְּנָעַן לִפְנֵי בְּנֵי יִשְׂרָאֵל׃
24 וַתֵּלֶךְ יַד בְּנֵי־יִשְׂרָאֵל הָלוֹךְ
וְקָשָׁה עַל יָבִין מֶלֶךְ־כְּנָעַן
עַד אֲשֶׁר הִכְרִיתוּ אֵת יָבִין
מֶלֶךְ־כְּנָעַן׃

v. 21. א׳ נחה

in indirect command, viz. 'he told her to stand.'

21. After giving the instruction in the previous verse, he fell asleep.

tent-pin. [Women used to drive the tent-pins into the earth when camp was pitched. It was one of the wooden pegs which fastened the tent-ropes to the ground.]

a hammer. This denotes a hammer having one pointed end, used to hew stones and to puncture. The other end is flat and is used in metal work (Kimchi, Shorashim).

into his temples. He must have been lying on his side.

for he was in a deep sleep. A circumstantial clause explaining how the act was possible without a struggle on Sisera's part (Metsudath David, Malbim).

22. *and, behold.* [The particle in the Hebrew seems to call attention to the co-incidence. We might render: 'and, behold, there was Barak, pursuing.']

Barak pursued. We must suppose, with Ralbag, that in the first instance he had followed the fleeing Canaanites to the gates of Harosheth-goiim (verse 16) but, not finding Sisera, concluded that he might be hiding somewhere nearer the scene of the battle; so he turned back to search for him.

24. *prevailed more and more.* After Sisera's defeat, the king and his followers were eventually humbled (Abarbanel).

Jabin king of Canaan. i.e. the dynasty of Jabin. (Daath Mikra).

5 CHAPTER V ה

1. Then sang Deborah and Barak the son of Abinoam on that day, saying:

2 When men let grow their hair in Israel,

When the people offer themselves willingly,

Bless ye the LORD.

3 Hear, O ye kings; give ear, O ye princes;

I, unto the LORD will I sing;

א וַתָּשַׁר דְּבוֹרָה וּבָרָק בֶּן־
אֲבִינֹעַם בַּיּוֹם הַהוּא לֵאמֹר׃
ב בִּפְרֹעַ פְּרָעוֹת בְּיִשְׂרָאֵל
בְּהִתְנַדֵּב עָם
בָּרְכוּ יְהֹוָה׃
ג שִׁמְעוּ מְלָכִים הַאֲזִינוּ רֹזְנִים
אָנֹכִי לַיהֹוָה אָנֹכִי אָשִׁירָה

CHAPTER V

DEBORAH'S TRIUMPHAL ODE

[THE Song of Deborah is universally acclaimed a literary masterpiece. For forcefulness of diction and brilliance of imagery and style it has few rivals. The message is clear, although the details are often obscured by the use of archaic words and expressions.]

1. *then sang Deborah and Barak.* Rabbinic commentators deduced from the order of the names that, as well as initiating the campaign which ended in victory, Deborah composed the ode, as did Moses his song, although it is stated. *Then sang Moses and the children of Israel* (Exod. xv. 1) (Ralbag, Abarbanel, Kimchi).

on that day. Not in the sense of 'at that time,' but literally on the day of victory (Daath Soferim, Daath Mikra).

2. *when men let grow their hair.* The difficulty of translating the phrase *biphroa' peraoth* has led to many conjectures. Rashi equates *para'* with *parats* and comments: when the heathens 'made breaches' among Israel as a punishment from God for his having forsaken Him, and when the people offered themselves willingly to repent, bless the LORD for the salvation He wrought. Kimchi associates it with revenge or retribution, explaining thus: Both for the retribution God performed against Israel for their sins and for their willingness to go to war and

defeat the foe, bless the LORD, i.e. both for the bad and the good we must thank God. Abarbanel and Metsudath David explain thus: Both for God's wreaking vengeance against the heathens through Israel and for inspiring the people to offer themselves willingly in battle despite great odds, bless the LORD. Ralbag assigns to the root the meaning 'to cease' and renders: 'when their strength ceased,' i.e. when they were too weak to resist the enemy, and, nevertheless, offered themselves willingly to battle, this was indeed a wondrous victory for which we must bless the LORD.

bless. Here with the meaning 'thank, praise.' The tenor of the verse is: at a time when havoc was wrought among the people of Israel (by the oppressing Canaanites) and the masses rallied voluntarily or enthusiastically (to fight them), thank the Lord (Metsudath David).

3. *O ye kings.* Addressed to the rulers of the nations who are summoned to listen to the praises of Israel's God (Kimchi); or they may be *the kings* mentioned in verse 19 (Targum).

princes. A poetical parallel to *kings* as in Hab. i. 10; Ps. ii. 2, etc. (Daath Mikra).

I. The pronoun is strongly emphasized: 'as for me, for my part' (Daath Soferim).

unto the LORD. In contrast to the kings who attribute Israel's victory to a natural occurrence, Deborah sings *unto the* LORD Who alone can decide the outcome of battles. A

I will sing praise to the Lord, the
   God of Israel.

4 Lord, when Thou didst go forth
   out of Seir,

   When Thou didst march out of
    the field of Edom,

   The earth trembled, the heavens
    also dropped,

   Yea, the clouds dropped water.

5 The mountains quaked at the
   presence of the Lord,

   Even yon Sinai at the presence of
    the Lord, the God of Israel.

6 In the days of Shamgar the son
   of Anath,

   In the days of Jael, the highways
   ceased,

אֲזַמֵּר לַיהוָה אֱלֹהֵי יִשְׂרָאֵל׃

4 יְהוָה בְּצֵאתְךָ מִשֵּׂעִיר
בְּצַעְדְּךָ מִשְּׂדֵה אֱדוֹם
אֶרֶץ רָעָשָׁה גַּם־שָׁמַיִם נָטָפוּ
גַּם־עָבִים נָטְפוּ מָיִם׃

5 הָרִים נָזְלוּ מִפְּנֵי יְהוָה
זֶה סִינַי מִפְּנֵי
יְהוָה אֱלֹהֵי יִשְׂרָאֵל׃

6 בִּימֵי שַׁמְגַּר בֶּן־עֲנָת
בִּימֵי יָעֵל חָדְלוּ אֳרָחוֹת

v. 4. קמץ בז״ק

manifest ring of triumphant exultation may
be discerned (Malbim).

I will sing. A different verb from *will I sing,*
'make melody.' The root *zimmer* is said to
denote originally 'singing to an accompani-
ment,' reproducing the hum of the notes
produced by a stringed instrument (see
Explanation and Index of Synonyms in the
Bible, Wertheimer).

4. The verse is reminiscent of Deut. xxxiii.
2. Sinai is regarded as situated in the land of
Seir (Edom). (See Ibn Ezra ad loc. quoting
Saadiah Gaon.)

go forth. To battle (see on ii. 15) (Kimchi
quoting Ibn Ezra).

out of Seir. Most commentators associate the
description in this verse with the Revelation
on Mount Sinai (Rashi, Kimchi). Others
think it alludes to the wars of Sihon and Og
(Ibn Ezra, Ralbag, Metsudath David).

march out. Note the *dagesh* in the Hebrew,
indicating that the word is an infinitive and
not a noun (Kimchi, Shorashim). [The root
signifies a stately march in 2 Sam. vi. 13.]

field. This is the literal meaning of the
Hebrew and is often used of a country in
general (Metsudath David).

Edom. Identical with Seir (cf. Gen. xxxvi.

8f.). It was the land assigned to Esau, and
comprised the mountain range stretching
east of a line from the southern end of the
Dead Sea to the Gulf of Akaba (See Rashi,
Deut. ii. 1).

dropped. The object of the verb is *water* in
the next clause (Daath Mikra).

yea, lit. 'also.' [Note the cumulative effect,
each clause in the verse adding another detail
to the total picture.]

5. *quaked.* This follows Targum. Others
render: 'flowed down,' depicting the mountains as though melting from fright (Rashi,
Ralbag).

6-8. These verses describe the precarious
conditions under which Israel lived before
Deborah's appearance on the scene. The
highways were infested with enemy bands,
and travellers were compelled to use the
less-frequented by-ways.

6. *Shamgar.* Cf. iii. 31. His exploits were
evidently insufficient to curb the enemy
(Metsudath David, Kimchi).

Jael. Rashi infers that she, too, was a judge.
Both she and Shamgar must have flourished
in the period immediately preceding Deborah. They were contemporaries, but Jael
apparently outlived Shamgar.

And the travellers walked through byways.

7 The rulers ceased in Israel, they ceased,

Until that thou didst arise, Deborah,

That thou didst arise a mother in Israel.

8 They chose new gods; Then was war in the gates; Was there a shield or spear seen Among forty thousand in Israel?

9 My heart is toward the governors of Israel,

That offered themselves willingly among the people. Bless ye the LORD.

10 Ye that ride on white asses,

וְהֹלְכֵי נְתִיבֹ֔ות יֵלְכ֖וּ
אֳרָח֖וֹת עֲקַלְקַלּֽוֹת׃
7 חָדְל֧וּ פְרָז֛וֹן בְּיִשְׂרָאֵ֖ל חָדֵ֑לּוּ
עַ֤ד שַׁקַּ֙מְתִּי֙ דְּבוֹרָ֔ה
שַׁקַּ֕מְתִּי אֵ֖ם בְּיִשְׂרָאֵֽל׃
8 יִבְחַר֙ אֱלֹהִ֣ים חֲדָשִׁ֔ים
אָ֖ז לָחֶ֣ם שְׁעָרִ֑ים
מָגֵ֤ן אִם־יֵֽרָאֶה֙ וָרֹ֔מַח
בְּאַרְבָּעִ֥ים אֶ֖לֶף בְּיִשְׂרָאֵֽל׃
9 לִבִּי֙ לְחוֹקְקֵ֣י יִשְׂרָאֵ֔ל
הַמִּֽתְנַדְּבִ֖ים בָּעָ֑ם
בָּרְכ֖וּ יְהֹוָֽה׃
10 רֹכְבֵי֩ אֲתֹנ֨וֹת צְחֹר֜וֹת

v. 7. 'הש בפתח

---

the highways. The roads used by wayfarers and caravans linking different parts of the country.

travellers. lit. 'they who walk along the paths,' persons who, for necessary reasons, had to travel in those dangerous times.

byways. lit. 'crooked ways,' winding and circuitous by-paths unfrequented by the enemy.

7. *open cities.* On the analogy of *perazoth* and *perazi,* all commentators, including Targum, render this as 'open cities,' i.e. cities of the plain, having neither fortifications nor walls (Rashi, Kimchi, Shorashim, Ralbag, Metsudath David). The clause means: the peasants deserted their exposed villages for the safety of the walled towns (Rashi).

that thou didst arise. The traditional translation is, that I Deborah arose. This condition persisted until I was chosen by the Almighty to govern Israel (Targum). Now that I have become leader of Israel, the safety of the open villages has been restored since we have won a complete victory over the enemies (Metsudath David).

I arose a mother. Like a mother, I prayed for them and was concerned about them (Meam Loez). Like a mother, I reproved them to correct their ways (Metsudath David). Like a mother, I had pity on them (Abarbanel).

8. The conditions in Israel as Deborah found them.

they chose new gods. The subject is the Israelites whose choice lost them the protection of God, and as a result, *there was war in the gates.* The enemy carried his predatory raids up to the city gates (Rashi).

a shield or spear. The Israelites were either totally unarmed, except for the rude weapons which each man could lay his hands on, or they were afraid of displaying the arms they possessed (Kimchi).

9. Having described the desperate plight of her people, she now turns to their deliverance.

my heart is. i.e. 'belongs, goes out' in gratitude (Rashi, Metsudath David).

10. *ye that ride on white asses.* viz. the rich merchants. A white ass was a mark of dis-

Ye that sit on rich cloths,
And ye that walk by the way,
tell of it;

11 Louder than the voice of archers,
by the watering-troughs!
There shall they rehearse the
righteous acts of the LORD,
Even the righteous acts of His
rulers in Israel.
Then the people of the LORD
went down to the gates.

12 Awake, awake, Deborah;
Awake, awake, utter a song;
Arise, Barak, and lead thy
captivity captive, thou son of
Abinoam.

יֹשְׁבֵי עַל־מִדִּין
וְהֹלְכֵי עַל־דֶּרֶךְ שִׂיחוּ׃
11 מִקּוֹל מְחַצְצִים בֵּין מַשְׁאַבִּים
שָׁם יְתַנּוּ צִדְקוֹת יְהֹוָה
צִדְקֹת פִּרְזוֹנוֹ בְּיִשְׂרָאֵל
אָז יָרְדוּ לַשְּׁעָרִים עַם־יְהֹוָה׃
12 עוּרִי עוּרִי דְּבוֹרָה
עוּרִי עוּרִי דַּבְּרִי־שִׁיר
קוּם בָּרָק
וּשֲׁבֵה שֶׁבְיְךָ בֶּן־אֲבִינֹעַם׃

v. 12. מלרע

tinction (Rashi). A form of the Hebrew for *white (tsechoroth)* occurs in Ezek. xxvii. 18 (Kimchi).

rich cloths. The noun *middin* is uncertain of meaning. A.J. is based on a derivation from *mad,* 'garment,' hence 'cloth' and so 'saddle-cloth' or 'rich cloth.' Most early commentators connect it with *din* and render 'ye that sit in judgment' (Targum, Rashi, Metsudath Zion). Some explain it as the name of a road known in those times (Kimchi from Mesorah, Ralbag).

tell. Or, 'speak of it,' as in Ps. cv. 2 (Metsudath Zion).

11. *instead of.* lit. 'from.' It is translated in this way to give sense to the sentence (Metsudath David).

archers. The word *mechatstsetsim* is rendered by A.J. as the denominative Piel from *chets,* arrow.' This follows Kimchi and Metsudoth. It may also be rendered as 'troops (Rashi, quoting Menachem),' or as 'pebbles' (Rashi). i.e. instead of fearing to make a sound when walking on the pebbles to the water-troughs.

there. At the watering-troughs.

the righteous acts. Referring perhaps to God's deeds in the past, rescuing His people from their peril (Malbim).

restoring open cities. The same noun as in

verse 7; i.e. He again made it safe to occupy unwalled villages without fear of enemy attack (Kimchi, Metsudath David).

then the people of the LORD, etc. After the victory, the Israelites went down to the Sanhedrin to study the Torah. The Sanhedrin is referred to as the 'gates' in Prov. xxxi. 23 and in Ruth iv. It may also be rendered as 'cities,' meaning that after the victory, the Israelites returned to their open cities (Ralbag).

12-22. The second part of the ode, after a brief introduction (verses 12f.), describes the lively response of certain tribes and the tardiness of others (verses 12-18), and then carries us, as it were, into the thick of the battle (verses 19-22).

19. *awake.* i.e. arouse your enthusiasm and praise the LORD. This is the simple explanation. The Rabbis of the Talmud (Pes. 66b) explained that, because Deborah said, *'Until that I Deborah arose,'* the Divine inspiration left her (cf. verse 7). Abarbanel adds that the listeners called to her, 'Awake, awake, Deborah; Awake, awake, utter a song.' When they saw that she did not respond, they turned to Barak, and said, 'Arise, Barak. . . .' Immediately, the Divine Spirit rested on him, and he commenced to sing.

captivity. A collective noun for 'captives.'

13 Then made He a remnant to have
   dominion over the nobles and
   the people;
   The LORD made me have dominion over the mighty.
14 Out of Ephraim came they whose
   root is in Amalek;
   After thee, Benjamin, among thy
   peoples;
   Out of Machir came down
   governors,
   And out of Zebulun they that
   handle the marshal's staff.

13 אָז יְרַד שָׂרִיד לְאַדִּירִים עָם
   יְהֹוָה יְרַד־לִי בַּגִּבּוֹרִים:
14 מִנִּי אֶפְרַיִם שָׁרְשָׁם בַּעֲמָלֵק
   אַחֲרֶיךָ בִנְיָמִין בַּעֲמָמֶיךָ
   מִנִּי מָכִיר יָרְדוּ מְחֹקְקִים
   וּמִזְּבוּלֻן מֹשְׁכִים בְּשֵׁבֶט סֹפֵר:

13. then. At the time when the national uprising began.

made He. etc. The subject in the Hebrew is not certain. Kimchi and Ralbag understand it to be God, whereas Rashi and Metsudath David understand it as Israel. The rendering would accordingly be: Then the remnant of Israel ruled over the mighty of the people.

a remnant. The remaining Israelites are the remnant mentioned (Kimchi, Abarbanel).

of the people. i.e. the powerful ones of the nation of Canaan (Metsudath David). It may also be rendered: 'over the powerful, over the nation,' denoting that the powerful nation was that of Jabin the king of Canaan (Kimchi and Ralbag).

14. Out of Ephraim, etc. The first half of this verse is very difficult. Translated literally, it reads: 'from Ephraim their root is in Amalek; after thee Benjamin in thy peoples.' Rashi, Kimchi, and Metsudath David translate 'against' instead of *in* and explain: from Ephraim, the root (viz. Joshua, prince of the tribe) fought against Amalek; and after him Benjamin, (viz. Saul, a Benjamite) will also fight after him. This interpretation implies a forecast of the future.

whose root was against Amalek. As mentioned above, this alludes to Joshua, the root, or prince of Ephraim, who subdued Amalek when Israel was attacked by them shortly after the Exodus (Exod. xvii. 13), as Scripture states: *'And Joshua weakened Amalek and his people by the edge of the sword.'* Rashi connects this verse with the preceding one, thus: The Lord made me have dominion over the mighty by sending Joshua to subdue Amalek.

after thee Benjamin. Deborah is addressing Ephraim. She says, 'After you, Ephraim, will come Saul the son of Kish, a scion of Benjamin who will come close to annihilating the Amalekite nation completely (1 Sam. xv.).

with thy peoples. She addresses Ephraim as representing Israel. Saul will attack Amalek with 20,000 soldiers recruited from all of Israel (Metsudath David). Alternatively, now she addresses Benjamin, saying 'you Benjamin with your recruited army will attack Amalek' (Kimchi). Rashi suggests that *ba'amamecha* is related to *omemoth,* dying embers, translating, 'with your abaters,' i.e. those who will reduce Amalek to dying embers.

Machir. i.e. the tribe of Manasseh of which Machir was the main branch (cf. Josh. xvii. 1). As mentioned there, Machir's territory was on the eastern bank of the Jordan.

governors. i.e. governors of high status participated in the war against the Amorites when Jair the son of Manasseh took it (Deut. iii. 14) (Rashi). Others explain that the descendants of Machir the son of Manasseh participated in the war against Sisera (Kimchi, Metsudath David).

handle. lit. 'draw'; for its use with the preposition *beth,* cf. 1 Kings xxii. 34.

the marshal's staff. lit. 'the rod of the scribe.' i.e. from Zebulun everyone participated in the battle, even the sages and the scribes, who were inexperienced in war. The rest of the population certainly responded to Barak's call (Kimchi, Ralbag, Metsudath David). Abarbanel points out that the Scripture does not call them *soferim,* scribes, but 'they that handle the pen of the scribe.' This

15 And the princes of Issachar were
with Deborah;
As was Issachar, so was Barak;
Into the valley they rushed forth
at his feet.
Among the divisions of Reuben
There were great resolves of
heart.

16 Why sattest thou among the
sheepfolds,
To hear the pipings for the
flocks?
At the divisions of Reuben
There were great searchings of
heart.

17 Gilead abode beyond the Jordan;

15 וְשָׂרַי בְּיִשָּׂשכָר עִם־דְּבֹרָה
וְיִשָּׂשכָר כֵּן בָּרָק
בָּעֵמֶק שֻׁלַּח בְּרַגְלָיו
בִּפְלַגּוֹת רְאוּבֵן
גְּדֹלִים חִקְקֵי־לֵב:
16 לָמָּה יָשַׁבְתָּ בֵּין הַמִּשְׁפְּתַיִם
לִשְׁמֹעַ שְׁרִקוֹת עֲדָרִים
לִפְלַגּוֹת רְאוּבֵן
גְּדוֹלִים חִקְרֵי־לֵב:
17 גִּלְעָד בְּעֵבֶר הַיַּרְדֵּן שָׁכֵן

refers to merchants who use the pen of the
scribe to record their accounts. Even they
left their business behind and responded to
Barak's call.

15. *the princes of Issachar*. lit. 'the princes in
Issachar'; the noun has the old plural suffix
(Kimchi).

as . . . Barak. Just as the entire tribe of Issachar followed Deborah, so did Barak (Kimchi, Ralbag). Rashi explains that the princes
of Issachar were the Sages who were always
occupied with Torah study and with astro-
nomical computations to determine the
occurrence of the New Moon and the inter-
calary years. They would always cooperate
with Deborah to teach Israel statutes and
laws. The rest of the people were faithful to
Barak to obey all his commands.

they rushed forth . . . his feet. The verb is lit.
'he was sent away,' the subject being am-
biguous. The sense is probably: the men of
Issachar at once answered the call and
impetuously followed Barak's leadership,
i.e. they ran eagerly to recruit an army to
follow Barak (Rashi). Alternatively, they followed Barak into the valley to battle with the
Canaanites (Metsudath David).

divisions. Unlike Issachar, the tribe of Reuben separated itself from its brethren by not
responding to Barak's summons to war
(Kimchi, Metsudath David). Daath Soferim
notes that *liflagoth* appears in the plural
form, denoting that this was not the first

time that Reuben separated himself from
the rest of his brethren, for their choice of
territory on the eastern bank of the Jordan
was also a separation from the rest of the
people.

resolves. Or *thoughts*; i.e. much thought
must be given to account for Reuben's
absence from the battle in which all Israel
participated (Kimchi, Metsudath David).
Rashi explains that Reuben's separation was
caused by his thoughts or plots, to refrain
from participation in the battle until they
would hear which side was winning, and
then join it.

16. Note the bitter taunt in the series of
questions that follows.

sheepfolds. An apt word in view of the pastoral character of the tribe. The noun *mishpe-
thaim* also occurs in Gen. xlix. 14 and
denotes an enclosure surrounded by a pal-
ing for the protection of the flocks. The
dual form is said to indicate that the folds
were divided into two parts (Kimchi). Other
commentators interpret it as 'boundaries,'
i.e. why did you choose your territory to
dwell on the eastern bank of the Jordan
between the border of Israel and the border
of the heathens if you are afraid of war?
(Metsudath David).

the pipings for the flocks. i.e. the shepherd's
call to the sheep. More probably the phrase
means 'the bleatings of the flocks,' a sarcas-
tic contrast to the stern call to battle. Did

And Dan, why doth he sojourn
by the ships?
Asher dwelt at the shore of the
sea,
And abideth by its bays.

18 Zebulun is a people that jeo-
parded their lives unto the
death,
And Naphtali, upon the high
places of the field.

19 The kings came, they fought;
Then fought the kings of Canaan,
In Taanach by the waters of
Megiddo;
They took no gain of money.

20 They fought from heaven,

וְדָ֗ן לָ֤מָּה יָגוּר֙ אֳנִיּ֔וֹת
אָשֵׁ֗ר יָשַׁב֙ לְח֣וֹף יַמִּ֔ים
וְעַֽל־מִפְרָצָ֖יו יִשְׁכּֽוֹן׃
18 זְבֻל֗וּן עַ֣ם חֵרֵ֥ף נַפְשׁ֛וֹ לָמ֖וּת
וְנַפְתָּלִ֑י עַ֖ל מְרוֹמֵ֥י שָׂדֶֽה׃
19 בָּ֤אוּ מְלָכִים֙ נִלְחָ֔מוּ
אָ֤ז נִלְחֲמוּ֙ מַלְכֵ֣י כְנַ֔עַן
בְּתַעְנַ֖ךְ עַל־מֵ֣י מְגִדּ֑וֹ
בֶּ֥צַע כֶּ֖סֶף לֹ֥א לָקָֽחוּ׃
20 מִן־שָׁמַ֖יִם נִלְחָ֑מוּ

v. 19. קמץ בז״ק

you not expect to go to war, dwelling in
such a location? Did you expect to sit back
and listen to the bleatings of the sheep?
(Metsudath David). Rashi and Targum explain it figuratively: Did you stay between
the boundaries to listen to the voices of the
warring armies, to hear who emits a cry of
victory and who emits a cry of defeat?

17. *Gilead.* The region east of the Jordan,
on both sides of the river Jabbok. The allusion is to the half-tribe of Manasseh which
had not settled in Canaan and did not
respond to Barak's call (Rashi). According
to Rashi, Machir was mentioned above (verse
14) in reference to the war with the Amorites, not the war with Sisera. Others explain
that Gilead did indeed participate in the
war. Deborah is presenting Gilead as an
example for Reuben, since they came
despite the fact that they dwelt on the other
side of the Jordan (Kimchi, Metsudath
David).

Dan. i.e. the part of the tribe settled in the
extreme north, and not the Danites in the
south-west. As with neither of them did the
territory reach the sea, Kimchi explains that
the ships here mentioned are not those
which sailed the Mediterranean but in
which the men of the tribe gathered their
wealth and fled across the Jordan from the
enemy (see also Rashi).

Asher dwelt at the shore of the sea. See Josh. xix.

24–31, where it is mentioned that Asher's
territory extended to the sea.

bays. The noun *miphrats* occurs only here.
Daath Mikra explains it as bays, places where
the sea breaks in. Earlier commentators
explain it as 'breaches,' i.e. vulnerable spots
where his cities can be attacked by the heathen neighbors (Kimchi, Metsudath David).
Hence, Asher's absence was excusable
(Rashi, Kimchi).

18. Zebulun and Naphtali are held up as a
laudable contrast to the unpatriotic or timid
eastern and northern tribes (Metsudath
David).

and Naphtali. i.e. this tribe also jeopardized
their lives (Metsudath David).

the high places of the field. i.e. Mount Tabor
(Rashi).

19. After the account of the attitude of the
tribes, the Ode proceeds to describe the
course of the battle.

the kings. Sisera evidently led a confederacy
of several kings against Israel (Ralbag).

came, they fought. The literary effect created
by the omission of the conjunction between
the two verbs is striking.

Taanach . . . Megiddo. See on Josh. xii. By *the
waters of Megiddo* is meant the Kishon and its
tributaries in the neighborhood of the city.

The stars in their courses fought
against Sisera.

21 The brook Kishon swept them
away,

That ancient brook, the brook
Kishon.

O my soul, tread them down
with strength.

22 Then did the horsehoofs stamp
By reason of the prancings, the
prancings of their mighty ones.

23 'Curse ye Meroz,' said the angel
of the LORD,

'Curse ye bitterly the inhabitants
thereof,

הַכּוֹכָבִים מִמְּסִלּוֹתָם
נִלְחֲמוּ עִם סִיסְרָא׃
21 נַחַל קִישׁוֹן גְּרָפָם
נַחַל קְדוּמִים נַחַל קִישׁוֹן
תִּדְרְכִי נַפְשִׁי עֹז׃
22 אָז הָלְמוּ עִקְּבֵי־סוּס
מִדַּהֲרוֹת דַּהֲרוֹת אַבִּירָיו׃
23 אוֹרוּ מֵרוֹז אָמַר מַלְאַךְ יְהֹוָה
אֹרוּ אָרוֹר יֹשְׁבֶיהָ

According to the Targum the text indicates
that the enemy's camp extended from
Taanach to Megiddo (so also Kimchi).

no gain. [The Hebrew *betsa* signifies 'piece,
bit.' The phrase does not mean that the
campaign was profitless because it was a
failure, or that they took no ransom from
the captive Israelites;] the implication is that
they refused hirelings' pay in their eagerness
to fight against Israel (Rashi, Ralbag, Metsudath David).

20. *they fought.* The verb is governed by the
stars in the next clause (Rashi).

from heaven. The victory of Israel was assured
because it depended not on Israel's prowess,
but on Divine intervention (Daath Soferim).

the stars. These, declared the Rabbis, were
the unpaid fighters whom God enlisted to
overcome the unpaid hirelings in the
Canaanite army (Rashi from Num. Rabbah 9).

in their courses. lit. 'from their highways,' the
paths which were allotted to them in the
skies; i.e. it was as though the stars were
waging war with the kings of Canaan. The
Rabbis said that the stars actually heated the
armor of the soldiers. In order to cool off,
they went into the brook where they were
swept away (Metsudath David).

21. *the brook Kishon.* See on iv. 7. In this
section of its course the Kishon is not a permanent or dangerous stream; but by God's
decree it swelled at the critical moment of
the battle (Metsudath David, Daath Mikra,
Daath Soferim).

that ancient brook. The Targum renders
'stream of the ancient,' i.e. where great
deeds were done in ancient times. Kimchi
explains that the brook was originally created to avenge Israel of their enemies.

tread them down with strength. The verb is
literally 'thou wilt tread.' According to this
translation, *them* refers to the waters of the
brook, explaining thus: The brook Kishon
swept them away, the brook Kishon where
originally, I could tread the water with
strength. This is to say that originally the
brook Kishon was so shallow that I could
tread the water with all my might (Ralbag,
Metsudath David). Others render: 'Tread
down, O my soul, [their] strength; referring
to the strength of the enemy (Rashi).

22. The precipitate flight of the enemy's
chariots.

stamp. The object to be understood is the
ground (Daath Mikra). Others interpret this
as an intransitive verb: 'Then were the horsehoofs pounded (Kimchi, Ralbag, Metsudath
David).

prancings. It may also be translated 'gallop-
ings.'

their mighty ones. The enemy's leaders; others
explain 'their magnificent steeds' (Kimchi).

23–31 SISERA'S FATE

This incident forms the subject of the third
section of the Ode which consists of two
parts: Sisera's flight and death, and the
scene at his house where his mother awaits
his return in triumph.

Because they came not to the
help of the Lord,
To the help of the Lord against
the mighty.'

24 Blessed above women shall Jael
be,
The wife of Heber the Kenite,
Above women in the tent shall
she be blessed.

25 Water he asked, milk she gave
him;
In a lordly bowl she brought him
curd.

26 Her hand she put to the tent-pin,
And her right hand to the workmen's hammer;

כִּי לֹא־בָאוּ לְעֶזְרַת יְהֹוָה
לְעֶזְרַת יְהֹוָה בַּגִּבּוֹרִים:
24 תְּבֹרַךְ מִנָּשִׁים יָעֵל
אֵשֶׁת חֶבֶר הַקֵּינִי
מִנָּשִׁים בָּאֹהֶל תְּבֹרָךְ:
25 מַיִם שָׁאַל חָלָב נָתָנָה
בְּסֵפֶל אַדִּירִים
הִקְרִיבָה חֶמְאָה:
26 יָדָהּ לַיָּתֵד תִּשְׁלַחְנָה
וִימִינָהּ לְהַלְמוּת עֲמֵלִים

23. *curse ye Meroz.* The command is
addressed to Israel. It is conjectured that
Meroz was a town along the road taken by
Sisera in his flight, where the inhabitants
failed to capture him. Its location is
unknown (Metsudath David, Kimchi).

the angel of the Lord. Rashi understands this
as a description of Barak who was perform-
ing God's mission.

curse ye bitterly. lit. 'curse ye cursing,' a common Hebrew idiom whereby the idea of a
verb is intensified by the addition of the
infinitive absolute (Daath Mikra).

to the help of the Lord. He who helps Israel is
as though he helped God (Rashi).

24. The effective aid rendered to Israel by
Jael the Kenite tent-dweller at a critical time
fully merited the gratitude of the nation's
leaders.

blessed above women. A Hebraic form of the
superlative: 'most blessed of women' (Daath
Mikra).

shall . . . be. Or, 'may Jael be.'

women in the tent. i.e. she shall be blessed
above other modest women who sit in the
tent (Kimchi). Alternatively, she shall be
blessed *by* the righteous, modest women
who sit in their tents (Metsudath David).
Rashi quotes the Midrashic interpretation
that 'women in the tent' refers to the
Matriarchs, each one of which is mentioned

in connection with a tent. Hence, Deborah
blesses Jael above the Matriarchs whose
descendents she saved from annihilation
(Gen. Rabbah 48).

25. With poetic artistry the scene in Jael's
tent is graphically depicted.

he asked. The allusion to Sisera is obvious
and more effective for not being specified.

lordly. i.e. fit for lords, or large size (Kimchi).

curd. Chemah, in post-Biblical Hebrew 'butter,' is artificially soured milk. It is a
refreshing drink made by shaking milk in
the skin-bottle in which it is stored, and fer-
menting it with the stale milk adhering to
the skin from previous processes.

26. The events which immediately followed, related in iv. 20, are not repeated.

hand. i.e. her left hand (Ralbag, Metsudath
David).

she put. The verb is plural and may be nothing more than poetic usage for the singular (Kimchi). Ralbag considers that *her hand*
is the object of the verb and the subject to
be understood as the forces in her which
controlled the hand.

the tent-pin. It is difficult to follow the
modern exegetes in their laborious attempt
to show that Jael used only one instrument,
and that *tent-pin* is here merely a poetic
parallel to *workmen's hammer* in the next
clause. The testimony of iv. 21 is decisive
against this interpretation.

And with the hammer she smote
Sisera, she smote through his
head,
Yea, she pierced and struck
through his temples.
27 At her feet he sunk, he fell, he
lay;
At her feet he sunk, he fell;
Where he sunk, there he fell
down dead.
28 Through the window she looked
forth, and peered,
The mother of Sisera, through
the lattice:
'Why is his chariot so long in
coming?
Why tarry the wheels of his
chariots?'
29 The wisest of her princesses
answer her,

וְתִלְמָה סִיסְרָא מֶחָקָה רֹאשׁ
וּמָחֲצָה וְחָלְפָה רַקָּתוֹ׃
27 בֵּין רַגְלֶיהָ כָּרַע נָפַל שָׁכֵב
בֵּין רַגְלֶיהָ כָּרַע נָפַל
בַּאֲשֶׁר כָּרַע שָׁם נָפַל שָׁדוּד׃
28 בְּעַד הַחַלּוֹן נִשְׁקְפָה וַתְּיַבֵּב
אֵם סִיסְרָא בְּעַד הָאֶשְׁנָב
מַדּוּעַ בֹּשֵׁשׁ רִכְבּוֹ לָבוֹא
מַדּוּעַ אֶחֱרוּ
פַּעֲמֵי מַרְכְּבוֹתָיו׃
29 חַכְמוֹת שָׂרוֹתֶיהָ תַּעֲנֶנָּה

v. 27. קמץ בז"ק

with the hammer she smote. [lit. 'she hammered.']

smote. The second *smote* is the rendering of a
different verb, *machak,* which does not occur
elsewhere in the Bible but in Mishnaic
Hebrew means 'scrape off, efface, remove
(Kimchi, Metsudath Zion, both of whom
explain it to mean that she removed his
head). Rashi, however, renders: 'pierced.'

struck through. The verb *chalaf* signifies to
pass away, vanish, pass through (Metsudath
Zion).

temples. The noun *rakkah* occurs again in
Song of Songs iv. 3; it denotes the thinnest
part of the skull (Kimchi, Shorashim).

27. *sunk.* [The verb *kara,* lit. 'knelt,' is used
here of the spasmodic drawing up of the
legs by Sisera when he received the death-
blow. This disposes of the theory favoured
by some modern scholars that Sisera,
according to the poetic version, was on his
feet drinking when he was struck.]

dead. Shadud is a rare word in such a context. It literally signifies being the victim of
an act of violence. The root is usually
applied to plundering, devastating (Metsudath Zion). [It may perhaps express the idea
of ignominy which was in those days
attached to the death of a soldier at the
hand of a woman (cf. ix. 54)].

28. *she.* The postponement of the subject
to the second part of the verse creates a
suspense which heightens the emotional
effect.

looked forth. The verb *shakaph* in the Niphal
conjugation means 'to look down on
something below,' since the one who looks
is likewise visible to the one upon whom he
is looking. In the Hiphil conjugation it is
used of God looking down from heaven
(Deut. xxvi. 15) since He is invisible to those
upon whom He looks (Kimchi, Shorashim;
Michlol Yofi).

peeved. The root *yibbeb* occurs only here in
the Bible. A.J. follows Rashi's interpretation. In Aramaic it denotes 'to sound a
trumpet, raise a clamor,' and in later
Hebrew 'to lament.' The basic idea appears
to be 'issue a shrill sound.' Kimchi and
Metsudoth render 'cried.'

lattice. A fitting in the opening of the window which admitted the cool air, but
screened the women of the household from
inquisitive eyes. The noun *eshnab* is found
again only in Prov. vii. 6 (Daath Mikra).

why . . . so long in coming? verb denotes tarry-
ing much longer than is to be expected
(Malbim). A similar construction occurs in
Exod. xxxii. 1 of Moses' delay in descending
from Sinai.

Yea, she returneth answer to
herself:

30 'Are they not finding, are they
not dividing the spoil?
A damsel, two damsels to every
man;
To Sisera a spoil of dyed garments,
A spoil of dyed garments of em-
broidery,
Two dyed garments of broidery
for the neck of every spoiler?'

31 So perish all Thine enemies, O
LORD;
But they that love Him be as the
sun when he goeth forth in his
might.
And the land had rest forty years.

אַף־הִיא תָּשִׁיב אֲמָרֶיהָ לָהּ:

30 הֲלֹא יִמְצְאוּ יְחַלְּקוּ שָׁלָל
רַחַם רַחֲמָתַיִם לְרֹאשׁ גֶּבֶר
שְׁלַל צְבָעִים לְסִיסְרָא
שְׁלַל צְבָעִים רִקְמָה
צֶבַע רִקְמָתַיִם לְצַוְּארֵי שָׁלָל:

31 כֵּן יֹאבְדוּ כָל־אוֹיְבֶיךָ יְהֹוָה
וְאֹהֲבָיו
כְּצֵאת הַשֶּׁמֶשׁ בִּגְבֻרָתוֹ
וַתִּשְׁקֹט הָאָרֶץ אַרְבָּעִים שָׁנָה:

| 6 | CHAPTER VI | ו |

1. And the children of Israel did that

1 וַיַּעֲשׂוּ בְּנֵי־יִשְׂרָאֵל הָרַע

wheels. The noun *pa'am* is never used in this
sense. It signifies 'beat' and probably
denotes here the 'hoof-beats' of the horses
attached to the chariot (probably Metsudath
Zion).

29. *the wisest.* An ironical touch is discernible in the reference to the 'wisdom' of these
women.

princesses. The ladies of high rank who
attended upon the mother of the comman-
der-in-chief (Daath Mikra).

yea . . . herself. The reason stated in the next
verse was given by *the wisest of her princesses*
and repeated with approval by Sisera's
mother (Kimchi, Ralbag).

30. *a damsel.* Women taken in war
belonged to their captors; the Hebrew law
on the subject is given in Deut. xxi. 10–14.
The noun *racham* has a derogatory connotation, 'a womb,' depicting the Israelite
women as sex objects by whom the soldiers
could satisfy their lust (Kimchi, Rashi, Daath
Mikra).

man. Better, 'warrior,' the Hebrew *geber*
denoting masculine strength (Wertheimer).

dyed garments. lit. 'colours.'

every spoiler. lit. 'for the neck of the spoil,'
i.e. the embroidered garments would be
placed at the head of the spoils to be given
to the general of the victorious army (Kimchi). Targum renders similar to the translation.

31. The Ode breaks off with effective suddenness, leaving in the reader's mind two
contrasting scenes: Sisera's lifeless body at
Jael's feet, and his mother with her attendants anxiously awaiting his triumphant
return.

so perish. Cf. Ps. lxviii. 3f. for a similar contrast. Deborah concludes the Ode with this
verse, as though to say, 'This is for her a
vain consolation, for so may all Thy
enemies perish, O LORD, just as he was
destroyed (Rashi from Siphre Num. xi. 7).

in his might. Just as the rays of the sun
become stronger and stronger until midday
when they are the strongest, so may Israel
become stronger and stronger (Kimchi, Ralbag, Metsudath David).

forty years. The period includes the years of
the Canaanite oppression (iv. 4). The rest
must therefore have amounted to no more
than twenty years (Metsudath David).

which was evil in the sight of the
LORD; and the LORD delivered them
into the hand of Midian seven years.
2. And the hand of Midian prevailed
against Israel; and because of
Midian the children of Israel made
them the dens which are in the
mountains, and the caves, and the
strongholds. 3. And so it was, when
Israel had sown, that the Midianites
came up, and the Amalekites, and
the children of the east; they came
up against them; 4. and they
encamped against them, and de-

בְּעֵינֵי יְהֹוָה וַיִּתְּנֵם יְהֹוָה בְּיַד־
מִדְיָן שֶׁבַע שָׁנִים: וַתָּעָז יַד־ ²
מִדְיָן עַל־יִשְׂרָאֵל מִפְּנֵי מִדְיָן
עָשׂוּ־לָהֶם ׀ בְּנֵי יִשְׂרָאֵל
אֶת־הַמִּנְהָרוֹת אֲשֶׁר
בֶּהָרִים וְאֶת־הַמְּעָרוֹת
וְאֶת־הַמְּצָדוֹת: וְהָיָה ³
אִם־זָרַע יִשְׂרָאֵל וְעָלָה
מִדְיָן וַעֲמָלֵק וּבְנֵי־קֶדֶם
וְעָלוּ עָלָיו: וַיַּחֲנוּ עֲלֵיהֶם ⁴

CHAPTER VI

THE CALL TO GIDEON

1–6 THE MIDIANITE OPPRESSION

1. *did.* The introductory formula here
differs from that of iv. 1 in omitting *again.*
Commenting on the omission, Rashi cites
the Midrash that, whereas before Deborah's
Song Israel's sins were cumulative, after it
their previous misdeeds were pardoned and
now they sinned afresh.

Midian. This nomad tribe shared blood kinship with Israel, being descended from
Abraham's concubine Keturah (Gen. xxv.
2). Its territory was in northern Hejaz, east
of Akabah, and probably extended to the
confines of Moab (Daath Mikra). During the
time of Moses, Midian was in the south of
Canaan, and when Joshua conquered the
land he also captured part of Midian (Josh.
xiii. 21). The captured Midianites remained
in the land of Israel, increased in number,
and at this time began to terrorize and
plunder Israel (Daath Soferim).

2. No attempt seems to have been made by
the Midianites to conquer the land; their
incursions were only of a predatory nature.

prevailed. The same verb was used of Othniel's supremacy (iii. 10).

and because. The conjunction is not in the

Hebrew and should be omitted in translation.

dens. The exact meaning of *minharoth* is
uncertain and, from the context, it can only
denote a place of hiding (Targum). The
commentators associate it with the root
nahor used in Aramaic to mean light. It is
used in this sense in Job iii. 3. Thus, it
denotes a cave with an inconspicuous peep-
hole (Rashi, Kimchi, Metsudath Zion). Ibn
Janach (Shorashim) interprets it as a lookout tower from which signals were sent.

caves. These abound all over Palestine and
serve as hide-outs and points for attacks
upon an unsuspecting foe.

strongholds. This denotes towers or mountain
strongholds (Shorashim, Kimchi; Shorashim, Ibn Janach). The root is *matzod,* and is
not related to *tzado,* which means *lying in
wait.* Rashi apparently understands it as a
stockade, made by clearing a wooded area
in the forest.

3. *and so it was.* lit. 'and it was'; the verb
introduces a recurring condition.

Amalekites. See on iii. 13.

children of the east. A comprehensive designa-
tion for the nomadic inhabitants of the
Syrian desert stretching from Ammon and
Moab to the banks of the Euphrates (cf.
Gen. xxix. 1 with Jer. xlix. 28 and Ezek. xxv.
4, 10).

stroyed the produce of the earth, till thou come unto Gaza, and left no sustenance in Israel, neither sheep, nor ox, nor ass. 5. For they came up with their cattle and their tents, and they came in as locusts for multitude; both they and their camels were without number; and they came into the land to destroy it. 6. And Israel was brought very low because of Midian; and the children of Israel cried unto the LORD.

7. And it came to pass, when the children of Israel cried unto the LORD because of Midian, 8. that the LORD sent a prophet unto the children of Israel; and he said unto them: 'Thus saith the LORD, the God of Israel: I brought you up

וַיַּשְׁחִ֨יתוּ֙ אֶת־יְב֣וּל הָאָ֔רֶץ
עַד־בּוֹאֲךָ֖ עַזָּ֑ה וְלֹא־יַשְׁאִ֤ירוּ
מִחְיָה֙ בְּיִשְׂרָאֵ֔ל וְשֶׂ֥ה וָשֽׁוֹר
5 וַחֲמֽוֹר׃ כִּ֣י הֵם֩ וּמִקְנֵיהֶ֨ם יַעֲל֜וּ
וְאָהֳלֵיהֶ֗ם יָבֹ֤אוּ כְדֵֽי־אַרְבֶּה֙
לָרֹ֔ב וְלָהֶ֥ם וְלִגְמַלֵּיהֶ֖ם אֵ֣ין
מִסְפָּ֑ר וַיָּבֹ֥אוּ בָאָ֖רֶץ לְשַׁחֲתָֽהּ׃
6 וַיִּדַּ֧ל יִשְׂרָאֵ֛ל מְאֹ֖ד מִפְּנֵ֣י מִדְיָ֑ן
וַיִּזְעֲק֥וּ בְנֵֽי־יִשְׂרָאֵ֖ל אֶל־
יְהֹוָֽה׃
7 וַיְהִ֕י כִּֽי־זָעֲק֥וּ בְנֵֽי־יִשְׂרָאֵ֖ל
אֶל־יְהֹוָ֑ה עַ֖ל אֹד֥וֹת מִדְיָֽן׃
8 וַיִּשְׁלַ֧ח יְהֹוָ֛ה אִ֥ישׁ נָבִ֖יא אֶל־
בְּנֵ֣י יִשְׂרָאֵ֑ל וַיֹּ֨אמֶר לָהֶ֜ם כֹּה־
אָמַ֤ר יְהֹוָה֙ ׀ אֱלֹהֵ֣י יִשְׂרָאֵ֔ל
אָנֹכִ֛י הֶעֱלֵ֥יתִי אֶתְכֶם֙

v. 5. ובאו ק׳

they came up against them. In order to avoid the redundancy of the verb, Malbim renders, 'and they came upon it,' i.e. they came upon the produce that the Israelites had sown.

4. *till thou come.* i.e. as far as but not including.

Gaza. The south-west limit of Israel's settlement (cf. 1 Kings v. 4).

5. *locusts.* [The figure is reminiscent of the eighth of the ten plagues brought on Egypt (Exod. x. 14f). It graphically describes the swarm of nomadic hordes that swooped down on the land.] The Hebrew for *locusts* is derived from a root meaning 'to multiply' and is connected with *larob, for multitude* (Kimchi, Shorashim; Ibn Janach, Shorashim).

6. *brought very low.* The root *dalal* denotes lack, usually of money or possessions, but sometimes used to denote lack of health or flesh (cf. Gen. xli. 19, 2 Sam. xiii. 4) (Chotham Tochnith, Ya'ir Or). Others explain it to denote poverty after previous wealth (Wertheimer).

7–10 A PROPHET POINTS THE MORAL

7. The purpose of the verse, which reproduces the second part of the preceding sentence, is to stress the point that no matter how grievously Israel may have sinned, when he cries to God in anguish, He has compassion upon his plight and intervenes on his behalf (Eliyahu Rabba 38).

8. *a prophet.* lit. 'a man, a prophet' (cf. iv. 4); perhaps it is in contradistinction to *angel of the* LORD in verse 11 (Malbim). Rabbinic tradition identifies the prophet, as it does the angel in ii. 1, with Phinehas (Rashi, Kimchi from Seder Olam).

from Egypt, and brought you forth out of the house of bondage; 9. and I delivered you out of the hand of the Egyptians, and out of the hand of all that oppressed you, and drove them out from before you, and gave you their land.   10. And I said unto you: I am the LORD your God; ye shall not fear the gods of the Amorites, in whose land ye dwell; but ye have not hearkened unto My voice.'

11. And the angel of the LORD came, and sat under the terebinth

מִמִּצְרַיִם וָאוֹצִיא אֶתְכֶם
9 מִבֵּית עֲבָדִים: וָאַצִּל אֶתְכֶם
מִיַּד מִצְרַיִם וּמִיַּד כָּל־
לֹחֲצֵיכֶם וָאֲגָרֵשׁ אוֹתָם
מִפְּנֵיכֶם וָאֶתְּנָה לָכֶם אֶת־
10 אַרְצָם: וָאֹמְרָה לָכֶם אֲנִי
יְהוָה אֱלֹהֵיכֶם לֹא תִירְאוּ
אֶת־אֱלֹהֵי הָאֱמֹרִי אֲשֶׁר אַתֶּם
יוֹשְׁבִים בְּאַרְצָם וְלֹא שְׁמַעְתֶּם
בְּקוֹלִי:
11 וַיָּבֹא מַלְאַךְ יְהוָה וַיֵּשֶׁב תַּחַת

I brought you up from Egypt, etc. The wording is reminiscent of the first commandment (Exod. xx. 2; Deut. v. 6). The great act of redemption is recalled here, as often by later prophets, to keep the people mindful of His infinite might and choice of Israel, but also of their duty to show their gratitude in loyal obedience (Meam Loez).

9. *I delivered you.* God had fulfilled His promise to Moses (Exod. iii. 8); but Israel had failed in his undertaking (cf. the end of verse 10).

out of the hands of the Egyptians. This is more than a repetition of *I brought you up from Egypt* in verse 8, and alludes to the deliverance at the Red Sea (Abarbanel).

all that oppressed you. viz. the peoples of Canaan, east and west of the Jordan. The same thought is expressed in ii. 18 and in 1 Sam. x. 18 (Metsudath David).

drove them out. To be connected with all that oppressed you (Kimchi).

gave. The verb in the Hebrew is more forceful (*waettenah* for *waetten*), but there is no equivalent in English for the energetic (cohortative) form used in the original (Gesenius).

10. *I said.* Here, too, the cohortative is employed.

I am, etc. Cf. Exod. xx. 2.

the gods of the Amorites. The phrase occurs in Josh. xxiv. 15. It is not surprising to find a prophet in the time of the judges familiar with the contents of the Book of Joshua.

but ye have not hearkened . . . voice. These few words convey the gist of the communication and explain why the people were suffering from the raids of the Midianites (Metsudath David).

11–24 GIDEON RECEIVES THE CALL

11. *angel of the* LORD. From verse 12 it may perhaps be inferred that as yet he was invisible to Gideon (see Abarbanel).

sat. If understood literally it suggests the picture of a wayfarer resting under a tree; but Kimchi renders 'tarried, stayed' (as in verse 18), and points out that angels invariably revealed themselves in an erect posture (cf. Gen. xviii. 2). According to Midrash, however, he was indeed sitting (Exodus Rabbah 25:1).

under the terebinth. He was apparently unobserved. The Midrash remarks that he

H   206

which was in Ophrah, that belonged unto Joash the Abiezrite; and his son Gideon was beating out wheat in the winepress, to hide it from the Midianites. 12. And the angel of the Lord appeared unto him, and said unto him: 'The Lord is with thee, thou mighty man of valour.' 13. And Gideon said unto him: 'Oh, my lord, if the Lord be with us,

הָאֵלָה אֲשֶׁר בְּעָפְרָה אֲשֶׁר
לְיוֹאָשׁ אֲבִי הָעֶזְרִי וְגִדְעוֹן בְּנוֹ
חֹבֵט חִטִּים בַּגַּת לְהָנִיס מִפְּנֵי
מִדְיָן: וַיֵּרָא אֵלָיו מַלְאַךְ יְהֹוָה 12
וַיֹּאמֶר אֵלָיו יְהֹוָה עִמְּךָ גִּבּוֹר
הֶחָיִל: וַיֹּאמֶר אֵלָיו גִּדְעוֹן בִּי 13
אֲדֹנִי וְיֵשׁ יְהֹוָה עִמָּנוּ וְלָמָּה

waited to hear the end of a conversation taking place between Gideon and his father in a winepress, where the two of them were threshing wheat. Gideon was saying, 'Father, you are too old for this work. Go home to rest and leave the threshing to me. If the Midianites come, I shall deal with them.' The angel, impressed by his display of filial affection and personal courage, decided that Gideon was the man most fitted by his qualities to be Israel's saviour (Kimchi and Abarbanel from obscure Midrashic source).

Ophrah. A place in the territory of Manasseh, believed to be Etaibeh, located south of Tul Kerem (Daath Mikra).

that belonged, etc. The words are added to differentiate this Ophrah from that of Benjamin (Josh. xviii. 23; 1 Sam. xiii. 17) (Kimchi). Metsudath David holds that the tree, and not the village, belonged to Joash.

Abiezrite. A sub-division of the tribe of Manasseh (cf. Josh. xvii 2).

Gideon. The name is derived from the root *gada,* 'to cut down,' and probably means 'the hewer.' He was evidently a man of extraordinary strength (cf. verse 12, Rashi).

beating out. The verb *chabat* denotes threshing with a stick as distinct from *dush,* with cattle (Kimchi). The method was more secretive and therefore employed in the dangerous circumstances.

winepress. The *gath* was a rectangular trough hewn out of the sloping of the rock. From it the juice of the grapes, after being pressed

out by treading, flowed into a similarly constructed receptacle (*yekeb*) a little lower down. In the restricted space of a winepress the wheat could only be threshed in small quantities (Daath Mikra).

to hide it. lit. 'to cause to flee.' The normal threshing-floor was on the exposed top of a hill to catch the wind, and it would not occur to the Midianites that a winepress was being used for the purpose (ibid.).

12. *appeared.* Consequently he must hitherto have been unseen (See Kimchi verse 11).

the Lord is with thee. As a common form of greeting it would have ordinarily conveyed a friendly wish: 'May the Lord be with thee.' Gideon understood it as an assertion and reacted with a bitter retort (See Rashi).

mighty man of valour. The expression occurs frequently in the Bible, but in this Book only here and xi. 1 of Jephthah. The addition of this compliment to the greeting made Gideon detect a deeper significance (See Kimchi).

13. Encouraged by the salutation, Gideon ventures to question the stranger whom he evidently recognizes as no ordinary individual (see on *have not I sent thee,* verse 14).

Oh. Hebrew *bi,* a deprecatory interjection which may be rendered; 'by your leave, please do not take offense at what I am about to say.' The term is often used in deferential speech (cf. Gen. xliii. 20, xliv. 18; Exod. iv. 10, 13) (Daath Mikra).

with us. In his modesty, he missed the

why then is all this befallen us? and where are all His wondrous works which our fathers told us of, saying: Did not the LORD bring us up from Egypt? but now the LORD hath cast us off, and delivered us into the hand of Midian.' 14. And the LORD turned towards him, and said: 'Go in this thy might, and save Israel from the hand of Midian; have not I sent thee?' 15. And he said unto him: 'Oh, my lord, wherewith shall I save Israel? behold, my family is

מְצָאַתְנוּ כָּל־זֹאת וְאַיֵּה
כָל־נִפְלְאֹתָיו אֲשֶׁר
סִפְּרוּ־לָנוּ אֲבוֹתֵינוּ לֵאמֹר
הֲלֹא מִמִּצְרַיִם הֶעֱלָנוּ יְהֹוָה
וְעַתָּה נְטָשָׁנוּ יְהֹוָה וַיִּתְּנֵנוּ בְּכַף
מִדְיָן: וַיִּפֶן אֵלָיו יְהֹוָה וַיֹּאמֶר 14
לֵךְ בְּכֹחֲךָ זֶה וְהוֹשַׁעְתָּ אֶת־
יִשְׂרָאֵל מִכַּף מִדְיָן הֲלֹא
שְׁלַחְתִּיךָ: וַיֹּאמֶר אֵלָיו בִּי 15
אֲדֹנָי בַּמָּה אוֹשִׁיעַ אֶת־

angel's point, *the* LORD *is with thee.* Hence the question which follows.

why. Gideon does not display ignorance of the cause of Israel's plight. He asks the speaker to reconcile his assertion with the facts of the situation, since it appeared to him that God had deserted the people and left them vulnerable to any happening (Malbim).

all this. He either means all that had been described earlier in the chapter, or he may have pointed to the winepress and the small portion of wheat he was engaged in beating out.

where are, etc. The question is asked not in a tone of scepticism, but of bewilderment (Metsudath David).

which our fathers told us. It is refreshing, amid the repeated admonitions in which the Book abounds, to have this testimony to the existence of a form of religious education. Despite the fact that many of the people worshipped idols, as did Gideon's father Joash, they still observed the *mitzvoth* in general and, in compliance with Deut. vi. 7, passed on the national traditions to their children (Daath Soferim).

hand. Hebrew *kaph,* 'palm,' a more emphatic term than *yad,* which conveys the idea of 'gripping' (Yair Or).

14. *the* LORD. Hitherto, the angel had been

speaking. Gideon's reply made him worthy to receive *direct* communication from God (Rashi). Others explain that the angel spoke in the name of God, interpreting the verse as 'And the [angel of the] LORD turned towards him (Abarbanel, Metsudath David).

this thy might. i.e. in the might with which God was endowing him for the accomplishment of the mission on which he was being sent (Kimchi). Others interpret this as referring to the merit he acquired by defending the Israelites (Rashi, Abarbanel, Metsudath David from Tanchuma Shofetim 4).

have not I sent thee? Alternatively 'indeed I have sent thee.' The word *halo* is used to strengthen the statement (Kimchi). Therefore, hasten to carry out your mission (Metsudath David). You may not hesitate; this is a command (Daath Soferim).

15. *Oh.* See on verse 13.

my lord. Gideon was not yet certain that he was addressing an angel of God. Despite the vowel signs, usually signifying the Name of God, it may still be rendered 'my lord,' with the plural form used out of respect for the person addressed. The *kamatz* under the *nun* is attributed to the pause (Kimchi). Targum, however, renders it as 'my LORD,' denoting that Gideon was already aware that he was speaking to an angel of God, or that God Himself was addressing him.

wherewith ... Israel? Such humility was

the poorest in Manasseh, and I am the least in my father's house.' 16. And the LORD said unto him: 'Surely I will be with thee, and thou shalt smite the Midianites as one man.' 17. And he said unto him: 'If now I have found favour in thy sight, then show me a sign that it is thou that talkest with me. 18. Depart not hence, I pray thee, until I come unto thee, and bring forth my present, and lay it before thee.' And he said: 'I will tarry until thou come back.' 19. And Gideon went in, and made ready a kid, and unleavened cakes of an ephah of meal; the flesh he put in a

יִשְׂרָאֵל הִנֵּה אַלְפִּי הַדַּל
בִּמְנַשֶּׁה וְאָנֹכִי הַצָּעִיר בְּבֵית
אָבִי: וַיֹּאמֶר אֵלָיו יְהוָֹה כִּי 16
אֶהְיֶה עִמָּךְ וְהִכִּיתָ אֶת־מִדְיָן
כְּאִישׁ אֶחָד: וַיֹּאמֶר אֵלָיו 17
אִם־נָא מָצָאתִי חֵן בְּעֵינֶיךָ
וְעָשִׂיתָ לִּי אוֹת שָׁאַתָּה מְדַבֵּר
עִמִּי: אַל־נָא תָמֻשׁ מִזֶּה עַד־ 18
בֹּאִי אֵלֶיךָ וְהֹצֵאתִי אֶת־
מִנְחָתִי וְהִנַּחְתִּי לְפָנֶיךָ וַיֹּאמַר
אָנֹכִי אֵשֵׁב עַד שׁוּבֶךָ: וְגִדְעוֹן 19
בָּא וַיַּעַשׂ גְּדִי־עִזִּים וְאֵיפַת־
קֶמַח מַצּוֹת הַבָּשָׂר שָׂם בַּסַּל

v. 17. הש׳ בקמץ

characteristic of Israel's leaders (cf. Exod iii. 11; Isa. vi. 5; Jer. i. 6; and in particular Jotham's parable, ix. 8ff.).

family. lit. 'thousand'; cf. the Saxon use of the word 'hundred.' This sub-division of the tribe, originally perhaps for military purposes, was itself made up of *mishpachoth* (families) and these in turn of 'fathers' houses.' This follows Targum. Others explain that each tribe was divided into thousands; each one governed by a leader (Rashi). Kimchi suggests that *alpi* is a derivation of *allufi*, 'my master' referring to his father.

poorest. Cf. 1 Sam. ix. 21 where Saul displays similar modesty. The implication is not that the family to which the speaker belongs is poor or insignificant in the absolute sense, but relatively in comparison with more powerful and numerous clans (Metsudath David).

16. *I will be with thee.* The same assurance as given to Moses (Exod. iii. 12). There are several details in the call to Gideon which are reminiscent of Moses' appointment to lead Israel out of Egypt.

as one man. Again in Num. xiv. 15; variously explained as 'at one blow, swiftly, completely so that there are no survivors (Daath Mikra, Metsudath David).

17. It was not unusual for a man who had received a Divine call to be given a sign as a guarantee that it was genuine (cf. xiii. 19ff.; Exod. iii. 12, iv. 1ff.; 1 Sam. x. 7). It is probably that the direct communication from God ended at this point and the dialogue between Gideon and the angel resumed (Daath Mikra).

show me a sign. More lit. 'perform for me a sign.' [i.e. forthwith and not in the future.]

it is thou that. This is a paraphrase to bring out the intention. The text is literally 'that thou talkest with me.'

18. *present.* See on iii. 15.

19. *went in.* To his tent.

kid. lit. 'kid of the goats.' Manoah did the same in similar circumstances (xiii. 15).

ephah. About a bushel.

basket, and he put the broth in a pot, and brought it out unto him under the terebinth, and presented it. 20. And the angel of God said unto him: 'Take the flesh and the unleavened cakes, and lay them upon this rock, and pour out the broth.' And he did so. 21. Then the angel of the LORD put forth the end of the staff that was in his hand, and touched the flesh and the unleavened cakes; and there went up fire out of the rock, and consumed the flesh and the unleavened cakes; and the angel of the LORD departed out of his sight. 22. And Gideon saw that he was the angel of the LORD; and Gideon said: 'Alas, O Lord GOD! forasmuch as I have seen the angel of the LORD face to face.' 23. And the LORD said unto him:

וְהַמָּרָק שָׂם בַּפָּרוּד וַיּוֹצֵא
אֵלָיו אֶל־תַּחַת הָאֵלָה וַיַּגַּשׁ:
20 וַיֹּאמֶר אֵלָיו מַלְאַךְ הָאֱלֹהִים
קַח אֶת־הַבָּשָׂר וְאֶת־הַמַּצּוֹת
וְהַנַּח אֶל־הַסֶּלַע הַלָּז וְאֶת־
21 הַמָּרָק שְׁפוֹךְ וַיַּעַשׂ כֵּן: וַיִּשְׁלַח
מַלְאַךְ יְהֹוָה אֶת־קְצֵה
הַמִּשְׁעֶנֶת אֲשֶׁר בְּיָדוֹ וַיִּגַּע
בַּבָּשָׂר וּבַמַּצּוֹת וַתַּעַל הָאֵשׁ
מִן־הַצּוּר וַתֹּאכַל אֶת־
הַבָּשָׂר וְאֶת־הַמַּצּוֹת וּמַלְאַךְ
22 יְהֹוָה הָלַךְ מֵעֵינָיו: וַיַּרְא
גִּדְעוֹן כִּי־מַלְאַךְ יְהֹוָה הוּא
וַיֹּאמֶר גִּדְעוֹן אֲהָהּ אֲדֹנָי יֱהֹוִה
כִּי־עַל־כֵּן רָאִיתִי מַלְאַךְ
23 יְהֹוָה פָּנִים אֶל־פָּנִים: וַיֹּאמֶר

פתח בס״ם v. 19.

20. pour out. Some explain this as 'pour away' as something unwanted. It is therefore not mentioned in the next verse (Daath Soferim, Daath Mikra). Others explain that he was to pour it on the rock to moisten it and make the subsequent miracle of the fire emanating therefrom even greater (Abarbanel, Metsudath Zion).

21. departed out of his sight. It is not clear whether the angel ascended in the flame, as happened with Manoah (xiii. 20), or suddenly vanished. The text merely states that he 'went away from his eyes.' Abarbanel compares the two, whereas Daath Soferim is inclined to believe that Manoah's revelation was greater than Gideon's.

22. that he was the angel of the LORD. Proved by his mysterious disappearance.

forasmuch as. Cf. the same phrase in a similar context in Gen. xxxiii. 10. Literally the expression means 'because therefore.' The clause beginning with this word and continuing to the end of the verse is not to be understood as a continuation of the exclamation, but the reason, spoken softly to himself as an aside, for having cried out. This is borne out by the phrase *the angel of the* LORD instead of 'Thy angel' at the end of the verse (Rashi).

I have seen, etc. The belief that Divine beings cannot be seen by living man was deep-seated in the Israelite mind and is expressed in the words *man shall not see Me and live* (Exod. xxxiii. 20). Consequently an experience such as here described was regarded as an omen of impending death (Abarbanel).

'Peace be unto thee; fear not; thou shalt not die.' 24. Then Gideon built an altar there unto the LORD, and called it 'Adonai-shalom'; unto this day it is yet in Ophrah of the Abiezrites.

25. And it came to pass the same night, that the LORD said unto him: 'Take thy father's bullock, and the second bullock of seven years old, and throw down the altar of Baal that thy father hath, and cut down the Asherah that is by it; 26. and build an altar unto the LORD thy God upon the top of this stronghold, in the ordered place, and take the

לְךָ יְהוָֹה שָׁלוֹם לְךָ אַל־תִּירָא
24 לֹא תָּמוּת: וַיִּבֶן שָׁם גִּדְעוֹן
מִזְבֵּחַ לַיהוָֹה וַיִּקְרָא־לוֹ
יְהוָֹה ׀ שָׁלוֹם עַד הַיּוֹם הַזֶּה
עוֹדֶנּוּ בְּעָפְרָת אֲבִי הָעֶזְרִי:
25 וַיְהִי בַּלַּיְלָה הַהוּא וַיֹּאמֶר
לוֹ יְהוָֹה קַח אֶת־פַּר־הַשּׁוֹר
אֲשֶׁר לְאָבִיךָ וּפַר הַשֵּׁנִי שֶׁבַע
שָׁנִים וְהָרַסְתָּ אֶת־מִזְבַּח
הַבַּעַל אֲשֶׁר לְאָבִיךָ וְאֶת־
הָאֲשֵׁרָה אֲשֶׁר־עָלָיו תִּכְרֹת:
26 וּבָנִיתָ מִזְבֵּחַ לַיהוָֹה אֱלֹהֶיךָ
עַל רֹאשׁ הַמָּעוֹז הַזֶּה
בַּמַּעֲרָכָה וְלָקַחְתָּ אֶת־הַפָּר

---

23. *peace be.* Some render, 'there is peace (see Malbim).'

24. *Adonai-shalom.* Meaning 'the LORD is peace,' the name perpetuating the words of encouragement which God had addressed to him (Metsudath David).

unto this day. Explained by some Jewish commentators as referring to the time of David, i.e. when Samuel composed the Book (Daath Mikra).

25–32 DESTRUCTION OF THE ALTAR OF BAAL

25. *the same night.* After the incidents just related.

bullock. lit. 'the bullock of the ox.' The tautology is explained by taking 'ox' as descriptive and understanding the phrase as 'a large ox,' 'an ox as big as a bullock' (Kimchi); or by supposing that the 'bullock of the ox' means 'the bullock born through the ox.' Ralbag, who favours the second alternative, maintains that the bullock had

been designated by Gideon's father as an idolatrous sacrifice from the moment of conception, and the same applies to *the second bullock.* Accordingly these animals had been designated as idolatrous sacrifices for seven years, in fact since the commencement of the Midianite oppression.

seven years old. This follows Kimchi. Targum renders: fattened for seven years.

Baal. See on ii. 13.

thy father hath. He was its custodian by proprietary right (Daath Mikra).

Asherah. See on iii. 7.

26. *this stronghold.* i.e. the rock on which he had offered the meat and unleavened bread (so Rashi and Kimchi). Some modern commentators suppose that it denotes a place of security, devised by Joash and his neighbours, to which they could withdraw on the approach of the Midianites (Daath Mikra).

the ordered place. The Hebrew word *ma'ara-*

second bullock, and offer a burnt-offering with the wood of the Asherah which thou shalt cut down.'
27. Then Gideon took ten men of his servants, and did as the LORD had spoken unto him; and it came to pass, because he feared his father's household and the men of the city, so that he could not do it by day, that he did it by night. 28. And when the men of the city arose early in the morning, behold, the altar of Baal was broken down, and the Asherah was cut down that was by it, and the second bullock was offered upon the altar that was built. 29. And they said one to another: 'Who hath done this thing?' And when they inquired and asked, they said: 'Gideon the son of Joash hath done this thing.' 30. Then the men of the city said unto Joash: 'Bring out thy son, that he may die; because he hath broken down the altar of Baal, and because he hath cut down the Asherah that was by it.' 31. And

הַשֵּׁנִי וְהַעֲלִיתָ עוֹלָה בַּעֲצֵי
27 הָאֲשֵׁרָה אֲשֶׁר תִּכְרֹת׃ וַיִּקַּח
גִּדְעוֹן עֲשָׂרָה אֲנָשִׁים מֵעֲבָדָיו
וַיַּעַשׂ כַּאֲשֶׁר דִּבֶּר אֵלָיו יְהֹוָה
וַיְהִי כַּאֲשֶׁר יָרֵא אֶת־בֵּית
אָבִיו וְאֶת־אַנְשֵׁי הָעִיר
מֵעֲשׂוֹת יוֹמָם וַיַּעַשׂ לָיְלָה׃
28 וַיַּשְׁכִּימוּ אַנְשֵׁי הָעִיר בַּבֹּקֶר
וְהִנֵּה נֻתַּץ מִזְבַּח הַבַּעַל
וְהָאֲשֵׁרָה אֲשֶׁר־עָלָיו כֹּרָתָה
וְאֵת הַפָּר הַשֵּׁנִי הֹעֲלָה עַל־
29 הַמִּזְבֵּחַ הַבָּנוּי׃ וַיֹּאמְרוּ אִישׁ
אֶל־רֵעֵהוּ כִּי עָשָׂה הַדָּבָר
הַזֶּה וַיִּדְרְשׁוּ וַיְבַקְשׁוּ וַיֹּאמְרוּ
גִּדְעוֹן בֶּן־יוֹאָשׁ עָשָׂה הַדָּבָר
30 הַזֶּה׃ וַיֹּאמְרוּ אַנְשֵׁי הָעִיר
אֶל־יוֹאָשׁ הוֹצֵא אֶת־בִּנְךָ
וְיָמֹת כִּי נָתַץ אֶת־מִזְבַּח
הַבַּעַל וְכִי כָרַת הָאֲשֵׁרָה
31 אֲשֶׁר־עָלָיו׃ וַיֹּאמֶר יוֹאָשׁ

---

chah means 'a row.' It might refer to the flat top of the rock, upon which the stones of the altar could be arranged in a row (Kimchi, Metsudath David). Alternatively, it may refer to the row of stones comprising the first altar he had built. He was to take the stones of the destroyed altar of the Baal and to build an altar atop the first one (Malbim).

27. Gideon carried out the Divine command at night because his act was in defiance of the commonly accepted rite of worship (Ralbag).

28. *the second bullock*. Kimchi supposes that the only purpose of taking the first bullock was to deprive the Abiezrites of it so that they might not offer it to Baal.

30. *bring out*. They thought that Joash still believed in idolatry and would be honoured to punish his rebellious son. The truth was that he had fully repented (Meam Loez).

Joash said unto all that stood against him: 'Will ye contend for Baal? or will ye save him? he that will contend for him, shall be put to death before morning; if he be a god, let him contend for himself, because one hath broken down his altar.' 32. Therefore on that day he was called Jerubbaal, saying: 'Let Baal contend against him, because he hath broken down his altar.'

33. Now all the Midianites and the Amalekites and the children of the east assembled themselves together; and they passed over, and pitched in the valley of Jezreel. 34. But the

לְכֹל אֲשֶׁר־עָמְדוּ עָלָיו
הַאַתֶּם ׀ תְּרִיבוּן לַבַּעַל אִם־
אַתֶּם תְּוֹשִׁיעוּן אוֹתוֹ אֲשֶׁר יָרִיב
לוֹ יוּמַת עַד־הַבֹּקֶר אִם־
אֱלֹהִים הוּא יָרֶב לוֹ כִּי נָתַץ
32 אֶת־מִזְבְּחוֹ: וַיִּקְרָא־לוֹ
בַיּוֹם־הַהוּא יְרֻבַּעַל לֵאמֹר
יָרֶב בּוֹ הַבַּעַל כִּי נָתַץ אֶת־
מִזְבְּחוֹ:
33 וְכָל־מִדְיָן וַעֲמָלֵק וּבְנֵי־
קֶדֶם נֶאֶסְפוּ יַחְדָּו וַיַּעַבְרוּ
34 וַיַּחֲנוּ בְּעֵמֶק יִזְרְעֶאל: וְרוּחַ

---

31. *against.* lit. 'upon,' which may mean 'near.'

will ye. The Hebrew is very emphatic.

contend for Baal. It is proper that you should contend on behalf of a god? It is presumption! (Ralbag)

or will ye save him? Is it for human beings to be avengers of an outraged deity? (Rashi)

shall be put to death. To impugn the divine character of a god, by questioning his power to defend himself against dishonour, made one liable to the death penalty (Ralbag).

before morning. lit. 'until morning.' Gideon's deed had been committed during the night and discovered the following day when the scene of this verse took place. The phrase therefore indicates 'by tomorrow morning' (Metsudath David).

let him contend for himself. Note the irony. If Baal cannot punish an insult, what sort of god is he! (Malbim)

32. *Jerubbaal.* i.e. 'let Baal contend.' [The derivation is not so much philological as

phonological. Assonance is a common source of Biblical names.]

33–35 PREPARATIONS FOR WAR

33. *assembled themselves.* For the periodic marauding expeditions described in verses 31ff. They were not organized on a warlike footing (Daath Soferim). He suggests that perhaps they planned to establish themselves there.

passed over. The Jordan is shallow at several points near Beth-shean where the crossing was made (Daath Mikra).

pitched. viz. their tents; the verb is regularly used of encampment by an army.

valley of Jezreel. Named after the city, on a spur of mount Gilboa. The valley extends from Carmel to Tabor where it branches off in three directions, the central and most important leading by Beth-shean to the Jordan valley; while of the other two, one runs along Little Hermon and the other below mount Gilboa. It has been throughout history the battlefield of Palestine. Today it is dotted with numerous Jewish settlements of agricultural and industrial workers (See Daath Mikra, Josh. xvii. 16).

spirit of the Lord clothed Gideon; and he blew a horn; and Abiezer was gathered together after him. 35. And he sent messengers throughout all Manasseh; and they also were gathered together after him; and he sent messengers unto Asher, and unto Zebulun, and unto Naphtali; and they came up to meet them. 36. And Gideon said unto God: 'If Thou wilt save Israel by my hand, as Thou hast spoken, 37. behold, I will put a fleece of wool on the threshing-floor; if there be dew on the fleece only, and it be dry upon all the ground, then shall I know that Thou wilt save Israel by my hand, as Thou hast spoken.' 38. And it was so; for he rose up early on the morrow, and pressed the fleece together, and wrung dew out of the fleece, a bowlful of water. 39. And Gideon said unto God: 'Let not

יְהוָ֖ה לָבְשָׁ֣ה אֶת־גִּדְע֑וֹן
וַיִּתְקַע֙ בַּשּׁוֹפָ֔ר וַיִּזָּעֵ֖ק אֲבִיעֶ֥זֶר
אַחֲרָֽיו׃ וּמַלְאָכִים֙ שָׁלַ֣ח 35
בְּכָל־מְנַשֶּׁ֔ה וַיִּזָּעֵ֖ק גַּם־ה֑וּא
אַחֲרָ֑יו וּמַלְאָכִ֣ים שָׁלַ֗ח בְּאָשֵׁ֤ר
וּבִזְבֻל֙וּן֙ וּבְנַפְתָּלִ֔י וַיַּעֲל֖וּ
לִקְרָאתָֽם׃ וַיֹּ֥אמֶר גִּדְע֖וֹן 36
אֶל־הָֽאֱלֹהִ֑ים אִם־יֶשְׁךָ֞
מוֹשִׁ֧יעַ בְּיָדִ֛י אֶת־יִשְׂרָאֵ֖ל
כַּאֲשֶׁ֥ר דִּבַּֽרְתָּ׃ הִנֵּ֣ה אָנֹכִ֗י 37
מַצִּ֛יג אֶת־גִּזַּ֥ת הַצֶּ֖מֶר בַּגֹּ֑רֶן
אִם־טַ֡ל יִהְיֶ֣ה עַֽל־הַגִּזָּ֣ה לְבַדָּ֗הּ
וְעַל־כָּל־הָאָ֥רֶץ חֹ֖רֶב וְיָדַעְתִּ֗י
כִּֽי־תוֹשִׁ֧יעַ בְּיָדִ֛י אֶת־יִשְׂרָאֵ֖ל
כַּאֲשֶׁ֥ר דִּבַּֽרְתָּ׃ וַיְהִי־כֵ֗ן 38
וַיַּשְׁכֵּם֙ מִֽמָּחֳרָ֔ת וַיָּ֖זַר אֶת־
הַגִּזָּ֑ה וַיִּ֤מֶץ טַל֙ מִן־הַגִּזָּ֔ה מְל֖וֹא
הַסֵּ֥פֶל מָֽיִם׃ וַיֹּ֤אמֶר גִּדְעוֹן֙ 39
אֶל־הָ֣אֱלֹהִ֔ים אַל־יִ֤חַר אַפְּךָ֙

v. 36. פתח בס״פ   v. 37. פ פתח בס״פ פתח בס״פ

34. *spirit of the* Lord. An accession of overwhelming vigour and courage (Targum, Rashi).

clothed. Rather, 'clothed itself with.' It took control of Gideon and enveloped him as one dons a garment.

blew a horn. See on iii. 27.

Abiezer. Gideon's clan, among whom he lived and over whom he ruled, was the first to rally to him, and no messengers had to be sent to him (Ralbag).

35. *Manasseh.* His own tribe was next summoned. The western half of the tribe is meant.

Asher, etc. Once again Issachar is omitted, as in chapter 1.

came up. In the military sense; marched against.

to meet them. viz. the tribes which had already taken the field.

36–40 THE DOUBLE SIGN

36. *as Thou has spoken.* In verse 16.

37. *I will put.* lit. 'I am putting.'

the threshing-floor. i.e. in the winepress in which he had previously beaten wheat. At this site, he had experienced prophecy when the angel appeared to him (Abarbanel).

Thine anger be kindled against me, and I will speak but this once: let me make trial, I pray Thee, but this once with the fleece; let it now be dry only upon the fleece, and upon all the ground let there be dew.' 40. And God did so that night; for it was dry upon the fleece only, and there was dew on all the ground.

בִּי וַאֲדַבְּרָה אַךְ הַפָּעַם
אֲנַסֶּה־נָּא רַק־הַפַּעַם בַּגִּזָּה
יְהִי־נָא חֹרֶב אֶל־הַגִּזָּה
לְבַדָּהּ וְעַל־כָּל־הָאָרֶץ
יִהְיֶה־טָּל: וַיַּעַשׂ אֱלֹהִים כֵּן 40
בַּלַּיְלָה הַהוּא וַיְהִי־חֹרֶב
אֶל־הַגִּזָּה לְבַדָּהּ וְעַל־כָּל־
הָאָרֶץ הָיָה טָל:

| 7 | CHAPTER VII | ז |

1. Then Jerubbaal, who is Gideon, and all the people that were with him, rose up early, and pitched beside En-harod; and the camp of Midian was on the north side of them, by Gibeath-moreh, in the valley.

2. And the LORD said unto Gideon: 'The people that are with thee are too many for Me to give the

וַיַּשְׁכֵּם יְרֻבַּעַל הוּא גִדְעוֹן 1
וְכָל־הָעָם אֲשֶׁר אִתּוֹ וַיַּחֲנוּ
עַל־עֵין חֲרֹד וּמַחֲנֵה מִדְיָן
הָיָה־לוֹ מִצָּפוֹן מִגִּבְעַת
הַמּוֹרֶה בָּעֵמֶק:
וַיֹּאמֶר יְהֹוָה אֶל־גִּדְעוֹן רַב 2

ב"א על v. 40. ב"א על v. 39.

39. *let not Thine anger,* etc. Reminiscent of Abraham's request (Gen. xviii. 32). Gideon was not testing God but seeking further assurance in a moment of grave crisis. The thought may have occurred to him that the ground, since it was hard, did not absorb the dew, as did the soft fleece; and so he asked for a more striking sign (Abarbanel, quoting R. Yedaiah Bedarschi).

only upon the fleece. This could only happen as the effect of a miracle, because in the ordinary way the ground would be dried much more quickly than the saturated wool by the wind (ibid.).

CHAPTER VII

1-8 REDUCTION IN THE SIZE OF GIDEON'S ARMY

1. *En-harod.* lit. 'well, or fountain, of

Harod.' The tribal name Harod occurs again in 2 Sam. xxiii. 25. The location of the place is uncertain, though it was obviously in the valley of Jezreel. It has been identified with Ain Jalud, a copious spring at the foot of Mount Gilboa, and was probably not far from the modern Jewish settlement which has been given the name (Daath Mikra).

Gibeath-moreh. Nowadays, the entire range east of Afula is known by this name (known by the Arabs as Jebel-Dahi and by others as 'the small Hermon'). However, since the Scripture calls it Gibeath-homoreh, *the hill of Moreh,* it is likely to refer to only one spur of this range, the volcanic hill, Tel-ajul, which overtowers the ancient Endor (Ibid.).

2. *too many for Me.* With so large a force there was danger that the coming victory would not be attributed to God's intervention, and He did not need so many to carry

Midianites into their hand, lest Israel vaunt themselves against Me, saying: Mine own hand hath saved me. 3. Now therefore make proclamation in the ears of the people, saying: Whosoever is fearful and trembling, let him return and depart early from mount Gilead.' And there returned of the people twenty and two thousand; and there remained ten thousand.

4. And the LORD said unto Gideon: 'The people are yet too many; bring them down unto the water, and I will try them for thee there; and it shall be, that of whom I say unto thee: This shall go with thee, the same shall go with thee;

הָעָם אֲשֶׁר אִתָּךְ מִתִּתִּי אֶת־
מִדְיָן בְּיָדָם פֶּן־יִתְפָּאֵר עָלַי
יִשְׂרָאֵל לֵאמֹר יָדִי הוֹשִׁיעָה
3 לִי: וְעַתָּה קְרָא נָא בְּאָזְנֵי
הָעָם לֵאמֹר מִי־יָרֵא וְחָרֵד
יָשֹׁב וְיִצְפֹּר מֵהַר הַגִּלְעָד וַיָּשָׁב
מִן־הָעָם עֶשְׂרִים וּשְׁנַיִם אֶלֶף
וַעֲשֶׂרֶת אֲלָפִים נִשְׁאָרוּ:
4 וַיֹּאמֶר יְהוָה אֶל־גִּדְעוֹן עוֹד
הָעָם רָב הוֹרֵד אוֹתָם אֶל־
הַמַּיִם וְאֶצְרְפֶנּוּ לְךָ שָׁם וְהָיָה
אֲשֶׁר אֹמַר אֵלֶיךָ זֶה | יֵלֵךְ
אִתָּךְ הוּא יֵלֵךְ אִתָּךְ וְכֹל

---

out His design. Cf. *There is no restraint to the* LORD *to save by many or by few* (1 Sam. xiv. 6).

vaunt themselves. For the idea, cf. Deut. viii. 17; Isa. x. 13. Important for Israel's future as the people of God was the understanding that not by the might of numbers or the strength of arms, but only through Divine aid was their salvation made possible (Daath Mikra).

3. *make proclamation.* This is the general procedure in an optional war. In a mandatory war, it is not recited. In this case, however, Gideon was expressly commanded to make this proclamation, to diminish his forces (Daath Soferim, Daath Mikra).

depart early. The verb *tsaphar* is otherwise unknown. The rendering given connects it with the Aramaic *tsaphra,* 'morning' (Rashi, Kimchi, Metsudath Zion). Others connect it with *tsephriah,* a crown, denoting something which goes around the head. Hence, here we would render 'go around' (Ibn Janach, Shorashim; suggested by Kimchi).

mount Gilead. [The most plausible explanation of the topographical difficulty created by the mention of this mountain which was in Transjordan is that, as some of Gilead's descendants lived on the western side of the Jordan, there may have been a mount called by that name in the Cananite portion of Manasseh's territory.] The Arabic name for En-harod, Ain-Jalud, and Nahr Jalud for the river flowing out of it are reminiscent of this name (Daath Mikra).

4. *yet too many.* And must be still further reduced if God's purpose was to be served.

the water. One of the wadis in the neighborhood, perhaps the well of Harod. No mention is made of a river, though some commentators take it for granted that the test was made by the bank of a river (Abarbanel).

try. The verb *tsaraph* signifies 'to remove dross' from a precious metal by smelting; hence remove the elements unfit to carry out the Divine plan (Kimchi).

and of whomsoever I say unto thee:
This shall not go with thee, the same
shall not go.' 5. So he brought
down the people unto the water;
and the LORD said unto Gideon:
'Every one that láppeth of the
water with his tongue, as a dog
lappeth, him shalt thou set by
himself; likewise every one that
boweth down upon his knees to
drink.' 6. And the number of them
that lapped, putting their hand to
their mouth, was three hundred
men; but all the rest of the people
bowed down upon their knees to
drink water. 7. And the LORD said
unto Gideon: 'By the three hundred
men that lapped will I save you, and
deliver the Midianites into thy

אֲשֶׁר־אֹמַר אֵלֶיךָ זֶה לֹא־
5 יֵלֵךְ עִמָּךְ הוּא לֹא־יֵלֵךְ: וַיּוֹרֶד
אֶת־הָעָם אֶל־הַמָּיִם וַיֹּאמֶר
יְהֹוָה אֶל־גִּדְעוֹן כֹּל אֲשֶׁר־
יָלֹק בִּלְשׁוֹנוֹ מִן־הַמַּיִם כַּאֲשֶׁר
יָלֹק הַכֶּלֶב תַּצִּיג אוֹתוֹ לְבָד
וְכֹל אֲשֶׁר־יִכְרַע עַל־בִּרְכָּיו
6 לִשְׁתּוֹת: וַיְהִי מִסְפַּר
הַמֲלַקְקִים בְּיָדָם אֶל־פִּיהֶם
שְׁלֹשׁ מֵאוֹת אִישׁ וְכֹל יֶתֶר
הָעָם כָּרְעוּ עַל־בִּרְכֵיהֶם
7 לִשְׁתּוֹת מָיִם: וַיֹּאמֶר יְהֹוָה
אֶל־גִּדְעוֹן בִּשְׁלֹשׁ מֵאוֹת
הָאִישׁ הַמֲלַקְקִים אוֹשִׁיעַ
אֶתְכֶם וְנָתַתִּי אֶת־מִדְיָן

v. 5. קמץ בז״ק

9–15 THE MIDIANITE SOLDIER'S

5. *lappeth.* [The text uses an onomatopoeic
root, *lakak*, similar to the English 'lick.' The
criterion between the chosen and rejected
was the act of kneeling which those who
lapped the water avoided.]

boweth down. lit. 'shall kneel.' Ralbag considers that they who knelt were indolent,
whereas the others were energetic. Kimchi
offers two explanations for the rejection of
the men who went down on their knees:
they betrayed the habit of genuflexion which
they had acquired in their worship of Baal,
or they were accustomed to worship their
reflection in the water. It is unlikely that the
choice of those who lapped rested on the fact
that they were men inured to warfare, whose
drinking in a more erect posture indicated
that they knew how to guard against a surprise attack by the enemy. The selection, as
appears from the context, was not to discover the men of physical fitness and bravery.

Josephus (*Antiquities V*, vi. 3) draws the opposite inference: 'Gideon was to esteem those
who bent down on their knees to be men of
courage; but for all those that drank hur-
riedly and noisily, to think that they did so
from fear of the enemies.' The miracle of the
victory would be magnified if the battle had
been fought by *the least fit* from the military
point of view.

6. *putting their hand to their mouth.* They
scooped up some water in the palm of the
hand and lapped it.

8. The food and horns of the rejected men
were taken from them for the use of the
small band that remained (Kimchi, Metsudath David).

victuals. The Hebrew noun has the absolute
state which Kimchi regards as equivalent to
the construct. This grammatical construction is found elsewhere in the Bible.

horns. To be sounded in the battle-charge
(Kimchi).

hand; and let all the people go every man to his place.' 8. So they took the victuals of the people in their hand, and their horns; and he sent all the men of Israel every man unto his tent, but retained the three hundred men; and the camp of Midian was beneath him in the valley.

9. And it came to pass the same night, that the LORD said unto him: 'Arise, get thee down upon the camp; for I have delivered it into thy hand. 10. But if thou fear to go down, go thou with Purah thy servant down to the camp. 11. And thou shalt hear what they say; and afterward shall thy hands be strengthened to go down upon the camp.' Then went he down with Purah his servant unto the outermost part of the armed men that were in the camp. 12. Now the Midianites and the Amalekites and all the children of the east lay along in the valley like locusts for

בְּיָדֶךָ וְכָל־הָעָם יֵלְכוּ אִישׁ
8 לִמְקֹמוֹ: וַיִּקְחוּ אֶת־צֵדָה
הָעָם בְּיָדָם וְאֵת שׁוֹפְרֹתֵיהֶם
וְאֵת כָּל־אִישׁ יִשְׂרָאֵל שִׁלַּח
אִישׁ לְאֹהָלָיו וּבִשְׁלֹשׁ־מֵאוֹת
הָאִישׁ הֶחֱזִיק וּמַחֲנֵה מִדְיָן
הָיָה לוֹ מִתַּחַת בָּעֵמֶק:
9 וַיְהִי בַּלַּיְלָה הַהוּא וַיֹּאמֶר
אֵלָיו יְהֹוָה קוּם רֵד בַּמַּחֲנֶה
10 כִּי נְתַתִּיו בְּיָדֶךָ: וְאִם־יָרֵא
אַתָּה לָרֶדֶת רֵד אַתָּה וּפֻרָה
11 נַעַרְךָ אֶל־הַמַּחֲנֶה: וְשָׁמַעְתָּ
מַה־יְדַבֵּרוּ וְאַחַר תֶּחֱזַקְנָה
יָדֶיךָ וְיָרַדְתָּ בַּמַּחֲנֶה וַיֵּרֶד
הוּא וּפֻרָה נַעֲרוֹ אֶל־קְצֵה
הַחֲמֻשִׁים אֲשֶׁר בַּמַּחֲנֶה:
12 וּמִדְיָן וַעֲמָלֵק וְכָל־בְּנֵי־
קֶדֶם נֹפְלִים בָּעֵמֶק כָּאַרְבֶּה

9–15 THE MIDIANITE SOLDIER'S DREAM

9. *the same night.* After the selection of the three hundred.

arise, get thee down. The command was not to reconnoitre, but to attack the enemy forthwith. This is indicated by the use of the preposition *beth*, translated *upon (the camp)*, which denotes an assault (as in I Sam. xxvi. 10), instead of *to (the camp)* in the next two verses (Malbim).

10. *if thou fear.* Despite his trust in God, Gideon displayed an understandable hesitation. He had never before led a warlike

expedition and his army was small, ill-armed, untrained and inexperienced.

11. *shall thy hands be strengthened.* The phrase occurs again in 2 Sam. ii. 7 and Zech. viii. 9, 13.

armed men. [The term *chamushim* is obviously connected with the numerical *chamesh*, 'five' and occurs elsewhere in the sense of 'men in fighting order.' It has been defined as groups of better armed and disciplined soldiers stationed in advance of the army to receive the initial assault; or the whole force was grouped in five divisions, viz. the vanguard, the centre, the two wings and the rear.]

multitude; and their camels were without number, as the sand which is upon the sea-shore for multitude. 13. And when Gideon was come, behold, there was a man telling a dream unto his fellow, and saying: 'Behold, I dreamed a dream, and, lo, a cake of barley bread tumbled into the camp of Midian, and came unto the tent, and smote it that it fell, and turned it upside down, that the tent lay flat.' 14. And his fellow answered and said: 'This is nothing else save the sword of Gideon the son of Joash, a man of Israel: into his hand God hath delivered Midian, and all the host.'

15. And it was so, when Gideon heard the telling of the dream, and

לָרֹב וְלִגְמַלֵּיהֶם אֵין מִסְפָּר
כַּחוֹל שֶׁעַל־שְׂפַת הַיָּם לָרֹב:
13 וַיָּבֹא גִדְעוֹן וְהִנֵּה־אִישׁ
מְסַפֵּר לְרֵעֵהוּ חֲלוֹם וַיֹּאמֶר
הִנֵּה חֲלוֹם חָלַמְתִּי וְהִנֵּה צְלוֹל
לֶחֶם שְׂעֹרִים מִתְהַפֵּךְ בְּמַחֲנֵה
מִדְיָן וַיָּבֹא עַד־הָאֹהֶל וַיַּכֵּהוּ
וַיִּפֹּל וַיַּהַפְכֵהוּ לְמַעְלָה וְנָפַל
14 הָאֹהֶל: וַיַּעַן רֵעֵהוּ וַיֹּאמֶר
אֵין זֹאת בִּלְתִּי אִם־חֶרֶב
גִּדְעוֹן בֶּן־יוֹאָשׁ אִישׁ יִשְׂרָאֵל
נָתַן הָאֱלֹהִים בְּיָדוֹ אֶת־מִדְיָן
וְאֶת־כָּל־הַמַּחֲנֶה:
15 וַיְהִי כִשְׁמֹעַ גִּדְעוֹן אֶת־מִסְפַּר

v. 13. צְלִיל ק

12. *lay along*. lit. 'were falling,' an expression of camping, as in Gen. xxv. 18 (Rashi, Metsudath Zion). It may be an expression denoting their imminent downfall (Meam Loez).

as the sand, etc. [This is doubtless said, not of the camels, but the entire enemy host.]

13. As Gideon approached the camp unnoticed in the darkness of the night, he overheard a soldier telling his comrade a dream he had had. It had significance for Gideon because dreams were believed to presage future events, especially in this case, since Gideon was divinely instructed concerning it (Meam Loez).

cake. The word *tselil* in this sense occurs only here and is usually explained as a 'circular' cake, probably flat and baked hard on ashes, hot stones or a small stove. Such can still be seen among the primitive Arabs (Targum, Rashi, Metsudath Zion).

barley. An inferior grain half the worth of wheat (cf. 2 Kings vii. 1). It may have sym-

bolized for the dreamer the impoverishment of Israel or the inferiority of Gideon (Rabbi Isaiah of Trani). Alternatively, the entire dream of the cake overturning the tent was an allusion to the weak Israelites defeating the powerful Midianites (Kimchi). The Rabbis take this as symbolic of the Omer sacrifice on Passover. In the merit of this mitzvah, the Israelites would defeat the Midianites and their allies (Rashi from Vayikra Rabbah).

the tent. i.e. the center of the camp, where the tents stood, surrounded by the armed men who were at the edge of the camp (Abarbanel, Malbim).

a man of Israel. This follows Ramban (Gen. ix. 20). Metsudath Zion, however, explains it as 'the great and prominent one.'

15–18 GIDEON'S PREPARATION FOR ATTACK

15. Encouraged by the dream and its interpretation, Gideon returned with the decision to attack at once.

the interpretation thereof, that he worshipped; and he returned into the camp of Israel, and said: 'Arise; for the LORD hath delivered into your hand the host of Midian.' 16. And he divided the three hundred men into three companies, and he put into the hands of all of them horns, and empty pitchers, with torches within the pitchers. 17. And he said unto them: 'Look on me, and do likewise; and, behold, when I come to the outermost part of the camp, it shall be that, as I do, so shall ye do. 18. When I blow the horn, I and all that are with me, then blow ye the horns also on every side of all the camp, and say: For the LORD and for Gideon!'

19. So Gideon, and the hundred men that were with him, came unto the outermost part of the camp in

הַחֲלוֹם וְאֶת־שִׁבְרוֹ וַיִּשְׁתָּחוּ
וַיָּשָׁב אֶל־מַחֲנֵה יִשְׂרָאֵל
וַיֹּאמֶר קוּמוּ כִּי־נָתַן יְהֹוָה
בְּיֶדְכֶם אֶת־מַחֲנֵה מִדְיָן:

16 וַיַּחַץ אֶת־שְׁלֹשׁ־מֵאוֹת הָאִישׁ
שְׁלֹשָׁה רָאשִׁים וַיִּתֵּן שׁוֹפָרוֹת
בְּיַד־כֻּלָּם וְכַדִּים רֵקִים
וְלַפִּדִים בְּתוֹךְ הַכַּדִּים:

17 וַיֹּאמֶר אֲלֵיהֶם מִמֶּנִּי תִרְאוּ
וְכֵן תַּעֲשׂוּ וְהִנֵּה אָנֹכִי בָא
בִּקְצֵה הַמַּחֲנֶה וְהָיָה כַאֲשֶׁר
18 אֶעֱשֶׂה כֵּן תַּעֲשׂוּן: וְתָקַעְתִּי
בַּשּׁוֹפָר אָנֹכִי וְכָל־אֲשֶׁר אִתִּי
וּתְקַעְתֶּם בַּשּׁוֹפָרוֹת גַּם־אַתֶּם
סְבִיבוֹת כָּל־הַמַּחֲנֶה
וַאֲמַרְתֶּם לַיהֹוָה וּלְגִדְעוֹן:

19 וַיָּבֹא גִדְעוֹן וּמֵאָה־אִישׁ
אֲשֶׁר־אִתּוֹ בִּקְצֵה הַמַּחֲנֶה

---

interpretation. lit. 'breaking.' The noun *sheber* is not found elsewhere in this sense. Kimchi comments that an uninterpreted dream is like a sealed package, and therefore the interpretation may be said to 'break' it open.

worshipped. Usually rendered 'bowed down' or 'prostrated himself.' This was in gratitude for the omen which he believed to be the work of God (Metsudath David).

16. The strategical plan was simple and effective. The sleeping enemy was to be surrounded on three sides, and the sudden burst of light accompanied by the trumpet-

blasts out of the blackness of the night would spread consternation in the camp (Abarbanel).

companies. lit. 'heads.' This term is used for divisions, both military divisions, as here, ix. 34; 1 Sam. xi. 11, xiii. 17 f.; Job i. 17, and tributaries of a river, as in Gen. ii. 10 (Metsudath Zion).

18. *all that are with me.* Defined in the next verse (Rashi).

for the LORD *and for Gideon.* The cry indicated their firm belief that the LORD would bring about victory through their leader, Gideon (Targum, Rashi, Metsudath David).

.he beginning of the middle watch,
when they had but newly set the
watch; and they blew the horns,
and broke in pieces the pitchers that
were in their hands. 20. And the
three companies blew the horns,
and broke the pitchers, and held
the torches in their left hands, and
the horns in their right hands
wherewith to blow; and they cried:
'The sword for the LORD and for
Gideon!' 21. And they stood every
man in his place round about the
camp; and all the host ran; and they
shouted, and fled.

22. And they blew the three
hundred horns, and the LORD set
every man's sword against his
fellow, even throughout all the
host; and the host fled as far as
Beth-shittah toward Zererah, as far

רֹאשׁ הָאַשְׁמֹרֶת הַתִּיכוֹנָה אַ֣ךְ
הָקֵם הֵקִ֖ימוּ אֶת־הַשֹּׁמְרִ֑ים
וַיִּתְקְעוּ֙ בַּשּׁוֹפָר֔וֹת וְנָפ֗וֹץ
הַכַּדִּ֖ים אֲשֶׁ֣ר בְּיָדָֽם׃ 20 וַֽיִּתְקְע֡וּ
שְׁלֹ֣שֶׁת הָרָאשִׁים֮ בַּשּֽׁוֹפָרוֹת֒
וַֽיִּשְׁבְּר֣וּ הַכַּדִּ֗ים וַיַּחֲזִ֤יקוּ בְיַד־
שְׂמֹאולָם֙ בַּלַּפִּדִ֔ים וּבְיַ֣ד־
יְמִינָ֔ם הַשֹּׁפָר֖וֹת לִתְק֑וֹעַ
וַֽיִּקְרְא֔וּ חֶ֥רֶב לַֽיהוָ֖ה וּלְגִדְעֽוֹן׃
21 וַיַּֽעַמְדוּ֙ אִ֣ישׁ תַּחְתָּ֔יו סָבִ֖יב
לַֽמַּחֲנֶ֑ה וַיָּ֧רָץ כָּל־הַֽמַּחֲנֶ֛ה
22 וַיָּרִ֥יעוּ וַיָּנֽוּסוּ׃ וַֽיִּתְקְעוּ֮
שְׁלֹשׁ־מֵא֣וֹת הַשּֽׁוֹפָרוֹת֒
וַיָּ֣שֶׂם יְהוָ֗ה אֵ֣ת חֶ֥רֶב אִ֛ישׁ
בְּרֵעֵ֖הוּ וּבְכָל־הַֽמַּחֲנֶ֑ה וַיָּ֨נָס
הַֽמַּחֲנֶ֜ה עַד־בֵּ֤ית הַשִּׁטָּה֙

19. *the middle watch.* The night, which was
reckoned as beginning at 6 p.m., was divided into three watches each of four hours. In
the Talmud (Ber. 3b) one Rabbi maintained
this view, while another argued that there
were four watches each of three hours, and
he explained the phrase *the middle watch* as
one of the two middle watches.

newly set the watch. The noun in the text signifies 'sentries.' This clause is added to explain why Gideon chose *the beginning* of the
watch. The sentries had just come on duty
and they were still drowsy (Abarbanel, Malbim).

20. *the sword for.* [Although not included in
verse 18, it formed part of the battle-cry as

exclaimed in the excitement of the attack.]

21. *in his place.* They had no need to
charge the enemy; the confusion they had
created would win the battle without further
action on their part (Daath Mikra).

22. *fled.* The general direction of the flight
was towards the Jordan (cf. verse 24), but
the places mentioned cannot be identified
with certainty. They probably lay along the
Plain of Jezreel and the Jordan valley
towards the middle of its course (Ibid.).

Beth-shittah. lit. 'house of acacia'; some
authorities identify the town with the
modern Shutta which lies between Shunem
and Beth-shean (Ibid.).

as the border of Abel-meholah, by Tabbath. 23. And the men of Israel were gathered together out of Naphtali, and out of Asher, and out of all Manasseh, and pursued after Midian. 24. And Gideon sent messengers throughout all the hill-country of Ephraim, saying: 'Come down against Midian, and take before them the waters, as far as Beth-barah, and also the Jordan.' So all the men of Ephraim were gathered together, and took the waters as far as Beth-barah, and also the Jordan. 25. And they took the two princes of Midian, Oreb and Zeeb; and they slew Oreb at the Rock of Oreb, and Zeeb they slew at the Winepress of Zeeb, and pursued Midian; and they brought

צְרֵרָתָה עַד שְׂפַת־אָבֵל
23 מְחוֹלָה עַל־טַבָּת: וַיִּצָּעֵק
אִישׁ־יִשְׂרָאֵל מִנַּפְתָּלִי וּמִן־
אָשֵׁר וּמִן־כָּל־מְנַשֶּׁה וַיִּרְדְּפוּ
24 אַחֲרֵי מִדְיָן: וּמַלְאָכִים שָׁלַח
גִּדְעוֹן בְּכָל־הַר אֶפְרַיִם
לֵאמֹר רְדוּ לִקְרַאת מִדְיָן
וְלִכְדוּ לָהֶם אֶת־הַמַּיִם עַד
בֵּית בָּרָה וְאֶת־הַיַּרְדֵּן וַיִּצָּעֵק
כָּל־אִישׁ אֶפְרַיִם וַיִּלְכְּדוּ
אֶת־הַמַּיִם עַד בֵּית בָּרָה
25 וְאֶת־הַיַּרְדֵּן: וַיִּלְכְּדוּ שְׁנֵי
שָׂרֵי מִדְיָן אֶת־עֹרֵב וְאֶת־
זְאֵב וַיַּהַרְגוּ אֶת־עוֹרֵב
בְּצוּר־עוֹרֵב וְאֶת־זְאֵב הָרְגוּ
בְיֶקֶב־זְאֵב וַיִּרְדְּפוּ אֶל־
מִדְיָן וְרֹאשׁ־עֹרֵב וּזְאֵב

Zererah. Some equate the name with Zarethan (see on Josh. iii. 16) (Daath Mikra).

Abel-meholah. The birthplace of Elisha (see 1 Kings xix. 16). Some believe it to be located about ten miles south of Beth-shean, perhaps the modern Ain Helweh (ibid.).

Tabbath. The site is unknown. The use of the preposition *al (by),* lit. 'upon,' may possibly indicate that it was the name given to a wadi or stream (see Daath Mikra).

23. News of the victory spread to the other northern tribes who joined in the pursuit.

24. The routed Midianites evidently fled southwards to the nearest fords of the Jordan, and at the summons of Gideon the Ephraimites came down from the hills to intercept their crossing.

the waters. The intervening watercourses besides the Jordan mentioned explicitly (Kimchi).

Beth-barah. Its location is doubtful; [perhaps the wadi Farah and Damieh.]

also the Jordan. Its main fords (Daath Mikra).

25. *Oreb . . . Zeeb.* The names mean 'raven' and 'wolf'; [they may have been designations given them to describe the fierce traits possessed by the two men.]

Rock of Oreb, etc. It is possible that these names were applied after the event to commemorate the fate of the princes (Ralbag, Kimchi). The memory of the defeat survived to the days of Isaiah (cf. Isa. x. 26). It is also mentioned in Ps. lxxxiii 12.

the heads of Oreb and Zeeb to Gideon beyond the Jordan.

הֵבִ֙יאוּ֙ אֶל־גִּדְע֔וֹן מֵעֵ֖בֶר לַיַּרְדֵּֽן׃

8   **CHAPTER VIII**   **ח**

1. And the men of Ephraim said unto him: 'Why hast thou served us thus, that thou didst not call us when thou wentest to fight with Midian?' And they did chide with him sharply. 2. And he said unto them: 'What have I now done in comparison with you? Is not the gleaning of Ephraim better than the

1 וַיֹּאמְר֨וּ אֵלָ֜יו אִ֣ישׁ אֶפְרַ֗יִם מָֽה־הַדָּבָ֤ר הַזֶּה֙ עָשִׂ֣יתָ לָּ֔נוּ לְבִלְתִּי֙ קְרֹ֣אות לָ֔נוּ כִּ֥י הָלַ֖כְתָּ לְהִלָּחֵ֣ם בְּמִדְיָ֑ן וַיְרִיב֥וּן אִתּ֖וֹ 2 בְּחָזְקָֽה׃ וַיֹּ֣אמֶר אֲלֵיהֶ֔ם מֶה־עָשִׂ֥יתִי עַתָּ֖ה כָּכֶ֑ם הֲלֹ֗א ט֛וֹב עֹלְל֥וֹת אֶפְרַ֖יִם מִבְצִ֥יר

v. 1. יתיר ר׳   v. 2. הב׳ רפה

---

beyond the Jordan. lit. 'from beyond'; the heads were brought to Gideon from the western side of the river. He had by then, as Rashi explains, crossed the Jordan in pursuit of the two kings of Midian, Zebah and Zalmunna (viii. 5).

CHAPTER VIII

1 1-3 COMPLAINT OF THE EPHRAIMITES

[As the most powerful tribe in the north, the Ephraimites were resentful of the usurpation by a lesser tribe of the hegemony in their area. Gideon, conscious of his inferior strength, silenced their protest with a tactful reply. They were met with sterner measures later when they raised a similar objection in the time of Jephthah (cf. xii. 1–7).]

1. *men.* The noun is used collectively; the verb is therefore in the plural (Daath Mikra).

why has thou served us thus. lit. 'what is this thing thou hast done to us?' [The resentment which they displayed throws a sidelight on the petty jealousies of the time which stood in the way of national unity.]

sharply. We may gather from xii. 1 the tone in which they addressed him.

2. Gideon's reply illustrates the proverb, *A soft answer turneth away wrath* (Prov. xv. 1).

in comparison with you. He asserts that his achievement was insignificant when compared with the daring exploits of the Ephraimites (Rashi, Metsudath David).

gleaning. The small grapes left over after the vintage. He implied that the part played by Ephraim (vii. 24f.), though less spectacular than the initial victory of Abiezer, was of decisive importance in the ultimate success of the campaign. There was some truth in Gideon's compliment, because if the fords of the Jordan had not been seized in time, the fruits of the first success would have been lost (Rashi, Kimchi). Some commentators think that the metaphor means, 'the weakest of the Ephraimites are better than the most heroic of the Abiezrites' (Targum, Ralbag).

vintage. The *dagesh* is omitted in the *beth,* which is rare. The effect is a softening of the sound and [may be intended to represent the mildness of Gideon's tone of voice.]

223

vintage of Abiezer? 3. God hath delivered into your hand the princes of Midian, Oreb and Zeeb; and what was I able to do in comparison with you?' Then their anger was abated toward him, when he had said that.

4. And Gideon came to the Jordan, and passed over, he, and the three hundred men that were with him, faint, yet pursuing. 5. And he said unto the men of Succoth: 'Give, I pray you, loaves of bread unto the people that follow me; for they are faint, and I am pursuing after Zebah and Zalmunna, the kings of Midian.' 6. And the princes of Succoth said: 'Are the hands of

3 אֲבִיעֶזֶר: בְּיֶדְכֶם נָתַן אֱלֹהִים
אֶת־שָׂרֵי מִדְיָן אֶת־עֹרֵב
וְאֶת־זְאֵב וּמַה־יָּכֹלְתִּי עֲשׂוֹת
כָּכֶם אָז רָפְתָה רוּחָם מֵעָלָיו
בְּדַבְּרוֹ הַדָּבָר הַזֶּה:

4 וַיָּבֹא גִדְעוֹן הַיַּרְדֵּנָה עֹבֵר
הוּא וּשְׁלֹשׁ־מֵאוֹת הָאִישׁ אֲשֶׁר

5 אִתּוֹ עֲיֵפִים וְרֹדְפִים: וַיֹּאמֶר
לְאַנְשֵׁי סֻכּוֹת תְּנוּ־נָא כִּכְּרוֹת
לֶחֶם לָעָם אֲשֶׁר בְּרַגְלָי כִּי־
עֲיֵפִים הֵם וְאָנֹכִי רֹדֵף אַחֲרֵי
זֶבַח וְצַלְמֻנָּע מַלְכֵי מִדְיָן:

6 וַיֹּאמֶר שָׂרֵי סֻכּוֹת הֲכַף זֶבַח

v. 6. סבירין ויאמרו

3. This verse explains the metaphor.

into your hand. In the Hebrew this comes at the beginning of the sentence for emphasis.

4–9 THE MEN OF SUCCOTH
REFUSE TO GIVE HELP

4. *and passed over.* lit. 'passing over'; the participle is more descriptive though less usual.

the three hundred men. His army had not increased, and he did not wish it to do so. The same small band who had put the Midianite host to flight continued the campaign to the end.

yet pursuing. To capture the Midianite kings, Zebah and Zalmunna, who were devastating the Israelite lands across the Jordan in the course of their flight (Rashi), and had apparently put Gideon's brothers to death (cf. verse 19).

5. *Succoth.* For the origin of the name ('booths'), cf. Gen. xxxiii. 17. Kimchi maintains that the word is connected with the Hebrew for 'thorns.' According to P.T. (Sheb. 9:2) it is identified with Deir Alla,

known today as Tel Deir Alla, on the northern bank of the Jabbok (see on Josh. xiii. 27) (Daath Mikra).

loaves. [Round, flat cakes; the word means 'circles.']

Zebah. The name, if Hebrew and not Midianite, means 'sacrifice' or 'slaughter.'

Zalmunna. [By a word-play the name is taken to signify 'shadow withheld', i.e. 'protection refused'; but it is doubtless of Midianite origin.]

6. *princes.* This is the usual rendering of the word; here it probably denotes 'officials,' the heads of the council of elders. Rashi's assertion that they were Israelites makes their refusal the more culpable, and indicates the deterioration that had set in among the Transjordanian tribes since Joshua's death. Perhaps they feared that the battle was not yet won, and they feared retaliations from the Midianites (Daath Soferim, Daath Mikra).

hands. lit. 'palm,' perhaps used figuratively for 'power.'

Zebah and Zalmunna now in thy power, that we should give bread unto thine army?' 7. And Gideon said: 'Therefore when the LORD hath delivered Zebah and Zalmunna into my hand, then I will tear your flesh with the thorns of the wilderness and with briers.' 8. And he went up thence to Penuel, and spoke unto them in like manner; and the men of Penuel answered him as the men of Succoth had answered. 9. And he spoke also unto the men of Penuel, saying: 'When I come back in peace, I will break down this tower.'

10. Now Zebah and Zalmunna were in Karkor, and their hosts with them, about fifteen thousand men, all that were left of all the host of the children of the east; for there fell a hundred and twenty thousand

וְצַלְמֻנָּע עַתָּה בְּיָדֶךָ כִּי־נִתֵּן
7 לִצְבָאֲךָ לָחֶם: וַיֹּאמֶר גִּדְעוֹן
לָכֵן בְּתֵת יְהֹוָה אֶת־זֶבַח
וְאֶת־צַלְמֻנָּע בְּיָדִי וְדַשְׁתִּי
אֶת־בְּשַׂרְכֶם אֶת־קוֹצֵי
הַמִּדְבָּר וְאֶת־הַבַּרְקֳנִים:
8 וַיַּעַל מִשָּׁם פְּנוּאֵל וַיְדַבֵּר
אֲלֵיהֶם כָּזֹאת וַיַּעֲנוּ אוֹתוֹ אַנְשֵׁי
פְנוּאֵל כַּאֲשֶׁר עָנוּ אַנְשֵׁי
9 סֻכּוֹת: וַיֹּאמֶר גַּם־לְאַנְשֵׁי
פְנוּאֵל לֵאמֹר בְּשׁוּבִי בְשָׁלוֹם
אֶתֹּץ אֶת־הַמִּגְדָּל הַזֶּה:
10 וְזֶבַח וְצַלְמֻנָּע בַּקַּרְקֹר
וּמַחֲנֵיהֶם עִמָּם כַּחֲמֵשֶׁת עָשָׂר
אֶלֶף כֹּל הַנּוֹתָרִים מִכֹּל מַחֲנֵה
בְנֵי־קֶדֶם וְהַנֹּפְלִים מֵאָה

that we should give. There is a note of derision in their refusal. They scoff at the idea of three hundred men overpowering the mighty kings of Midian (DM).

7. tear. lit. 'thresh,' i.e. strike with violence (Kimchi and Rashi). Others explain that he threatened to throw them naked into a bed of thorns and trample them together, like grain on the threshing-floor (ibid.).

briers. The cognate noun in Arabic denotes a plant with thorny heads. Gideon's sharp retort showed that, when occasion demanded, he could be as stern as he had been conciliatory with Ephraim.

8. Penuel. Cf. Gen. xxxii. 31f. This was a place of importance rebuilt by Jeroboam (1 Kings xii. 25). It lay farther from the Jordan than Succoth and higher up in the hills. It is variously sought at Tulul ed-Dahab, cone-shaped hills about 250 feet above the Jabbok valley, or at Kalat or Rabat (ibid.).

9. tower. The stronghold which formed a refuge in time of danger for the inhabitants of unwalled cities (Metsudath David, Daath Mikra).

10–12 CAPTURE OF ZEBAH AND ZALMUNNA

10. Karkor. It is believed to be Karkar in the south-east in the valley of Sirhan, approximately 230 kilometers from the middle of the Dead Sea to the east (Daath Mikra).

for there fell. More accurately, 'and those that had fallen.'

men that drew sword. 11. And Gideon went up by the way of them that dwelt in tents on the east of Nobah and Jogbehah, and smote the host; for the host was secure. 12. And Zebah and Zalmunna fled; and he pursued after them; and he took the two kings of Midian, Zebah and Zalmunna, and discomfited all the host. 13. And Gideon the son of Joash returned from the battle from the ascent of Heres. 14. And he caught a young man of the men of Succoth, and inquired of him; and he wrote down for him the princes of Succoth, and the elders

וְעֶשְׂרִים אֶלֶף אִישׁ שֹׁלֵף
11 חָרֶב: וַיַּעַל גִּדְעוֹן דֶּרֶךְ
הַשְּׁכוּנֵי בָאֳהָלִים מִקֶּדֶם
לְנֹבַח וְיָגְבְּהָה וַיַּךְ אֶת־
הַמַּחֲנֶה וְהַמַּחֲנֶה הָיָה בֶטַח:
12 וַיָּנֻסוּ זֶבַח וְצַלְמֻנָּע וַיִּרְדֹּף
אַחֲרֵיהֶם וַיִּלְכֹּד אֶת־שְׁנֵי |
מַלְכֵי מִדְיָן אֶת־זֶבַח וְאֶת־
צַלְמֻנָּע וְכָל־הַמַּחֲנֶה
13 הֶחֱרִיד: וַיָּשָׁב גִּדְעוֹן בֶּן־
יוֹאָשׁ מִן־הַמִּלְחָמָה מִלְמַעֲלֵה
14 הֶחָרֶס: וַיִּלְכָּד־נַעַר מֵאַנְשֵׁי
סֻכּוֹת וַיִּשְׁאָלֵהוּ וַיִּכְתֹּב אֵלָיו
אֶת־שָׂרֵי סֻכּוֹת וְאֶת־זְקֵנֶיהָ

v. 10. כצ״ל

a hundred and twenty thousand. The extent of the overwhelming victory is thus vividly revealed.

11. *the way of them that dwelt in tents.* Archaeologists claim to have established that 'the way of the tent-dwellers' corresponds with the route now called 'the road of the nomads' which passes through the 'gateway' between the south-west spurs of the Hauran and the broken hills in which the river Zerka has its source. The Hebrew phrase presents several grammatical difficulties, and the rendering given is an attempt at making sense. If the translation is correct, the reference can only be to the Bedouin, but the meaning still remains uncertain (Daath Mikra).

Nobah. A city in the territory of Manasseh (cf. Num. xxxii. 42).

Jogbehah. A city of Gad (cf. Num. xxxii. 35); identified with Khirbet el-Jubeihat, north-west of Amman and about midway between it and es-Salt (Daath Mikra).

secure. Because of the distance which now separated them from Gideon and his men (Metsudath David).

12. *discomfited.* lit. 'terrified'; he inspired fresh panic in the bewildered warriors.

3–17 PUNISHMENT OF SUCCOTH AND PENUEL

13. *returned.* The battle was over and won. With the capture of the two kings, Gideon's purpose was accomplished. On the homeward journey he executed his threat against those who had refused his men aid.

the ascent of Heres. Early commentators render: 'before the sun set' (Targum, Rashi, Kimchi) or 'after the sun rose' (Kimchi, Abarbanel) (cf. xiv. 18). If indeed it is a city, its place has not been identified.

14. *wrote down.* [That a knowledge of writing was widespread at that time is proved by archaeological discoveries.]

thereof, seventy and seven men.
15. And he came unto the men of
Succoth, and said: 'Behold Zebah
and Zalmunna, concerning whom
ye did taunt me, saying: Are the
hands of Zebah and Zalmunna now
in thy power, that we should give
bread unto thy men that are weary?'
16. And he took the elders of the
city, and thorns of the wilderness
and briers, and with them he taught
the men of Succoth. 17. And he
broke down the tower of Penuel, and
slew the men of the city. 18. Then
said he unto Zebah and Zalmunna:
'Where are the men whom ye slew
at Tabor?' And they answered:
'As thou art, so were they; of one

15 שִׁבְעִים וְשִׁבְעָה אִישׁ: וַיָּבֹא
אֶל־אַנְשֵׁי סֻכּוֹת וַיֹּאמֶר הִנֵּה
זֶבַח וְצַלְמֻנָּע אֲשֶׁר חֵרַפְתֶּם
אוֹתִי לֵאמֹר הֲכַף זֶבַח
וְצַלְמֻנָּע עַתָּה בְּיָדֶךָ כִּי נִתֵּן
16 לַאֲנָשֶׁיךָ הַיְּעֵפִים לָחֶם: וַיִּקַּח
אֶת־זִקְנֵי הָעִיר וְאֶת־קוֹצֵי
הַמִּדְבָּר וְאֶת־הַבַּרְקֳנִים וַיֹּדַע
17 בָּהֶם אֵת אַנְשֵׁי סֻכּוֹת: וְאֶת־
מִגְדַּל פְּנוּאֵל נָתָץ וַיַּהֲרֹג אֶת־
18 אַנְשֵׁי הָעִיר: וַיֹּאמֶר אֶל־
זֶבַח וְאֶל־צַלְמֻנָּע אֵיפֹה
הָאֲנָשִׁים אֲשֶׁר הֲרַגְתֶּם בְּתָבוֹר
וַיֹּאמְרוּ כָּמוֹךָ כְמוֹהֶם אֶחָד

---

seventy and seven men. [The number seems to
indicate some form of council similar to the
seventy elders of earlier and later days.]

15. *he came.* As no mention is made of an
assault, it has been inferred that the city was
unprotected and offered no resistance.

16. *he taught.* The implied object is 'a lesson.' This form of punishment (see on verse
7) is described in Plato's *Republic* as one
inflicted upon the worst offenders.

17. *slew the men of the city.* The context suggests that he subjected the inhabitants of
Penuel to severer punishment than the men
of Succoth. Since they had a tower in which
to take shelter, they had no excuse that they
feared the Midianites (Malbim).

18–21 EXECUTION OF ZEBAH
AND ZALMUNNA

18. *where are the men.* From the answer it
may be deduced that the question was more

than an inquiry as to the whereabouts of the
victims. It probably included a demand to
produce the bodies for identification or,
failing that, to describe the victims in sufficient detail to establish their identity. Hence
the Midianites' answer and Gideon's subsequent remark (see Abarbanel).

Tabor. If mount Tabor is intended, the difficulty arises as to what Gideon's brothers
had been doing so far away from their
homes. In the absence of details all explanations are merely conjecture.

one. The word, in the context, is difficult.
Some connect with what precedes and render as an adverbial accusative: 'thy likeness
was their likeness, all one' (Kimchi). Others,
connecting with what follows, render: 'each
one resembled,' or 'one of them had the
appearance' (Targum). When we bear in
mind that the speakers were not Hebrews, a
degree of ambiguity in expression is understandable.

form with the children of a king.'
19. And he said: 'They were my
brethren, the sons of my mother; as
the LORD liveth, if ye had saved them
alive, I would not slay you.' 20. And
he said unto Jether his first-born:
'Up, and slay them.' But the youth
drew not his sword; for he feared,
because he was yet a youth. 21.
Then Zebah and Zalmunna said:
'Rise thou, and fall upon us; for as
the man is, so is his strength.' And
Gideon arose, and slew Zebah and
Zalmunna, and took the crescents
that were on their camels' necks.

22. Then the men of Israel said

19 כְּתֹאַר בְּנֵי הַמֶּלֶךְ: וַיֹּאמֶר
אַחַי בְּנֵי־אִמִּי הֵם חַי־יְהֹוָה
לוּ הַחֲיִתֶם אוֹתָם לֹא הָרַגְתִּי
20 אֶתְכֶם: וַיֹּאמֶר לְיֶתֶר בְּכוֹרוֹ
קוּם הֲרֹג אוֹתָם וְלֹא־שָׁלַף
הַנַּעַר חַרְבּוֹ כִּי יָרֵא כִּי עוֹדֶנּוּ
21 נָעַר: וַיֹּאמֶר זֶבַח וְצַלְמֻנָּע
קוּם אַתָּה וּפְגַע־בָּנוּ כִּי כָאִישׁ
גְּבוּרָתוֹ וַיָּקָם גִּדְעוֹן וַיַּהֲרֹג
אֶת־זֶבַח וְאֶת־צַלְמֻנָּע וַיִּקַּח
אֶת־הַשַּׂהֲרֹנִים אֲשֶׁר בְּצַוְּארֵי
גְמַלֵּיהֶם:
22 וַיֹּאמְרוּ אִישׁ־יִשְׂרָאֵל אֶל־

form. In the sense of 'figure, stature, physical appearance' (Kimchi).

19. *sons of my mother.* They were my brothers, not my sons. Therefore, they were not responsible for my rebellion and should not have been slain (Malbim).

as the LORD liveth. lit. 'the LORD is living.'

if ye had saved them. By slaying his brothers, the Midianites had imposed the duty of blood-revenge upon Gideon (cf. Deut. xix. 6) (Malbim, Daath Mikra).

I would not slay you. It was prevalent not to kill a captured king unless he was brought to justice (Malbim).

20. *Jether.* The name appears as a form of Jethro, the Midianite father-in-law of Moses (Exod. iv. 18). It was borne by the father of Amasa (1 Kings ii. 5) and by men of Judah and Asher (1 Chron. ii. 32, iv. 17, vii. 38).

up, and slay them. To avenge the blood of his father's brothers (Malbim).

he feared. i.e. he feared them (Rashi). Because of his youth, he did not realize that they were completely at his mercy, and, therefore, feared to kill them (Metsudath David). Daath Soferim explains that this indicates the pure character of the children of Israel; even the son of the mighty Gideon was reluctant to shed blood.

21. The Midianite chiefs were not afraid to die. What they wished to avoid was the agony of a protracted death by an inexperienced hand (Kimchi, Metsudath David).

crescents. Hebrew *saharon,* a collar with attachments of metal moon-shaped ornaments (connected with *sahar,* Aramaic and Syriac for 'moon'). It was worn by men (verse 26) and women (Isa. iii. 18) (Rashi, Kimchi).

22–23 FIRST ATTEMPT TO
ESTABLISH KINGSHIP IN ISRAEL

23. *the men of Israel.* This term is said to connote the body of 'freemen' who formed the army (cf. vii. 1, ix. 55) (Daath Mikra).

unto Gideon: 'Rule thou over us, both thou, and thy son, and thy son's son also; for thou hast saved us out of the hand of Midian.' 23. And Gideon said unto them: 'I will not rule over you, neither shall my son rule over you; the LORD shall rule over you.' 24. And Gideon said unto them: 'I would make a request of you, that ye would give me every man the ear-rings of his spoil.'—For they had golden ear-rings, because they were Ishmaelites. 25. And they answered: 'We will willingly give them.' And they spread a garment, and did cast therein every man the ear-rings of his spoil. 26. And the weight of the golden ear-rings that he requested was a thousand and seven hundred

גִּדְעוֹן מְשָׁל־בָּנוּ גַּם־אַתָּה
גַּם־בִּנְךָ גַּם בֶּן־בְּנֶךָ כִּי
הוֹשַׁעְתָּנוּ מִיַּד מִדְיָן: וַיֹּאמֶר 23
אֲלֵהֶם גִּדְעוֹן לֹא־אֶמְשֹׁל אֲנִי
בָּכֶם וְלֹא־יִמְשֹׁל בְּנִי בָּכֶם
יְהוָה יִמְשֹׁל בָּכֶם: וַיֹּאמֶר 24
אֲלֵהֶם גִּדְעוֹן אֶשְׁאֲלָה מִכֶּם
שְׁאֵלָה וּתְנוּ־לִי אִישׁ נֶזֶם
שְׁלָלוֹ כִּי־נִזְמֵי זָהָב לָהֶם כִּי
יִשְׁמְעֵאלִים הֵם: וַיֹּאמְרוּ נָתוֹן 25
נִתֵּן וַיִּפְרְשׂוּ אֶת־הַשִּׂמְלָה
וַיַּשְׁלִיכוּ שָׁמָּה אִישׁ נֶזֶם שְׁלָלוֹ:
וַיְהִי מִשְׁקַל נִזְמֵי הַזָּהָב אֲשֶׁר 26
שָׁאָל אֶלֶף וּשְׁבַע־מֵאוֹת זָהָב

v. 26. קמץ בז"ק

---

rule. Though the word 'reign' is not used, it is obvious that hereditary leadership was intended (cf. ix. 8ff.). Already the need for mutual support was becoming increasingly felt among the tribes (Abarbanel).

23. *the LORD shall rule over you.* [This magnificent act of self-abnegation was the crowning glory of Gideon's career. To have achieved a decisive victory and restored national independence, gained the loyalty and confidence of his people, and yet retain his simplicity and humility is evidence of true greatness. With prophetic insight he saw that Israel's destiny was bound up with God's Sovereignty and not with temporal kingship.]

24–27 THE EPHOD MADE BY GIDEON

In his desire to leave a monument which would perpetuate the memory of the miraculous deliverance of which he had been the Divine instrument, Gideon asked for a portion of the gold that the Israelites had taken as spoil. Out of this he made an ephod which afterwards became an object of worship (Kimchi).

24. *ear-rings.* This is probably the meaning of *nezem* in this passage; it can also denote 'nose-ring' worn by women (as explained by Metsudath Zion).

Ishmaelites. Not in the sense of 'descendants of Ishmael,' but close relatives of Ishmael, since the Midianites were descended from Keturah (Gen. xxv. 2), who, according to the Rabbis, was identified with Hagar, the mother of Ishmael (Kimchi).

25. *a garment.* [The *simlah* was a wide outer wrapper which could readily be converted into a sack by tying the corners together (cf. Exod. xii. 34). The text is literally 'the garment'; for the definite article, see on vii. 13.]

26. [The value of the shekels was about seventy pounds sterling.]

shekels of gold; beside the crescents,
and the pendants, and the purple
raiment that was on the kings of
Midian, and beside the chains that
were about their camels' necks.
27. And Gideon made an ephod
thereof, and put it in his city, even
in Ophrah; and all Israel went astray
after it there; and it became a snare
unto Gideon, and to his house.
28. So Midian was subdued before
the children of Israel, and they lifted
up their heads no more. And the
land had rest forty years in the days
of Gideon.

לְבַד מִן־הַשַּׂהֲרֹנִים וְהַנְּטִיפוֹת
וּבִגְדֵי הָאַרְגָּמָן שֶׁעַל מַלְכֵי
מִדְיָן וּלְבַד מִן־הָעֲנָקוֹת
27 אֲשֶׁר בְּצַוְּארֵי גְמַלֵּיהֶם: וַיַּעַשׂ
אוֹתוֹ גִדְעוֹן לְאֵפוֹד וַיַּצֵּג אוֹתוֹ
בְעִירוֹ בְּעָפְרָה וַיִּזְנוּ כָל־
יִשְׂרָאֵל אַחֲרָיו שָׁם וַיְהִי
לְגִדְעוֹן וּלְבֵיתוֹ לְמוֹקֵשׁ:
28 וַיִּכָּנַע מִדְיָן לִפְנֵי בְּנֵי יִשְׂרָאֵל
וְלֹא יָסְפוּ לָשֵׂאת רֹאשָׁם
וַתִּשְׁקֹט הָאָרֶץ אַרְבָּעִים שָׁנָה
בִּימֵי גִדְעוֹן:

pendants. The noun netiphoth is also found
in Isa. iii. 19. The translation is based on
the etymology from nataph, 'to drip.' The
Targum translates 'diadems, chaplets.' Some
scholars connect it with nataph, 'stacte' (cf.
Exod. xxx. 34), and explain it as capsules in
which this sweet-smelling gum was worn
(Kimchi, Ralbag). Others interpret it as a
pendant hanging over the heart (Metsudath
Zion) or attached to other ornaments, such
as ear-rings or necklaces. The glistening
pearl or metal bead gave the appearance of
a drop, hence the name netiphoth (Daath
Mikra).

the purple raiment. The badge of royalty. The
colour, a red purple, was extremely costly
(ibid.).

the chains, etc. In the Orient animals are still
adorned in this manner.

27. ephod. It was to serve as a memorial
(Rashi). Associated, as it was, with the vest-
ments of the High Priest (cf. Exod. xxviii.
6), it was but natural that the object should
come to be considered as something sacred.
It frequently appears in the Bible as an
object of worship (cf. xvii. 5, xviii. 14; Hos.
iii. 4) and a means of ascertaining the Divine
will (1 Sam. xxiii. 9).

Ophrah. See on vi. 11.

after it. Rashi and Kimchi qualify this statement as meaning that they strayed after
Gideon's death, not during his lifetime (cf.
verse 33).

unto Gideon, and to his house. It was, remark
Jewish expositors, the cause of the deaths of
most of his sons (ix. 5) (Metsudath David).

28. PEACE IN THE LAND

lifted up their heads no more. [The Midianite
defeat must have been very severe to warrant the addition of this statement, which
does not occur in connection with the victories gained by the other judges. After this
period the Midianites scarcely appear in the
sacred literature.]

29. And Jerubbaal the son of Joash went and dwelt in his own house. 30. And Gideon had three-score and ten sons of his body begotten; for he had many wives. 31. And his concubine that was in Shechem, she also bore him a son, and he called his name Abimelech. 32. And Gideon the son of Joash died in a good old age, and was buried in the sepulchre of Joash his father, in Ophrah of the Abiezrites.

33. And it came to pass, as soon as Gideon was dead, that the children of Israel again went astray after the Baalim, and made Baal-berith their god. 34. And the children of Israel remembered not

29 וַיֵּלֶךְ יְרֻבַּעַל בֶּן־יוֹאָשׁ וַיֵּשֶׁב
30 בְּבֵיתוֹ: וּלְגִדְעוֹן הָיוּ שִׁבְעִים
בָּנִים יֹצְאֵי יְרֵכוֹ כִּי־נָשִׁים
31 רַבּוֹת הָיוּ לוֹ: וּפִילַגְשׁוֹ אֲשֶׁר
בִּשְׁכֶם יָלְדָה־לּוֹ גַם־הִיא בֵּן
וַיָּשֶׂם אֶת־שְׁמוֹ אֲבִימֶלֶךְ:
32 וַיָּמָת גִּדְעוֹן בֶּן־יוֹאָשׁ בְּשֵׂיבָה
טוֹבָה וַיִּקָּבֵר בְּקֶבֶר יוֹאָשׁ
אָבִיו בְּעָפְרָה אֲבִי הָעֶזְרִי:
33 וַיְהִי כַּאֲשֶׁר מֵת גִּדְעוֹן וַיָּשׁוּבוּ
בְּנֵי יִשְׂרָאֵל וַיִּזְנוּ אַחֲרֵי
הַבְּעָלִים וַיָּשִׂימוּ לָהֶם בַּעַל
34 בְּרִית לֵאלֹהִים: וְלֹא זָכְרוּ

29–32 THE FAMILY OF GIDEON AND HIS DEATH

29. *dwelt in his own house.* Since the land was peaceful, he concentrated on his household and on raising a family (see next verse) (Metsudath David). Although Gideon did not desire to exercise leadership over Israel, he should, nevertheless, have passed through the land to maintain order rather than settle down in his house (Daath Soferim. Cf. 1 Sam. vii. 15ff.).

30. *sons of his body begotten.* This denotes that they were actually his sons, not his grandsons (ibid.).

many wives. This was to his degradation, for a leader of Israel, as a king, should not have so many wives (Deut. xvii. 17) (Meam Loez, Daath Soferim).

31. *he called.* lit. 'he put, assigned' (again in 2 Kings xvii. 34; Neh. ix. 7). Daath Soferim explains that this verb denotes not the name given to a child at birth, but conferred upon him at a later stage of his life. Upon recognizing his kingly behavior and talents, he gave him this name.

Abimelech. A regal name, common among the kings of Canaan (cf. Gen. xx., xxvi) (Daath Mikra). This name indicated that he was destined to become a king (Abarbanel).

32. *sepulchre.* [The existence of family sepulchres is evidence that the Israelites were settled in the land.]

33–35 NATIONAL APOSTASY

33. *again went astray.* As they had done after the death of previous judges. The seductive influence of the Canaanite cults was, in the absence of the restraining rule of the judge, too strong to resist.

Baal-berith. Appears in ix. 46 as *El-berith,* the god of Shechem, where a shrine in its name flourished (cf. also ix. 4). The name, 'Baal (lord) of a covenant,' is said to denote their love and allegiance to this deity (Rashi, Shab. 83b). It is most unlikely that the entire nation went astray such a short time after they had completely forsaken paganism. There were, however, a large number that worshipped idols, and were left unpunished (Daath Soferim).

the LORD their God, who had delivered them out of the hand of all their enemies on every side; 35. neither showed they kindness to the house of Jerubbaal, namely Gideon, according to all the goodness which he had shown unto Israel.

בְּנֵי יִשְׂרָאֵל אֶת־יְהֹוָה אֱלֹהֵיהֶם הַמַּצִּיל אוֹתָם מִיַּד כָּל־אֹיְבֵיהֶם מִסָּבִיב: וְלֹא־ 35 עָשׂוּ חֶסֶד עִם־בֵּית יְרֻבַּעַל גִּדְעוֹן כְּכָל־הַטּוֹבָה אֲשֶׁר עָשָׂה עִם־יִשְׂרָאֵל:

9   CHAPTER IX   פ

1. And Abimelech the son of Jerubbaal went to Shechem unto his mother's brethren, and spoke with them, and with all the family of the house of his mother's father, saying:

וַיֵּלֶךְ אֲבִימֶלֶךְ בֶּן־יְרֻבַּעַל 1 שְׁכֶמָה אֶל־אֲחֵי אִמּוֹ וַיְדַבֵּר אֲלֵיהֶם וְאֶל־כָּל־מִשְׁפַּחַת בֵּית־אֲבִי אִמּוֹ לֵאמֹר:

35. *kindness.* What this lack of kindness meant is perhaps to be deduced from ix. 16–18 (Rashi).

CHAPTER IX

THE CAREER OF ABIMELECH

That this chapter does not begin with the usual formula, 'and the children of Israel did that which was evil in the sight of the Lord,' is accounted for by the circumstances that the subject of the narrative was not a judge raised by God in response to the cry of the oppressed people. He was an upstart who established his rule by violence.

1–6 HOW ABIMELECH BECAME RULER IN SHECHEM

The leaders of Shechem were persuaded by Abimelech to set aside the claims of Gideon's other sons and proclaim him ruler. With the help of money obtained from the treasury of the heathen shrine he hired a band of *vain and light fellows*, and killed all the sons of his father except the youngest who escaped by hiding.

1. *Abimelech.* He was the son of Gideon's concubine (viii. 31), and his right to succeed his father was inferior to that of his half-brothers.

Jerubbaal. This name is perhaps used throughout the chapter with the deliberate intention of emphasizing the irony of the situation. The son of the hero, whose name betokened the defeat of Baal (vi. 32), raised himself to power with the aid of men who worshipped it and with money that came from its shrine!

went. Presumably from his father's house at Ophrah (Daath Soferim).

Shechem. This being his mother's town (viii. 31), he could count on the support of his Canaanite kinsmen (ibid.).

mother's brethren. i.e. the nearest relatives. His mother seems to have belonged to a Canaanite family of influence.

house. Like *family* the 'fathers' house' was a distinct unit in the social composition of a tribe or people in the ancient world.

2. 'Speak, I pray you, in the ears of all the men of Shechem: Which is better for you, that all the sons of Jerubbaal, who are threescore and ten persons, rule over you, or that one rule over you? remember also that I am your bone and your flesh.' 3. And his mother's brethren spoke of him in the ears of all the men of Shechem all these words; and their hearts inclined to follow Abimelech; for they said: 'He is our brother.' 4. And they gave him threescore and ten pieces of silver out of the house of Baal-berith, wherewith Abimelech

2 דַּבְּרוּ־נָא בְּאָזְנֵי כָל־בַּעֲלֵי שְׁכֶם מַה־טּוֹב לָכֶם הַמְשֹׁל בָּכֶם שִׁבְעִים אִישׁ כֹּל בְּנֵי יְרֻבַּעַל אִם־מְשֹׁל בָּכֶם אִישׁ אֶחָד וּזְכַרְתֶּם כִּי־עַצְמְכֶם וּבְשַׂרְכֶם אָנִי: 3 וַיְדַבְּרוּ אֲחֵי־אִמּוֹ עָלָיו בְּאָזְנֵי כָל־בַּעֲלֵי שְׁכֶם אֵת כָּל־הַדְּבָרִים הָאֵלֶּה וַיֵּט לִבָּם אַחֲרֵי אֲבִימֶלֶךְ כִּי אָמְרוּ אָחִינוּ הוּא: 4 וַיִּתְּנוּ־לוֹ שִׁבְעִים כֶּסֶף מִבֵּית בַּעַל בְּרִית וַיִּשְׂכֹּר בָּהֶם

2. [This verse reveals that Abimelech's accession to power was not due to popular choice based upon his personal qualifications, but was the result of intrigue.]

men. lit. 'lords,' perhaps 'free men' or 'citizens.' It cannot be said with certainty whether they were Canaanites or Israelites. Both views have much in their favour; but Abimelech's claim to be of their own flesh and blood, in contrast to the other sons of Jerubbaal, lends support to the former (Daath Mikra).

threescore and ten persons. As recorded in viii. 30. The purpose of his remark was: if the leadership passed into the hands of Jerubbaal's numerous sons, the effect was sure to be dissension between them with harmful consequences to the people. One ruler was surely preferable to a large body of rulers. (ibid.). We have no indication that Abimelech's initial plan was to murder his brothers (Daath Soferim).

your bone and your flesh. In modern parlance, 'your flesh and blood.' Being half-Canaanite, he insinuated that it was in their interest that they should support him.

3. spoke of him. Abimelech's kinsmen used his argument when they discussed the matter with their fellow-townsmen (Metsudath Zion).

our brother. Abimelech was related to all the inhabitants of Shechem (Metsudath David).

4. threescore and ten pieces of silver. In itself not a large amount, but it is an indication that the shrines in those days possessed treasuries to which devotees made contributions. Some of the heathen sanctuaries in ancient times were depositories of vast wealth. The Temple of Solomon, too, had its treasury (cf. 1 Kings vii. 51). The riches so accumulated were often put to uses for which they were never intended by the donors (cf. 2 Kings xvi. 8). They were also at times a centre of attraction for the greed of foreign conquerors (cf. 2 Kings xxiv. 13). Abarbanel explains that they gave Abimelech the seventy shekels to suggest that his seventy brothers be slain, which they were. Others explain that this equals the tribute everyone would have had to pay to each of Gideon's sons. Now, they would give it all to Abimelech (Meam Loez).

Baal-berith. See on viii. 33.

hired vain and light fellows, who followed him. 5. And he went unto his father's house at Ophrah, and slew his brethren the sons of Jerubbaal, being threescore and ten persons, upon one stone; but Jotham the youngest son of Jerubbaal was left; for he hid himself.

6. And all the men of Shechem assembled themselves together, and all Beth-millo, and went and made Abimelech king, by the terebinth of the pillar that was in Shechem.

אֲבִימֶלֶךְ אֲנָשִׁים רֵיקִים

5 וּפֹחֲזִים וַיֵּלְכוּ אַחֲרָיו: וַיָּבֹא בֵית־אָבִיו עָפְרָתָה וַיַּהֲרֹג אֶת־אֶחָיו בְּנֵי־יְרֻבַּעַל שִׁבְעִים אִישׁ עַל־אֶבֶן אֶחָת וַיִּוָּתֵר יוֹתָם בֶּן־יְרֻבַּעַל הַקָּטֹן כִּי נֶחְבָּא:

6 וַיֵּאָסְפוּ כָּל־בַּעֲלֵי שְׁכֶם וְכָל־בֵּית מִלּוֹא וַיֵּלְכוּ וַיַּמְלִיכוּ אֶת־אֲבִימֶלֶךְ לְמֶלֶךְ עִם־אֵלוֹן מֻצָּב אֲשֶׁר בִּשְׁכֶם:

vain. lit. 'empty' (cf. the Talmudic word *reka*). Metsudath Zion renders 'devoid of virtues.' It is usually understood as men with idle hands, empty stomachs and a disinclination to earn an honest livelihood. Jephthah gathered a similar band (cf. xi. 3). Daath Mikra interprets it as men devoid of family ties and property.

light. Rashi explains that they were precipitate men who acted upon impulse without reflection. Kimchi regards them as people moving from place to place to earn a livelihood. According to variant versions of the Targum, it means licentious, cowherds, or contemptible (Kimchi).

who followed him. Acting as his bodyguard and prepared to obey his orders whatever they might be.

5. *upon one stone.* They were all in the house together, mourning their father's death. Or, they were together deciding how to divide the judgeship (Abarbanel). Daath Mikra explains that Abimelech took his

brothers completely unawares. Since they had no intention to compete for the leadership, they were not on guard against him.

was left. Of the seventy. Though not excluded from the number, it is still correct to speak in round numbers of 'seventy' slain (Kimchi).

6. *Beth-millo.* Several explanations have been offered; *Millo* was the name of Abimelech's maternal grandfather; *Beth-millo* is identical with *the tower of Shechem,* mentioned in verses 46f.; it is a term signifying 'rampart,' because it consisted of walls 'filled in' with rubble, stones and earth. *Millo,* without *Beth,* occurs in 2 Sam. v. 9 and elsewhere to denote a fortification. King Joash was murdered at a place called Beth-millo (2 Kings xii. 21). The name may, however, be of Canaanite origin.

terebinth of the pillar. Some commentators follow the Targum in rendering: 'a plain in which there were pillars (Kimchi). According to one theory it was the sanctuary of

7. And when they told it to Jotham, he went and stood in the top of mount Gerizim, and lifted up his voice, and cried, and said unto them: 'Hearken unto me, ye men of Shechem, that God may hearken unto you. **8.** The trees went forth on a time to anoint a king over them; and they said unto the olive-tree: Reign thou over us. **9.** But the olive-tree said unto them: Should I leave my fatness, seeing that by me they honour God and man, and go to hold sway over the trees? **10.** And the trees said to the fig-tree: Come thou, and reign over us. **11.** But the fig-tree said unto them:

7 וַיַּגִּדוּ לְיוֹתָם וַיֵּלֶךְ וַיַּעֲמֹד בְּרֹאשׁ הַר־גְּרִזִים וַיִּשָּׂא קוֹלוֹ וַיִּקְרָא וַיֹּאמֶר לָהֶם שִׁמְעוּ אֵלַי בַּעֲלֵי שְׁכֶם וְיִשְׁמַע 8 אֲלֵיכֶם אֱלֹהִים: הָלוֹךְ הָלְכוּ הָעֵצִים לִמְשֹׁחַ עֲלֵיהֶם מֶלֶךְ וַיֹּאמְרוּ לַזַּיִת מָלְוכָה עָלֵינוּ: 9 וַיֹּאמֶר לָהֶם הַזַּיִת הֶחֳדַלְתִּי אֶת־דִּשְׁנִי אֲשֶׁר־בִּי יְכַבְּדוּ אֱלֹהִים וַאֲנָשִׁים וְהָלַכְתִּי לָנוּעַ 10 עַל־הָעֵצִים: וַיֹּאמְרוּ הָעֵצִים לַתְּאֵנָה לְכִי־אַתְּ מׇלְכִי 11 עָלֵינוּ: וַתֹּאמֶר לָהֶם הַתְּאֵנָה

מלה ק' v. 8.

Shechem, a natural spot from which to proclaim a new king. This may have been the tree under which Jacob buried the idolatrous trinkets of his household (Gen. xxxv. 4), and there Joshua set up a monument as a witness (Josh. xxiv. 26f). Apparently a pillar stood beneath the tree.

7–15 JOTHAM'S FABLE

7. *top.* Since the height of the mountain was over 900 feet above the valley, commentators consider it unlikely that Jotham stood on the summit. There is a triangular platform projecting from the mountain-side which overlooks the town and the valley and it has been suggested that Jotham addressed the people from this natural pulpit. It has been pointed out that the voice of a person speaking on Gerizim can be distinctly heard both on Ebal and in the valley between.

8. *the trees went forth.* The parable has ever been a most effective means of arresting and holding the attention, not only of children and primitive peoples, but also of the mature minds of all generations.

on a time. This is expressed in the Hebrew by the infinite absolute added to the finite verb.

the olive-tree. A particularly apt choice of metaphor for a scene set in the fertile valley of Shechem where, even today, beautiful groves of olive-trees flourish.

9. *should I leave,* etc. The point of the reply is the unwillingness of really able men to abandon the tasks in which they are interested for rank and power.

honour God and man. The oil produced from the olive provided illumination in the Tabernacle and the home, as well as the unguent used in anointing kings and High Priests (Kimchi, Metsudath David). The olive was also part of the people's diet (Kimchi).

hold sway. lit. 'sway.' To the imaginative mind, the swaying of the tree in the breeze readily conjures up the picture of a monarch nodding approval of his subjects' actions. The preposition *over* favours this interpretation against the alternative 'stag-

Should I leave my sweetness, and my good fruitage, and go to hold sway over the trees? 12. And the trees said unto the vine: Come thou, and reign over us. 13. And the vine said unto them: Should I leave my wine, which cheereth God and man, and go to hold sway over the trees? 14. Then said all the trees unto the bramble: Come thou, and reign over us. 15. And the bramble said unto the trees: If in truth ye **anoint me king over you, then come and take refuge in my shadow; and if not, let fire come out of the**

הֶחֳדַ֫לְתִּי אֶת־מְתָקִי וְאֶת־
תְּנוּבָתִי הַטּוֹבָה וְהָלַכְתִּי לָנ֫וּעַ
עַל־הָעֵצִים׃ וַיֹּאמְרוּ הָעֵצִים 12
לַגָּ֑פֶן לְכִי־אַתְּ מָלְכִי עָלֵינוּ׃
וַתֹּ֫אמֶר לָהֶם הַגֶּ֫פֶן הֶחֳדַ֫לְתִּי 13
אֶת־תִּירוֹשִׁי הַמְשַׂמֵּחַ אֱלֹהִים
וַאֲנָשִׁים וְהָלַכְתִּי לָנ֫וּעַ עַל־
הָעֵצִים׃ וַיֹּאמְרוּ כָל־הָעֵצִים 14
אֶל־הָאָ֑טָד לֵךְ אַתָּה מְלָךְ־
עָלֵינוּ׃ וַיֹּאמֶר הָאָטָד אֶל־ 15
הָעֵצִים אִם בֶּאֱמֶת אַתֶּם
מֹשְׁחִים אֹתִי לְמֶ֫לֶךְ עֲלֵיכֶם
בֹּ֫אוּ חֲסוּ בְצִלִּי וְאִם־אַ֫יִן תֵּצֵא
אֵשׁ מִן־הָאָטָד וְתֹאכַל אֶת־

v. 12. מלכי ק׳

ger, shake, wander. Early commentators, however, render, 'to wander because of the trees' (Abarbanel, Metsudath David).

11. *my sweetness.* The fig has a delicious sweetness both when fresh and dried.

fruitage. The Hebrew denotes 'produce' and has been rendered 'crop.' Kimchi in Shorashim explains it as 'the emerging of the fruits and vegetables and their development.' The yield of the fig-tree may be as much as two or three crops in a year.

13. *wine.* The noun used here, *tirosh*, is not always synonymous with *yayin*, the common word for 'wine.' In Hos. iv. 11 it is differentiated in the Hebrew and translated *new wine.* Kimchi *ad loc.* interprets it as newly fermented wine which people drink readily and become intoxicated. *Yayin* is the stronger, aged variety.

cheereth. With reference to God the verb can only be regarded as a figure of speech. The Jewish commentators understand it to allude to the joy which God, so to speak,

derives from the intonation of the appropriate Psalms which were sung over offerings in which wine played a part (Rashi, Kimchi, Metsudath David from Ber. 35a). As for wine cheering man, cf. Ps. civ. 14.

14. *bramble.* Having failed to tempt the useful types, the trees, as a last resort, offer the crown to the lowest grade of plant, the bramble. It is found in the neighborhood of Shechem clinging to the rocks. Jotham may actually have pointed to it as he spoke, so adding emphasis to his denunciation.

15. *if in truth.* The bramble finds it hard to believe that the offer is made to it seriously. He therefore asks, 'If in truth, not in derision, ye anoint me . . .' (Metsudath David).

in my shadow. Put your faith in me and trust to my care. The irony must have been evident to those who heard the fable. The thought of the stately trees seeking protection beneath the contemptible bramble was an absurdity (see Abarbanel).

let fire come out. The dry and leafless thorn,

bramble, and devour the cedars of Lebanon. 16. Now therefore, if ye have dealt truly and uprightly, in that ye have made Abimelech king, and if ye have dealt well with Jerubbaal and his house, and have done unto him according to the deserving of his hands—17. for my father fought for you, and adventured his life, and delivered you out of the hand of Midian; 18. and ye are risen up against my father's house this day, and have slain his sons, threescore and ten persons, upon one stone, and have made Abimelech, the son of his maidservant, king over the men of Shechem, because he is your brother —19. if ye then have dealt truly and uprightly with Jerubbaal and with

16 אַרְזֵי הַלְּבָנוֹן: וְעַתָּה אִם־
בֶּאֱמֶת וּבְתָמִים עֲשִׂיתֶם
וַתַּמְלִיכוּ אֶת־אֲבִימֶלֶךְ
וְאִם־טוֹבָה עֲשִׂיתֶם עִם־
יְרֻבַּעַל וְעִם־בֵּיתוֹ וְאִם־
כִּגְמוּל יָדָיו עֲשִׂיתֶם לוֹ:
17 אֲשֶׁר־נִלְחַם אָבִי עֲלֵיכֶם
וַיַּשְׁלֵךְ אֶת־נַפְשׁוֹ מִנֶּגֶד וַיַּצֵּל
18 אֶתְכֶם מִיַּד מִדְיָן: וְאַתֶּם
קַמְתֶּם עַל־בֵּית אָבִי הַיּוֹם
וַתַּהַרְגוּ אֶת־בָּנָיו שִׁבְעִים אִישׁ
עַל־אֶבֶן אֶחָת וַתַּמְלִיכוּ אֶת־
אֲבִימֶלֶךְ בֶּן־אֲמָתוֹ עַל־
בַּעֲלֵי שְׁכֶם כִּי אֲחִיכֶם הוּא:
19 וְאִם־בֶּאֱמֶת וּבְתָמִים עֲשִׂיתֶם
עִם־יְרֻבַּעַל וְעִם־בֵּיתוֹ הַיּוֹם

useless in itself, was liable in the hot Mesopotamian summer to catch fire and set corn-fields and forests ablaze.

the cedars of Lebanon. The noblest tree in Palestine and one of the most famous in the world, the cedar presented a vivid contrast to the bramble. As a metaphor it must have been extremely flattering to the leaders of Shechem.

16–21 APPLICATION OF THE PARABLE

16. The verse introduces a threefold protasis, followed in verses 17 and 18 by a parenthesis, in which the speaker drives home with bitter resentment the forgotten service rendered by Jerubbaal and the baseness of the ingratitude displayed by his former followers.

uprightly. Sincerely, in good faith. The strong appeal to truth and sincerity evidences a conviction that eventually truth must triumph and Divine retribution was a reality.

17. *adventured his life.* lit. 'cast away his soul to a distance,' as something of no consequence to him when the welfare of his people was involved.

18. *have slain.* The men of Shechem, by providing the means wherewith Abimelech hired the assassins, were accomplices in the crime (cf. verse 24).

he is your brother. Cf. verses 2f.

19. *if.* This resumes the protasis in the second half of verse 16 (Malbim).

his house this day, then rejoice ye in Abimelech, and let him also rejoice in you. 20. But if not, let fire come out from Abimelech, and devour the men of Shechem, and Beth-millo; and let fire come out from the men of Shechem, and from Beth-millo, and devour Abimelech.' 21. And Jotham ran away, and fled, and went to Beer, and dwelt there, for fear of Abimelech his brother.

22. And Abimelech was prince over Israel three years. 23. And God sent an evil spirit between Abimelech and the men of Shechem; and the men of Shechem dealt treacherously with Abimelech; 24.

הֱיֵה שְׂמַחוּ בַּאֲבִימֶלֶךְ וְיִשְׂמַח
20 גַּם־הוּא בָּכֶם: וְאִם־אַיִן
תֵּצֵא אֵשׁ מֵאֲבִימֶלֶךְ וְתֹאכַל
אֶת־בַּעֲלֵי שְׁכֶם וְאֶת־בֵּית
מִלּוֹא וְתֵצֵא אֵשׁ מִבַּעֲלֵי שְׁכֶם
וּמִבֵּית מִלּוֹא וְתֹאכַל אֶת־
21 אֲבִימֶלֶךְ: וַיָּנָס יוֹתָם וַיִּבְרַח
וַיֵּלֶךְ בְּאֵרָה וַיֵּשֶׁב שָׁם מִפְּנֵי
אֲבִימֶלֶךְ אָחִיו:
22 וַיָּשַׂר אֲבִימֶלֶךְ עַל־יִשְׂרָאֵל
23 שָׁלֹשׁ שָׁנִים: וַיִּשְׁלַח אֱלֹהִים
רוּחַ רָעָה בֵּין אֲבִימֶלֶךְ וּבֵין
בַּעֲלֵי שְׁכֶם וַיִּבְגְּדוּ בַעֲלֵי־
24 שְׁכֶם בַּאֲבִימֶלֶךְ: לָבוֹא חֲמַס

rejoice. There is a tone of sarcasm in the expression (Daath Soferim).

20. *but if not.* And what Jotham now says is the truth (Malbim).

let fire come out from the men of Shechem. i.e. the same fire from Abimelech which would consume his subjects. The belief in just retribution on the principle of 'measure for measure' is here again illustrated.

21. *Beer.* There is no indication which of the many places bearing this name (meaning 'well') is intended. Some suppose that it was Beer-sheba, a suitable place of retreat from the point of view of distance. Some suggest Beeroth (Josh. ix. 17; 2 Sam. iv. 2), three hours' journey north of Jerusalem (Daath Soferim); and others again Khirbet el-Bireh, a village eight miles north of Beth-shean (Daath Mikra).

22–25 FRICTION BETWEEN ABIMELECH AND HIS SUBJECTS

22. *was prince.* The root *sur* is used in pre-

ference to *malach* (reigned) because he seized the rulership by force (Rashi, Kimchi). The latter adds that this is also due to the fact that he did not rule over all Israel.

over Israel. His sway must therefore have extended beyond Shechem and Beth-millo. Daath Mikra suggests that, since Shechem was the most prominent and wealthiest city in the region, his sphere of influence must have spread throughout the center of the country.

23. *an evil spirit.* i.e. mutual hatred and mistrust. Compare the evil spirit of Saul (1 Sam. xvi. 14) and Ahab's prophets (I Kings xxii. 21f.). In Hebraic thought the good and bad emanate ultimately from God (cf. Isa. xiv. 7); yet *the ways of the LORD are right, and the just do walk in them; but transgressors do stumble therein* (Hos. xiv. 10).

dealt treacherously. As predicted by Jotham (verse 20) only three years before.

24. This verse explains the dissension and

that the violence done to the threescore and ten sons of Jerubbaal
might come, and that their blood
might be laid upon Abimelech their
brother, who slew them, and upon
the men of Shechem, who strengthened his hands to slay his brethren.
25. And the men of Shechem set
liers-in-wait for him on the tops of
the mountains, and they robbed all
that came along that way by them;
and it was told Abimelech.

26. And Gaal the son of Ebed
came with his brethren, and went
on to Shechem; and the men of
Shechem put their trust in him.
27. And they went out into the field,
and gathered their vineyards, and
trod the grapes, and held festival,

שִׁבְעִים בְּנֵי־יְרֻבַּעַל וְדָמָם
לָשׂוּם עַל־אֲבִימֶלֶךְ אֲחִיהֶם
אֲשֶׁר הָרַג אוֹתָם וְעַל בַּעֲלֵי
שְׁכֶם אֲשֶׁר־חִזְּקוּ אֶת־יָדָיו
25 לַהֲרֹג אֶת־אֶחָיו: וַיָּשִׂימוּ לוֹ
בַעֲלֵי שְׁכֶם מְאָרְבִים עַל
רָאשֵׁי הֶהָרִים וַיִּגְזְלוּ אֵת כָּל־
אֲשֶׁר־יַעֲבֹר עֲלֵיהֶם בַּדָּרֶךְ
וַיֻּגַּד לַאֲבִימֶלֶךְ:
26 וַיָּבֹא גַּעַל בֶּן־עֶבֶד וְאֶחָיו
וַיַּעַבְרוּ בִּשְׁכֶם וַיִּבְטְחוּ־בוֹ
27 בַּעֲלֵי שְׁכֶם: וַיֵּצְאוּ הַשָּׂדֶה
וַיִּבְצְרוּ אֶת־כַּרְמֵיהֶם וַיִּדְרְכוּ
וַיַּעֲשׂוּ הִלּוּלִים וַיָּבֹאוּ בֵּית

resultant catastrophe as no mere accident,
but the effect of the working of Divine retribution (Kimchi, Metsudath David).

25. *for him.* viz. Abimelech; the ambush
was placed in a position to give warning of
his approach (Abarbanel). Others translate
lo 'to his damage' and assume that the
ambush waylaid those who were bringing
tribute to him, or reduced the revenues by
making the roads unsafe for travellers
(Daath Mikra).

it was told. The expression lends colour to
the suggestion that Abimelech's seat of
government was not in Shechem, which is
supported by what is related in verse 31 (see
Daath Soferim).

26–41 REBELLION AGAINST ABIMELECH

26. A foreign upstart named Gaal arrives
with some confederates at Shechem and succeeds in winning the confidence of the
citizens.

Gaal the son of Ebed. His name is associated

with the root *ga'al,* 'to abhor' and that of his
father denotes 'slave.' In spite of his name,
'the abhorrent one, son of a slave,' he has
been described by modern scholars as a
shrewd demagogue.

went on to. lit. 'passed in'; perhaps 'moved
into, went over.' It is not clear from the text
whether the rebels entered the city or wandered about the outskirts.

put their trust in him. They reckoned on his
help in the revolt they were planning against
Abimelech (Metsudath David).

27. The purpose of the verse is to inform us
that whereas up to then the citizens were
afraid to celebrate the vintage publicly, they
now openly defied Abimelech; or a public
celebration of this kind was an occasion
which brought to the surface the latent
discontent with Abimelech's rule (Abarbanel).

festival. The noun *hillulim* occurs again only
in Lev. xix. 24 where it is translated *giving*

and went into the house of their god, and did eat and drink, and cursed Abimelech. 28. And Gaal the son of Ebed said: 'Who is Abimelech, and who is Shechem, that we should serve him? is not he the son of Jerubbaal? and Zebul his officer? serve ye the men of Hamor the father of Shechem; but why should we serve him? 29. And would that this people were under my hand! then would I remove Abimelech.' And he said to Abimelech: 'Increase thine army, and come out.' 30. And when Zebul the ruler of the city heard the words of Gaal the son of Ebed, his anger was kindled. 31. And he sent messengers unto Abimelech

אֱלֹהֵיהֶם וַיֹּאכְלוּ וַיִּשְׁתּוּ
וַיְקַלְלוּ אֶת־אֲבִימֶלֶךְ:
28 וַיֹּאמֶר I גַּעַל בֶּן־עֶבֶד מִי־
אֲבִימֶלֶךְ וּמִי־שְׁכֶם כִּי
נַעַבְדֶנּוּ הֲלֹא בֶן־יְרֻבַּעַל
וּזְבֻל פְּקִידוֹ עִבְדוּ אֶת־אַנְשֵׁי
חֲמוֹר אֲבִי שְׁכֶם וּמַדּוּעַ
29 נַעַבְדֶנּוּ אֲנָחְנוּ: וּמִי יִתֵּן אֶת־
הָעָם הַזֶּה בְּיָדִי וְאָסִירָה אֶת־
אֲבִימֶלֶךְ וַיֹּאמֶר לַאֲבִימֶלֶךְ
30 רַבֶּה צְבָאֲךָ וָצֵאָה: וַיִּשְׁמַע
זְבֻל שַׂר הָעִיר אֶת־דִּבְרֵי
גַעַל בֶּן־עֶבֶד וַיִּחַר אַפּוֹ:
31 וַיִּשְׁלַח מַלְאָכִים אֶל־

praise. It is unnecessary to assume that the celebration here described was a perverted form of the festival as ordained by Moses in Leviticus. All nations of antiquity gave vent to their joyous emotions at the time of vintage. Hence, this was the Canaanite vintage festival (Daath Mikra).

their god. The Israelites in that region were devotees of the idolatrous cults of Canaan. It is also possible that the people of Shechem were the descendants of the original Hivites who inhabited Shechem in ancient time (Daath Mikra).

cursed. Perhaps the sense here is 'spoke lightly of.' According to the Targum, however, they actually cursed him.

28. With the citizens of Shechem in hilarious and defiant mood, Gaal calls for the overthrow of Abimelech's regime.

who is Abimelech. That he should be prince over the city of Shechem (Rashi).

and who is Shechem, etc. Why should the citizens of Shechem be under the rule of Abimelech? He is *the son of Jerubbaal,* an

alien who came from an Israelite district, Ophrah of Abiezer, and has no right to be ruler (Rashi).

and Zebul, his officer. He, too, has as little claim to office as Abimelech. If you are seeking a prince over yourselves, let him be one of the men of Hamor who was ruler over the city of ancient times (cf. Gen. xxxiii. 19, xxxiv. 2) (Rashi).

why should we serve him? viz. Abimelech (Metsudath David).

29. *would that,* etc. If only he exercised control over the people, he would soon depose Abimelech. For the sense of *remove,* cf. 1 Kings xv. 13 (Rabbi Joseph Kara).

he said to Abimelech. Gaal did not, of course, throw out his challenge in the presence of Abimelech. The words were reported to Zebul, who communicated them to the king (Rashi).

increase thine army. A message of boastful defiance (Daath Mikra).

come out. From wherever you may be and give battle (Rashi).

in Tormah, saying: 'Behold, Gaal the son of Ebed and his brethren are come to Shechem; and, behold, they will incite the city against thee. 32. Now therefore, up by night, thou and the people that are with thee, and lie in wait in the field. 33. And it shall be, that in the morning, as soon as the sun is up, thou shalt rise early, and set upon the city; and, behold, when he and the people that are with him come out against thee, then mayest thou do to them as thou shalt be able.'

34. And Abimelech rose up, and all the people that were with him, by night, and they lay in wait against Shechem in four companies. 35. And Gaal the son of Ebed went out, and stood in the entrance of the gate of the city; and Abimelech rose up, and the people that were with him, from the ambushment. 36. And when Gaal saw the people, he said to Zebul: 'Behold, there come people down from the tops of the mountains.' And Zebul said unto him:

אֲבִימֶלֶךְ בְּתָרְמָה לֵאמֹר הִנֵּה נַעַל בֶּן־עֶבֶד וְאֶחָיו בָּאִים שְׁכֶמָה וְהִנָּם צָרִים אֶת־הָעִיר 32 עָלֶיךָ: וְעַתָּה קוּם לַיְלָה אַתָּה וְהָעָם אֲשֶׁר־אִתָּךְ וֶאֱרֹב 33 בַּשָּׂדֶה: וְהָיָה בַבֹּקֶר כִּזְרֹחַ הַשֶּׁמֶשׁ תַּשְׁכִּים וּפָשַׁטְתָּ עַל־ הָעִיר וְהִנֵּה־הוּא וְהָעָם אֲשֶׁר־אִתּוֹ יֹצְאִים אֵלֶיךָ וְעָשִׂיתָ לּוֹ כַּאֲשֶׁר תִּמְצָא יָדֶךָ: 34 וַיָּקָם אֲבִימֶלֶךְ וְכָל־הָעָם אֲשֶׁר־עִמּוֹ לָיְלָה וַיֶּאֶרְבוּ עַל־שְׁכֶם אַרְבָּעָה רָאשִׁים: 35 וַיֵּצֵא נַעַל בֶּן־עֶבֶד וַיַּעֲמֹד פֶּתַח שַׁעַר הָעִיר וַיָּקָם אֲבִימֶלֶךְ וְהָעָם אֲשֶׁר־אִתּוֹ 36 מִן־הַמַּאְרָב: וַיַּרְא־נַעַל אֶת־הָעָם וַיֹּאמֶר אֶל־ זְבֻל הִנֵּה־עָם יוֹרֵד מֵרָאשֵׁי הֶהָרִים וַיֹּאמֶר אֵלָיו זְבֻל אֶת

v. 33. למדנחאי אל

---

30. *ruler of the city.* He was the governor of Shechem under Abimelech's direction.

31. *In Tormah.* This translation equates the place with *Arumah* (verse 41), following Ralbag, Abarbanel and an alternative offered by Kimchi. According to the Targum and Rashi, we should render 'privily' or 'craftily.'

will incite, etc. A free rendering of a difficult Hebrew phrase which is literally 'are besieging the city against thee,' i.e. to prevent you from entering (Kimchi, Metsudath David).

32. The strategy which Zebul proposed was put into operation as described in verses 34f.

33. *set upon.* lit. 'spread out upon,' an apt verb to describe the deployment of troops (Metsudath Zion).

as thou shalt be able. lit. 'as thy hand will find,' i.e. either kill or capture Gaal (Metsudath David).

34. *four companies.* The usual manner was three (cf. vii. 16; 1 Sam. xi. 11, xiii. 17).

'Thou seest the shadow of the mountains as if they were men.' 37. And Gaal spoke again and said: 'See, there come people down by the middle of the land, and one company cometh by the way of Elon-meonenim.' 38. Then said Zebul unto him: 'Where is now thy mouth, that thou saidst: Who is Abimelech, that we should serve him? is not this the people that thou hast despised? go out now, I pray, and fight with them.' 39. And Gaal went out before the men of Shechem, and fought with Abimelech. 40. And Abimelech chased him, and he fled before him, and there fell many wounded, even unto the entrance of the gate. 41. And Abimelech dwelt at Arumah; and Zebul drove out Gaal and his brethren, that they should not dwell in Shechem.

42. And it came to pass on the morrow, that the people went out into the field; and it was told Abimelech. 43. And he took the

צֵל הֶהָרִים אַתָּה רֹאֶה

37 כְּאֲנָשִׁים: וַיֹּסֶף עוֹד גַּעַל
לְדַבֵּר וַיֹּאמֶר הִנֵּה־עָם
יוֹרְדִים מֵעִם טַבּוּר הָאָרֶץ
וְרֹאשׁ־אֶחָד בָּא מִדֶּרֶךְ אֵלוֹן

38 מְעוֹנְנִים: וַיֹּאמֶר אֵלָיו זְבֻל
אַיֵּה אֵיפוֹא פִיךָ אֲשֶׁר תֹּאמַר
מִי אֲבִימֶלֶךְ כִּי נַעַבְדֶנּוּ הֲלֹא
זֶה הָעָם אֲשֶׁר־מָאַסְתָּה בּוֹ
צֵא־נָא עַתָּה וְהִלָּחֶם בּוֹ:

39 וַיֵּצֵא גַעַל לִפְנֵי בַּעֲלֵי שְׁכֶם

40 וַיִּלָּחֶם בַּאֲבִימֶלֶךְ: וַיִּרְדְּפֵהוּ
אֲבִימֶלֶךְ וַיָּנָס מִפָּנָיו וַיִּפְּלוּ
חֲלָלִים רַבִּים עַד־פֶּתַח

41 הַשָּׁעַר: וַיֵּשֶׁב אֲבִימֶלֶךְ
בָּארוּמָה וַיְגָרֶשׁ זְבֻל אֶת־גַּעַל
וְאֶת־אֶחָיו מִשֶּׁבֶת בִּשְׁכֶם:

42 וַיְהִי מִמָּחֳרָת וַיֵּצֵא הָעָם

43 הַשָּׂדֶה וַיַּגִּדוּ לַאֲבִימֶלֶךְ: וַיִּקַּח

---

36. *thou seest,* etc. The mocking tone in which this is said is more apparent to the reader than it was to Gaal (Kimchi).

37. *middle.* lit. 'navel,' i.e. the central hill in the district (Metsudath Zion).

Elon-meonenim. the name signifies 'oak of the diviners.'

38. *thy mouth.* i.e. thy boastful language (Kimchi).

40. *unto the entrance.* Abimelech did not storm the city since Gaal and his forces were inside (Malbim).

41. *dwelt.* This follows Metsudath David.

Malbim, however, prefers to translate 'abode,' explaining that he only stayed there for that night.

Arumah. An unidentified place in the vicinity of Shechem; the modern el-Ormah, south-east of that city, has been suggested (Daath Mikra).

42–45 ABIMELECH AVENGES HIMSELF ON SHECHEM

42. *the people.* The inhabitants of Shechem (Rashi).

went out. To attend to their usual work (Rashi). They felt certain that Abimelech

people, and divided them into three companies, and lay in wait in the field; and he looked, and, behold, the people were coming forth out of the city; and he rose up against them, and smote them. 44. And Abimelech, and the companies that were with him, rushed forward, and stood in the entrance of the gate of the city; and the two companies rushed upon all that were in the field, and smote them. 45. And Abimelech fought against the city all that day; and he took the city, and slew the people that were therein; and he beat down the city, and sowed it with salt.

46. And when all the men of the tower of Shechem heard thereof, they entered into the hold of the house of El-berith. 47. And it was told Abimelech that all the men of

אֶת־הָעָם וַיֶּחֱצֵם לִשְׁלֹשָׁה
רָאשִׁים וַיֶּאֱרֹב בַּשָּׂדֶה וַיַּרְא
וְהִנֵּה הָעָם יֹצֵא מִן־הָעִיר
וַיָּקָם עֲלֵיהֶם וַיַּכֵּם׃

44 וַאֲבִימֶלֶךְ וְהָרָאשִׁים אֲשֶׁר
עִמּוֹ פָּשְׁטוּ וַיַּעַמְדוּ פֶּתַח שַׁעַר
הָעִיר וּשְׁנֵי הָרָאשִׁים פָּשְׁטוּ
עַל־כָּל־אֲשֶׁר בַּשָּׂדֶה

45 וַיַּכּוּם׃ וַאֲבִימֶלֶךְ נִלְחָם
בָּעִיר כֹּל הַיּוֹם הַהוּא וַיִּלְכֹּד
אֶת־הָעִיר וְאֶת־הָעָם אֲשֶׁר־
בָּהּ הָרָג וַיִּתֹּץ אֶת־הָעִיר
וַיִּזְרָעֶהָ מֶלַח׃

46 וַיִּשְׁמְעוּ כָּל־בַּעֲלֵי מִגְדַּל
שְׁכֶם וַיָּבֹאוּ אֶל־צְרִיחַ בֵּית

47 אֵל בְּרִית׃ וַיֻּגַּד לַאֲבִימֶלֶךְ

would not attack two days in succession (Abarbanel).

44. *the companies that were with him.* This rendering is against Kimchi and others who translate the word here as 'chiefs,' since Abimelech led only one company. Metsudath David, however, explains it as 'one of the companies.'

rushed forward. The same Hebrew word is rendered *set upon* in verse 33 and *rushed upon* in the second part of this verse. The modern equivalent is 'deployed.'

stood in the entrance. To cut off the retreat of those who were *in the field,* i.e. outside the city, and prevent help reaching them from the city (Rashi, Metsudath David).

45. *sowed it with salt.* Cf. Jer. xvii. 6; Ps. cvii. 34; Job xxxix. 6. It was a means of ensuring desolation. Yet the city soon rose out of its ruins (cf. 1 Kings xii. 1).

46–49 THE MEN AND WOMEN IN THE TOWER OF SHECHEM BURNT TO DEATH

46. *men of the tower of Shechem.* Kimchi conjectures that they were the 'lords' of Shechem who were absent from the city at the time of the assault and now fled to the tower for refuge. The *tower* was probably not part of the city but near-by and the site of the shrine.

hold. The noun *tseriach* is unknown and occurs again only in verse 49 and 1 Sam. xiii. 6 in the plural. As a verb, it means to shout, or raise the voice (cf. Zeph. 1. 14, Isa. xlii. 13).It is, therefore, believed to be a raised building or a tower upon which the lookout stands to shout his warning (Kimchi, Shorashim; Metsudath Zion). Rashi understands it as a forest.

the tower of Shechem were gathered together. 48. And Abimelech got him up to mount Zalmon, he and all the people that were with him; and Abimelech took an axe in his hand, and cut down a bough from the trees, and took it up, and laid it on his shoulder; and he said unto the people that were with him: 'What ye have seen me do, make haste, and do as I have done.' 49. And all the people likewise cut down every man his bough, and followed Abimelech, and put them to the hold, and set the hold on fire upon them; so that all the men of the tower of Shechem died also, about a thousand men and women. 50. Then went Abimelech to Thebez, and encamped against Thebez, and took it. 51. But there was a strong tower within the city, and thither fled all the men and women, even all they of the city, and shut themselves in, and got them up to the roof of the tower. 52. And Abimelech came unto the tower, and fought against it, and

כִּי הִתְקַבְּצוּ כָּל־־בַּעֲלֵי

48 מִגְדַּל־שְׁכֶם: וַיַּעַל אֲבִימֶלֶךְ
הַר־צַלְמוֹן הוּא וְכָל־הָעָם
אֲשֶׁר־־אִתּוֹ וַיִּקַּח אֲבִימֶלֶךְ
אֶת־הַקַּרְדֻּמּוֹת בְּיָדוֹ וַיִּכְרֹת
שׂוֹכַת עֵצִים וַיִּשָּׂאֶהָ וַיָּשֶׂם עַל־
שִׁכְמוֹ וַיֹּאמֶר אֶל־הָעָם
אֲשֶׁר־עִמּוֹ מָה רְאִיתֶם עָשִׂיתִי

49 מַהֲרוּ עֲשׂוּ כָמוֹנִי: וַיִּכְרְתוּ
גַם־כָּל־הָעָם אִישׁ שׂוֹכֹה
וַיֵּלְכוּ אַחֲרֵי אֲבִימֶלֶךְ וַיָּשִׂימוּ
עַל־הַצְּרִיחַ וַיַּצִּיתוּ עֲלֵיהֶם
אֶת־הַצְּרִיחַ בָּאֵשׁ וַיָּמֻתוּ גַּם
כָּל־אַנְשֵׁי מִגְדַּל־שְׁכֶם כְּאֶלֶף
אִישׁ וְאִשָּׁה:

50 וַיֵּלֶךְ אֲבִימֶלֶךְ אֶל־תֵּבֵץ וַיִּחַן
51 בְּתֵבֵץ וַיִּלְכְּדָהּ: וּמִגְדַּל־עֹז
הָיָה בְתוֹךְ־הָעִיר וַיָּנֻסוּ שָׁמָּה
כָּל־הָאֲנָשִׁים וְהַנָּשִׁים וְכֹל
בַּעֲלֵי הָעִיר וַיִּסְגְּרוּ בַּעֲדָם
52 וַיַּעֲלוּ עַל־גַּג הַמִּגְדָּל: וַיָּבֹא
אֲבִימֶלֶךְ עַד־הַמִּגְדָּל וַיִּלָּחֶם

---

48. *mount Zalmon.* The hill has not been identified. It is believed to be the north-east incline of mount Gerizzim (Daath Mikra).

an axe. lit. 'the axes'; [the plural has been explained grammatically as a *constructio pregnans,* referring to the axes which he and the others were holding.]

50–57 ATTACK ON THEBEZ:
DEATH OF ABIMELECH

50. *Thebez.* Identified with the modern Tubas about thirteen miles north of Shechem. Presumably this city was also involved in the rebellion (Daath Mikra).

51. *strong tower.* lit. 'tower of strength.'

went close unto the door of the tower to burn it with fire. 53. And a certain woman cast an upper millstone upon Abimelech's head, and broke his skull. 54. Then he called hastily unto the young man his armour-bearer, and said unto him: 'Draw thy sword, and kill me, that men say not of me: A woman slew him.' And his young man thrust him through, and he died. 55. And when the men of Israel saw that Abimelech was dead, they departed every man unto his place. 56. Thus God requited the wickedness of Abimelech, which he did unto his father, in slaying his seventy brethren; 57. and all the wickedness of the men of Shechem did God requite upon their heads; and upon them came the curse of Jotham the son of Jerubbaal.

בּוֹ וַיִּגַּשׁ עַד־פֶּתַח הַמִּגְדָּל

53 לְשָׂרְפוֹ בָאֵשׁ: וַתַּשְׁלֵךְ אִשָּׁה אַחַת פֶּלַח רֶכֶב עַל־רֹאשׁ אֲבִימֶלֶךְ וַתָּרִץ אֶת־גֻּלְגָּלְתּוֹ:

54 וַיִּקְרָא מְהֵרָה אֶל־הַנַּעַר | נֹשֵׂא כֵלָיו וַיֹּאמֶר לוֹ שְׁלֹף חַרְבְּךָ וּמוֹתְתֵנִי פֶּן־יֹאמְרוּ לִי אִשָּׁה הֲרָגָתְהוּ וַיִּדְקְרֵהוּ

55 נַעֲרוֹ וַיָּמֹת: וַיִּרְאוּ אִישׁ־ יִשְׂרָאֵל כִּי־מֵת אֲבִימֶלֶךְ

56 וַיֵּלְכוּ אִישׁ לִמְקֹמוֹ: וַיָּשֶׁב אֱלֹהִים אֵת רָעַת אֲבִימֶלֶךְ אֲשֶׁר עָשָׂה לְאָבִיו לַהֲרֹג אֶת־

57 שִׁבְעִים אֶחָיו: וְאֵת כָּל־רָעַת אַנְשֵׁי שְׁכֶם הֵשִׁיב אֱלֹהִים בְּרֹאשָׁם וַתָּבֹא אֲלֵיהֶם קִלֲלַת יוֹתָם בֶּן־יְרֻבָּעַל:

---

53. *a certain woman.* The incident is quoted in 2 Sam. xi. 21.

upper millstone. The upper revolving stone of a handmill, circular in shape, a foot or so in diameter and several inches thick with a handle for the person who grinds. These stones were as much as twenty-seven pounds in weight.

54. *armour-bearer.* Men of rank were usually accompanied in battle by an attendant (cf. vii. 11; 1 Sam. xiv. 6, xvi. 21, xxxi. 4).

a woman slew him. [To a warrior the most ignoble death was that inflicted by the hand of a woman.]

55. *the men of Israel.* These words lend support to the view that the rebels against whom Abimelech fought were Canaanites. The inhabitants of Shechem and Thebez were doubtless mixed.

56. *requited.* The ignominious death of Abimelech was a just punishment for his crime against his family. Like a golden thread there runs through the whole Scriptural narrative the doctrine that wickedness is never allowed to go unpunished.

57. *the curse of Jotham.* Cf. verse 20.

10   CHAPTER X

1. And after Abimelech there arose to save Israel Tola the son of Puah, the son of Dodo, a man of Issachar; and he dwelt in Shamir in the hill-country of Ephraim. 2. And he judged Israel twenty and three years, and died, and was buried in Shamir.

3. And after him arose Jair, the Gileadite; and he judged Israel twenty and two years. 4. And he had thirty sons that rode on thirty ass colts, and they had thirty cities, which are called Havvoth-jair unto

1 וַיָּקָם אַחֲרֵי אֲבִימֶלֶךְ לְהוֹשִׁיעַ
אֶת־יִשְׂרָאֵל תּוֹלָע בֶּן־פּוּאָה
בֶּן־דּוֹדוֹ אִישׁ יִשָּׂשכָר וְהוּא־
יֹשֵׁב בְּשָׁמִיר בְּהַר אֶפְרָיִם:
2 וַיִּשְׁפֹּט אֶת־יִשְׂרָאֵל עֶשְׂרִים
וְשָׁלֹשׁ שָׁנָה וַיָּמָת וַיִּקָּבֵר
בְּשָׁמִיר:
3 וַיָּקָם אַחֲרָיו יָאִיר הַגִּלְעָדִי
וַיִּשְׁפֹּט אֶת־יִשְׂרָאֵל עֶשְׂרִים
4 וּשְׁתַּיִם שָׁנָה: וַיְהִי־לוֹ שְׁלֹשִׁים
בָּנִים רֹכְבִים עַל־שְׁלֹשִׁים
עֲיָרִים וּשְׁלֹשִׁים עֲיָרִים לָהֶם
לָהֶם יִקְרְאוּ ׀ חַוֹּת יָאִיר עַד

CHAPTER X

1–2 JUDGESHIP OF TOLA

1. *after.* The word does no more than indicate sequence in time; and there is no need to infer with Kimchi that the implication is that Abimelech was also among those who saved Israel (Malbim).

Tola. The name was given to a son of *Issachar* (Gen. xlvi. 13) who founded a clan (Num. xxvi. 23). This judge, accordingly, bore the name of his ancestor.

Puah. In the passages cited in the preceding note the name is borne by Tola's brother. It is to be inferred that Tola and Puah were common names in the families of Issachar.

Dodo. As a proper noun it occurs in the Bible (2 Sam. xxiii. 9, 24; 1 Chron. xi. 12, 26) and in the Amarna Letters. The ancient versions render 'his uncle,' the Vulgate referring the pronoun to Abimelech. This is an error, since Abimelech was of the tribe of Manasseh (Malbim).

Shamir. Not identical with the place of the same name in Josh. xv. 48. Its location is uncertain, but it was probably the north-eastern part of the highlands of Ephraim, not far from Jezreel.

3–5 JUDGESHIP OF JAIR

3. *Jair.* It was the name of Manasseh's son (Num. xxxii. 41; Deut. iii. 14; 1 Kings iv. 13). The judge belonged to that tribe.

Gileadite. He therefore came from east of the Jordan.

4. *ass colts.* An indication of their owner's rank and affluence in the East (Kimchi).

cities. Hebrew *ayarim,* the same noun as for *ass colts*; an intentional play on words. (Kimchi)

Havvoth-jair. i.e. 'the villages of Jair' (see on Josh. xiii. 30). Besides Havvoth-jair in Gilead (mentioned again in 1 Kings iv. 13), there was another in Bashan (Deut. iii. 13f; Josh. xiii. 30), the latter consisting of sixty

this day, which are in the land of
Gilead.   5. And Jair died, and was
buried in Kamon.

6. And the children of Israel again
did that which was evil in the sight
of the LORD, and served the Baalim,
and the Ashtaroth, and the gods of
Aram, and the gods of Zidon, and
the gods of Moab, and the gods of
the children of Ammon, and the gods
of the Philistines; and they forsook
the LORD, and served Him not.
7. And the anger of the LORD was
kindled against Israel, and He gave
them over into the hand of the
Philistines, and into the hand of the
children of Ammon.   8. And they
oppressed and crushed the children

הַיּוֹם הַזֶּה אֲשֶׁר בְּאֶרֶץ
5 הַגִּלְעָד׃ וַיָּמָת יָאִיר וַיִּקָּבֵר
בְּקָמוֹן׃
6 וַיֹּסִפוּ ׀ בְּנֵי יִשְׂרָאֵל לַעֲשׂוֹת
הָרַע בְּעֵינֵי יְהֹוָה וַיַּעַבְדוּ אֶת־
הַבְּעָלִים וְאֶת־הָעַשְׁתָּרוֹת
וְאֶת־אֱלֹהֵי אֲרָם וְאֶת־אֱלֹהֵי
צִידוֹן וְאֵת ׀ אֱלֹהֵי מוֹאָב וְאֵת
אֱלֹהֵי בְנֵי־עַמּוֹן וְאֵת אֱלֹהֵי
פְלִשְׁתִּים וַיַּעַזְבוּ אֶת־יְהֹוָה
7 וְלֹא עֲבָדוּהוּ׃ וַיִּחַר־אַף
יְהֹוָה בְּיִשְׂרָאֵל וַיִּמְכְּרֵם בְּיַד
פְּלִשְׁתִּים וּבְיַד בְּנֵי עַמּוֹן׃
8 וַיִּרְעֲצוּ וַיְרֹצְצוּ אֶת־בְּנֵי

v. 8. חצי הספר בפסוקים

cities. That was the original Havvoth-jair
after which this one was named (Daath
Mikra).

5. *Kamon.* Perhaps the modern Kumen,
east of the Jordan (Daath Mikra). Josephus
(Antiquities V, vii. 6) describes it as 'a city of
Gilead.'

6–9 ISRAEL AGAIN SINS
AND SUFFERS

6.   The broadening of their contact with the
surrounding nations led the Israelites to
adopt forms of worship practised not only in
the immediate neighbourhood, but also in
lands farther afield. Rashi points out that
seven types of idolatry are enumerated.

Baalim . . . Ashtaroth. See on ii. 11, 13.

gods of Aram. The best known were Haddad,
Ramman (Rimmon in the Bible) and Athar.

gods of Zidon. i.e. of Phoenicia. Their worship was later promoted by Ahab under the
influence of Jezebel (1 Kings xvi. 31f).

gods of Moab. The chief of these was Chemosh (Num. xxi. 29; 1 Kings xi. 7).

gods of the children of Ammon. Notably Molech
(1 Kings xi. 7).

gods of the Philistines. e.g. Dagon and Baal-
zebub (1 Sam. v. 2–7; 2 Kings i. 2f.).

forsook . . . served Him not. The apparent
tautology signifies that the Israelites did not
even serve God in conjunction with these
idols (Rashi, Kimchi).

7. *children of Ammon.* Theirs was formerly
the land across the Jordan between the
rivers Jabbok and Arnon. They were forced
eastwards by the Amorites from whom in
time the Israelites wrested the territory (Jud.
xi. 12–23).

of Israel that year; eighteen years [oppressed they] all the children of Israel that were beyond the Jordan in the land of the Amorites, which is in Gilead. 9. And the children of Ammon passed over the Jordan to fight also against Judah, and against Benjamin, and against the house of Ephraim, so that Israel was sore distressed. 10. And the children of Israel cried unto the LORD, saying: 'We have sinned against Thee, in that we have forsaken our God, and have served the Baalim.' 11. And the LORD said unto the children of Israel: 'Did not I save you from the Egyptians, and from the Amorites, from the children of Ammon, and from the Philistines? 12. The Zidonians also, and the Amalekites, and the Maonites, did oppress you;

יִשְׂרָאֵל בַּשָּׁנָה הַהִיא שְׁמֹנֶה
עֶשְׂרֵה שָׁנָה אֶת־כָּל־בְּנֵי
יִשְׂרָאֵל אֲשֶׁר בְּעֵבֶר הַיַּרְדֵּן
בְּאֶרֶץ הָאֱמֹרִי אֲשֶׁר בַּגִּלְעָד׃
9 וַיַּעַבְרוּ בְנֵי־עַמּוֹן אֶת־
הַיַּרְדֵּן לְהִלָּחֵם גַּם־בִּיהוּדָה
וּבְבִנְיָמִין וּבְבֵית אֶפְרָיִם
10 וַתֵּצֶר לְיִשְׂרָאֵל מְאֹד׃ וַיִּזְעֲקוּ
בְּנֵי יִשְׂרָאֵל אֶל־יְהֹוָה לֵאמֹר
חָטָאנוּ לָךְ וְכִי עָזַבְנוּ אֶת־
אֱלֹהֵינוּ וַנַּעֲבֹד אֶת־
11 הַבְּעָלִים׃ וַיֹּאמֶר יְהֹוָה אֶל־
בְּנֵי יִשְׂרָאֵל הֲלֹא מִמִּצְרַיִם
וּמִן־הָאֱמֹרִי מִן־בְּנֵי עַמּוֹן
12 וּמִן־פְּלִשְׁתִּים׃ וְצִידוֹנִים
וַעֲמָלֵק וּמָעוֹן לָחֲצוּ אֶתְכֶם

8. *that year.* i.e. in which Jair died (Rashi). The difficulty of the phrase that follows is overcome by some commentators by explaining the *beth* as equivalent to *mem* and rendering 'from that year' (Kimchi).

that were beyond the Jordan. These Israelites bore the brunt of the oppression (Rashi, Metsudath David).

the land of the Amorites. The territory of Sihon and Og.

9. The Ammonites seem to have followed the same route as that taken earlier by the Moabites (cf. iii. 12ff.) but penetrated deeper into the Land of Israel.

10–18 REPENTANCE AND PREPARATION FOR RESISTANCE

11. *the* LORD *said.* The message was delivered by a prophet (Kimchi).

save you. This is not in the text, but has to be inserted to complete the sentence.

from the Egyptians. Seven deliverances are enumerated in this passage corresponding to the seven forms of idolatry they had worshipped (Rashi).

from the Amorites. Above i. 34.

from the children of Ammon. They joined in the Moabite oppression (iii. 13).

from the Philistines. In the days of Shamgar (iii. 31).

12. *the Zidonians.* i.e. the Phoenicians; probably in the oppression of Jabin (iv. 13) (Daath Mikra).

the Amalekites. Who were allied to Eglon (iii. 13).

the Maonites. There is no record of oppres-

and ye cried unto Me, and I saved you out of their hand. 13. Yet ye have forsaken Me, and served other gods; wherefore I will save you no more. 14. Go and cry unto the gods which ye have chosen; let them save you in the time of your distress.' 15. And the children of Israel said unto the LORD: 'We have sinned; do Thou unto us whatsoever seemeth good unto Thee; only deliver us, we pray Thee, this day.' 16. And they put away the strange gods from among them, and served the LORD; and His soul was grieved for the misery of Israel.

17. Then the children of Ammon were gathered together, and encamped in Gilead. And the children of Israel assembled themselves together, and encamped in Mizpah. 18. And the people, the princes of Gilead, said one to another: 'What

וַתִּצְעֲקוּ אֵלַי וָאוֹשִׁיעָה אֶתְכֶם
13 מִיָּדָם: וְאַתֶּם עֲזַבְתֶּם אוֹתִי
וַתַּעַבְדוּ אֱלֹהִים אֲחֵרִים לָכֵן
לֹא־אוֹסִיף לְהוֹשִׁיעַ אֶתְכֶם:
14 לְכוּ וְזַעֲקוּ אֶל־הָאֱלֹהִים
אֲשֶׁר בְּחַרְתֶּם בָּם הֵמָּה יוֹשִׁיעוּ
15 לָכֶם בְּעֵת צָרַתְכֶם: וַיֹּאמְרוּ
בְנֵי־יִשְׂרָאֵל אֶל־יְהֹוָה חָטָאנוּ
עֲשֵׂה־אַתָּה לָנוּ כְּכָל הַטּוֹב
בְּעֵינֶיךָ אַךְ הַצִּילֵנוּ נָא הַיּוֹם
16 הַזֶּה: וַיָּסִירוּ אֶת־אֱלֹהֵי
הַנֵּכָר מִקִּרְבָּם וַיַּעַבְדוּ אֶת־
יְהֹוָה וַתִּקְצַר נַפְשׁוֹ בַּעֲמַל
יִשְׂרָאֵל:
17 וַיִּצָּעֲקוּ בְּנֵי עַמּוֹן וַיַּחֲנוּ בַּגִּלְעָד
וַיֵּאָסְפוּ בְּנֵי יִשְׂרָאֵל וַיַּחֲנוּ
18 בַּמִּצְפָּה: וַיֹּאמְרוּ הָעָם שָׂרֵי
גִלְעָד אִישׁ אֶל־רֵעֵהוּ מִי

sion by this people during the period reviewed. The LXX reads 'Midian.'

15. *we have sinned.* True repentance begins with confession of sin. It must, however, be followed by abandonment of the evil and a return to the ways of righteousness (Rambam, Repentance 1:1). This happened in the present instance (cf. verse 16).

whatsoever seemeth good unto Thee. It was better to throw themselves upon the mercy of God than to be the victims of human cruelty (cf. 2 Sam. xxiv. 14) (Malbim).

16. *His soul was grieved.* An anthropomorphism. Maimonides (*Guide* I, 41)

defined the noun *nephesh* in such a connection as 'will'; the Divine will was that Israel's sufferings should cease (Kimchi).

17. *were gathered together.* lit. 'cried together,' i.e. by means of a proclamation. They seemed to have dispersed when they realized that an Israelite army had assembled at Mizpah to offer resistance (Kimchi).

assembled. Fortified by a feeling of Divine protection. All they required now was a leader.

18. *the people, the princes.* The construction is explained grammatically as 'restrictive apposition.'

man is he that will begin to fight against the children of Ammon? he shall be head over all the inhabitants of Gilead.'

הָאִישׁ אֲשֶׁר יָחֵל לְהִלָּחֵם בִּבְנֵי
עַמּוֹן יִהְיֶה לְרֹאשׁ לְכֹל יֹשְׁבֵי
גִלְעָד:

11   CHAPTER XI   יא

1. Now Jephthah the Gileadite was a mighty man of valour, and he was the son of a harlot; and Gilead begot Jephthah. 2. And Gilead's wife bore him sons; and when his wife's sons grew up, they drove out Jephthah, and said unto him: 'Thou shalt not inherit in our father's house; for thou art the son of another woman.' 3. Then Jephthah fled from his brethren, and dwelt in the land of Tob; and there were

וְיִפְתָּח הַגִּלְעָדִי הָיָה גִּבּוֹר
חַיִל וְהוּא בֶּן־אִשָּׁה זוֹנָה וַיּוֹלֶד
גִּלְעָד אֶת־יִפְתָּח: וַתֵּלֶד
אֵשֶׁת־גִּלְעָד לוֹ בָּנִים וַיִּגְדְּלוּ
בְנֵי־הָאִשָּׁה וַיְגָרְשׁוּ אֶת־
יִפְתָּח וַיֹּאמְרוּ לוֹ לֹא־תִנְחַל
בְּבֵית־אָבִינוּ כִּי בֶּן־אִשָּׁה
אַחֶרֶת אָתָּה: וַיִּבְרַח יִפְתָּח
מִפְּנֵי אֶחָיו וַיֵּשֶׁב בְּאֶרֶץ טוֹב

v. 1. הפטרת חקת

---

what man is he, etc. The words form an introduction to the story of Jephthah which follows.

CHAPTER XI

JEPHTHAH

1–11 HIS APPOINTMENT AS LEADER

1. *Jephthah.* It appears as a place-name in the Book of Joshua: Iphtah (xv. 43) and Iphtahel (xix. 15).

mighty man of valour. The same quality was ascribed to Gideon (vi. 12); later to Kish, the father of Saul (1 Sam. ix. 1) and the Syrian general Naaman (2 Kings v. 1).

a harlot. Tradition declares that she was a concubine, and is called a *harlot* because she lived with her husband Gilead without betrothal and marriage-contract (Kimchi). According to the Targum she was an innkeeper, like Rahab (see on Josh. ii. 1).

Gilead. There is nothing unusual in a child being given the name of the land in which he was born.

2. *drove out.* This action was illegal, because by law, as Kimchi remarks, the son of a concubine had a share in the inheritance.

another woman. An opprobrious term for a concubine.

3. *Tob.* Jewish commentators regard this as the name of the lord of the land. We find a person bearing the same name in Ruth iii. 13 (see the Soncino ed. *ad loc.*). The land adjoined Syria and is usually located northeast of Gilead. It is mentioned again in 2 Sam. x. 6, 8 in alliance with the Ammonites in their war against David. It may be identical with Tubin in 1 Macc. v. 13 and Tubieni in 2 Macc. xii. 17 (see Daath Soferim).

were gathered. The text does not use the ordinary verb *asaph* but *lakat*, associated

gathered vain fellows to Jephthah, and they went out with him.

4. And it came to pass after a while, that the children of Ammon made war against Israel. 5. And it was so, that when the children of Ammon made war against Israel, the elders of Gilead went to fetch Jephthah out of the land of Tob. 6. And they said unto Jephthah: 'Come and be our chief, that we may fight with the children of Ammon.' 7. And Jephthah said unto the elders of Gilead: 'Did not ye hate me, and drive me out of my father's house? and why are ye come unto me now when ye are in distress?' 8. And the elders of Gilead said unto Jephthah: 'Therefore are we returned to thee now, that thou mayest

וַיִּתְלַקְּטוּ אֶל־יִפְתָּח אֲנָשִׁים רֵיקִים וַיֵּצְאוּ עִמּוֹ:

4 וַיְהִי מִיָּמִים וַיִּלָּחֲמוּ בְנֵי־עַמּוֹן

5 עִם־יִשְׂרָאֵל: וַיְהִי כַּאֲשֶׁר־ נִלְחֲמוּ בְנֵי־עַמּוֹן עִם־יִשְׂרָאֵל וַיֵּלְכוּ זִקְנֵי גִלְעָד לָקַחַת אֶת־

6 יִפְתָּח מֵאֶרֶץ טוֹב: וַיֹּאמְרוּ לְיִפְתָּח לְכָה וְהָיִיתָה לָּנוּ לְקָצִין וְנִלָּחֲמָה בִּבְנֵי עַמּוֹן:

7 וַיֹּאמֶר יִפְתָּח לְזִקְנֵי גִלְעָד הֲלֹא אַתֶּם שְׂנֵאתֶם אוֹתִי וַתְּגָרְשׁוּנִי מִבֵּית אָבִי וּמַדּוּעַ בָּאתֶם אֵלַי עַתָּה כַּאֲשֶׁר צַר

8 לָכֶם: וַיֹּאמְרוּ זִקְנֵי גִלְעָד אֶל־יִפְתָּח לָכֵן עַתָּה שַׁבְנוּ

with 'gleaning.' It probably conveys the idea of a slow recruitment man by man.

vain. See on ix. 4.

went out with him. They lived by carrying out raids (Ralbag).

4. This verse picks up the thread of the story in x. 17.

after a while. lit. 'from days.' It was eighteen years after the beginning of the oppression (x. 8) (Malbim).

5. *made war.* Ammonite oppression (x. 8) developed into a military campaign against Israel which had to be resisted.

the elders of Gilead. viz. the heads of the families including the *father's house* of Jephthah; hence his remark in verse 7 (Abarbanel).

6. *be our chief.* They were not asking him to act as a hired leader only for the duration of the war. The term *katsin* is used in Josh. x.

24 where it signifies a military commander, though it is also applied to a civil ruler (cf. Isa. i. 10, iii. 6ff).

7. *did not hate me.* Cf. Isaac's answer to Abimelech in Gen. xxvi. 27.

drive me out. The question was addressed to the delegation because they were indirectly responsible for his expulsion which, as rulers of the city, they could have prevented; also because among them were members of his father's family who had perpetrated the deed (Abarbanel, Metsudath David).

when ye are in distress. He reproaches them, not so much for coming to him when they needed his aid, but for not coming to his help when he needed them. 'If you were not prepared to help me in my trouble,' he says in effect, 'why do you expect me to help you in yours?' (Metsudath David).

8. *therefore.* Because we have wronged you (Abarbanel, Malbim).

go with us, and fight with the children of Ammon, and thou shalt be our head over all the inhabitants of Gilead.' 9. And Jephthah said unto the elders of Gilead: 'If ye bring me back home to fight with the children of Ammon, and the LORD deliver them before me, I will be your head.' 10. And the elders of Gilead said unto Jephthah: 'The LORD shall be witness between us; surely according to thy word so will we do.' 11. Then Jephthah went with the elders of Gilead, and the people made him head and chief over them; and Jephthah spoke all his words before the LORD in Mizpah.

12. And Jephthah sent messengers unto the king of the children of Ammon, saying: 'What hast thou to do with me, that thou art come unto me to fight against my land?' 13. And the king of the children of

אֵלַיִךְ וְהָלַכְתָּ עִמָּנוּ וְנִלְחַמְתָּ
בִּבְנֵי עַמּוֹן וְהָיִיתָ לָּנוּ לְרֹאשׁ
9 לְכֹל יֹשְׁבֵי גִלְעָד: וַיֹּאמֶר
יִפְתָּח אֶל־זִקְנֵי גִלְעָד אִם־
מְשִׁיבִים אַתֶּם אוֹתִי לְהִלָּחֵם
בִּבְנֵי עַמּוֹן וְנָתַן יְהֹוָה אוֹתָם
לְפָנָי אָנֹכִי אֶהְיֶה לָכֶם
10 לְרֹאשׁ: וַיֹּאמְרוּ זִקְנֵי־גִלְעָד
אֶל־יִפְתָּח יְהֹוָה יִהְיֶה שֹׁמֵעַ
בֵּינוֹתֵינוּ אִם־לֹא כִדְבָרְךָ כֵּן
11 נַעֲשֶׂה: וַיֵּלֶךְ יִפְתָּח עִם־זִקְנֵי
גִלְעָד וַיָּשִׂימוּ הָעָם אוֹתוֹ
עֲלֵיהֶם לְרֹאשׁ וּלְקָצִין וַיְדַבֵּר
יִפְתָּח אֶת־כָּל־דְּבָרָיו לִפְנֵי
יְהֹוָה בַּמִּצְפָּה:
12 וַיִּשְׁלַח יִפְתָּח מַלְאָכִים אֶל־
מֶלֶךְ בְּנֵי־עַמּוֹן לֵאמֹר מַה־
לִּי וָלָךְ כִּי־בָאתָ אֵלַי לְהִלָּחֵם
13 בְּאַרְצִי: וַיֹּאמֶר מֶלֶךְ בְּנֵי־

---

9. *I will be your head.* i.e. if I am victorious, I will inevitably be your head whether you agree or not (Abarbanel, Malbim).

10. *witness.* lit. 'listening.' What they implied was that God would be a witness to their agreement (Metsudath David).

11. *the people made him head.* The choice was approved by all the people; cf. the election of Saul (1 Sam. xi. 15), Rehoboam (1 Kings xii. 1) and Jeroboam (1 Kings xii. 20).

all his words. This doubtless refers to the agreement he had come to with the elders

(verses 9f.). His purpose was to add religious sanction to the compact; hence *before the* LORD (Kimchi).

Mizpah. In Gilead where the people had assembled (x. 17).

12–28 JEPHTHAH'S NEGOTIATIONS
WITH THE AMMONITES

12. *Jephthah sent messengers.* He at once acts as the official leader of the nation (Malbim).

what hast thou to do with me. lit. 'what to me and thee?', i.e. what do you want of me? (Metsudath David)

Ammon answered unto the messengers of Jephthah: 'Because Israel
took away my land, when he came
up out of Egypt, from the Arnon
even unto the Jabbok, and unto the
Jordan; now therefore restore those
cities peaceably.' 14. And Jephthah
sent messengers again unto the king
of the children of Ammon; 15. and
he said unto him: 'Thus saith
Jephthah: Israel took not away the
land of Moab, nor the land of the
children of Ammon. 16. But when
they came up from Egypt, and Israel
walked through the wilderness unto
the Red Sea, and came to Kadesh;
17. then Israel sent messengers unto
the king of Edom, saying: Let me,
I pray thee, pass through thy land;
but the king of Edom hearkened not.

עַמּוֹן אֶל־מַלְאֲכֵי יִפְתָּח יַעַן כִּי־
לָקַח יִשְׂרָאֵל אֶת־אַרְצִי
בַּעֲלוֹתוֹ מִמִּצְרַיִם מֵאַרְנוֹן
וְעַד־הַיַּבֹּק וְעַד־הַיַּרְדֵּן
וְעַתָּה הָשִׁיבָה אֶתְהֶן בְּשָׁלוֹם:
14 וַיּוֹסֶף עוֹד יִפְתָּח וַיִּשְׁלַח
מַלְאָכִים אֶל־מֶלֶךְ בְּנֵי עַמּוֹן:
15 וַיֹּאמֶר לוֹ כֹּה אָמַר יִפְתָּח
לֹא־לָקַח יִשְׂרָאֵל אֶת־אֶרֶץ
מוֹאָב וְאֶת־אֶרֶץ בְּנֵי עַמּוֹן:
16 כִּי בַּעֲלוֹתָם מִמִּצְרָיִם וַיֵּלֶךְ
יִשְׂרָאֵל בַּמִּדְבָּר עַד־יַם־
17 סוּף וַיָּבֹא קָדֵשָׁה: וַיִּשְׁלַח
יִשְׂרָאֵל מַלְאָכִים ׀ אֶל־מֶלֶךְ
אֱדוֹם לֵאמֹר אֶעְבְּרָה־נָּא
בְאַרְצֶךָ וְלֹא שָׁמַע מֶלֶךְ אֱדוֹם

13. *The Arnon.* This river flows into the
Dead Sea half-way down on the eastern
shore. It marked the southern boundary of
the disputed territory (Daath Mikra).

the Jabbok. Called by the Arabs Zerka, 'blue
river,' it empties itself in the Jordan near
the city Adam (Josh. iii. 16). This marked the
northern boundary of the land to which the
Ammonites laid claim (ibid.).

restore those cities. The land was Ammonite,
belonging at the time of the Israelite conquest
to the Amorites (Num. xxi. 21ff.). The claim was
apparently based on the fact that Sihon, the
Amorite king, has wrested the territory from
Moab (Num. xxi. 26). The Ammonites had now
merged with the Moabites (cf. *Chemosh thy god*
in verse 24, the chief god of Moab), and so
demanded the restoration of the cities which
had belonged to Moab (ibid.).

those cities. lit. 'them.'

peaceably. Without resort to war (Metsudath
David).

15. *took not away.* God had strictly forbidden them to do so (cf. Deut. ii. 9).

the land of Moab. The introduction into the
discussion of the apparently irrelevant
Moab is explained by Kimchi as emphasizing the fact that the king of Ammon was
claiming Moabite territory which had been
conquered by the Amorites before passing
into Israel's possession. Therefore Israel
had not taken anything even from Moab,
much less from Ammon.

16. *Kadesh.* According to Ibn Ezra, Num.
xx. 14, this is not Kadesh-barnea.

17. *the king of Edom.* Cf. Num. 14ff. Evidently the early history of Israel was carefully handed down from generation to
generation.

And in like manner he sent unto the king of Moab; but he would not; and Israel abode in Kadesh. 18. Then he walked through the wilderness, and compassed the land of Edom, and the land of Moab, and came by the east side of the land of Moab, and they pitched on the other side of the Arnon; but they came not within the border of Moab, for the Arnon was the border of Moab. 19. And Israel sent messengers unto Sihon king of the Amorites, the king of Heshbon; and Israel said unto him: Let us pass, we pray thee, through thy land unto my place. 20. But Sihon trusted not Israel to pass through his border; but Sihon gathered all his people together, and pitched in Jahaz, and fought against Israel. 21. And the Lord, the God of Israel, delivered Sihon and all his people into the hand of Israel, and they smote them; so Israel possessed all

וְגַם אֶל־מֶלֶךְ מוֹאָב שָׁלַח
וְלֹא אָבָה וַיֵּשֶׁב יִשְׂרָאֵל
18 בְקָדֵשׁ: וַיֵּלֶךְ בַּמִּדְבָּר וַיָּסָב
אֶת־אֶרֶץ אֱדוֹם וְאֶת־אֶרֶץ
מוֹאָב וַיָּבֹא מִמִּזְרַח־שֶׁמֶשׁ
לְאֶרֶץ מוֹאָב וַיַּחֲנוּן בְּעֵבֶר
אַרְנוֹן וְלֹא־בָאוּ בִּגְבוּל מוֹאָב
19 כִּי אַרְנוֹן גְּבוּל מוֹאָב: וַיִּשְׁלַח
יִשְׂרָאֵל מַלְאָכִים אֶל־סִיחוֹן
מֶלֶךְ־הָאֱמֹרִי מֶלֶךְ חֶשְׁבּוֹן
וַיֹּאמֶר לוֹ יִשְׂרָאֵל נַעְבְּרָה־נָּא
20 בְאַרְצְךָ עַד־מְקוֹמִי: וְלֹא־
הֶאֱמִין סִיחוֹן אֶת־יִשְׂרָאֵל
עֲבֹר בִּגְבֻלוֹ וַיֶּאֱסֹף סִיחוֹן
אֶת־כָּל־עַמּוֹ וַיַּחֲנוּ בְּיָהְצָה
21 וַיִּלָּחֶם עִם־יִשְׂרָאֵל: וַיִּתֵּן
יְהֹוָה אֱלֹהֵי־יִשְׂרָאֵל אֶת־
סִיחוֹן וְאֶת־כָּל־עַמּוֹ בְּיַד
יִשְׂרָאֵל וַיַּכּוּם וַיִּירַשׁ יִשְׂרָאֵל

---

the king of Moab. This is not explicitly recorded; but see the next note.

he would not. This is inferred from the words of Moses (Deut. ii. 29): *As the children of Esau that dwell in Seir, and the Moabites that dwell in Ar, did unto me*; as Edom did not allow the Israelites to pass through, so also Moab (Rashi).

Israel abode in Kadesh. Cf. Num. xx. 1.

18. *he walked through the wilderness.* The Israelites made a circuit round Edom and Moab, going south along the western frontier of Edom to the Red Sea and then through the desert northwards to the east of Edom and Moab (Rashi).

the other side. i.e. at the extreme northern end of Moab where the territory of Sihon and Og began (Rashi).

19. *Heshbon.* The modern Hesban, about sixteen miles east of the Jordan (Daath Mikra).

my place. i.e. the land they were making for, Canaan (Metsudath David).

20. *Jahaz.* See on Josh. xiii. 18.

the land of the Amorites, the inhabitants of that country. 22. And they possessed all the border of the Amorites, from the Arnon even unto the Jabbok, and from the wilderness even unto the Jordan. 23. So now the LORD, the God of Israel, hath dispossessed the Amorites from before His people Israel, and shouldest thou possess them? 24. Wilt not thou possess that which Chemosh thy god giveth thee to possess? So whomsoever the LORD our God hath dispossessed from before us, them will we possess. 25. And now art thou any thing better than Balak the son of Zippor, king of Moab? did he ever strive against Israel, or did he ever fight against them? 26. While Israel dwelt in Heshbon and its towns, and in Aroer and its towns, and in all the cities that are along by the side

אֶת כָּל־אֶרֶץ הָאֱמֹרִי יוֹשֵׁב
22 הָאָרֶץ הַהִיא: וַיִּירְשׁוּ אֵת
כָּל־גְּבוּל הָאֱמֹרִי מֵאַרְנוֹן
וְעַד־הַיַּבֹּק וּמִן־הַמִּדְבָּר
23 וְעַד־הַיַּרְדֵּן: וְעַתָּה יְהוָה |
אֱלֹהֵי יִשְׂרָאֵל הוֹרִישׁ אֶת־
הָאֱמֹרִי מִפְּנֵי עַמּוֹ יִשְׂרָאֵל
24 וְאַתָּה תִּירָשֶׁנּוּ: הֲלֹא אֵת אֲשֶׁר
יוֹרִישְׁךָ כְּמוֹשׁ אֱלֹהֶיךָ אוֹתוֹ
תִירָשׁ וְאֵת כָּל־אֲשֶׁר הוֹרִישׁ
יְהוָה אֱלֹהֵינוּ מִפָּנֵינוּ אוֹתוֹ
25 נִירָשׁ: וְעַתָּה הֲטוֹב טוֹב אַתָּה
מִבָּלָק בֶּן־צִפּוֹר מֶלֶךְ מוֹאָב
הֲרֹב רָב עִם־יִשְׂרָאֵל אִם־
26 נִלְחֹם נִלְחַם בָּם: בְּשֶׁבֶת
יִשְׂרָאֵל בְּחֶשְׁבּוֹן וּבִבְנוֹתֶיהָ
וּבְעַרְעוֹר וּבִבְנוֹתֶיהָ וּבְכָל־
הֶעָרִים אֲשֶׁר עַל־יְדֵי אַרְנוֹן

22. The delimitation of boundaries in this verse leaves no room for the Ammonites, except perhaps in the desert.

23. *shouldest thou possess them?* Would the Ammonites presume to undo the work of God? (Metsudath David).

24. *Chemosh.* Commentators recognize the anomaly of introducing the national god of Moab into the present context. Kimchi points out the biting sarcasm of Jephthah's words: 'You are demanding land which belonged to Moab whose god was unable to save it from falling into the hands of the Amorites. Take, then, possession of the land which Chemosh does give to you!'

25. *better.* Superior in military power (Ramban, Num. xxii. 4).

Balak. Cf. Num. xxiff.

did he ever fight against them? Balak did not venture to meet Israel in battle, but instead called in the aid of a soothsayer who failed him. Would, then, the king of Ammon, with the weaker forces at his disposal, dare to attempt what Balak was afraid to do?

26. *Aroer.* The modern Ara'ir on the bank of the Arnon; the southernmost city of Israel east of the Jordan. The text has the variant *Ar'or*.

of the Arnon, three hundred years; wherefore did ye not recover them within that time? 27. I therefore have not sinned against thee, but thou doest me wrong to war against me; the LORD, the Judge, be judge this day between the children of Israel and the children of Ammon.' 28. Howbeit the king of the children of Ammon hearkened not unto the words of Jephthah which he sent him.

29. Then the spirit of the LORD came upon Jephthah, and he passed over Gilead and Manasseh, and passed over Mizpeh of Gilead, and from Mizpeh of Gilead he passed over unto the children of Ammon. 30. And Jephthah vowed a vow unto the LORD and said: 'If Thou wilt indeed deliver the children of Ammon into my hand, 31. then it shall be, that whatsoever cometh forth of the doors of my house to

שְׁלֹשׁ מֵאוֹת שָׁנָה וּמַדּוּעַ לֹא־
27 הִצַּלְתֶּם בָּעֵת הַהִיא: וְאָנֹכִי
לֹא־חָטָאתִי לָךְ וְאַתָּה עֹשֶׂה
אִתִּי רָעָה לְהִלָּחֶם בִּי יִשְׁפֹּט
יְהֹוָה הַשֹּׁפֵט הַיּוֹם בֵּין בְּנֵי
28 יִשְׂרָאֵל וּבֵין בְּנֵי עַמּוֹן: וְלֹא
שָׁמַע מֶלֶךְ בְּנֵי עַמּוֹן אֶל־
דִּבְרֵי יִפְתָּח אֲשֶׁר שָׁלַח אֵלָיו:
29 וַתְּהִי עַל־יִפְתָּח רוּחַ יְהֹוָה
וַיַּעֲבֹר אֶת־הַגִּלְעָד וְאֶת־
מְנַשֶּׁה וַיַּעֲבֹר אֶת־מִצְפֵּה
גִלְעָד וּמִמִּצְפֵּה גִלְעָד עָבַר
30 בְּנֵי עַמּוֹן: וַיִּדַּר יִפְתָּח נֶדֶר
לַיהֹוָה וַיֹּאמַר אִם־נָתוֹן תִּתֵּן
31 אֶת־בְּנֵי עַמּוֹן בְּיָדִי: וְהָיָה
הַיּוֹצֵא אֲשֶׁר יֵצֵא מִדַּלְתֵי בֵיתִי

---

three hundred years. From the conquest by Joshua to the time of Jephthah. The computation in years is as follows: Joshua 28, Othniel 40 (including 7 of Kushan-risha-thaim), Ehud 80 (including 18 of Eglon). Deborah 40, seven years of the Midianite oppression, Gideon 40, Abimelech 3, Tola 23, Jair 22 (one of his years overlapped Tola), 18 under Ammon, making a total of 300 (Rashi quoting the Seder Olam). Kimchi gives a slightly different calculation.

27. *I.* Jephthah speaking on behalf of Israel.

29–33 DEFEAT OF THE AMMONITES

29. *the spirit of the* LORD. See on iii. 10.

he passed over. He journeyed through the areas named to collect troops before return-

ing to his headquarters at Mizpah.

30. *Jephthah vowed.* As Jacob had done before him (cf. Gen. xxviii. 20), and as Hannah (1 Sam. i. 11) and Absalom (2 Sam. xv. 8) were to do after him.

31. *whatsoever.* Not the vow, but the form it took, was culpable. According to the Talmud (Taan. 4a), Jephthah was one of three men who framed a vow carelessly. He did not foresee the possibility that it might be an unclean animal and unfit for sacrifice which would be the first to meet him, and so he was punished by the tragedy of his daughter. Some modern commentators conclude from the phrase *the doors of my house* that he did not exclude the thought of a human sacrifice, but expected it to be a slave. Kimchi, Ralbag, and Abarbanel, on

meet me, when I return in peace from the children of Ammon, it shall be the LORD's, and I will offer it up for a burnt-offering.' 32. So Jephthah passed over unto the children of Ammon to fight against them; and the LORD delivered them into his hand. 33. And he smote them from Aroer until thou come to Minnith, even twenty cities, and unto Abel-cheramim, with a very great slaughter. So the children of Ammon were subdued before the children of Israel.

34. And Jephthah came to Mizpah unto his house, and, behold, his daughter came out to meet him with timbrels and with dances; and she was his only child; beside her he had neither son nor daughter. 35. And it came to pass, when he saw her,

לִקְרָאתִי בְּשׁוּבִי בְשָׁלוֹם מִבְּנֵי
עַמּוֹן וְהָיָה לַיהֹוָה וְהַעֲלִיתִיהוּ
עוֹלָה: וַיַּעֲבֹר יִפְתָּח אֶל־בְּנֵי 32
עַמּוֹן לְהִלָּחֶם בָּם וַיִּתְּנֵם יְהֹוָה
בְּיָדוֹ: וַיַּכֵּם מֵעֲרוֹעֵר וְעַד־ 33
בּוֹאֲךָ מִנִּית עֶשְׂרִים עִיר וְעַד
אָבֵל כְּרָמִים מַכָּה גְּדוֹלָה
מְאֹד וַיִּכָּנְעוּ בְּנֵי עַמּוֹן מִפְּנֵי
בְּנֵי יִשְׂרָאֵל:
וַיָּבֹא יִפְתָּח הַמִּצְפָּה אֶל־ 34
בֵּיתוֹ וְהִנֵּה בִתּוֹ יֹצֵאת
לִקְרָאתוֹ בְתֻפִּים וּבִמְחֹלוֹת
וְרַק הִיא יְחִידָה אֵין־לוֹ מִמֶּנּוּ
בֵּן אוֹ־בַת: וַיְהִי כִרְאוֹתוֹ 35

v. 33. ע״כ   v. 34. סבירין ממנת

the other hand, interpret: *it shall be the LORD's* if it is something which cannot be offered on the altar, and then it shall be dedicated to God and never be put to secular use; if, however, it is something that can be a sacrifice, *I will offer it up*. They translate *and I will offer it* as 'or I will offer it.'

32. *passed over,* etc. Jephthah took the initiative and carried the war into enemy territory (see Daath Mikra).

33. *Aroer.* Not the town on the Arnon (verse 26) but east of Rabbath-ammon (see Josh. xiii. 25) (Daath Mikra).

Minnith. Perhaps the site of Rujem-el-Mesaffar, east of Rabbath-ammon, the Ammonite city farthest east on the border of the permanent agriculture settlements. Past this are only villages and nomads. Therefore, Jephthah turned northward (ibid.).

Abel-cheramim. Meaning 'meadow of vineyards' (Targum, Rashi). At the northern edge of the Ammonite settlement, perhaps Horbath Wad'ah, at the bend of the Jabbok (Daath Mikra).

34–40 JEPHTHAH'S DAUGHTER

34. *with timbrels and with dances.* As was usual with women after a victory (cf. Exod. xv. 20; 1 Sam. xviii. 6).

only child. As explained below, she was actually his only child (see Gen. xxii. 2).

beside her. The literal meaning of the text is 'from him.' Kimchi conjectures that Jephthah was married to a widow with children whom he had adopted as his own, but that 'from himself' he had only this daughter. Malbim explains that even the maiden was his step-daughter and he was childless; the text is to be understood: *from himself he had neither son nor daughter.*

that he rent his clothes, and said: 'Alas, my daughter! thou hast brought me very low, and thou art become my troubler; for I have opened my mouth unto the LORD, and I cannot go back.' 36. And she said unto him: 'My father, thou hast opened thy mouth unto the LORD; do unto me according to that which hath proceeded out of thy mouth; forasmuch as the LORD hath taken vengeance for thee of thine enemies, even of the children of Ammon.' 37. And she said unto her father: 'Let this thing be done for me: let me alone two months,

אוֹתָהּ וַיִּקְרַע אֶת־בְּגָדָיו
וַיֹּאמֶר אֲהָהּ בִּתִּי הַכְרֵעַ
הִכְרַעְתִּנִי וְאַתְּ הָיִית בְּעֹכְרָי
וְאָנֹכִי פָּצִיתִי פִי אֶל־יְהוָֹה
36 וְלֹא אוּכַל לָשׁוּב: וַתֹּאמֶר
אֵלָיו אָבִי פָּצִיתָה אֶת־פִּיךָ
אֶל־יְהוָֹה עֲשֵׂה לִי כַּאֲשֶׁר יָצָא
מִפִּיךָ אַחֲרֵי אֲשֶׁר עָשָׂה לְךָ
יְהוָֹה נְקָמוֹת מֵאֹיְבֶיךָ מִבְּנֵי
37 עַמּוֹן: וַתֹּאמֶר אֶל־אָבִיהָ
יֵעָשֶׂה לִּי הַדָּבָר הַזֶּה הַרְפֵּה
מִמֶּנִּי שְׁנַיִם חֳדָשִׁים וְאֵלְכָה

---

35. *rent his clothes.* A mark of grief (Gen. xxxvii. 29, 34; 2 Sam. xiii. 19, 31; Job. i. 20). Rending the garment is still practised by Jews as a sign of bereavement (M.K. 15a).

brought me very low. Perhaps better, 'struck me down,' lit. 'caused me to kneel,' figuratively took the strength out of my legs so that I am forced to my knees (Metsudath Zion).

thou art become. [In the text *thou* is emphatic: thou of all people.]

I cannot go back. Kimchi remarks that legally the vow is invalid and could have been annulled. The Midrash Rabbah (Leviticus, end) relates that he should have gone to Phinehas or the High Priest should have gone to him and had the vow annulled. Each stood on his dignity and waited for the other to take action, and between the obstinacy of the two the maiden suffered. Both were punished: the Divine Presence departed from Phinehas and leprosy struck Jephthah.

36. [Although the nature of the vow had not been told to her, she felt instinctively that it seriously involved her. This she

gathered from the words of Jephthah *I have opened my mouth unto the* LORD, and the anguish evident in his voice and the expression on his face.]

my father. In her innocence, she does not believe that there is any way out of her predicament. She surrenders herself to God's will and harms Jephthah even more by requesting only two months (Daath Soferim).

forasmuch as the LORD *hath taken vengeance.* Both of them think that since this came about, it is definitely God's will that accompanied him in battle, that he fulfill his vow (ibid.).

do unto me, etc. The words make it evident that a dreadful fate was in store for her. What exactly it was is not told. Expositors differ on the point; but that she became a human sacrifice is by no means certain. The Israelite ethical code was strictly opposed to it; yet, according to the Talmud (Taan. 4a) and other Rabbinic sources, including the Targum, she was indeed sacrificed. As mentioned above, Jephthah and Phinehas were at fault. Cf. Ramban, Lev. xxvii. 29.

that I may depart and go down upon the mountains, and bewail my virginity, I and my companions.' 38. And he said: 'Go.' And he sent her away for two months; and she departed, she and her companions, and bewailed her virginity upon the mountains. 39. And it came to pass at the end of two months, that she returned unto her father, who did with her according to his vow which he had vowed; and she had not known man. And it was a custom in Israel, 40. that the daughters of Israel went yearly to lament the daughter of Jephthah the Gileadite four days in a year.

וָאֵֽרְדָה עַל־הֶֽהָרִים וְאֶבְכֶּה
עַל־בְּתוּלַי אָנֹכִי וְרֵעוֹתָֽי:
38 וַיֹּאמֶר לֵכִי וַיִּשְׁלַח אוֹתָהּ שְׁנֵי
חֳדָשִׁים וַתֵּלֶךְ הִיא וְרֵעוֹתֶיהָ
וַתֵּבְךְּ עַל־בְּתוּלֶיהָ עַל־
39 הֶהָרִים: וַיְהִי מִקֵּץ | שְׁנַיִם
חֳדָשִׁים וַתָּשָׁב אֶל־אָבִיהָ
וַיַּעַשׂ לָהּ אֶת־נִדְרוֹ אֲשֶׁר
נָדָר וְהִיא לֹא־יָדְעָה אִישׁ
וַתְּהִי־חֹק בְּיִשְׂרָאֵל:
40 מִיָּמִים | יָמִימָה תֵּלַכְנָה בְּנוֹת
יִשְׂרָאֵל לְתַנּוֹת לְבַת־יִפְתָּח
הַגִּלְעָדִי אַרְבַּעַת יָמִים בַּשָּׁנָה:

12   CHAPTER XII   יב

1. And the men of Ephraim were gathered together, and passed to

1 וַיִּצָּעֵק אִישׁ אֶפְרַיִם וַיַּעֲבֹר
---
v. 37. ורעותי ל׳

37. *go down.* The Jewish commentators see in the verb in such a connection the sense of 'weeping' (Rashi Kimchi).

upon the mountains. To be in seclusion (Daath Mikra).

virginity. [To die childless was a source of grief and reproach among most nations of old.]

39. *according to his vow.* A veil is drawn over the final scene. Jephthah is said to have built a house for her in which she lived a solitary life until she died (Kimchi).

it was a custom in Israel. Some commentators prefer to take the noun *chok* in its literal sense of 'statute,' and explain that a decree was ordained making the deed illegal for the future (Targum, Rashi). Others join the clause with the next verse (Kimchi).

40. *lament.* [In v. 11 the verb is rendered *rehearse.* The meaning may be that they celebrated her heroic self-sacrifice in song.]

CHAPTER XII

1–6 WAR WITH EPHRAIM

1. *the men of Ephraim were gathered together.* As the Ephraimites resented Gideon's action in ignoring them when he fought against Midian (cf. viii. 1), they were similarly offended that Jephthah took the field against Ammon without asking for their aid. Gideon and Jephthah were of different temperament; the former appeased them, the latter took stern action (Ralbag). [*Were gathered together* indicates that their intention was hostile, since the meaning is 'were mustered.']

Zaphon; and they said unto Jephthah: 'Wherefore didst thou pass over to fight against the children of Ammon, and didst not call us to go with thee? we will burn thy house upon thee with fire.' 2. And Jephthah said unto them: 'I and my people were at great strife with the children of Ammon; and when I called you, ye saved me not out of their hand. 3. And when I saw that ye saved me not, I put my life in my hand, and passed over against the children of Ammon, and the LORD delivered them into my hand; wherefore then are ye come up unto me this day, to fight against me?' 4. Then Jephthah gathered together all the men of Gilead, and

צָפֿוֹנָה וַיֹּאמְרוּ לְיִפְתָּח מַדּוּעַ ׀
עָבַרְתָּ ׀ לְהִלָּחֵם בִּבְנֵי־עַמּוֹן
וְלָנוּ לֹא קָרָאתָ לָלֶכֶת עִמָּךְ
בֵּיתְךָ נִשְׂרֹף עָלֶיךָ בָּאֵשׁ: 2 וַיֹּאמֶר יִפְתָּח אֲלֵיהֶם אִישׁ
רִיב הָיִיתִי אֲנִי וְעַמִּי וּבְנֵי־
עַמּוֹן מְאֹד וָאֶזְעַק אֶתְכֶם
וְלֹא־הוֹשַׁעְתֶּם אוֹתִי מִיָּדָם: 3 וָאֶרְאֶה כִּי־אֵינְךָ מוֹשִׁיעַ
וָאָשִׂימָה נַפְשִׁי בְכַפִּי וָאֶעְבְּרָה
אֶל־בְּנֵי עַמּוֹן וַיִּתְּנֵם יְהֹוָה
בְּיָדִי וְלָמָה עֲלִיתֶם אֵלַי הַיּוֹם
הַזֶּה לְהִלָּחֶם בִּי: 4 וַיִּקְבֹּץ
יִפְתָּח אֶת־כָּל־אַנְשֵׁי גִלְעָד

---

passed. Better, 'crossed' the Jordan.

Zaphon. A place in the Jordan valley near Succoth, on the east side of the river (cf. Josh. xiii. 27). The Palestinian Talmud (Shevi. 38d) identifies it with Amathus, the modern Amateh, north of the Jabbok (D.M.). Some commentators translate the word 'northward' (so Targum and Rashi), and explain that, after crossing the Jordan, they turned north into Gilead.

didst not call us. Regarding themselves as the most powerful of the tribes, the Ephraimites interpreted Jephthah's neglect of them as a deliberate slight (Malbim).

we will burn thy house. For a similar threat, cf. xiv. 15.

2. *I and my people were at great strife.* lit. 'a man of strife was I, and my people and the children of Ammon, very much.' [The Hebrew is awkward, but may represent the unpolished language of a warrior like Jephthah.] What he evidently meant was that he and his people were in dire straits

because of Ammon's aggressiveness (Abarbanel, Metsudath David).

when I called you. This is not recorded, and the Jewish commentators understand the statement as an additional piece of information. The course of events was, they suppose: During Jephthah's stay in the land of Tob, he was plagued constantly by the Ammonites. He turned in vain to the Ephraimites for help (Metsudath David). Others conjecture that during the eighteen years of Ammonite oppression, the Gileadites had turned to the Ehpraimites for help many times, but in vain (Abarbanel, Malbim). Now that war was inevitable, he recruited those tribes upon whom he felt he could rely (xi. 29).

3. *the LORD delivered them into my hand.* He disclaimed the victory as due to his generalship; it was God's doing. Therefore the hostility of the Ephraimites towards him personally was unjustified (Metsudath David).

4. *gathered together.* It is to be deduced that

fought with Ephraim; and the men of Gilead smote Ephraim, because they said: 'Ye are fugitives of Ephraim, ye Gileadites, in the midst of Ephraim, and in the midst of Manasseh.' 5. And the Gileadites took the fords of the Jordan against the Ephraimites; and it was so, that when any of the fugitives of Ephraim said: 'Let me go over,' the men of Gilead said unto him: 'Art thou an Ephraimite?' If he said: 'Nay'; 6. then said they unto him: 'Say now Shibboleth'; and he said 'Sibboleth'; for he could not frame to pronounce it right; then they laid hold on him, and slew him at the fords of the Jordan; and there fell at that time of Ephraim forty and two thousand.

7. And Jephthah judged Israel six

וַיִּלָּחֶם אֶת־אֶפְרַיִם וַיַּכּוּ אַנְשֵׁי
גִלְעָד אֶת־אֶפְרַיִם כִּי אָמְרוּ
פְּלִיטֵי אֶפְרַיִם אַתֶּם גִּלְעָד
בְּתוֹךְ אֶפְרַיִם בְּתוֹךְ מְנַשֶּׁה:
5 וַיִּלְכֹּד גִּלְעָד אֶת־מַעְבְּרוֹת
הַיַּרְדֵּן לְאֶפְרָיִם וְהָיָה כִּי
יֹאמְרוּ פְּלִיטֵי אֶפְרַיִם
אֶעֱבֹרָה וַיֹּאמְרוּ לוֹ אַנְשֵׁי־
גִלְעָד הַאֶפְרָתִי אַתָּה וַיֹּאמֶר
6 לֹא: וַיֹּאמְרוּ לוֹ אֱמָר־נָא
שִׁבֹּלֶת וַיֹּאמֶר סִבֹּלֶת וְלֹא יָכִין
לְדַבֵּר כֵּן וַיֹּאחֲזוּ אוֹתוֹ
וַיִּשְׁחָטוּהוּ אֶל־מַעְבְּרוֹת
הַיַּרְדֵּן וַיִּפֹּל בָּעֵת הַהִיא
מֵאֶפְרַיִם אַרְבָּעִים וּשְׁנַיִם
7 אָלֶף: וַיִּשְׁפֹּט יִפְתָּח אֶת־

Jephthah's army had been disbanded and was now recalled to meet this new danger from within.

because they said, etc. The words spoken were obviously a cutting taunt on the part of the Ephraimites which the men of Gilead deeply resented. The precise meaning of the phraseology is difficult to determine.

ye are fugitives, etc. Modern expositors abandon the attempt to interpret the passage. Based on the Targum, Jewish commentators explain: You Gileadites (who think yourselves to be brave soldiers) are comparable with the most despicable of the Ephraimites (who desert in the time of war) to be found in the tribes of Ephraim and Manasseh (Metsudath David).

5. *took the fords.* To cut off the retreat of the fleeing Ephraimites (cf. iii. 28, vii. 24) (ibid).

the fugitives of Ephraim. The phrase used by the Ephraimites in the previous verse with contempt now became applicable to them.

6. *Shibboleth.* The noun has two meanings, viz. 'ear of corn' (Gen. xli. 5f.) and 'flood of a stream' (Ps. lxix. 3). The latter was more probably in the questioners' mind, since the locality was the ford of the river. Rashi thinks that the fugitives were asked to say, 'Let me pass over the flood of the river.'

Sibboleth. The existence of dialectical variations even at that early period among the Israelites is not surprising.

could not frame. The verb meaning 'to establish,' i.e. they could not pronounce it correctly (Metsudath David).

forty and two thousand. The Ephraimites had been taught a sharp lesson, and in the subsequent history we do not again hear of their arrogant claims.

years. Then died Jephthah the Gileadite, and was buried in one of the cities of Gilead.

8. And after him Ibzan of Bethlehem judged Israel. 9. And he had thirty sons, and thirty daughters he sent abroad, and thirty daughters he brought in from abroad for his sons. And he judged Israel seven years. 10. And Ibzan died, and was buried at Beth-lehem.

11. And after him Elon the Zebulunite judged Israel; and he judged Israel ten years. 12. And Elon the Zebulunite died, and was buried in Aijalon in the land of Zebulun.

יִשְׂרָאֵל שֵׁשׁ שָׁנִים וַיָּמָת יִפְתָּח
הַגִּלְעָדִי וַיִּקָּבֵר בְּעָרֵי גִלְעָד:
8 וַיִּשְׁפֹּט אַחֲרָיו אֶת־יִשְׂרָאֵל
אִבְצָן מִבֵּית לָחֶם:
9 וַיְהִי־לוֹ שְׁלֹשִׁים בָּנִים
וּשְׁלֹשִׁים בָּנוֹת שִׁלַּח הַחוּצָה
וּשְׁלֹשִׁים בָּנוֹת הֵבִיא לְבָנָיו
מִן־הַחוּץ וַיִּשְׁפֹּט אֶת־יִשְׂרָאֵל
10 שֶׁבַע שָׁנִים: וַיָּמָת אִבְצָן
וַיִּקָּבֵר בְּבֵית לָחֶם:
11 וַיִּשְׁפֹּט אַחֲרָיו אֶת־יִשְׂרָאֵל
אֵילוֹן הַזְּבוּלֹנִי וַיִּשְׁפֹּט אֶת־
12 יִשְׂרָאֵל עֶשֶׂר שָׁנִים: וַיָּמָת
אֵילוֹן הַזְּבוּלֹנִי וַיִּקָּבֵר בְּאַיָּלוֹן
בְּאֶרֶץ זְבוּלֻן:

7 DEATH OF JEPHTHAH

one of the cities of. The text has 'in the cities of.' The Midrash (to Gen. xxiv. 13f.) explains that he was stricken with leprosy as punishment (see on xi. 35). His death was lingering, and he lost his limbs one by one as in elephantiasis in the course of his movements through the land; they were buried where they happened to drop off. Ralbag maintains that parts of his body were, at his request, buried in the different cities where he had achieved victories against the Ammonites. His purpose was to leave behind him a memorial of his deeds, seeing that he had no children to perpetuate his memory.

8–10 JUDGESHIP OF IBZAN

8. *Ibzan.* The name occurs only in this passage. Rabbinic tradition identifies him with Boaz (B.B. 91a).

Beth-lehem. Josephus (*Antiquities* V, vii. 13)

places it in Judah. Modern commentators prefer to locate it, without proof, in Zebulun (Josh. xix. 15) and equate it with the village of Beit-lahm about seven miles north-west of Nazareth.

9. *sent abroad.* In marriage with men of other tribes (Daath Soferim).

brought in. As wives for his sons. It is perhaps to be understood that he adopted this policy to extend his influence over a wide area (ibid).

judged. Probably in a civil capacity only. The decisive victory of Jephthah secured a lengthy period of peace.

11–12 JUDGESHIP OF ELON

11. *Elon.* The name occurs as a son of Zebulun (Gen. xli. 14; Num. xxvi. 26).

12. *Aijalon.* The Hebrew consonants are identical with the name *Elon*. The place is distinct from the Aijalon in Dan (Josh. x. 12).

13. And after him Abdon the son of Hillel the Pirathonite judged Israel. 14. And he had forty sons and thirty sons' sons, that rode on threescore and ten ass colts; and he judged Israel eight years. 15. And Abdon the son of Hillel the Pirathonite died, and was buried in Pirathon in the land of Ephraim, in the hill-country of the Amalekites.

וַיִּשְׁפֹּט אַחֲרָיו אֶת־יִשְׂרָאֵל 13
עַבְדּוֹן בֶּן־הִלֵּל הַפִּרְעָתוֹנִי:
וַיְהִי־לוֹ אַרְבָּעִים בָּנִים 14
וּשְׁלֹשִׁים בְּנֵי בָנִים רֹכְבִים
עַל־שִׁבְעִים עֲיָרִם וַיִּשְׁפֹּט
אֶת־יִשְׂרָאֵל שְׁמֹנֶה שָׁנִים:
וַיָּמָת עַבְדּוֹן בֶּן־הִלֵּל 15
הַפִּרְעָתוֹנִי וַיִּקָּבֵר בְּפִרְעָתוֹן
בְּאֶרֶץ אֶפְרַיִם בְּהַר
הָעֲמָלֵקִי:

13   CHAPTER XIII   יג

1. And the children of Israel again did that which was evil in the sight of the LORD; and the LORD delivered them into the hand of the Philistines forty years.

2. And there was a certain man of Zorah, of the family of the Danites,

וַיֹּסִפוּ בְּנֵי יִשְׂרָאֵל לַעֲשׂוֹת 1
הָרַע בְּעֵינֵי יְהוָה וַיִּתְּנֵם יְהוָה
בְּיַד־פְּלִשְׁתִּים אַרְבָּעִים
שָׁנָה:
וַיְהִי אִישׁ אֶחָד מִצָּרְעָה 2

v. 2. הפטרת נשא

13–14 JUDGESHIP OF ABDON

13. *Abdon*. The name is found in the genealogical list of Benjamin (1 Chron. viii. 23, 30).

Hillel. Only here in the Bible. It was later the name of two famous Rabbis.

Pirathonite. Pirathon in Ephraim (verse 15) was the home of one of David's heroes (2 Sam. xxiii. 30; 1 Chron. xi. 31, xxvii. 14). It is generally identified with Fer'ata, six miles south of Shechem (Daath Mikra).

14. *rode on . . . ass colts.* A sign of wealth and rank (cf. v. 10) (Kimchi, Metsudath David).

15. *hill-country of the Amalekites.* The name

of the Amalekites may have come to be associated with the district as the result of an intrusion and temporary occupation, or because of an early settlement.

CHAPTER XIII

SAMSON'S BIRTH

1. *forty years.* Beginning before Samson's judgeship and continuing until the days of Eli the Priest (Metsudath David).

2. *Zorah.* A border city between Dan and Judah (see on Josh. xv. 33), now Surah, about seventeen miles west of Jerusalem (Daath Mikra).

whose name was Manoah; and his wife was barren, and bore not. 3. And the angel of the LORD appeared unto the woman, and said unto her: 'Behold now, thou art barren, and hast not borne; but thou shalt conceive, and bear a son. 4. Now therefore beware, I pray thee, and drink no wine nor strong drink, and eat not any unclean thing. 5. For, lo, thou shalt conceive, and bear a son; and no razor shall come upon his head; for the child shall be a Nazirite unto God from the womb; and he shall begin to save Israel out of the hand of the Philistines.' 6. Then the woman came and told her husband, saying: 'A man of God came unto me, and his countenance was like the countenance of the angel of God, very terrible;

מִמִּשְׁפַּחַת הַדָּנִי וּשְׁמוֹ מָנוֹחַ וְאִשְׁתּוֹ עֲקָרָה וְלֹא יָלָדָה:

3 וַיֵּרָא מַלְאַךְ־יְהוָה אֶל־הָאִשָּׁה וַיֹּאמֶר אֵלֶיהָ הִנֵּה־נָא אַתְּ־עֲקָרָה וְלֹא יָלַדְתְּ וְהָרִית

4 וְיָלַדְתְּ בֵּן: וְעַתָּה הִשָּׁמְרִי נָא וְאַל־תִּשְׁתִּי יַיִן וְשֵׁכָר וְאַל־

5 תֹּאכְלִי כָּל־טָמֵא: כִּי הִנָּךְ הָרָה וְיָלַדְתְּ בֵּן וּמוֹרָה לֹא־יַעֲלֶה עַל־רֹאשׁוֹ כִּי־נְזִיר אֱלֹהִים יִהְיֶה הַנַּעַר מִן־הַבָּטֶן וְהוּא יָחֵל לְהוֹשִׁיעַ אֶת־יִשְׂרָאֵל מִיַּד פְּלִשְׁתִּים:

6 וַתָּבֹא הָאִשָּׁה וַתֹּאמֶר לְאִישָׁהּ לֵאמֹר אִישׁ הָאֱלֹהִים בָּא אֵלַי וּמַרְאֵהוּ כְּמַרְאֵה מַלְאַךְ

family. i.e. clan (Kimchi).

Manoah. The name signifies 'rest' or 'resting-place'; it is borne by no other Biblical character.

barren. Throughout Scripture the child of a marriage long unfruitful is in a peculiar sense the gift of God destined to accomplish His purpose (Daath Soferim).

3. It is noteworthy that the angel appeared to the woman, an indication of her high place in the community (Num. Rabbah 10).

4. *wine . . . strong drink.* Rashi defines the terms as new and old wine respectively. According to some authorities, *shechar,* when combined with *yayin,* includes all varieties of intoxicating liquor, made from fruits, honey, etc. According to halacha, however, a Nazirite was permitted to drink intoxicating liquors other than wine. Only products of the vine were interdicted for him (Rambam, Neziruth 5:1).

unclean thing. viz. those forbidden to a Nazirite (cf. Num. vi. 3ff.) (Kimchi).

5. *shalt conceive.* lit. 'art with child.'

razor. The noun *morah* is found again in xvi. 17 and 1 Sam. i. 11; its etymology is obscure. Rashi derives it from a root *yarah,* 'to cast away,' an instrument which removes the hair.

Nazirite . . . from the womb. He was to be a Nazirite throughout his life, as distinct from a man who submits himself to the restrictions under a vow for a stated period.

begin to save. He will not effect a complete deliverance as other judges had done, but will only *begin* what later leaders will fulfil. By his blows against the Philistines he weakened their power (Kimchi, Abarbanel, Metsudath David).

6. *countenance.* Better, 'appearance.'

terrible. In the sense of awe-inspiring.

and I asked him not whence he was, neither told he me his name; 7. but he said unto me: Behold, thou shalt conceive, and bear a son; and now drink no wine nor strong drink, and eat not any unclean thing; for the child shall be a Nazirite unto God from the womb to the day of his death.'

8. Then Manoah entreated the LORD, and said: 'Oh, LORD, I pray Thee, let the man of God whom Thou didst send come again unto us, and teach us what we shall do unto the child that shall be born.' 9. And God hearkened to the voice of Manoah; and the angel of God came again unto the woman as she sat in the field; but Manoah her husband was not with her. 10. And the woman made haste, and ran, and told her husband, and said unto him: 'Behold, the man hath appeared unto me, that came unto me that day.' 11. And Manoah arose, and went after his wife, and came to the

הָאֱלֹהִים נוֹרָא מְאֹד וְלֹא
שְׁאִלְתִּיהוּ אֵי־מִזֶּה הוּא וְאֶת־
7 שְׁמוֹ לֹא־הִגִּיד לִי: וַיֹּאמֶר
לִי הִנָּךְ הָרָה וְיֹלַדְתְּ בֵּן וְעַתָּה
אַל־תִּשְׁתִּי ׀ יַיִן וְשֵׁכָר וְאַל־
תֹּאכְלִי כָּל־טֻמְאָה כִּי־נְזִיר
אֱלֹהִים יִהְיֶה הַנַּעַר מִן־הַבֶּטֶן
עַד־יוֹם מוֹתוֹ:

8 וַיֶּעְתַּר מָנוֹחַ אֶל־יְהֹוָה וַיֹּאמַר
בִּי אֲדוֹנָי אִישׁ הָאֱלֹהִים אֲשֶׁר
שָׁלַחְתָּ יָבוֹא־נָא עוֹד אֵלֵינוּ
וְיוֹרֵנוּ מַה־נַּעֲשֶׂה לַנַּעַר
9 הַיּוּלָּד: וַיִּשְׁמַע הָאֱלֹהִים
בְּקוֹל מָנוֹחַ וַיָּבֹא מַלְאַךְ
הָאֱלֹהִים עוֹד אֶל־הָאִשָּׁה
וְהִיא יוֹשֶׁבֶת בַּשָּׂדֶה וּמָנוֹחַ
10 אִישָׁהּ אֵין עִמָּהּ: וַתְּמַהֵר
הָאִשָּׁה וַתָּרָץ וַתַּגֵּד לְאִישָׁהּ
וַתֹּאמֶר אֵלָיו הִנֵּה נִרְאָה אֵלַי
הָאִישׁ אֲשֶׁר־בָּא בַיּוֹם אֵלָי:
11 וַיָּקָם וַיֵּלֶךְ מָנוֹחַ אַחֲרֵי אִשְׁתּוֹ

v. 8. מלא ר   v. 8. הל' בדגש

---

7. behold, thou shalt conceive. A Rabbi (Midrash Rabbah to Numbers x. 5) pointed out that in reporting the angel's words the woman omitted thou art barren, and hast not borne, because she did not want her husband to know that their childlessness was due to her.

to the days of his death. She rightly inferred this from the angel's words in verse 5 though he may not have explicitly said so (Abarbanel).

8. that shall be born. The angel's instructions had been to the woman, apart from the child's hair remaining uncut. Manoah therefore requested more details about the child's special upbringing (Metsudath David).

10. that day. lit. 'on the day,' the memorable day (Metsudath David).

11. went after his wife. Followed her advice (Rashi).

man, and said unto him: 'Art thou
the man that spokest unto the
woman?' And he said: 'I am.'
12. And Manoah said: 'Now when
thy word cometh to pass, what shall
be the rule for the child, and what
shall be done with him?' 13. And
the angel of the LORD said unto
Manoah: 'Of all that I said unto the
woman let her beware. 14. She
may not eat of any thing that cometh
of the grape-vine, neither let her
drink wine or strong drink, nor eat
any unclean thing; all that I commanded her let her observe.' 15.
And Manoah said unto the angel of
the LORD: 'I pray thee, let us detain
thee, that we may make ready a kid
for thee.' 16. And the angel of the
LORD said unto Manoah: 'Though
thou detain me, I will not eat of thy
bread; and if thou wilt make ready
a burnt-offering, thou must offer it
unto the LORD.' For Manoah knew
not that he was the angel of the

וַיָּבֹא אֶל־הָאִישׁ וַיֹּאמֶר לוֹ
הַאַתָּה הָאִישׁ אֲשֶׁר־דִּבַּרְתָּ
אֶל־הָאִשָּׁה וַיֹּאמֶר אָנִי׃
12 וַיֹּאמֶר מָנוֹחַ עַתָּה יָבֹא דְבָרֶיךָ
מַה־יִּהְיֶה מִשְׁפַּט הַנַּעַר
13 וּמַעֲשֵׂהוּ׃ וַיֹּאמֶר מַלְאַךְ יְהֹוָה
אֶל־מָנוֹחַ מִכֹּל אֲשֶׁר־
אָמַרְתִּי אֶל־הָאִשָּׁה תִּשָּׁמֵר׃
14 מִכֹּל אֲשֶׁר־יֵצֵא מִגֶּפֶן הַיַּיִן
לֹא תֹאכַל וְיַיִן וְשֵׁכָר אַל־
תֵּשְׁתְּ וְכָל־טֻמְאָה אַל־
תֹּאכַל כֹּל אֲשֶׁר־צִוִּיתִיהָ
15 תִּשְׁמֹר׃ וַיֹּאמֶר מָנוֹחַ אֶל־
מַלְאַךְ יְהֹוָה נַעְצְרָה־נָּא
אוֹתָךְ וְנַעֲשֶׂה לְפָנֶיךָ גְּדִי
16 עִזִּים׃ וַיֹּאמֶר מַלְאַךְ יְהֹוָה
אֶל־מָנוֹחַ אִם־תַּעְצְרֵנִי לֹא־
אֹכַל בְּלַחְמֶךָ וְאִם־תַּעֲשֶׂה
עֹלָה לַיהֹוָה תַּעֲלֶנָּה כִּי לֹא־
יָדַע מָנוֹחַ כִּי־מַלְאַךְ יְהֹוָה

---

12. *rule.* lit. 'judgment'; how shall we act
towards him? (Rashi from Targum).

13. *of all that I said,* etc. Apparently the
angel ignored Manoah's request as regards
the child, but the reply is to be inferred
from the context. It amounted to this: for
the present you need no instruction about
the child; the important point is that the
mother should obey the command that I
gave her (Metsudath David).

15. *let us detain thee.* Come into the house
and accept our hospitality, the verb express-

ing the urgency of the invitation (Metsudath
Zion). Rashi renders, 'let us bring you in.'

16. *bread.* In the wider sense of 'food'
(Kimchi).

unto the LORD. Because many of his comtem-
poraries were offering to idols. Hence the
warning (Kimchi).

for. Had Manoah been certain that he was
speaking to an angel, he would not have
offered him food (Metsudath David). [Per-
haps Manoah made the request to assure

17 הוּא: וַיֹּאמֶר מָנוֹחַ אֶל־
מַלְאַךְ יְהֹוָה מִי שְׁמֶךָ כִּי־יָבֹא
18 דְבָרְיךָ וְכִבַּדְנוּךָ: וַיֹּאמֶר לוֹ
מַלְאַךְ יְהֹוָה לָמָּה זֶּה תִּשְׁאַל
19 לִשְׁמִי וְהוּא פֶלִאי: וַיִּקַּח מָנוֹחַ
אֶת־גְּדִי הָעִזִּים וְאֶת־הַמִּנְחָה
וַיַּעַל עַל־הַצּוּר לַיהֹוָה
וּמַפְלִא לַעֲשׂוֹת וּמָנוֹחַ וְאִשְׁתּוֹ
20 רֹאִים: וַיְהִי בַעֲלוֹת הַלַּהַב
מֵעַל הַמִּזְבֵּחַ הַשָּׁמַיְמָה וַיַּעַל
מַלְאַךְ־יְהֹוָה בְּלַהַב הַמִּזְבֵּחַ
וּמָנוֹחַ וְאִשְׁתּוֹ רֹאִים וַיִּפְּלוּ
21 עַל־פְּנֵיהֶם אָרְצָה: וְלֹא־
יָסַף עוֹד מַלְאַךְ־יְהֹוָה לְהֵרָאֹה
אֶל־מָנוֹחַ וְאֶל־אִשְׁתּוֹ אָז יָדַע
מָנוֹחַ כִּי־מַלְאַךְ יְהֹוָה הוּא:
22 וַיֹּאמֶר מָנוֹחַ אֶל־אִשְׁתּוֹ מוֹת
נָמוּת כִּי אֱלֹהִים רָאִינוּ:
23 וַתֹּאמֶר לוֹ אִשְׁתּוֹ לוּ חָפֵץ
יְהֹוָה לַהֲמִיתֵנוּ לֹא־לָקַח
מִיָּדֵנוּ עֹלָה וּמִנְחָה וְלֹא הֶרְאָנוּ

v. 17. יתיר י׳   v. 18. יתיר א׳

LORD. 17. And Manoah said unto the angel of the LORD: 'What is thy name, that when thy words come to pass we may do thee honour?' **18.** And the angel of the LORD said unto him: 'Wherefore askest thou after my name, seeing it is hidden?' **19.** So Manoah took the kid with the meal-offering, and offered it upon the rock unto the LORD; and [the angel] did wondrously, and Manoah and his wife looked on. **20.** For it came to pass, when the flame went up toward heaven from off the altar, that the angel of the LORD ascended in the flame of the altar; and Manoah and his wife looked on; and they fell on their faces to the ground. **21.** But the angel of the LORD did no more appear to Manoah or to his wife. Then Manoah knew that he was the angel of the LORD. **22.** And Manoah said unto his wife: 'We shall surely die, because we have seen God.' **23.** But his wife said unto him: 'If the LORD were pleased to kill us, He would not have received a burnt-offering and a meal-offering at our hand, neither would He have shown

---

himself on the point, and then used a further test by inquiring about his name.]

17. *what.* lit. 'who,' the person being equated with his name (Kimchi).

do thee honour. By the bestowal of a handsome reward; the verb *kibbed* is employed similarly in Num. xxii. 17 (Daath Mikra).

18. *hidden.* Ineffable and incomprehensible (cf. Gen. xxxii. 30) (Kimchi).

20. *when the flame went up.* Cf. vi. 21.

21. *then.* When Manoah saw the angel ascend in the flame (Kimchi).

22. *surely die.* See on vi. 22.

us all these things, nor would at this time have told such things as these.'

24. And the woman bore a son, and called his name Samson; and the child grew, and the LORD blessed him. 25. And the spirit of the LORD began to move him in Mahaneh-dan, between Zorah and Eshtaol.

אֶת־כָּל־אֵלֶּה וְכָעֵת לֹא
הִשְׁמִיעָנוּ כָּזֹאת:
24 וַתֵּלֶד הָאִשָּׁה בֵּן וַתִּקְרָא אֶת־
שְׁמוֹ שִׁמְשׁוֹן וַיִּגְדַּל הַנַּעַר
25 וַיְבָרְכֵהוּ יְהֹוָה: וַתָּחֶל רוּחַ
יְהֹוָה לְפַעֲמוֹ בְּמַחֲנֵה־דָן בֵּין
צָרְעָה וּבֵין אֶשְׁתָּאֹל:

---

14   CHAPTER XIV   יד

1. And Samson went down to Timnah, and saw a woman in Timnah of the daughters of the Philistines. 2. And he came up, and told his father and his mother, and

1 וַיֵּרֶד שִׁמְשׁוֹן תִּמְנָתָה וַיַּרְא
אִשָּׁה בְּתִמְנָתָה מִבְּנוֹת
2 פְּלִשְׁתִּים: וַיַּעַל וַיַּגֵּד לְאָבִיו

v. 25. ע״כ

---

23. *told such things as these.* viz. the rearing of the child which will be their responsibility; this would be impossible if they were to die (ibid.).

24. *Samson.* The etymology of the name is doubtful, the most probable being a derivation from *shemesh*, 'sun,' perhaps 'the sunny one' (Meam Loez).

25. *the spirit of the* LORD. An irresistible impulse accompanied by unusual physical strength, see Kimchi.

move. lit. 'strike as a bell'; the meaning is 'agitate, influence' (ibid., from Sotah 9b).

Mahaneh-dan. Near Kiriath-jearim. According to Kimchi, it was the spot where the Danites camped on their way to take Laish.

Zorah. See on verse 2.

Eshtaol. Often associated with Zorah (cf. Josh. xv. 33, xix. 41); nearly two miles to the east of it on the borders of Dan and Judah (Metsudath David, Daath Mikra).

CHAPTER XIV

SAMSON'S MARRIAGE

1. *went down.* Coming from his home in Zorah, which was situated on a higher elevation, Samson had to descend to Timnah (Kimchi from Sot. 10a).

Timnah. Generally identified with the ruined site of Tibneh, near the modern village of that name, about three and a half miles south-west of Zorah. It is 740 feet above sea-level. The place is mentioned in Gen. xxxviii. 12ff.; Josh. xv. 10, xix. 43; 2 Chron. xxviii. 18 (see Daath Mikra).

saw a woman. Apparently the Philistine women were not veiled when they walked abroad.

Philistines. At this period the weakening of Egyptian authority enabled them to develop a spirit of independence which led to a clash with Israel.

2. *told his father and his mother.* Marriage was negotiated by the parents, especially the father (cf. Gen. xxi. 21, xxiv. 4, xxxiv. 8; Exod. xxi. 9) (Daath Mikra).

said: 'I have seen a woman in Timnah of the daughters of the Philistines; now therefore get her for me to wife.' 3. Then his father and his mother said unto him: 'Is there never a woman among the daughters of thy brethren, or among all my people, that thou goest to take a wife of the uncircumcised Philistines?' And Samson said unto his father: 'Get her for me; for she pleaseth me well.' 4. But his father and his mother knew not that it was of the Lord; for he sought an occasion against the Philistines. Now at that time the Philistines had rule over Israel.

5. Then went Samson down, and his father and his mother, to

וּלְאִמּוֹ וַיֹּאמֶר אִשָּׁה רָאִיתִי
בְתִמְנָתָה מִבְּנוֹת פְּלִשְׁתִּים
וְעַתָּה קְחוּ־אוֹתָהּ לִי לְאִשָּׁה׃
3 וַיֹּאמֶר לוֹ אָבִיו וְאִמּוֹ הַאֵין
בִּבְנוֹת אַחֶיךָ וּבְכָל־עַמִּי
אִשָּׁה כִּי־אַתָּה הוֹלֵךְ לָקַחַת
אִשָּׁה מִפְּלִשְׁתִּים הָעֲרֵלִים
וַיֹּאמֶר שִׁמְשׁוֹן אֶל־אָבִיו
אוֹתָהּ קַח־לִי כִּי־הִיא יָשְׁרָה
4 בְעֵינָי׃ וְאָבִיו וְאִמּוֹ לֹא יָדְעוּ
כִּי מֵיְהֹוָה הִיא כִּי־תֹאֲנָה
הוּא־מְבַקֵּשׁ מִפְּלִשְׁתִּים
וּבָעֵת הַהִיא פְּלִשְׁתִּים מֹשְׁלִים
בְּיִשְׂרָאֵל׃
5 וַיֵּרֶד שִׁמְשׁוֹן וְאָבִיו וְאִמּוֹ

---

to wife. The Rabbis held that before the marriage the woman became a proselyte. They considered it unthinkable that a Nazirite should live with a heathen wife (Kimchi on xii. 4, Metsudath David).

3. *among the daughters of thy brethren.* The objection to intermarriage was deep rooted.

daughters of thy brethren ... my people. The former probably denotes blood-relations and the latter Israelites in general (Malbim).

uncircumcised. The epithet seems to have been applied exclusively to the Philistines. The Canaanites, with the exception of the Shechemites (cf. Gen. xxxiv. 14), are thought to have practised circumcision (Daath Mikra).

pleaseth me well. lit. 'is right in my eyes'; the same idiom, with a condemnatory implica-

tion, occurs in xxi. 25. The more usual expression is 'find favour in one's eyes.'

4. *for he sought an occasion against.* lit. 'that he (would be) seeking an occasion from.' Modern commentators define *he* as God; but it is contrary to Hebraic thought that God required an *occasion* in the circumstances here described. A.J. is correct in making Samson the subject, but the phrase should be given its literal translation. The Philistines exercised dominion over Israel, and if Samson as the representative of his people attacked some of them, a counter-attack would certainly be the sequel. The text states that it was ordained by God that Samson should suffer a personal affront at the hand of some Philistines upon whom he would take revenge as a wronged individual (Abarbanel, Metsudath David, Malbim).

Timnah, and came to the vineyards of Timnah; and, behold, a young lion roared against him. 6. And the spirit of the LORD came mightily upon him, and he rent him as one would have rent a kid, and he had nothing in his hand; but he told not his father or his mother what he had done. 7. And he went down, and talked with the woman; and she pleased Samson well. 8. And after a while he returned to take her, and he turned aside to see the carcass of the lion; and, behold, there was a swarm of bees in the body of the

תִּמְנָ֑תָה וַיָּבֹ֙אוּ֙ עַד־כַּרְמֵ֣י
תִמְנָ֔תָה וְהִנֵּה֙ כְּפִ֣יר אֲרָי֔וֹת
6 שֹׁאֵ֖ג לִקְרָאתֽוֹ׃ וַתִּצְלַ֨ח עָלָ֜יו
ר֣וּחַ יְהֹוָ֗ה וַֽיְשַׁסְּעֵ֙הוּ֙ כְּשַׁסַּ֣ע
הַגְּדִ֔י וּמְא֖וּמָה אֵ֣ין בְּיָד֑וֹ וְלֹ֤א
הִגִּיד֙ לְאָבִ֣יו וּלְאִמּ֔וֹ אֵ֖ת אֲשֶׁ֥ר
7 עָשָֽׂה׃ וַיֵּ֖רֶד וַיְדַבֵּ֣ר לָֽאִשָּׁ֑ה
8 וַתִּישַׁ֖ר בְּעֵינֵ֥י שִׁמְשֽׁוֹן׃ וַיָּ֤שׇׁב
מִיָּמִים֙ לְקַחְתָּ֔הּ וַיָּ֥סַר לִרְא֖וֹת
אֵ֚ת מַפֶּ֣לֶת הָֽאַרְיֵ֔ה וְהִנֵּ֞ה עֲדַ֧ת
דְּבֹרִ֛ים בִּגְוִיַּ֥ת הָאַרְיֵ֖ה וּדְבָֽשׁ׃

5. *a young lion.* The Hebrew *kephir* signifies a full-grown cub. Kimchi explains that the lion is known by different Hebrew words at the various stages of its growth. Beginning as *gur*, it becomes successively *kephir, aryeh, labi* and *layish.* The older it grows the fiercer it becomes.

against him. Not 'against them,' Samson having in his eagerness gone ahead of his parents or taken a by-path through the vineyards, while they walked along the high-road (Kimchi).

6. *came mightily.* Samson felt himself endowed with supernatural strength (Targum, Kimchi).

rent him. The root *shasa'* appears in the phrase *cloven-hoofed* (Lev. xi. 3).

he had nothing in his hand. The intention is to give the information that he rent the lion with his bare hands as evidence of his strength. It is not necessary to suppose that the Philistines had imposed a prohibition on the Israelites against carrying arms (Malbim).

he told not, etc. When he met his parents before reaching Timnah (see on verse 5), he did not tell them of his adventure because

he did not consider it a great accomplishment (Metsudath David).

7. *with the woman.* This rendering accords Kimchi against the Targum followed by Rashi who understands the text as 'concerning the woman,' i.e. discussed his proposed marriage with her. Metsudath David and Malbim explain that Samson had conversation with her to find out whether she was intelligent, since hitherto he had only seen her; hence the continuation *she pleased Samson well.*

8. *he returned.* He had presumably gone home after the interview recorded in the last verse. Now he went back to contract the marriage (Metsudath David).

he turned aside. An indication that when he met the lion he was not on the high-road (see Metsudath Zion).

the carcass. lit. 'that which had fallen.' Metsudath Zion adds, 'in the place where it had fallen.'

in the body. It is reported by travellers in the Arabian desert that the heat in summer dries up the moisture of dead bodies within twenty-four hours, turning them into mummies which do not emit a bad odour. Bees will not approach a putrid carcass.

lion, and honey. 9. And he scraped it out into his hands, and went on, eating as he went, and he came to his father and mother, and gave unto them, and they did eat; but he told them not that he had scraped the honey out of the body of the lion. 10. And his father went down unto the woman; and Samson made there a feast; for so used the young men to do. 11. And it came to pass, when they saw him, that they brought thirty companions to be with him. 12. And Samson said unto them: 'Let me now put forth a riddle unto you; if ye can declare it me within the seven days of the feast, and find it out, then I will give you thirty linen garments and

9 וַיִּרְדֵּהוּ אֶל־כַּפָּיו וַיֵּלֶךְ הָלוֹךְ
וְאָכֹל וַיֵּלֶךְ אֶל־אָבִיו וְאֶל־
אִמּוֹ וַיִּתֵּן לָהֶם וַיֹּאכֵלוּ וְלֹא־
הִגִּיד לָהֶם כִּי מִגְּוִיַּת הָאַרְיֵה
10 רָדָה הַדְּבָשׁ׃ וַיֵּרֶד אָבִיהוּ
אֶל־הָאִשָּׁה וַיַּעַשׂ שָׁם שִׁמְשׁוֹן
מִשְׁתֶּה כִּי כֵּן יַעֲשׂוּ הַבַּחוּרִים׃
11 וַיְהִי כִּרְאוֹתָם אוֹתוֹ וַיִּקְחוּ
שְׁלֹשִׁים מֵרֵעִים וַיִּהְיוּ אִתּוֹ׃
12 וַיֹּאמֶר לָהֶם שִׁמְשׁוֹן אָחוּדָה־
נָּא לָכֶם חִידָה אִם־הַגֵּד
תַּגִּידוּ אוֹתָהּ לִי שִׁבְעַת יְמֵי
הַמִּשְׁתֶּה וּמְצָאתֶם וְנָתַתִּי לָכֶם
שְׁלֹשִׁים סְדִינִים וּשְׁלֹשִׁים

9. *scraped.* Or 'separated.' This is an expression of separating anything which is clinging, as bread clinging to an oven. In this sense, the verb *radah* is used frequently in Mishnaic Hebrew (Rashi, Kimchi).

he came to his father and mother. Who were journeying with Samson for the marriage. He left them temporarily to visit the place where he had slain the lion.

he told them not, etc. Thus he felt secure that no one knew his secret when he proposed the riddle to the Philistines (see verse 12) (Daath Mikra).

10. *his father went down.* To complete the negotiations before the marriage took place (Malbim).

so used the young men to do. Among the Philistines but not the Israelites; otherwise no explanation would have been necessary (Daath Mikra).

11. *companions.* To act as groomsmen (Rashi). Some commentators make the far-fetched suggestion that the thirty men were attached to him by the Philistines to keep watch over his movements, since his strong appearance caused them apprehension.

12. *put forth a riddle.* lit. 'riddle a riddle.' The word *chidah* is derived from a root denoting a hidden thing. Hence, I will put forth a statement the meaning of which is hidden (Kimchi, Sefer Hashorashim). Others explain it as a legend or a tale. Hence, I will tell you a story, which you will be expected to interpret (Ibn Janach, Sefer Hashorashim): As a source of entertainment the riddle was much loved in all ages. (See 1 Kings x. 1; Ezek. xvii. 2.)

the seven days of the feast. The custom of continuing marriage festivities for seven days is already mentioned in Gen. xxix. 27 as having been practised in Patriarchal times in Mesopotamia. We practise it today because it is a Rabbinical enactment (Keth. 7).

linen garments. The noun *sadin* occurs again in Isa. iii. 23 and Prov. xxxi 24. It was made of fine linen, rectangular in shape and of considerable size, worn either as an under-

thirty changes of raiment; 13. but if ye cannot declare it me, then shall ye give me thirty linen garments and thirty changes of raiment.' And they said unto him: 'Put forth thy riddle, that we may hear it.' 14. And he said unto them:

Out of the eater came forth food,
And out of the strong came forth sweetness.

And they could not in three days declare the riddle. 15. And it came to pass on the seventh day, that they said unto Samson's wife: 'Entice thy husband, that he may declare unto us the riddle, lest we burn thee and thy father's house with fire; have ye called us hither to impoverish us?' 16. And Samson's wife wept before him, and said: 'Thou dost but hate me, and lovest me not; thou hast put forth a riddle unto the children of my people, and wilt thou not tell it

13 חֲלִפֹת בְּגָדִים: וְאִם־לֹא
תוּכְלוּ֙ לְהַגִּיד לִי וּנְתַתֶּם אַתֶּם
לִי שְׁלֹשִׁים סְדִינִים וּשְׁלֹשִׁים
חֲלִיפוֹת בְּגָדִים וַיֹּאמְרוּ לוֹ
חוּדָה חִידָתְךָ וְנִשְׁמָעֶנָּה:
14 וַיֹּאמֶר לָהֶם
מֵהָאֹכֵל יָצָא מַאֲכָל
וּמֵעַז יָצָא מָתוֹק
וְלֹא יָכְלוּ לְהַגִּיד הַחִידָה
15 שְׁלֹשֶׁת יָמִים: וַיְהִי | בַּיּוֹם
הַשְּׁבִיעִי וַיֹּאמְרוּ לְאֵשֶׁת־
שִׁמְשׁוֹן פַּתִּי אֶת־אִישֵׁךְ
וְיַגֶּד־לָנוּ אֶת־הַחִידָה פֶּן־
נִשְׂרֹף אוֹתָךְ וְאֶת־בֵּית אָבִיךְ
בָּאֵשׁ הַלְיָרְשֵׁנוּ קְרָאתֶם לָנוּ
16 הֲלֹא: וַתֵּבְךְּ אֵשֶׁת שִׁמְשׁוֹן
עָלָיו וַתֹּאמֶר רַק־שְׂנֵאתַנִי
וְלֹא אֲהַבְתָּנִי הַחִידָה חַדְתָּה
לִבְנֵי עַמִּי וְלִי לֹא הִגַּדְתָּה

garment next to the body or as an outer robe to cover the ordinary clothes (Kimchi, Shorashim).

changes of raiment. Chaliphoth denotes festive garments as against working garb, often costly and presented as a mark of favour (cf. Gen. xlv. 22; 2 Kings v. 5, 22f.) (Targum).

14. *they could not.* Their inability to solve the riddle was not surprising, because it was based on an incident of which they had no knowledge.

15. *on the seventh day.* viz. of the week, not

of the feast (Rashi). The riddle was propounded on Wednesday, and by Saturday they knew that the solution was beyond them.

lest we burn thee, etc. That this was no idle threat is seen from xv. 6; cf. the similar threat to Jephthah (xii. 1).

hither. This is the translation of the Targum, as if instead of *halo* the text had *halom* which some Hebrew MSS. read. Metsudath David gives *halo* its usual meaning 'is it not so?'

16. *before him.* lit. 'upon him.'

me?' And he said unto her: 'Behold, I have not told it my father nor my mother, and shall I tell thee?' 17. And she wept before him the seven days, while their feast lasted; and it came to pass on the seventh day, that he told her, because she pressed him sore; and she told the riddle to the children of her people. 18. And the men of the city said unto him on the seventh day before the sun went down:

What is sweeter than honey?

And what is stronger than a lion?

And he said unto them:

If ye had not plowed with my heifer,

Ye had not found out my riddle.

19. And the spirit of the LORD came mightily upon him, and he went down to Ashkelon, and smote thirty men of them, and took their spoil, and gave the changes of raiment unto them that declared the riddle. And his anger was kindled, and he went up to his father's house.

וַיֹּ֣אמֶר לָ֗הּ הִנֵּ֤ה לְאָבִי֙ וּלְאִמִּי֙

17 לֹ֣א הִגַּ֔דְתִּי וְלָ֖ךְ אַגִּ֑יד וַתֵּ֤בְךְּ

עָלָיו֙ שִׁבְעַ֣ת הַיָּמִ֔ים אֲשֶׁר־

הָיָ֥ה לָהֶ֖ם הַמִּשְׁתֶּ֑ה וַיְהִ֣י | בַּיּ֣וֹם

הַשְּׁבִיעִ֗י וַיַּגֶּד־לָהּ֙ כִּ֣י

הֱצִיקַ֔תְהוּ וַתַּגֵּ֥ד הַחִידָ֖ה לִבְנֵ֥י

18 עַמָּֽהּ׃ וַיֹּ֣אמְרוּ לוֹ֩ אַנְשֵׁ֨י הָעִ֜יר

בַּיּ֤וֹם הַשְּׁבִיעִי֙ בְּטֶ֣רֶם יָבֹ֣א

הַחַ֔רְסָה

מַה־מָּת֣וֹק מִדְּבַ֔שׁ

וּמֶ֥ה עַ֖ז מֵאֲרִ֑י

וַיֹּ֣אמֶר לָהֶ֔ם

לוּלֵא֙ חֲרַשְׁתֶּ֣ם בְּעֶגְלָתִ֔י

לֹ֥א מְצָאתֶ֖ם חִידָתִֽי׃

19 וַתִּצְלַ֨ח עָלָ֜יו ר֣וּחַ יְהֹוָ֗ה וַיֵּ֣רֶד

אַשְׁקְל֣וֹן וַיַּ֣ךְ מֵהֶ֣ם | שְׁלֹשִׁ֣ים

אִ֗ישׁ וַיִּקַּח֙ אֶת־חֲלִ֣יצוֹתָ֔ם וַיִּתֵּן֙

הַחֲלִיפ֔וֹת לְמַגִּידֵ֖י הַחִידָ֑ה

וַיִּ֣חַר אַפּ֔וֹ וַיַּ֖עַל בֵּ֥ית אָבִֽיהוּ׃

---

my father, etc. It is deduced that parents were regarded as standing in a more intimate and affectionate relationship than the wife.

shall I tell thee? An exclamatory question to which the intended reply is self-evident.

17. *the seven days.* i.e. what remained of the week from the fourth day onwards (Rashi).

18. *before the sun went down.* At sunset a new day began. They waited until the last minute to enhance the zest of their triumph (Daath Mikra).

plowed with my heifer. i.e. used devious methods. By *heifer* he made a scornful reference to his wife who had betrayed his secret. The reply in the Hebrew has the form of a rhymed couplet (see Rabbi Jos. Kara).

19. *the spirit . . . upon him.* As verse 6.

Ashkelon. On the Palestine coast between Gaza and Ashdod, about two days' journey from Timnah (see D.M. on Josh. xiii. 3).

his anger was kindled. Against his wife and he left her (Metsudath David).

20. But Samson's wife was given to his companion, whom he had had for his friend.

כ וַתְּהִי אֵשֶׁת שִׁמְשׁוֹן לְמֵרֵעֵהוּ אֲשֶׁר רֵעָה לוֹ:

15   CHAPTER XV   טו

1. But it came to pass after a while, in the time of wheat harvest, that Samson visited his wife with a kid; and he said: 'I will go in to my wife into the chamber.' But her father would not suffer him to go in. 2. And her father said: 'I verily thought that thou hadst utterly hated her; therefore I gave her to thy companion; is not her younger sister fairer than she? take her, I pray thee, instead of her.' 3. And Samson said unto them: 'This time shall I be quits with the Philistines, when I do them a mischief.' 4. And Samson went and caught three hundred foxes, and took torches, and

א וַיְהִי מִיָּמִים בִּימֵי קְצִיר־חִטִּים וַיִּפְקֹד שִׁמְשׁוֹן אֶת־אִשְׁתּוֹ בִּגְדִי עִזִּים וַיֹּאמֶר אָבֹאָה אֶל־אִשְׁתִּי הֶחָדְרָה וְלֹא־נְתָנוֹ אָבִיהָ לָבוֹא: ב וַיֹּאמֶר אָבִיהָ אָמֹר אָמַרְתִּי כִּי־שָׂנֹא שְׂנֵאתָהּ וָאֶתְּנֶנָּה לְמֵרֵעֶךָ הֲלֹא אֲחוֹתָהּ הַקְּטַנָּה טוֹבָה מִמֶּנָּה תְּהִי־נָא לָךְ תַּחְתֶּיהָ: ג וַיֹּאמֶר לָהֶם שִׁמְשׁוֹן נִקֵּיתִי הַפַּעַם מִפְּלִשְׁתִּים כִּי־ ד עֹשֶׂה אֲנִי עִמָּם רָעָה: וַיֵּלֶךְ שִׁמְשׁוֹן וַיִּלְכֹּד שְׁלֹשׁ־מֵאוֹת שׁוּעָלִים וַיִּקַּח לַפִּדִים וַיֶּפֶן

---

20. *companion.* i.e. one of the groomsmen mentioned in verse 11 (Rashi, Kimchi).

CHAPTER XV

SAMSON'S EXPLOITS

1. *after a while.* lit. 'from days.' The precise interval of time is not known. It may also mean 'after a year' (Metsudath Zion).

wheat harvest. About May; this is mentioned because of what is related in verse 5 (Rabbi Joseph Kara).

a kid. Intended as a conciliatory gift. Kids were customarily sent as gifts of affection (see Gen. xiii. 17) (Daath Mikra).

2. *utterly hated her.* Because she had obtained the answer to his riddle and disclosed it to the Philistines (Metsudath David).

3. *said unto them.* i.e. to his father-in-law and to the other Timnites gathered there (Daath Mikra).

this time. [In contrast to the occasion when he killed thirty innocent Philistines (xiv. 19).]

be quits. He felt that his action was justified since he had been wronged (Rashi, Kimchi, Ralbag, Metsudath David).

4. *foxes.* Some render 'jackals.' The Hebrew word *shu'al* is, through the Persian *shagal*, the origin of the English 'jackal.'

turned tail to tail, and put a torch in
the midst between every two tails.
5. And when he had set the torches
on fire, he let them go into the
standing corn of the Philistines, and
burnt up both the shocks and the
standing corn, and also the oliveyards. 6. Then the Philistines said:
'Who hath done this?' And they said:
'Samson, the son-in-law of the
Timnite, because he hath taken his
wife, and given her to his companion.' And the Philistines came
up, and burnt her and her father
with fire. 7. And Samson said unto
them: 'If ye do after this manner,
surely I will be avenged of you, and
after that I will cease.' 8. And
he smote them hip and thigh with a
great slaughter; and he went down
and dwelt in the cleft of the rock of
Etam.

זָנָב אֶל־זָנָב וַיָּשֶׂם לַפִּיד אֶחָד
בֵּין־שְׁנֵי הַזְּנָבוֹת בַּתָּוֶךְ:
5 וַיַּבְעֶר־אֵשׁ בַּלַּפִּידִים וַיְשַׁלַּח
בְּקָמוֹת פְּלִשְׁתִּים וַיַּבְעֵר
מִגָּדִישׁ וְעַד־קָמָה וְעַד־כֶּרֶם
6 זָיִת: וַיֹּאמְרוּ פְלִשְׁתִּים מִי
עָשָׂה זֹאת וַיֹּאמְרוּ שִׁמְשׁוֹן חֲתַן
הַתִּמְנִי כִּי לָקַח אֶת־אִשְׁתּוֹ
וַיִּתְּנָהּ לְמֵרֵעֵהוּ וַיַּעֲלוּ
פְלִשְׁתִּים וַיִּשְׂרְפוּ אוֹתָהּ וְאֶת־
7 אָבִיהָ בָּאֵשׁ: וַיֹּאמֶר לָהֶם
שִׁמְשׁוֹן אִם־תַּעֲשׂוּן כָּזֹאת כִּי
אִם־נִקַּמְתִּי בָכֶם וְאַחַר
8 אֶחְדָּל: וַיַּךְ אוֹתָם שׁוֹק עַל־
יָרֵךְ מַכָּה גְדוֹלָה וַיֵּרֶד וַיֵּשֶׁב
בִּסְעִיף סֶלַע עֵיטָם:

v. 6. נ״א ואת־בית אביה   v. 8. נ״א וילך

---

torches. Pieces of wood wrapped in absor-
bent material and soaked in oil (Daath
Mikra).

5. *let them go.* A similar practice has been
recorded in Ovid (*Fasti* IV. 681ff.); and it has
been suggested that the Romans borrowed
it from the Phoenicians among whom it kept
alive the incident narrated in this passage.

6. *her father.* A number of Hebrew MSS.
agree with the LXX and Peshitta in reading
'the house of her father' (cf. xiv. 15).

7. *if ye do after this manner.* i.e. if this is the
way you act. Various interpretations have
been placed on the clause: giving a man's
wife to another (Rashi); not compensating
me with money for the loss of my wife and
burning her (Malbim); you did not punish

her and her father for wronging me, but
took revenge on them for what I have done
(see Alshich).

cease. Leave you alone.

8. *hip and thigh.* lit. 'hip upon thigh'; an
idiomatic expression for complete discomfiture. Its origin is doubtful. Kimchi explains
it either as 'footmen and horsemen' (so the
Targum), or the fleeing and falling multitude; when a fugitive falls head over heels
his thigh is above his hip.

cleft of the rock. For the phrase, cf. Isa. ii. 21,
lvii. 5.

Etam. A town in Judah, as appears from the
following verses. The rock was doubtless
close by the town of Etam (cf. 2 Chron. xi.

9. Then the Philistines went up, and pitched in Judah, and spread themselves against Lehi. 10. And the men of Judah said: 'Why are ye come up against us?' And they said: 'To bind Samson are we come up, to do to him as he hath done to us.' 11. Then three thousand men of Judah went down to the cleft of the rock of Etam, and said to Samson: 'Knowest thou not that the Philistines are rulers over us? what then is this that thou hast done unto us?' And he said unto them: 'As they did unto me, so have I done unto them.' 12. And they said unto him: 'We are come down to bind thee, that we may deliver thee into the hand of the Philistines.' And Samson said unto them: 'Swear unto me, that ye will not fall upon me yourselves.' 13. And they spoke unto him, saying: 'No; but we will bind thee fast, and deliver thee into

9 וַיַּעֲלוּ פְלִשְׁתִּים וַיַּחֲנוּ בִּיהוּדָה
10 וַיִּנָּטְשׁוּ בַּלֶּחִי: וַיֹּאמְרוּ אִישׁ
יְהוּדָה לָמֶה עֲלִיתֶם עָלֵינוּ
וַיֹּאמְרוּ לֶאֱסוֹר אֶת־שִׁמְשׁוֹן
עָלִינוּ לַעֲשׂוֹת לוֹ כַּאֲשֶׁר עָשָׂה
11 לָנוּ: וַיֵּרְדוּ שְׁלֹשֶׁת אֲלָפִים
אִישׁ מִיהוּדָה אֶל־סְעִיף סֶלַע
עֵיטָם וַיֹּאמְרוּ לְשִׁמְשׁוֹן הֲלֹא
יָדַעְתָּ כִּי־מֹשְׁלִים בָּנוּ
פְלִשְׁתִּים וּמַה־זֹּאת עָשִׂיתָ לָּנוּ
וַיֹּאמֶר לָהֶם כַּאֲשֶׁר עָשׂוּ לִי
12 כֵּן עָשִׂיתִי לָהֶם: וַיֹּאמְרוּ לוֹ
לֶאֱסָרְךָ יָרַדְנוּ לְתִתְּךָ בְּיַד־
פְלִשְׁתִּים וַיֹּאמֶר לָהֶם שִׁמְשׁוֹן
הִשָּׁבְעוּ לִי פֶּן־תִּפְגְּעוּן בִּי
13 אַתֶּם: וַיֹּאמְרוּ לוֹ לֵאמֹר לֹא
כִּי־אָסֹר נֶאֱסָרְךָ וּנְתַנּוּךָ

6), about half an hour's journey south of Beth-lehem. A different Etam is mentioned in 1 Chron. iv. 32 (Daath Mikra).

9. *spread themselves.* In small detachments searching for Samson (Rashi, Metsudath Zion).

Lehi. Nearer the Philistine border than Etam (cf. verse 14); the site is unknown (Daath Mikra).

10. *why are ye come up against us?* The Judahites feared an attack; and conscious of no action by them to warrant it, they ask the reason for the appearance of the armed bands (see Rashi).

to bind. i.e. that you, the Judahites, should bind Samson and surrender him (Rashi).

11. *three thousand men.* Samson's strength, in their estimation, must have been extraordinary to require this number (Daath Mikra).

what then is this . . . unto us? By exposing us to attack through your dealings with the Philistines (Metsudath David).

12. *that we may deliver thee.* Since the Philistines demand that you be surrendered to them, and you are liable to death according to the law of the land, and you are endangering our people, we may deliver you into their hands (Malbim).

their hand; but surely we will not kill thee.' And they bound him with two new ropes, and brought him up from the rock.   14. When he came unto Lehi, the Philistines shouted as they met him; and the spirit of the LORD came mightily upon him, and the ropes that were upon his arms became as flax that was burnt with fire, and his bands dropped from off his hands. 15. And he found a new jawbone of an ass, and put forth his hand, and took it, and smote a thousand men therewith.   16. And Samson said:

With the jawbone of an ass, heaps upon heaps,

With the jawbone of an ass have I smitten a thousand men.

17. And it came to pass, when he had made an end of speaking, that he cast away the jawbone out of his hand; and that place was called Ramath-lehi.   18. And he was sore athirst, and called on the LORD, and said: 'Thou hast given this great

בְּיָדָם וְהָמֵת לֹא נְמִיתֶךָ
וַיַּאַסְרֻהוּ בִּשְׁנַיִם עֲבֹתִים
חֲדָשִׁים וַיַּעֲלוּהוּ מִן־הַסָּלַע:

14 הוּא־בָא עַד־לֶחִי וּפְלִשְׁתִּים
הֵרִיעוּ לִקְרָאתוֹ וַתִּצְלַח עָלָיו
רוּחַ יְהֹוָה וַתִּהְיֶינָה הָעֲבֹתִים
אֲשֶׁר עַל־זְרוֹעוֹתָיו כַּפִּשְׁתִּים
אֲשֶׁר בָּעֲרוּ בָאֵשׁ וַיִּמַּסּוּ

15 אֲסוּרָיו מֵעַל יָדָיו: וַיִּמְצָא
לְחִי־חֲמוֹר טְרִיָּה וַיִּשְׁלַח יָדוֹ
וַיִּקָּחֶהָ וַיַּךְ־בָּהּ אֶלֶף אִישׁ:

16 וַיֹּאמֶר שִׁמְשׁוֹן
בִּלְחִי הַחֲמוֹר חֲמוֹר חֲמֹרָתָיִם
בִּלְחִי הַחֲמוֹר
הִכֵּיתִי אֶלֶף אִישׁ:

17 וַיְהִי כְּכַלֹּתוֹ לְדַבֵּר וַיַּשְׁלֵךְ
הַלְּחִי מִיָּדוֹ וַיִּקְרָא לַמָּקוֹם
18 הַהוּא רָמַת לֶחִי: וַיִּצְמָא מְאֹד
וַיִּקְרָא אֶל־יְהֹוָה וַיֹּאמַר אַתָּה

---

yourselves. He demanded a pledge that they would only bind him and not hand him over dead; otherwise he would not be able to defend himself, since his wondrous strength was powerless against his fellow Jews (Daath Mikra).

13. *new ropes.* As in xvi. 11. They were used apparently because of their superior strength to old ropes. Scripture tells us this so that we may understand more clearly the incident depicted in the following verse, that even though Samson was bound with new ropes, they 'became as flax that was burnt with fire' (Daath Mikra).

14. *as flax.* Cf. xvi. 9.

dropped. lit. 'melted.'

15. *new.* lit. 'fresh'; it was therefore heavy and tough. When dry it becomes light and brittle (Rabbi Joseph Kara).

jawbone. It was the first weapon to hand. In the East parts of dead animals may often be seen lying about in the open.

16. *heaps upon heaps.* lit. 'a heap, two heaps.' There is a word-play since *chamor* is used both for 'an ass' and 'a heap' (after the Targum).

17. *was called.* lit. 'he called,' the subject being indefinite.

Ramath-lehi. lit. 'the hill of the jaw-bone' (Ralbag).

deliverance by the hand of Thy servant; and now shall I die for thirst, and fall into the hand of the uncircumcised?' 19. But God cleaved the hollow place that is in Lehi, and there came water thereout; and when he had drunk, his spirit came back, and he revived; wherefore the name thereof was called En-hakkore, which is in Lehi unto this day. 20. And he judged Israel in the days of the Philistines twenty years.

נָתַתָּ בְיַד־עַבְדְּךָ אֶת־
הַתְּשׁוּעָה הַגְּדֹלָה הַזֹּאת וְעַתָּה
אָמוּת בַּצָּמָא וְנָפַלְתִּי בְּיַד
הָעֲרֵלִים: וַיִּבְקַע אֱלֹהִים 19
אֶת־הַמַּכְתֵּשׁ אֲשֶׁר־בַּלֶּחִי
וַיֵּצְאוּ מִמֶּנּוּ מַיִם וַיֵּשְׁתְּ וַתָּשָׁב
רוּחוֹ וַיֶּחִי עַל־כֵּן | קָרָא שְׁמָהּ
עֵין הַקּוֹרֵא אֲשֶׁר בַּלֶּחִי עַד
הַיּוֹם הַזֶּה: וַיִּשְׁפֹּט אֶת־ 20
יִשְׂרָאֵל בִּימֵי פְלִשְׁתִּים
עֶשְׂרִים שָׁנָה:

---

16   CHAPTER XVI   טז

1. And Samson went to Gaza, and saw there a harlot, and went in unto her. 2. [And it was told] the Gazites, saying: 'Samson is come

וַיֵּלֶךְ שִׁמְשׁוֹן עַזָּתָה וַיַּרְא־שָׁם 1
אִשָּׁה זוֹנָה וַיָּבֹא אֵלֶיהָ:
לְעַזָּתִים | לֵאמֹר בָּא שִׁמְשׁוֹן 2

---

18. *for thirst.* If I stay here (Metsudath David).

and fall into the hands of the uncircumcised. Better, 'or fall.' If I go to the nearest city for water, I will surely fall into the hands of the Philistines.

uncircumcised. See on xiv. 3.

19. *the hollow place.* The noun *machtesh* means a 'mortar.' In this case it is used for a cleft in a rock resembling a mortar (Kimchi and Ralbag).

that is in Lehi. This follows Ralbag. Kimchi renders 'that was under the jawbone.' Rashi explains it as 'the socket that is in the jawbone.'

En-hakkore. i.e. 'the spring of him that calls,' viz. to God for help (Rashi based on Targum Jonathan). Alternatively, 'the eye [of God] is upon him that calls.' The name was given to commemorate the miracle per-

formed for Samson, since he was a judge of Israel (Malbim).

which is in Lehi unto this day. With the same name (Metsudath David).

20. *in the days of.* i.e. when the Philistines were the overlords of Israel (Kimchi).

CHAPTER XVI

LAST YEARS OF SAMSON

1–3 HIS EXPLOITS AT GAZA

1. *Gaza.* [This Philistine city, situated about two miles from the coast to the south, was thirty miles from Samson's hometown.] He demonstrated his fearlessness by entering this heavily fortified city lodging in the house of a harlot (Malbim).

a harlot. See on Josh. ii. 1. In such a house, he was less likely to be detected. Moreover, by doing so, he separated himself from the

hither.' And they compassed him in, and lay in wait for him all night in the gate of the city, and were quiet all the night, saying: 'Let be till morning light, then we will kill him.' 3. And Samson lay till midnight, and arose at midnight, and laid hold of the doors of the gate of the city, and the two posts, and plucked them up, bar and all, and put them upon his shoulders, and carried them up to the top of the mountain that is before Hebron.

4. And it came to pass afterward, that he loved a woman in the valley of Sorek, whose name was Delilah. 5. And the lords of the Philistines came up unto her, and said unto her: 'Entice him, and see wherein his

הִנֵּה וַיָּסֹבּוּ וַיֶּאֶרְבוּ־לוֹ כָל־
הַלַּיְלָה בְּשַׁעַר הָעִיר
וַיִּתְחָרְשׁוּ כָל־הַלַּיְלָה לֵאמֹר
עַד־אוֹר הַבֹּקֶר וַהֲרַגְנֻהוּ:
3 וַיִּשְׁכַּב שִׁמְשׁוֹן עַד־חֲצִי
הַלַּיְלָה וַיָּקָם ׀ בַּחֲצִי הַלַּיְלָה
וַיֶּאֱחֹז בְּדַלְתוֹת שַׁעַר־הָעִיר
וּבִשְׁתֵּי הַמְּזוּזוֹת וַיִּסָּעֵם עִם־
הַבְּרִיחַ וַיָּשֶׂם עַל־כְּתֵפָיו
וַיַּעֲלֵם אֶל־רֹאשׁ הָהָר אֲשֶׁר
עַל־פְּנֵי חֶבְרוֹן:
4 וַיְהִי אַחֲרֵי־כֵן וַיֶּאֱהַב אִשָּׁה
בְּנַחַל שׂוֹרֵק וּשְׁמָהּ דְּלִילָה:
5 וַיַּעֲלוּ אֵלֶיהָ סַרְנֵי פְלִשְׁתִּים
וַיֹּאמְרוּ לָהּ פַּתִּי אוֹתוֹ וּרְאִי

Israelites, who were not accustomed to such behavior. Thus, the Philistines could not blame the Israelites for his actions (Daath Soferim).

2. *saying.* Rashi understands the unusual Hebrew form as signifying 'it was told,' while Kimchi prefers to assume that the phrase 'it was told' is implied.

they compassed him in. They arranged for their men to cover the gateways of the city so that he could not leave without their knowing it. Apparently they were unaware in which house he was staying, and they made no attempt to search for him in the night (Ralbag).

3. *plucked them up.* The two wings of the gate were flanked by posts and turned on pins which moved in sockets in the sill and lintel. The bar ran across the whole breadth of the leaves from post to post. Samson pulled it all up and carried it to the top of the hill.

bar. It was probably of metal (cf. 1 Kings iv. 13).

that was before Hebron. A distance of nearly forty miles.

4–22 SAMSON AND DELILAH

4. *afterward.* The word forms a loose chronological connection with the preceding story.

Sorek. The Hebrew denotes a choice variety of the vine (cf. Gen. xlix. 11; Isa. v. 2; Jer. ii. 21) which may have given its name to the valley. The location seems to be the Wadi es-Surar which starts fifteen miles west of Jerusalem and runs to the coastal plain (Daath Mikra).

Delilah. This woman did not convert and retained her Philistine name (Malbim). Intuitively, she was called Delilah, which, in Hebrew, denotes that she uprooted his strength, his heart, and his actions (Sot. 9b).

5. *lords.* See on iii. 3.

great strength lieth, and by what
means we may prevail against him,
that we may bind him to afflict him;
and we will give thee every one of
us eleven hundred pieces of silver.'
6. And Delilah said to Samson: 'Tell
me, I pray thee, wherein thy great
strength lieth, and wherewith thou
mightest be bound to afflict thee.'
7. And Samson said unto her: 'If
they bind me with seven fresh
bowstrings that were never dried,
then shall I become weak, and be as
any other man.'   8. Then the lords
of the Philistines brought up to her
seven fresh bowstrings which had
not been dried, and she bound him
with them.   9. Now she had liers-
in-wait abiding in the inner chamber.
And she said unto him: 'The
Philistines are upon thee, Samson.'
And he broke the bowstrings as a

בַּמֶּה כֹּחוֹ גָדוֹל וּבַמֶּה נוּכַל
לוֹ וַאֲסַרְנֻהוּ לְעַנּוֹתוֹ וַאֲנַחְנוּ
נִתַּן־לְךָ אִישׁ אֶלֶף וּמֵאָה
כָסֶף: 6 וַתֹּאמֶר דְּלִילָה אֶל־
שִׁמְשׁוֹן הַגִּידָה־נָּא לִי בַּמֶּה
כֹּחֲךָ גָדוֹל וּבַמֶּה תֵאָסֵר
לְעַנּוֹתֶךָ: 7 וַיֹּאמֶר אֵלֶיהָ
שִׁמְשׁוֹן אִם־יַאַסְרֻנִי בְּשִׁבְעָה
יְתָרִים לַחִים אֲשֶׁר לֹא־חֹרָבוּ
וְחָלִיתִי וְהָיִיתִי כְּאַחַד הָאָדָם:
8 וַיַּעֲלוּ־לָהּ סַרְנֵי פְלִשְׁתִּים
שִׁבְעָה יְתָרִים לַחִים אֲשֶׁר
לֹא־חֹרָבוּ וַתַּאַסְרֵהוּ בָּהֶם:
9 וְהָאֹרֵב יֹשֵׁב לָהּ בַּחֶדֶר
וַתֹּאמֶר אֵלָיו פְּלִשְׁתִּים עָלֶיךָ
שִׁמְשׁוֹן וַיְנַתֵּק אֶת־הַיְתָרִים

v. 5. התי בפתח

wherein his great strength lieth. lit. 'by what
means his strength is great.' They realized
that it must be due to a supernatural cause.
It has been pointed out that Samson is
never described as a giant, which made his
strength appear the more remarkable (Liku-
tei Yekarim, Meam Loez).

to afflict him. This was a promise that they
would not kill him, which they kept, since
they only blinded him (Malbim). Even
Delilah would not betray Samson to such an
extent to endanger his life (Daath Soferim).

we will give. The pointing of the verb is unusual, being the third person singular masculine of the Niphal conjugation (Kimchi).

every one of us. Each of the five Philistine
lords promised her payment (Daath Mikra).

6. tell me. [It is to be presumed that her
question was not asked abruptly, but she

gradually worked up to it. Nevertheless it is
impossible to believe that Samson was so
stupid as not to have his suspicions aroused.
One of his weaknesses was his excessive self-
assurance; he felt that he could amuse himself at her expense as long as he pleased. He
tried once too often.]

7.   seven. [A magical number.]

fresh. In that condition they would be tough
and more firmly tied into knots.

bowstrings. Either cords made from the intes-
tines of animals (Daath Mikra) or from moist
flexible branches (Kimchi).

as any other man. lit. 'as one of the (ordinary)
men.'

8.   bound him. While he was awake (Metsudath David, verse 14).

9.   abiding. They did not come out even

string of tow is broken when it toucheth the fire. So his strength was not known. 10. And Delilah said unto Samson: 'Behold, thou hast mocked me, and told me lies; now tell me, I pray thee, wherewith thou mightest be bound.' 11. And he said unto her: 'If they only bind me with new ropes wherewith no work hath been done, then shall I become weak, and be as any other man.' 12. So Delilah took new ropes, and bound him therewith, and said unto him: 'The Philistines are upon thee, Samson.' And the liers-in-wait were abiding in the inner chamber. And he broke them from off his arms like a thread. 13. And Delilah said unto Samson: 'Hitherto thou hast mocked me, and told me lies; tell me wherewith thou mightest be bound.' And he said unto her: 'If thou weavest the seven locks of my head with the web.' 14. And she fastened it with the pin, and said

כַּאֲשֶׁר יִנָּתֵק פְּתִיל־הַנְּעֹרֶת
בַּהֲרִיחוֹ אֵשׁ וְלֹא נוֹדַע כֹּחוֹ:
10 וַתֹּאמֶר דְּלִילָה אֶל־שִׁמְשׁוֹן
הִנֵּה הֵתַלְתָּ בִּי וַתְּדַבֵּר אֵלַי
כְּזָבִים עַתָּה הַגִּידָה־נָּא לִי
11 בַּמֶּה תֵּאָסֵר: וַיֹּאמֶר אֵלֶיהָ
אִם־אָסוֹר יַאַסְרוּנִי
בַּעֲבֹתִים חֲדָשִׁים אֲשֶׁר לֹא־
נַעֲשָׂה בָהֶם מְלָאכָה וְחָלִיתִי
12 וְהָיִיתִי כְּאַחַד הָאָדָם: וַתִּקַּח
דְּלִילָה עֲבֹתִים חֲדָשִׁים
וַתַּאַסְרֵהוּ בָהֶם וַתֹּאמֶר אֵלָיו
פְּלִשְׁתִּים עָלֶיךָ שִׁמְשׁוֹן
וְהָאֹרֵב יֹשֵׁב בֶּחָדֶר וַיְנַתְּקֵם
13 מֵעַל זְרֹעֹתָיו כַּחוּט: וַתֹּאמֶר
דְּלִילָה אֶל־שִׁמְשׁוֹן עַד־הֵנָּה
הֵתַלְתָּ בִּי וַתְּדַבֵּר אֵלַי כְּזָבִים
הַגִּידָה לִּי בַּמֶּה תֵּאָסֵר וַיֹּאמֶר
אֵלֶיהָ אִם־תַּאַרְגִי אֶת־שֶׁבַע
מַחְלְפוֹת רֹאשִׁי עִם־
14 הַמַּסָּכֶת: וַתִּתְקַע בַּיָּתֵד

---

after he was bound, but waited to see whether the cords would hold (Metsudath David).

toucheth. lit. 'smells.'

11. *new ropes.* Made of three strands (Kimchi). For *new,* see on xv. 13.

wherewith no work had been done. Defining new; if they had been put to use, they would have lost their strength.

12. *like a thread.* Used in sewing which can easily be broken asunder.

13. *the web.* The woven cloth with which she interwove his hair (Kimchi). The apodosis of the sentence, though unexpressed, is obvious.

14. *fastened it.* i.e. she fastened the piece of weaving in the loom to prevent its slipping out, weaving his hair into her work as she would do with ordinary threads (Metsudath David).

unto him: 'The Philistines are upon
thee, Samson.' And he awoke out
of his sleep, and plucked away the
pin of the beam, and the web.
15. And she said unto him: 'How
canst thou say: I love thee, when
thy heart is not with me? thou hast
mocked me these three times, and
hast not told me wherein thy great
strength lieth.' 16. And it came to
pass, when she pressed him daily
with her words, and urged him, that
his soul was vexed unto death.
17. And he told her all his heart, and
said unto her: 'There hath not come
a razor upon my head; for I have
been a Nazirite unto God from my
mother's womb; if I be shaven, then
my strength will go from me, and
I shall become weak, and be like any
other man.' 18. And when Delilah
saw that he had told her all his
heart, she sent and called for the
lords of the Philistines, saying:
'Come up this once, for he hath told

וַתֹּאמֶר אֵלָיו פְּלִשְׁתִּים עָלֶיךָ
שִׁמְשׁוֹן וַיִּיקַץ מִשְּׁנָתוֹ וַיִּסַּע
אֶת־הַיְתַד הָאֶרֶג וְאֶת־
15 הַמַּסָּכֶת: וַתֹּאמֶר אֵלָיו אֵיךְ
תֹּאמַר אֲהַבְתִּיךְ וְלִבְּךָ אֵין
אִתִּי זֶה שָׁלֹשׁ פְּעָמִים הֵתַלְתָּ
בִּי וְלֹא־הִגַּדְתָּ לִּי בַּמֶּה כֹּחֲךָ
16 גָדוֹל: וַיְהִי כִּי־הֵצִיקָה לּוֹ
בִדְבָרֶיהָ כָּל־הַיָּמִים
וַתְּאַלֲצֵהוּ וַתִּקְצַר נַפְשׁוֹ
17 לָמוּת: וַיַּגֶּד־לָהּ אֶת־כָּל־
לִבּוֹ וַיֹּאמֶר לָהּ מוֹרָה לֹא־
עָלָה עַל־רֹאשִׁי כִּי־נְזִיר
אֱלֹהִים אֲנִי מִבֶּטֶן אִמִּי אִם־
גֻּלַּחְתִּי וְסָר מִמֶּנִּי כֹחִי וְחָלִיתִי
18 וְהָיִיתִי כְּכָל־הָאָדָם: וַתֵּרֶא
דְלִילָה כִּי־הִגִּיד לָהּ אֶת־
כָּל־לִבּוֹ וַתִּשְׁלַח וַתִּקְרָא
לְסַרְנֵי פְלִשְׁתִּים לֵאמֹר עֲלוּ
הַפַּעַם כִּי־הִגִּיד לָהּ אֶת־

v. 18. הל׳ רפה   v. 16. לי ק׳

web. The cloth with which his hair had been woven (Kimchi).

15. *heart.* The word is not employed here in the sense of affection, but signifies what resides in the heart, viz. according to Hebrew psychology, thought (see verse 17).

16. *was vexed.* lit. 'shortened'; sick to death.

17. *all his heart.* He revealed his secret knowledge (Metsudath David).

if I be shaven. Not that his strength lay in his hair, but as long as the symbol of his sacred calling remained, the Divine gift with which he had been endowed would be with him (Daath Soferim).

18. *all his heart.* This time she instinctively felt that he had spoken the truth. Some authorities are of the opinion that she inferred the veracity of his statement from the fact that he mentioned God's name in connection with it (Sot. 9b).

me all his heart.' Then the lords of the Philistines came up unto her, and brought the money in their hand. 19. And she made him sleep upon her knees; and she called for a man, and had the seven locks of his head shaven off; and she began to afflict him, and his strength went from him. 20. And she said: 'The Philistines are upon thee, Samson.' And he awoke out of his sleep, and said: 'I will go out as at other times, and shake myself.' But he knew not that the LORD was departed from him. 21. And the Philistines laid hold on him, and put out his eyes; and they brought him down to Gaza, and bound him with fetters of brass; and he did grind in the prison-house. 22. Howbeit the hair of his head began to grow again after he was shaven.

כָּל־לִבּוֹ וְעָלוּ אֵלֶיהָ סַרְנֵי
פְלִשְׁתִּים וַיַּעֲלוּ הַכֶּסֶף בְּיָדָם:
19 וַתְּיַשְּׁנֵהוּ עַל־בִּרְכֶּיהָ וַתִּקְרָא
לָאִישׁ וַתְּגַלַּח אֶת־שֶׁבַע
מַחְלְפוֹת רֹאשׁוֹ וַתָּחֶל לְעַנּוֹתוֹ
20 וַיָּסַר כֹּחוֹ מֵעָלָיו: וַתֹּאמֶר
פְּלִשְׁתִּים עָלֶיךָ שִׁמְשׁוֹן וַיִּקַץ
מִשְּׁנָתוֹ וַיֹּאמֶר אֵצֵא כְּפַעַם
בְּפַעַם וְאִנָּעֵר וְהוּא לֹא יָדַע
21 כִּי יְהוָה סָר מֵעָלָיו: וַיֹּאחֲזוּהוּ
פְלִשְׁתִּים וַיְנַקְּרוּ אֶת־עֵינָיו
וַיּוֹרִידוּ אוֹתוֹ עַזָּתָה וַיַּאַסְרוּהוּ
בַּנְחֻשְׁתַּיִם וַיְהִי טוֹחֵן בְּבֵית
22 הָאֲסִירִים: וַיָּחֶל שְׂעַר־
רֹאשׁוֹ לְצַמֵּחַ כַּאֲשֶׁר גֻּלָּח:

v. 21. האסורים ק׳

19. *a man.* The Hebrew means 'the man'; the agent specifically appointed by the Philistine lords (Rashi).

and had . . . shaven off. The text reads: 'and she shaved off,' which Metsudath David explains as 'she ordered (the man) to shave off.' This usage is common in the Bible; cf. *the house which king Solomon built for the* LORD (1 Kings vi. 2), which means that he gave orders to build.

20. *go out.* Without restriction.

shake myself. To get rid of the drowsiness of sleep (Kimchi); but modern expositors prefer the explanation: from his bonds (Daath Mikra). Nothing, however, is mentioned of Samson being tied up in any way on this occasion, so they suppose that this was done to discover whether his strength had been sapped.

he knew not. Either because he was not fully awake and did not realize the change that had taken place in him; or he hoped that, despite the cutting of his hair, God would not abandon him (Kimchi).

21. *put out.* lit. 'bored' a form of mutilation common in ancient times (cf. 1 Sam. xi. 2; 2 Kings xxv. 7).

his eyes. The Rabbis remarked that the eyes are the agents of sin. Samson's eyes had lusted after Philistine women, and that part of his body suffered punishment (Sot. 9b).

fetters. The Hebrew noun has the dual form, perhaps denoting that they were fastened to his hands and feet (Daath Mikra).

he did grind. The Philistines humiliated him by imposing upon him work normally performed by slave-women (cf. Exod. xi. 5; Isa. xlvii. 2).

23. And the lords of the Philistines gathered them together to offer a great sacrifice unto Dagon their god, and to rejoice; for they said: 'Our god hath delivered Samson our enemy into our hand.' 24. And when the people saw him, they praised their god; for they said: 'Our god hath delivered into our hand our enemy, and the destroyer of our country, who hath slain many of us.' 25. And it came to pass, when their hearts were merry, that they said: 'Call for Samson, that he may make us sport.' And they called for Samson out of the prison-house; and he made sport before them; and they set him between the pillars. 26. And Samson said unto the lad that held him by the hand: 'Suffer me that I may feel the pillars whereupon the house resteth, that

כג וְסַרְנֵי פְלִשְׁתִּים נֶאֶסְפוּ לִזְבֹּחַ
זֶבַח־גָּדוֹל לְדָגוֹן אֱלֹהֵיהֶם
וּלְשִׂמְחָה וַיֹּאמְרוּ נָתַן אֱלֹהֵינוּ
בְּיָדֵנוּ אֵת שִׁמְשׁוֹן אוֹיְבֵנוּ:
כד וַיִּרְאוּ אֹתוֹ הָעָם וַיְהַלְלוּ אֶת־
אֱלֹהֵיהֶם כִּי אָמְרוּ נָתַן אֱלֹהֵינוּ
בְיָדֵנוּ אֶת־אוֹיְבֵנוּ וְאֵת
מַחֲרִיב אַרְצֵנוּ וַאֲשֶׁר הִרְבָּה
כה אֶת־חֲלָלֵינוּ: וַיְהִי כִּי טוֹב
לִבָּם וַיֹּאמְרוּ קִרְאוּ לְשִׁמְשׁוֹן
וִישַׂחֶק לָנוּ וַיִּקְרְאוּ לְשִׁמְשׁוֹן
מִבֵּית הָאֲסִירִים וַיְצַחֵק
לִפְנֵיהֶם וַיַּעֲמִידוּ אוֹתוֹ בֵּין
כו הָעַמּוּדִים: וַיֹּאמֶר שִׁמְשׁוֹן
אֶל־הַנַּעַר הַמַּחֲזִיק בְּיָדוֹ
הַנִּיחָה אוֹתִי וַהֲימִשֵׁנִי אֶת־
הָעַמֻּדִים אֲשֶׁר הַבַּיִת נָכוֹן

v. 25. כטוב ק׳.   v. 25. האסורים ק׳.   v. 26. והמישני ק׳

23–31 SAMSON'S DEATH

23. *Dagan.* A deity of the Philistines with a temple to his worship in Ashdod (1 Sam. v. 2ff.). The name has been associated with *dag,* 'a fish' (Rashi, Kimchi, Abarbanel on 1 Sam. v. 2), or *dagan,* 'corn,' and thought of as half man and half fish or a god of agriculture (Daath Mikra). The data point to his being a Semite god worshipped even in Babylonia. A place-name *Beth-dagon* occurs in Josh. xv. 41, xix. 27, and Sennacherib's Prism Inscription mentions a *Bit-daganna* near Jaffa.

24. *they said.* What follows is a song based upon a fivefold repetition of the rhyme-ending *-nu.* This form of song is common in Arabic.

destroyer of our country. They had in mind the episode related in xv. 4f.

25. *make us sport.* Not 'play the buffoon'; the appearance of the man, formerly possessed of superhuman strength but now blind and feeble, would give the drunken mob cause to laugh and jeer (Daath Soferim).

26. *suffer me.* lit. 'give me rest,' i.e. leave me alone (Metsudath David).

that I may feel. Rather, 'and cause me to feel.' (Rashi, Metsudath David from Targum).

the pillars. The two middle columns which supported the hall where the more distinguished people were assembled.

l may lean upon them.' 27. Now the house was full of men and women; and all the lords of the Philistines were there; and there were upon the roof about three thousand men and women, that beheld while Samson made sport. 28. And Samson called unto the LORD, and said: 'O Lord GOD, remember me, I pray Thee, and strengthen me, I pray Thee, only this once, O God, that I may be this once avenged of the Philistines for my two eyes.' 29. And Samson took fast hold of the two middle pillars upon which the house rested, and leaned upon them, the one with his right hand, and the other with his left. 30. And Samson said: 'Let me die with the Philistines.' And he bent with all his might; and the house fell upon the lords, and upon all the people that were therein. So the dead that he slew at his death were more than they that

עֲלֵיהֶ֑ם וָאֶשָּׁעֵ֖ן עֲלֵיהֶֽם׃

27 וְהַבַּ֤יִת מָלֵא֙ הָאֲנָשִׁ֣ים וְהַנָּשִׁ֔ים וְשָׁ֕מָּה כֹּ֖ל סַרְנֵ֣י פְלִשְׁתִּ֑ים וְעַל־הַגָּ֗ג כִּשְׁלֹ֤שֶׁת אֲלָפִים֙ אִ֣ישׁ וְאִשָּׁ֔ה הָרֹאִ֖ים בִּשְׂח֥וֹק

28 שִׁמְשֽׁוֹן׃ וַיִּקְרָ֥א שִׁמְשׁ֛וֹן אֶל־ יְהֹוָ֖ה וַיֹּאמַ֑ר אֲדֹנָ֣י יֱהֹוִ֡ה זָכְרֵ֣נִי נָ֣א וְחַזְּקֵ֣נִי נָ֩א אַ֨ךְ הַפַּ֜עַם הַזֶּ֗ה הָאֱלֹהִ֔ים וְאִנָּקְמָ֛ה נְקַם־אַחַ֥ת

29 מִשְּׁתֵ֥י עֵינַ֖י מִפְּלִשְׁתִּֽים׃ וַיִּלְפֹּ֨ת שִׁמְשׁ֜וֹן אֶת־שְׁנֵ֣י ׀ עַמּוּדֵ֣י הַתָּ֗וֶךְ אֲשֶׁ֤ר הַבַּ֙יִת֙ נָכ֣וֹן עֲלֵיהֶ֔ם וַיִּסָּמֵ֖ךְ עֲלֵיהֶ֑ם אֶחָ֥ד בִּימִינ֖וֹ

30 וְאֶחָ֥ד בִּשְׂמֹאלֽוֹ׃ וַיֹּ֣אמֶר שִׁמְשׁ֗וֹן תָּמ֣וֹת נַפְשִׁי֮ עִם־ פְּלִשְׁתִּים֒ וַיֵּ֣ט בְּכֹ֔חַ וַיִּפֹּ֤ל הַבַּ֙יִת֙ עַל־הַסְּרָנִ֔ים וְעַל־כָּל־הָעָ֖ם אֲשֶׁר־בּ֑וֹ וַיִּהְי֤וּ הַמֵּתִים֙ אֲשֶׁר־ הֵמִ֣ית בְּמוֹת֔וֹ רַבִּ֕ים מֵאֲשֶׁ֥ר

v. 28. התי׳ רפה

---

27. The hall was open to a great court with a flat roof as is usual in the East, upon which the mass of the people sat and stood in a crowd.

38. O LORD God. The pathos of the situation, with Samson's plea to God in what he intends to be his last moments, is overwhelming.

this once avenged, etc. The text is capable of the more effective rendering: 'the vengeance of one of my two eyes.' He feels that the vengeance which he contemplates taking

will only be partial, but it is all he can accomplish in the circumstances (Daath Mikra).

29. took fast hold of. The meaning of laphat is 'to grasp with a twisting movement' (Kimchi, Ibn Janach).

30. me. lit. 'my soul,' the breathing part of my body (Metsudath David).

bent. Standing between the columns, he exerted all his strength and pushed them apart (ibid.).

he slew in his life. 31. Then his brethren and all the house of his father came down, and took him, and brought him up, and buried him between Zorah and Eshtaol in the burying-place of Manoah his father. And he judged Israel twenty years.

31 הֵמִית בְּחַיָּיו׃ וַיֵּרְדוּ אֶחָיו
וְכָל־בֵּית אָבִיהוּ וַיִּשְׂאוּ אֹתוֹ
וַיַּעֲלוּ ׀ וַיִּקְבְּרוּ אוֹתוֹ בֵּין
צָרְעָה וּבֵין אֶשְׁתָּאֹל בְּקֶבֶר
מָנוֹחַ אָבִיו וְהוּא שָׁפַט אֶת־
יִשְׂרָאֵל עֶשְׂרִים שָׁנָה׃

17   CHAPTER XVII   יז

1. Now there was a man of the hill-country of Ephraim, whose name was Micah. 2. And he said unto his mother: 'The eleven hundred

1 וַיְהִי־אִישׁ מֵהַר־אֶפְרָיִם
2 וּשְׁמוֹ מִיכָיְהוּ׃ וַיֹּאמֶר לְאִמּוֹ
אֶלֶף וּמֵאָה הַכֶּסֶף אֲשֶׁר

v. 1. קמץ בטרחא

---

31. *brethren.* His kinsmen (Meam Loez).

house of his father. See on ix. 1.

took him. In the confusion which followed the disaster, many Philistines searched among the debris for lost relatives, and consequently the Hebrews were not noticed when they came to look for Samson's body.

Zorah . . . Eshtaol. See on xiii. 2, 25.

he judged Israel twenty years. Rabbinic exegesis explains that the clause is not a repetition of xv. 20, but provides the information that the fear which Samson had aroused among the Philistines during the twenty years of his judgeship lingered for twenty years after his death. The task of the judge, to obtain security for the people, was accordingly discharged by Samson for forty years (Kimchi from P.T. Sot. i. 8; Num. Rabbah, Naso 14).

CHAPTER XVII

MICAH'S SHRINE

THE Rabbis placed the incidents of Micah and the concubine (xix–xxi) in the age of Othniel. The reason for the juxtaposition of the Micah story and the career of Samson is twofold: It deals with the Danites from which tribe Samson originated (Ralbag),

and it mentions the sum of eleven hundred shekels, the identical sum paid Delilah by each of the Philistine lords for his betrayal (xvi. 5; see on verse 2). In both cases, the money was given for wicked purposes (Rashi).

1–6 THE IDOL MADE BY MICAH

A man from mount Ephraim, named Micah, who had stolen eleven hundred shekels of silver from his mother, on hearing that she had pronounced a curse upon the known thief, returned the money. His mother gave two hundred pieces to the silversmith to make an idol for Micah's house.

1. *hill-country of Ephraim.* See ii. 9. We are not told more precisely where he lived.

Micah. Heb. *Michayehu*, 'who is like God.' From verse 4 on, he is called by the shortened form of the name. Malbim explains that originally he was righteous and was called Michayehu. After he commenced to worship idols, however, the letters of God's name were omitted from his name, and he was called Micah.

2. *his mother.* According to some Jewish authorities she was Delilah, on the supposition that the sum of money stolen was received by her from the Philistines. Rashi

pieces of silver that were taken from thee, about which thou didst utter a curse, and didst also speak it in mine ears, behold, the silver is with me; I took it.' And his mother said: 'Blessed be my son of the LORD.' 3. And he restored the eleven hundred pieces of silver to his mother, and his mother said: 'I verily dedicate the silver unto the LORD from my hand for my son, to make a graven image and a molten image; now therefore I will restore it unto thee.' 4. And when he restored the money unto his mother, his mother took two hundred pieces of silver, and gave them to the founder, who made thereof a graven image and a molten image; and it was in the house of Micah. 5. And the man Micah had a house of God, and he made an ephod, and teraphim, and consecrated one of his

לְקַח־לָךְ וְאַתְּ אֵלִית וְגַם אָמַרְתְּ בְּאָזְנַי הִנֵּה־הַכֶּסֶף אִתִּי אֲנִי לְקַחְתָּיו וַתֹּאמֶר אִמּוֹ

3 בָּרוּךְ בְּנִי לַיהֹוָה: וַיָּשֶׁב אֶת־ אֶלֶף־וּמֵאָה הַכֶּסֶף לְאִמּוֹ וַתֹּאמֶר אִמּוֹ הַקְדֵּשׁ הִקְדַּשְׁתִּי אֶת־הַכֶּסֶף לַיהֹוָה מִיָּדִי לִבְנִי לַעֲשׂוֹת פֶּסֶל וּמַסֵּכָה

4 וְעַתָּה אֲשִׁיבֶנּוּ לָךְ: וַיָּשֶׁב אֶת־ הַכֶּסֶף לְאִמּוֹ וַתִּקַּח אִמּוֹ מָאתַיִם כֶּסֶף וַתִּתְּנֵהוּ לַצּוֹרֵף וַיַּעֲשֵׂהוּ פֶּסֶל וּמַסֵּכָה וַיְהִי

5 בְּבֵית מִיכָיְהוּ: וְהָאִישׁ מִיכָה לוֹ בֵּית אֱלֹהִים וַיַּעַשׂ אֵפוֹד וּתְרָפִים וַיְמַלֵּא אֶת־יַד אַחַד

v. 2. ואת ק׳

rejects this view, however, since the Seder Olam places these incidents at the time of Othniel (see above).

taken. The thief avoids the stronger verb 'stolen' (Daath Mikra).

from thee. lit. 'to thee' (Rashi).

utter a curse. Upon the thief if he did not restore the money. The power of the curse was believed to be very real, and a parent's curse was the most potent of all (Daath Mikra).

blessed be, etc. The curse could not be unsaid, but she neutralized it by a blessing. She secured her son for confessing and offering to return the money (Metsudath David).

3. *graven image . . . molten image.* The noun *pesel* signifies 'a carving' of an idol in wood or stone; then generally an image, even of metal. The *massechah* was an idol cast in metal, usually gold or silver. The two hundred pieces of silver were given to pay the founder, who made the images with the

remaining nine hundred pieces of silver (Kimchi, Metsudath David).

4 *and when.* The adverb is inserted in translation to overcome the difficulty of the apparent repetition. Kimchi and Ralbag hold that the money was returned a second time, while Rashi thinks that in verse 3 Micah had only declared his intention to restore it.

the founder. lit. 'the refiner,' the silversmith. In the Bible he is mostly a maker of idols (cf. Isa. xl. 19; Jer. x. 9, 14).

5. *a house of idolatry.* Wherever the name *Elohim* is mentioned in this chapter, it is profane since it refers to Micah's idol (Rashi from Shebu. 35b).

ephod. See on viii. 27.

teraphim. The precise nature of this idolatrous object in Hebrew plural in form, is not certain. It seems to have been, partially or wholly, of human shape (cf. 1 Sam. xix. 13).

sons, who became his priest. 6. In those days there was no king in Israel; every man did that which was right in his own eyes.

7. And there was a young man out of Beth-lehem in Judah—in the family of Judah—who was a Levite, and he sojourned there. 8. And the man departed out of the city, out of Beth-lehem in Judah, to sojourn where he could find a place; and he came to the hill-country of Ephraim to the house of Micah, as he journeyed. 9. And Micah said unto him: 'Whence comest thou?' And he said unto him: 'I am a Levite of Beth-lehem in Judah, and I go to sojourn where I may find a place.' 10. And Micah said unto him: 'Dwell with me, and be unto me a father and a priest, and I will give thee ten pieces of silver by the year, and a suit of apparel, and thy victuals.' So the Levite went in. 11. And the Levite was content to dwell with the man; and the young man was unto him as one of his sons.

6 מִבָּנָיו וַיְהִי־לוֹ לְכֹהֵן: בַּיָּמִים הָהֵם אֵין מֶלֶךְ בְּיִשְׂרָאֵל אִישׁ הַיָּשָׁר בְּעֵינָיו יַעֲשֶׂה:

7 וַיְהִי־נַעַר מִבֵּית לֶחֶם יְהוּדָה מִמִּשְׁפַּחַת יְהוּדָה וְהוּא לֵוִי

8 וְהוּא גָר־שָׁם: וַיֵּלֶךְ הָאִישׁ מֵהָעִיר מִבֵּית לֶחֶם יְהוּדָה לָגוּר בַּאֲשֶׁר יִמְצָא וַיָּבֹא הַר־ אֶפְרַיִם עַד־בֵּית מִיכָה

9 לַעֲשׂוֹת דַּרְכּוֹ: וַיֹּאמֶר־לוֹ מִיכָה מֵאַיִן תָּבוֹא וַיֹּאמֶר אֵלָיו לֵוִי אָנֹכִי מִבֵּית לֶחֶם יְהוּדָה וְאָנֹכִי הֹלֵךְ לָגוּר בַּאֲשֶׁר

10 אֶמְצָא: וַיֹּאמֶר לוֹ מִיכָה שְׁבָה עִמָּדִי וֶהְיֵה־לִי לְאָב וּלְכֹהֵן וְאָנֹכִי אֶתֶּן־לְךָ עֲשֶׂרֶת כֶּסֶף לַיָּמִים וְעֵרֶךְ בְּגָדִים וּמִחְיָתֶךָ

11 וַיֵּלֶךְ הַלֵּוִי: וַיּוֹאֶל הַלֵּוִי לָשֶׁבֶת אֶת־הָאִישׁ וַיְהִי הַנַּעַר

---

consecrated. lit. 'filled his hand,' a technical term apparently derived from the rite of filling the priest's hand with sacrificial gifts on his induction (quoted by Ramban, Exod. xxviii. 41).

7–13 A LEVITE APPOINTED AS PRIEST

A Levite of Beth-lehem, in search of a home, calls at Micah's house and is persuaded to stay and officiate as priest.

7. *Beth-lehem in Judah.* To distinguish it from other places of the same name (see on Josh. xix. 15) (Kimchi).

the family of Judah. i.e. he belonged to the family of Judah from his father's side (Rashi).

Levite. Rashi explains that he was a Levite on his mother's side. Kimchi says that he was a Levite from both sides. He lived, however, in Beth-lehem which belonged to the family of Judah. According to Rabbinical interpretation, he was related to the family of Judah in his actions, which resembled those of King Manasseh (B.B. 109b).

8. *as he journeyed.* lit. 'to make his way.' i.e. while continuing on the way he was travelling. He had no intention of remaining at Micah's house (Rashi, Kimchi).

10. *a father.* i.e. a teacher and an instructor (Metsudath Zion) (See Gen. xlv. 8; 2 Kings vi. 21).

12. And Micah consecrated the Levite, and the young man became his priest, and was in the house of Micah. 13. Then said Micah: 'Now know I that the LORD will do me good, seeing I have a Levite as my priest.'

לֹ֤ו כְּאַחַ֣ד מִבָּנָ֑יו וַיְמַלֵּ֞א 12
מִיכָה֙ אֶת־יַ֣ד הַלֵּוִ֔י וַיְהִי־ל֥וֹ
הַנַּ֖עַר לְכֹהֵ֑ן וַיְהִ֖י בְּבֵ֥ית
מִיכָֽה׃ וַיֹּ֣אמֶר מִיכָ֗ה עַתָּ֤ה 13
יָדַ֙עְתִּי֙ כִּֽי־יֵיטִ֣יב יְהֹוָ֖ה לִ֑י כִּ֧י
הָֽיָה־לִ֛י הַלֵּוִ֖י לְכֹהֵֽן׃

---

18   CHAPTER XVIII   יח

1. In those days there was no king in Israel; and in those days the tribe of the Danites sought them an inheritance to dwell in; for unto that day there had nothing been allotted unto them among the tribes of Israel for an inheritance. 2. And the children of Dan sent of their family five men from their whole number, men of valour, from Zorah, and from Eshtaol, to spy out the land, and to search it; and they said unto them: 'Go, search the land;

בַּיָּמִ֣ים הָהֵ֔ם אֵ֥ין מֶ֖לֶךְ 1
בְּיִשְׂרָאֵ֑ל וּבַיָּמִ֣ים הָהֵ֗ם שֵׁ֤בֶט
הַדָּנִ֜י מְבַקֶּשׁ־ל֤וֹ נַחֲלָה֙ לָשֶׁ֔בֶת
כִּי֩ לֹא־נָ֨פְלָה לּ֜וֹ עַד־הַיּ֣וֹם
הַה֗וּא בְּתוֹךְ־שִׁבְטֵ֥י־יִשְׂרָאֵ֖ל
בְּנַחֲלָֽה׃ וַיִּשְׁלְח֣וּ בְנֵי־דָ֣ן ׀ 2
מִמִּשְׁפַּחְתָּ֡ם חֲמִשָּׁ֣ה אֲנָשִׁ֣ים
מִקְצוֹתָם֩ אֲנָשִׁ֨ים בְּנֵי־חַ֜יִל
מִצָּרְעָ֣ה וּמֵאֶשְׁתָּאֹ֗ל לְרַגֵּ֤ל
אֶת־הָאָ֙רֶץ֙ וּלְחָקְרָ֔הּ וַיֹּאמְר֣וּ
אֲלֵהֶ֗ם לְכ֛וּ חִקְר֥וּ אֶת־הָאָ֖רֶץ

---

went in. lit. 'went,' i.e. followed the advice of Micah (Rashi).

13. *now know I,* etc. His optimism proved somewhat premature, as revealed in the next chapter. Micah had committed evil although intending to serve God, and punishment followed.

CHAPTER XVIII

THE DANITES FIND A NEW HOME

1–10 THE DANITE PROSPECTING PARTY

THE Danites, settled around Zorah and

Eshtaol, find themselves cramped for living space, and unable to secure for themselves a permanent hold, send out a party to prospect who, on their way, come to Micah's house.

1. *no king.* Hence the idolatry related in the chapter (Malbim).

an inheritance. A hereditary possession in the land.

2. *from their whole number.* i.e. from all parts of the tribe so that the mission might be representative (Daath Mikra). Ehrlich adopts the explanation of Metsudath David: from their leading men.

Zorah . . . Eshtaol. See on xiii. 2, 25.

and they came to the hill-country of
Ephraim, unto the house of Micah,
and lodged there. 3. When they
were by the house of Micah, they
knew the voice of the young man
the Levite; and they turned aside
thither, and said unto him: 'Who
brought thee hither? and what doest
thou in this place? and what hast
thou here?' 4. And he said unto
them: 'Thus and thus hath Micah
dealt with me, and he hath hired me,
and I am become his priest.' 5. And
they said unto him: 'Ask counsel,
we pray thee, of God, that we may
know whether our way which we are
going shall be prosperous.' 6. And
the priest said unto them: 'Go in
peace; before the LORD is your way
wherein ye go.'

7. Then the five men departed,

וַיָּבֹ֙אוּ֙ הַר־אֶפְרַ֔יִם עַד־בֵּ֥ית
3 מִיכָ֖ה וַיָּלִ֥ינוּ שָֽׁם: הֵ֚מָּה עִם־
בֵּ֣ית מִיכָ֔ה וְהֵ֣מָּה הִכִּ֗ירוּ
אֶת־ק֛וֹל הַנַּ֥עַר הַלֵּוִ֖י וַיָּס֣וּרוּ
שָׁ֔ם וַיֹּ֣אמְרוּ ל֔וֹ מִֽי־הֱבִיאֲךָ֣
הֲלֹ֔ם וּמָֽה־אַתָּ֥ה עֹשֶׂ֖ה בָּזֶ֑ה
4 וּמַה־לְּךָ֖ פֹּֽה: וַיֹּ֣אמֶר אֲלֵהֶ֗ם
כָּזֹ֚ה וְכָזֶ֙ה עָ֣שָׂה לִ֣י מִיכָ֔ה
וַיִּשְׂכְּרֵ֕נִי וָאֱהִי־ל֖וֹ לְכֹהֵֽן:
5 וַיֹּ֣אמְרוּ ל֗וֹ שְׁאַל־נָ֣א בֵֽאלֹהִ֑ים
וְנֵ֣דְעָ֔ה הֲתַצְלִ֣יחַ דַּרְכֵּ֔נוּ אֲשֶׁ֥ר
אֲנַ֖חְנוּ הֹלְכִ֣ים עָלֶֽיהָ:
6 וַיֹּ֧אמֶר לָהֶ֛ם הַכֹּהֵ֖ן לְכ֣וּ
לְשָׁל֑וֹם נֹ֣כַח יְהֹוָ֔ה דַּרְכְּכֶ֖ם
אֲשֶׁ֥ר תֵּֽלְכוּ־בָֽהּ:
7 וַיֵּלְכוּ֙ חֲמֵ֣שֶׁת הָֽאֲנָשִׁ֔ים וַיָּבֹ֖אוּ

---

unto the house. They arrived at the house, but
did not enter it (cf. the next verse) (Kimchi,
Metsudath David).

lodged. Stayed the night.

3. *they knew the voice.* The Levite had perhaps made their acquaintance on a previous
occasion. How and where are not stated;
but it may be inferred from xvii. 8 that the
young man had wandered about the
country. While so doing, he had met many
persons among whom were these Danites
(Daath Mikra). Alternatively, since the lad
was from the family of Kohath, whose Levitical cities were in the tribe of Dan, they
recognized him (Malbim). Since he was pray-
ing aloud at the time, they heard and recognized his voice (Daath Mikra).

hither. The same word, *halom,* was used in

God's address to Moses (Exod. iii. 5); so the
Midrash comments that the Danites
employed the word deliberately to hint that,
as a descendant of Moses, the Levite had no
right to be officiating at an idolatrous shrine
(Rashi from B.B. 110a).

4. *thus and thus.* As related in xvii. 10ff.
(Metsudath David).

5. *ask counsel . . . God.* As in i. 1. They did
not appreciate that the ephod, through
which the enquiry would be made, was used
for an idolatrous purpose (Kimchi following
the Targum). As mentioned above, according to many authorities, this is profane,
since it refers to the teraphim (Rashi, Kimchi following the Talmud).

6. The men proceed northwards and find a
city called Laish, situated in an isolated and
undefended position amid fertile fields.

and came to Laish, and saw the
people that were therein, how they
dwelt in security, after the manner
of the Zidonians, quiet and secure;
for there was none in the land,
possessing authority, that might put
them to shame in any thing, and
they were far from the Zidonians,
and had no dealings with any man.
8. And they came unto their
brethren to Zorah and Eshtaol; and
their brethren said unto them:
'What say ye?' 9. And they said:
'Arise, and let us go up against them;
for we have seen the land, and,
behold, it is very good; and are ye
still? be not slothful to go and to

לְיְשָׁה וַיִּרְאוּ אֶת־הָעָם אֲשֶׁר־
בְּקִרְבָּהּ יוֹשֶׁבֶת לָבֶטַח
כְּמִשְׁפַּט צִדֹנִים שֹׁקֵט | וּבֹטֵחַ
וְאֵין־מַכְלִים דָּבָר בָּאָרֶץ
יוֹרֵשׁ עֶצֶר וּרְחוֹקִים הֵמָּה
מִצִּידֹנִים וְדָבָר אֵין־לָהֶם
עִם־אָדָם: 8 וַיָּבֹאוּ אֶל־
אֲחֵיהֶם צָרְעָה וְאֶשְׁתָּאֹל
וַיֹּאמְרוּ לָהֶם אֲחֵיהֶם מָה
אַתֶּם: 9 וַיֹּאמְרוּ קוּמָה וְנַעֲלֶה
עֲלֵיהֶם כִּי רָאִינוּ אֶת־
הָאָרֶץ וְהִנֵּה טוֹבָה מְאֹד וְאַתֶּם
מַחְשִׁים אַל־תֵּעָצְלוּ לָלֶכֶת

Laish. Also called *Leshem* (Josh. xix. 47); not
far from Lebanon and the sources of the
Jordan. The name Tel el-Kadi ('mount of
the judge') preserves the later name *Dan*
('judge'). It lay in the valley belonging to
Beth-rehob (verse 28) (Daath Mikra, verse
29).

dwelt. The Hebrew has a feminine form. On
the analogy of Exod. v. 16 and Jer. viii. 5
the subject may be *the people* (Kimchi), or the
feminine word 'city' understood (Daath
Mikra).

Zidonians. i.e. the Phoenicians. The deduction has been drawn that the locality was the
site of a settlement not of the Canaanites,
and that the Phoenicians were a peace-lov-
ing community averse to war (Kimchi).

possessing authority. The phrase *yoresh etser*
occurs nowhere else and its meaning is
uncertain. The literal translation seems to
be 'one who inherits (power of) restraint'
and it may signify 'heir to the throne.' Rashi
explains that heirs were restricted in number; and were they to die, there would be

no others to fight anybody who took possession of their land.

put them to shame in any thing. Another
obscure phrase. Kimchi and Ralbag con-
strue it as a parallel to the preceding; one
who instructs and rebukes. Rashi quotes an
explanation he had heard: no one had
occasion to ask help of his neighbour with
the possibility of being offended by a refusal, because the district was exceptionally
fertile (cf. verse 10).

from the Zidonians. Who would consequently
not be concerned to defend them if the
Danites appropriated their land (Rashi).

had no dealings. They had no treaty of mutual
aid with any neighbouring people (ibid.).

8. *what say ye?* lit. 'what you?' what have
you to report (cf. *who art thou?* in Ruth iii.
16 which may be understood similarly)
(Rashi, Kimchi).

9. *are ye still?* Inactive (Kimchi), dallying
(Rashi).

enter in to possess the land. 10. When ye go, ye shall come unto a people secure, and the land is large; for God hath given it into your hand; a place where there is no want; it hath every thing that is in the earth.'

11. And there set forth from thence of the family of the Danites, out of Zorah and out of Eshtaol, six hundred men girt with weapons of war. 12. And they went up, and encamped in Kiriath-jearim, in Judah; wherefore that place was called Mahaneh-dan unto this day; behold, it is behind Kiriath-jearim. 13. And they passed thence unto the hill-country of Ephraim, and came unto the house of Micah. 14. Then answered the five men that went to spy out the country of Laish, and said unto their brethren: 'Do ye know that there is in these houses an

לָבֹא לָרֶשֶׁת אֶת־הָאָרֶץ:

10 כְּבֹאֲכֶם תָּבֹאוּ ׀ אֶל־עַם בֹּטֵחַ וְהָאָרֶץ רַחֲבַת יָדַיִם כִּי־נְתָנָהּ אֱלֹהִים בְּיֶדְכֶם מָקוֹם אֲשֶׁר אֵין־שָׁם מַחְסוֹר כָּל־דָּבָר אֲשֶׁר בָּאָרֶץ:

11 וַיִּסְעוּ מִשָּׁם מִמִּשְׁפַּחַת הַדָּנִי מִצָּרְעָה וּמֵאֶשְׁתָּאֹל שֵׁשׁ־מֵאוֹת אִישׁ חָגוּר כְּלֵי מִלְחָמָה:

12 וַיַּעֲלוּ וַיַּחֲנוּ בְּקִרְיַת יְעָרִים בִּיהוּדָה עַל־כֵּן קָרְאוּ לַמָּקוֹם הַהוּא מַחֲנֵה־דָן עַד הַיּוֹם הַזֶּה הִנֵּה אַחֲרֵי קִרְיַת

13 יְעָרִים: וַיַּעַבְרוּ מִשָּׁם הַר־אֶפְרָיִם וַיָּבֹאוּ עַד־בֵּית

14 מִיכָה: וַיַּעֲנוּ חֲמֵשֶׁת הָאֲנָשִׁים הַהֹלְכִים לְרַגֵּל אֶת־הָאָרֶץ לַיִשׁ וַיֹּאמְרוּ אֶל־אֲחֵיהֶם

---

10. *large.* lit. 'broad of hands'; stretching wide to the right and left, not cooped up among hills (Metsudath David).

11–26 SEIZURE OF THE TERAPHIM

The Danites set out, six hundred armed warriors, accompanied by their women and children, their flocks and all their belongings. They encamp near Kiriath-jearim and pass on to mount Ephraim where was the home of Micah. Having taken possession of Micah's images, they persuaded the Levite to accompany them. Micah protests in vain.

12. *Kiriath-jearim.* Meaning 'city of forests,' now identified with Khurbet 'Erma, about

four miles east of Beth-shemesh. It was a city of the Gibeonites which escaped destruction through the deception played on Joshua (Josh. ix. 17). In the time of Samuel, the ark remained there for a period (1 Sam. vii. 1ff.).

Mahaneh-dan. 'The camp of Dan' (cf. xiii. 25).

behind. i.e. west of.

14. *answered.* The verb *anah* sometimes means 'to speak.' It is so rendered here by Metsudath Zion.

these houses. Micah's home consisted of several buildings (Daath Mikra).

ephod, and teraphim, and a graven image, and a molten image? now therefore consider what ye have to do.' 15. And they turned aside thither, and came to the house of the young man the Levite, even unto the house of Micah, and asked him of his welfare. 16. And the six hundred men girt with their weapons of war, who were of the children of Dan, stood by the entrance of the gate. 17. And the five men that went to spy out the land went up, and came in thither, and took the graven image, and the ephod, and the teraphim, and the molten image; and the priest stood by the entrance of the gate with the six hundred men girt with weapons of war. 18. And when these went into Micah's house, and fetched the graven image of the ephod, and the teraphim, and the molten image, the priest said unto them: 'What do ye?' 19. And they said unto him: 'Hold thy peace, lay thy hand upon thy

הַיְדַעְתֶּם כִּי יֵשׁ בַּבָּתִּים הָאֵלֶּה
אֵפוֹד וּתְרָפִים וּפֶסֶל וּמַסֵּכָה
וְעַתָּה דְּעוּ מַה־תַּעֲשׂוּ׃
15 וַיָּסֻרוּ שָׁמָּה וַיָּבֹאוּ אֶל־בֵּית־
הַנַּעַר הַלֵּוִי בֵּית מִיכָה
וַיִּשְׁאֲלוּ־לוֹ לְשָׁלוֹם׃
16 וְשֵׁשׁ־מֵאוֹת אִישׁ חֲגוּרִים
כְּלֵי מִלְחַמְתָּם נִצָּבִים פֶּתַח
17 הַשָּׁעַר אֲשֶׁר מִבְּנֵי דָן׃ וַיַּעֲלוּ
חֲמֵשֶׁת הָאֲנָשִׁים הַהֹלְכִים
לְרַגֵּל אֶת־הָאָרֶץ בָּאוּ שָׁמָּה
לָקְחוּ אֶת־הַפֶּסֶל וְאֶת־
הָאֵפוֹד וְאֶת־הַתְּרָפִים וְאֶת־
הַמַּסֵּכָה וְהַכֹּהֵן נִצָּב פֶּתַח
הַשַּׁעַר וְשֵׁשׁ־מֵאוֹת הָאִישׁ
18 הֶחָגוּר כְּלֵי הַמִּלְחָמָה׃ וְאֵלֶּה
בָּאוּ בֵּית מִיכָה וַיִּקְחוּ אֶת־
פֶּסֶל הָאֵפוֹד וְאֶת־הַתְּרָפִים
וְאֶת־הַמַּסֵּכָה וַיֹּאמֶר אֲלֵיהֶם
הַכֹּהֵן מָה אַתֶּם עֹשִׂים׃
19 וַיֹּאמְרוּ לוֹ הַחֲרֵשׁ שִׂים־יָדְךָ

15. *of his welfare.* lit. 'for peace.' They gave him the conventional greeting.

16. *gate.* Of the city.

17. According to Metsudath David the course of events was as follows: the five investigators left Micah's house with the Levite (described in anticipation as *the priest*) to consult with the six hundred men at the gate; they left the Levite with these men and returned to the house to take the graven image, etc.

18. *graven image of the ephod.* Kimchi infers that there were images without an ephod, but Micah's had one.

19. *lay thy hand upon thy mouth.* The gesture of one who forces himself to keep silent (cf. Job. xxix. 9, xl. 4) (Metsudath David).

mouth, and go with us, and be to us a father and a priest; is it better for thee to be priest unto the house of one man, or to be priest unto a tribe and a family in Israel?' 20. And the priest's heart was glad, and he took the ephod, and the teraphim, and the graven image, and went in the midst of the people. 21. So they turned and departed, and put the little ones and the cattle and the goods before them. 22. When they were a good way from the house of Micah, the men that were in the houses near to Micah's house were gathered together, and overtook the children of Dan. 23. And they cried unto the children of Dan. And they turned their faces, and said unto Micah: 'What aileth thee, that thou comest with such a company?' 24. And he said: 'Ye have taken away my god which I made, and the priest, and are gone away, and what

עַל־פִּ֙יךָ֙ וְלֵ֣ךְ עִמָּ֔נוּ וֶהְיֵה־לָ֖נוּ לְאָ֣ב וּלְכֹהֵ֑ן הֲט֣וֹב ׀ הֱיוֹתְךָ֣ כֹהֵ֗ן לְבֵית֙ אִ֣ישׁ אֶחָ֔ד א֚וֹ הֱיוֹתְךָ֣ כֹהֵ֔ן לְשֵׁ֥בֶט וּלְמִשְׁפָּחָ֖ה
20 בְּיִשְׂרָאֵֽל׃ וַיִּיטַב֙ לֵ֣ב הַכֹּהֵ֔ן וַיִּקַּח֙ אֶת־הָ֣אֵפ֔וֹד וְאֶת־הַתְּרָפִ֖ים וְאֶת־הַפָּ֑סֶל וַיָּבֹ֖א
21 בְּקֶ֥רֶב הָעָֽם׃ וַיִּפְנ֖וּ וַיֵּלֵ֑כוּ וַיָּשִׂ֨ימוּ אֶת־הַטַּ֧ף וְאֶת־הַמִּקְנֶ֛ה וְאֶת־הַכְּבוּדָּ֖ה
22 לִפְנֵיהֶֽם׃ הֵ֥מָּה הִרְחִ֖יקוּ מִבֵּ֣ית מִיכָ֑ה וְהָאֲנָשִׁ֗ים אֲשֶׁ֤ר בַּבָּתִּים֙ אֲשֶׁ֣ר עִם־בֵּ֣ית מִיכָ֔ה נִזְעֲק֔וּ וַיַּדְבִּ֖יקוּ אֶת־בְּנֵי־
23 דָֽן׃ וַיִּקְרְאוּ֙ אֶל־בְּנֵי־דָ֔ן וַיַּסֵּ֖בּוּ פְּנֵיהֶ֑ם וַיֹּאמְר֣וּ לְמִיכָ֔ה
24 מַה־לְּךָ֖ כִּ֥י נִזְעָֽקְתָּ׃ וַיֹּ֡אמֶר אֶת־אֱלֹהַ֣י אֲשֶׁר־עָשִׂ֩יתִי֩ לְקַחְתֶּ֨ם וְאֶת־הַכֹּהֵ֖ן וַתֵּלֵ֑כוּ

20. *was glad.* He accepted their invitation with alacrity (Daath Mikra).

21. *the little ones.* So sure were they of victory that they took their children with them. It must be presumed that the women also accompanied them although this is not mentioned (Kimchi).

the goods. The noun *kebuddah,* derived from the root *kabed,* 'to be heavy,' and not found elsewhere, means 'burdens, impediments' (Rashi, Kimchi).

before them. To safeguard them against attack

from · the rear (Abarbanel, Metsudath David).

22. *the men . . . Micah's house.* The loss of the images and the priest affected also Micah's neighbours, since they believed that their welfare was endangered (Daath Mikra).

overtook. lit. 'caused to cleave' (cf. Gen. xix. 19).

23. *they turned.* The subject is the Danites (Rashi).

what aileth thee . . . company? lit. 'what to thee that thou art mustered?'

have I more? and how then say ye unto me: What aileth thee?' 25. And the children of Dan said unto him: 'Let not thy voice be heard among us, lest angry fellows fall upon you, and thou lose thy life, with the lives of thy household.' 26. And the children of Dan went their way; and when Micah saw that they were too strong for him, he turned and went back unto his house. 27. And they took that which Micah had made, and the priest whom he had, and came unto Laish, unto a people quiet and secure, and smote them with the edge of the sword; and they burnt the city with fire. 28. And there was no deliverer, because it was far from Zidon, and they had no dealings with any man; and it was in the valley that lieth by Beth-rehob. And they built the city, and dwelt

וּמַה־לִּי עוֹד וּמַה־זֶּה תֹּאמְרוּ

25 אֵלַי מַה־לָּךְ: וַיֹּאמְרוּ אֵלָיו
בְּנֵי־דָן אַל־תַּשְׁמַע קוֹלְךָ
עִמָּנוּ פֶּן־יִפְגְּעוּ בָכֶם אֲנָשִׁים
מָרֵי נֶפֶשׁ וְאָסַפְתָּה נַפְשְׁךָ וְנֶפֶשׁ

26 בֵּיתֶךָ: וַיֵּלְכוּ בְנֵי־דָן
לְדַרְכָּם וַיַּרְא מִיכָה כִּי־
חֲזָקִים הֵמָּה מִמֶּנּוּ וַיִּפֶן וַיָּשָׁב

27 אֶל־בֵּיתוֹ: וְהֵמָּה לָקְחוּ אֵת
אֲשֶׁר־עָשָׂה מִיכָה וְאֶת־
הַכֹּהֵן אֲשֶׁר הָיָה־לוֹ וַיָּבֹאוּ
עַל־לַיִשׁ עַל־עַם שֹׁקֵט וּבֹטֵחַ
וַיַּכּוּ אוֹתָם לְפִי־חָרֶב וְאֶת־

28 הָעִיר שָׂרְפוּ בָאֵשׁ: וְאֵין מַצִּיל
כִּי רְחוֹקָה־הִיא מִצִּידוֹן
וְדָבָר אֵין־לָהֶם עִם־אָדָם
וְהִיא בָּעֵמֶק אֲשֶׁר לְבֵית־
רְחוֹב וַיִּבְנוּ אֶת־הָעִיר וַיֵּשְׁבוּ

---

24. *what have I more?* You have deprived me of these, so what is left to me?

25. *angry fellows.* lit. 'embittered of soul'; men of nasty temper (Rashi).

lose. lit. 'gather in (to thy people).'

26. *too strong.* There was no king in Israel to administer justice, and so they had to yield to superior force.

27–31 CAPTURE OF LAISH

27. *burnt the city with fire.* The reason for this drastic action may have been that it was defiled by idolatry (Kimchi); or to strike terror into the hearts of the surviving inhabitants so that they would not counter-attack (ibid.); or to implant fear in the surrounding villages and towns (Ralbag).

28. *it was far from Zidon,* etc. See on verse 7.

lieth by. Or 'belongeth to, leadeth to.'

Beth-rehob. Supposed by some authorities to be Jebel Hunin, south-west of Tel el-kadi (Dan). It cannot be the *Rehob* of i. 31, but is possibly the same as the town mentioned in Num. xiii. 21. In the tenth century B.C.E. Beth-rehob was an Aramean city (cf. 2 Sam. x. 6, 8) (see Daath Mikra).

therein. 29. And they called the name of the city Dan, after the name of Dan their father, who was born unto Israel; howbeit the name of the city was Laish at the first. 30. And the children of Dan set up for themselves the graven image; and Jonathan, the son of Gershom, the son of Manasseh, he and his sons were priests to the tribe of the Danites until the day of the captivity of the land. 31. So they set them up Micah's graven image which he made, all the time that the house of God was in Shiloh.

29 בָּהּ׃ וַיִּקְרְאוּ שֵׁם־הָעִיר דָּן
בְּשֵׁם דָּן אֲבִיהֶם אֲשֶׁר יוּלַּד
לְיִשְׂרָאֵל וְאוּלָם לַיִשׁ שֵׁם־
30 הָעִיר לָרִאשֹׁנָה׃ וַיָּקִימוּ לָהֶם
בְּנֵי־דָן אֶת־הַפָּסֶל וִיהוֹנָתָן
בֶּן־גֵּרְשֹׁם בֶּן־מְנַשֶּׁה הוּא
וּבָנָיו הָיוּ כֹהֲנִים לְשֵׁבֶט הַדָּנִי
31 עַד־יוֹם גְּלוֹת הָאָרֶץ׃ וַיָּשִׂימוּ
לָהֶם אֶת־פֶּסֶל מִיכָה אֲשֶׁר
עָשָׂה כָּל־יְמֵי הֱיוֹת בֵּית־
הָאֱלֹהִים בְּשִׁלֹה׃

---

19   CHAPTER XIX   יט

1. And it came to pass in those days,   וַיְהִי בַּיָּמִים הָהֵם וּמֶלֶךְ אֵין

v. 29.   v. 30. הל׳ בדגש ב׳ תלויה

---

29. *who was born unto Israel.* This fact is mentioned to remove a possible impression that the Dan, after whom the place was named, was the father of the group of settlers and not the ancestor of the tribe.

Laish. Cf. Josh. xix. 48, where it is called *Leshem.* Cf. Gen. xiv. 14, where the city is called Dan as early as the time of Abraham. Kesseth Hasofer theorizes that these were two different cities, one named Dan in ancient times, and the other originally named Laish, or Leshem, and renamed by the tribe of Dan. Daath Soferim concurs.

30. *Jonathan.* He was the aforementioned Levite (Metsudath David).

Manasseh. The Rabbis declared that the suspended letter *nun* in the Hebrew text indicates that the name is really Moses who was the father of Gershom (Exod. ii. 22). The alteration was made from respect for the great leader, so as not to associate his name with a grandson who ministered to idols (Rashi from B.B. 109b).

the captivity of the land. Commentators differ as to the captivity which is intended. Rashi refers it to the exile of the northern tribes by Sennacherib (2 Kings xv. 29), and Kimchi, connecting this verse with the next, to the exile of the ark from Shiloh (1 Sam. iv. 11). Ralbag understands it as the exile of the Danites alone, and places the captivity in the time of Jabin king of Canaan (iv. 2f.).

31. *Shiloh.* The modern Seilum, situated on a low hill enclosed on all sides by higher ground, nine and a half miles north-east of Bethel (Daath Mikra on Josh. xviii. 1).

CHAPTER XIX

THE OUTRAGE AT GIBEAH

A LEVITE of mount Ephraim took a concubine from Bethlehem of Judah. She deserted him and returned home. After a time the man paid her a visit, was welcomed by her

when there was no king in Israel, that there was a certain Levite sojourning on the farther side of the hill-country of Ephraim, who took to him a concubine out of Beth-lehem in Judah. 2. And his concubine played the harlot against him, and went away from him unto her father's house to Beth-lehem in Judah, and was there the space of four months. 3. And her husband arose, and went after her, to speak kindly unto her, to bring her back, having his servant with him, and a couple of asses; and she brought him into her father's house; and

בְּיִשְׂרָאֵל וַיְהִי | אִישׁ לֵוִי גָּר
בְּיַרְכְּתֵי הַר־אֶפְרַיִם וַיִּקַּח־
לוֹ אִשָּׁה פִילֶגֶשׁ מִבֵּית לֶחֶם
2 יְהוּדָה: וַתִּזְנֶה עָלָיו פִּילַגְשׁוֹ
וַתֵּלֶךְ מֵאִתּוֹ אֶל־בֵּית אָבִיהָ
אֶל־בֵּית לֶחֶם יְהוּדָה וַתְּהִי־
שָׁם יָמִים אַרְבָּעָה חֳדָשִׁים:
3 וַיָּקָם אִישָׁהּ וַיֵּלֶךְ אַחֲרֶיהָ
לְדַבֵּר עַל־לִבָּהּ לַהֲשִׁיבָהּ
וְנַעֲרוֹ עִמּוֹ וְצֶמֶד חֲמֹרִים
וַתְּבִיאֵהוּ בֵּית אָבִיהָ וַיִּרְאֵהוּ

v. 3. להשיבה ק׳

father, and persuaded her to go back with him. On the return journey they were overtaken by darkness and decided to spend the night in Gibeah, a Benjamite city, where a kindly man invited them into his house. The inhabitants surrounded the house and insisted that the stranger be handed over to them. The law of hospitality demanded that his guest be protected, and the man offered the crowd his own daughter as well as the concubine. The offer was refused, and to save himself the Levite thrust the woman out of the house. She was outraged and found dead in the morning. He took the body home, cut it into twelve pieces which he sent to all the tribes with an account of the outrage. The nation was roused to violent indignation.

1–9 A LEVITE VISITS BETH-LEHEM

1. *no king in Israel*. See on xviii. 1.

the farther side. On the northern part of the central highland on the more retired portion. No town is mentioned (cf. xvii. 1).

took to him a concubine. Better, 'he took to him a woman as concubine' (Daath Mikra).

Beth-lehem in Judah. The preceding narrative

was also connected with a Levite and Beth-lehem (Abarbanel).

2. *against him*. lit. 'upon him, an unparalleled preposition with the verb *played the harlot*. Kimchi explains as: while still with him.

the space of four months. lit. 'days, four months.' Often *yamim* denotes 'year,' and according to Kimchi the text should either be rendered as though the conjunction 'and' stood before *four*, making the phrase mean 'a year and four months'; or the term *four months* is in apposition to *yamim* and the phrase is to be understood as '(a number of) days, viz. four months.' Cf. the Hebrew text of Gen. xxiv. 55.

3. The man's attitude recalls that of the prophet Hosea.

kindly. lit. 'on her heart'; the idea is to exert persuasion. Cf. Gen. xxxiv. 3, l. 21, etc. (Metsudath David).

a couple of asses. Carrying provisions and gifts, and providing transport (see Metsudath David).

into her father's house. Evidently the first meeting took place elsewhere, perhaps in, or near, the women's quarters (Kimchi).

when the father of the damsel saw him, he rejoiced to meet him. 4. And his father - in - law, the damsel's father, retained him; and he abode with him three days; so they did eat and drink, and lodged there. 5. And it came to pass on the fourth day, that they arose early in the morning, and he rose up to depart; and the damsel's father said unto his son-in-law: 'Stay thy heart with a morsel of bread, and afterward ye shall go your way.' 6. So they sat down, and did eat and drink, both of them together; and the damsel's father said unto the man: 'Be content, I pray thee, and tarry all night, and let thy heart be merry.' 7. And the man rose up to depart; but his father-in-law urged him, and he lodged there again. 8. And he arose early in the morning on the fifth day to depart; and the damsel's father said: 'Stay thy heart, I pray thee, and tarry ye until the day declineth'; and they did eat,

אֲבִי הַנַּעֲרָה וַיִּשְׂמַח לִקְרָאתוֹ:

4 וַיֶּחֱזַק־בּוֹ חֹתְנוֹ אֲבִי הַנַּעֲרָה וַיֵּשֶׁב אִתּוֹ שְׁלֹשֶׁת יָמִים וַיֹּאכְלוּ

5 וַיִּשְׁתּוּ וַיָּלִינוּ שָׁם: וַיְהִי בַּיּוֹם הָרְבִיעִי וַיַּשְׁכִּימוּ בַבֹּקֶר וַיָּקָם לָלֶכֶת וַיֹּאמֶר אֲבִי הַנַּעֲרָה אֶל־חֲתָנוֹ סְעָד לִבְּךָ פַּת־

6 לֶחֶם וְאַחַר תֵּלֵכוּ: וַיֵּשְׁבוּ וַיֹּאכְלוּ שְׁנֵיהֶם יַחְדָּו וַיִּשְׁתּוּ וַיֹּאמֶר אֲבִי הַנַּעֲרָה אֶל־ הָאִישׁ הוֹאֶל־נָא וְלִין וְיִטַב

7 לִבֶּךָ: וַיָּקָם הָאִישׁ לָלֶכֶת וַיִּפְצַר־בּוֹ חֹתְנוֹ וַיָּשָׁב וַיָּלֶן

8 שָׁם: וַיַּשְׁכֵּם בַּבֹּקֶר בַּיּוֹם הַחֲמִישִׁי לָלֶכֶת וַיֹּאמֶר | אֲבִי הַנַּעֲרָה סְעָד־נָא לְבָבְךָ וְהִתְמַהְמְהוּ עַד־נְטוֹת הַיּוֹם

v. 5. הע׳ בקמץ

4. *retained.* lit. 'took hold of'; the verb almost suggests the use of physical restraint. The woman's father, as the following verses show, was reluctant to let him go (Daath Mikra).

5. *stay thy heart,* etc. Gen. xviii. 5. When the stomach is full, it presses against the diaphragm and so against the heart which rests upon it, and is accordingly literally 'supported.' The phrase occurs in Latin and is more than a metaphor.

a morsel of bread. Oriental hospitality was modest in its claims but lavish in its execution (cf. Gen. xviii. 5).

6. *be content.* Better, 'consent.'

let thy heart be merry. i.e. enjoy yourself. The phrase is used of the effect of a feast, especially of wine-drinking (cf. xvi. 25).

7. *rose.* i.e. he rose to leave despite his father-in-law's invitation to stay the night.

8. *tarry ye until the day declineth.* The request to stay until the day declined is strange, since it would be dangerous for a traveller to set out towards evening. That the host was aware of this is seen from verse 9. Perhaps by the 'decline of the day' he meant after noon when the sun begins to incline towards the west, or the shadow on the dial declines (Kimchi). Alternatively, the verb translated *and tarry ye* may be the third per-

both of them. **9.** And when the man rose up to depart, he, and his concubine, and his servant, his father-in-law, the damsel's father, said unto him: 'Behold, now the day draweth toward evening; tarry, I pray you, all night; behold, the day groweth to an end; lodge here, that thy heart may be merry; and to-morrow get you early on your way, that thou mayest go home.' **10.** But the man would not tarry that night, but he rose up and departed, and came over against Jebus—the same is Jerusalem; and there were with him a couple of asses saddled; his concubine also was with him. **11.** When they were by Jebus—the day was far spent—the servant said unto his master: 'Come, I pray thee, and let us turn aside into this city of the Jebusites, and lodge in it.' **12.** And his master said unto him: 'We will not turn aside into the city of a foreigner, that is not of the children of Israel; but we will pass

9 וַיֹּאכְלוּ שְׁנֵיהֶם: וַיָּקָם הָאִישׁ
לָלֶכֶת הוּא וּפִילַגְשׁוֹ וְנַעֲרוֹ
וַיֹּאמֶר לוֹ חֹתְנוֹ אֲבִי הַנַּעֲרָה
הִנֵּה־נָא רָפָה הַיּוֹם לַעֲרוֹב
לִינוּ־נָא הִנֵּה חֲנוֹת הַיּוֹם לִין
פֹּה וְיִיטַב לְבָבֶךָ וְהִשְׁכַּמְתֶּם
מָחָר לְדַרְכְּכֶם וְהָלַכְתָּ
10 לְאֹהָלֶךָ: וְלֹא־אָבָה הָאִישׁ
לָלוּן וַיָּקָם וַיֵּלֶךְ וַיָּבֹא עַד־
נֹכַח יְבוּס הִיא יְרוּשָׁלַ͏ִם וְעִמּוֹ
צֶמֶד חֲמוֹרִים חֲבוּשִׁים
11 וּפִילַגְשׁוֹ עִמּוֹ: הֵם עִם־יְבוּס
וְהַיּוֹם רַד מְאֹד וַיֹּאמֶר הַנַּעַר
אֶל־אֲדֹנָיו לְכָה־נָּא וְנָסוּרָה
אֶל־עִיר־הַיְבוּסִי הַזֹּאת וְנָלִין
12 בָּהּ: וַיֹּאמֶר אֵלָיו אֲדֹנָיו לֹא
נָסוּר אֶל־עִיר נָכְרִי אֲשֶׁר
לֹא־מִבְּנֵי יִשְׂרָאֵל הֵנָּה

---

son plural with the ordinary conjunction and should be rendered 'and they tarried' (Metsudath David).

9. *draweth.* lit. 'hath weakened.' The expression 'the day has weakened' has its origin in the synonymous use of 'day' and 'sun,' and signifies that the sun has weakened or lost its heat (Rashi, Kimchi, Metsudath David). Cf. the cuneiform sign for 'day' (UD) which is the same as for 'sun.'

toward evening. This was true, because after they had travelled about two hours night fell (verse 10).

groweth to an end. lit. 'the camping of,' i.e. the time when men rest (Kimchi).

THE SCENE AT GIBEAH

10. *Jebus.* A name given to Jerusalem (cf. 1 Chron. xi. 4f.) probably with reference to its non-Israelite population, the Jebusites (Daath Mikra).That it was not the older name of the city is manifest from the Amarna Letters (*c.* 1400 B.C.E.) where *u-ru-sa-lim* is often found (Kesseth Hasofer, Gen. xiv. 14).

11. *by.* lit. 'with.'

far spent. lit. 'gone down exceedingly.' The uncommon form *rad* for *yarad* is explained as having belonged to the Hebrew language of the period.

12. *the city of a foreigner.* He would rather spend the night among Israelites. His

299

over to Gibeah.' 13. And he said unto his servant: 'Come and let us draw near to one of these places; and we will lodge in Gibeah, or in Ramah.' 14. So they passed on and went their way; and the sun went down upon them near to Gibeah, which belongeth to Benjamin. 15. And they turned aside thither, to go in to lodge in Gibeah; and he went in, and sat him down in the broad place of the city; for there was no man that took them into his house to lodge. 16. And, behold, there came an old man from his work out of the field at even; now the man was of the hill-country of Ephraim, and he sojourned in Gibeah; but the men of the place were Benjamites. 17. And he lifted up his eyes, and saw the wayfaring man in the broad place of the city; and the old man said: 'Whither

13 וְעָבַרְנוּ עַד־גִּבְעָה: וַיֹּאמֶר
לְנַעֲרוֹ לְךָ וְנִקְרְבָה בְּאַחַד
הַמְּקֹמוֹת וְלַנּוּ בַגִּבְעָה אוֹ
14 בְרָמָה: וַיַּעַבְרוּ וַיֵּלֵכוּ וַתָּבֹא
לָהֶם הַשֶּׁמֶשׁ אֵצֶל הַגִּבְעָה
15 אֲשֶׁר לְבִנְיָמִן: וַיָּסֻרוּ שָׁם
לָבוֹא לָלוּן בַּגִּבְעָה וַיָּבֹא
וַיֵּשֶׁב בִּרְחֹב הָעִיר וְאֵין אִישׁ
מְאַסֵּף־אוֹתָם הַבַּיְתָה לָלוּן:
16 וְהִנֵּה | אִישׁ זָקֵן בָּא מִן־
מַעֲשֵׂהוּ מִן־הַשָּׂדֶה בָּעֶרֶב
וְהָאִישׁ מֵהַר אֶפְרַיִם וְהוּא־גָר
בַּגִּבְעָה וְאַנְשֵׁי הַמָּקוֹם בְּנֵי
17 יְמִינִי: וַיִּשָּׂא עֵינָיו וַיַּרְא אֶת־
הָאִישׁ הָאֹרֵחַ בִּרְחֹב הָעִיר
וַיֹּאמֶר הָאִישׁ הַזָּקֵן אָנָה תֵלֵךְ

v. 13. חסר ה׳

reliance for safety on his own people exposes the villainy of the Benjamites the more glaringly (Meam Loez).

Gibeah. lit. 'hill,' a name borne by many towns. This was of Benjamin (verse 14), identified with Tel el-ful, a hill nearly three thousand feet above sea-level, about four miles north of Jerusalem (Daath Mikra).

13. *Ramah.* The modern er-Ram, about five miles from Jerusalem (ibid.).

14. *the sun went down.* In the East the interval between sunset and darkness is very brief; therefore they did not proceed as far as Ramah, but sought accomodation in Gibeah.

15. *they turned aside.* The verb is appropriate, because the village lay to one side of the main road.

sat him down. There were no inns in the town and travellers had to depend on offers of hospitality.

the broad place. Located just within the city-gate in the center of the city (Daath Mikra).

took. lit. 'gathered.'

16. *of the hill-country of Ephraim.* Hospitality was not offered by a Benjamite, but by a man who sojourned there. This is one of several features of resemblance between the incident and the experience of the angels in Sodom (Gen. xix). This man was too old and conditioned to be influenced by his bad neighbours. Moreover, he remained aloof from the Benjamites both by his awareness that he was a stranger, and by the fact that he was occupied with his work most of the day (Meam Loez).

goest thou? and whence comest thou?' 18. And he said unto him: 'We are passing from Beth-lehem in Judah unto the farther side of the hill-country of Ephraim; from thence am I, and I went to Beth-lehem in Judah, and I am now going to the house of the LORD; and there is no man that taketh me into his house. 19. Yet there is both straw and provender for our asses; and there is bread and wine also for me, and for thy handmaid, and for the young man that is with thy servants; there is no want of any thing.' 20. And the old man said: 'Peace be unto thee; howsoever let all thy wants lie upon me; only lodge not in the broad place.' 21. So he brought him into his house, and gave the asses fodder; and they washed their feet, and did eat and drink. 22. As they were making their hearts merry, behold, the men of the city, certain base fellows, beset the house round about, beating at the door; and they

18 וּמֵאַ֣יִן תָּב֑וֹא וַיֹּ֣אמֶר אֵלָ֔יו עֹבְרִ֣ים אֲנַ֗חְנוּ מִבֵּֽית־לֶ֨חֶם יְהוּדָה֮ עַד־יַרְכְּתֵ֣י הַר־ אֶפְרַ֒יִם֒ מִשָּׁ֣ם אָנֹ֔כִי וָאֵלֵ֕ךְ עַד־ בֵּ֥ית לֶ֨חֶם֙ יְהוּדָ֔ה וְאֶת־בֵּ֤ית יְהוָה֙ אֲנִ֣י הֹלֵ֔ךְ וְאֵ֣ין אִ֔ישׁ

19 מְאַסֵּ֥ף אוֹתִ֖י הַבָּֽיְתָה׃ וְגַם־ תֶּ֤בֶן גַּם־מִסְפּוֹא֙ יֵ֣שׁ לַחֲמוֹרֵ֔ינוּ וְ֠גַם לֶ֣חֶם וָיַ֤יִן יֶשׁ־לִי֙ וְלַֽאֲמָתֶ֔ךָ וְלַנַּ֖עַר עִם־עֲבָדֶ֑יךָ אֵ֥ין

20 מַחְס֖וֹר כָּל־דָּבָֽר׃ וַיֹּ֨אמֶר הָאִ֤ישׁ הַזָּקֵן֙ שָׁל֣וֹם לָ֔ךְ רַ֚ק כָּל־מַחְסֽוֹרְךָ֖ עָלָ֑י רַ֥ק

21 בָּרְח֖וֹב אַל־תָּלַֽן׃ וַיְבִיאֵ֣הוּ לְבֵית֔וֹ ויָּ֖בָול לַחֲמוֹרִ֑ים וַֽיִּרְחֲצוּ֙ רַגְלֵיהֶ֔ם וַיֹּֽאכְל֖וּ וַיִּשְׁתּֽוּ׃

22 הֵ֘מָּה֮ מֵיטִיבִ֣ים אֶת־ לִבָּם֒ וְהִנֵּה֩ אַנְשֵׁ֨י הָעִ֜יר אַנְשֵׁ֣י בְנֵֽי־בְלִיַּ֗עַל נָסַ֙בּוּ֙ אֶת־הַבַּ֔יִת מִֽתְדַּפְּקִ֖ים עַל־הַדָּ֑לֶת

v. 21. ויבל ק׳   v. 20. פתח בס״ס

---

17. *whither goest thou?* etc. Arabs still ask the same questions of a stranger.

18. *the house of the* LORD. i.e. to Shiloh (Rashi).

19. *there is both straw,* etc. He meant that he required nothing but shelter (Metsudath David).

20. *peace be unto thee.* The implication of the words is 'do not worry' (ibid.).

21. *washed their feet.* Cf. Gen. xviii. 4, xix.

2, etc. To do this was very welcome to men who wore sandals.

22-28 DEATH OF THE CONCUBINE

22. *base fellows.* lit. 'men of the sons of worthlessness. The grammatical construction is explained as the substitution of a genitive for the apposition (Michlol Yofi).

beating. The Hithpael conjugation instead of the Kal may denote an unseemly eagerness.

301

spoke to the master of the house, the old man, saying: 'Bring forth the man that came into thy house, that we may know him.' 23. And the man, the master of the house, went out unto them, and said unto them: 'Nay, my brethren, I pray you, do not so wickedly; seeing that this man is come into my house, do not this wanton deed. 24. Behold, here is my daughter a virgin, and his concubine; I will bring them out now, and humble ye them, and do with them what seemeth good unto you; but unto this man do not so wanton a thing.' 25. But the men would not hearken to him; so the man laid hold on his concubine, and brought her forth unto them; and they knew her, and abused her all the night until the morning; and when the day began to spring, they let her go. 26. Then came the woman in the dawning of the day, and fell down at the door of the man's house where her lord was, till it was light. 27. And her lord rose up in the morning, and opened

וַיֹּאמְרוּ אֶל־הָאִישׁ בַּעַל
הַבַּיִת הַזָּקֵן לֵאמֹר הוֹצֵא אֶת־
הָאִישׁ אֲשֶׁר־בָּא אֶל־בֵּיתְךָ
וְנֵדָעֶנּוּ: וַיֵּצֵא אֲלֵיהֶם הָאִישׁ 23
בַּעַל הַבַּיִת וַיֹּאמֶר אֲלֵהֶם
אַל־אַחַי אַל־תָּרֵעוּ נָא אַחֲרֵי
אֲשֶׁר־בָּא הָאִישׁ הַזֶּה אֶל־
בֵּיתִי אַל־תַּעֲשׂוּ אֶת־הַנְּבָלָה
הַזֹּאת: הִנֵּה בִתִּי הַבְּתוּלָה 24
וּפִילַגְשֵׁהוּ אוֹצִיאָה־נָּא אוֹתָם
וְעַנּוּ אוֹתָם וַעֲשׂוּ לָהֶם הַטּוֹב
בְּעֵינֵיכֶם וְלָאִישׁ הַזֶּה לֹא
תַעֲשׂוּ דְּבַר הַנְּבָלָה הַזֹּאת:
וְלֹא־אָבוּ הָאֲנָשִׁים לִשְׁמֹעַ לוֹ 25
וַיַּחֲזֵק הָאִישׁ בְּפִילַגְשׁוֹ וַיֹּצֵא
אֲלֵיהֶם הַחוּץ וַיֵּדְעוּ אוֹתָהּ
וַיִּתְעַלְּלוּ־בָהּ כָּל־הַלַּיְלָה
עַד־הַבֹּקֶר וַיְשַׁלְּחוּהָ בַּעֲלוֹת
הַשָּׁחַר: וַתָּבֹא הָאִשָּׁה לִפְנוֹת 26
הַבֹּקֶר וַתִּפֹּל פֶּתַח בֵּית־
הָאִישׁ אֲשֶׁר־אֲדוֹנֶיהָ שָּׁם עַד־
הָאוֹר: וַיָּקָם אֲדֹנֶיהָ בַּבֹּקֶר 27

v. 25. כעלות ק׳

---

we may know him. The citizens were addicted to unnatural vice (Rashi, Kimchi).

24. The resemblance of this verse to Gen. xix. 8 is striking.

25. *brought her forth.* Thinking that the men would be attracted by her beauty. It was a

dastardly act to save himself in this manner (Abarbanel).

when the day began to spring. lit. 'in the ascent of the dawn'; when the first trace of light appeared in the sky (Metsudath David).

26. *the dawning of the day.* lit. 'as the turning of the morning.'

the doors of the house, and went out to go his way; and, behold, the woman his concubine was fallen down at the door of the house, with her hands upon the threshold. 28. And he said unto her: 'Up, and let us be going'; but none answered; then he took her up upon the ass; and the man rose up, and got him unto his place. 29. And when he was come into his house, he took a knife, and laid hold on his concubine, and divided her, limb by limb, into twelve pieces, and sent her throughout all the borders of Israel. 30. And it was so, that all that saw it said: 'Such a thing hath not happened nor been seen from the day that the children of Israel came up out of the land of Egypt unto this day; consider it, take counsel, and speak.'

וַיִּפְתַּח דַּלְתוֹת הַבַּיִת וַיֵּצֵא לָלֶכֶת לְדַרְכּוֹ וְהִנֵּה הָאִשָּׁה פִילַגְשׁוֹ נֹפֶלֶת פֶּתַח הַבַּיִת
28 וְיָדֶיהָ עַל־הַסַּף: וַיֹּאמֶר אֵלֶיהָ קוּמִי וְנֵלֵכָה וְאֵין עֹנֶה וַיִּקָּחֶהָ עַל־הַחֲמוֹר וַיָּקָם
29 הָאִישׁ וַיֵּלֶךְ לִמְקֹמוֹ: וַיָּבֹא אֶל־בֵּיתוֹ וַיִּקַּח אֶת־הַמַּאֲכֶלֶת וַיַּחֲזֵק בְּפִילַגְשׁוֹ וַיְנַתְּחֶהָ לַעֲצָמֶיהָ לִשְׁנֵים עָשָׂר נְתָחִים וַיְשַׁלְּחֶהָ בְּכֹל גְּבוּל
30 יִשְׂרָאֵל: וְהָיָה כָל־הָרֹאֶה וְאָמַר לֹא־נִהְיְתָה וְלֹא־ נִרְאֲתָה כָּזֹאת לְמִיּוֹם עֲלוֹת בְּנֵי־יִשְׂרָאֵל מֵאֶרֶץ מִצְרַיִם עַד הַיּוֹם הַזֶּה שִׂימוּ־לָכֶם עָלֶיהָ עֻצוּ וְדַבֵּרוּ:

---

20   CHAPTER XX   כ

1. Then all the children of Israel

1 וַיֵּצְאוּ כָּל־בְּנֵי יִשְׂרָאֵל

27. *to go his way.* It is not to be assumed that he meant to leave the town without recovering the woman.

28. *up, and let us be going.* He evidently thought that she was alive (Metsudath David).

none answered. There was no response from her (Metsudath Zion).

the man rose up. He returned to his home taking the body with him.

29. *limb by limb.* lit. 'according to her bones.'

sent her. As Saul did with the oxen (1 Sam. xi. 7).

throughout all the borders. To rouse the horror and indignation of all Israel (Abarbanel).

30. *hath not happened.* viz. the brutal treatment of the woman.

CHAPTER XX

WAR WITH BENJAMIN

A GENERAL assembly of the tribes was held at Mizpah and an army mustered to go on a punitive expedition against Benjamin. The demand that the perpetrators of the crime be given up was rejected by the Benjaminites who prepared to resist. War was

went out, and the congregation was assembled as one man, from Dan even to Beer-sheba, with the land of Gilead, unto the LORD at Mizpah. 2. And the chiefs of all the people, even of all the tribes of Israel, presented themselves in the assembly of the people of God, four hundred thousand footmen that drew sword.—3. Now the children of Benjamin heard that the children of Israel were gone up to Mizpah.— And the children of Israel said: 'Tell us, how was this wickedness brought to pass?' 4. And the Levite, the husband of the woman that was murdered, answered and said: 'I came into Gibeah that belongeth to Benjamin, I and my

וַתִּקָּהֵל הָעֵדָה כְּאִישׁ אֶחָד
לְמִדָּן וְעַד־בְּאֵר שֶׁבַע וְאֶרֶץ
הַגִּלְעָד אֶל־יְהֹוָה הַמִּצְפָּה:
2 וַיִּתְיַצְּבוּ פִּנּוֹת כָּל־הָעָם כֹּל
שִׁבְטֵי יִשְׂרָאֵל בִּקְהַל עַם
הָאֱלֹהִים אַרְבַּע מֵאוֹת אֶלֶף
3 אִישׁ־רַגְלִי שֹׁלֵף חָרֶב: וַיִּשְׁמְעוּ
בְּנֵי בִנְיָמִן כִּי־עָלוּ בְנֵי־
יִשְׂרָאֵל הַמִּצְפָּה וַיֹּאמְרוּ בְּנֵי
יִשְׂרָאֵל דַּבְּרוּ אֵיכָה נִהְיְתָה
4 הָרָעָה הַזֹּאת: וַיַּעַן הָאִישׁ
הַלֵּוִי אִישׁ הָאִשָּׁה הַנִּרְצָחָה
וַיֹּאמֶר הַגִּבְעָתָה אֲשֶׁר לְבִנְיָמִן

v. 2. כצ״ל

declared and fierce fighting followed. After a series of defeats, the tribes prepared a stratagem which succeeded and the Benjamites were all but exterminated.

1–11 THE ASSEMBLY AND ITS DECISION

1. *went out.* [To prepare for war.]

congregation. [*Edah* is a technical term for the whole people.]

as one man. See on vi. 16. [Here the meaning is 'without exception.]

from Dan even to Beer-sheba. The extreme northern and southern limits of the country (Metsudath David). For *Dan,* see on xviii. 7, and for Beer-sheba, on Josh. xv. 28.

Gilead. All the tribes east of the Jordan, with the single exception of the men of Jabesh (xxi. 8) (Daath Mikra).

Mizpah. In Benjamin (Daath Mikra). They gathered there because of its memorable associations with the great victory of Joshua's day (Kimchi). See on Josh. xviii. 26.

2. *chiefs.* lit. 'corners (Rashi and Kimchi

following the Targum).' Others interpret this literally, viz. each tribe stood in its own individual corner (Abarbanel, Metsudath David).

that drew sword. Ready to punish the offending tribe, in battle if need be. The assembly was of a military character but charged with a moral mission; hence the phrase the people of God (Daath Mikra).

3. *now the children of Benjamin heard,* etc. This is a parenthetical insert describing Benjamin's reaction to the gathering. Although Benjamin knew that Israel had gathered, they did not care to punish the guilty nor did they come to clarify their position (Kimchi, Metsudath David, Malbim). Others explain that, although the Benjamites knew of the gathering, they were not officially summoned. Therefore, the Israelites were punished (Ramban on Gen. xix. 8).

tell us. lit. 'speak.'

4. *Gibeah.* [In the Hebrew it stands at the beginning of the clause for emphasis.]

concubine, to lodge. 5. And the men of Gibeah rose against me, and beset the house round about upon me by night; me they thought to have slain, and my concubine they forced, and she is dead. 6. And I took my concubine, and cut her in pieces, and sent her throughout all the country of the inheritance of Israel; for they have committed lewdness and wantonness in Israel. 7. Behold, ye are all here, children of Israel, give here your advice and counsel.' 8. And all the people arose as one man, saying: 'We will not any of us go to his tent, neither will we any of us turn unto his house. 9. But now this is the thing which we will do to Gibeah: we will go up against it by lot; 10. and we will take ten men of a hundred throughout all the tribes of Israel, and a hundred of a thousand, and a thousand out of ten thousand, to fetch victuals for the people, that they may do, when they come to Gibeah of Benjamin, according to all the wantonness that they have

בָּאתִי אֲנִי וּפִילַגְשִׁי לָלוּן׃
5 וַיָּקֻמוּ עָלַי בַּעֲלֵי הַגִּבְעָה
וַיָּסֹבּוּ עָלַי אֶת־הַבַּיִת לָיְלָה
אוֹתִי דִּמּוּ לַהֲרֹג וְאֶת־פִּילַגְשִׁי
6 עִנּוּ וַתָּמֹת׃ וָאֹחֵז בְּפִילַגְשִׁי
וָאֲנַתְּחֶהָ וָאֲשַׁלְּחֶהָ בְּכָל־
שְׂדֵה נַחֲלַת יִשְׂרָאֵל כִּי עָשׂוּ
7 זִמָּה וּנְבָלָה בְּיִשְׂרָאֵל׃ הִנֵּה
כֻלְּכֶם בְּנֵי יִשְׂרָאֵל הָבוּ לָכֶם
8 דָּבָר וְעֵצָה הֲלֹם׃ וַיָּקָם כָּל־
הָעָם כְּאִישׁ אֶחָד לֵאמֹר לֹא
נֵלֵךְ אִישׁ לְאָהֳלוֹ וְלֹא נָסוּר
9 אִישׁ לְבֵיתוֹ׃ וְעַתָּה זֶה הַדָּבָר
אֲשֶׁר נַעֲשֶׂה לַגִּבְעָה עָלֶיהָ
10 בְגוֹרָל׃ וְלָקַחְנוּ עֲשָׂרָה
אֲנָשִׁים לַמֵּאָה לְכֹל שִׁבְטֵי
יִשְׂרָאֵל וּמֵאָה לָאֶלֶף וְאֶלֶף
לָרְבָבָה לָקַחַת צֵדָה לָעָם
לַעֲשׂוֹת לְבוֹאָם לְגֶבַע בִּנְיָמִן
כְּכָל־הַנְּבָלָה אֲשֶׁר עָשָׂה

5. *men.* lit. 'lords' (see on ix. 2).

thought to have slain. That such was their intention in xix. 22 may naturally be inferred from the fate which befell his concubine (Malbim).

7. *your advice and counsel.* lit. 'a word and counsel'; i.e. express your view on what to do about this atrocious incident (ibid.).

9. *we will go up.* The verb is not in the

Hebrew and is inferred from the context (Kimchi, Metsudath David).

by lot. The purpose of the lot is explained in the next verse.

10. A tenth of the fighting force, to be selected by lot, will be detailed to supply the army with provisions.

they may do. They alludes to *the people,* the fighting men (Rashi, Metsudath David).

Gibeah. The form in the Hebrew is *Geba.*

wrought in Israel.' 11. So all the men of Israel were gathered against the city, knit together as one man.

12. And the tribes of Israel sent men through all the tribe of Benjamin, saying: 'What wickedness is this that is come to pass among you? 13. Now therefore deliver up the men, the base fellows that are in Gibeah, that we may put them to death, and put away evil from Israel.' But the children of Benjamin would not hearken to the voice of their brethren the children of Israel. 14. And the children of Benjamin gathered themselves together out of their cities unto Gibeah, to go out to battle against the children of Israel. 15. And the children of Benjamin numbered on that day out of the cities twenty and six thousand men that drew sword,

11 בְּיִשְׂרָאֵל: וַיֵּאָסֵף כָּל־אִישׁ
יִשְׂרָאֵל אֶל־הָעִיר כְּאִישׁ
אֶחָד חֲבֵרִים:
12 וַיִּשְׁלְחוּ שִׁבְטֵי יִשְׂרָאֵל אֲנָשִׁים
בְּכָל־שִׁבְטֵי בִנְיָמִן לֵאמֹר מָה
הָרָעָה הַזֹּאת אֲשֶׁר נִהְיְתָה
13 בָּכֶם: וְעַתָּה תְּנוּ אֶת־
הָאֲנָשִׁים בְּנֵי־בְלִיַּעַל אֲשֶׁר
בַּגִּבְעָה וּנְמִיתֵם וּנְבַעֲרָה רָעָה
מִיִּשְׂרָאֵל וְלֹא אָבוּ ‬ בִנְיָמִן
לִשְׁמֹעַ בְּקוֹל אֲחֵיהֶם בְּנֵי־
14 יִשְׂרָאֵל: וַיֵּאָסְפוּ בְנֵי־בִנְיָמִן
מִן־הֶעָרִים הַגִּבְעָתָה לָצֵאת
לַמִּלְחָמָה עִם־בְּנֵי יִשְׂרָאֵל:
15 וַיִּתְפָּקְדוּ בְנֵי בִנְיָמִן בַּיּוֹם
הַהוּא מֵהֶעָרִים עֶשְׂרִים וְשִׁשָּׁה
אֶלֶף אִישׁ שֹׁלֵף חָרֶב לְבַד

v. 13. בני קרי ולא כתיב

---

they have wrought. The subject is the Benjamites.

11. *the city.* Gibeah (Abarbanel, Metsudath David).

knit together. lit. 'companions'; the root signifies 'to join together.' i.e. not as individual tribes, but as one man (Abarbanel).

12–16 THE BENJAMITE FORCE

12. *tribe of Benjamin.* The Hebrew means 'tribes' as in 1 Sam. ix. 21, and the plural is explained as denoting the families comprising the tribe (cf. Gen. xlvi. 21). Such a subdivision is described as a 'tribe' in Num. iv. 18 (Rashi, Kimchi, Metsudath David).

come to pass. The same verb as in verse 3 and xix. 30; it perhaps expresses unexpected-

ness and bewilderment. In English the corresponding phrase would be: 'what has come over you?'

13. *put away evil.* Better, 'extirpate' (cf. Deut. xiii. 6). The same verb is used of the complete removal of leaven on the Passover eve.

the children of. Not in the text; this is one of ten instances of a *kere* without a *kethib* (Minchath Shai).

14. *unto Gibeah.* To join their compatriots in the city.

15. *twenty and six thousand.* The total casualties in the final battle were twenty-five thousand (verse 46). Kimchi suggests that the remaining thousand may have died in the earlier skirmishes (verses 21, 25).

besides the inhabitants of Gibeah, who numbered seven hundred chosen men. 16. All this people, even seven hundred chosen men, were left-handed; every one could sling stones at a hair-breadth, and not miss.

17. And the men of Israel, beside Benjamin, numbered four hundred thousand men that drew sword; all these were men of war. 18. And the children of Israel arose, and went up to Beth-el, and asked counsel of God; and they said: 'Who shall go up for us first to battle against the children of Benjamin?' And the LORD said: 'Judah first.' 19. And the children of Israel rose up in the morning, and encamped against Gibeah. 20. And the men of Israel went out to battle against Benjamin; and the men of Israel set the battle in array against them at Gibeah. 21. And the children of Benjamin

מִיֹּשְׁבֵי הַגִּבְעָה֙ הִתְפָּקְד֔וּ שְׁבַע
16 מֵא֥וֹת אִ֖ישׁ בָּח֑וּר׃ מִכֹּ֣ל ׀
הָעָ֣ם הַזֶּ֗ה שְׁבַ֤ע מֵאוֹת֙ אִ֣ישׁ
בָּח֔וּר אִטֵּ֖ר יַד־יְמִינ֑וֹ כָּל־זֶ֗ה
קֹלֵ֧עַ בָּאֶ֛בֶן אֶל־הַֽשַּׂעֲרָ֖ה וְלֹ֥א
יַחֲטִֽא׃
17 וְאִ֤ישׁ יִשְׂרָאֵל֙ הִתְפָּֽקְד֔וּ לְבַ֖ד
מִבִּנְיָמִ֔ן אַרְבַּ֥ע מֵא֛וֹת אֶ֖לֶף
אִ֣ישׁ שֹׁ֣לֵֽף חָ֑רֶב כָּל־זֶ֖ה אִ֥ישׁ
18 מִלְחָמָֽה׃ וַיָּקֻ֜מוּ וַיַּעֲל֣וּ בֵֽית־
אֵ֗ל וַיִּשְׁאֲל֣וּ בֵֽאלֹהִים֮ וַיֹּֽאמְרוּ֙
בְּנֵ֣י יִשְׂרָאֵ֔ל מִ֚י יַעֲלֶה־לָּ֣נוּ
בַתְּחִלָּ֔ה לַמִּלְחָמָ֖ה עִם־בְּנֵ֣י
בִנְיָמִ֑ן וַיֹּ֥אמֶר יְהֹוָ֖ה יְהוּדָ֥ה
19 בַתְּחִלָּֽה׃ וַיָּק֥וּמוּ בְנֵֽי־יִשְׂרָאֵ֖ל
בַּבֹּ֑קֶר וַיַּחֲנ֖וּ עַל־הַגִּבְעָֽה׃
20 וַיֵּצֵא֙ אִ֣ישׁ יִשְׂרָאֵ֔ל לַמִּלְחָמָ֖ה
עִם־בִּנְיָמִ֑ן וַיַּעַרְכ֨וּ אִתָּ֤ם
אִֽישׁ־יִשְׂרָאֵל֙ מִלְחָמָ֔ה אֶל־
21 הַגִּבְעָֽה׃ וַיֵּצְא֥וּ בְנֵֽי־בִנְיָמִ֖ן

---

16. *seven hundred.* Not those mentioned in the previous verse as coming from Gibeah (Daath Mikra).

left-handed. Everyone of the seven hundred (Rashi). See on iii. 15

sling stones. The skill of the Benjamites in this method of warfare is recorded in 1 Chron. xii. 2f. Its deadliness was proved in the battles that ensued.

hair-breadth. lit. 'to the hair.'

17–28 TWO DEFEATS OF THE ISRAELITES

18. *the children of Israel.* They were probably representatives chosen from the people.

who shall go up, etc. Cf. i. 1f. They omitted to enquire whether they would be victorious (Rashi).

came forth out of Gibeah, and destroyed down to the ground of the Israelites on that day twenty and two thousand men. 22. And the people, the men of Israel, encouraged themselves, and set the battle again in array in the place where they set themselves in array the first day. 23. And the children of Israel went up and wept before the LORD until even; and they asked of the LORD, saying: 'Shall I again draw nigh to battle against the children of Benjamin my brother?' And the LORD said: 'Go up against him.'

24. And the children of Israel came near against the children of Benjamin the second day. 25. And Benjamin went forth against them out of Gibeah the second day, and destroyed down to the ground of the children of Israel again eighteen thousand men; all these drew the

מִן־הַגִּבְעָה וַיַּשְׁחִיתוּ בְיִשְׂרָאֵל
בַּיּוֹם הַהוּא שְׁנַיִם וְעֶשְׂרִים
22 אֶלֶף אִישׁ אָרְצָה: וַיִּתְחַזֵּק
הָעָם אִישׁ יִשְׂרָאֵל וַיֹּסִפוּ
לַעֲרֹךְ מִלְחָמָה בַּמָּקוֹם אֲשֶׁר
עָרְכוּ־שָׁם בַּיּוֹם הָרִאשׁוֹן:
23 וַיַּעֲלוּ בְנֵי־יִשְׂרָאֵל וַיִּבְכּוּ
לִפְנֵי־יְהוָֹה עַד־הָעֶרֶב
וַיִּשְׁאֲלוּ בַיהוָֹה לֵאמֹר
הַאוֹסִיף לָגֶשֶׁת לַמִּלְחָמָה
עִם־בְּנֵי בִנְיָמִן אָחִי וַיֹּאמֶר
יְהוָֹה עֲלוּ אֵלָיו:
24 וַיִּקְרְבוּ בְנֵי־יִשְׂרָאֵל אֶל־בְּנֵי
25 בִנְיָמִן בַּיּוֹם הַשֵּׁנִי: וַיֵּצֵא בִנְיָמִן
ו לִקְרָאתָם מִן־הַגִּבְעָה בַּיּוֹם
הַשֵּׁנִי וַיַּשְׁחִיתוּ בִבְנֵי יִשְׂרָאֵל
עוֹד שְׁמֹנַת עָשָׂר אֶלֶף אִישׁ

21. destroyed. The defeat was, according to tradition (Sanh. 103b), punishment for their failure to show equal zeal in suppressing the idolatry in the shrine of Micah.

down to the ground. [i.e. hewed them down to the ground and left them lying there.]

22. and set the battle, etc. They continued to trust in their own strength and were already stationed for battle. After this, they sent the elders to obtain permission to advance upon Benjamin. In verse 26, however, all of Israel gathered to repent, and they properly asked of God whether they should continue to conduct the war (Malbim).

23. the children of Israel. Not the people, the men of Israel, as in the previous verse, but a selected number (Malbim).

my brother. The addition of these words is significant. They showed that they were not asking for revenge for the thousands that fell in battle. Rather, their objective was to correct Benjamin from their evil ways (Abarbanel).

go up against him. Note the difference in verse 28 where the enquiry was added or shall I cease? and the assurance is given I will deliver him into thy hand.

sword. 26. Then all the children of
Israel, and all the people, went up,
and came unto Beth-el, and wept,
and sat there before the LORD, and
fasted that day until even; and they
offered burnt-offerings and peace-
offerings before the LORD. 27. And
the children of Israel asked of the
LORD—for the ark of the covenant
of God was there in those days,
28. and Phinehas, the son of
Eleazar, the son of Aaron, stood
before it in those days—saying:
'Shall I yet again go out to battle
against the children of Benjamin my
brother, or shall I cease?' And the
LORD said: 'Go up; for to-morrow
I will deliver him into thy hand.'
29. And Israel set liers-in-wait
against Gibeah round about.

30. And the children of Israel went
up against the children of Benjamin
on the third day, and set themselves

אַרְצָה כָּל־אֵלֶּה שֹׁלְפֵי חָרֶב׃

26 וַיַּעֲלוּ כָל־בְּנֵי יִשְׂרָאֵל וְכָל־
הָעָם וַיָּבֹאוּ בֵית־אֵל וַיִּבְכּוּ
וַיֵּשְׁבוּ שָׁם לִפְנֵי יְהֹוָה וַיָּצוּמוּ
בַיּוֹם־הַהוּא עַד־הָעָרֶב
וַיַּעֲלוּ עֹלוֹת וּשְׁלָמִים לִפְנֵי

27 יְהֹוָה׃ וַיִּשְׁאֲלוּ בְנֵי־יִשְׂרָאֵל
בַּיהֹוָה וְשָׁם אֲרוֹן בְּרִית
הָאֱלֹהִים בַּיָּמִים הָהֵם׃

28 וּפִינְחָס בֶּן־אֶלְעָזָר בֶּן־
אַהֲרֹן עֹמֵד | לְפָנָיו בַּיָּמִים
הָהֵם לֵאמֹר הַאוֹסִף עוֹד
לָצֵאת לַמִּלְחָמָה עִם־בְּנֵי־
בִנְיָמִן אָחִי אִם־אֶחְדָּל וַיֹּאמֶר
יְהֹוָה עֲלוּ כִּי מָחָר אֶתְּנֶנּוּ

29 בְיָדֶךָ׃ וַיָּשֶׂם יִשְׂרָאֵל אֹרְבִים
אֶל־הַגִּבְעָה סָבִיב׃

30 וַיַּעֲלוּ בְנֵי־יִשְׂרָאֵל אֶל־בְּנֵי
בִנְיָמִן בַּיּוֹם הַשְּׁלִישִׁי וַיַּעַרְכוּ

---

26. *Beth-el.* Not the city of that name but,
in view of the following verse, literally 'the
house of God' in Shiloh (Kimchi). Cf.
Meshech Chochmah, Deut. xii. 8.

and wept. The feeling of contrition was now
more intense than on the first occasion
(verse 23). They knew that something must
be wrong when an expedition, having as its
purpose, the punishment of a foul crime,
met with repeated disaster (Abarbanel).

27. The first half of the verse is continued
in the next with the word *saying.* The
remaining half of verse 27 and the first part

of verse 28, ending with *in those days,* are in
parenthesis (Metsudath David).

the ark. This is the only reference to the ark
in the Book.

29–44 THE FINAL BATTLE

29. *liers-in-wait.* Cf. ix. 32. The same strategy had proved successful in the second
battle for Ai (Josh. viii. 4). The nature of
the country was such that, both here and at
Ai, the city could only be taken by drawing
the defenders from their vantage-ground by
means of a feigned flight.

in array against Gibeah, as at other times. 31. And the children of Benjamin went out against the people, and were drawn away from the city; and they began to smite and kill of the people, as at other times, in the field, in the highways, of which one goeth up to Beth-el, and the other to Gibeah, about thirty men of Israel. 32. And the children of Benjamin said: 'They are smitten down before us, as at the first.' But the children of Israel said: 'Let us flee, and draw them away from the city unto the highways.' 33. And all the men of Israel rose up out of their place, and set themselves in array at Baal-tamar; and the liers-in-wait of Israel broke forth out of their place, even out of Maareh-geba. 34. And there came over against Gibeah ten thousand chosen men out of all Israel, and

אֶל־הַגִּבְעָה כְּפַעַם בְּפָעַם:
31 וַיֵּצְאוּ בְנֵי־בִנְיָמִן לִקְרַאת
הָעָם הָנְתְּקוּ מִן־הָעִיר וַיָּחֵלּוּ
לְהַכּוֹת מֵהָעָם חֲלָלִים
כְּפַעַם ׀ בְּפַעַם בַּמְסִלּוֹת אֲשֶׁר
אַחַת עֹלָה בֵית־אֵל וְאַחַת
גִּבְעָתָה בַּשָּׂדֶה כִּשְׁלֹשִׁים אִישׁ
32 בְּיִשְׂרָאֵל: וַיֹּאמְרוּ בְּנֵי בִנְיָמִן
נִגָּפִים הֵם לְפָנֵינוּ כְּבָרִאשֹׁנָה
וּבְנֵי יִשְׂרָאֵל אָמְרוּ נָנוּסָה
וּנְתַקְנֻהוּ מִן־הָעִיר אֶל־
33 הַמְסִלּוֹת: וְכֹל ׀ אִישׁ יִשְׂרָאֵל
קָמוּ מִמְּקוֹמוֹ וַיַּעַרְכוּ בְּבַעַל
תָּמָר וְאֹרֵב יִשְׂרָאֵל מֵגִיחַ
34 מִמְּקֹמוֹ מִמַּעֲרֵה־גָבַע: וַיָּבֹאוּ
מִנֶּגֶד לַגִּבְעָה עֲשֶׂרֶת אֲלָפִים
אִישׁ בָּחוּר מִכָּל־יִשְׂרָאֵל

v. 31.   v. 32. הק׳ דגושה   הל׳ דגושה

---

30. *as at other times.* A change of tactics discernible by the Benjamites would have aroused their suspicion.

31. *smite and kill.* lit. 'smite slain men'; this idiom is known as a proleptic figure of speech.

at other times. On the two previous occasions (Metsudath David).

the field. i.e. the open country.

the highways. Possibly two roads joined or crossed at this point (ibid.).

33. *rose up.* The main army abandoned their original position and reformed their ranks at another point.

Baal-tamar. The place is otherwise unknown. Tradition identifies it with Attara, a ruin near Gibeah. The 'palm-tree' (*tamar*) suggested to the Targum the Plain of Jericho, to others the palm-tree of Deborah (iv. 5).

broke forth. The verb *giach* is generally used of water gushing forth; but in Aramaic it means 'to attack, make war upon.'

Maareh-geba. The Hebrew is best understood as a compound place-name. The first half, connected with *arah*, 'be bare,' possibly denotes a clearing in a wooded district which would be used as the hiding-place of an ambush (Daath Mikra).

34. *there came.* viz. the men who had secreted themselves (Metsudath David).

the battle was sore; but they knew
not that evil was close upon them.
35. And the LORD smote Benjamin
before Israel; and the children of
Israel destroyed of Benjamin that
day twenty and five thousand and
a hundred men; all these drew the
sword.

36. So the children of Benjamin
saw that they were smitten. And
the men of Israel gave place to
Benjamin, because they trusted unto
the liers-in-wait whom they had set
against Gibeah.—37. And the liers-
in-wait hastened, and rushed upon
Gibeah; and the liers-in-wait drew
forth, and smote all the city with the
edge of the sword. 38. Now there
was an appointed sign between the
men of Israel and the liers-in-wait,
that they should make a great beacon
of smoke rise up out of the city.—
39. And the men of Israel turned in
the battle, and Benjamin began to
smite and kill of the men of Israel

וְהַמִּלְחָמָה כָּבֵדָה וְהֵם לֹא
יָדְעוּ כִּי־נֹגַעַת עֲלֵיהֶם
35 הָרָעָה: וַיִּגֹּף יְהֹוָה ׀ אֶת־בִּנְיָמִן
לִפְנֵי יִשְׂרָאֵל וַיַּשְׁחִיתוּ בְנֵי
יִשְׂרָאֵל בְּבִנְיָמִן בַּיּוֹם הַהוּא
עֶשְׂרִים וַחֲמִשָּׁה אֶלֶף וּמֵאָה
אִישׁ כָּל־אֵלֶּה שֹׁלֵף חָרֶב:
36 וַיִּרְאוּ בְנֵי־בִנְיָמִן כִּי
נִגָּפוּ וַיִּתְּנוּ אִישׁ־יִשְׂרָאֵל
מָקוֹם לְבִנְיָמִן כִּי בָטְחוּ
אֶל־הָאֹרֵב אֲשֶׁר שָׂמוּ
37 אֶל־הַגִּבְעָה: וְהָאֹרֵב הֵחִישׁוּ
וַיִּפְשְׁטוּ אֶל־הַגִּבְעָה וַיִּמְשֹׁךְ
הָאֹרֵב וַיַּךְ אֶת־כָּל־הָעִיר
38 לְפִי־חָרֶב: וְהַמּוֹעֵד הָיָה
לְאִישׁ יִשְׂרָאֵל עִם־הָאֹרֵב
הֶרֶב לְהַעֲלוֹתָם מַשְׂאַת הֶעָשָׁן
39 מִן־הָעִיר: וַיַּהֲפֹךְ אִישׁ־
יִשְׂרָאֵל בַּמִּלְחָמָה וּבִנְיָמִן
הֵחֵל לְהַכּוֹת חֲלָלִים בְּאִישׁ־

they knew not. The subject is the Benjamites
(Metsudath David).

evil was done. Disaster was imminent; again
in verse 41 (ibid.).

36. Having given a general account of the
battle, the writer proceeds to describe events
in greater detail (ibid.).

gave place. They allowed the Benjamites to
escape into Gibeah (Rashi).

37. drew forth. lit. 'drew.' Rashi and Kimchi

understand the verb as 'draw out a sound'
on trumpets (cf. Exod. xix. 13; Josh. vi. 5);
others as 'advanced' (see on iv. 6) (Targum).

38. an appointed sign. So Rashi; Kimchi
prefers the more usual meaning 'a fixed
time.'

they should make a great beacon. lit. 'to multiply
to their causing an uprising of the smoke to
ascend' (Rashi).

39. turned. In pretended flight (Kimchi).

about thirty persons; for they said: 'Surely they are smitten down before us, as in the first battle.' 40. But when the beacon began to arise up out of the city in a pillar of smoke, the Benjamites looked behind them, and, behold, the whole of the city went up in smoke to heaven. 41. And the men of Israel turned, and the men of Benjamin were amazed; for they saw that evil was come upon them. 42. Therefore they turned their backs before the men of Israel unto the way of the wilderness; but the battle followed hard after them; and they that came out of the city destroyed them in the midst of the men of Israel. 43. They inclosed the Benjamites round about and chased them, and overtook them at their resting-place, as far as over against Gibeah toward the sunrising. 44. And there fell of Benjamin eighteen thousand men;

יִשְׂרָאֵל כִּשְׁלֹשִׁים אִישׁ כִּי
אָמְרוּ אַךְ נִגּוֹף נִגָּף הוּא
לְפָנֵינוּ כַּמִּלְחָמָה הָרִאשֹׁנָה:

40 וְהַמַּשְׂאֵת הֵחֵלָּה לַעֲלוֹת מִן־
הָעִיר עַמּוּד עָשָׁן וַיִּפֶן בִּנְיָמִן
אַחֲרָיו וְהִנֵּה עָלָה כְלִיל־

41 הָעִיר הַשָּׁמָיְמָה: וְאִישׁ
יִשְׂרָאֵל הָפַךְ וַיִּבָּהֵל אִישׁ
בִּנְיָמִן כִּי רָאָה כִּי־נָגְעָה עָלָיו

42 הָרָעָה: וַיִּפְנוּ לִפְנֵי אִישׁ
יִשְׂרָאֵל אֶל־דֶּרֶךְ הַמִּדְבָּר
וְהַמִּלְחָמָה הִדְבִּיקָתְהוּ וַאֲשֶׁר
מֵהֶעָרִים מַשְׁחִיתִים אוֹתוֹ

43 בְּתוֹכוֹ: כִּתְּרוּ אֶת־בִּנְיָמִן
הִרְדִיפֻהוּ מְנוּחָה הִדְרִיכֻהוּ
עַד נֹכַח הַגִּבְעָה מִמִּזְרַח־

44 שָׁמֶשׁ: וַיִּפְּלוּ מִבִּנְיָמִן שְׁמֹנָה־

---

40. *whole.* The noun *kalil* is the term for an offering wholly burned on the altar (e.g. Lev. vi. 15f.). Of a city it appears again in Deut. xiii. 17.

41. *amazed.* Or, 'terrified.'

42. *the way of the wilderness.* The ravines and uncultivated steep descents of the broken Ephraimite hill-country which extend east of Gibeah down to the Jordan valley (Daath Mikra).

the city. lit. 'the cities,' which Rashi interprets as the men of the towns along the line of flight who came out to assist the Benjamites. The translation would then be: 'them that came out of the cities (the Israelites) destroyed.'

in the midst of the men of Israel. The Hebrew is 'in the midst of it.' Some refer to the suffix to 'the city' (Rashi); others to the two contingents of the Israelite army (Targum).

43. *inclosed.* Or, 'encircled' (cf. s. xxii. 13) (Rashi, Kimchi).

chased. lit. 'caused to pursue' (Rashi Kimchi); the Hiphil of this verb does not occur elsewhere.

their resting-place. The noun *menuchah* may possibly be a place-name; cf. Janoah from the same root. (Josh. xvi. 7; 2 Kings xv. 29). Perhaps Manahath, a Benjamite city mentioned in 1 Chron. xiii (Daath Mikra).

all these were men of valour.
45. And they turned and fled toward
the wilderness unto the rock of
Rimmon; and they gleaned of them
in the highways five thousand men;
and followed hard after them unto
Gidom, and smote of them two
thousand men. 46. So that all who
fell that day of Benjamin were
twenty and five thousand men that
drew the sword; all these were men
of valour. 47. But six hundred men
turned and fled toward the wilderness unto the rock of Rimmon, and
abode in the rock of Rimmon four
months. 48. And the men of Israel
turned back upon the children of
Benjamin, and smote them with the
edge of the sword, both the entire
city, and the cattle, and all that they
found; moreover all the cities which
they found they set on fire.

עֲשָׂר אֶלֶף אִישׁ אֶת־כָּל־
45 אֵלֶּה אַנְשֵׁי חָיִל: וַיִּפְנוּ וַיָּנֻסוּ
הַמִּדְבָּרָה אֶל־סֶלַע הָרִמּוֹן
וַיְעֹלְלֻהוּ בַּמְסִלּוֹת חֲמֵשֶׁת
אֲלָפִים אִישׁ וַיַּדְבִּיקוּ אַחֲרָיו
עַד־גִּדְעֹם וַיַּכּוּ מִמֶּנּוּ אַלְפַּיִם
46 אִישׁ: וַיְהִי כָל־הַנֹּפְלִים
מִבִּנְיָמִן עֶשְׂרִים וַחֲמִשָּׁה אֶלֶף
אִישׁ שֹׁלֵף חֶרֶב בַּיּוֹם הַהוּא
47 אֶת־כָּל־אֵלֶּה אַנְשֵׁי־חָיִל:
וַיִּפְנוּ וַיָּנֻסוּ הַמִּדְבָּרָה אֶל־
סֶלַע הָרִמּוֹן שֵׁשׁ מֵאוֹת אִישׁ
וַיֵּשְׁבוּ בְּסֶלַע רִמּוֹן אַרְבָּעָה
48 חֳדָשִׁים: וְאִישׁ יִשְׂרָאֵל שָׁבוּ
אֶל־בְּנֵי בִנְיָמִן וַיַּכּוּם
לְפִי־חֶרֶב מֵעִיר מְתֹם עַד־
בְּהֵמָה עַד כָּל־הַנִּמְצָא גַּם
כָּל־הֶעָרִים הַנִּמְצָאוֹת
שִׁלְּחוּ בָאֵשׁ:

44. *all these.* In the text the accusative particle precedes with the purpose of adding
prominence to what follows; again in verse
46.

45–48 A REMNANT OF THE
BENJAMITES ESCAPES

45. *they turned.* The subject is the survivors
of the Benjamite force.

Rimmon. The modern Rumman situated on a
rocky hill about three miles east of Beth-el,
on the verge of the hill-country described in
the note on verse 42 (Daath Mikra). The
fleeing army made for the safety of this rock,
but only a small proportion of their

number reached the place of refuge (cf.
verse 47).

gleaned. Like the small grapes plucked after
the main vintage (Rashi, Kimchi).

Gidom. The place is mentioned nowhere else
and is unknown.

48. *turned back.* From pursuing the rest of
the fugitives (Daath Mikra).

the children of Benjamin. viz. the population of
the other cities of that tribe.

the entire city. For *methom* (*entire*) many
Hebrew MSS. read *methim*, 'the city of men,'
the inhabited city (cf. Deut. ii. 34). Minchath
Shai rejects this reading.

21   CHAPTER XXI   כא

1. Now the men of Israel had sworn in Mizpah, saying: 'There shall not any of us give his daughter unto Benjamin to wife.' 2. And the people came to Beth-el, and sat there till even before God, and lifted up their voices, and wept sore. 3. And they said: 'O LORD, the God of Israel, why is this come to pass in Israel, that there should be to-day one tribe lacking in Israel?' 4. And it came to pass on the morrow that the people rose early, and built there an altar, and offered burnt-offerings and peace-offerings. 5. And the children of Israel said: 'Who is there among all the tribes of Israel that came not up in the assembly unto the LORD?' For they had made a great oath concerning him that

1 וְאִישׁ יִשְׂרָאֵל נִשְׁבַּע בַּמִּצְפָּה
לֵאמֹר אִישׁ מִמֶּנּוּ לֹא־יִתֵּן
2 בִּתּוֹ לְבִנְיָמִן לְאִשָּׁה: וַיָּבֹא
הָעָם בֵּית־אֵל וַיֵּשְׁבוּ שָׁם עַד־
הָעֶרֶב לִפְנֵי הָאֱלֹהִים וַיִּשְׂאוּ
קוֹלָם וַיִּבְכּוּ בְּכִי גָדוֹל:
3 וַיֹּאמְרוּ לָמָה יְהֹוָה אֱלֹהֵי
יִשְׂרָאֵל הָיְתָה זֹּאת בְּיִשְׂרָאֵל
לְהִפָּקֵד הַיּוֹם מִיִּשְׂרָאֵל שֵׁבֶט
4 אֶחָד: וַיְהִי מִמָּחֳרָת וַיַּשְׁכִּימוּ
הָעָם וַיִּבְנוּ־שָׁם מִזְבֵּחַ וַיַּעֲלוּ
5 עֹלוֹת וּשְׁלָמִים: וַיֹּאמְרוּ בְּנֵי
יִשְׂרָאֵל מִי אֲשֶׁר לֹא־עָלָה
בַקָּהָל מִכָּל־שִׁבְטֵי יִשְׂרָאֵל
אֶל־יְהֹוָה כִּי הַשְּׁבוּעָה

CHAPTER XXI

PRESERVATION OF THE TRIBE OF BENJAMIN

1-5 AFTERMATH OF THE WAR

THE Israelites had sworn not to give their daughters in marriage to the Benjamites. The decision was regretted when it was realized that the tribe was threatened with extinction, and a method was devised whereby this danger was averted.

1. *had sworn in Mizpah.* i.e. when they had assembled in Mizpah before going out to war against Benjamin. This act is not recorded. It is now reported because its implications dawned upon the people (Abarbanel, Metsudath David).

2. *came to Beth-el.* Cf. xx. 18, 26. Some Jewish commentators also interpret here as the 'house of God' in Shiloh (Metsudath David. See Kimchi).

sore. lit. 'a great weeping.' The reason for the lamentation is stated in the next verse.

3. *why is this come to pass,* etc. They complained of the circumstances which had led to the present situation. What mysterious working of Providence allowed such a tragedy to happen? (Abarbanel)

4. *an altar.* They erected a new altar, that being part of the process of seeking guidance of God (Kimchi).

5. *they had made,* etc. lit. 'the great oath was concerning.'

came not up unto the LORD to
Mizpah, saying: 'He shall surely be
put to death.' 6. And the children
of Israel repented them for Benjamin
their brother, and said: 'There is one
tribe cut off from Israel this day.
7. How shall we do for wives for
them that remain, seeing we have
sworn by the LORD that we will not
give them of our daughters to wives?'
8. And they said: 'What one is there
of the tribes of Israel that came not
up unto the LORD to Mizpah?'
And, behold, there came none to
the camp from Jabesh-gilead to the
assembly. 9. For when the people
were numbered, behold, there were
none of the inhabitants of Jabesh-
gilead there. 10. And the congregation sent thither twelve thousand men of the valiantest, and
commanded them, saying: 'Go and
smite the inhabitants of Jabesh-
gilead with the edge of the sword,
with the women and the little ones.
11. And this is the thing that ye shall
do: ye shall utterly destroy every

הַגְּדוֹלָ֑ה הָיְתָ֕ה לַאֲשֶׁ֨ר לֹא־
עָלָ֧ה אֶל־יְהֹוָ֛ה הַמִּצְפָּ֖ה
‎6 לֵאמֹ֖ר מ֣וֹת יוּמָֽת׃ וַיִּנָּֽחֲמוּ֙
בְּנֵ֣י יִשְׂרָאֵ֔ל אֶל־בִּנְיָמִ֖ן אָחִ֑יו
וַיֹּ֣אמְר֔וּ נִגְדַּ֥ע הַיּ֛וֹם שֵׁ֥בֶט אֶחָֽד
‎7 מִיִּשְׂרָאֵֽל׃ מַה־נַּעֲשֶׂ֥ה לָהֶ֛ם
לַנּוֹתָרִ֖ים לְנָשִׁ֑ים וַאֲנַ֗חְנוּ
נִשְׁבַּ֤עְנוּ בַֽיהֹוָה֙ לְבִלְתִּ֜י תֵּת־
לָהֶ֥ם מִבְּנוֹתֵ֖ינוּ לְנָשִֽׁים׃
‎8 וַיֹּ֣אמְר֔וּ מִ֗י אֶחָד֙ מִשִּׁבְטֵ֣י
יִשְׂרָאֵ֔ל אֲשֶׁ֛ר לֹא־עָלָ֥ה אֶל־
יְהֹוָ֖ה הַמִּצְפָּ֑ה וְ֠הִנֵּה לֹ֣א בָא־
אִ֧ישׁ אֶל־הַֽמַּחֲנֶ֛ה מִיָּבֵ֥ישׁ
‎9 גִּלְעָ֖ד אֶל־הַקָּהָֽל׃ וַיִּתְפָּקֵ֖ד
הָעָ֑ם וְהִנֵּ֤ה אֵֽין־שָׁם֙ אִ֔ישׁ
‎10 מִיּוֹשְׁבֵ֖י יָבֵ֥שׁ גִּלְעָֽד׃ וַיִּשְׁלְחוּ־
שָׁ֣ם הָעֵדָ֗ה שְׁנֵים־עָשָׂ֥ר אֶ֛לֶף
אִ֖ישׁ מִבְּנֵ֣י הֶחָ֑יִל וַיְצַוּ֨וּ אוֹתָ֜ם
לֵאמֹ֗ר לְכ֨וּ וְהִכִּיתֶ֜ם אֶת־
יוֹשְׁבֵ֨י יָבֵ֤שׁ גִּלְעָד֙ לְפִי־חֶ֔רֶב
‎11 וְהַנָּשִׁ֖ים וְהַטָּֽף׃ וְזֶ֥ה הַדָּבָ֖ר
אֲשֶׁ֣ר תַּעֲשׂ֑וּ כָּל־זָכָ֗ר וְכָל־

---

6. *repented them.* The phrase means that
they had second thoughts (Metsudath Zion).

8. *Jabesh-gilead.* Appears again in Biblical
history in 1 Sam. xi. 1ff., xxxi. 11ff.; 2 Sam.
ii. 4f., xxi. 12. The place is supposed by
some authorities to be the modern Meri-
amin, about seven miles from Pella, near a
stream which is still called Wadi Yabis. Kaf-

tor Vaferach, however, maintains that Wadi
Yabis is some distance from Jabesh-gilead.
He was informed that *Wadi Yabis* is a cor-
ruption of *Wadi Al Yas,* the Arabic name of
Elijah, hence Elijah's stream. Jabesh-gilead
is directly east of Beth-shean, approximately a three day journey. It is called *Goffen* by
the Arabs, meaning 'dry,' corresponding to
the Hebrew *yabesh.*

male, and every woman that hath lain by man.' 12. And they found among the inhabitants of Jabesh-gilead four hundred young virgins, that had not known man by lying with him; and they brought them unto the camp to Shiloh, which is in the land of Canaan.

13. And the whole congregation sent and spoke to the children of Benjamin that were in the rock of Rimmon, and proclaimed peace unto them. 14. And Benjamin returned at that time; and they gave them the women whom they had saved alive of the women of Jabesh-gilead; and yet so they sufficed them not. 15. And the people repented them for Benjamin, because that the LORD had made a breach in the tribes of Israel.

16. Then the elders of the congregation said: 'How shall we do for wives for them that remain, seeing the women are destroyed out of Benjamin?' 17. And they said: 'They that are escaped must be as an inheritance for Benjamin, that a

אִשָּׁה יֹדַעַת מִשְׁכַּב־זָכָר

12 תַּחֲרִימוּ: וַיִּמְצְאוּ מִיּוֹשְׁבֵי ׀ יָבֵישׁ גִּלְעָד אַרְבַּע מֵאוֹת נַעֲרָה בְתוּלָה אֲשֶׁר לֹא־יָדְעָה אִישׁ לְמִשְׁכַּב זָכָר וַיָּבִאוּ אוֹתָם אֶל־הַמַּחֲנֶה שִׁלֹה אֲשֶׁר בְּאֶרֶץ כְּנָעַן:

13 וַיִּשְׁלְחוּ כָּל־הָעֵדָה וַיְדַבְּרוּ אֶל־בְּנֵי בִנְיָמִן אֲשֶׁר בְּסֶלַע רִמּוֹן וַיִּקְרְאוּ לָהֶם שָׁלוֹם:

14 וַיָּשָׁב בִּנְיָמִן בָּעֵת הַהִיא וַיִּתְּנוּ לָהֶם הַנָּשִׁים אֲשֶׁר חִיּוּ מִנְּשֵׁי יָבֵשׁ גִּלְעָד וְלֹא־מָצְאוּ לָהֶם

15 כֵּן: וְהָעָם נִחָם לְבִנְיָמִן כִּי־עָשָׂה יְהוָה פֶּרֶץ בְּשִׁבְטֵי יִשְׂרָאֵל:

16 וַיֹּאמְרוּ זִקְנֵי הָעֵדָה מַה־נַּעֲשֶׂה לַנּוֹתָרִים לְנָשִׁים כִּי־נִשְׁמְדָה מִבִּנְיָמִן אִשָּׁה:

17 וַיֹּאמְרוּ יְרֻשַּׁת פְּלֵיטָה לְבִנְיָמִן

---

12. *to Shiloh.* See on verse 2.

which is in the land of Canaan. The geographical note stresses the fact that the unmarried women were brought across the Jordan.

14. *sufficed them not.* There were only four hundred brides for six hundred men. For the root *matsa*, 'to suffice' (lit. 'find') cf. Num. xi. 22; Josh. xvii. 16 (Targum).

15. *repented them.* Of the war which they had conducted against Benjamin (Metsudath David).

16–24 WIVES ARE PROVIDED FOR THE UN-MARRIED BENJAMITES

16. *the women are destroyed.* This is not explicitly recorded and has to be deduced from xx. 48.

17. *they that are escaped,* etc. The difficult Hebrew construction is literally 'an inheritance of escape to Benjamin.' Kimchi construes it as a *constructio pregnans*: 'there ought to be an inheritance of escape for Benjamin'; it is their inherited right, on the ground of the promise given to Jacob that he would be

tribe be not blotted out from Israel.
18. Howbeit we may not give them
wives of our daughters.' For the
children of Israel had sworn, saying:
'Cursed be he that giveth a wife to
Benjamin.' 19. And they said:
'Behold, there is the feast of the
LORD from year to year in Shiloh,
which is on the north of Beth-el, on
the east side of the highway that
goeth up from Beth-el to Shechem,
and on the south of Lebonah.'
20. And they commanded the
children of Benjamin, saying: 'Go
and lie in wait in the vineyards;
21. and see, and, behold, if the
daughters of Shiloh come out to
dance in the dances, then come ye
out of the vineyards, and catch you
every man his wife of the daughters
of Shiloh, and go to the land of
Benjamin. 22. And it shall be,
when their fathers or their brethren
come to strive with us, that we will

וְלֹא־יִמָּחֶה שֵׁבֶט מִיִּשְׂרָאֵל׃
18 וַאֲנַחְנוּ לֹא־נוּכַל לָתֶת־לָהֶם
נָשִׁים מִבְּנוֹתֵינוּ כִּי־נִשְׁבְּעוּ
בְנֵי־יִשְׂרָאֵל לֵאמֹר אָרוּר
19 נֹתֵן אִשָּׁה לְבִנְיָמִן׃ וַיֹּאמְרוּ
הִנֵּה חַג־יְהֹוָה בְּשִׁלוֹ מִיָּמִים ׀
יָמִימָה אֲשֶׁר מִצְּפוֹנָה לְבֵית־
אֵל מִזְרְחָה הַשֶּׁמֶשׁ לִמְסִלָּה
הָעֹלָה מִבֵּית־אֵל שְׁכֶמָה
20 וּמִנֶּגֶב לִלְבוֹנָה׃ וַיְצַוּ אֶת־
בְּנֵי בִנְיָמִן לֵאמֹר לְכוּ
21 וַאֲרַבְתֶּם בַּכְּרָמִים׃ וּרְאִיתֶם
וְהִנֵּה אִם־יֵצְאוּ בְנוֹת־שִׁילוֹ
לָחוּל בַּמְּחֹלוֹת וִיצָאתֶם מִן־
הַכְּרָמִים וַחֲטַפְתֶּם לָכֶם אִישׁ
אִשְׁתּוֹ מִבְּנוֹת שִׁלוֹ וַהֲלַכְתֶּם
22 אֶרֶץ בִּנְיָמִן׃ וְהָיָה כִּי־יָבֹאוּ
אֲבוֹתָם אוֹ אֲחֵיהֶם לָרִוב ׀

v. 20. וְיַצַו ק׳   v. 22. לָרִיב ק׳

the ancestor of twelve tribes. Other Jewish
commentators explain: the women who survived out of Jabesh-gilead have been
assigned to the Benjamites, so a tribe will
not be blotted out from Israel (Metsudath
David).

18. *sworn*. Cf. verses 1, 7.

19. *feast*. Or 'celebration.' Kimchi conjectures that this celebration took place on
one of the three pilgrim festivals, or, perhaps, on Yom Kippur, as we find the practice in the time of the Second Temple
(Ta'an. 26b). Abarbanel conjectures that it
took place on Sukkoth, referred to in the
Talmud as *chag*. The root from which this
noun is derived signifies 'to dance.' It is also

used as an occasion for sacrifice. Hence,
sacrifices were offered in Shiloh at this occasion (Metsudath David).

north, etc. According to Kimchi, the topographical details relate, not to the position
of Shiloh, but to the place where the dancing was to take place.

Lebonah. The modern el-Lubban, about
three miles north-west of Shiloh (Daath
Mikra).

21. *to dance*. Religious festivals were, in
ancient times, associated with dancing
(ibid.).

go to the land of Benjamin. The escape was easy
because the Benjamite border was only
about two hours' journey distant.

say unto them: Grant them graciously unto us; because we took not for each man of them his wife in battle; neither did ye give them unto them, that ye should now be guilty.' 23. And the children of Benjamin did so, and took them wives, according to their number, of them that danced, whom they carried off; and they went and returned unto their inheritance, and built the cities, and dwelt in them. 24. And the children of Israel departed thence at that time, every man to his tribe and to his family, and they went out from thence every man to his inheritance. 25. In those days there was no king in Israel; every man did that which was right in his own eyes.

אֵלֵ֫ינוּ וְאָמַ֫רְנוּ אֲלֵיהֶם חָנ֫וּנוּ
אוֹתָם כִּי לֹא לָקַ֫חְנוּ אִישׁ אִשְׁתּ֫וֹ
בַּמִּלְחָמָה כִּי לֹא אַתֶּ֫ם נְתַתֶּ֫ם

23 לָהֶם כָּעֵת תֶּאְשָׁ֫מוּ: וַיַּעֲשׂוּ־
כֵן בְּנֵי בִנְיָמִ֫ן וַיִּשְׂא֫וּ נָשִׁים
לְמִסְפָּרָ֫ם מִן־הַמְּחֹֽלֲל֫וֹת
אֲשֶׁר גָּזָ֫לוּ וַיֵּלְכ֫וּ וַיָּשׁ֫וּבוּ אֶל־
נַחֲלָתָ֫ם וַיִּבְנוּ֫ אֶת־הֶעָרִ֫ים

24 וַיֵּשְׁב֫וּ בָּהֶ֫ם: וַיִּתְהַלְּכ֫וּ מִשָּׁ֫ם
בְּנֵי־יִשְׂרָאֵל בָּעֵת הַהִ֫יא אִ֫ישׁ
לְשִׁבְט֫וֹ וּלְמִשְׁפַּחְתּ֫וֹ וַיֵּצְא֫וּ

25 מִשָּׁ֫ם אִ֫ישׁ לְנַחֲלָתֽוֹ: בַּיָּמִ֫ים
הָהֵ֫ם אֵ֫ין מֶ֫לֶךְ בְּיִשְׂרָאֵ֑ל אִ֫ישׁ
הַיָּשָׁ֫ר בְּעֵינָ֫יו יַעֲשֶֽׂה:

חזק

22. *to strive with us.* Over their daughters who had been kidnapped at the feast.

grant them graciously. Give them to us as a personal favour (Kimchi).

neither did ye give them unto them. The Benjamites having taken the brides by force, the Israelites would not have violated their oath (Kimchi, Rashi, Metsudath David).

24. *departed.* The Hithpael conjugation is used in the text perhaps with the meaning 'went in different directions,' 'dispersed.'

thence. viz. from Shiloh. The second *from thence* means from the territory of Benjamin and did not usurp their property (Metsudath David).

25 THE MORAL STATE OF THE PEOPLE

A sad comment on the history of the eventful period which is now brought to a close. It repeats xvii. 6, xviii. 1, xix. 1. This serves also to introduce the following Book of Samuel, telling us that until his time, there was no king in Israel (Kimchi).

Authorities quoted

Terms and abbreviations

Index

AUTHORITIES QUOTED

Abarbanel, Isaac (1437–1509).

Aboth—*Pirkë Aboth, Sayings of the Fathers*: Mishnaic tractate.

Alshich, Moses (sixteenth century) *Maroth Hazovoth.*

Azulai, Chaim Joseph David (1727–1807) *Homath Anach.*

Daath Mikra (1970, Contemporary Jewish Commentary) Mosad HaRav Kook.

Daath Soferim (1975, Contemporary Jewish Commentary), by Chaim D. Rabinowitz.

Elijah of Wilna (1720–1797, Annotator of the Bible and Talmud).

Hershcovitz and Zidman (Jewish Bible Commentator), *The Book of Joshua* (in Hebrew).

Isaiah of Trani (thirteenth century).

Josephus, Flavius (Jewish Historian, 1st century C.E.).

Kara, Joseph (1060–1130).

Kimchi, David (1160–1235), Bible Commentator).

K'li Y'kar (1603, Commentary on Early Prophets) Samuel Laniado.

Maimonides, Moses (1135–1204), *Guide for the Perplexed.*

Malbim, Meyer Leibush (1809–1879, famed Biblical Commentator).

Mechilta—Ancient Rabbinical Commentary on Exodus.

Metsudath David ('Tower of David'), Hebrew Commentary on Books of the Bible by David Altschul (17th century).

Midrash—Rabbinical homilies on the Pentateuch, etc.

Mishnah—Codification on Jewish law (c. 200 C.E.).

Peshitta—Syriac Translation of the Bible (2nd century C.E.).

Pesikta—Midrashic compilation.

Pirkë—Midrashic compilation.

Porath Joseph (Enoch Zundel, Anthology on Joshua).

Ralbag (Rabbi Levi ben Gershon, 1288–1344, Commentator and Philosopher).

Rashi (Rabbi Solomon ben Isaac, 1040–1105, Commentator).

Seder Olam—Early Jewish Chronicle.

Septuagint—Greek Translation of the Bible, begun in the third century B.C.E.

Siphrë—Ancient Rabbinical Commentary on Numbers and Deuteronomy.

Talmud—Corpus of Jewish Law and Thought (compiled at the end of the fifth century C.E.).

Tanchuma—Midrashic Commentary on the Pentateuch (original version 4th century C.E.).

Targum—Aramaic Translation of the Bible (1st and 2nd centuries C.E.).

Yalkut Me'am Loez (1973, Anthology of Commentaries on the Bible) Joshua and Judges by Samuel Yerushalmi.

Yalkut Shimoni—Midrashic compilation (13th century).

TERMS AND ABBREVIATIONS

ad loc.   At that place.

A.J.   American Jewish Translation of the Scriptures.

A.V.   Authorized Version.

B.B.   *Baba Bathra*, Talmudic tractate.

B.C.E.   Before the Christian era.

c.   About.

C.E.   Common era.

Cf.   Compare, refer to.

D.M.   Daath Mikra.

Ecclus.   Apocryphal Book of Ecclesiasticus.

ed.   Edition, or edited by.

e.g.   For example.

Erub.   *Erubin*, Talmudic tractate.

etc.   And so forth.

f.   Following verse or chapter (plural ff.).

i.e.   That is.

j.   Jerusalem (or, Palestinian) Talmud.

kerë.   The Hebrew as it is read according to the Masoretes.

Keth.   *Kethuboth*, Talmudic tractate.

kethib.   The Hebrew as it is written according to tradition.

lit.   Literally.

loc. cit.   At the place quoted.

Macc.   Apocryphal Book of Maccabees.

Mak.   *Makkoth*, Talmudic tractate.

Meg.   *Megillah*, Talmudic tractate.

Men.   *Menachoth*, Talmudic tractate.

MS.   Manuscript (plural MSS.).

M.T.   Masoretic text.

R.V.   Revised Version.

Sanh.   *Sanhedrin*, Talmudic tractate.

Sec.   Section.

Shebi.   *Shebiith*, Talmudic tractate.

Sot.   *Sotah*, Talmudic tractate.

Suk.   *Sukkah*, Talmudic tractate.

Taan.   *Taanith*, Talmudic tractate.

viz.   Namely.

Yeb.   *Yebamoth*, Talmudic tractate.

INDEX

INDEX

I. Names and Subjects.

A

Aaron, 144
Abdon (city), 128
Abdon son of Hillel, 263
Abel-cheramim, 257
Abel-meholah, 202
Abiezrites, 99, 207, 211, 214, 224, 231
Abimelech son of Gideon, 231, 232ff.
Abraham, 143f.
Acco, 166
Achan, 32ff., 135
Achor, the valley of, 38, 86
Achsah daughter of Caleb, 89, 159
Achshaph, 63, 72, 114
Achzib, 93, 115, 166
Adadah, 90
Adam (city), 16
Adamah, 117
Adami-nekeb, 116
Addar, 85
Adithaim, 92
Adonai-shalom, 211
Adoni-bezek, king, 157
Adoni-zedek, king, 52f.
Adullam, 71, 92, 107
Adummim, the ascent of, 86
Ahiman, 88, 159
Ahlab, 166
Ai, 33ff., 40ff., 71
Aijalon, 118, 127, 167, 262; the valley of, 56
Ain, 92, 110, 126
Akrabbim, the ascent of, 85, 167
Allammelech, 114
Almon, 126
Altar, built by Gideon, 211, by Joshua, 45, by the two and a half tribes, 133; idolatrous, 168, 211f.; in Bethel, 314
Amad, 114
Amalekites, the, 179, 197, 204, 213, 218, 248, 263
Amam, 91
Amarna Letters, the, quoted, 8, 52, 163, 166, 172, 176, 299
Ammonites, the, 69, 76, 79, 179, 247, 248, 249f., 251ff.
Amorites, the, 167, 248, 254f.
Anab, 67, 94

B

Anaharath, 113
Anak(im), 67f., 84, 88, 125, 162
Anathoth, 126
Angels, 26, 27, 167, 169, 200, 206f., 210, 264ff.
Anim, 94
Anthropomorphism, 249
Aphek, 72, 74, 115, 166
Aphekah, 94
Arab (city), 94
Arabah, the, 16, 42, 63, 66, 69, 71, 107; sea of, 69
Arad, 71, 161
Aram, 247
Aram-naharaim, 177
Arba, 84, 88, 125
Archites, the, 96
Arnon, river, 253, 254, 255, 256; valley of, 68, 69, 76, 77
Aroer, 69, 76, 77, 79, 255, 257
Arumah, 242
Ashan, 93, 110
Ashdod, 68, 74, 93f.
Asherites, the, aided Gideon, 222; allotment to, 114f.; failed to aid Deborah, 199; inactive in subduing the Canaanites, 166; summoned by Gideon, 214
Asherah (-oth), 177, 211f.
Ashkelon, 74, 162, 273
Ashnah, 92, 93
Ashtaroth, 49, 70, 76, 80, 172, 247
'As one man,' meaning of, 209
Asriel, 99
Asses, white, 195
Ataroth, 96, 97
Atroth-addar, 97, 106
Avvim (city), 108
Avvim, the, 74
Azekah, 55, 92
Azmon, 85
Aznoth-tabar, 116

B

Baal(im), 171f., 177, 213, 231, 247; altar of, 211f.
Baalah, 87, 91; the mount of, 88
Baal-berith, 231, 233
Baal-gad, 66, 70, 75

324

INDEX

Baal-hermon, 176

Baal-tamar, 310

Baalath, 118

Baalath-beer, 110

Balaam, 78, 145

Balah, 110

Balak, king, 145, 255

Bamoth-baal, 77

Ban, the, 29f.

Barak son of Abinoam, 187ff., 196, 198

Bashan, 49, 69, 70, 76, 80, 98, 100, 127, 132

Bealoth, 90

Beer (city), 238

Beeroth, 50, 108

Beer-sheba, 91, 110, 304

Beeshterah, 127

Bene-berak, 118

Benjamites, the, allotment to, 106f.; attacked by the Israelites, 304ff.; oppressed by the Ammonites, 248; outrage committed by, 300ff.; provided with wives, 316ff.; shared Jerusalem with the Jebusites, 162f.; skill in stone-slinging, 307

Beten, 114

Beth-anath, 117, 166

Beth-anoth, 95

Beth-arabah, 86, 95, 108

Beth-aven, 33

Beth-baal-meon, 77

Beth-barah, 222

Beth-dagon, 93, 114

Bethel, 33, 40ff., 71, 72, 96, 106, 108, 110, 163, 187, 307, 309, 310, 314, 317

Bethel-luz, 96

Beth-emek, 114

Beth-haram, 79

Beth-hoglah, 86, 107, 108

Beth-horon, the nether, 96, 106; the upper, 55, 97, 127

Beth-jeshimoth, 69, 78

Beth-lebaoth, 110

Beth-lehem, 112, 262, 288, 297, 301

Beth-marcaboth, 110

Beth-millo, 234, 238

Beth-nimrah, 79

Beth-pazez, 113

Beth-pelet, 91

Beth-peor, 78

Beth-rehob, 295

Beth-shean, 101, 102, 164

Beth-shemesh, 88, 113, 117, 126, 166

Beth-shittah, 221

Beth-tappuah, 94

Beth-zur, 95

Betonim, 79

Bezek, 156f.

Bezer, 122, 129

Biziothiah, 91

Bochim, 168, 169

Bohan, the Stone of, 86, 107

Bozkath, 93

Burnt-offering, 45, 136, 137f., 257, 266, 309, 314

C

Cabbon, 93

Cabul, 114

Caleb son of Jephunneh, 83ff., 88f., 125, 159f., 162

Canaan, the nations inhabiting, 14

Captain, of the host of the Lord, 25f.

Carmel (city), 94

Carmel, mount, 72, 114

Chamber, upper, 181

Chemosh, Moabite god, 255

Chephar-ammonah, 180

Chephirah, 50, 108

Chesalon, 88

Chesil, 91

Chesulloth, 113

'Children of the east,' 204

Chinnereth (-oth), 63, 117; sea of, 69, 79

Chisloth-tabor, 111

Chithlish, 93

Circumcision, of the Israelites, 22ff.

'City of palm trees,' 161, 179

Clothes, rending the, in mourning, 258

Confession of sin, 37, 38

Corn, parched, 25

Covenant, ark of the, 12ff., 27f., 34, 46

Cushan-rishathaim, king, 177f.

D

Dabbesheth, 111

Dagon, 284

Dan (city), 119, 296, 304

Danites, the, allotment to, 117ff.; failed to aid Deborah, 199; inactive in subduing the Canaanites, 167; seek territory, 289, 292f., 295f.

Dannah, 94

Debir, 61, 67, 71, 86, 89, 94, 126, 159

325

INDEX